OXFORD MEDICAL PUBLICATIONS
Mind, Meaning, and Mental Disorder

MIND, MEANING, AND MENTAL DISORDER

The Nature of Causal Explanation In Psychology And Psychiatry

DEREK BOLTON
Institute of Psychiatry and
Maudsley Hospital, London

and

JONATHAN HILL
University of Liverpool and
Royal Liverpool
Children's Hospital

Oxford New York Tokyo
Oxford University Press
1996

Oxford University Press, Walton Street, Oxford OX2 6DP

Oxford New York
Athens Auckland Bangkok Bombay
Calcutta Cape Town Dar es Salaam Delhi
Florence Hong Kong Istanbul Karachi
Kuala Lumpur Madras Madrid Melbourne
Mexico City Nairobi Paris Singapore
Taipei Tokyo Toronto
and associated companies in
Berlin Ibadan

Oxford is a trade mark of Oxford University Press

Published in the United States
by Oxford University Press Inc., New York

© Derek Bolton and Jonathan Hill, 1996

A catalogue record for this book is available from the British Library

Library of Congress Cataloging in Publication Data
Bolton, Derek.
Mind, meaning, and mental disorder: the nature of causal
explanation in psychology and psychiatry/Derek Bolton and Jonathan Hill.
p. cm. – (Oxford medical publications)
Includes bibliographical references and index.
ISBN 0–19–261504–1 (hbk.)
1. Mental illness–Philosophy. 2. Mental illness–Etiology.
3. Philosophy of mind. 4. Intentionality (Philosophy)
5. Causation. 6. Mind and body. 7. Meaning (Philosophy)
I. Hill, Jonathan, Prof. II. Title. III. Series.
[DNLM: 1. Mental Disorders–etiology. 2. Philosophy.
3. Neuropsychology. WM 140 B694m 1996]
RC437.5.B65 1996
616.89'001–dc20
DNLM/DLC
for Library of Congress 95–39306 CIP

ISBN 0 19 261504 1

Typeset by Hewer Text Compsition Services, Edinburgh
Printed in Great Britain by
Bookcraft Ltd, Avon

Foreword

Chris R. Brewin, Research Professor, Department of
Psychology, Royal Holloway, University of London

In the period from 1950 to the mid-1970s behaviour therapists developed clearly
defined procedures such as desensitization and response prevention that could readily
be described and taught. These techniques required little investigation of the individual,
only a careful description of the behaviour, its antecedents, and its consequents.
However, their usefulness tended to be restricted to the treatment of fairly circumscribed
disorders such as specific phobias and compulsions. When behaviour therapists came to
address depression and more generalized anxiety disorders, the significance of personal
meanings assumed great importance. The investigation of individual thought processes,
as recommend by Albert Ellis and Aaron Beck, became the cornerstone of the new
cognitive–behavioural approaches.

These new techniques were not embraced, however, without a prolonged period
of soul-searching by behaviour therapists. There was great anxiety that investigating
individual cognitions was not as 'scientific' or methodologically rigorous as purely
behavioural approaches. The new approaches were eventually adopted because they
worked, but many expressed unease. The fear was frequently expressed that, in
taking this step, behaviour therapy could no longer be so clearly differentiated from
psychoanalysis. It was perceived that the project of creating a truly 'scientific' type
of therapy was being abandoned for ever in favour of an explicit search for personal
meaning.

These fears and uncertainties about the scientific status of psychotherapy, particularly
when contrasted with the status of biological psychiatry, are still very much with us. It
is hard for the identification of pathogenic personal meanings, no matter how plausible
and no matter how successful the outcome, to appear as valuable scientifically as
identifying the existence of too large or too small quantities of a neurotransmitter.
These issues contribute not only to individual unease, but also to external perceptions
of the mental health sciences to internal demarcations, and to decisions about how best
to spend limited research funds. This book therefore addresses a topic that is of central
importance to all those working in mental health.

Bolton and Hill's important and far-reaching analysis goes right to the heart of these
controversial issues. By approaching the problem from the standpoint of the philosophy
of science and the philosophy of mind, they avoid the taking of sides and any sterile
argument about what is 'better'. Rather, they oblige the reader to see the problem
in a wholly new way, one which distinguishes the causality inherent in physics and
chemistry from the causality inherent in biological systems that have inbuilt goals and
are constantly working towards more or less well specified objectives.

As they point out, explanations that are couched in terms of meaning or intention are extremely powerful in biology and psychology. They also show convincingly that these explanations work just as well for many examples of abnormal behaviour as they do for normal behaviour that follows predictable rules. The divide between the biological and the psychosocial approach to mental illness is shown to be profoundly misleading — instead, Bolton and Hill argue, the divide is between intentional explanations and non-intentional explanations. According to intentional explanations, symptoms arise because normally functioning biological and psychological systems are attempting to deal with information that is either internally inconsistent or is inconsistent with the person's goals. According to non-intentional explanations, the biological or psychological systems are themselves malfunctioning, probably as a result of some disease process. Both types of explanation may apply at different times, and both are equally 'scientific'.

This analysis, while not minimizing the inherent difficulties, clearly defines the unique contribution of psychotherapy and explains why the psychiatric problems of the majority of sufferers will never be explicable in terms of biological or psychological malfunctioning arising from non-intentional causes. From this perspective, all psychotherapies aim to specify what information is in the system, how accurate this is, and whether there is conflict with the person's goals. Where they differ is in their methods of assessment and in their techniques for resolving conflict.

As well as placing psychotherapy within a broader context of the explanation of psychiatric disorder, Bolton and Hill's analysis also defines a scientific project of categorizing and describing regularities in the personal meanings attached to psychiatric symptoms. Although ambitious, its completion is probably considerably more achievable than that of mapping the entire human genome. This book suggests that, as far as the majority of psychiatric patients are concerned, it will also be of considerably more value.

Preface

Philosophical ideas about the mind, brain, and behaviour can seem theoretical and unimportant when placed alongside the urgent questions of mental distress and disorder. However, there is a need to give attempts to answer these questions some direction. On the one hand, a substantial research effort is going into the investigation of brain processes and the development of drug treatments for psychiatric disorders, and, on the other, a wide range of psychotherapies and forms of counselling are becoming available to adults and children with mental health problems. These two strands reflect a long Western tradition of dividing body and mind, and attempting to resolve questions of the explanation of disturbance either in favour of the malfunctioning brain, or the disordered psyche. It is crucial in determining the direction of research and clinical practice to clarify whether these are competing incompatible perspectives, or whether they are complementary and in need of integration.

However, it is unlikely that philosophical ideas will illuminate central questions in psychology and psychiatry without themselves being informed by the concepts and findings from areas such as learning theory, developmental psychology, artificial intelligence, and psychoanalysis. The book therefore starts with a review of key issues in the philosophy of mind and philosophy of science as they relate to questions of cognition, emotion, and behaviour. Intentionality emerges as a central concept in human functioning, but we go on to make the case that it is a distinguishing feature of biological systems in general. Human psychological faculties then emerge as particularly sophisticated elaborations of intentional processes, which create the conditions both for intelligence and culture, and also for instability and disorder.

Throughout the discussion philosophical theories are brought to bear on the particular questions of the explanation of behaviour, the nature of mental causation, and eventually the origins of major disorders, including depression, anxiety disorders, schizophrenia, and personality disorder.

The book has been written for philosophers and academic and clinical psychologists and psychiatrists, but we would be delighted if anyone whose business or interest is to understand human behaviour were to make use of it. In that it presents a particular thesis it is aimed at a postgraduate readership, but the advanced undergraduate will find that many contemporary themes in philosophy, psychology, and psychiatry are covered, and provided the ideas proposed are treated with some caution under exam conditions, the more innovative content may not prove too hazardous.

The authors came to have an interest in philosophical problems in psychology and psychiatry by different routes. Before training as a clinical psychologist D. B. read philosophy and researched on Wittgenstein. J. H. read natural sciences before training in medicine, psychiatry, and family therapy. Both of us were undergraduates at Cambridge University where our belief in the value of ideas and cross-disciplinary thinking was reinforced and informed. We published papers independently about 12 years ago which overlapped in subject-matter—meanings, reasons, and causes—and conclusions, whence came our idea of co-writing a book. During the 1980s we were very fortunate to be part of a group of people working at the Institute of Psychiatry and the Maudsley Hospital in London that met regularly to present papers and discuss philosophical issues in relation to psychology and psychiatry. This provided a containing and critical setting in which to try out new ideas, many of which appear in this book, and we are very pleased to acknowledge and thank the other members of that group, Jim Birley who particularly encouraged its formation, Adrian Grounds, Peter Hobson, Alan Lee and Digby Tantam.

The book as a whole is co-written, although some chapters were written mainly by one or other of us. Chapters 1–4 were written mainly by D. B., 5 and 7 mainly by J. H., while 6, 8, and 9 have been co-written.

D. B.'s contribution was written partly during tenure of a Jacobsen Research Fellowship in Philosophy at University College London during 1989–91, and he gratefully acknowledges this support. A different kind of support came from Stacia, Henry, and Matthew, who for many years gave his attempts to make time to write the book their whole-hearted backing.

J. H. would like to thank his father for teaching him the value of asking questions and his mother for her insight that they cannot all be answered. He is very grateful to his wife Judy, and his children Susannah, Jessie, and Rosalind for their support, and belief that this book would be completed. Alison Richards helped in the ordering of the ideas, and David Lyon provided valuable assistance in the use of clear language. Dudley Ankerson and Bernard Wood provided inspiration on broader but equally important fronts.

Both authors would like to thank friends and colleagues for their comments and advice on all or parts of the work at various stages of completion, including Simon Baron-Cohen, Chris Brewin, Andy Clark, Bill Fulford, Sebastian Gardner, Peter Hobson, David Papineau, and Mick Power.

D. B., *London*
J. H., *Liverpool*
1995

mental states) are causal, but they are in critical respects different from causal explanations of the sort found in the physical sciences. In this way we draw a distinction between two varieties of causal explanation, which we call the *intentional* and the *non-intentional*. This distinction obviously differs from the distinction between meaning and causality because it is not drawn in terms of what is or is not causal. But also, the distinction we propose appears at a different place in the spectrum of the sciences, not between the 'hard' natural sciences and the 'soft' cultural sciences, but rather between the natural sciences of physics and chemistry, and the (equally natural) biological sciences. In the biological sciences we find concepts of function, design, rules, information, and information-processing, which are the essential ingredients of intentional-causal explanation as understood here. Marking the distinction at this point, between the pre-biological and the biological sciences, has the effect of assimilating biology to psychology, and indeed to the cultural sciences. Our point can be put briefly by saying that meaning is akin to, or is on a continuum with, the information that pervades biological systems and functioning. This proposal stands in contrast to those that, in one way or another, endorse a radical distinction between the meaning of mind, language and culture, and anything to be found in the natural sciences, biological or otherwise. These alternative positions, which otherwise of course vary greatly among themselves, include materialism and hermeneutics, and the views of such contemporary philosophers as Quine and Davidson.

For psychiatry, which seeks models of aetiology and intervention, the exploration of meaningful processes is of interest only in so far as meanings are causes. Once this claim, in the form outlined above, is defined and established in the first part of the essay, through chapters 1–6, we turn in the second part of the essay, chapters 7–9, to explore breakdown of intentionality, and the nature and limits of intentional explanations of psychological disorder. The notion of breakdown of intentionality is also relevant to the first part of the essay, however. Intentional-causal explanations, our whole way of conceiving the phenomena that they explain, are permeated by concepts involving normative distinctions, such as function, and hence dysfunction, design more-or-less suited to the environment and task, normal as opposed to abnormal environmental conditions, true/false belief, adaptive as opposed to maladaptive behaviour, and so on. In this sense themes concerning disorder and its explanation run through all of the chapters.

While the philosophy of psychology has a long and familiar history, and is currently flourishing, the philosophy of psychiatry has been relatively neglected. The most thorough and influential analysis of the philosophical foundations of psychiatry was Jaspers', and there the distinction between meaningful and causal connections was fundamental. Since Jaspers, it would be fair to say that philosophical study of general psychiatry has been in limbo. Philosophers have perhaps been wary of tackling the problems of psychiatry because of unfamiliarity. In part this would be modesty appropriate in the philosophy of any science, art, or scholarly discipline, but a further factor here is probably the one identified by Foucault, that in the modern age 'madness' became alienated from culture, delegated then solely to the psychiatric profession. This has been a result detrimental to all concerned. While the philosophical foundations of psychiatry suffered from inevitable neglect, attention focused rather on the two broad areas referred to earlier: the scientific status or otherwise of psychoanalytic theory, and the diverse 'anti-psychiatry' critiques. The former debate did not concern primarily the concept of disorder, nor, a related point, psychiatry in general. The latter debates certainly were about psychiatry and the notion of 'mental illness', but their problems were social, political, and historical, not primarily philosophical. Controversy about the scientific status of psychoanalytic theory continues (Grünbaum 1984, 1986), and mainstream, medical psychiatry had, and continues, to defend itself against the radical critiques (Clare 1976; Wing 1978; Roth and Kroll 1986; Reznek 1991).

We do not attempt in this essay to weigh into these well-known debates. Our aim is rather as stated above, to examine some philosophical aspects of the problem of meaning and causality, in the light of contemporary theory in philosophy of mind and cognitive psychology, and its bearing on the concepts of mental order and disorder. This examination is relevant to the controversies surrounding psychoanalytic theory, and the notion of mental illness, but these are not the main focus. If the essay can claim allegiance to any 'tradition' in the philosophy of psychiatry, it would be to that represented by Jaspers. That said, we have no pretensions to follow Jaspers in the non-philosophical direction of his work, concerned with the details of psychiatric phenomenology and its classification. This emphasis belonged with the idea that meaningful phenomena have no causal role: all that was to be done, in this case, was to describe and classify them. By contrast, in so far as meaningful phenomena are implicated in causal processes, the task is to try to explicate some basic principles of their operation.

There are various reasons why the time is right for increased communication between philosophy and psychiatry; in particular, the divide between philosophy and psychology has become more flexible, with shared interest in the nature of mind and of psychological explanation. One upshot of this increased flexibility is that problems of mental disorder and its explanation are more available to philosophy. Several books on the philosophy of psychiatry have appeared in recent years, compared with few or none in previous decades. Fulford (1988) emphasized the value-laden, normative nature of concepts in psychiatry, and Hundert (1989) identified disorder in the forms of interaction between subject and object, organism and environment. Themes of these kinds are also prominent in the present essay.

REFERENCES

Clare, A. (1976). *Psychiatry in dissent*. Tavistock Publications, London.
Foucault, M. (1965). *Madness and civilization*. Random House, New York.
Fulford, K. W. M. (1988). *Moral theory and medical practice*. Cambridge University Press, Cambridge.
Grünbaum, A. (1984). *The foundations of psychoanalysis: a philosophical critique*. University of California Press, Berkeley.
Grünbaum, A. (1986). Precis of *The foundations of psychoanalysis: a philosophical critique*, with peer commentary. *The Behavioral and Brain Sciences*, **9**, 217–84.
Habermas, J. (1971). *Knowledge and human interests* (trans. J. J. Shapiro). Beacon Press, Boston.

Hundert, E. M. (1989). *Philosophy, psychiatry, and neuroscience.* Oxford University Press, Oxford.

Jaspers, K. (1923). *Allgemeine Pychopathologie.* Springer Verlag, Berlin. (English translation: Hoenig, J. and Hamilton, M. W. (1963) *General Psychopathology.* Manchester University Press, Manchester.)

Klein, G. S. (1976). *Psychoanalytic theory.* International Universities Press, New York.

Laing, R. D. (1960). *The divided self.* Penguin, Harmondsworth, Middlesex.

Reznek, L. (1991). *The philosophical defence of psychiatry.* Routledge, London.

Ricoeur, P. (1970). *Freud and philosophy.* Yale University Press, New Haven, Connecticut.

Roth, M. and Kroll, J. (1986). *The reality of mental illness.* Cambridge University Press, Cambridge.

Schafer, R. (1976). *A new language for psychoanalysis.* Yale University Press, New Haven, Connecticut.

Szasz, T. (1961). *The myth of mental illness: foundations of a theory of personal conduct.* Harper and Row, New York.

von Wright, G. H. (1971). *Explanation and understanding.* Routledge and Kegan Paul, London.

Wing, J. (1978). *Reasoning about madness.* Oxford University Press, Oxford.

1
Mind, meaning,
and the explanation of action

1.1 MAIN IDEA OF THE CHAPTER

The main idea of this chapter is that explanations of behaviour in terms of meaningful, mental states have theory-driven predictive power. Three sections work out various aspects of this idea. Section 1.2 looks at its expression in psychological science, specifically in the cognitive paradigm which superceded behaviourism. Section 1.3 works around the meaning of meaning and related concepts including intentionality and information. Section 1.4 examines aspects of the theory of mind. These sections, the substantial part of the chapter, deal with issues central to current philosophy of mind and psychological theory, and are intended to be of interest in their own right. But they also serve to substantiate the claim that meaningful, mental explanations of action are good at prediction. From this main claim of the chapter is then derived, in Section 1.5, its main conclusion, that such explanations are *causal*.

This conclusion has practical significance for psychological theory: in seeking causal explanations of action, we should construct models that refer to meaningful, mental states. On the other hand, the significance of all this, both the conclusion and its implication, owes much to historical considerations. The *problem* here, and hence the solution, is hard to understand in isolation from the history of ideas. The relevant history includes the emergence of the *Geisteswissenschaften* and the problem of meaning in the late nineteenth century, this against the background of dualism and the problematic status of mind which was axiomatic to the modern science of the seventeenth century, and the effects of both problematics on the development of a scientific psychology.

In the absence of this context, it is hard to see the problem or the interest in the solution. The problem of whether mental, meaningful explanations are causal or not is a typically philosophical one, apparent only at a highly theoretical level. Typically, observation and experiment do not touch it at all. The question is not about the phenomena, not even about this or that theory of the phenomena, but concerns rather the status of a particular kind of psychological theory, whether it is causal or not, and hence, for example, whether it belongs within the domain of the empirical sciences. It is also hard to grasp what the problem is, or that there is a problem at all, within the terms of common sense. Common sense and ordinary language have no difficulty with the idea that meaningful, mental states are causes, in the sense that explanations which invoke beliefs, desires, and so on, typically use terms such as 'because', 'cause', etc. The problem is not apparent here. It becomes apparent only in relation to preconceptions about the nature of mind, its relation to the body, and about the nature of meaning and causality. The problem has relatively little to do with common sense, and not much to do with this or that theory, but is much more to do with background philosophical assumptions. These assumptions have been constructed during the few hundred years or so since the beginnings of modern Western thought. Both mind, and then later meaning, have been correctly regarded as highly problematic from the point of view of the methodological assumptions of the natural sciences.

Dualism is discussed at the beginning of subsection 1.2.1 and some historical aspects of the problem of meaning in subsection 1.3.8. These historical discussions are relatively brief: for the most part the chapter concentrates on contemporary issues in philosophy of mind and psychological theory.

The argument is, as indicated, from the (theory-driven) predictive power of explanation of action in terms of mind and meaning to the causal status of such explanation. There are various other positions and pathways in this area well-known in the contemporary philosophical literature. One very influential position quite distinct from what is proposed here is due to Davidson. While Davidson assumes that reason-giving explanations are causal, he does not derive this from the premise that they belong to a theory with predictive power, and he sees them as discontinuous with the endeavour of empirical science (for example, Davidson 1963, 1970; Evnine 1991; Malpas 1992). In this respect Davidson's work is in the tradition of the dichotomy between '*verstehen*' and '*erklären*', and between meaning and causality, which this essay aims to deconstruct. Dennett and Fodor, both of whom will be discussed frequently in this essay, have each emphasized the predictive power of the kind of explanation in question. Fodor (for example 1987) infers causality, but links it to a strong version of mind/meaning–brain identity theory which will be discussed and rejected in the second chapter. Dennett (for example 1988) steers away from the question of causality, perhaps linked to his wanting to avoid a problematic realism, such as Fodor's, about mind and meaning. The problem of realism here, the question of what mental states are, particularly if they are to be credited with causal power, will be discussed in the second and third chapters. Many problems arise once we embrace the conclusion that mental, meaningful states are causal, and these will occupy us through many subsequent chapters. In this chapter we lay the foundations for the conclusion, by spelling out how such states figure in theories that predict.

1.2 THE 'COGNITIVE PARADIGM' IN PSYCHOLOGICAL SCIENCE

1.2.1 Previous paradigms defined by dualism

Since the beginnings of the modern scientific view of the world, mind and its place in nature have been problematic. The problems were expressed by Cartesian dualism, the theory of two quite distinct substances, *res extensa* and *res cogitans*, which accompanied the development of the scientific world-picture. As Burtt argued in his classic study, Cartesian dualism accompanied the growth of the modern scientific world-picture not only in time, but was an inevitable complement to it (Burtt 1932; see also Bolton 1979, pp. 51–3, for a summary of philosophical themes in Burtt's argument). The world described by the new physics was spatial (geometrical), material, independent, and objective. Mind, by contrast, was immaterial, non-spatial, and essentially subjective. This modern dualism effectively split the human being in two. The human body was conceived as matter like the rest of nature, and then mind comprised everything human that could not be construed as material. In this way not only was the spiritual, or rational, soul distinguished from the body and from nature, but so also sensation, perception, appetite, and will, which would seem so clearly to be bodily qualities and functions, except in so far as the body, like the rest of nature, had been stripped of all sensitivity and life. Modern dualism split the *natural* human being in two; in this respect it was a new conception, distinct from the various kinds of dualism found in ancient and scholastic thought (Burtt 1932, pp. 113ff.; Copleston 1960, pp. 120ff.).

The modern distinction between matter and mind raised very many problems, including the problem of causal interaction. It always was unclear how mental processes, being immaterial, could causally influence matter, specifically the body and the brain, or vice versa. Furthermore, in so far as the material universe constituted a closed system in which energy remained constant, it seemed impossible that events within it should be affected by, or should affect, events in a different reality altogether. In brief, it was apparently impossible for Cartesian mental events to cause material events; in particular, they apparently could not be causes of behaviour. From here it may be seen that if explanations of behaviour in terms of mental events are causal, the mental events in question are unlikely to be of the sort defined by Cartesian dualism; and, in turn, the implication would then be that the behaviour to be explained would not be of the sort defined by Cartesian dualism, either. The Cartesian concepts of mind and matter (including the body and behaviour) stand or fall together.

In positing two such distinct substances as mind and matter, modern dualism made the prospect of relation between them irredeemably problematic. So far as concerned mind and body in particular, a relatively straightforward sign of the problem was the apparent impossibility of causal interaction between the two. But the same underlying difficulty gave rise to a variety of problems concerning the expression of mind in behaviour, among which was the 'problem of knowledge of other minds'.

Cartesian mind was private: mental states, according to dualism, are known directly in one's own case, but otherwise they can be known only indirectly, by problematic inference from behaviour and speech. This epistemological problem did not arise at the start. The great seventeenth-century epistemological problem was not knowledge of other minds, but knowledge of the reality posited by the new physics. It should be emphasized that this reality was not the familar one apparent in perception. Rather, the epistemological problem followed on the distinction between the world of sensory appearance and the *absolute* reality 'behind' it, a distinction fundamental to seventeenth-century science and made explicit in Cartesian dualism (Burtt 1932). The problem of knowledge of the external world (nature itself) remained the 'scandal of philosophy' until Kant. Within the Cartesian (seventeenth century) metaphysics, matter and mind were both problematic, each in their own, though interdependent, ways. Within this context, however, there was no problem of knowledge of other minds. This question, as to how one subject can know another, was beside the point, indeed could not arise, while there remained the problem of the (one) subject's knowledge of object. Rather, the problem of intersubjectivity began to make its appearance, through the nineteenth century, within post-Kantian idealism, as the subject came to be seen as embodied, within nature, and among others (Bolton 1982; Mensch 1988).

The problem of knowledge of mind, that is to say, of 'other minds', arose in a particularly stark form within the foundations of psychological science in the latter decades of the nineteenth century. The possibilities and the problems of the new science were defined by dualism. Given acceptance of the Cartesian concept of mind, scientific psychology confronted two main tasks: study of mental phenomena (consciousness, sensation, perception, memory, and so on), and study of their relation to physical events. The first programme constituted the core of psychology, the second was the subsidiary psychophysiology. Both required a method of observing mental events, and the methodology implied by dualism was clear: mental phenomena are observed directly by their subject in introspection, while they are known only indirectly by others, on the basis, primarily, of the subject's introspective reports. However, this introspectionist methodology was problematic on various counts, such as reliability and its restrictive reliance on language-use. Behind such practical disadvantages lay the fundamental problem that Cartesian mental states were epistemically private, inaccessible to public observation and verification. This privacy, and the ontological status of mind as distinct from matter, were thoroughly problematic from the point of view of science method.

New options were needed. An alternative was indeed available within dualism, for inherent in it was the possibility of an alternative methodology concerned exclusively with the material world, and to what is accessible to public observation, namely, *behaviour*. While behaviourism represented a radically new approach to psychological science, still it operated within the thought-space defined by Cartesian dualism. Behaviourism was defined by dualism, negatively and positively. Dualism defined what it was that behaviourism was excluding as irrelevant to science, namely, the Cartesian mind. Further, and positively, Cartesian dualism bequethed to behaviourism its general model of the topic of the new science, according to which the body, as Cartesian matter, is fundamentally non-intelligent, or *mechanical*, in particular, governed by the operation of reflex arcs. Behaviourism as a methodology eschewed reference to mental states for the purpose of explaining behaviour. Without a role in explanation, mental states were, from the point of view of psychological science, non-existent: there was no reason to posit them. Explanation of behaviour confined itself to causes in the environment, to stimuli affecting the agent. There was, however, available to methodological behaviourism a limited notion of something going on within the organism, namely, direct causal connections between stimuli and responses. These direct stimulus–response connections could be innately wired in, as anticipated in the Cartesian notion of the reflex arc, or made in learning procedures, according to the principles of association, in classical or operant conditioning. (On the early development of modern psychological science see, for example, Zangwill 1950; Robinson 1976; Gardner 1985; Baars 1986; Brennan 1986; Leahey 1994.)

1.2.2 Explanation of behaviour in terms of cognitive states

Methodological behaviourism combined with stimulus–response psychology domi-nated animal learning theory in the first decades of the twentieth century. There were signs of dissent even within animal learning theory, however, as psychologists in the 1930s and 1940s sought to model 'higher' forms of behaviour, and apparently found the need to invoke cognitive states and processes. Two related features of behaviour were particularly important here. First, animal behaviour is characteristically *purposive*, or *goal-directed*, and secondly, that this purposive behaviour is frequently *plastic*, that is to say, is flexible according to circumstances. One kind of example of plasticity is that of rats which, having learnt to run through a maze to the goal-box will, if the maze is flooded, swim to it (Macfarlane 1930). Flexible, purposive behaviour exhibits certain *higher-order invariants* which are not evident at the level of simple, physical (geometrical) descriptions of behaviour. Distinct sequences of behaviour can have in common that they lead to the same goal, and also, as in the example above, two behavioural sequences can follow the same path. It is then plausible to suppose that behaviour exhibits these invariants because the relevant features of the environment are *represented in (encoded in)* the animal. This is to say, what the animal acquires in the learning process is a 'map' of the maze, and an 'expectancy' of the goal. In this way plastic, purposive behaviour lends itself to cognitive modes of description and explanation, while non-purposive, or uniform, stereotyped behaviour, does not. Many experiments were devised to demonstrate the purposive nature of behaviour, and, in particular, various types of plasticity of means to end.[1]

Cognitive learning theory stands in contrast to the more straightforward stimulus–re-sponse model. According to the former, associations between stimuli are acquired, not only associations between stimuli and responses. The contrast here can be expressed in various ways. One is to say that the cognitive model posits *representations* of the environment, something like a 'mental map', the most simple form of which would be patterns of stimulus–stimulus associations. On the other hand, it is worthwhile noting that the stimulus–response model can be construed as positing a kind of representation: stimuli are represented at least in the sense that they cause specific responses. The connection between representation of the environment and the behaviour it gives rise to is very clear in stimulus–response theory. In fact, however, the connection is made too close, so that the difference between representation and the behaviour caused collapses, and we are left only with the latter. What happens in cognitive theory is that representations of stimuli are allowed *to interact with one another* before the production of behaviour. This feature of the theory accomodates the fact that there is (in 'higher' behaviour) no one–one link between particular stimuli and particular responses. Hence also the frequently cited characterization of cognitive as opposed to stimulus–response theory, namely, that it explains behaviour as a response to *interpretations* of stimuli, not to stimuli immediately; or again, that the connection between stimuli and responses is mediated by representations.

Another way of making out the difference between the cognitive paradigm and the earlier stimulus–response psychology uses the term *information*. According to the cognitive model, information is picked up from the environment, processed, which processing includes assimilation into pre-existing cognitive maps, and states carrying processed information mediate between between stimulus and response. Stimulus–response explanation, on the other hand, needs a notion of information defined only in terms of the S–R linkage, a notion so minimal that it does not require separate consideration.

Stimulus–response psychology belonged with behaviourist methodology, as noted above, and so naturally the theoretical move towards the cognitive paradigm implied also a methodological shift. The methodological question is: what is required for an adequate explanation of behaviour? Given Cartesian preconceptions according to which mental states are immaterial and causally irrelevant, it follows readily enough that they will have no role in the explanation of behaviour, that our methodological presuppositions should be confined to environmental stimuli, and their direct causal effect on behaviour. The question, then, was whether this alone could do all the required explanatory work. And the answer seemed to be 'no' in the case of explanation of the goal-directed and plastic characteristics of higher animal behaviour. And in so far as these characteristics require for their explanation the postulate of representations, or information-carrying states, then this postulate becomes a methodological presupposition.

In the background of this move away from behaviourism is an epistemological change on a large scale. A fundamental reason why early psychological science eschewed mental states was that they were epistemically private, accessible only to the subject, by introspection. The issues in animal learning theory, however, were already well removed from this Cartesian concept of mind. The issues, of course, had nothing to do with rats introspecting mental states, but rather concerned what was needed in theory for the explanation of behaviour and, together with that, for predictive power. In psychological science, mental states are introduced into the picture, if they are introduced at all, if theory requires them for the purposes of explanation and prediction of behaviour. As already indicated, their role in theory is essentially a matter of carrying information, used in the control of action. This use of the notion of mental states is quite different from the Cartesian. In the Cartesian framework the definition of mental states is fundamentally epistemological: mental states are known immediately, infallibly, by their subject. It is precisely this property that makes mental states so far irrelevant to psychological science. Mental states become relevant to psychological science in so far as postulating them facilitates the purposes of scientific theory, these being, briefly, explanation and prediction. This handle on the notion of mental states presupposes, indeed is, an epistemology. The theory of knowledge of mental states is, in very broad terms, as follows: mental states are known (beliefs about them are evaluated) with reference to the predictive power and success of theory which postulates them.

Two features of this new epistemology may be noted here. First, it suits primarily a third-person perspective, and owes an account of any special characteristics of first-person (subjective) knowledge of mental states. The position here is exactly the opposite to the Cartesian. Secondly, the new epistemology of mental states, with its appeal to theory as opposed to direct observation, belongs with a more general 'post-empiricist' epistemology. These two points, concerning post-empiricist epistemology, and knowledge of one's own mental states, will be taken up later in the chapter, in section 1.4.

There was much to be said on either side of the debate within animal learning theory between the stimulus–response and cognitive approaches, but as is well-known, and as just implied, the issue was not at all just a local one. A paradigm shift in and around psychological science was beginning. The debate within animal learning theory came to be settled decisively in favour of the cognitive model, largely under the influence of external developments, which showed up inadequacies in the concepts of stimulus–response theory, and which replaced rigidly construed behavioural methodology by methodologies explicitly employing cognitive concepts. These developments were particularly in linguistics, artificial intelligence and mathematical information theory, and they promoted what has come to be called the 'cognitive revolution' in psychology in the 1950s and 1960s. Let us review briefly these external influences.[2]

We consider first Chomsky's well-known critique (1959) of Skinner's project of explaining language learning and use in terms of the concepts and principles of stimulus–response theory. Chomsky's criticisms illustrate the points discussed above concerning the weaknesses of stimulus–response theory and its accompanying strict behavioural methodology. Early in the paper Chomsky remarks on the reason why Skinner's programme appears so 'bold and remarkable' (Chomsky 1959, pp. 48–49, original italics):

> It is not primarily the fact that he has set functional analysis as his problem, or that he limits himself to study of *observables*, i.e., input–output relations. What is so surprising is the particular limitations he has imposed on the way in which the observables of behaviour are to be studied, and, above all, the particularly simple nature of the *function* which, he claims, describes the causation of behaviour. One would naturally expect that prediction of the behavior of a complex organism (or machine) would require, in addition to information about external stimulation, knowledge of the internal structure of the organism, the ways in which it processes input information and organizes its own behavior.

Such reference to 'internal' structure and processes was precisely what Skinner wished to avoid, emphasizing rather external factors, such as stimulus, reinforcement, etc. Chomsky proceeded to argue, however, that these (and related) fundamental concepts of conditioning theory, while they may be given relatively specific operational definitions in the experimental paradigms of animal learning theory, come to lose clear meaning outside of these contexts, and the principles (laws) which employ them become vacuous or trivial. On the notion of *stimulus-control* of an utterance, for example, Chomsky writes (Chomsky 1959, p. 52, original italics):

> A typical example . . . would be the response to a piece of music with the utterance *Mozart* or to a painting with response *Dutch*. These responses are asserted to be 'under the control of extremely subtle properties' of the physical object or event [Skinner 1957, p. 108]. Suppose instead of saying *Dutch* we had said *Clashes with the wall-paper, I thought you liked abstract work, Never saw it before, Tilted, Hanging too low, Beautiful, Hideous, Remember our camping trip last summer?*, or whatever else might come into our minds when looking at the picture . . . Skinner could only say that each of these responses is under the control of some other stimulus property of the physical object. If we look at a red chair and say *red*, the response is under the stimulus control of the stimulus *redness*; if we say *chair*, it is under the control of the collection of properties *chairness* . . ., and similarly for any other response. This device is as simple as it is empty.

The point at issue here is that in complex behaviour, such as speaking a language, there is plasticity in response: we can respond in many ways to the same stimulus. Or better, in many ways to the same stimulus *as described in physical terms*. To say in *these* terms that behaviour is under stimulus-control is false. On the other hand, we can adopt an alternative way of characterizing the stimulus, namely, the stimulus *as represented by*, or, *as described by*, the subject; but then, we lose complete objectivity in the description, and rely on the familiar concepts of common-sense, mentalistic psychology. And to say in *these* terms that behaviour is under stimulus-control may well be true, but if so, trivially. Thus, Chomsky continues (ibid.):

> Since properties are free for the asking . . . we can account for a wide class of responses in terms of Skinnerian functional analysis by identifying the *controlling stimuli*. But the word *stimulus* has lost all objectivity in this usage. Stimuli are no longer part of the outside physical world; they are driven back into the organism. We identify the stimulus when we hear the response. It is clear from such examples, which abound, that the talk of stimulus control simply disguises a complete retreat to mentalistic psychology.

The problem for the claim that utterances are under stimulus control can be put briefly as follows. Either the stimulus is identified independently of the meaning of the utterance (e.g. in physical terms) or its identification depends on the meaning of the utterance. But on the first reading the claim is false, and on the second it is vacuous. What is vacuous here is any purported explanation of uttering sentences with this or that meaning.

The same general obstacle faces the attempt to define the meaningful content of information-carrying states in terms of their causes. Such a proposal goes under the name of causal semantics; it will be discussed in Chapter 4 and faced with a line of argument similar to Chomsky's against Skinner. We anticipated these sorts of issues earlier in the discussion of the cognitive paradigm in contrast with stimulus–response psychology, concluding that, at least in the psychological explanation of higher behaviour, the content of representation cannot be defined primarily in terms of the stimuli represented, but rather with reference to the activity which, in interaction with other representations, it regulates.

Related problems are encountered in the definition of *response*. One problem pointed out by Chomsky is that Skinner does not attempt to specify what kind of similarity in form is required for two physical events to be considered instances of the same operant. Chomsky, as Skinner, is concerned here of course with identifying units of verbal behaviour, but the problem of *criteria of identification of responses* is a general one for operant theory. Consider an example that is not to do with language: the movement, physically defined, of lifting one's arm. This could count as a variety of actions (or behaviours), such as stretching, greeting, holding up the traffic, surrendering, depending on the context, internal and external. The same physical event (bodily movement) can be many behaviours. But also vice versa: the same behaviour (or action) can be instanced by a variety of bodily movements. In this critical sense the notions of *same behaviour*, and of *behaviour* itself, await definition. As Chomsky observes in connection with linguistic utterances, 'extrapolation' of the definition of response from the limited experimental paradigms is of no use: operational definitions cannot (by definition) be applied to a different class of phenomena (Chomsky p. 1959, 53).

The issue here is nothing less than the nature of the *explanandum* for psychological theory, and it can be usefully expressed in terms of 'intentionality', a concept that will be discussed in Section 1.3. Stimulus–response theory is most happy with the response being understood as being a physically defined movement of the body. Behaviour in this sense has no intentionality—in brief, it is not about anything—and is likely not to require any posit of regulation by intentional states for its explanation. But on the other hand, and of course, it is also taken for granted that the behaviour of interest to (any) psychological theory does have intentionality, whether the behaviour be, for example, bar-pressing, or speech production. Typically, as Chomsky observes, S–R theory trades on ambiguity between construing behaviour as being non-intentional on the one hand and intentional on the other, with the heavy reliance on operational definition in terms of experimental paradigms allowing and obscuring this ambiguity. The significance of this is that what is required in theory critically depends on the nature of the behavioural *explanandum*. While non-intentional behaviour can be regarded as the effects of non-intentional causes, explanation of intentional behaviour, with its characteristic goal-directedness and adapativeness, requires the notion of regulation by intentional states. Aspects of this point have been considered earlier in this section, and it is discussed further below (subsection 1.3.6).

The correspondence between behavioural movements and the actions thereby performed is a loose and variable one. Here we see an expression of the plasticity which causes profound trouble for behaviourism and S–R theory. There is no simple one–one mapping between physically defined stimuli and stimuli that control behaviour, and none either between physically defined bodily movements and behaviour. The (considerable) slack between physically defined events and the behavioural phenomena is precisely what is taken up with reference to internal, cognitive processes. And so, in attempting to make plausible his operant theory, Skinner repeatedly lapses into (for him) illicit reliance on mentalistic concepts. This happens again, Chomsky notes (1959, pp. 53–4), in the case of response-strength, defined as 'probability of emission': Skinner's detailed treatment of examples relies on appeal to concepts such as *interest, intention, belief.*

The trouble with Skinner's notion of reinforcement, and the law of effect which invokes it, is even more acute. Since reinforcement is defined as a stimulus capable of increasing response-strength, the claim of the Law of Effect, that reinforcement increases response-strength, is patently a tautology. Skinner is forced into this trivialization because of the impossibility of finding a non-vacuous characterization of reinforcement, that is, colloquially, of what living beings are motivated to work for. Of course, examples abound, but can they be captured without reference to what living creatures in fact do work for? Presumably not. And consequently, the so-called law of effect is doomed to vacuousness, or, at the very least, it has no advantages over our common-sense, mentalistic explanations. Having reviewed many of Skinner's examples of reinforcement, Chomsky concludes (Chomsky pp. 1959, 56–7, original italics):

> The phrase 'X is reinforced by Y . . .' is being used for a cover term for 'X wants Y', 'X likes Y', 'X wishes that Y were the case', etc. Invoking the term *reinforcement* has no explanatory force, and any idea that this paraphrase introduces any new clarity or objectivity into the description of wishing, liking, etc., is a serious delusion. . . . A mere terminological revision, in which a term borrowed from the laboratory is used with the full vagueness of the ordinary vocabulary, is of no conceivable interest.

Following his critique of Skinner's programme, Chomsky outlined a positive way forward, namely, consideration of the syntactic structure of language, and of the way in which knowledge of grammer, internalized in the speaker, contributes to verbal behaviour. In this way the notion of *internalized structures and rules* became central to a cognitive, non-behavioural, theory of language learning and use. The details, however, of Chomsky's new linguistics are not our concern in the present argument. The relevant points may be summarized as follows: that stimulus–response psychology, and the concepts of conditioning on which it is based, are inadequate for the explanation of complex, plastic behaviour; that its systematic attempt to down-play the subject's contribution in such behaviour becomes combined with implicit and illicit reliance on the mentalistic concepts of common sense; and that an explicit theory of the subjective contribution to complex behaviour typically postulates internalized structures and rules. This latter idea became pivotal in the new 'cognitive revolution' in psychology.

A second major influence contributing to this revolution in the 1950s and 1960s was the application in psychology of methods and models from the new discipline of artificial intelligence (AI), that is, the construction of machines, computers, real or ideal, which can simulate aspects of (natural) intelligence. The relevance of AI methodology to cognitive psychology is profound. It provides ways of conceiving and modelling mental processes, such as (obviously) computation, and (less obviously) attention and perception, which, on the one hand, permit experimental investigation and test, and which, on the other, carry no implication that these mental processes operate within some non-physical medium. In these ways the new methodology removed two major obstacles to the scientific study of the mind, obstacles that had given rise, inevitably but temporarily, to behaviourism. AI terminology and methodology greatly influenced the theory of and research into particular cognitive capactites: attention, perception, memory, language comprehension, etc. (Neisser 1967; Anderson 1983; Johnson-Laird 1988; Boden 1988). But in addition to this influence in faculty-specific research, and of course related to it, the new AI gave new and powerful form to cognitive theories of behaviour. It endorsed and elaborated the idea that cognitive processes are involved in the organization and regulation of complex, plastic, rule-guided behaviour (Miller *et al.* 1960). It is this contribution of AI which is of particular relevance to the present theme.

It may be remarked immediately, however, that the AI model of cognitive processes at work in the mediation of behaviour raises as well as solves conceptual problems. As noted in the above discussion of cognitive theories of animal learning, what seems to be required for the explanation of complex behaviour is the concept of a *representation of the environment*. Now while AI offers a model of internal processes which underlie intelligent behaviour, the model is essentially one of *computations*, that is, roughly, rule-following manipulations of (transformations of) symbols; but there is apparently no mention yet of anything like *representation of the environment*. This is to say, the concepts in AI pertain, at least in the first instance, to the *syntax* of symbols, but they do not yet explicate their *semantics*, that is, their meaning, or their representational properties. This indeed has been regarded as one of the major inadequacies of AI models of mental processes. Or, the argument can be turned the other way round: success of computational models of mind can be used to cast doubt on the legitimacy of concepts of mind which invoke meaning. These issues are taken up in the next chapter.

Let us finally mention briefly a third major influence contributing to the cognitive revolution in psychology, mathematical communication theory (MCT) (Shannon and Weaver 1949). MCT is concerned with certain statistical quantities associated with 'sources', 'channels', and 'receivers'. When a particular condition is realized at a source, and there are other conditions which could have been realized, the source can be regarded as a *generator of information*. For example, in throwing a dice the result reduces six possibilities to one actuality, and therefore generates information, quantified as log (2) 6, = 2.6 bits. The amount of information generated is relative to a receiver, in particular, to the amount of information already in the receiver about the source; in the example above it is assumed that prior to the throw we know only that six results are equally possible. Various applications of MCT to psychology were made, for example in psychophysical models (Miller 1953; Attneave 1959; Garner 1962).

However, in addition to specific applications of details of MCT, it reinforced use of the information-processing terminology which has come to pervade cognitive psychology and the cognitive sciences generally. The terminology can be used to formulate the basic tenets of cognitive psychology such as the following: information is picked up from the environment, by the sense-receptors, processed (transformed, encoded) in certain ways, including into representations of the environment, which then serve in the organization and regulation of complex (purposive, plastic, rule-guided) behaviour.

On the other hand, it must be noted that the concept of information used in this way is quite distinct from, though related to, the concept as used in MCT. The concept required in cognitive psychology is, as we have already seen, a semantic one: we are interested in the fact that particular signals carry information from (and about) the environment, that this informational content is employed in the production of representations and the regulation of organism/environment interactions. The idea of informational content does not, however, figure in MCT. The mathematical theory is concerned with *how much* information is carried, not with *what* information is carried. Indeed, it does not deal with particular signals at all, hence not with their content, but with classes of signals, and the statistical averages of the amounts of information carried. In this sense the mathematical theory is of no immediate relevance in explicating the concept of semantic information which underpins theorizing in cognitive psychology, and cognitive explanations of behaviour in particular.[3]

Following this partial and brief survey of some of the major influences on the cognitive revolution in psychology, let us return to the issue with which we began, the conflict within psychology between cognitive and stimulus–response learning theories. The characteristics of animal behaviour cited in order to introduce the concepts of cognition were its goal-directedness and its plasticity. Traditionally, behaviours with these characteristics have been contrasted with behaviours, such as salivation, for which stimulus–response theory seems adequate. From a biological point of view, however, there is every reason to say that the systems serving responses such as salivation are goal-directed. Furthermore, the information-processing paradigm of course applies here. So the distinction between behaviour explicable in terms of stimulus–response connections, and 'higher' behaviour of the sort emphasized by the cognitive learning theories cannot be brought out in terms of goal-directness and information-processing. The notion of 'higher' here requires explication in some other way, and the implication of the above considerations is that it has to do with *plasticity*.

Plasticity is of two basic types: first, in cases where the same response is made to a variety of stimuli, secondly in cases where a variety of responses are made to the same stimulus. In brief, the S–R relation is not one–one, but is one–many or many–one. Both these types of plasticity occur in the context of goal-directed behaviour, and they have the function precisely to serve in the attainment of the relevant goal. The goal is constant, but if it is to be achieved under varying patterns of environmental conditions, the behaviour of the living being has to be adaptive, plastic in one or other or both of the ways described. Adaptive behaviour thus exhibits *invariants* across physically distinct stimuli, responses, and sequences of interaction. It is in this respect that we distinguish 'higher' animal behaviour (such as flexible route-finding, problem-solving) from conditioned behaviour, and even more so from the operation of biological subsystems, which, though goal-directed and mediated by information, exhibit no, or relatively less, plasticity.

The above remarks suggest a connection between behavioural plasticity and the nature of informational content. In the absence of plasticity, it is plausible to say that patterns of information are already in the environment, requiring only to be picked up and used (acted upon) by an appropriately designed system. But to the extent that there is plasticity, patterns of information already in the environment are not of the kind apparently at work in the regulation of behaviour. Rather, what regulates behaviour has to be considered the result of work done within the living being. The information has to be more 'processed'. For example, two physically distinct stimuli, or two physically distinct sequences of behaviour, have to come to be treated as the same. The conclusion is, then, that information-processing systems are more complex, 'higher', indeed increasingly 'cognitive', to the degree that the result of processing which regulates behaviour of the system is different from the information being received. Or again: to the degree that behaviour is determined by 'subjective' as well as 'objective' factors.

All these considerations, concerning plasticity, informational content, the importance of contribution of the agent, the distinction between lower and higher forms of cognition, will recur repeatedly in one context or another throughout this essay.

We consider next what the cognitive psychology paradigm has to say about two large topics: consciousness and affect. These brief discussions are included to make more adequate the characterization of the cognitive paradigm used here, with particular attention to points directly relevant to the main themes of the essay, concerning the explanation of behaviour in terms of meaningful, mental states.

1.2.3 In living beings cognition is already affective

It is obvious enough, given the formative influence of such disciplines as transformational linguistics, AI modelling, and mathematical communication theory, that cognitive psychology erred on the side of saying little about affect. Producers of syntactic strings of symbols, computers, and mathematically defined signal exchangers are, so far, unemotional. On the other hand, and as made prominent in the presentation in the preceding section, fundamental to cognitive psychology was the project of explaining animal behaviour in terms of cognitive states. The cognitive theory of action has to posit at least goals, methods of achieving them, and means of determining success or failure, and these elements are enough to provide a basis for the concept of affect (Miller *et al.* 1960; Pfeifer 1988; Oatley 1988). The absence of the notion from the models that helped to form cognitive psychology was connected to the fact that these critical elements were more or less obviously absent. The production of well-formed syntax so far has no point, except itself. Neither does information exchange between mathematically defined systems. Computers can be made to perform tasks, but they don't mind whether they achieve them or not, and in this sense the tasks, and the notions of success and failure, are ours rather than theirs. The notions of goals, and success and failure in achieving them, belong primarily to biological systems, for which success as opposed to failure *matters*.

Living beings depend for their survival on achieving certain outcomes and avoiding others. They show a definite preference for success in these tasks, and hence interest in the environment and the results of their actions. We refer here to the activity of the living being as a whole, but the notions of goals, success, and failure can be applied secondarily to biological subsystems, in so far as their normal functioning is essential for the integrity of the whole. The adaptiveness and plasticity of action is designed precisely for the achievement of goals in the face of variation and adversity. The position for living as opposed to inanimate systems is that they strive to achieve whatever is required for their integrity. Adaptiveness, plasticity, urgency, rest, and motion are examples of the kind of behavioural characteristics that the notion of 'striving to achieve' seeks to capture and interpret.

This is the context in which the notion of affect starts to work. States of affairs have a 'valency' for the living being, positive or negative, according to whether they promote or disrupt its integrity and capacity for action. Perception of states of affairs as being in this sense positive or negative is linked closely to plans for appropriate action, such as approach or avoidance. In this way affective responses to situations are associated with motives for action. Commonly cited as basic emotions are happiness, anger, fear, sadness, and disgust. With the possible exception of the latter, these emotions involve perceptions of situations as affecting integrity and action, and are closely linked to behavioural responses. Happiness is linked to achievement of goals and perhaps temporary absence of others; anger is a response to being hurt, and includes the impulse to retaliate, fear includes perception of threat and leads to fleeing or fighting, sadness follows loss of what is valued, and involves yearning, and so on. The notion of 'basic emotions' here belongs to biology and evolutionary theory in particular, but also to the a priori (philosophical) theory of action. There is a close link between these two kinds of theory, exploited throughout the essay, in so far as each seeks to define what is fundamental to action.[4]

Cognition and affect are both defined in terms of action: cognition serves action by processing information; affect signifies the point of it all. But these are interwoven, aspects of one activity. The goals of action have to be represented, and its methods have to have an aim. From the point of view of the philosophy and psychology of action, emotion has cognitive structure and content, and cognition is in the service of achieving aims, and hence involves affect.

These principles will recur in a variety of contexts as we proceed. They affirm close links between cognition and emotion, but this is not to say that the two are indistinguishable. Clearly they are, to some extent, depending on the type of case in hand. Cognitive processing can be relatively affect-less, in the absence of any real goal or, again, if divorced from action. How far processing here is typical of cognition in everyday life is open to doubt, and this is reflected in the increasing shift of focus in cognitive psychology from articifical experimental paradigms to those with more ecological (and biological) validity. Also, emotion may be in various ways independent of cognition, and this is exploited in research on the effects of mood on cognition. It is, for example, possible to make someone unhappy by giving her information (e.g. about a loss) and then to study what effects this negative mood state has on memory, for example that she remembers negative events, such as previous losses. Clearly, this kind of interaction does not count against the general principle that emotions are cognitive and cognitions emotional.[5]

On the other hand, emotion may be experienced in the apparent absence of appropriate cognition. However, assuming that the emotion is salient (intense, persistent, with effects on behaviour), the apparent absence of appropriate cognition raises the question of abnormal function. A possible explantion is that the emotion has been caused not by the processing of information but by lower-level interference to the physiological structures and processes which serve the emotions, for example by naturally occurring biochemical imbalance. Another kind of explanation is that emotion and cognition have become dissociated for psychological reasons: the object of the emotion may be intolerable to the person, for example. In the same way there are, broadly speaking, two ways of explaining cognition in the apparent absence of the appropriate emotion. One posits lower-level disruption of information-processing, the other invokes rules at the level of the information-carrying states themselves. The distinction between these two kinds of causal pathway, and their roles in the generation of disorder, will be developed as major themes in the essay, and need not detain us here. For now the main point is simply that the apparent absence of connection between (strong) emotion and appropriate cognition so far suggests a breakdown in normal functioning, and in this sense such cases are exceptions that prove the rule.

The interwoven nature of cognition and emotion in living beings may be expressed by saying that cognitive states, to the extent that they are emotionally charged, are already sources of energy, specifically motivators of action. The formulation is relevant to the conclusion drawn in this chapter, that explanations which invoke mental, meaningful states are causal, and to the claim worked out through chapters 4 and 5 that information-processing, or intentionality, is the basis of a distinctive form of causal explanation.

1.2.4. Consciousness: empirical questions and philosophical problems

We turn now to consider the role of consciousness in the cognitive psychology paradigm. Cognitive states are posited as representations (information-carrying states) involved in the regulation of action. This conception, or definition, of cognition stands in marked contrast to the Cartesian. In Cartesian dualism, cognition is a feature of mind, as opposed to matter, and the defining characteristic of mind is that it is known indubitably to the subject. In this conception, it is not at all part of the definition of cognition that it serves action, nor indeed that it represents anything external: Cartesian mind could, in principle, be just as it is even in the absence of the body and of the rest of the external, material world. The absence in the Cartesian famework of any role for mind in the running of behaviour shows up clearly in its conception of behaviour as mechanical, as 'non-intelligent'. But just as the Cartesian conception has little to say about those features of mind, cognition and behaviour, which are treated as axiomatic in cognitive psychology, so conversely, cognitive psychology has some difficulty encompassing what is fundamental in Cartesian dualism: subjective awareness, or consciousness. This is to say, these concepts are not built into the foundations of the theory, historically or logically.

Within the cognitive psychology paradigm, the essential function of cognitive states is to serve in the regulation of action, and it does not belong to their definition that they are known to the subject. Indeed, and this is the point already implicit in the paragraph above, the paradigm so far has nothing to say about cognitive states 'being known to the subject'. Cognitive psychology can accomodate the notions of consciousness and subjective awareness in its own terms, that is, in so far as they have a role in explanation of certain features of information-processing and (ultimately) the regulation of action. These features would include selective attention, high levels of analysis (processing), executive control, and the subjective report in language of information-processing and information-carrying states. It is typically for the purpose of explaining phenomena of these kinds that cognitive psychological models invoke the notion of consciousness. A corollary, unsuprising in the context sketched above, is that in terms of these sorts of criteria of consciousness, most information-processing is pre-conscious or unconscious. Conscious states and processes are a subset of those that regulate behaviour, for example, as already indicated, those with an executive role, and/or closely linked (in language-users) to verbal report.

In this general context many kinds of question arise, more or less connected to one another. One immediate issue is whether the external criteria of consciousness can diverge. Can there be cognitive states which regulate behaviour but which are, in principle, inaccessible to conscious reporting? Do unconscious cognitive states use something other than language-like symbolism? Are they linked particularly with drives, or emotions? Can conscious and unconscious regulations of action come into conflict, with the implication of disorder in case they do? Aspects of some of these issues will be considered later, for example conflict and disorder in subsection 1.4.3 and Chapter 8, and distinction between kinds of encoding in AI models in the next chapter (Section 2.2). Otherwise, we leave aside details of the distinction between conscious and unconscious in terms of the cognitive psychology paradigm, making only the general observation that in the paradigm what is essential to cognitive states is regulation of behaviour, as opposed to 'subjective awareness'. This general conception permits subsequent distinctions between conscious and unconscious modes of cognition and the formulation of empirical questions about them as indicated above.[6]

We shall return to the role of consciousness later, in a developmental context (Section 6.4), but before leaving the topic at this stage we may note that philosophical as well as empirical questions surround the concept. These 'philosophical problems' derive from the Cartesian concept of mind and the deep theory change involved in its replacement by the cognitive-behavioural paradigm. The dualism between mind and matter in seventeenth-century philosophy, as formulated by Descartes, was overdetermined, being many distinctions at once. Mind was equivalent to consciousness, to appearance, and to representation (thought), in contrast to matter, which was the reality represented by thought. The seventeenth-century picture as a whole was highly and irredeemably problematic, mainly because the postulated reality lay beyond the appearances and could be not be known directly, or at all, by the subject of thought, the *cogito*. But notwithstanding this major anomaly, the theory stood, supported by fundamental assumptions. As already indicated (subsection 1.2.1), a major assumption of the modern world-view was that the material world described by the new philosophy of nature (physics) was absolute, and therefore had to be distinguished from the objects given in sense-appearances, which are relative objects, tainted by subjectivity.

Moving beyond this original seventeenth-century metaphysics, a more superficial dualism takes for granted the material world, including (human) bodies, and then wonders whether these bodies (other than one's own) have immaterial minds. This 'problem of other minds' has already been mentioned (in subsection 1.2.1) as implicated in methodological behaviourism. It is essentially a hotchpotch problem, a transitionary thought-stage between the original Cartesian dualism and the non-dualist idea that mind is revealed in the activity of the human body (being), an idea which in turn permits knowledge of one subject by another. The view that mental processes regulate higher activity, and hence can be inferred on the basis of that activity, has become commonplace, and, accordingly, scepticism about other minds has become out of date, a 'philosophical' problem only, or one belonging to the early history of psychological science.

However, the hotchpotch problem still lives on, just about, in a still more emaciated form, as the (or one of the) 'philosophical' problems of *consciousness*. Do living beings, or some of them, have conscious states (sometimes called 'qualia'), or some special quality of awareness, over and above particular forms of information-processing, undetectable by any means known to man or woman? What can be detected, from the outside, are (only), we are inclined to say, *signs* of consciousness, of particular forms of information-processing, such as selective attention and self-report. But consciousness itself, so this line of thought continues, seems unknowable, except in one's own case. But then—and here we have the feeling of a typically philosophical conundrum—in one's own case one seems to be aware of *nothing but* objects of consciousness. After all—and here we remind ourselves of the original Cartesian problem (subsection 1.2.1)—what one knows in one's own case are conscious sense-experiences (sights, sounds, touch, etc.), not any material substance over and above (or underneath) these.

The correct inference here is that consciousness cannot be thought of as something separable from the objects of empirical knowledge. There is, however, a distinction to be drawn between the subject's knowledge of objects and the subject's knowledge of other subjects. In the former, consciousness is indistinguishable from the experience of reality. In the latter, consciousness in another subject is indistinguishable from its appearances in the person's activity, and this is the methodological assumption suited to cognitive science.[7]

1.2.5 'Folk psychology' within the paradigm

The cognitive paradigm in psychological science posits cognitive, information-carrying states for the purpose of explaining and predicting complex behaviour. Now it is apparent—when looked at in this way—that folk psychology does the same sort of thing.

Explanation of behaviour in terms of the mental states of the agent are familiar in everyday discourse. In order to explain why a person is acting in such-and-such a way we suppose that she has, at least, certain beliefs and a desire: beliefs about current circumstances and about the effects of her actions, and desire for a particular result. This form of psychological explanation is apparently used in all cultures including our own, and prior to any psychological science, and it has come to be called in the recent literature 'folk psychology' (Stich 1983; Fodor 1987; Astington *et al.* 1988; Mele 1992). A critical point here is that folk psychology does not serve only the hermeneutic purpose of making sense of the phenomena retrospectively, but also facilitates the prediction of action. This may be made by a detached observer, but prediction here also, and most importantly, means the mutual anticipation which is a condition of social life.

Folk psychology includes explanations of action in terms of beliefs and desires, but also accounts of the origin of beliefs in terms of experience, of experience in terms of reality, and of desire in terms of need. These sorts of explanation are characteristic of folk psychology, but they are also used in the social sciences and in some branches of psychology, such as social, developmental, and clinical psychology, especially in the psychoanalytic tradition.

Crucial to folk psychological mental states is their so-called meaningful content, typically specified by propositional clauses of natural languages, referring to actual or possible states of affairs. A person has the belief that such-and-such is the case, or the desire that it should be the case; and so on. The meaning of mental states is critical to the interconnections among them, and to their relation to action.

The at least superficial similarity between cognitive-behavioural psychology and folk psychology may give rise to surprise and consternation. The surprise is that while scientifically respectable paradigms, such as conditioning theory and physiological psychology, say little or nothing about mind and meaning, these being matters for the unscientific folk, including the pseudo-scientific psychoanalytic theorists, we now have a scientifically respectable paradigm, the successor to conditioning theory, and compatible with an up-dated physiological psychology, which essentially posits something like mental, meaningful, intervening states for the purpose of explaining behaviour. Then the consternation: so does not the cognitive paradigm here come up against all that looked problematic about this sort of alleged explanation? How can there be a 'science' of mind, or of meaning? One response then is to back-peddle: cognitive psychology does not really posit anything like meaningful, mental states, after all. This skirmish will be discussed later (in subsection 1.3.8, and again in Section 4.4), but first we turn in the next section to work around the problem of meaning, specifically bringing out its intimate link with action (interaction) and hence its fundamental role in psychological theory.

1.3 INTENTIONALITY AND MEANING: THE MARK OF MIND AND ACTION

1.3.1 Some (rough) definitions

Intentionality is a concept much used in current philosophy of mind and psychological theory. It has two main aspects. First, it refers to *aboutness* (or *directedness*). To say that a belief (or fear, or hope, or any other information-carrying state) has intentionality means partly that it is *about something*, typically an object, or state of affairs. Furthermore, and this is the second aspect of intentionality, it is not necessary that this 'something', that which, for example, the belief is about, exists in reality. One can believe that such-and-such is the case, when it is not; one can fear something that does not exist; and so on. The proposal that intentionality is the defining characteristic of mind, credited to Brentano (1874), has become the focus of many issues in contemporary philosophical and theoretical psychology.[8]

Readers unfamiliar with this term of philosophical art should note that intentionality as meant here has nothing specifically to do with intentions in the everyday sense, except in so far as intentions, like any other mental states, have intentionality, and the concept has still less to do with conscious, verbally expressed intentions.

A philosophical term of art distinct though connected to *intentionality* is *intensionality* (spelt with an 's' rather than a 't'). It may be thought of as applying directly to sentences, and secondarily to the states they describe. Two characterizations of intensionality may be given, though they can be made into one. One of the characterizations is plainly close to the definition of intentionality: a compound sentence is intensional if its truth-value does not depend on the truth-value of its component. Thus, it may be true that John believes that angels exist irrespective of whether they do.

The second way of characterizing the intensionality of sentences is as follows: a sentence is intensional if its truth-value is not preserved by substitution of co-extensive terms. John may want the biggest teddy bear in the room, though he still may not want Jill's teddy, even if . . ., etc. We can also take an example relevant to attempts to define informational content in terms of evolutionary theory, discussed at length in Chapter 4 (Section 4.5). Frogs snap at flies but also at small, ambient black dots which are not flies. What is the content of the informational states driving the behaviour: 'fly' or '(any) ambient black dot'? In effect we are asking here about the nature of the intentional object of the information-carrying state and of the behaviour that it regulates, and this can usefully be understood as a question about the appropriate intensional description.

Most mental states are described by sentences that are intensional in one or both of the above senses. Implications include that we can believe and want things that do not exist, and that we may believe or want certain things under some descriptions but not under others. These are, of course, enormously important facts about us, about our mentality in particular, to which we shall return in various ways throughout the essay. The main point may be stated briefly by saying that the mental states are about reality conceived in specific ways, in certain ways rather than others, and may be about what in reality does not exist.

Concepts closely linked to intentionality (and intensionality), include thought, representation, meaning, and information. All of these are essentially to do with 'aboutness' and 'inexistence' in the senses outlined above. The link between intentionality and thought (or thinking) suggests that Brentano's thesis is to some extent anticipated in the Cartesian idea that the *cogito* defines the mind. The close link between intentionality and meaning is expressed in the fact that intentional objects may also be called the meaning, or the meaningful content, of the intentional states. Information, too, seems to have intentionality: signals carry information about, for example, relative spatial position, or the information *that* such-and-such, etc., and it is also possible for informational content to be in *error*.

A main theme in the essay will be that intentionality, in the technical sense defined above, in terms of *aboutness* and 'inexistence', characterizes the 'information' invoked in cognitive psychological models, and indeed also that invoked in the information-processing models that permeate biology (subsection 1.3.7; Chapter 5). It is obviously critical to these lines of thought that intentionality is understood in the technical sense and is not restricted by definition to conscious, verbally expressed states of mind.

One way of expressing the line of argument to be developed later, referred to in the preceding paragraph, is to say that it extends Brentano's thesis downwards, the proposal being that intentionality characterizes not only states of mind, but more generally, the information-carrying states in functional, biological systems.

The connection between intentionality, activity, and function will be discussed briefly below (subsections 1.3.3, 1.3.4), and in more detail in chapters 4 and 5. We begin by discussing in the next subsection what the proposed view stands opposed to, this being, briefly, that intentionality (representation, thought, meaning) is a matter of being something like a picture of reality.

1.3.2 An old theory: resemblance (pictures)

In cognitive-behavioural psychology mental states are attributed to an agent, and on this basis action is explained and predicted. An essential feature of at least some of these mental states is that they carry information about the environment, about the scene of action. Such information-carrying, meaningful states are variously known as perceptions, beliefs, representations, mental models, and so on.

At this stage many questions arise. What is a representation? How does anything represent anything else, and some particular thing? How can a meaningful sign serve in the generation of action? These questions are all very closely linked together: the answer to any one of them already fixes the terms of answers to the others. Before considering them, it should be remarked that the issues are general ones, independent of the vehicle by which meaning is carried. Many kinds of item can carry information: mental states, but also pictures, words, written and spoken, and presumably states of the brain. In what follows we approach the problems of representation and meaning in relation to pictures and language. Questions as to how and in what sense the brain is a semantic system will occupy us throughout Chapter 2.

First consider the question: 'What is a representation?' It may be noticed straightaway that the word 'represent' apparently has the connotation that something (some object or state of affairs) is being in some sense *replicated*, presented again, in the sign. This in turn belongs with the idea, of which more later, that a representation must be in some sense like a picture, or image. Not all of the terms that require explication have this connotation; not, for example, 'belief' or 'information-carrying state'. But, in any case, the line of thought that links representations to pictures and images is a very powerful one. It belongs, however, to a past paradigm (to seventeenth-century philosophy, including Cartesianism and empiricism), not to the present.

The idea that representation is a matter of one item (the sign, or model) copying another (reality) has a very long history. It was conscripted into use in seventeenth-century philosophy, in the context of Cartesian dualism, but it has other origins and applications. In its most clear and strong form the idea is simply this: A represents (means) B by being a *resemblance of* B. This account looks most plausible in the case of pictures and images, and has therefore been applied primarily to mental representation, in which pictures and images seem to play a role. The account seems less well-suited to that other paradigm of meaning and representation, language.

At the start, Plato saw (in the *Cratylus*), that words apparently do not *sound like* what they represent. Characteristically, Plato was concerned with spoken language rather than with written. But it is equally true that written language does not *look like* what it represents. If the resemblance theory of meaning and representation is to be made to work for language, it has to be argued that in *some sense* 'beneath the surface', despite appearances, there is indeed a resemblance between language and the world. Plato considered, without enthusiasm, the possibility that resemblance could be found in the history (etymology) of words. In the twentieth century, a very different form of resemblance theory for language was constructed by Wittgenstein in his *Tractatus* (1921). The proposal was that propositions are pictures of states of affairs, though the pictorial form of language is beneath the surface, to be revealed by logical analysis.

Neither Plato nor Wittgenstein were led to a resemblance theory for language because of superficial plausibility, which indeed it conspicuously lacks. They were led to it rather under pressure from a profound argument, concerning the fact that language can, like other forms of representation, be *true or false* of the world. The problem is to explain how signs can be meaningful (can represent something in reality) without thereby being true; or again, it is to explain how a meaningful sign can be false. The problem can be posed as a paradox: if a sign is meaningful (is a *sign* at all), then it must stand for something in reality—but false signs correspond to nothing. The theory of meaning as resemblance serves to resolve this paradox of the false proposition. As we shall see later, in section 4.3, causal accounts of meaning have great difficulty accounting for the fact that a meaningful, information-carrying state can be false as well as true. The solution offered by the resemblance theory, expressed as in the *Tractatus*, runs briefly as follows: a picture is meaningful because its parts stand for objects in reality, but can nevertheless be false, if the objects signified do not stand in the relationship shown in the picture. Conversely, the proposition as picture is true if it is *like* the state of affairs depicted.

This theory of representation as resemblance gives clear expression to the idea of *truth as correspondence with reality*. The implication is that once the resemblance theory of representation is abandoned, we shall require an account of truth and falsity which is not based in the notions of correspondence and failure of correspondence between signs and reality. Aspects of this implication will be pursued in later chapters.

The picture theory of language encounters many problems, not the least of which is the one already mentioned, that sentences simply do not look like pictures of what they mean. However, this problem, like others, can be handled by appropriate saving devices, including particularly the notion of a logical form hidden beneath surface grammar. The overthrow of the picture theory required not only pressure from anomalies, but primarily the construction of a radically different theory of language and meaning.

Wittgenstein went on to propose a new theory in his later period. The proposal was, in brief, that *the meaning of a sign is given by its use in human activity*. Wittgenstein's account is simple on the surface but is philosophically exceedingly complex. It pervades all the works of his later period, being introduced for example in the first pages of the *Philosophical Investigations* (Wittgenstein 1953, §§1–37; with commentaries in, for example, Folgelin 1976; Bolton 1979; Pears 1988). Wittgenstein's theory of meaning as use in activity is thoroughly conducive to the proposals worked through in this essay, and will be referred to frequently. In the next subsection we note that Wittgenstein's account clearly endorses the proposal that runs though this chapter, that there are strong connections between concepts such as meaning and intentionality, and action. Wittgenstein's later-period theory of meaning is also invoked explicitly in Chapter 2, in defining the sense in which the brain encodes meaning (Section 2.6). The theory is explored further in Chapter 3, when we consider Wittgenstein's account of what it means to follow a rule (Section 3.3).

1.3.3 Intentionality based in action

The present essay adopts the view that intentionality (meaning, thought, representation) is grounded in activity. So far, following the general method of cognitive behavioural science, we have introduced meaningful mental states essentially in relation to the explanation and prediction of action. It is to be expected that the theory of meaning which belongs with this approach will likewise affirm a fundamental connection between meaning and action—and this is what Wittgenstein's later-period account does.

Broadly speaking it would be fair to say that the link between intentionality and action is relatively clear in psychological theory, in the context of its aim of explaining behaviour. The link was already apparent in the primitive stimulus–response theoretical definition of meaning (Skinner 1957; see also subsection 1.2.2, on Chomsky's critique). It is fundamental to the whole enterprise of explaining behaviour by appeal to cognitive states, as already noted, and it remains explicit in contemporary psychological theorizing (for example Looren de Jong 1991; Vedeler 1991).

On the other hand, in philosophy there is no general acceptance of the idea that there is a conceptual link between intentionality or meaning and action. It would be fair to say that since the *Tractatus* philosophers have abandoned the idea that language represents by virtue of resemblance, or, what comes more or less to the same, the idea that the truth of a proposition consists of a quasi-spatial matching between (complex) sign and state of affairs. So-called causal theories of meaning, in which the connection between meaning and activity generally does not appear as fundamental, have largely taken its place. The definition of meaning in terms of causal relations makes meaning dynamic as opposed to static, and in this sense moves away from the resemblance/picture theory and towards the connection with action. However, it fails to capture the normative distinctions essential to meaning, in this sense achieving less than the older theory, and it fails to grasp the various kinds of *creativity* involved in meaning. Making good these shortfalls leads us in effect to the link between meaning and action, in so far as action is activity which admits of normative distinctions and which is creative in various connected senses. Action as the creation of order is discussed in the context of rule-following in Chapter 3 (Section 3.3), and the weaknesses of causal semantics and the need for a functional, action-based semantics are discussed in the fourth chapter (Sections 4.3 and 4.5).

The account of meaning as being use in practice applies to signs generally, not just to those of language. Consider those signs which are paradigms for the resemblance theory of representation: pictures and images. It is plausible to suppose that we represent kinds, for example triangles or horses, in the form of mental pictures or images which resemble the items in question. But even in these most favourable cases the details are problematic. We would want to suppose that the representing mental image was like all the instances of the kind. The difficulty is, however, that instances of a kind are generally not all like one another, so that a particular mental image would have to be like some instances but not others. As Berkeley observed in connection with Locke's doctrine of general ideas, it is hard to conceive how we could form in our minds the idea of a triangle which is neither oblique nor right-angled, etc. (Berkeley 1710, p. 13). The underlying problem is that instances of a kind generally do not exhibit a common feature; rather, they are united by what Wittgenstein called 'family resemblances' (1953, §66). The absence of a common feature, in analogue or verbal form, has given rise in contemporary cognitive psychology to more sophisticated models of the representation of classes (Rosch and Mervis 1975; Fodor *et al.* 1980; Smith and Medin 1981; with recent review in Eysenck and Keane 1990, for example).

The fact that, in a plain sense, instances of a given kind generally do not all look alike disrupts the idea, fundamental to the resemblance theory of representation, that the meaning of a sign is fixed by the nature of the sign. This idea serves to make the use of a sign in practice a result of, rather than the origin of, its meaning. But it does not work. A picture of a chair, say, does not mean 'chair' by virtue of looking like all chairs; nothing can look like all (and only) chairs. Moreover, a picture of a particular chair can (be used to) mean various things, not only 'chair', but also, for example, 'antique chair', 'something to sit on', etc. Pictures determine no unique meaning. Rather, what is critical is not the nature of the picture itself, but the *use* to which it is put, for example its use in sorting out *these* items from *these*. In general, pictures can be used in a variety of ways, and their meaning varies with their use (Wittgenstein 1953, for example §139). In so far as meaning is determined by use, there is as yet no need to distinguish signs that resemble things from those, such as words, that do not. Resemblance then no longer appears as a fundamental concept in the theory of meaning and representation. What is fundamental to representation is not the nature of the sign, but is rather the way the sign is used in activity.

Typical of Wittgenstein's critique would be something like the following line of argument (cf. Wittgenstein 1953, for example sections *c.* §191–239; commentary in, for example, Folgelin 1976, Bolton 1979, Pears 1988). How can a person sort out items into categories, for example according to shape? Well, she uses cards with shapes drawn on, and consults these as she goes. So how does she know how to use the cards, when this or that item is close enough to the sample, or that size doesn't matter, and so on? Now the answer here can't come in the form of appeals to more samples. This is clear enough in the case of cards held in the hands, but then we are tempted by the idea of samples in the mind, which of course have special *mental properties*, so that in particular they don't need interpreting (they can be used in only one way). The explanation short-circuits. It admits that ordinary samples do very little work. Witness this also by 'giving' cards to a cat, for example. The cat simply has no idea what to do with them, or what we are requiring of it. So we presuppose a great deal when we think that the sorting procedure makes use of samples, in particular we presuppose that the person can participate in the procedure, in this 'form of life'. Make sense of this ability to participate, and then by all means add that samples on cards might sometimes be helpful—but these are the last and a relatively small part of the story.

Activity is obscured by appeal to resemblance between sample and items in the class. The various theories of universals, and the empiricist doctrine of abstract ideas, all have the effect of denying the role of creative activity in classification. It is as if the sample (the universal or abstract idea) does all the work of classifying, so that the activity of sorting this with that is irrelevant, or at most the acting out of an order (a classification) that already exists.

1.3.4 Rules and regulations

The notion of resemblance has been used to explicate the ordering of particulars into classes. We saw earlier (subsection 1.3.2) that it has also been used to provide a solution to the problem of true-or-false representation. The implication of abandoning the resemblance theory is that this solution also is abandoned. We can say that the use of signs, whether in classifying, or representation of states of affairs, is true or false, correct or incorrect. As Wittgenstein saw, this normative feature of our use of signs can be expressed using the concepts of *rules* and *rule-following*. In saying that someone is using a sign we are supposing that its use in practice is governed by a rule, that particular applications of it are correct as opposed to incorrect, or vice versa. What is required then is an account of what it means for a sign (or any representation) to be used correctly or incorrectly, according to a rule. These issues will be taken up in later parts of the essay, mainly in Chapters 3 and 4.

Another aspect of what is essentially the same point is that representations serve in the regulation of behaviour, in its direction according to a rule. The notion of regulation is central to the theory of action, and generally to cybernetics and the theory of (functional) systems (Wiener 1948; von Bertalanffy 1968; Sayre 1976; Varela 1979).

The notions of rules and regulation are introduced into explanations of systemic activity at a very abstract (philosophical) level. They capture the fundamental idea that activity (interaction with the environment) is 'right' or 'wrong'. But there is no commitment here yet to the idea that representations as rules are *objects*. It may be that ordered activity involves the use of object-like items, various 'expressions of rules', in the form of language or pictures, but this is so far speculation, philosophical or empirical. What has to be guarded against particularly is philosophical pressure to suppose that there *must be* object-like representations, hidden in the mind or brain, if not evident in the hands. As we have seen, this supposition belongs primarily with the idea that representation is something done by objects, whereas the conception of representation as a rule belongs with the idea that representation is achieved by activity. These issues surface again in the second chapter (Section 2.2), when we consider various models of how reality is represented (how information is encoded) in the brain.

It may be noted that the account of meaning in terms of rule-following practice makes transparent what remains obscure according to the resemblance theory, namely, the intimate connection between meaning and the prediction of action. Theories which invoke meaningful (information-carrying) states are effective in the prediction of action because they attribute to the agent the propensity to follow certain rules, and therefore they can be used to predict, rightly or wrongly, what the agent will do.

1.3.5 The intentional stance

In this section we consider a framework proposed by Dennett (1979, 1987, 1988), which clarifies the logic of mentalistic explanations of behaviour, their predictive power, and their relation to other forms of explanation. The framework is fruitful not only in the philosophy of psychology generally, but also in the philosophy of psychiatry.

Dennett proposed that three stances can be used in the prediction of behaviour: the physical stance, the design stance, and the intentional stance. He illustrated these in application to what is apparently the simplest case, artificial intelligence, taking the chess-playing computer as an example (Dennett 1979). The moves of the computer could be, in principle, predicted from knowledge of the physical constitution of the machine and of the physical laws governing its operation. This would be prediction from the physical stance. Prediction of the computer's moves could also be based on knowledge of the design of the machine, including its program. This would be prediction from the design stance. It requires no knowledge of the physical constitution of the machine. Dennett argues that while the physical and design stances can, in principle, be used for prediction, they are in practice inapplicable in the case of the more sophisticated chess-playing computers. There is, however, a third possibility, one that requires neither knowledge of the physical constitution of the machine and covering physical laws, nor knowledge of the program. It consists, simply, in predicting that the computer will make the most 'rational' move! This is prediction from the intentional stance. In the intentional stance we attribute to the computer, in scare quotes, certain 'beliefs' and 'desires'. This is to say, we attribute regulation by intentional states, carrying information about the state of play, and about goals.[9]

Dennett's framework is relevant to many themes of the present essay, concerning the mind–body relation, the power of explanations that invoke information-carrying states, and the concept of psychological disorder. The relevance of the framework to these issues may be summarized as follows.

Dennett brings out the fact that a form of explanation at least akin to that familiar in folk psychology as applied to human beings is applicable also to artificial intelligent systems. The implication is that some aspects of folk psychological explanation, in particular those concerned with prediction of behaviour, do not invoke dualist concepts of mind. There is no (not much) temptation to suppose that computers have immaterial mental states. This move away from dualism is, of course, one of the main philosophical implications of the new discipline of artificial intelligence, and it opens up possibilities of relationship between mind and body which were excluded by the dualist dichotomy.

Dennett's elucidation of the intentional stance reinforces one of the main points of the present chapter, that explanation in terms of meaningful states is efficient in prediction of behaviour. Further, it suggests that such explanation is the best we have for the purpose, at present, and indeed for the foreseeable future. Prediction of human behaviour from the physical stance would require at least knowledge of brain processes far exceeding what is currently available in neuroscience. Similarly, prediction from the design stance would await at least major developments in cognitive psychology. In the meantime, we use folk psychology. But furthermore, even supposing that neuroscience and cognitive psychology progressed to the point of being able, in principle, to predict behaviour as efficiently as explanation in terms of meaningful mental states, it would still be doubtful whether, for practical purposes of prediction, either could replace folk psychology. If Dennett is right, even in the case of chess-playing computers, for which we already have adequate theories of hardware and software, the complexity of explanations involving them prohibit their use for the prediction of moves. And the complexity of human behaviour, of its physical basis and underlying information-processing, exceeds that of the chess-playing computer by orders of magnitude.

There remains, on the other hand, the theoretical question of whether the intentional stance could, in principle, be eliminated in favour eventually of the physical stance. An argument against this supposition is proposed later in this chapter (subsection 1.4.3), and is developed in various contexts in later chapters (sections 2.4.2, 2.5.6, 5.5).

Dennett's framework is also relevant to analysis of the concept of psychological disorder. Dennett makes the plausible suggestion, in passing, that in order to explain breakdown of function, for example in the chess-playing computer, we have to drop to the physcial stance, there to appeal to short-circuits, overheating or blown fuses, for example (Dennett 1979, pp. 4–5). The point behind this suggestion is that when function fails we have to abandon the intentional stance, with its reference to rules, strategies, etc. and look instead for physically defined causes.

A priori inference of this kind lends support, in the case of psychological disorder, to the 'medical model' in psychiatry, in so far as it favours theories of organic aetiology. Psychological disorder is the breakdown of psycho-logic, that is, of meaning, rationality, and so on, and beyond this limit we apparently have to abandon our normal intentional forms of explanation (the theory of mind) and posit instead causal processes at the biological level which disrupt normal processes. However, the supposition that breakdown of function can be explained only from the physical stance is invalid, even in the relatively simple case of the chess-playing computer. There are options from within the design stance, and also some from within the intentional stance, although these are more complicated. Dennett, by the way, does not develop these other options, since they lie outside his primary concerns, but they are not incompatible with his account.

Consider first the option of explaining disorder from the design stance. The chess-playing computer makes irrational moves, inappropriate to winning the game, because it follows the wrong rules (for this purpose). Here we envisage a causal pathway to breakdown of function in which there is no physical disruption to information-processing, but rather use of inappropriate rules. Contemporary models of major psychological disorders such as autism or schizophrenia, discussed in Chapter 9, may be seen in Dennett's terms as making use of the design stance as well as, or instead of, the cruder physical stance. On the other hand, as will be discussed later (subsection 7.2.2), the notion of 'design' is considerably more complex, and problematic, in the case of living beings as compared with computers.

As to the possibility of explaining disorder from within the intentional stance, this seems to be ruled out a priori—at least at first sight. Apparently disorder is precisely the breakdown of intentionality, and hence it does not admit of explanation in terms of intentional processes. In the psychological case, the concept of disorder signifies the point at which there is (serious) breakdown of meaning: disorder means, roughly, (serious) breakdown in meaningful connections. Hence it cannot be explained in terms of such connections. This simple and powerful line of thought is fundamental to the problems with which we are concerned, the role of meaning in the causal explanation of order and disorder. Its simplicity and power derive primarily, however, from limiting consideration to systems which have only one function. We are in fact concerned with complex systems with many goals and subgoals, routines and subroutines, and in this case there are several possibilities that avoid the apparent contradiction in explaining breakdown of intentionality in terms of intentional processes. One possibility is that two or more sets of rules come into conflict, leading to disorder in action. Another is that one goal can be abandoned in order to achieve a higher goal; that in this sense one function will be sacrificed, but as part of an intentional strategy. In these kinds of ways intentional processes can be implicated in breakdown, and they are elaborated on in later chapters (7, 8, and 9).

Having described Dennett's framework and its relevance to the present essay, we should remark on a major divergence of emphasis between Dennett's theorizing and ours, on the fundamental issue of how the intentional stance and the intentional systems to which it applies are to be defined. Dennett tends to define the intentional stance in terms of the assumption of rationality, and intentional systems (trivially) as those to which the intentional stance can be usefully applied (Dennett 1987, Chapter 2, 1988). The way taken here is different. We begin by defining intentional systems in terms of the behavioural characteristics already discussed in subsection 1.2.2 as supporting cognitive as opposed to S–R models of animal behaviour. These characteristics are, briefly, goal-directedness and flexibility according to circumstances. The intentional stance is then seen to explain and predict the behaviour of systems with these characteristics precisely because it posits regulation by states which carry information about goals and the current environment (or organism–environment interactions).

These differences in definition have several consequences. Dennett's approach suggests that the intentional stance is restricted in application to 'rational' systems. Rationality is a high-level cognitive capacity of human beings, some other relatively advanced animals, and artificial simulators. The behavioural definition of intentional systems proposed here, by contrast, has to do only with ends and means, and applies far down the phylogenetic scale, and to biological subsystems as well. Secondly, and connected, Dennett's approach apparently does not envisage the intentional stance being used for predicting irrational behaviour. But it can be. We may learn for example that the chess-playing computer prefers its black bishop to its queen (systematically moves in such a way as to retain the former rather than the latter given these alternative outcomes), and this rule is as useful for prediction as the more rational opposite. What matters to the use of the intentional stance is that some or other identifiable strategy is being used to achieve some identifiable end-state; it is not also necessary that the strategy or the end-state is reasonable. This point is of course critical to the problem tackled later in the essay, concerning the role of intentional processes in disorder. A third consequence of Dennett's approach is that by understating in the foundations of the theory the role of behavioural criteria in warranting attributions of intentionality, their objectivity looks less secure than it might otherwise. The problem of objectivity, with reference to Dennetts' remarks on it, is discussed in Section 3.4.

1.3.6 The intentional stance predicts intentional behaviour

The behavioural characteristics that warrant use of the intentional stance, goal-directness and plasticity, are invariants which are not apparent at the level of physical or geometrical description of the behaviour. This point may be expressed briefly, though with caution, by saying that the characteristics are not apparent at the 'behavioural' level, where 'behavioural' here refers to spatially–defined movements of the body. In general there is no one–one correspondence between behavioural descriptions (in this restricted sense) and intentional descriptions. For example, two distinct behavioural sequences may have in common that they lead to the same goal.

Connected with this point is that intentional predictions can, and frequently do, show an indeterminacy relative to behaviour as physically defined. For example, if I know that Jack plans to meet Jill in Clapham at 2.15, I can predict that at 2 o'clock he will be making his way there, but I may not be able to predict whether is proceeding by foot, bus, or car. My prediction, though indeterminate, is nevertheless informative: many possibilities are excluded. In order to make a more precise behavioural prediction, I require more information. Similarly, in the case of the chess-playing computer: I may predict that the computer will develop an attack on the queen's side, without knowing exactly how it will do so. Nevertheless, the prediction is that some moves, or patterns of moves, are more likely than others.

The intentional stance is effective in the prediction of behaviour. The predicted behaviour is, in general, not defined in physical or geometrical terms, but is rather brought under intentional descriptions. The distinction here between behavioural movements and (intentional) action has been much discussed in the philosophical literature (Anscombe 1957; Davidson 1971; Hornsby 1986). The kind of behaviour predicted by intentional psychology is behaviour that itself has significance, meaning, and intentionality. It may be noted that actions have intentionality in the same sense as applies to the cognitive states that regulate them (subsection 1.3.1). That is to say, actions are typically object-directed, and this 'object' may not exist in reality. For example, an animal trying to find food searches in the same way whether or not there is any food to find.

The point at issue here is not simply that 'we can describe behaviour in two ways', that is as physical movement and as intentional. Behind this contrast are the important issues concerning the point of modes of description, and what practices they belong to. Specifically, intentional, in contrast with non-intentional, characterizations of behaviour belong with the aim of trying to capture, to understand, explain, and predict, complex interaction between living beings and their environment. Further, because this interaction is what we are trying to explain, the mental states we invoke have intentionality, or meaning. Intentionality and meaning, which can seem utterly mysterious or suspect, or both, in fact appear as clear and inevitable in the context of this simple connection. Let us consider this point further.

What is it that explanations of behaviour seek to explain? It is true, just about, that we can describe behaviour narrowly, without mentioning the environment, as bodily movements. Supposing the *explanandum* to be of this kind, it would presumably follow that the *explanans* also would not require reference to the environment. Explanation in terms of inner processes would then not invoke information, or meaning. But of course behaviour in this restricted sense is precisely not what interests us. We don't want to know, for example, why Jones moved his arm in such-and-such a geometrically defined way; we want to know why he picked up the cup; why and how the rat found found its way round the maze to the goal-box, etc. The behavioural *explanandum*, that is to say, is typically an (invariant in the) interaction between the living being and its environment. This being so, it is not surprising that, indeed it has to be the case that, the *explanans* cites facts about the agent, facts about the environment, and (primarily) facts about the interactions between the two. We say, for example, Jones saw the cup, wanted a drink, so picked it up; the rat learnt that the sequence L–R–L leads to food, etc.

Such explanations cite features, actual or possible, of the environment, but these as being represented, stored, or encoded within the subject. They are applicable in both psychology and biology: in the former semantic or representational properties are attributed to mental states, in the latter to material processes in the brain. The mind/matter distinction is less critical here than the fact that in both types of explanation of behaviour the concepts of information-processing are fundamental. The contents of information-bearing states, mental or material, have to be characterized by reference to environmental features precisely in so far as they are invoked to explain behaviour as interaction between the organism and its environment.

Information-processing concepts are justified by their role in providing adequate causal explanation of interactions between the living being and its environment. A fundamental concept here is that information about the environment is stored (in some code) within the agent. One simple aspect of the logic of such attribution can be brought out by comparison with the notion of stored or potential energy in physics. Explanations of clockwork, for example, invoke the concept of potential energy stored within the spring-mechanism, in order to explain why energy expended in interaction between the mechanism and something else, during winding of the clock, affects the behaviour of the mechanism at a later time. The concept of energy storage serves here at least to preserve the principle that causation is spatio-temporally local. The same general logic underlies the notion of information-storage in biology and psychology. It is invoked at least in order to explain how information picked up in interaction between the living being (or biological subsystem) and its environment at one time can affect its behaviour at a later time.

The fact that the bio-psychological concept of information, and even more so of highly processed information, is more complex that the concept of energy in physics is connected, of course, with the complexity of the behaviour of living beings as compared with, for example, clockwork. There are diverse relations between input and output, stimulus and response; there is evidence of interpretation, construal of a stimulus as a this or a that, of success or failure in relation to apparent goals, of behaviour based on error, or on imagination; and so on. To cut a long but familiar story very short: it is the 'intelligent' behaviour of livings beings in their environment, its evidence of learning, variety, plasticity, creativity, goal-directedness, etc. which underlies attribution to the living being of information-carrying states with particular, more or less processed, contents.

It may be noted that there is a qualified argument here for the impossibility of eliminating the concept of intentionality or meaning from behavioural science. It is perfectly possible to manage without intentional concepts, but what can then be predicted is only non-intentional behaviour. *If* the goal is explanation and prediction of intentional behaviour (complex organism–environment interactions), *then* the methodological assumption has to be that the agent is regulated by information about the environment, that is, by intentional states, either mental, or encoded in the brain, or both.

This line of thought is invoked repeatedly through Chapter 2, as we consider various objections to the claim that information (or meaning) is encoded in the brain. For example, it runs counter to the widely held assumption that brain states cannot encode so-called 'broad' content (subsection 2.5.6).

1.3.7 Cognitive psychological information and folk psychological meaning

As discussed in subsection 1.2.5, there are evidently strong connections between the relatively recent paradigm of cognitive psychology, and our familiar folk psychology.

Both are committed to the fundamental idea that cognitive or mental states are involved in the organization and regulation of behaviour. Folk psychology formulates explanations of behaviour in terms of beliefs, desires, etc., while cognitive psychology uses specialist terms concerning information-processing, and end-(goal-) states, as well as borrowing fairly freely from folk psychology colloquial notions such as plans, decisions, etc. Further, the meaningful content that characterizes folk psychological mental states apparently has a counterpart in the information-content carried by cognitive psychological states. Both sorts of state have the critical property of *intentionality*: they are about something, and they may be in error. It is reasonable to say that intentionality is a, or the, fundamental feature of meaningful states, but this feature also belongs to the information-carrying states which are fundamental to the cognitive psychology paradigm. That there is a close connection between cognitive psychology and our familiar folk psychology might seem obvious enough, but there are difficult issues concealed here, particularly to do with the possible commitment of cognitive psychology to the notion of meaning, which has long been regarded as problematic and probably irrelevant from a scientific point of view. We shall consider these issues in the next subsection, but first let us define in more detail the relation between the notion of information as it is used in cognitive psychology, and the folk psychological notion of meaning.[10]

The first point to make is that the folk psychological notion of meaningful content does not cover all the kinds of informational content invoked in cognitive psychology. Rather, and this is the main proposal of this subsection, the folk psychological notion refers particularly to that highly processed information which is involved in the regulation of action. The cognitive psychology paradigm applied to human action requires the concept of highly processed information which serves in the regulation of that action. The proposal is that the concept required here is captured by the familiar common-sense notion of belief with meaningful content. In brief: the information regulating action is typically specified by statements of the form 'S believes that p'. Such statements play a role in explanations of action roughly as follows: 'A person S is doing such and such because S believes that p is the case, wants it to be that q, and believes that by performing the action in question in context p, the result will be that q'. This form of complex proposition can, of course, also be adapted to make a prediction that S will perform the action in question in the said circumstances given the requisite beliefs and desire, other things being equal.

We take it that cognitive psychology as part of behavioural science aspires to be of use in the prediction of behaviour. For this purpose, according to the information-processing paradigm, it is necessary to include among the posited conditions of action, specification of the information involved in its regulation. Our proposal is that it is at this point that the theory requires the notion of meaningful content familiar in everyday usage.

However and of course, cognitive psychology has aims other than the prediction of action. In particular, it seeks to determine methods of information pick-up and processing which precede the use of information in action. On these issues folk psychology has conspicuously little to say. Its grasp of perception, for example, is pretty well exhausted by the simple description 'S sees that p', a description that refers to the result of much processing. In general what matters to folk psychology is not the input side of information-processing, but rather the end-result: highly processed, meaningful states involved in the organization and regulation of action. This is what matters to folk psychology, because the prediction of such action is what matters to the folk.

A further point to make by way of clarification of the main proposal is that the information invoked in cognitive psychology is not restricted to what is or to what can be encoded in linguistic form. In the early stages of sensory information-processing, as in visual perception for example, coding structures are non-linguistic, and it is plausibly only the later stages of perception, approaching production of the conscious perceptual image, which can be described as aquisition of a belief specifiable in words. There is evidence that analogical structures, such as spatial images, as well as propositional descriptions in linguistic form, are implicated in some thinking and problem-solving, and there may also be a more generic, non-propositional form of encoding meaning. The representations regulating action may themselves be sensorimotor in form.[11]

In proposing that the informational content regulating action is specified by the meaningful content of belief, the intention is not to deny any of the above points. It is true that beliefs are typically identified by propositional clauses of natural languages. However, attribution of a belief identified in this way does not presuppose that the belief is encoded in language. This is evident in the fact that we attribute beliefs to living beings that have no language, such as very young children or animals. The grounds of such attribution is intelligent behaviour which, we suppose, is mediated by perceptual and other non-linguistic images. Neither is our concept of belief restricted in the case of language users to the precise words they use to express beliefs. We can attribute to someone the belief 'that p' without supposing that the person has uttered or indeed ever could utter the expression 'p'; the person may speak another language for example. In general, our concepts of belief and meaningful content exhibit an appropriate neutrality with respect to the particular form in which information regulating action is encoded, notwithstanding the fact that specifying informational content *in words* inevitably requires words, particular words of a particular language.

The main argument of this section is, then, that the concept of belief with meaningful content is (or is very closely connected to) the concept of informational content regulating action, such as is required by the cognitive psychology paradigm. The connection is between folk psychology and that aspect of cognitive psychology concerned with the prediction of behaviour. Folk psychology has little or nothing to say about the stages of information-processing prior to regulation of action, but in description of the informational content involved in regulation folk psychology comes into its own. It is in this respect that folk psychology, with its concepts of mental states with meaningful contents, has got matters just about right. Unless this claim is correct, it is hard to see, indeed, how folk psychology could be as effective as it is in the prediction of action. Its success would be a mystery.

The proposed account of the relation between cognitive psychology and folk psychology stands opposed to the idea, to be considered further in the following subsection, that folk psychology is only a relatively weak, pre-scientific theory, the key concepts of which, and the notion of meaning in particular, await replacement by a mature cognitive psychology. This view implies that the domain of interest of the two theories coincide, with the scientific, naturally enough, doing better than the pre-scientific. The account proposed here is rather that folk psychological theory is a proper subset of cognitive psychological theory, namely, that part dealing with the regulation of action by meaningful mental states. This account implies that cognitive psychology not only will win, but always has won hands down, over the business of defining information pick-up and processing prior to the regulation of action by meaningful mental states: folk psychology never was a contender here. The proposed account implies, on the other hand, that the more cognitive psychology attempts to define the information-carrying states involved in the regulation of action (particularly action with ecological validity), the more it is bound to draw on the familar concepts and contents of folk psychology.

1.3.8 Cognitive science and meaning: the historical problem

The above conclusion involves accepting, notwithstanding conceptual problems familiar in the recent history of ideas, that meaning after all has a role in scientific theory. The problems, already referred to in the Introduction, may be sketched as follows.

The last decades of the nineteenth century saw the emergence of new sciences, particularly history and social science, which had as their subject-matter the expression of mind in society. To the extent that these new *Geisteswissenschaften* had their roots in German idealism, rather than in the seventeenth-century dichotomy between mind and matter, knowledge of mind was not a problem for them: the activity of mind in culture and society was a given. But there arose then a fundamentally new problem, which remains ours, namely, that knowledge of mind and its expression in activity does not conform readily to the methodological assumptions and rules of the natural sciences. The tension found expression in the celebrated distinctions between *meaning* and *causality*, and between *understanding* and *explaining* (see von Wright 1971 for an historical, critical review). Human activity is permeated by meaning, understanding of which is a fundamental aim of the cultural sciences. Meaningful phenomena, however, and the way they are known, seem to be different in fundamental ways from the subject-matter and methods of the natural sciences. One contrast is that meaningful phenomena (such as an historical event, or a cultural practice) are singular or even unique, whereas natural science deals (mostly) with repeated and/or repeatable phenomena. Another, connected contrast is that physics seeks and uses general causal laws in its explanations, while the cultural sciences produce diverse meaningful accounts of diverse events. A third contrast is more explicitly epistemological: understanding plausibly draws on empathy, is subjective, and varies between subjects, while the methods of observation in the natural sciences are objective, and the results should be the same for all.

The problems of mind and meaning have to do with a tension between meaningful phenomena and scientific method, the method used by the hugely successful paradigm of knowledge, modern natural science. They are distinct from the problems of mind and body, concerning the apparent impossibility of causal interaction, and the epistemological privacy of mind. As already remarked, the roots of the two sets of difficulties are distinguishable: the new cultural sciences grew within the context of nineteenth-century idealism, which had already left seventeenth-century dualism behind. On the other hand, of course, it was inevitable that the two problematics became muddled up. This is perhaps specially true for psychology, where both the mind/body issues and the problems of meaning and scientific method are of fundamental relevance. The Cartesian framework remained enormously influential, in philosophy and in the sciences, including the new psychology. The older Cartesian problems of mind and body then overlapped and combined with the new problems of mind, meaning, and scientific method, both contributing to the idea that meaningful mental (immaterial) states, and the meaningful activity which they allegedly produce, were thoroughly problematic within the scientific world-picture.

Conflict-resolution was achieved by splitting: causality as opposed to meaning, explanation as opposed to understanding, behavioural science as opposed to hermeneutic non-science. This solution becomes undermined, however, in so far as cognitive psychology, the legitimate heir to experimental behavioural psychology, is committed to anything like meaningful states.

This has been a major problematic for cognitive science from the beginning. The paradigm was, and continues to be, surrounded by controversy about the status, definition, and role of meaning. We referred above (subsection 1.2.2) to three external influences which helped to bring about the cognitive revolution in psychology: transformational linguistics, AI, and the mathematical theory of communication (information theory). It is remarkable and significant that all three in fact explicitly eschewed reference to meaning. The exclusion of meaning was already noted above in connection with AI and information theory, but the same point applies in the case of transformational linguistics: Chomsky's theory was about syntax, not semantics (Chomsky 1957; Katz and Fodor 1963). The fact that these three paradigms of the new cognitive science all, for one reason or another, excluded semantics reinforced the pre-existing scepticism about meaning from the point of view of science, expressed in the turn-of-the-century distinction between meaningful and causal connections.

While linguistics, AI models, and the mathematical theory of communication could, all for different reasons and in different ways, exclude semantics, the same is apparently not true of the cognitive theory of behaviour, which now lies at the centre of behavioural science. The cognitive theory which replaced stimulus–response theory invokes regulation by information-carrying states for the purpose of explaining and predicting behaviour. The states involved in the regulation of behaviour, that is, in the regulation of interactions between the living being and the environment, carry information about those interactions. The notion of information at work here is, and has to be, a semantic one, involving the characteristic intentional properties of directness, and the possibility of error. That the cognitive states invoked by cognitive theory have semantic, intentional properties is essential to the theory, not just incidental, at least in so far as it is being used to explain and predict organism/environment interactions. And it seems then that we are marginally close to saying that the cognitive theory of behaviour has to invoke meaning.

The idea that cognitive psychology can manage without meaning was given a good run for its money by Stich in his well-known *From folk psychology to cognitive science* (1983). Stich proposed that cognitive psychology can and should eschew the notion of meaningful content fundamental to folk psychology (Stich 1983, Chapter 1, *et passim*). The advantage to be gained from this manoeuvre is that cognitive psychology would not be saddled with those features of meaning which are problematic from the point of view of scientific method, such as vagueness, context-dependence and observer-relativity (Stich 1983, Chapter 5). But is the exclusion of meaning from cognitive psychology possible? Stich argues that it is not only possible but mandatory. His argument concerns the problem of supervenience of meaningful states on states of the brain (Stich 1983, pp. 164ff.). This kind of argument will be discussed and rejected in the next chapter (Section 2.5). For now the point to be made is simply that Stich apparently fails to consider whether the baby—the cognitive psychological notion of information—would not be thrown out along with the bathwater—the folk psychological notion of meaning. It would seem that Stich's position is tenable only under either or both of the following assumptions: that the notions of meaningful content and informational content are fundamentally distinct, and/or that cognitive psychology requires no notion of informational content. As to this latter claim, it is not at all obvious how the information-processing models of cognitive psychology could manage without the notion of information (or informational content) being processed. The basis of the former claim is also unclear. Rather, as noted above, the information-carrying states posited by cognitive psychology share fundamental characteristics with the meaningful states posited by folk psychology. In particular, both are invoked in the explanation and prediction of complex behaviour, and both have the features characteristic of intentionality: they are about reality, and its interaction with the living being, and they can be in error.

In so far as the cognitive states posited by cognitive psychology have meaningful content, then apparently scientific explanation and meaning have to be compatible after all. This conclusion implies that we have to find answers to a number of difficult questions: What do explanations of behaviour in terms of meaning have to do with those with face scientific validity, namely, explanations in terms of brain processes? Secondly, how do we accomodate within the theory of scientific explanation the subjectivity which characterizes attributions of meaning? These two questions are tackled in the following two chapters. And further, to be considered in chapters 4 and 5, there is the problem defined explicitly in the distinction between meaningful and causal connections: Are meaningful explanations after all causal? And if so, in what sense?

1.4 THEORY AND THEORY OF MIND

1.4.1 The idea of theory in post-empiricist epistemology

The assumption that psychological explanation of behaviour, scientific or folk, is embedded in a theory has been made throughout the chapter so far. Further aspects of the 'theory of mind' are considered later in this section, but first we consider in general terms the notion of 'theory' and its role in post-empiricist epistemology. As we shall see, this topic interacts with many of the themes in this chapter and in the essay as a whole.

Empiricism was a major theory of knowledge from the seventeenth-century onwards. It began life, in Locke and Hume, as much psychology as philosophy, and it assumed a central role in the development of psychological science towards the end of the nineteenth century. Also, during the nineteenth century, empiricism increasingly dominated conceptions of the physical sciences. In philosophy empiricism assumed a new form in the first decades of the twentieth century, as logical empiricism, or logical positivism, which applied some empiricist assumptions to the theory of meaning (of language). Throughout the twentieth century, however, in very many and diverse ways, empiricism has been deconstructed, and we are now the owners and users of a different kind of theory of knowledge, at its most clear, perhaps, when defined in contrast to what it replaces. Post-empiricist epistemology interacts with so many themes of this essay, and will be used or referred to so frequently, that a statement of some principles in this one place will prove useful.[12]

Empiricist epistemology supposed that all knowledge (except of the logical truths) is based in experience. This implies a one–one or one–many mapping between beliefs and experiences, and it presupposes that experience is given as independent of beliefs, as so-called 'hard' (uninterpreted, infallible) data. These empiricist assumptions have been dismantled in the twentieth century. It has been recognized that empirical beliefs form a theory in which there is no mapping of the required kind between individual beliefs and experience, and that there is no sharp distinction between theory and empirical data. This latter point is usually expressed by saying that all observation is theory-laden. The fundamental idea of empiricism is that knowledge is derived from sense-experience, conceived as an absolute (unconditional) given. Sense-experience is, on this view, essentially passive, involving no activity on the part of the subject, but only simple 'awareness'. By contrast, once the subject is an agent, perception has to be active, in various senses. Sense-data have to be processed into information relevant to action, to its aims and methods, in the context of information already held. Sense-experience involves cognitive activity. Another aspect of the same point is that perception is fundamentally in the service of action, in the sense of activity of the living being as a whole. Hence also, when perception is conscripted into use for planning action, it essentially involves hypotheses (expectations) about the scene and outcomes of action. Beyond a certain level of complexity, these hypotheses assume the form of a systematic theory.

The above characterization of post-empiricism runs together two themes: first, a set of interrelated claims about theory and experience (that theory is systemic in relation to experience, that the distinction between the two is not sharp, etc.), and secondly, that sense-experience (and cognition generally) is in the service of action. The first is the most familiar theme in post-empiricism. We suggest, however, that the second also belongs to the epistemology which replaces empiricism. Fundamental to empiricism was the view of sense-experience as being a passive reflection of reality, whereas, by contrast, experience in post-empiricism is active, in various senses but including that experience (and cognition generally) is essentially in the service of action. This same view of cognition is, of course, also axiomatic in biology, evolutionary theory, and cognitive-behavioural psychology. Philosophical and bio-psychological theory coincide here.

In order to make as clear as possible the context for, and relevance of, what is inevitably a much oversimplified and very partial discussion of empiricism and post-empiricism, let us list their points of contact with issues discussed elsewhere in the essay. The list is of some of the more obvious points only, and they are all connected with one another.

First, as already noted, empiricism belonged with the idea that the subject is a passive observer of ready-made images, whereas post-empiricism, by contrast, posits activity in many connected senses. The assumption that cognition is essentially involved in the regulation of action, axiomatic to cognitive-behavioural psychology, is typical of post-empiricist epistemology. The present essay is based on this assumption, and invokes it througout. The sixth point to be made below also directly concerns the active nature of cognition.

Secondly, Locke's empiricism was closely linked to the Cartesian concept of mind (discussed above, subsection 1.2.1), in particular to the theory of introspection, that is the Cartesian theory of first-person knowledge of mental states, the inference being that post-empiricism implies a new kind of account of self-knowledge (subsection 1.4.3).

Thirdly, Hume's empiricism comprised a theory of learnt connections between mental states, one which relied heavily on the notion of *association*. This notion re-appeared within psychological science, in particular in the theory of conditioning. Association (in space and time) has nothing much to do with *content*. The implication is that post-empiricist psychology will invoke connections between mental states other than (mere) association, and in particular connections which depend on semantic content. This is linked to the shift from conditioning to cognitive psychological theories discussed in subsection 1.2.2, and also directly to the problem of causality and meaning, which is the next point.

Fourthly, Hume's analysis of causality turns precisely on association only and not internal connections between events (subsection 4.2.1). The implication is that post-empiricism can envisage a different kind of causality, involving internal, content-based connections. Such a form of causal explanation will be explicated through chapters 4 and 5.

Fifthly, empiricism promotes a particular view of psychological science, namely, that is seeks generalizations over hard empirical data (e.g. movements of the body). Post-empiricism envisages a more theoretical view of hypotheses, and indeed of the data. This is reflected in psychology in liberation from behaviourism by the cognitive paradigm (subsection 1.2.2). But along with this shift in the methodological assumptions of psychological science there is a corresponding shift in the conception of its subject-matter.

As a sixth point, empiricism implies that the subjects under study in psychological science are in the business of learning generalizations over (associations between) hard empirical data (R–S or S–S links, etc.). In contrast, post-empiricist psychology envisages that subjects, at any rate beyond a certain level of cognitive development, are engaged in a task more like theory-building. The capacity of cognitive psychology to handle cognitive processing more complex than conditioning (subsection 1.2.2) is a sign of its close relation to post-empiricism. A connected point is that within the cognitive paradigm, the role of cognitive states in mediating between sensory data and action is a function not only of the sensory data but also of interaction among the cognitive states themselves. The mediating role of cognitive states is thus systemic, in a sense consistent with post-empiricist epistemology. There is no simple one–one mapping between what presents to the senses and the cognition, or behaviour, to which it gives rise.

Finally, among the higher-level theories envisaged by post-empiricism would be one for the explanation and prediction of behaviour in terms of mental states, the theme of this chapter. Such a theory can be called a 'theory of mind' (subsection 1.4.2). We move away here from the Cartesian idea that mental events are inaccessible, ghostly processes, towards regarding them as something more like theoretical constructs, which is the kind of status they have in cognitive psychology.

In brief, the shift from empiricist epistemology to post-empiricism interacts at various levels with many issues relevant to psychology and addressed in this essay. Furthermore, the issues concern not only mind, causality, and the nature of explanation, as indicated above, but also mental disorder. This implication will be brought out in subsection 1.4.4. Essential background to that discussion are those parts of post-empiricist epistemology which deal with the preservation of theoretical order. The issues here have been well worked through in the philosophy of science. They are of central importance in many contexts and we turn next to consider them briefly.

As already discussed, empiricism implies that particular beliefs correspond to particular conditions of experience. The claim can be expressed by saying: in the case of any proposition (which purports to represent reality) we should, in principle, be able to say what conditions of experience would make it true or would make it false, or, would lead to its acceptance or rejection. The kind of claim was presupposed in Popper's attempt to distinguish science from non-science using the principle of falsifiability. The principle seemed to presuppose that all propositions in scientific theory could be unambiguously falsified by certain experimental data. This supposition is apparently empiricist in the sense outlined above, and in so far as this is so, it would be correct to say that Popper's principles of falsifiability and demarcation were among the last expression of empiricist dogma. The principles were applied in various ways, including in highly influential criticism of psychoanalytic theory, for being non-falsifiable non-science.[13]

Subsequent work in the philosophy and history of science, in particular Lakatos's classic paper (1970), dismantled these remaining empiricist assumptions. It became clear that there was no definite mapping between observations and theoretical propositions. If a theory as a whole made empirical predictions that turned out to be false, diagnosis of error in the theory was so far ambigous: it could be inferred that there was error somewhere in the system, but not yet where. Further, some propositions within the theory were likely to be protected from refutation, to be in this sense treated as unfalsifiable. These would be propositions fundamental to the theory as a whole, typically referring to 'unobservables' and the principles governing their causal interactions. Such propositions constitute the 'core' of the scientific theory. Further, however, the theory as a whole has to contain a more or less explicit theory of observation, which in effect links the theoretical, unobservable processes to the instruments and procedures of measurement. Observation and experiment, at least in so far as it is taken to be relevant to (confirming or disconfirming) theory, has to be interpreted by the theory of observation. The notion of hard, theory-free, incorrigible data is undermined in this way.

The history of science is replete with cases in which the theory ostensibly under test has been saved from anomalies by adjustment within the theory of observation. An example cited by Lakatos (1970, p. 130n) is the Newtonian theory of gravitation applied to lunar motion, which was at first incompatible with the observations made by the first Astronomer Royal at Greenwich: Newton corrected Flamsteed's data for the effects of atmospheric refraction, and the amended observations were, after all, as predicted by the gravitational theory. This is, of course, a remarkable and famous example of success. It illustrates that adjustments that save a theory from anomalies can be desirable, in fact can constitute advance in knowledge. The ammended theory turns anomalies into confirmations, but it achieves this by increasing the scope and predictive power of the theory. This type of move is called by Lakatos a progressive theory-change, and it stands in contrast to degenerating changes, which preserve theory by restricting its predictive power (Lakatos 1970, pp. 118f.). There are diverse ways in which the predictive power of theories can degenerate: for example, by multiplication of *ad hoc* hypotheses, or by stretching the definition and application of key explanatory terms.

Lakatos makes clear the ways in which scientific theory can degenerate. These problems and issues are familiar in psychological theorizing. Consider the charge referred to above, that psychoanalytic theory is unfalsifiable. Even if the charge of intrinsic unfalsifiability is misconceived, the criticism can stand in the form: in some respects psychoanalytic theory may have *come to be used* unfalsifiably, hedged about by so many possibilities and qualifications that it becomes a match for any phenomena we can imagine, so that it predicts everything and excludes nothing. Over-elaboration is certainly a particular hazard for an elaborate theory, particularly one that deals in unconscious mental states and mechanisms. The opposite kind of risk exists for theory that errs on the side of parsimony. For example, as discussed in subsection 1.2.2, Chomsky showed that operant theory applied to language learning stretches the meaning of its few key terms to the point of vacuity.

It should be emphasized that the tendency to protect core theory from refutation, even at high cost, is not adequately explained by appeal to such as whim, pride, or perversity. There is a methodological principle at work here, which has logical and psychological justification. The core theory, defining the underlying phenomena and causal principles, is essential for making predictions. For this reason it cannot (psychologically) and should not (logically) be given up easily. Without it we would not be able to make any predictions, and therefore neither would we know how to act: action would so far cease. In scientific investigation this means: we would have no reason to set up an experiment, since there would be nothing to put to the test. The implication is that fundamental theories generally are not given up even if experience apparently contradicts them. Indeed, as Lakatos observed, theories in science are typically launched amidst an array of anomalies, and they stay afloat notwithstanding the apparent contradictions: the anomalies are either ignored, or it is assumed that they can be handled by the theory, somehow or other.

In general, theories are not abandoned under the weight of counter-evidence, in so far as the counter-evidence can be deflected away from what is essential to the theory. This raises the issue of what more is required for radical theory change. The general answer is that a new theory has to be on offer, one that can replace the old one and that can, in particular, make sense of, explain and predict, what were anomalies for the old theory (Lakatos 1970). Large-scale changes of this kind may be described as 'paradigm-shifts' (Kuhn 1962). They can be seen throughout the history of the sciences, for example, the change from the Ptolemeic to the Copernican view of the Earth's place in the solar system; the change from Newtonian to relativistic mechanics; and in psychology recently, the change from behaviourist to cognitive psychology.

The above considerations concern scientific theory and practice (experimentation), but they apply equally to the epistemology of daily life. The implication is that the knowledge or belief used in daily life has the form of theories. In the remainder of this section we consider how this applies to activities generally, to the knowledge-base of interaction with other social beings (subsection 1.4.2), and indeed to knowledge of one's own actions (subsection 1.4.3). The section ends with discussion of 'core' beliefs fundamental to the possibility of action as such, a matter which brings us to the interplay between psychological order and disorder, a principal theme of the essay as a whole (subsection 1.4.4).

Before proceeding to apply the insight of post-empiricism, that knowledge and belief in daily life have the form of theories, two caveats or complications should be noted. To the extent that the term 'theory' connotes only propositional knowledge (knowledge expressed in sentence-like structures), the claim that all knowledge is theoretical neglects various forms of analogical representation. Qualifications along these lines are discussed for example by Feyerabend (1988). In the particular case of the theory of mind, to be discussed in subsection 1.4.2, analogical knowledge would involve something like mental simulation, or empathy, and this epistemology will be discussed in the third chapter (Section 3.2).

A further complication is the fact that a person's behaviour, or indeed an animal's behaviour, may be best predicted by attribution of a theory, an interconnected set of beliefs and desires, not withstanding the fact that the person (still less the animal) does not, or could not, come up with any such theory. This consideration has led to distinctions between 'explicit' and 'tacit' theory, and between explicit and tacit knowledge generally.[14] Broadly speaking, the assumption we make in this chapter and throughout the essay is that attribution of a theory to a person or animal is warranted in so far as it facilitates prediction of their behaviour. It is certainly a further issue whether the agent can or does articulate such a theory. The capacity to give an account of oneself plausibly depends on language, and hence is uniquely human, and it matures relatively late even in human cognitive development, during adolescence (subsection 6.5.3). Furthermore, even when a person formulates a theory about the beliefs and desires regulating his or her own actions, it may not be the one that best predicts those actions. In this sense the person's explicit theory may be partial or false, and as we shall see, these kinds of failure of self-knowledge can generate psychological difficulties (subsection 1.4.3).

So far in this section we have considered mainly scientific theories and experimentation, but post-empiricist epistemology has a quite general application. Practice is guided by systems of belief, pictures or models of the world in which action takes place. They define the preconditions of action, its nature and its consequences. This context determines the significance (meaning) of what we do, and the beliefs that define it are brought to bear in the planning and execution of courses of action. Human practices are endless in number, and boundless in diversity and complexity: farming, marrying, teaching, travelling, painting, calculating, experimenting, praying, and so forth. The order in an activity finds expression in the beliefs belonging to it; order concerning the various presuppositions of the activity, the variety in the course of action, and its purpose. Agriculture, for example, is a way of life dependent on many things in nature and in human beings, and comprises many stages, and this complexity is mirrored in interconnected beliefs, concerning such things as seeds, soil, sun, rain, and the importance of right timing. There may be theories also about crop rotation, about the breeding of new strains, and in magical cultures, theories about the collaboration of spirits, and so on. So it is that within and around practices we have systems of belief, in agriculture, as in making machinery, conducting a scientific experiment, making friends, etc. The systematic nature of belief corresponds to the systematic nature of activity. One belief in isolation prompts no single action, but from a combination of beliefs action does follow, indeed many interwoven and interrelated actions. As a point about predicting practices of another agent, the implication is that the mental states and meanings which are attributed have the form of a theory, corresponding to the systematic nature of what is being predicted.

The strong links between theory and practice are reflected in the intimate connection between theory and experience emphasized in post-empiricism. These are two aspects of the same point, since experience is action, from the point of view of the agent.

Thus, experience is completely interwoven with beliefs about the reality that we are experiencing, with the former conditioning the latter, but also the latter the former. Among our beliefs are those that state fundamental convictions about the world in which we act; these beliefs define the world, and therefore the content of experience itself. Preconceptions determine what can be experienced, so far as we are concerned. What we *really see*, as opposed to imagine, or simply 'feel in ourselves', depends on what we believe is there to be seen. For example, if the world-picture excludes spirits, then, it will be said, there is no experience of spirits, but at most only hallucinations of them, or mistaken inferences from what is really seen. Our ideas concerning reality influence experience, or at least our interpretation of experience.

The notion of interpretation here, though valid, does not imply that there is an absolute, uninterpreted experience. All experience, at least by the time it is used for action, is interpreted, and it is generally possible to construct various interpretations. Further, to speak of interpretation here, though legitimate, is to speak from the outside: it acknowledges the role of thought in the formation of intelligible experience; it is perhaps to compare one system of thought with an alternative. Seen from within, however, one's beliefs do not 'interpret' experience, they define what one's experience *is*; perceptions and thought, including thought in language, form a unified experience of reality.

Empiricism was right to join together the concepts of experience and idea. But it wrongly gave priority to the one (experience) over the other (idea). Further, it conceived both too narrowly, in terms only of qualities given immediately in the five modes of sensation. Most importantly, empiricism conceived both in absolute terms, independently of activity and interpretation.

1.4.2 Theory of action in terms of mind

We may bring together the idea that intentional concepts are useful in explanation and prediction of action, and post-empiricist epistemology, fundamental to which is the notion of theory. Combining these two themes we are led to the idea that we explain and predict action using a theory of intentional states and processes. In brief, we are led to the idea of a 'theory of mind', and to a particular way of looking at our familiar folk psychology.

Folk psychology, our familiar language of mental states and processes, admits of several interpretations. Within the framework of Cartesian metaphysics, the language refers to a private, immaterial realm, independent of the body. Part of this picture is that first-person knowledge of mind is direct and certain, while third-person knowledge is indirect and (probably irredeemably) uncertain. This whole problematic, inherited from seventeenth-century philosophy, was played out in the first decades of psychological science, with introspectionism followed by behaviourism. The philosophical work of dismantling the Cartesian interpretation of mind was accomplished, for example, by Wittgenstein (1953) and by Ryle (1949). These philosophers were able to show that mental concepts do not refer to some private process running parallel to behaviour, but are intimately (logically) linked to behaviour itself. It would be fair to say that in these writers the negative part of the argument, the deconstruction, was clearer than the positive part. It became clear what mentalistic language was *not* doing. But then, what *was* it doing? What is it for?

The answer to this post-Cartesian question emerged clearly first in experimental psychology, naturally so given its nature, briefly as follows: mental states are invoked in psychological theory as regulators of action, for the purpose of explaining and predicting complex forms of behaviour. In other words, the post-Cartesian response in psychological science has been the cognitive paradigm.

There are striking similarities, as well as differences, between cognitive psychological science and our familiar folk psychology (subsection 1.3.7). Given the similarities, it is natural enough to suppose that folk psychology is also in the business of, among other things, explaining and predicting behaviour, and is in this sense a (quasi-scientific) theory. Hence we arrive at the idea of the 'theory of mind'.

Another theme in the same movement of thought is this. As behavioural scientists became accustomed to the explicit and deliberate use of mentalistic concpets in explanation and prediction of the behaviour of their experimental subjects, it becames possible to think that those participants might be using a similar theory to make sense of and anticipate social behaviour, including, indeed, interactions with the experimenters. It was in fact in this kind of context, interplay between the subject, a chimpanzee, and the scientist, that the expression 'theory of mind' was created (Premack and Woodruff 1978). The implication for our familiar folk psychological language is then that it is an explicit formulation of a 'theory of mind' (Stich 1983; Fodor 1987; Whiten 1991).

The idea that folk psychology is a scientific-like theory for the explanation and prediction of behaviour is thus new. Its appearance required not only the dismantling of Cartesian assumptions, but also firm familiarity with the cognitive paradigm in behavioural science. Previous to this the idea is conspicuous by its absence. For example, Piaget studied development of the child's theories of many things, from the physical world to morality, but not yet development of the child's theory of mind. This is now, however, a flourishing topic in developmental psychology (Astington *et al.* 1988; Harris 1989; Wellman 1990; Butterworth *et al.* 1991; Bennett 1993).

The idea that propositions about mental states serve in the explanation and prediction of action is fundamental to the post-Cartesian cognitive paradigm. It is taken as the starting-place for the present essay, and runs through most of its themes and arguments. That propositions about mind have a form of a theory, in the sense of post-empiricist epistemology, is an (inevitable) corollary of the basic idea, and is explicitly explored and used in various places as we proceed.

In the next section, knowledge of one's own mind, as well as knowledge of the other's mind, is construed as having the form of a theory. In Chapter 4 (Section 4.6) we discuss the status of theoretical generalizations over meaningful mental states. In Chapter 8 we explore further a topic to be introduced below (Subsection 1.4.4), that there are aspects of the theory of the self in relation to the world which are essential to action, such that action and thought itself are threatened if they are threatened.

The notion of a theory of mind draws attention to certain features of explanation of behaviour in terms of mental states: the explanations 'go beyond' immediately known phenomena; they can be used to make sense of, and predict, what is observable; they function within a hierarchically organized system of propositions; etc. In brief, knowledge of mind is being understood in a typically post-empiricist way. The contrast is basically with *direct* acquaintance with the objects of knowledge. In the case of mental objects this direct acquaintance would be introspection, though it always appeared problematic in the third person case. The point of the shift to post-empiricism is not, however, that we can imagine giving up the theory that other people have minds, as if it were a disposable option. Such a claim is dubious psychology (Hobson 1991), and dubious philosophy. It has already been argued (in subsection 1.3.6), that the intentional stance is mandatory, while the purpose is prediction of intentional activity.

1.4.3 Self-knowledge, error, and disorder

The considerations so far in this chapter have concerned primarily the attribution of intentional states on the basis of 'intelligent' (goal-directed, plastic) behaviour, seen in human beings, but also in animals and even artificial intelligent systems. In this subsection we move on to consider a capacity which is uniquely human, namely, the ability to give an account of one's own intentional states. We have the capacity to give an account of the beliefs, desires, plans, and so on, according to which we act. This is a very high-level cognitive capacity, perhaps the highest of all, one inimately involved in concepts such as self-consciousness, autonomy, freedom, and responsibility.[15]

The capacity to give an account of one's own cognitive states may be called the capacity for second-order intentionality. Intentionality consists in the possession of cognitive states such as beliefs and desires. Second-order intentionality consists in the possession of beliefs about those beliefs and desires, or desires about desires, etc. It is expressed in propositions of the form: 'I believe that I believe (or desire) that p'.

The capacity to give an account of oneself is of great importance, and so, therefore, is the matter of its failure. It is no surprise to find that the capacity is characteristically—although not universally—disrupted in cases of what we call psychological or psychiatric disorder. A person experiences a strong emotion, or finds herself engaged in some course of action, but has no idea of the reason why. Typically the person feels ignorant, perplexed, and overwhelmed. Another kind of case is that in which the person has an account, but it is 'irrational', in the opinion of others, and perhaps even in his or her own. Of course, ignorance, or an irrational account of the beliefs and desires regulating one's action, is not sufficient for 'disorder'. There are many aspects of daily action of which we have no account: we simply act, respond in the way we do, without preoccupation as to the reasons. Or again, we may have a whimsical account, bordering on the eccentric. However, in so far as an activity or mood is salient for us, especially if it is disruptive or distressing in frequency and/or intensity, then generally we do seek a valid understanding of why it is occurring, at least so that it becomes predictable, and perhaps manageable. Apart from problems of clinical severity, we are all more or less familiar with difficulties in making sense of problematic patterns of behaviour and feeling, such as in personal relations, or in attitudes to work. Disruption in self-knowledge is thus involved in psychological difficulties of clinical severity, and in 'problems of living', to adopt Szasz's (1961) phraze. So the issues here are relevant to the main themes of this essay.

The account of self-knowledge that has dominated philosophy and psychology since about the seventeenth century through to relatively recently, may be called the traditional theory of introspection. The main idea is that mental states are immediately manifest to the self. This metaphor has three specific implications: completeness, infallibility, and 'priviledged access'. The self knows *all* of its own mental states, it *cannot make a mistake* about them, and its knowledge of them is direct, qualitatively superior to the indirect, inferential knowledge (or belief) possible for another subject.

This seventeenth-century conception of self-knowledge has collapsed with the appearance of the cognitive psychological paradigm, from Freud onwards, in which the defining characteristic of mental states is their regulation of behaviour, not their appearance in consciousness (or self-report) (see Subsection 1.2.4). It is evident within this paradigm that people sometimes make mistakes about, or have no idea about, the intentional processes regulating their behaviour.

What replaces the theory of introspection, broadly speaking, is the idea that self-knowledge *has the form of a theory*. A version of this new epistemology was proposed by Nisbett and Wilson in their well-known paper (1977), and will be discussed further below. The proposal that self-knowledge has the form of a theory has the immediate advantages of accomodating the phenomena which are anomalous for the traditional theory of introspection, namely, ignorance and error. Theories in general are partial, as opposed to complete, and they are subject to error, as opposed to infallible. These features of self-knowledge become comprehensible, if self-knowledge is construed as a theory.

The construal of self-knowledge as a theory extends the notion of 'theory of mind', discussed in the previous subsection, to one's own case: knowledge of one's own mind is seen as having the same form as knowledge of other minds, namely, the form of a theory. In the context of post-empiricist epistemology generally, the point is that knowledge of the self has the same or similar form to knowledge of reality in general. This suggestion was indeed already in classical empiricism. Locke grouped together introspection ('reflection') with the 'external' senses, assimilating knowledge of the internal world to knowledge of the external (1690, Book II, Chapter 1, §4).

The construal of self-knowledge as a theory is plausible in the contexts of current theories of the mind and knowledge, but it is also somewhat counter-intuitive. Is it true that knowledge of one's own mind is just like one's knowledge of someone else's? Is it true that in reporting one's mental states one is invoking a theory ranging over unobservables? Certainly we would be very far from the notion of introspection; in fact too far.

There are empirical and philosophical reasons for making certain qualifications to the idea that self-knowledge is theoretical. These qualifications concern two features of self-knowledge which are highlighted by, though overstated by, the traditional theory of introspection: infallibility and priviledged access. (Nothing remains, by the way, of the third claim of the theory, completeness, once we adopt the model of cognitive psychology.) Let us consider the issues of priviledged access and infallibility in connection with Nisbett and Wilson's (1977) proposal that self-knowledge has the form of a theory.

Nisbett and Wilson emphasize that a feature of their account is first person/third person symmetry in knowledge of (beliefs about) mental states: an observer has the same source of belief about my mental states as I do, namely theory. On the other hand, Nisbett and Wilson allow that the subject has 'indeed direct access to a great storehouse of private knowledge', or at least knowledge 'quantitatively superior' to that of any observer, such as concerning personal historical facts, the focus of current attention, current sensations, also emotions, evaluations, and plans (Nisbett and Wilson 1977, p. 255). This qualification by Nisbett and Wilson to their generally anti-introspectionist stance is exploited and elaborated by Ericsson and Simon, who add to Nisbett and Wilson's catalogue: awareness of on-going processes (Ericsson and Simon 1980, p.245). They propose that priviledged subjective information of the above sorts is in, or can be retrieved into, short-term memory, whence it is available for verbal reports (loc. cit. *et passim*). Ericsson and Simon cite (interpretations of) much experimental evidence in support of the conclusion that subjective reports of mental states and processes, in so far as they draw on information of the above kinds held in short-term memory, do indeed show high degrees of accuracy as judged by behavioural criteria. In brief, introspection can indeed be a direct, reliable source of knowledge about the mental states and processes regulating our behaviour.

The implication is that we have to qualify the proposal of first-person/third-person epistemological symmetry. While it may be true that both subject and observer alike draw on theory, the observer has as information only behaviour (including speech), while the subject has maybe that, but in any case also priviledged information of the sort described above, roughly, what is conscious in perception and short-term memory.

The issue of priviledged access is connected to the issue of infallibility in the reporting of subjective states. There are circumstances in which the statement 'I believe that p', even when sincerely made, can be wrong. For example, a social psychologist may demonstrate to me, following controlled observation of my behaviour in a selection procedure, that I discriminate on the basis of sex or ethnic group, even though I was not only unaware of this, but sincerely believed the opposite. The general point, illustrated in various contexts in Nisbett and Wilson's review (1977), is that first-person reporting of mental states is fallible in so far as it may conflict with the person's actions.[16]

On the other hand, there is a way in which sincerely made statements of belief can be infallible. In so far as I resolve to act in accord with a belief—in so far as, as we colloquially say, I 'make a point of it'—then in general my behaviour will indeed accord with that belief. In the circumstances envisaged above, the psychologist's demonstration would have the effect, we may suppose, of ensuring that I do not continue making the same mistake. Nisbett and Wilson make the point that if subjects in experimental situations were to be (made) aware of being influenced by (what they would regard as) factors irrelevant to the task, then they would probably correct for them (Nisbett and Wilson 1977, pp. 239, 247). This is connected to another point made by Nisbett and Wilson, that when we consciously, deliberately apply rules for decision-making, then the verbal report of these rules will indeed accurately predict behaviour (1977, p. 244). The position in such a case could be described by saying that we have a correct *theory about* what is regulating behaviour, but it would be better to say instead, or as well, that the theory *serves in* the regulating procedure. In these circumstances the verbal expression is not so much a (true or false) report of a mental process, but is rather an affirmation of the intent to follow such-and-such a procedure. Hence there is (in normal circumstances) no possibility of error.

Analogous points apply in the case of desire. The assertion 'I desire that p' may be false, as judged by concurrent behaviour incompatible with that desire, or as judged by the speaker's disillusionment on achieving its object. Nevertheless, the assertion (assuming it is sincere) is likely to be true in the sense that (at least some of) the speaker's behaviour is, or would be in appropriate circumstances, appropriate to the expressed desire. The expression of desire, as of belief, can be the expression of intent.

Nisbett and Wilson emphasize the fallible use of self-report, in which, for example, 'I believe that p' is offered, perhaps mistakenly, as the best explanatory account of the speaker's behaviour. But Nisbett and Wilson tend to neglect the infallible usage of first-person statements of belief and desires, in which they are more akin to expressions of intent. Related arguments were proposed in early commentaries on Nisbett and Wilson's paper, particularly by Morris (1981) and by Shotter (1981). The critical point in the present context is that infallibility of self-reports is being explained by supposing that they function not only as (true-or-false) descriptions but also as expressions of states of mind and inclinations to action.

Neglect of the expression of intention has the effect of neglecting also an important consequence of being in error. According to the simplest version of the proposal that self-knowledge has the form of a theory, the issue of correctness or incorrectness in reports of one's own mental states is just the same as in other theoretical explanations, a matter of criteria familiar in the philosophy of science: predictive efficacy, coherence, parsimony, etc. If we make a mistake then so be it; we adjust the theory. While this may be an adequate model of correctness/incorrectness so far as concerns precisely the theoretical aspects of statements of beliefs and desires, we need another kind of model in relation to their use as expressions of commitment to a course of action. In so far as sincere statements of belief express the intention to act in accord with that belief, even when there is behavioural evidence of a contrary belief at work, so that the expressed belief is in that sense mistaken, then the consequence of being mistaken is not simply that the subject happens to be wrong; it is rather that there are *two conflicting systems* of belief, in fact two conflicting systems of belief–desire–behaviour complexes.

Verbally expressed beliefs and desires regulate certain actions. This set of beliefs, desires, and actions is either congruent with (consistent with) other relevant actions, and the beliefs and desires which (we suppose) regulate them; or they are not. If the two sets are consistent, then second-order intentional statements, of the form 'I believe that I believe that, or desire that, p' are indistinguishable from the first-order statements

'I believe that, desire that, p'. But if the two sets are inconsistent, then first-order and second-order intentionality have fallen apart. In the first case, the person 'knows herself': what she is doing and why. In the second case the person is in a (more or less serious) muddle, engaged in two incompatible courses of action. There is failure of self-knowledge, long recognized as the source of much of our trouble.

Knowledge of one's own mind, like knowledge of other minds, has the form of a theory. This post-empiricist formulation has a surprising, radically non-Cartesian result, namely, that self-knowledge is closely interwoven with the social. This follows from the fact that the theory of mind, like theories generally, has essentially social origins. Let us explore this point further.

Post-empiricist epistemology is defined by at least the negative claim, that knowledge is not derived from experience (alone), but also by the positive claim that knowledge, in the form of theory, is acquired in education, broadly conceived. Knowledge is acquired as it were by 'revelation', by all means no longer divine, but given in the teachings of social groups. Underlying this change in epistemological emphasis from individual experience to social teaching is a shift in the idea of thought itself. In empiricism thoughts are something like mental images, and hence they are plausibly derived from experience. Post-empiricism, by contrast, characteristically for the twentieth century, emphasizes language as a fundamental medium of thought; and language is manifestly social, acquired in education.

Post-empiricist epistemology thus emphasizes that knowledge of mind is theoretical, and further, that the source of the theory is social. This applies to knowledge of one's own mind, just as much as to knowledge of someone else's.

The theory of mind as acquired in education, including one's theory about one's own mind, is essentially partial, and more or less right or more or less wrong. There is truth or error here, in our view of ourselves, depending on the way we have been taught.

It is, on the other hand, possible to steer away from the idea that socially constructed theory can be in error. This tendency is inherent in post-empiricism. To the extent that experience is conditioned by socially constructed theory, it cannot be an independent measure of the theory's truth or falsity. Then perhaps the distinction between true or false theory collapses altogether, or, less drastically, it seems to turn on distinction between agreement and disagreement, so that truth comes to be seen as a matter of *consensus*. Emphasis on the theoretical and hence social origins of theory as opposed to its empirical basis, inevitably leads to the drawing of a strong link between being right and being in accord with the relevant social group. This line of thought, in connection with the theory of mind, is apparently followed by Nisbett and Wilson in the following quotation (1977, p. 255):

> In general we may say that people will be accurate in reports about the causes of their behaviour and evaluations whenever the culture, or a subculture, specifies clearly what stimuli should produce which responses, and especially where there is continuing feedback from the culture or subculture concerning the extent to which the individual is following the prescribed rules for input and output.

Nisbett and Wilson make this generalization from experiments in which trained experts (stockbrokers and clinical psychologists) can say what decision procedures they are following. Now we have seen that, in general, when people follow an explicit rule then some, at least, of their behaviour will accord with the explicit rule. But we have also remarked that even so they may be following other, contrary rules, without being aware of it. In the experiments cited by Nisbett and Wilson this was presumably not the case. But if it is the case, then the explicit rule is *not* an accurate representation of the underlying psychological processes: it fails to explain and predict that behaviour which accords with the contrary rules. Further, and of course, this misrepresentation can occur *whether or not* the explicit rule is socially prescribed. For the point here is simply that not only individuals, but also cultures and subcultures can be in error about the cognitive and affective states which mediate between stimuli and behaviour.

Rejection of the idea that there is any essential connection between accuracy of self-reports and consensus follows simply on the assumption, used throughout this essay, that attribution of mental states generally serves to predict behaviour, and is accurate or inaccurate according as to whether it does so correctly or otherwise. The distinction here is not a matter of agreement as opposed to disagreement. If a person reports that she is following such-and-such a rule, then (in the normal case) she will indeed be following it and the report will be, in this respect, right. This applies whether the rule in question is socially prescribed or idiosyncratic. Further, and in either case, the self-report may be wrong in the sense that it fails to account for other, conflicting patterns of behaviour.

Our intention here is not to understate the role of social learning, and indeed of consensus, in acquisition of the theory of mind. The point being made is rather, and just, that truth of the theory and of particular judgements within it cannot be defined in those terms. It is important to press this point because otherwise it would seem that self-knowledge is achieved whenever we follow socially prescribed rules, whereas the reality is that this method is just as likely to be lead us into error.

The theory of mind includes hypotheses of the following kinds: as to what kind of experiences should give rise to what beliefs and feelings, and conversely, as to what such-and-such beliefs and feelings are the result of; as to what behaviour appropriately belongs with what beliefs and emotions; as to what people do desire, or do rationally desire, etc. The fact is that we are not omniscient about such matters, not at all. A given psychological theory (individual or social) has a partial range, like any theory, so that it is silent on, for example, the emotions caused by such-and-such a type of experience. Further, it will have false components, for example that such-and-such a belief is an unreasonable response to such-and-such an experience, when in fact the link between them is entirely inevitable. The individual acquires such a theory, with all its blind spots and errors, and applies it in his own case, with, let us suppose, due social reinforcement, and he will then be—like his fellows—quite out of touch with what is actually going on in him, that is, with his relation to experience and his own actions.

Examples of inadequate or incorrect psychological theory, more or less contentious, abound. The following are intended only to illustrate what seems obvious, that groups just as much as individuals can get psychological theory thoroughly wrong. At the cultural level there is much to be said for Foucault's general indictment of the modern European age for its excessive use of Reason and its systematic ignorance, denial, or disqualification of other psychological forces (Foucault 1965). A connected point is that if Freud was right, the common-sense psychology of his time was woefully inadequate.

The above are plausible examples of inadequate or false theory at the cultural level. The smallest subcultural unit, the family, is of particular interest because it is here that the child learns most immediately such psychological theory as is on offer. Children's ability to recognize emotions, say, depends on family discourse about emotional states, their causes and their effects (Brown and Dunn 1991; Dunn *et al.* 1991*a,b*).

Partiality and error are occupational hazards. In the clinic can be seen examples, often of course extreme, of what happens in general: children being taught inadequate or plainly wrong accounts of (mental) life. No connection is made for the child between, say, withdrawal and feeling angry, or depressed, or between the experience of loss and sadness. Or false theories are proposed, such as: father never gets angry (so his withdrawal cannot be a sign of anger); we are a happy family (so whatever misgivings you may have are illegitimate); crying is wrong (so is not an appropriate response to loss); whatever mother does, she is beyond criticism (or beyond praise); mother loves you totally (so whatever else you are suffering from, it isn't lack of love). Such theories, or lack of theory, are passed on to the child and adherence to them is ensured by positive and negative feedback to the child's contributions. Often, as is the case with other types of theory, they are the product of more than one generation (cf. the family therapy literature on 'family myths', for example Byng-Hall 1973). In these ways, the child acquires no good theory as to the relation between experience, cognitive and affective states, and behaviour.

The above considerations point to many themes central to the essay. This is because, as remarked at the beginning of the subsection, self-knowledge in the sense explicated here belongs with the highest mental functions, and is thereby crucially implicated in human psychological order and disorder. The capacity to affirm in language the intentionality of one's own activity brings with it, as the other side of the coin, the possibility of conflict between deliberate, rule-guided activity and the cognitive states which otherwise regulate affect and behaviour.

Regardless of whether a psychological theory acquired in education, and in the family specifically, is adequate, once acquired ('internalized'), it generates behaviour appropriate to it. In the case of error, as emphasized earlier, the problem is not just that the child has the wrong theory; it is rather that she tries to live according to rules that run counter to her natural inclinations. For example, the child may ignore—or believe she should be able to ignore—a significant loss, so she might not cry, or otherwise grieve. Or again, a child will generally tend to feel miserable, even despairing, if left alone (for too long), but it may be a rule in the family, implicit and explicit, that everyone should be, providing they are normal, happy. Following this rule, as well as her natural inclinations, the child will be both miserable and happy at the same time, or in succession. Either way the emotions, and the actions to which they would give rise, are inhibited.

In this simple example can be seen the characteristic point that one of the conflicting mental states is not given the right name. Happiness is correctly named, but misery is given no name, or is misnamed. The 'right' name here means: use of the name leads to expectations that are fulfilled. As generally, the use of intentional language is justified by its success in prediction. The child learns that happiness is associated with feelings such as of satisfaction and gratitude, and with the natural expressions of these feelings. But if the word is applied in cases in which the child is neglected, then so far she is unprepared for her feelings and inclinations; they make no sense. So far the child does not know what she is believing, feeling, or inclined to do.

Psychological disorder can result from acquisition of a false or inadequate theory of mind. The shortcomings in theory which we have been considering have to do with the *content* of mental states and the relations between contents, as opposed to their *form*. Let us explore the contrast further. Folk psychology has a form, defined by attribution of intentional states and connections between them, of increasing theoretical complexity. It is plausible to say that this form is relatively constant across cultures, perhaps that it is innately conditioned rather than learnt, and that disorder in the capacity to use this form of theory is likely to be drastic. On this last point, it has been hypothesized that failure in development of the theory of mind, of certain of its formal features beyond a certain level of complexity, is implicated in one of the major developmental psychological disorders, autism (Baron-Cohen *et al.* 1993). The failures of theory considered in this subsection concern content rather than form in this sense. Content, in contrast to form, is relatively culture-sensitive, and, a connected point, is presumably learnt rather than innately determined. Given that a child is prepared to develop a complex theory of cognitive-affective states in application to others and to the self, she relies on adults to teach her the content of such states in particular cases, and here there is room for error. The more serious the error, the more it has to do with conditions fundamental to action, the more serious would be the confusion and conflict to which it gives rise.

A sense of 'form' used by logicians, and distinct from that indicated above, concerns adherence to logical principles, such as non-contradiction. The 'laws of logic' of course do not turn on content. Arguably, however, their acquisition and use are sensitive to the vagaries of education. Communications to children can include more or less subtle contradictions, which can be expected to inhibit development of the capacity to think (straight). This line of thought found expression in the hypothesis that contradictory communication, in the special (inescapable) form of so-called 'double-binds', is implicated in the genesis of the major cognitive disorder, schizophrenia (Bateson *et al.* 1956; and, for discussion, Hirsch and Leff 1975. Cf. subsection 8.2.2, p. 308 and section 9.2). The form/content distinction is complicated and many-sided, and hence also is its relevance to psychological disorder.

The intimate link between failure of self-knowledge and psychological disorder is evident in the fact that some of the major pioneering work of dismantling the Cartesian theory of introspection, hence in effect the Cartesian concept of mind, has been in the area of psychological disorder, specifically by Freud. The view of self-knowledge sketched in this subsection reaffirms the close connection between ignorance about ourselves and disorder, but in other general respects it apparently differs markedly from Freudian theory. First, Freud viewed the processes involved in self-knowledge and ignorance as intrapsychic, whereas the view outlined here emphasizes their interpersonal nature. Secondly, one of Freud's crucial observations was that failure of self-knowledge typically serves a defensive function, protecting the self from intolerable intentional states, such as beliefs, memories, feelings, or impulses. By contrast, in the account given so far here nothing has been said about failure of self-knowledge having a defensive function; ignorance appears so far as no more than a failure of education. These differences are more superficial than deep, however. As will be suggested in various places as we proceed, the intrapsychic and the interpersonal, although distinguishable, are interwoven (subsection 3.3.3, sections 6.3 and 6.4); as are ignorance, or distortion of reality, and defence (subsections 1.4.4 and 8.2.3).

In the following subsection, continuing explication of post-empiricist epistemology, we consider the question of rules (beliefs) that are fundamental to action and cognition. This is linked to the issues raised above concerning the definition and role of logic in psychological order, and in the defence against disorder.

1.4.4 Fundamental rules: logic and psychologic

The post-empiricist perspective allows us to see that theories have a 'core' of fundamental beliefs, or rules, which cannot be given up without the threat that thought and action itself fall into disarray (subsection 1.4.1). Thus, if the chemical theory embodied in the periodic table of elements, or particular hypotheses essential to it, were to be given up, in the absence of a viable alternative, the cost would be confusion in, and cessation of, chemical experimentation and thinking. We would not know what to think, or what to do. This kind of point is well recognized and (relatively) well understood in application to scientific theory. Its applications to psychology and clinical psychology are of interest here. The critical point is that some theory is essential to us, either because it belongs with activities we cannot do without, or because it belongs with action as such. We apparently do not have to continue with chemistry, for example, so we could carry on despite the demise of current theory, and do something else instead. Though of course even this point is relative and needs qualification: it might not apply to someone whose identity as a chemist was fundamental to the person's view of him or herself. There are cultural and individual differences in what are taken to be essential practices and beliefs. It can be said, on the other hand, that some very general beliefs are essential to action as such, though again, what this amounts to may vary from individual to individual, and between cultures and subcultures. But insofar as there are such convictions, they maintain psychological order: what lies beyond them is breakdown.

Issues of this kind were explored philosophically by Wittgenstein in *On certainty* (1969). Wittgenstein saw that knowledge, or certainty, was intimately linked to what we need in order to act. For example, at §414 Wittgenstein writes:

> How do I *know* that it is my hand? Do I even here know what it means to say it is my hand?—When I say 'how do I know' I do not mean that I have the least *doubt* of it. What we have here is a foundation for all my action.

Again, at §411:

> If I say '*we assume* that the earth has existed for many years past' (or something similar), then of course it sounds strange that we should *assume* such a thing. But in the entire system of our language-games it belongs to the foundations. The assumption, one might say, forms the basis of action, and therefore, naturally, of thought.

An implication of these and many other passages in *On certainty* is that the foundations of knowledge coincide with the foundations of thought and meaning. We have to know, or at least be certain of, judgement itself. In this general respect Wittgenstein's proposal follows the original Cartesian epistemology: the method *de omnibus dubitandum* came to an end precisely at the *Cogito*. But while in Descartes thought consisted of (subjective) mental events, such as images of perception, thought in Wittgenstein's philosophy pertains essentially to action. Hence the conclusion that the foundations of certainty are what is required for action.

The connection between these points and the empiricist theory of knowledge may be brought out in the following way. Empiricism acknowledged that the truths of logic were (alone) not based in experience. 'Logic' here refers to what is essential to thought. In the philosophical tradition logic variously comprised the law of identity and the laws of the syllogism, later elaborated into the propositional and predicate calculi. In post-empiricism, however, logic acquires a significance broader than these formalities. It comes to include core assumptions within systems of belief which serve as rules for the interpretation of experience, as opposed to beliefs which might be overthrown by experience. Further, the boundary line here between logic and empirical belief is no longer clear-cut. Wittgenstein brings out such points in the following passages, for example, at §§94–8:

I did not get my picture of the world by satisfying myself of its correctness; nor do I have it because I am satisfied of its correctness. No: it is the inherited background against which I distinguish between true and false.

The propositions describing this world-picture might be part of a kind of mythology. And their role is like that of rules of a game; and the game can be learned purely practically, without learning any explicit rules.

It might be imagined that some propositions, of the form of empirical propositions, were hardened and functioned as channels for such empirical propositions as were not hardened but fluid; and that this relation altered with time, in that fluid propositions hardened, and hard ones became fluid.

. . . But if someone were to say 'So logic too is an empirical science, he would be wrong. Yet this is right: the same proposition may get treated at one time as something to test by experience, at another as a rule of testing.

A similar point is made at §319:

But wouldn't one have to say then, that there is no sharp boundary between propositions of logic and empirical propositions? The lack of sharpness *is* that of the boundary between *rule* and empirical proposition.

If core propositions, or rules, within the system of belief were to be questioned, then the entire system would be under threat. Reference to the law of identity in this connection is made at §494:

'I cannot doubt this proposition without giving up all judgement'.
But what sort of proposition is that? (It is reminiscent of what Frege said about the law of identity.) It is certainly no empirical proposition. It does not belong to psychology. It has rather the character of a rule.

A strange consequence of this broadening of the scope of logic is brought out, and softened, at §628:

> When we say 'Certain propositions must be excluded from doubt', it sounds as if I ought to put these propositions—for example that I am called L. W.—into a logic-book. For if it belongs to the description of a language-game, it belongs to logic. But that I am called L. W. does not belong to any such description. The language-game that operates with people's names can certainly exist even if I am mistaken about my name,—but it does presuppose that it is nonsensical to say that the majority of people are mistaken about their names.

But it may be added here that even though the language-game certainly continues given radical error or doubt by one person, that person's participation may well come to an end. At §§613–14, for example:

> But what could make me doubt whether this person here is N. N., whom I have known for years? Here a doubt would seem to drag everything with it and plunge it into chaos.
> That is to say: If I were contradicted on all sides and told that this person's name was not what I had always known it was (and I use 'know' here intentionally), then in that case the foundation of all judging would be taken away from me.

Given these high stakes, the point is precisely that we are hardly inclined to give up core beliefs. Under pressure, their rule-like function takes over: counter-evidence is deflected away. Thus, at §516, for example:

> If something happened (such as someone telling me something) calculated to make me doubtful of my own name, there would certainly also be something that made the grounds of these doubts themselves seem doubtful, and I could therefore decide to retain my old belief.

A similar point is made at §§360–2 (with allusion perhaps to the Cartesian appeal to divine good faith):

> I KNOW that this is my foot. I could not accept any experience as proof to the contrary.—That may be an exclamation; but what *follows* from it? At least that I shall act with a certainty that knows no doubt, in accordance with my belief.
> But I might also say: it has been revealed to me by God that it is so. God has taught me that this is my foot. And therefore if anything happened that seemed to conflict with this knowledge I should have to regard *that* as deception.
> But doesn't it come out here that knowledge is related to a decision?

The notion of revealed truth, antithetical to empiricism, ironically re-appears, in mundane not divine form, in the post-empiricist epistemology. Theories are passed on to the individual in education, as remarked already in the preceding subsection in the case of 'theory of mind'. Particularly for the child, belief in adults is essential to learning. On this, Wittgenstein (1969) writes, for example:

> §160. The child learns by believing the adult. Doubt comes *after* belief.

Belief in the teacher has to be one of the child's fundamental rules. Allow us to give an anecdote that illustrates this point specifically in relation to the current theme concerning logic. A child (aged 5) of one of the authors came home from school saying that he had been learning about shapes, and had learned among other things that a rectangle was not a rectangle. Gentle scepticism and suggestions of alternatives were met with the firm and repeated declaration that Miss had said so. For this 5-year-old, when it came to a choice between what Miss said and the law of identity, the law of identity came a clear second.

The question arises as to what those propositions are that we claim to know for certain, and which ones form the basis of our judgement. The general answer is just that they are those propositions that we need in order to act and to think. We can give extreme generalities, but beyond those we are limited to giving examples.

In *On certainty* Wittgenstein makes much reference to the work of G. E. Moore. In papers aimed at defending common sense against scepticism Moore cited examples of certainties that define extremely general conditions of our action (life): the body, the hand in particular, space and time, experience, and other human beings (Moore 1925, 1939). The level of generality here is appropriately philosophical. Other examples of certainties cited by Wittgenstein include somewhat less general facts, of for example history, geography, and biology, as well as judgements made by a person about his or her personal history and circumstances. It is evident here that the examples that could be given are endless. There is great diversity between cultures, sub-cultures, and individuals, and variation through time. So we can cite more or less general, and more or less particular cases of propositions which have the property of logical certainty, but it is not possible to define the conditions of thought and action once and for all.

It has been implicit in the discussion so far that there is an intimate connection between propositions that define our picture of the world, and mental order. Doubt or error concerning fundamental rules raises the issue of breakdown of psychological function. The connection here is of central concern to the themes of the present essay.

While our certainty has foundations in logic, these foundations are not absolute. There is no suggestion that our knowledge is infallible. It is possible for a person to be in doubt about, or in error about, even fundamental things. But in such cases, doubt arises as to the person's soundness of mind. Wittgenstein makes this point throughout *On certainty*. For example, at §71:

> If my friend were to imagine one day that he had been living for a long time past in such and such a place, etc. etc., I should not call this a *mistake*, but rather a mental disturbance (Geistesstorung), perhaps a transient one.

And at §155, concerning Moore's 'common-sense' propositions:

> In certain circumstances a man cannot make a *mistake*. ('Can' is here used logically, and the proposition does not mean that a man cannot say anything false in those circumstances.) If Moore were to pronounce the opposite of those propositions which he declares certain, we should not just not share his opinion: we should regard him as demented (geistesgestort).

Certain false judgements cast doubt on the speaker's state of mind. The inference would be that there is something wrong with the person's capacity to make judgements. The nature of the impairment would be so far unclear; it may involve perception, memory, language-comprehension, or reason itself. That there are judgements which define the capacity for judgement is presupposed in neurological and psychiatric examination. When a clinician asks a patient questions such as: 'How many fingers am I holding up?' or, 'Where are we now?', the aim is not to elicit information, but is rather to test the measure.

These considerations bring out the nature of certainty. A person can say: 'I *must* be right about this (for example that this is my hand), providing I am able to make judgements at all'. Of course, from the person's point of view this qualification can hardly be doubted: what lies on the other side is chaos (madness).

The philosophical theory of judgement and knowledge has to include an account of radical error, which will be 'mental disorder'. This link between philosophical theory and the notion of mental disorder is clear in Wittgenstein's work in post-empiricist epistemology, but in the previous tradition it was submerged beneath the weight of the problem of knowledge (of the external world). At the beginning of modern thought Descartes made the connection between error in fundamental matters and madness. In pursuing the method of doubt beyond the bounds of common sense, beyond what is apparently beyond rational doubt—for example that he has a body—Descartes in his *First meditation* observes that he has to cite circumstances in which contrary, bizarre beliefs can occur, in particular in insanity and in dreaming (1641, p. 145). But it then becomes an insoluble problem to distinguish wakefulness from sleep (ibid. p. 146); or again, we could add, to distinguish sanity from delusion. Descartes continues (loc. cit.):

> Now let us assume that we are asleep and that all these particulars, e.g. that we open our eyes, shake our head, extend our hands, and so on, are but false delusions; and let us reflect that possibly neither our hands nor our whole body are such as they appear to us to be.

The Cartesian problem can be formulated in terms of mental disorder, or dreaming, but the real problem had nothing much to do with either. Rather, as has been suggested (subsection 1.2.1), the real problem in the modern world-picture was how absolute objects could be known on the basis of relative, subjective experience. The Cartesian problem belonged to an age in which subjective experience (delusional or otherwise) was more certain than (absolute) objectivity. For us, on the other hand, the common, though not absolute, world of objects is obvious enough, so that it hardly needs affirmation. The issue remains relevant in psychiatry, however, since in mental disorder even what appears obvious to us all is brought into question.

In *On certainty* Wittgenstein examined the certainty that we attach to some beliefs of a factual nature, general or personal. In focusing on factual beliefs, Wittgenstein followed traditional theory of knowledge, the originality being the characteristically post-empiricist insight that certainty in such beliefs was a matter of their being essential to action, and hence to judgement itself. But the acknowledgement of the fundamental connection between certainty and action opens up a different area, concerning beliefs that are actually about the self's activity, and in particular about what is essential to it. Such beliefs constitute what can be called the core of the theory of action.

Action presupposes at least the following core beliefs, or expectations: that the self is competent (enough) to act, that the world is predictable (enough), and that the world provides (enough) satisfaction of needs. Such expectations have to be preserved if activity is to continue. If they were to be abandoned, action would appear to be either impossible or pointless: there would be, so far, no reason to act.

Beliefs of this kind have a special epistemological and logical role. They will be expressed, if they are expressed at all, with certainty. Or again, the agent will be extremely reluctant to abandon them, on pain, so far, of abandoning action itself. This means, for example, that any experience that seems to contradict them will, if at all possible, be re-interpreted in such a way as to preserve the beliefs, and hence action itself.

Another way of bringing out the special epistemological and logical role of such propositions is to describe them as a priori. This has various connotations. The involvement of such beliefs in the regulation of action follows from the definition of (belongs to the concept of) action itself. Further, such beliefs are not based in experience, but rather serve in the interpretation of experience: counter-evidence will tend to be re-construed so as to remove threat to the core beliefs. It is possible also that such beliefs or expectations are a priori in the sense of being innate, designed in at birth. It is at least plausible to suppose that living beings are designed by evolutionary selection so as to expect such as predictability and satisfaction of needs, these expectations being preconditions of attempts to act. Another sign of the special status of these beliefs and expectations, one which directly links the philosophical and psychological senses of being a priori (or innate) is the fact that their attribution is valid providing the subject is acting at all, regardless of the particular nature of the action.

It is true that we rarely have occasion to articulate or attribute core assumptions of action explicitly. Typically, fundamental principles may remain implicit, until the theory is faced with repeated recalcitrant experiences. The presuppositions of action show up when they apparently fail to apply. Thus, for example, in the learned helplessness experimental paradigm animals apparently give up the expectation that what they do makes a difference, and consequently they do nothing (Seligman 1975). It is evident in this example that fundamental rules underlying action can be (are) attributed to animals, such as rats, which have no language. The only presuppositions are those that underlie the attribution of mental (cognitive) states generally. Core beliefs or expectations can be attributed to a living being in so far as they best explain and predict intentional activity. And so also, as in the case of learned helplessness just cited, the negation of such beliefs or expectations can be attributed in so far as they best explain and predict the giving up of intentional activity.

It belongs to post-empiricism that action is regulated by cognitive states in the form of a theory, which has a core, essential to the enterprise, which will be protected more or less at any cost, by whatever resources the living, cognitive being has at its disposal. Beliefs at the core of the theory are essential for action, but also essential for thought (cognition) itself. Their opposites are not possible thoughts, or at least, not ones that can be used in the planning of action. In this sense the belief that the world is enough for life is a 'logical truth': its negation cannot be thought. The implication here, which belongs both to philosophy (logic) and to psychology, is that major assaults on the core of the theory of action not only require drastic defensive manoeuvres, but they also, at the same time, have profoundly adverse effects on the capacity for thought.

These issues will be taken up later, in Chapter 8, under the headings of psychological trauma and psychic defences.

1.5 THEORY-DRIVEN PREDICTIVE POWER IMPLIES CAUSALITY

1.5.1 Introduction

Throughout this chapter we have explored various aspects of the fact that explanations of behaviour in terms of intentional states have predictive power. In this section we draw the conclusion that such explanations are causal. This conclusion is relatively less surprising in the case of explanations in cognitive-behavioural psychology, with their scientific credentials and terminology, but is more contentious when applied to folk psychological explanations. This is because folk psychology is often thought of as pre-, merging into non-scientific, and because its central notion of meaning has been regarded as nothing to do with science generally or with causal explanation in particular. We consider some of these issues concerning folk psychology first, before moving on to the connection between predictive power and causal explanation.

1.5.2 Folk psychology as a theory for prediction

Cognitive psychology had more explanatory and predictive power than the paradigm that it replaced, S–R theory (Subsection 1.2.1), as one would expect of a scientific paradigm-shift. Folk psychology too, however, can be, and is, used for prediction. Using our familiar method of understanding in terms of mental states, we anticipate actions and reactions, by all means fallibly, but generally with remarkable accuracy. Any kind of course of action and its separable components, whether it be, to chose at random from countless possible types of example, playing a game, making friends, building a house, conducting an experiment, is understood by us according to the beliefs, motives, and strategies of the participants. And generally, notwithstanding ample scope for misunderstanding, we anticipate what goes on with enough success, enough of the time. To the extent that we make mistakes, then our grasp of the activity, and our own participation, is confounded.

That folk psychology has predictive power is from one point of view not surprising at all. Predictive power is closely linked to practical utility, and given that the folk have practical concerns, it makes sense that they should have developed a theory which has predictive power. On the other hand, response to this line of thought probably depends on which examples of folk theories we have in mind. We can think of, say, folk physics in support of it, but as against it, examples such as astrology and magic, as cited by Churchland (1988). It may be that the appraisal of folk theories generally depends on their compatibility with current scientific paradigms.

Here we come across a consideration specific to folk psychology, that its characteristic posits, mental states and their meaning, have been thoroughly problematic from the point of view of modern science, and resisted within psychological science particularly (subsections 1.2.1, 1.3.8). Against this background, our familiar ordinary explanations of people's actions in terms of such as beliefs, desires, motives, and plans, with examples obvious to the point of being trite, may be dismissed as *merely* 'folk psychology', with little or no relevance to hard psychological science, whether behavioural or neurophysiological.

Nevertheless it has become clear recently, as folk psychology has come to be regarded as a theory akin to cognitive psychology, that there is a decisive objection to simply dismissing it as scientifically invalid or irrelevant. The objection, as we have anticipated, is just that folk psychology generates powerful predictions. Fodor has made this point with particular force.[17]

Predictive efficacy, of course, is one of the fundamental aims of scientific theory. The point is exactly not that folk psychology is being praised for such as literary or poetic qualities, which might indeed be regarded as irrelevant to its scientific value.

This is connected with the fact that the same considerations also count against 'hermeneutic' vindications of the discourse of mind and meaning, which would endorse and make a virtue of its non-scientific status. According to the line of argument adopted here, the language of mind and meaning has at least one fundamental feature in common with scientific theory, namely predictive function. This function is critical to the scientific endeavour, and to the extent that it belongs also to our understanding of mind and meaning, the dichotomy between these two forms of discourse deconstructs.

1.5.3 The inference to causal explanation

Explanations of action in terms of meaningful mental states are effective in prediction. The point to be made at this stage is just that there is a close relation between predictive efficacy and causal explanation. It is relatively uncontroversial to say that predictive power is a necessary condition for an explanation to be causal. It is not by itself, however, a sufficient condition. Accidental connections (for example between being a swan and being white) can be used for prediction, without being causal. It is characteristic of accidental generalizations that their truth is accidentally restricted in space and/or time (in the example just cited restricted to Europe, before zoos), and also that they do not belong to or follow from a systematic theory. Neither of these points applies in the case of explanation of behaviour in terms of mind and meaning. There are various plausible responses to the apparent fact that attribution of mental states predicts behaviour, but supposition that the connection is mere coincidence is not among them. The next possibility is more interesting.

Generalization may be reliable, and may indeed signify causal connection, but the associated phenomena may be linked by a common cause, rather than one kind being a cause of the other. An example would be the association between migrating behaviour of birds in different parts of the world. Typically we construe an association as signifying a common cause in case we have, or can at least envisage, a theory that would specify the causal mechanisms and hence the connection between the several sets of phenomena. It is possible to look at the connection between mental states and behaviour in this way. The idea would be: there are reliable connections between mental states of certain kinds and behaviour of certain kinds, such that the former predict the latter, but mental states are not causes of behaviour, rather they are both products of a common cause, the most likely candidate for which role is activity of the brain. This is a reasonable answer but it is out of date: it is reasonable only in the context of assumptions that have been replaced in current theory. The assumptions are Cartesian, or neo-Cartesian, namely, that mental events are immaterial processes, running in parallel to material events, neural or bodily, and that there is no essential connection between the mental and the material. The Cartesian dual-process theory has no role in cognitive psychology or cognitive science generally, including AI in particular. To put the point another way, we are beyond the stage at which the predictive power of the theory of mind can be understood in these terms.

The situation is rather that the pressure mounts to adopt some form of mind/brain identity theory, the main idea being that mental events are *in some sense* brain events and (therefore can be) *in some sense* causes of behaviour. Subsequent chapters are dedicated to making sense of the italicized phrases in this solution! These chapters, particularly 2, 4, and 5, are in this sense elaborations of the conclusion reached at this point.

Although it awaits explication, the conclusion stands that explanation of action in terms of mental states and their meaningful contents is causal, and it collapses the traditional dichotomy between meaningful and causal explanations.

1.6 SUMMARY

The main idea of this chapter is that explanations of behaviour in terms of meaningful, mental states have theory-driven predictive power. Three sections, 1.2–1.4, work out various aspects of this idea, and the conclusion is then drawn in 1.5 that such explanations are *causal*.

Section 1.2 concerned psychological science. The section began (1.2.1) with a sketch of dualism and the problematic role of mind in seventeenth-century science. The ill-fit between mind and science became starkly apparent at the turn of the nineteenth century with attempts to construct a science of the mind, leading first to a methodologically weak introspectionism and then to the other alternative within the framework of Cartesian dualism, behaviourism. The logic of cognitive explanations of behaviour and influences on the cognitive revolution in psychology were discussed in subsection 1.2.2. Cognitive animal learning theory drew attention to the fact that the behaviour of man and of higher animals is 'intelligent' (goal-directed and plastic), apparently not only a matter of mechanical conditioning, and proposed that cognitive processes are implicated in the organization and regulation of such behaviour. The following two subsections considered briefly the role within the cognitive paradigm of two major psychological faculties: affect and consciousness. The cognitive paradigm can look, especially from the point of view of some its formative influences, affectless. But this appearance is misleading: affect, or emotion, is essential to cognition, in so far as it regulates the activity of living beings (1.2.3). On the other hand, it is true that the concept of consciousness is not essential to the general paradigm. It assumes importance for the explanation of certain high-level features of action, most, though not all, of which are characteristically human (1.2.4). The section closed (1.2.5) by remarking on similarities between cognitive and folk psychology, a theme that recurs throughout the chapter.

In Section 1.3 we began a task that will occupy us throughout the essay, clarification of that family of concepts that includes notions such as intentionality, representation, meaning, and information. After some preliminary definitions (subsection 1.3.1), we considered the attractive idea, which has a very long history, that such concepts are grounded in *resemblance* between sign and signified (subsection 1.3.2). We saw reasons to reject the resemblance theory, however, in favour of the view that signs have meaning (represent, have intentionality, carry information) in so far as they are used in activity (subsection 1.3.3). Such use is subject to normative descriptions (right/wrong, etc.), and can in this sense be described as rule-following (subsection 1.3.4). The intimate connection between concepts of meaning and rule-following begins to clarify a central theme in this chapter, that explanations that invoke meaningful states are effective in prediction: they attribute propensity to follow rules, and hence serve to predict what the agent will do. The predictive power of intentional explanations is emphasized by Dennett. In Subsection 1.3.5 we considered his notion of the intentional stance for the explanation of systemic, functional behaviour, in comparison and contrast with the design and physical stances. The intentional stance predicts intentional behaviour, a feat that cannot be accomplished from the lower-level physical stance (subsection 1.3.6). This is an argument for the ineliminability of intentional explanations of action. It is argued in subsection 1.3.7 that there is a strong connection between the folk psychological notion of meaning and the cognitive psychological notion of (semantic) information. Folk psychological attributions of belief seek specifically to identify the highly processed information involved in the regulation of action. By contrast, folk psychology has little or nothing to say about earlier stages of information-processing. The implication of this argument is that folk psychology has a share of the scientific legitimacy of cognitive psychology, but also that the cognitive psychology paradigm inherits the traditional problems of meaning from the point of view of scientific assumptions and methods (subsection 1.3.8). It was not only Cartesian mind that was problematic in the modern scientific world-picture. As attention came to focus on the meaningful character of mind, this too was recognized as problematic from the point of view of science. Meaningful phenomena were seen to involve subjectivity, and were apparently not among the causes envisaged by the natural sciences. Hence the pressure to keep meaningful phenomena, including meaningful mental states, out of psychological science.

In Section 1.4 we noted that various themes so far and to follow throughout the essay interact strongly with the shift from empiricist to post-empiricist epistemology. Critical to post-empiricism is the idea that knowledge is not derived directly from unconditionally given experience, but is mediated by theory, hierarchically organized systems of belief (subsection 1.4.1). We went on to consider the currently influential idea that we use a 'theory of mind' to predict behaviour (subsection 1.4.2). In subsection 1.4.3 we considered our capacity to represent our own mental states, to hold beliefs about the states of mind regulating our own action. It was argued that this second-order intentionality has two aspects. On the one hand, it is similar to the third-person case: a person can have a theory about her own mental states, just as she has a theory about those of another. A person's theory about herself, like theories generally, can be wrong. On the other hand, (sincere) statements of belief and desire, can function more like expressions of intention. Even if they incorrectly identify the mental states at work in a particular course of behaviour, nevertheless they tend to generate actions and affect appropriate to what is avowed. In such circumstances, there is conflict within the system. Rule-conflict generally is critical in psychological disorder, and we return to the notion in that context in later chapters. Of the many and various connections between post-empiricism and themes of the essay, one concerns the boundary between order and disorder (subsection 1.4.4): the theory underlying action has a core which is essential to action, such that its breakdown would threaten action itself.

The effectiveness of explanations in terms of meaningful, mental states in delivering predictions of behaviour points to the conclusion that such explanations are causal. This inference was drawn in Section 1.5. The argument is indeed relatively straightforward. The problem is not so much the argument but making sense of its conclusion. At its starkest, the conclusion is that meaningful mental states are causes of action (or behaviour). The conclusion, however, raises many problems, immediately two: 'What is the ontological status of mental states?' and, 'What is the nature of mental causation?'. A third problem, pressing from the direction of the theory of knowledge is this: causal processes are surely within, or have, objective reality, but meanings are notoriously tainted by subjectivity. The ontological problem will be addressed in Chapter 2, the epistemological issues in Chapter 3, and the special nature of meaningful, mental causation in chapters 4 and 5.

NOTES

1. For accounts of animal learning theory see, for example, Hilgard and Bower (1966) and Mackintosh (1983). The brief discussion in the text of early cognitive theory refers mainly to the work of Tolman (1932, 1948). Brewer (1974) and Dulany (1974) provide helpful, brief critiques of the transition from conditioning to cognitive learning models.

2. The following review is very partial as well as brief. It omits theories within psychology which, as well as cognitive learning theory, anticipated the cognitive paradigm, Piaget's developmental psychology, and Heider's attribution theory. For comprehensive treatments of the cognitive revolution in psychology see Gardner (1985) and Baars (1986).

3. For discussion of the relation between the concept of information in MCT and in cognitive psychology see Dretske (1981, 1983). Dretske's main aim in these works was to work out a causal theory of semantics, a topic to be discussed in Chapter 4.

4. Classic philosophical studies of the emotions include Aristotle's *De Anima*, and Spinoza's *Ethics* Part III. The biological/evolutionary theoretic approach to the emotions was elaborated by Darwin (1872). The close connection between affect, cognition, and action is apparent conceptually and in psychological theory (Gordon 1987; Oatley 1988; Barnard and Teasdale 1991). The central role of affect can also be defined using cybernetic theory, e.g. Ciompi 1991. On the notion of valency and basic emotions in current cognitive psychology see, for example, Davidson (1992) and other papers in Stein and Oatley (1992). Oatley and Johnson-Laird (1987)

have proposed that emotions are linked specifically to the managing of multiple goals, an issue that occupies us in Chapter 6 (Section 6.4).

5. The early statement of the problem of ecological validity for cognitive psychology was Neisser's (1976), with recent discussion in relation to memory including Conway (1991) and Ceci and Bronfenbrenner (1991). The question of independence of emotion from cognition was hotly debated in the 1980s (Zajonc 1980, 1984; Zajonc *et al.* 1982; Lazarus 1982, 1984; Mandler 1982), with eventually a degree of consensus that emotion *can be* independent of *conscious* cognitive processing, though normally involves unconscious processing (Mandler 1982; Brewin 1988; Williams *et al.* 1988). This conclusion is compatible with what is proposed in the text. The literature on influence of mood on cognitive processing is reviewed in Williams *et al.* (1988) and Brewin (1988). Recent theorizing about the links between cognition and emotion include, in philosophy, Greenspan (1988) and Nash (1989) and, in psychology, the very detailed model proposed by Barnard and Teasdale (Barnard and Teasdale 1991; Teasdale and Barnard 1993).

6. This is the briefest allusion to a complicated, contentious, and expanding area of cognitive psychological research (see, for example, Lycan 1987; Gillett 1988; Marcel and Bisiach 1988; Clark 1990; Pickering and Skinner 1990; Velmans 1991; Baddeley 1992; Davies and Humphreys 1992; Smith 1992; Baddeley and Weiskrantz 1993). An excellent review of the issues from the point of view of clinical psychology, which emphasizes connections between current cognitive science and early work by theorists such as Freud and Janet, is given by Power and Brewin (1991).

7. The distinction here is often drawn in terms of first-and third-person perspectives on the objects of knowledge and on mental states in particular (see, for example, Nagel 1986; Dennett 1987). Various recent approaches to consciousness work to break the down the Cartesian distinction between reality and consciousness, from the point of view of cognitive psychology (Velmans 1990), in relation to quantum mechanics (Lockwood 1989; see also Goertzel 1992), and by, for example, Davidson (1989) and Dennett (1991) in the philosophy of mind. Philosophical problems of consciousness are discussed also by, for example, Hannay (1990), Searle (1990, 1992), Flanagan (1992), and in Davies and Humphreys (1992).

8. The definition of *intentionality* given here, and the definition of *intensionality* to be given below in the text, while sufficient for our purposes, are rough and ready, and readers seeking detailed accuracy are advised to consult the account of Brentano's thesis and some of its more recent formulations and versions in Dennett (1969); see also Searle (1983). Full discussions of intentionality in relation to modern philosophical psychology are given by Lyons in his series of articles (1990, 1991, 1992). These articles consider various approaches to intentionality, exemplified by Carnap and Dennett (in the first article), by Chomsky and Fodor (in the second), and by the teleological semantics (in the third article). Lyons's range is reflected in the present essay. Dennett's approach is discussed in subsection 1.3.5, Fodor's language of thought hypothesis is discussed in Chapter 2, Section 2.2, and causal and teleological (or functional) semantics throughout Chapter 4.

9. Dennett's analysis raises the question whether it is possible or necessary to distin-

guish between systems such as computers which have merely 'derived' intentionality from those like ourselves who have 'intrinsic' or 'original' intentionality (Dennett 1987; Newton 1992) The issues under this heading are diverse and complicated. They include the problem of defining when such systems are 'in error', which is considered at length throughout Chapter 4. Another issue discussed under this heading concerns the ways in which intentional systems are 'designed': computers by human beings, human beings by evolution. We touch on aspects of this issue in Chapter 5, arguing that the intentionality of biological systems specifically is characterized by a range of connected structural and functional features. Generally speaking, however, nothing in the present essay relies heavily on any distinction between 'derived' and 'intrinsic' (or 'original') intentionality.

10. This is a complex topic, only some aspects of which will be addressed in the text; see also, for example, Dretske (1981, 1983, 1988), Jackendoff (1987), Bogdan (1988), Israel (1988), Greenwood (1991), Cummins (1991), and Hanson (1990). Information and meaning together are the topics for causal and functional semantics, to be discussed in Chapter 4.

11. A discussion of the relation between language and the various levels of visual information-processing described by Marr (1982) can be found in Jackendoff (1987). The issue of analogical as opposed to propositional and linguistic representation has been the subject of much research and debate, for example Shepard and Metzler (1971), Kosslyn and Pomerantz (1977), Kosslyn (1981), Pylyshyn (1981), Johnson-Laird (1983), Weiskrantz (1988), Finke (1989), and Tye (1991). Barnard's interacting cognitive subsystems framework posits nine types of information and two levels of meaning, specific propositional coding and a more generic level (Barnard 1985; Barnard and Teasdale 1991; Teasdale and Barnard 1993). The question of symbolic encoding of information as it arises in AI models is discussed in section 2.2, and the grounding of meaning in sensorimotor representations is discussed in Section 2.3. Recent philosophical commentary on the relation between thought and language includes Gillett (1992). The problem of linguistic as opposed to non-linguistic specification of mental contents is excellently discussed by Clark (1990).

12. Source material for empiricism includes Locke (1690) and Hume (1777). On logical empiricism see, for example, Ayer (1936, 1959). Major statements of post-empiricism include Quine (1953), Feyerabend (1965), Wittgenstein (1969), and Lakatos (1970). Aspects of these last two works are discussed in subsection 1.4.4 and in this subsection, respectively.

13. On the demarcation criterion, see Popper (1959), Kuhn (1962), Lakatos and Musgrave (1970), including particularly Lakatos (1970) and Feyerabend (1975), with commentary in O'Hear (1989). On its application to psychoanalytic theory, see Popper (1962, 1974), and for commentary Grünbaum (1984, 1986, 1993).

14. These distinctions are many-sided, complex, and controversial. They arose early in cognitive science (Chomsky 1965; Fodor 1968; Turvey 1974), and remain influential in contemporary theorizing (Chomsky 1980; Evans 1985; Stich and Nichols 1992). The simple position adopted in this essay is stated below in the text.

15. 'Self-knowledge' has various meanings, of which the capacity to give an account

of one's own intentional states is one. For critical discussion of the varieties of self-knowledge see, for example, Neisser (1988) and Cassam (1994).

16. This way of qualifying first-person infallibility and authority, in terms of possible conflict with the person's actions, is quite distinct from another method currently popular in the philosophical literature, in which the qualification appeals to the so-called 'broad' content of mental states (Davidson 1984, 1987; Burge 1988; Boghossian 1989; McKinsey 1991). The notion of broad content invoked here derives from Putnam's (1975) argument that 'meaning ain't in the head', and will be discussed at length in the next chapter (Section 2.5).

   Both ways of qualifying first-person authority have in common the critical point that self-reports of mental states are committed to the existence of something 'non-subjective', and hence can be wrong. In the account proposed here this something non-subjective is the person's (objective) behaviour, while in the other account it is typically some independently defined feature of the external world. Criticisms of the generally accepted notion of broad content are made in subsection 2.5.4 from the standpoint of a behavioural criterion of content, and those criticisms are of a piece with the behavioural criterion of failure of self-knowledge proposed here.

   An advantage of this behavioural criterion is that it can deliver an account not only of possible error in first-person reports, but also of 'infallible' uses of such reports. The approach to infallibility, based on the fact that self-reports normally regulate action, is considered below in the text.

17. See, for example, Fodor (1987, Chapter 1). Much recent discussion has concerned the role in folk psychological explanation and prediction of *ceteris paribus* clauses (that is, of qualifying clauses to the effect: 'other things being equal'), and particularly the question whether reliance on such clauses invalidates the alleged explanations and predictive power (for example, Fodor 1987, 1991; Schiffer 1991). We assume here that this is not the case. Indeed, it will be argued later, in Chapters 4 and 5, that one particular type of folk psychological (and cognitive psychological) *ceteris paribus* clause, referring in some way to 'normal' psychological function, is critical to the logic of explanations which invoke intentional states, and to their special causal status.

REFERENCES

Anderson, J. R. (1983). *The architecture of cognition*. Harvard University Press, Cambridge, Mass.

Anscombe, G. E. M. (1957). *Intention*. Blackwell, Oxford.

Astington, J. W., Harris, P. L. and Olson, D. R. (ed.) (1988). *Developing theories of mind*. Cambridge University Press, Cambridge.

Attneave, F. (1959). *Applications of information theory to psychology: a summary of basic concepts, methods and results*. Henry Holt, New York.

Ayer, A. J. (1936). *Language, truth and logic*. Gollanz, London. (2nd edn, revised, 1946.)

Ayer, A. J. (ed.) (1959). *Logical positivism.* The Free Press, Glencoe, Illinois.

Baars, B. (1986). *The cognitive revolution in psychology.* Guildford, New York.

Baddeley, A. (1992). Editorial: Consciousness and working memory. *Consciousness and Cognition*, 1, 3–6.

Baddeley, A. and Weiskrantz, L. (ed.) (1993). *Attention: selection, awareness, and control.* Oxford University Press, Oxford.

Barnard, P. (1985). Interacting cognitive subsystems: a psycholinguistic approach to short-term memory. In *Progress in the psychology of language*, (ed. A. Ellis), Vol. 2, pp. 197–258. Lawrence Erlbaum Associates, London.

Barnard, P. and Teasdale, J. (1991). Interacting cognitive subsystems: a systemic approach to cognitive-affective interaction and change. *Cognition and Emotion*, 5, 1–39.

Baron-Cohen, S., Tager-Flusberg, H., and Cohen, D. (ed.) (1993). *Understanding other minds: perspectives from autism.* Oxford University Press, Oxford.

Bateson, G., Jackson, D., Haley, J., and Weakland, J. (1956). Toward a theory of schizophrenia. *Behavioral Science*, 1, 251–64.

Bennett, M. (ed.) (1993). *The child as psychologist.* Harvester, Sussex.

Berkeley, G. (1710). The principles of human knowledge. In *The works of George Berkeley*, (ed. A. A. Luce and T. E. Jessop), Vol. ii. Thomas Nelson and Sons, London, 1949.

Boden, M. (1988). *Computer models of mind.* Cambridge University Press, Cambridge.

Bogdan, R. J. (1988). Information and cognition: an ontological account. *Mind and Language*, 3, 81–122.

Boghossian, P. (1989). Content and self-knowledge. *Philosophical Topics*, 17, 5–26.

Bolton, D. (1979). *An approach to Wittgenstein's philosophy.* Macmillan, London.

Bolton, D. (1982). Life-form and idealism. In *Idealism, past and present*, (ed. G. Vesey), pp. 269–84. Cambridge University Press, Cambridge.

Brennan, J. F. (1986). *History and systems of psychology*, (3rd edn). Prentice Hall, Englewood Cliffs, NJ.

Brentano, F. (1874). *Psychologie vom empirischen standpunkt*, Vol. I. Leipzig.

Brewer, W. (1974). There is no convincing evidence for operant or classical conditioning in adult humans. In *Cognition and the symbolic processes*, (ed. W. B. Weimer and D. S. Palermo), pp. 1–42. Lawrence Erlbaum Associates, Hillsdale, NJ.

Brewin, C. R. (1988). *Cognitive foundations of clinical psychology.* Lawrence Erlbaum, Hove.

Brown, J. and Dunn, J. (1991). 'You can cry, mum': the social and developmental implications of talk about internal states. *British Journal of Developmental Psychology*, 9, 237–56.

Burge, T. (1988). Individualism and self-knowledge. *Journal of Philosophy*, 85, 649–63.

Burtt, E. A. (1932). *The metaphysical foundations of modern physical science*, (2nd edn). Routledge and Kegan Paul, London.

Butterworth, G., Harris, P., Leslie, A., and Wellman, H. (ed.) (1991). *Perspectives on the child's theory of mind.* Oxford University Press, Oxford.

Byng-Hall, J. (1973). Family myths used as defence in conjoint family therapy. *British Journal of Medical Psychology*, 46, 239–49.

Cassam, Q. (ed.) (1994). *Self-knowledge.* Oxford University Press, Oxford.

Ceci, S. J. and Bronfenbrenner, U. (1991). On the demise of everyday memory. *American Psychologist,* **46,** 27–31.

Chomsky, N. (1957) *Syntactic structures.* Mouton, The Hague.

Chomsky, N. (1959). Review of B. F. Skinner's *Verbal behavior. Language,* 35, 26–58. (Reprinted in Block, N. (ed.) (1980). *Readings in philosophy of psychology,* Vol. I, pp. 48–63. Methuen, London. Page references to this volume.

Chomsky, N. (1965). *Aspects of the theory of syntax.* MIT Press, Cambridge, Mass.

Chomsky, N. (1980). Rules and representations. With peer commentary. In *The Behavioral and Brain Sciences,* 3, 1–61.

Churchland, P. M. (1988). *Matter and consciousness.* MIT Press, Cambridge, Mass. (1984, revised 1988.)

Ciompi, L. (1991). Affects as central organizing and integrating factors. *British Journal of Psychiatry,* **159,** 97–105.

Clark, A. (1990). Belief, opinion and consciousness. *Philosophical Psychology,* 3, 139–54.

Conway, M. A. (1991). In defense of everyday memory. *American Psychologist,* **46,** 19–26.

Copleston, F. (1960). *A history of philosophy,* Vol. iv. Burns and Oates, London.

Cummins, R. (1991). The role of mental meaning in psychological explanation. In *Dretske and his critics,* (ed. B. McLaughlin), pp. 102–17. Blackwell, Oxford.

Darwin, C. (1872). *The expression of the emotions in man and animals.* Reprinted by University of Chicago Press, 1965.

Davidson, D. (1963). Actions, reasons, and causes. Reprinted in Davidson, D. (1980). *Essays on actions and events,* pp. 3–19. Clarendon Press, Oxford.

Davidson, D. (1970). Mental events. In *Experience and theory,* (ed. L. Foster and J. Swanson). MIT Press, Cambridge, Mass. (Reprinted in Davidson, D. (1980). *Essays on actions and events,* pp. 207–27. Clarendon Press, Oxford.)

Davidson, D. (1971). *Agency.* In *Agent, action, and reason,* (ed. R. Binkley, R. Bronaugh, and A. Marras). University of Toronto Press, Toronto. (Reprinted in Davidson, D. (1980). *Essays on actions and events,* pp. 43–61. Clarendon Press, Oxford.)

Davidson, D. (1984). 1st Person Authority. *Dialectica,* 38, 101–11.

Davidson, D. (1987). Knowing one's own mind. *Proceedings and Addresses of the American Philosophical Association,* 60, 441–58.

Davidson, D. (1989). The myth of the subjective. In *Relativism: interpretation and confrontation,* (ed. M. Krausz, pp. 159–72. Notre Dame University Press, Notre Dame, Ind.

Davidson, R. J. (1992). Prolegomenon to the structure of emotion: Gleanings from neuropsychology. In *Basic emotions,* (ed. N. L. stein and K. Oatley), pp. 245–68. Lawrence Erlbaum Associates, Hove.

Davies, M. and Humphreys, G. W. (ed.) (1992). *Consciousness.* Blackwell, Oxford.

Dennett, D. (1969). *Content and consciousness.* Routledge and Kegan Paul, London.

Dennett, D. (1979). *Brainstorms: philosophical essays on mind and psychology.* Harvester, Sussex.

Dennett, D. (1987). *The intentional stance.* MIT Press, Cambridge, Mass.

Dennett, D. (1988). Precis of *The intentional stance* with peer commentary. *The Behavioral and Brain Sciences*, 11, 495–546.

Dennett, D. (1991). *Consciousness explained*. Penguin, Harmondsworth.

Descartes, R. (1641). *Meditations on first philosophy*. (Quotations from and page references to *The philosophical works of Descartes*, trans. E. S. Haldane and G. R. T. Ross, Cambridge University Press, Cambridge, 1911, reprinted 1967.)

Dretske, F. (1981). *Knowledge and the flow of information*. MIT Press, Cambridge, Mass.

Dretske, F. (1983). Precis of *Knowledge and the flow of information*, with peer commentary. *Behavioral and Brain Sciences*, 6, 55–63.

Dretske, F. (1988). Commentary: Bogdan on information. *Mind and Language*, 3, 141–44.

Dulany, D. (1974). On the support of cognitive theory in opposition to behaviour theory: a methodological problem. In *Cognition and the symbolic processes*, (ed. W. B. Weimer and D. S. Palermo), pp. 43–56. Lawrence Erlbaum Associates, Hillsdale, NJ.

Dunn, J., Brown J., and Beardsall, L. (1991a). Family talk about feeling states and children's later understanding of others' emotions. *Developmental Psychology*, 27, 448–55.

Dunn, J., Brown J., Slomkowski, C., Tesla, C., and Youngblade, L. (1991b). Young children's understanding of other people's feelings and beliefs: individual differences and their antecedents. *Child Development*, 62, 1352–66.

Ericsson, K. A. and Simon, H. A. (1980). Verbal reports as data. *Psychological Review*, 87, 215–51.

Evans, G. (1985). Semantic theory and tacit knowledge. In *Collected papers*, (ed. G. Evans), pp. 322–42. Oxford University Press, Oxford.

Evnine, S. (1991). *Donald Davidson*. Polity Press, Cambridge.

Eysenck, M. W. and Keane, M. T. (1990). *Cognitive psychology. A student's handbook*. Lawrence Erlbaum Associates, Hove.

Feyerabend, P. (1965). Problems of empiricism. In *Beyond the edge of certainty*, (ed. R. Colodny), Prentice Hall, Englewood Cliffs.

Feyerabend, P. (1975). *Against method*. New Left Books, London.

Feyerabend, P. (1988). Knowledge and the role of theories. *Philosophy and Social Sciences*, 18, 157–78.

Finke, R. A. (1989). *Principles of mental imagery*. MIT Press, Cambridge, Mass.

Flanagan, O. (1992). *Consciousness reconsidered*. MIT Press, Cambridge, Mass.

Fodor, J. (1968). The appeal to tacit knowledge in psychological explanation. *Journal of Philosophy*, 65, 627–40.

Fodor, J. (1987). *Psychosemantics*. MIT Press, Cambridge, Mass.

Fodor, J. (1991). You can fool some of the people all of the time, everything else being equal; hedged laws and psychological explanation. *Mind*, 100, 19–34.

Fodor, J., Garrett, M. F., Walker, E. C. T., and Parkes, C. H. (1980). Against definitions. *Cognition*, 8, 263–367.

Folgelin, R. (1976). *Wittgenstein*. Routledge and Kegan Paul, London.

Foucault, M. (1965). *Madness and civilization*. Random House, New York.

Gardner, H. (1985). *The mind's new science: A history of the cognitive revolution*.

Basic Books. (Reprinted 1987 with new epilogue.)

Garner, W. R. (1962). *Uncertainty and structure as psychological concepts.* Wiley, London.

Gillett, G. (1988). Consciousness and brain function. *Philosophical Psychology,* **1,** 327–41.

Gillett, G. (1992) *Representation, meaning, and thought.* Clarendon Press, Oxford.

Goertzel, B. (1992). Quantum theory and consciousness. *Journal of Mind and Behavior,* **13,** 29–36.

Gordon, R. M. (1987). *The structure of emotions: investigations in cognitive philosophy.* Cambridge University Press, Cambridge.

Greenspan, P. S. (1988). *Emotions and reasons: an inquiry into emotional justification.* Routledge, New York.

Greenwood, J. (ed.) (1991). *The future of folk psychology: Intentionality and cognitive science.* Cambridge University Press, Cambridge.

Grünbaum, A. (1984). *The foundations of psychoanalysis: A philosophical critique.* University of California Press, California.

Grünbaum, A. (1986). Precis of *The foundations of psychoanalysis: A philosophical critique,* with peer commentary. *The Behavioral and Brain Sciences,* **9,** 217–84.

Grünbaum, A. (1993). *Validation in the clinical theory of psychoanalysis.* International Universities Press, Madison, CT.

Hannay, A. (1990). *Human consciousness.* Routledge, New York.

Hanson, P. (ed.) (1990). *Information, language, and cognition.* University of British Columbia Press, Vancouver.

Harris, P. L. (1989). *Children and emotion: the development of psychological understanding.* Blackwell, Oxford.

Hilgard, E. R. and Bower, G. H. (1966). *Theories of learning,* (3rd edn). Appleton-Century-Crofts, New York.

Hirsch, S. and Leff, J. (1975). *Abnormalities in parents of schizophrenics,* Maudsley Monographs 22. Oxford University Press, Oxford.

Hobson, P. (1991). Against the theory of 'Theory of Mind'. *British Journal of Developmental Psychology,* **9,** 33–51.

Hornsby, J. (1986). Physicalist thinking and conceptions of behaviour. In *Subject, thought and context,* (ed. P. Pettit and J. McDowell), pp. 95–115. Clarendon, Oxford.

Hume, D. (1777). *An enquiry concerning human understanding,* (ed. L. A. Selby-Bigge, 1902, (2nd edn)). Oxford University Press, Oxford.

Israel, D. (1988). Commentary: Bogdan on information. *Mind and Language,* **3,** 123–40.

Jackendoff, R. (1987). *Consciousness and the computational mind.* MIT Press, Cambridge, Mass.

Johnson-Laird, P. (1983). *Mental models: towards a cognitive science of language, inference and consciousness.* Cambridge University Press, Cambridge.

Johnson-Laird, P. (1988). *The computer and the mind.* Cambridge University Press, Cambridge.

Katz, J. and Fodor, J. (1963). The structure of a semantic theory. *Language,* **39,** 170–210.

Kosslyn, S. M. (1981). The medium and the message in mental imagery: a theory. *Psychological Review*, 88, 44–66.

Kosslyn, S. M. and Pomerantz, J. R. (1977). Imagery, propositions, and the form of internal representations. *Cognitive Psychology*, 9, 52–76.

Kuhn, T. S. (1962). *The structure of scientific revolutions*. University of Chicago Press, Chicago.

Lakatos, I. (1970). Falsification and the methodology of scientific research programmes. In *Criticism and the growth of knowledge*, (ed. I. Lakatos and A. Musgrave), pp. 91–196. Cambridge University Press, Cambridge.

Lakatos, I. and Musgrave, A. (ed.) (1970). *Criticism and the growth of knowledge*. Cambridge University Press, Cambridge.

Lazarus, R. G. (1982). Thoughts on the relation between emotion and cognition. *American Psychologist*, 37, 1019–24.

Lazarus, R. G. (1984). On the primacy of cognition. *American Psychologist*, 39, 124–9.

Leahey, T. H. (1994). *A history of modern psychology*, (2nd edn). Prentice Hall, Englewood Cliffs, NJ.

Locke, J. (1690). *An essay concerning human understanding*, (ed. P. H. Nidditch, 1975). Oxford University Press, Oxford.

Lockwood, M. (1989). *Mind, brain and quantum*. Blackwell, Oxford.

Looren de Jong, H. (1991). Intentionality and the ecological approach. *Journal for the Theory of Social Behavior*, 21, 91–109.

Lycan, W. G. (1987). *Consciousness*. MIT Press, Cambridge, Mass.

Lyons, W. (1990). Intentionality and modern philosophical psychology, I: The modern reduction of intentionality. *Philosophical Psychology*, 3, 247–69.

Lyons, W. (1991). Intentionality and modern philosophical psychology, II: The return to representation. *Philosophical Psychology*, 4, 83–102.

Lyons, W. (1992). Intentionality and modern philosophical psychology, III: The appeal to teleology. *Philosophical Psychology*, 5, 309–26.

Macfarlane, D. A. (1930). The role of kinesthesis in maze learning. *University of California Publications in Psychology*, 4, 277–305.

McKinsey, M. (1991). Anti-individualism and privileged access. *Analysis*, 51, 9–16.

Mackintosh, N. J. (1983). *Conditioning and associative learning*. Oxford University Press, New York.

Malpas, J. E. (1992). *Donald Davidson and the mirror of meaning: holism, truth, interpretation*. Cambridge University Press, Cambridge.

Mandler, J. (1982). The structure of value: accounting for taste. In *Affect and cognition*, (ed. M. S. Clarke and S. T. Fiske), pp. 3–36. Lawrence Erlbaum, Hillsdale NJ.

Marcel, A. J. and Bisiach, E. (ed.) (1988). *Consciousness in contemporary science*. Clarendon, Oxford.

Marr, D. C. (1982). *Vision: a computational investigation into the human representation and processing of visual information*. Freeman, San Francisco.

Mele, A. R. (1992). *Springs of action: understanding intentional behavior*. Oxford University Press, New York.

Mensch, J. R. (1988). *Intersubjectivity and transcendental idealism*. SUNY Press, Albany.

Miller, G. A. (1953). What is information measurement? *American Psychologist*, 8, 3–11.

Miller, G. A., Gallanter, E., and Pribram, K. (1960). *Plans and the structure of behavior*. Holt, Rinehart and Winston, New York.

Moore, G. E. (1925). A defence of common sense. (Reprinted in Moore, G. E. (1959). *Philosophical papers*, pp. 32–59. George Allen and Unwin, London.)

Moore, G. E. (1939). Proof of an external world. (Reprinted in Moore, G. E. (1959). *Philosophical papers*, pp. 127–50. George Allen and Unwin, London.)

Morris, P. (1981). The cognitive psychology of self-reports. In *The psychology of ordinary explanations of social behaviour*, (ed. C. Antaki) pp. 183–203. Academic Press, London.

Nagel, T. (1986). *The view from nowhere*. Oxford University Press, Oxford.

Nash, R. (1989). Cognitive theories of emotion. *Nous*, 23, 481–504.

Neisser, U. (1967) *Cognitive psychology*. Appleton-Century-Crofts, New York.

Neisser, U. (1976). *Cognition and reality*. Freeman, San Francisco.

Neisser, U. (1988). Five kinds of self-knowledge. *Philosophical Psychology*, 1, 35–59.

Newton, N. (1992). Dennett on Intrinsic Intentionality. *Analysis*, 52, 18–23.

Nisbett, R. and Wilson, T. (1977). Telling more than we can know: verbal reports on mental processes. *Psychological Review*, 84, 31–59.

Oatley, K. (1988). Plans and the communicative function of emotions: a cognitive theory. In *Cognitive perspectives on emotion and motivation*, (ed. V. Hamilton, G. Bower, and N. Frijda), pp. 345–64. Kluwer, Dordrecht.

Oatley, K. and Johnson-Laird, P. (1987). Towards a cognitive theory of emotions. *Cognition and Emotion*, 1, 29–50.

O'Hear, A. (1989). *An introduction to the philosophy of science*. Oxford University Press, Oxford.

Pears, D. (1988). *The false prison: A study of the development of Wittgenstein's philosophy*, Vol. 2. Clarendon Press, Oxford.

Pfeifer, R. (1988). Artificial intelligence models of emotion. In *Cognitive perspectives on emotion and motivation, (ed. V. Hamilton, G. Bower, and N. Frijda), pp. 287–320. Kluwer, Dordrecht.*

Pickering, J. and Skinner, M. (1990). *From sentience to symbols: readings on consciousness*. Harvester, Sussex.

Popper, K. (1959). *The logic of scientific discovery*. Hutchinson, London.

Popper, K. (1962). *Conjectures and refutations*. Routledge and Kegan Paul, London.

Popper, K. (1974). Replies to my critics. In *The philosophy of Karl Popper*, (ed. P. A. Schilpp), Book II, pp. 961–1197. Open Court, Lasalle, Illinois.

Power, M. and Brewin, C. (1991). From Freud to cognitive science: a contemporary account of the unconscious. *British Journal of Clinical Psychology*, 30, 289–310.

Premack, D. and Woodruff, G. (1978). Does the chimpanzee have a theory of mind?. *The Behavioral and Brain Sciences*, 4, 515–26.

Putnam, H. (1975). The meaning of 'meaning'. In *Mind, language and reality*, pp. 215–71. Cambridge University Press, Cambridge.

Pylyshyn, Z. (1981). The imagery debate: analogue media versus tacit knowledge. *Psychological Review*, 88, 16–45.

Quine, W. V. O. (1953). Two Dogmas of empiricism. In *From a logical point of view*, (ed. W. V. O. Quine), pp. 20–46. Harvard University Press, Cambridge, Mass.

Robinson, D. N. (1976). *An intellectual history of psychology*. Macmillan, New York.

Rosch, E. and Mervis, C. B. (1975). Family resemblances: studies in the internal structure of categories. *Cognitive psychology*, 7, 573–605.

Ryle, G. (1949). *The concept of mind*. Hutchinson, London.

Sayre, K. M. (1976). *Cybernetics and the philosophy of mind*. Routledge and Kegan Paul, London.

Schiffer, S. (1991). *Ceteris paribus clauses*. Mind, 100, 1–17.

Searle, J. R. (1983). *Intentionality: an essay in the philosophy of mind*. Cambridge University Press, Cambridge.

Searle, J. R. (1990). Consciousness, explanatory inversion and cognitive Science. *Behavioral and Brain Sciences*, 13, 585–642.

Searle, J. R. (1992). *The rediscovery of the mind*. MIT Press, Cambridge, Mass.

Seligman, M. (1975). *Helplessness: on depression, development, and death*. W. H. Freeman, San Francisco.

Shannon, C. and Weaver, W. (1949). *The mathematical theory of communication*. University of Illinois Press, Urbana.

Shepard, R. N. and Metzler, J. (1971). Mental rotation of three-dimensional objects. *Science*, 171, 1–17.

Shotter, J. (1981). Telling and reporting: prospective and retrospective uses of self-ascriptions. In *The psychology of ordinary explanations of social behaviour*, (ed. C. Antaki), pp. 157–81. Academic Press, London.

Skinner, B. (1957). *Verbal behaviour*. Appleton-Century-Crofts, New York.

Smith, D. W. (1992). Consciousness in action. *Synthese*, 90, 119–43.

Smith, E. E. and Medin, D. L. (1981). *Categories and concepts*. Harvard University Press, Cambridge, Mass.

Stein, N. L. and Oatley, K. (ed.). (1992). *Basic emotions*. Lawrence Erlbaum Associates, Hove.

Stich, S. (1983). *From folk psychology to cognitive science*. MIT Press, Cambridge, Mass.

Stich, S. and Nichols, S. (1992). Folk psychology: simulation or tacit theory? *Mind and Language*, 7, 35–71.

Szasz, T. S. (1961). *The myth of mental illness: Foundations of a theory of personal conduct*. Harper and Row, New York.

Teasdale, J. and Barnard, P. (1993). *Affect, cognition and change*. Lawrence Erlbaum Associates, Hove.

Tolman, E. C. (1932). *Purposive behavior in animals and men*. Appleton-Century-Crofts, New York.

Tolman, E. C. (1948). Cognitive maps in rats and men. *Psychological Review*, 55, 189–208.

Turvey, M. T. (1974). Constructive theory, perceptual systems, and tacit knowledge. In *Cognition and the symbolic processes, (ed. W. B. Weimer and D. S. Palermo), pp. 165–80. Lawrence Erlbaum Associates, Hillsdale, NJ*.

Tye, M. (1991). *The imagery debate*. MIT Press, Cambridge, Mass.

Varela, F. (1979). *Principles of biological autonomy*. North Holland, New York.

Vedeler, D. (1991). Infant intentionality as object directness: an alternative to representationalism. *Journal for the Theory of Social Behavior*, 21, 431–48.

Velmans, M. (1990). Consciousness, brain and the physical world. *Philosophical Psychology*, 3, 77–99.

Velmans, M, (1991). Is human information processing conscious? *Behavioral and Brain Sciences*, 14, 651–726.

von Bertalanffy, L. (1968). *General systems theory: foundations, developments, applications*. George Braziller, New York.

von Wright, G. H. (1971). *Explanation and understanding*. Routledge and Kegan Paul, London.

Weiskrantz, L. (ed.) (1988). *Thought without language*. Clarendon Press, Oxford.

Wellman, H. (1990). *The child's theory of mind*. MIT Press, Cambridge, Mass.

Whiten, A. (ed.) (1991). *Natural theories of mind: evolution, development and simulation of everyday mindreading*. Blackwell, Oxford.

Wiener, N. (1948). *Cybernetics of control and communication in the animal and the machine*. MIT Press, Cambridge, Mass.

Williams, J. M. G., Watts, F. N., Macleod, C., and Matthews, A. (1988). *Cognitive psychology and emotional disorders*. Wiley, Chichester.

Wittgenstein, L. (1921). *Tractatus logico-philosophicus*. (Trans. D. F. Pears and B. F. McGuiness (1961). Routledge and Kegan Paul, London.

Wittgenstein, L. (1953). *Philosophical investigations*, (ed. G. E. M. Anscombe and R. Rhees, trans. G. E. M. Anscombe). Blackwell, Oxford.

Wittgenstein, L. (1969). *On certainty*, (ed. G. E. M. Anscombe and G. H. von Wright, trans. D. Paul and G. E. M. Anscombe). Blackwell, Oxford.

Zajonc, R. B. (1980). Feeling and thinking: preferences need no inferences. *American Psychologist*, 35, 151–75.

Zajonc, R. B. (1984). On the primacy of affect. *American Psychologist*, 39, 117–23.

Zajonc, R., Pietromonaco, P., and Bargh, J. (1982). Independence and interaction of affect and cognition. In *Affect and cognition*, (ed. M. S. Clarke and S. T. Fiske), pp. 211–27. Lawrence Erlbaum Associates, Hillsdale, NJ.

Zangwill, O. L. (1950). *An introduction to modern psychology*. Methuen, London.

2
Mind, Meaning, and Neural Causation

2.1 THE PROBLEM, AND A FAMILIAR SOLUTION: THE BRAIN ENCODES MEANING

2.1.1 Mind–brain identity as a quick solution

It was concluded in the first chapter that explanations of action in terms of meaningful, mental states are causal; or again, that such states are causes of (intentional) behaviour.

This conclusion raises many questions, including the following: 'How do meaningful mental states cause behaviour?'; 'What are such states, that they *can* cause behaviour?'; and 'How do they relate to brain states, which we suppose (also) cause behaviour?'[1]

Mental states now appear in the best scientific theory we have of complex, higher behaviour. The problem of the causal status of mind is therefore not only of philosophical relevance (or irrelevance); it presses hard in science itself. On the other hand, the issues here are inevitably entangled with long-standing philosophical controversies. These include the traditional problems of dualism: the apparent causal powerlessness of mind, and its incompatibility generally with materialist assumptions in the natural sciences (subsection 1.2.1). Given the forced choice between dualism and materialism, any new science of behaviour apparently has no choice but to opt for the latter. It should be recalled that in the considerations in the preceding chapter there was no commitment to dualism. The argument emphasized the functional role of mental states as mediating causes between stimuli and behaviour, without reference to their ontological status. A tempting response at this stage is to suppose that mental events are just material events in the brain, and that this is how and why they have causal influences on behaviour.

In brief, the materialist theory of mind can be derived from two premises: first, that mental processes mediate causally between stimuli and behaviour; and secondly, that the causal processes which mediate between stimuli and behaviour are material processes in the brain. The first premise can plausibly be construed either as a basic postulate of cognitive psychology or as a conceptual presumption of folk psychology, or as both. The second premise is plausibly construed as derived from two claims, one a priori the other a posteriori. The former is to the effect that all causes of material events are material, while the empirical claim is that the material causes of behaviour are, in fact, in the brain. Hence we infer that mental events, as causes of behaviour, are contingently (as a matter of empirical fact) identical with brain events.

This move, identifying the mind with the brain, would apparently solve the problem of mental causation at one stroke, in terms highly satisfactory to materialism and natural science.

2.1.2 The legacy of Cartesianism: inevitable problems

Predictably enough, however, the philosophical problem cannot be disposed of so fast. Philosophical problems typically have the form of forced choice dichotomies, which have their origins in genuine tensions and contradictions in deep theory. Dogmatic statements of one side or another of the split express rather than solve the underlying conflicts. In the present case, identifying the mind with the material brain encounters difficulties which are all variations of the fact that the material brain lacks properties of the mind.

The problematic here derives largely from seventeenth-century philosophy, which, as outlined in the previous chapter (subsection 1.2.1), stripped 'matter' of all but the primary (mathematical, absolute) qualities, consigning the rest to 'the mind', which hence became the container for all sensibility. To say that the mind is identical with the brain will not work if the brain is understood in the spirit of seventeenth-century dualism, as being matter with only physically defined properties. Cartesian mind was defined in various ways: as a thinking substance, conscious, subjective, known with certainty, and as immaterial. These characteristics all are bound to present as problems to be deconstructed or resolved before mind–brain identity theory or any post-Cartesian concept of mind can be made to work. But, certainly, no theory is going to be adequate which just affirms one or other half of Cartesian dualism. If there is going to be an adequate materialism, it will have to envisage the brain as being something like the Cartesian mind, not as non-mental Cartesian matter. This is the very general idea, expressed in historical terms, which we will be working around in this chapter.

The materialist theory of mind has been subject to various kinds of objection. One kind of objection rests on the fact that mental states have properties which material states do not (such as manifestation in consciousness, epistemic privacy), and vice versa (such as spatial location). Since, according to Liebniz' 'law of identity' two identical things have all properties in common, it would follow that mental states cannot be material states. However, it has been argued, controversially, that the thesis of contingent identity, as opposed to conceptual or analytic identity, can avoid or otherwise cope with problems of this sort. These issues have been much debated in the philosophical literature (for example Boyd 1980, and other papers in Block 1980 *a*, Part Two).

We already considered briefly in the first chapter (subsection 1.2.2) the distinction between first-person (subjective) and third-person (objective) perspectives on the mind. In large part the obvious objections to the materialist theory have to do with the 'subjective' aspects of mind: mind as viewed by the subject. From this point of view mental states are manifest in consciousness, and have phenomenal qualities, but neither of these characteristics obviously belongs to brain states. However, we shall focus here on problems for the materialist theory that arise from the objective, or scientific perspective. This is, after all, the context in which mind–brain identity is inferred: the claim never was grounded in introspection. From the objective perspective, mental states make their appearance as posits in the theory of behaviour, as mediators between stimulus and response. The question is whether from this external, scientific point of view mental states can be identified with material states of the brain. In effect we are questioning here the fast derivation of the materialist theory of mind with which we concluded the preceding subsection.

In considering inadequacies of mind–brain identity from the objective, scientific perspective, we are in one sense already far removed from Cartesianism, which viewed mind from a subjective point of view only. On the other hand, a (or the) defining attribute of Cartesian mind was *thinking*, which is closely linked to representation, meaning, and intentionality, and these are none other than the characteristics of mental states which are essential for the purposes of cognitive explanations of behaviour. The explanation of action in terms of mental states depends on the fact that mental states are about the scene of action, and about agent–environment interactions (subsection 1.3.6). So it turns out that what was essential to the Cartesian mind is essential also to mind as posited by cognitive-behavioural explanations. This means that the latter will not be satisfied with any definition of mental states that makes them 'material' *as opposed to* 'thoughtful'. Put the other way round, from the point of view of the explanation of behaviour in terms of mental states, if mind is going to be identified with the material brain, then the material brain will have to be—like Cartesian mind—a 'thinking substance'.

2.1.3 On the irreducibility of mind and meaning

The language of mind and meaning used in the description and explanation of action is, no doubt, vastly different from the language used to describe the material processes in the brain. As discussed in the first chapter, the mental states that have to do with action have meaningful content, or intentionality; they are subject to normative descriptions, pertaining to rules, to distinctions such as right/wrong, reasonable/unreasonable, etc.; they are attributed to the agent 'holistically', in the form of a theory about many (meaningfully) connected states. These are the characteristics of mental states as invoked in the explanation and prediction of behaviour, and they apparently have no counterpart in brain states, at least when physically defined. The implication is that the mind cannot be identified with the material brain, or, at least, that mental state descriptions cannot be reduced to descriptions of the brain. The various, related meaningful aspects of mental states prohibit any (simple) reduction of the mental to the physical, since, to put it briefly, meaning would be lost in the reduction.[2]

An aid to understanding the attractiveness of the mind–brain identity theory and the problems that it conceals is provided by Hornsby (1986). She presents two pictures of the mediation between 'inputs' and 'outputs': one is the intentional psychological, the other is the neurophysiological. As follows (Hornsby 1986, p. 95):

subject of beliefs, desires, etc.

objects of perception → — — — — — — — PERSON — — — — — — — → desired effects of action

— — → — — — events at sensory surfaces — — → — BRAIN — — → — movements of the body — — → — — —

subject of neurophysiological

→ — — — the direction of causation

Hornsby observes (loc. cit.) that one has only to look at these two pictures to be tempted to make a superimposition. She proceeds to argue that such superimposition is invalid, in particular at the 'output' end. One theme in Hornsby's argument is that intentional actions do not map on to, and cannot be identified with, bodily movements. This lack of correspondence has been referred to already in the first chapter (subsection 1.3.6). The general problem with the superimposition at the 'input' end is that the objects of perception and of belief typically cannot be captured by physical descriptions because, in brief, they carry more and different kinds of meaning (information). This critical point has been considered already in the preceding chapter (subsection 1.2.2), will be discussed later in this chapter (subsection 2.5.4) and at length in Chapter 4 (sections 4.3 and 4.4).

The main question for this chapter concerns the superimposition of the 'central' mediating states. Can mental states be identified with neurophysiological states? In so far as there is no identity between the *relata* of these two kinds of central states, it can be expected that the answer to this question is negative, and further, that the reasons are closely related to those in the cases of inputs and outputs; they concern the *meaning* carried by mental states. The conclusion is, in brief, that the meaning of mental states prohibits their being identified with neural states.

2.1.4 The brain encodes meaning

However, while there is something correct about the preceding line of thought, it is not difficult to see a way of softening the implied contrast between mind and brain. At its starkest, the problem may be expressed by saying that mental states have meaning—carry information—while neural states do not. But, of course, the reply is then simply that this is not true: neural states do carry information. It is axiomatic in the area of overlap between cognitive science and neuroscience that information-processing is implemented by the brain. In brief: neural states encode, and process, information. In what follows, this will sometimes be called the 'encoding thesis' for short.

The question under consideration is whether from the external point of view, in the context of explaining behaviour in terms of mental states, these states can be identified with material states of the brain. The answer is that it is possible, provided that the latter are described in terms of informational content and processing. If, on the other hand, neural states and processes are described in a lower-level, non-intentional language, without reference to information, then it is a mistake to make the identification, for an essential feature of mental states is not captured in these lower-level descriptions.

In the historical terms sketched in subsection 2.1.2 the point can be expressed in the following way: from the point of view of the cognitive-behavioural sciences, the theory of mind–brain identification can be made to work, but on condition that the brain is doing the kind of thing that was done by the Cartesian mind, in particular *thinking* (or representing). In contemporary terms this proposal is the familiar one, that the brain is an information-processing system.

It should be exphasized that the concept of information required in the present context has to be a *semantic* one, linked to meaning, intentionality, representation, etc. The context in question is the modelling of, and hence the explanation and prediction of, organism–environment interactions. In this context, for this purpose, the information processed by the brain has to be *about* something (it has to *represent* something), namely, actual or possible states of the environment, results of action, etc. When brain function is described in these terms, in terms of intentionality, it is in effect being regarded as functioning like the mind.

This proposal is not most happily expressed by saying that mental (or meaningful) states and processes *are identical with* brain states and processes. It is better expressed using terms such as 'are realized by'. This shift in terminology signifies a relationship which is not static, but which is more like that between process and function. It is recommended already by the functionalist theory of mental states, which defines them in terms of their causes and effects. The functionalist theory can be used to derive the theory of mind–brain identity, along the lines of the argument given at the beginning of the section, but it can also be turned against a strong version of the identity theory.

The objection emphasizes precisely function rather than composition: functional states in general can be 'realized' in a variety of ways, so they cannot be identified with a particular material structure or process. The functional states of computing systems, for example, can be realized in diverse kinds of hardware. In biology it is familiar that the same function can be served by a variety of structures and processes in different species. Similarly, the argument proceeds, mental states as functional states cannot be identified with the material states that realize them. According to this argument, the valid sense of 'identity' here would have to be that in which functional states are 'realized by', 'served by', or 'implemented by' material processes. It may be that, as a matter of fact, the same kind of mental state is realized in different cases by different neural structures and processes. The same belief as a functionally defined state may be realized in one way in human beings, in another in cats, or in different ways in different members of the same species, or even differently in the same person at different times. Considerations of this sort have led to a distinction between *type* and *token* mind–brain identity theories. (These terms are taken from philosophical logic: 'type' means kind, 'token' means instance. Thus, the following quotation marks, 'A A', contain one letter type and two letter tokens.) Type identity theory proposes that each type of mental event is identical with a type of brain event. This strong version of the identity theory has come to be regarded as mistaken, for the kind of reasons adduced above, and has been replaced by token identity theory. According to this weaker version, each token mental event is identical with (in the sense of realized by) some token brain event. Token identity theory acknowledges that it cannot be assumed that kinds of mental event correspond to kinds of brain events. Thus, functional characterization of mental states, whether in terms of causal role, or in terms of carrying information, or both, requires that the mind–brain identity theory be ammended to read as follows: each mental event (token) is realized by (and in this sense only 'is identical with') some (token) brain event.[3]

Let us summarize some steps of the argument so far. Causation by mental states can be reconciled with material, neural causation, by adopting a materialist theory of mind, according to which mental states are identical with states of the brain. However, the theory immediately runs up against objections that mental states have properties brain states do not. Some of the peculiarly mental properties have to do with the mind as subjectively experienced, but others are postulated from the perspective of the scientific observer, pertaining to the role of mental states in the production of behaviour, and it is this which is primarily the concern of the present essay. We saw in the first chapter that for the purposes of explaining and predicting complex, higher action (organism–environment interactions) the cognitive psychology paradigm supposes that such activity is regulated by mental states of the living being which have intentionality (which carry information, or meaning). The question is then this: can these mental states be identified with the neural states that cause behaviour?; and the answer is a relatively simple 'yes': the intentional states which regulate behaviour are states of the brain. Certainly, and essentially, this proposed relatively simple solution presupposes that brain states have semantic properties, or again, that intentional states are 'realized in' brain states. The proposed solution can be expressed in the terms characteristic of the interface between cognitive psychology and neuroscience by saying that neural states 'encode' information (or meaning). The implication here is that the causal role of information-carrying neural states in the regulation of organism–environment interactions depends on the information they encode. This critical point will be expanded below in subsections 2.5.5–6, and developed through chapters 4 and 5.

It should be emphasized that the proposed solution makes no commitment to causation by meaningful states *in addition to* causation by neural states. The first kind of causal explanation essentially makes use of intentional concepts (it runs in terms of information-processing). But the point is that causal explanation of action which invokes neural states and processing *also* uses intentional concepts, is run in these same terms. In other words, the distinction between causation by intentional states and causation by non-intentional states does not signify a distinction between causation by non-material states (whatever that might be) and causation by material states. Rather, there are two forms of causal explanation, one of which does and one of which does not invoke intentional states, but both invoke material as opposed to immaterial states (whatever they might be). Hence this proposal undermines the Cartesian mind/matter distinction rather than endorsing one side of it (matter) at the expense of the other (mind). Both kinds of causal explanation invoke material states, but in one of them material states are credited with properties of the Cartesian mind, namely, representation ('thought'). The distinction between, and definition of, the two forms of causality being proposed here will be taken up later, in chapters 4 and 5.

There is no commitment here to dualism, to the idea that there is a mental (meaningful) substance in addition to matter. The point would be rather than there are two forms of description of the material brain. One form of description employs intentional concepts, in particular the concept of information, while the other uses only non-intentional concepts, drawn from basic sciences such as physics and chemistry. The proposal is in effect that the irreducibility of meaning does not signify a dichotomy between mind and matter, but rather a distinction between meaningful (intentional) descriptions and non-meaningful (non-intentional) descriptions. Material processes in the brain can be described in either way, and are described in both ways at the interface between cognitive psychology and neuroscience. In particular, when the purpose is to explain interactions between the organism and the environment, neural processes are described as being concerned precisely with the pick-up, processing, and utilization of information (or meaning).

It follows that intentional language in the brain sciences is essential, and cannot be eliminated in favour of non-intentional descriptions, *for certain purposes, specifically the explanation and prediction of organism–environment interactions.* This is to say, what is known in psychology as cognitive-behavioural science, and in philosophy as the theory of action, will not be able to manage without intentional concepts, and, to make a point of more philosophical interest, it is a philosphical error to think that they could or should be run in non-intentional terms. As anticipated in the first chapter (Subsection 1.3.6), these points are fundamental to the issues addressed in this chapter, and will recur through it.

The solution proposed here to the problem of reconciling mental, meaningful, and material causation includes what Kim (1991) has usefully called the 'dual explanandum strategy'. Kim formulates the problem as follows: 'Given that every physical event has a physical cause, how is a mental cause also possible?' (Kim 1991, p. 57). He points out that a promising general strategy is just to say that there are two behavioural *explananda*, and that there is therefore no problem about there being two kinds of *explanans*. This is the approach adopted here, the critical distinctions being drawn in terms of the presence or absence of intentionality. Kim's main concern is with Dretske's version of the dual explanadum strategy, different from the one proposed here, but he argues that a general point about the strategy is that it requires commitment to dualism, specifically to non-physical causes (Kim 1991, pp. 59–60). But as argued above, the dual explanadum strategy, at least in the version proposed here, and particularly in combination with the encoding thesis, does not imply dualism. Let us take for granted that there are only physical causes, and specifically that the behaviour of a system has physical causes within the system. Even so, when we wish to explain and predict intentional (functional, goal-directed) system–environment interactions, we have to attribute to those physical causes encoded intentionality.

2.1.5 Review of objections, 1–5

The proposed solution to the problem of reconciling meaningful/ mental causation with material causation by the brain is simply that the neural states that cause behaviour encode meaning, with the implication that the causal role of these states is a function of the meaning (or information) they encode.

This familiar idea, however, runs up against a number of powerful and influential theoretical objections, at least five. They are all more or less directly to the effect that mental states with meaningful content, at least as characterized in ordinary language and folk psychology, cannot be construed as being encoded in the brain, and hence not as causes of behaviour. If this conclusion were valid, we would have to preserve something like the turn-of-the-century distinction between meaning and causality. The five objections to the proposed solution, which will be considered in the next five sections of this chapter, may be characterized briefly as follows:

1. The hypothesized encoding is incompatible with connectionist models of psychological function.
2. You can't get semantics out of syntax (not even neural syntax).
3. In any case, it would be the neural syntax doing the causing, and the alleged causal role of semantics drops out as irrelevant.
4. Meanings ain't in the head. (They don't supervene on brain states.)
5. It ascribes to brains what properly belongs to people (and relationships, and culture).

The first objection is based mainly on powerful computer models of mental function, the second is a practically an axiom of philosophical logic, the third is combination of much the same point with plausible assumptions about causality, the fourth is a highly influential line of thought deriving from Putnam linked to a materialist definition of content, and the fifth objection has strong Wittgensteinian credentials. In any circumstances this would be a curious alliance of disparate views, and it is remarkable that they converge in objecting in one way or another to the proposal that meaning is encoded in the brain and thereby has a causal role.

The proposal, on the other hand, has much to be said for it. As already indicated, it manages to reconcile in a relatively straightforward way the role of meaning in the explanation of action, explored in the previous chapter, with the idea that the brain controls behaviour. Cognitive psychology and neuroscience readily use the idea that the brain encodes information (meaning), which in effect defuses conflict between the regulating role of information (or meaning) and the regulating role of the brain. It seems possible, then to combine the claims that ascriptions of meaningful, intentional states provide powerful explanations of behaviour; that such states are causes of behaviour; and that the causes of behaviour are in the brain, specifically, neural states that encode information (meaning). In this combination of claims, fundamental tenets of folk psychology, cognitive psychology, and of neuroscience appear as compatible, indeed as complementary. What is critical in the reconciliation is the apparently simple idea that the brain can encode meaning. This is what in effect collapses dichotomies in deep theory: matter/mind, matter/intentionality, and causality/ meaning.

2.2 OBJECTIONS TO THE PROPOSED SOLUTION, 1: 'ARE THERE "SENTENCES IN THE HEAD"?'

2.2.1 The language of thought hypothesis

It is an axiom of folk psychology, and arguably of cognitive psychology, that behaviour is caused by (regulated by) meaningful states, which are typically identified by propositional clauses of natural languages. Take this as a first (composite) premise. Take as second premise: behaviour is caused by neural states. Plausible conclusion: brain states are (encode) meaningful states, with the implication that brain states must be something like propositional clauses of natural languages. In brief: there must be 'sentences in the head'.

Following this line of thought we come to the area of Fodor's so-called language of thought hypothesis. This hypothesis is sophisticated and complicated, comprising many interrelated components, among which are the following: mental states with meaningful content have an articulated syntactic structure (analogous to the syntactic structure of sentences of natural languages); the causal role of a mental state in relation to other mental states and to behaviour is determined by its syntactic structure; mental states are realized in neural states, which also have 'syntactic' structure; the causal role of such neural states is determined by their 'syntactic' structure (Fodor 1975, and for critical commentary see, for example, Clark 1989; Warmbrod 1989; Maloney 1990; Loewer and Rey 1991; as well as below).

In a more recent work Fodor introduces the language of thought (LOT) hypothesis as follows (Fodor 1987, p. 135):

> LOT wants to construe propositional-attitude tokens as relations to symbol tokens. According to standard formulations, to believe that P is to bear a certain relation to a token of a symbol which means that P. (It is generally assumed that tokens of the symbol in question are neural objects, . . .). Now, symbols have intentional contents and their tokens are physical in all the known cases. And—qua physical—symbol tokens are the rights sorts of things to exhibit causal roles.

The language of thought hypothesis (in its full form not recorded here) is the most rigorous working out of the view that mental, meaningful causality is equivalent to, or reducible to, the material causality of the brain, and is much admired for this reason.

The hypothesis can also be understood as giving a particularly literal interpretation to the claim, endorsed in general terms in this chapter, that meaningful mental states are encoded in brain states. The implied interpretation is that if, for example, a person believes that p, then this meaningful mental state is encoded in the person's brain in the sense that there is in the brain a neural state, with a syntactic structure, which has the same meaning as the sentence 'p'. There are, literally, meaningful sentence-like structures in the brain.

The language of thought hypothesis claims that the neural states that realize cognitive functions have the syntactic structure of sentences of natural language. This apparently amounts to an empirical claim about the 'cognitive architecture' of the states which realize cognitive functions, and as such interacts with the theory of artificial intelligence (AI).

AI, with its theoretical and working models of machines, computers, which can perform intelligent functions, has been among the most powerful influences in the development of cognitive psychology (subsection 1.2.2). It constructs models of how intelligent performance can be achieved, and hence perhaps of how it is in fact achieved by the brain. By providing such models, AI theory has helped to make cognitive function accessible to psychological theory and experiment, to free psychology from the confines of behaviourism, which notoriously had little or nothing to say about internal processes mediating stimulus and response, about processes inside the so-called 'black box'. Our interest in AI modelling in the present context has to do with its implications for the problem of mental causation generally and the neural encoding of meaning in particular.[4]

AI constructs models of the structures that serve mental functions, so what do these models have to say about the claim that there are sentence-like structures in the head? In brief, although the position becomes much more complicated, the claim is endorsed by 'good old-fashioned', symbolic, AI models, but is apparently incompatible with the more recent connectionist models of neural structure and function.

The language of thought hypothesis is closely connected, via the so-called computational theory of mind (on which more below, subsection 2.3.1) to the classical (von Neumann–Turing) theory of computation. In this classical theory, computation is performed on symbol systems, symbols, and strings of symbols, and these, and the rules that govern their manipulation, are defined in terms of syntactic form only. Syntactic form is some physical characteristic of a symbol, such as the shape. In the case of computation in the brain, syntax would be a matter of some physical property of the brain, such as electromagnetic characteristics of neuronal activity. When applied in AI models of cognition, the classical theory of computation gives rise to two sorts of issues. First, there is the problem whether and how syntactically defined states and operations have anything to do with *meaning*. This problem is relevant to our themes of mind, meaning, and material states as they are formulated within AI theory, and we shall consider it in Section 2.3. Secondly, it may be that the brain is not a classically defined computer, and this is the point of the connectionist alternatives, to which we now turn.

2.2.2 Objections based on connectionist models

Fodor's language of thought hypothesis belongs with traditional, symbolic AI models of the sort based in the classical theory of computation. In these models explicitly stored formal-synatic rules are applied to explicit and localizable symbolic structures, including structures with the syntactic form of sentences. If a computing device can be ascribed the information that p, the ascribed state can be identified with a localized state of the device.

However, and on the other hand, connectionist models of 'computation' (now in scare quotes) typically do not involve operations on discrete structures that can be identified as symbols. The representational or symbolic features of connectionist systems are embodied as parallel patterns of activity among subsymbolic units, distributed over the system as a whole. There is no physical (hardware) counterpart to a symbol, or sentence.[5]

There is thus apparent conflict between traditional, symbolic AI models and connectionist models, and hence also conflict between theories of cognitive function that appeal to the one or to the other. Assuming this incompatibility, it is possible to construct the following argument: if connectionist models of neural structure and function are correct, then there are no sentence-like structures in the brain of the sort presupposed by folk psychology, and explicitly posited by the language of thought hypothesis, and the brain does not encode the meaningful states envisaged in folk psychology. Whence:

(1) folk psychology and the language of thought hypothesis can be eliminated; and

(2) neural causation has nothing to do with 'meaningful causation', which notion goes the same way as its folk psychological origin.

An argument along these lines has been proposed by Ramsey *et al.* (1990). They write:

> The crucial folk psychological tenets in forging the link between connectionism and eliminativism are the claims that propositional attitudes are *functionally discrete, semantically interpretable*, states that play a *causal role* in the production of behaviour. (Ramsey *et al.* 1990, p. 121.)

The proposal that folk psychology is committed to functional discreteness is implausible given the systemic, holistic nature of attribution of the propositional attitudes (referred to above, subsection 2.1.3; cf. also 1.4.1–2). This is linked to the reasons why the argument proposed by these authors turns out to be unsatisfactory, but for the present let us continue with the development of their argument. Ramsey *et al.* proceed to describe connectionist models which are apparently incompatible with the assumptions in question (1990, pp. 128–9):

> In many connectionist networks it is not possible to localize propositional representation beyond the input layer. That is, there are no particular features or states of the system which lend themselves to a straightforward semantic evaluation. ... It is connectionist networks of this sort ... that we have in

mind when we talk about the encoding of information in the biases, weights and hidden nodes being *widely distributed* rather than *localist*.

... It is often plausible to view such networks as collectively or holistically encoding a set of propositions, although none of the hidden units, weights or biases are comfortably viewed as *symbols*. When this is the case we will call the strategy of representation invoked in the model *subsymbolic*.

Ramsey *et al.* then draw their conclusion that a particular kind of connectionist model is incompatible with what they take to be fundamental to folk psychology (1990, p. 141):

The connectionist models in question are those which are offered as models at the *cognitive* level, and in which the encoding of information is widely distributed and subsymbolic. In such models ... there are no *discrete, semantically interpretable* states that play a *causal role* in some cognitive episodes but not others. Thus there is, in these models, nothing with which the propositional attitudes of common sense psychology can plausibly be identified. If these models turn out to offer the best accounts of human belief and memory, we will be confronting an *ontologically radical* theory change—the sort of theory change that will sustain the conclusion that propositional attitudes, like caloric and phlogiston, do not exist.

In brief, the argument is that if connectionism is right about neural structure, folk psychology is wrong, and is up for 'elimination'. No loss, it will be added, by those who believe that the idea of mental, meaningful causation belongs peculiarly to a pre-scientific, out-of-date, folk psychology. (For related arguments for eliminativism see also, for example, Churchland, P.M. 1989 and Churchland, P.S. 1986.)

In reply to this kind of argument there are several points to be made. First, the conclusion—that folk psychology may turn out to be simply wrong—looks false in the light of its predictive efficacy, discussed in the first chapter. Secondly, the incompatibility between connectionist and traditional AI models is probably less sharp than the argument supposes. Thirdly, in any case there is nothing in connectionist models incompatible with the general idea, endorsed and defended in this chapter, that information (meaning) is encoded in the brain; on the contrary, the models aim to show *how* this could be achieved. And finally, such strength as the argument has derives from the fact that it credits (saddles) folk psychology with an unnecessarily strong claim about the neural encoding of meaning. These four points are discussed in turn below.

Arguments of the kind described in the first chapter counsel against the dismissal (supposed eliminability) of folk psychology. Folk psychology has predictive power, but this fact would apparently be a mystery if it were simply a false theory. Moreover, it is not just folk psychology that is at issue here. As argued (in subsection 1.3.7), the cognitive psychology paradigm, based as it is on the notion of information-processing, is committed to something very like the folk psychological meaningful mental states. The suggestion that this commitment is simply wrong mystifies the predictive power of models within this cognitive psychology paradigm, as well as that of folk psychology. This is the basic reason for suspecting the soundness of any argument that concludes that explanation of behaviour in terms of meaningful mental states is invalid.

What can be said in reply, then, to the claim that such states fail to show up in powerful connectionist models of mental function? The distinction between symbolic AI models, based on the classical theory of computation, and connectionist models is valid, but in various ways blurred. Connectionist models can be (and are) implemented by traditional computers using symbol-based programmes. This fact, however, is of doubtful relevance to understanding the implementation of cognitive function in the brain, since it is likely that if the brain is a computing system at all, it is a massive parallel distributed, connectionist system, not a digital, serial computer. Connectionist theories have aimed explicitly at compatibility with what is known of the micro-structure and -function of the brain. Of more relevance to cognitive psychology and neuroscience is the possibility that symbolic programs could be implemented in connectionist hardware. If this is possible, the conflict between symbolic AI models of cognitive function and connectionist models of brain function would be lessened. The position would be that while the latter are valid models of implementation in the brain, the former are valid models of 'emergent' properties of the system, namely, of manipulation of (meaningful) symbols according to rules. This idea receives support from the fact that there are statistical cluster analyses of connectionist networks the results of which do admit of semantic labelling. On the other hand, certain cognitive tasks, particularly those involving reasoning and inference with symbols, are most readily modelled in the traditional symbolic programs, while others, including sensori- and motor-functions, are most readily modelled in connectionist programs. This fact points to a different way of reconciling the two kinds of model. It may be that the brain is engaged in both types of processing, serial-symbolic, and parallel-connectionist, with interactions between them.[6]

Be that (the relation between traditional and connectionist AI models), as it may, the claim that meaning (information) is encoded in the brain is unaffected. This, to recall, is the main idea endorsed and defended in the present chapter, proposed as a solution to the problem of reconciling meaningful/mental causation with the causation of behaviour by the brain. But of course, connectionism has no objections to the idea, fundamental to the cognitive neuroscience enterprise, that the brain processes, and hence has to encode, information about the environment. There is no question about *whether* the brain encodes and processes information, but only about *how* it does so. In connectionist systems information is stored as parallel patterns of activity among subsymbolic units, not in symbols. It can be seen in the second quotation above from Ramsey *et al.* (1990, pp. 128–9), that they apparently have no problem with the idea that connectionist networks encode information, even 'sets of propositions'.

To repeat, the issue between connectionist and traditional AI models of brain function is not *whether* the brain encodes information (meaning), but *how*. It is usual and valid to say that the traditional models invoke symbols, while the connectionist models do not. The notion of symbol at work here is basically a syntactic one, to be understood superficially by way of examples such as letters and numerals, and defined formally within the so-called classical theory of computation, (referred to in subsection 2.2.1, and in more detail in subsection 2.3.1). An equally valid conception of symbolism, however, is the semantic one. According to this, a symbol may be defined as *whatever carries meaning* (information). In *this* sense, which to repeat is valid though distinct from that in classical computation theory, connectionist models do indeed envisage 'symbols', namely, as patterns of activity within the system. It can be seen that this conception of neural symbolism is broadly consistent with there being a fundamental link between the meaning of a sign and its use in activity, an idea adopted in the first chapter (subsections 1.3.2–4) and applied throughout the essay. Issues in the definition of symbolism and syntax, and their relation to semantics are of course critical to the concept of 'encoded meaning' and will be addressed further in subsequent sections.

We have been considering the argument proposed by Ramsey *et al.* (1990) which would eliminate folk psychology on connectionist grounds, and we suggested above that such strength as the argument has derives from the fact that it credits (saddles) folk psychology with an unnecessarily strong presupposition about the neural encoding of meaning. The argument assumes that attribution of mental states with (linguistically identified) meaning presupposes that there are in-the-head items similar to such states. Fodor's language of thought hypothesis, we should note and emphasize, makes just this same assumption. As is quite characteristic of philosophical claims and counter-claims, the two opposed positions here, Fodor's on the one hand, and Ramsey *et al.*'s on the other, the one vindicating folk psychological explanation, the other which would eliminate it, in fact share critical preconceptions. In this case the critical shared assumption is roughly as follows, that meaningful mental states are real, and causal, only if they correspond to discrete, localizable micro-states of the brain. Under this assumption it will indeed appear as though Fodor's language of thought hypothesis is the only way of saving the validity of folk psychology, and equally, that folk psychology, like Fodor's hypothesis, may well fall foul of connectionist models of brain function. However, it is by no means obvious that common sense does or should make the kind of assumption in question. We consider in the next subsection reasons for saying that both the hypothesized language of thought vindication of folk psychological explanation and the arguments that would eliminate folk psychological explanation mistake its logic and hence its ontological commitments.

2.2.3 Reply: there don't have to be such sentences

Let us leave questions as to what is in the brain and how it does what it does, whatever that is, and return to a relatively clear position, where we started the essay, with what is open to view, namely, that theory-driven attribution of psychological states with meaningful content, whether in folk or scientific theory, is based in and predicts behaviour.

For example, we describe a rat as having acquired (by normal learning procedures) information about a maze including a goal-box containing food, and as being hungry (on the grounds that it hasn't eaten for a while), then we can predict, other things being equal (including 'normal'), that the rat, given free run of the maze, will run along to the goal-box and eat. Attribution of the psychological states is based on observation of behavioural patterns, and it predicts further behavioural patterns. But the question under consideration is whether these attributions are valid only if there are discrete and localizable micro-states of the brain which correspond to such terms as 'information about the maze', or 'expectation of food in the goal-box'. The general problem here concerns the relation between descriptions that are based on patterns of behavioural interaction, and descriptions that refer to states and events inside what is behaving. Clark (1988) clarifies the issues here by use of analogy with descriptions of cars.

Clark notes that cars admit of (at least) two general kinds of description. One kind may be called 'performance' descriptions: they refer to how the car performs (behaves) when driven in particular ways in particular conditions. They include descriptions concerning such as road-holding while cornering, acceleration, and fuel consumption. A second type of description concerns what may be called 'engineering' characteristics, such as weight-distribution, wheel-size, gear-ratios. Three connected points are apparent about the relation between performance and engineering descriptions. First, the same performance description, such as 'corners well at high speeds', can apply to cars with very different engineering characteristics. Secondly, in any particular car, a performance feature does not correspond to an isolated engineering characteristic, but rather to the interaction of many such characteristics, and moreover, to these in interaction with the conditions in which the car is driven. In this sense performance features are 'emergent' properties; a particular performance feature appears precisely when a car (with any one of a variety of engineering profiles) is performing, that is, when it is being driven in such-and-such conditions. Thirdly, and again related, terms used in describing performance may have no analogues in terms used in describing engineering features; for example neither the expression 'holds the road badly in the wet' nor any expression with similar meaning will appear in description of the car's engineering profile. In summary of these three points, it may be concluded that performance descriptions do not 'map on to' engineering characteristics.

Clark (1988) goes on to apply this simple analysis to the case of psychological propositions. Such propositions attribute properties to the agent, semantic properties essentially defined as being about the environment, and on the basis of such attribution we make predictions about interactions between the agent and the environment. In these ways psychological propositions are akin to performance descriptions. (In terms of the car analogy, performance features are attributed to a car, these features are defined explicitly or implicitly with reference to (environmental) driving conditions, and such attribution enables prediction of how the car will behave in such-and-such conditions.) But performance descriptions refer to 'emergent' characteristics, to characteristics that appear in the course, precisely, of performance. And we have seen that, at least in the case of cars, it is a mistake to suppose that such emergent characteristics map on to internal mechanisms. So it is at least questionable to assume that psychological propositions, as performance descriptions, map on to internal, neural states and processes, still more so to assume that the validity of such propositions presupposes such a mapping.

The above considerations suggest that there are two distinct though related types of explanation of behaviour. The first is concerned with behaviour considered essentially as interaction with the environment. It proceeds on the basis of observation of regularities in interactions, and it constructs explanations and predictions of such regularities by attributing to the agent states which are 'about the environment' (that is, semantic, meaningful, information-carrying states). Folk psychology is the paradigm of this type of explanation, and it generally works well (enough) for the purposes of daily life. The same basic method is used, with extensions and refinements for particular purposes, by various forms of 'cognitive-behavioural' science. The second type of explanation of behaviour concerns the neural mechanisms and processes that underlie the behavioural capacities. The link between these two types of explanation is provided (currently) by AI models of neural function, which seek to explicate how 'intelligent' behaviour is produced by the brain.

The language of thought hypothesis clarifies and explicitly endorses, with its use of the symbolic AI model, the claim that the two types of explanation described above will coincide: the hypothesis is that states with the same structure as meaningful states, as described in ordinary language, will be found in the brain. The problem is that, if the brain is indeed correctly modelled as a connectionist system, the hypothesis is false, at least at a micro-level of analysis.

However, there is no need to suppose, and there is good reason not to suppose, that the two types of explanation must coincide. In particular, the validity of the first type, explanation of behaviour in terms of cognitive, meaningful states, does not require that such states are manifest in the micro-structure and -function of the brain, and in particular, therefore, it is not undermined by connectionist models of neural function. What is required is rather that the explanations correspond to at least emergent characteristics of neural processing. We have indicated above several ways in which this requirement is met. First, to the extent that connectionist systems admit of higher-level descriptions in terms of symbolic processing. Secondly, that statistical analysis of micro-function in connectionist systems reveals clusters that admit of semantic labelling. Thirdly, that attributions of mental states with content are 'performance' descriptions, based in observation of regularities, and in this sense they correspond to emergent characteristics of the agent, to characteristics that appear in the course of action. The first two senses in which psychological propositions are valid concerns particularly AI modelling of neural function. But the third runs free of an scientific discovery concerning the the way in which behaviour is generated by the brain. It locates the subject-matter of psychological propositions in action (in interaction), not inside the brain.

While folk psychological descriptions are not committed to the existence of corresponding in-the-head items, it would be fair to say that they presuppose that there is *some 'mechanism' or other* in the person which can produce intelligent, intentional behaviour. What this presupposition is taken to amount to will depend on background metaphysics. In the Cartesian framework, the assumption is more or less only that of immaterial mind. In our post-dualist age, neural mechanisms of the appropriate kinds are required, as modelled currently in AI.

On the basis of the above understanding of psychological descriptions, it remains possible to say that they provide causal explanations, and possible to say also that the states they invoke are encoded in the brain.

By all means, the notions of causality and of encoding require particular interpretations. The nature of encoding will continue to occupy us through this chapter, and causality will be discussed at length in chapters 4 and 5, but some points are apparent here. Characteristics of a system which appear in interaction with the environment can be cited in causal explanations. In the case of cars, for example, a performance characteristics such as poor road-holding can be cited in causal explanation of (and in prediction of) a crash. It may be noted that engineering characteristics will serve such a purpose only in so far as they contribute to, in such-and-such circumstances, performance characteristics. This is, in a very simple way, analogous to the fact that neural states explain intentional behaviour only in so far as they encode intentional states. In the psychological case, for example, a rat's behaviour in a maze, expectation that there is food in the goal-box, neurally encoded, can be cited in causal explanation of (and in prediction of) running to the box. The performance characteristics cannot be identified with, and do not necessarily correspond to, internal, physically defined states. In this case we have to envisage a form of causal explanation that does not consist in saying that one material state gives rise to another, and, in particular, that is not based in observation of constant conjunction between the cause and the effect. In other words, while psychological propositions are causal, they are not captured by physicalist descriptions, nor by the Humean analysis. Chapters 4 and 5 will be occupied with the task of identifying a non-physicalist, non-Humean concept of causality appropriate to the explanation of action.

2.3 OBJECTIONS TO THE PROPOSED SOLUTION, 2: '(NEURAL) SYNTAX ISN'T ENOUGH FOR SEMANTICS'

2.3.1 Searle and the computational theory of mind

As noted in the previous section, the language of thought hypothesis is closely connected to the so-called computational theory of mind, which in turn is based in the classical (von Neumann–Turing) theory of computation. According to classical theory, computation is performed on symbol systems, physical tokens (of some kind), and strings of tokens; the rules that govern their manipulation are defined in terms of shape, in terms of syntatic form only. In particular, computation is defined without reference to meaning; symbols may be 'interpreted' as having meaning, as representing objects and states of affairs, but this is not essential to the definition or to the practice of computation. If this classical, 'symbolic' theory of computation is applied to cognitive psychology, the result is the so-called computational theory of mind, according to which, in brief, cognitive states and processes are defined in terms of syntax, not (essentially) in terms of meaning (Fodor 1975; Newell 1980; Pylyshyn 1980, 1984).

The claim that cognition can be adequately characterized as computational in the sense of classical theory, which seemed to be the assumption behind AI, and which was spelt out in the computational theory of mind, has been the subject of much debate in the cognitive science literature. The debate was sparked by Searle in the early 1980s by his 'Chinese room argument' in support of the conclusion that symbol manipulation cannot be sufficient for understanding (or meaning, or intentionality). The argument is very well known and for our purposes a very brief formulation will suffice.

Imagine you are handed Chinese symbols and asked to manipulate (transform) them according to a rule book, then no matter how efficiently you receive symbols at inputs, follow the rules, and dispose of the symbols produced as outputs, still this process of symbol-manipulation is compatible with you having no understanding whatsoever of the meaning of the symbols. Human beings with brains, however, do understand the meaning of symbols. So if AI theory says that cognitive activity of the brain is symbol-manipulation only, then it's wrong.

In a recent formulation of the argument, Searle draws out his main point about the Chinese room as follows (1987, p. 214):

> The point of the story is to remind us of a conceptual truth that we knew all along; namely, that there is a distinction between manipulating the syntactical elements of languages and actually understanding the language at a semantic level. What is lost in the AI *simulation of* cognitive behaviour is the distinction between syntax and semantics. . . . In the case of actually understanding a language, we have something more than a formal or syntactical level. We have a semantics. We do not just shuffle uninterpreted formal symbols, we actually know what they mean.

Searle's Chinese room argument, together with its strengths and weaknessness, and proposed solutions to the problems it raises, have been much discussed in the literature (Searle 1980, 1982, 1984, 1987; and, among others Russow 1984; Rey 1986; Gray 1987; Newton 1988; Harnad 1989, 1990). In what follows we draw out some points directly related to biology and psychology.

A recurring theme in criticisms of the attempt to analyse cognitive processes in terms of syntax alone, and of the computational theory of mind in particular, is that it is insufficiently biological. In his discussions of the Chinese room argument Searle (1987) makes such a point by saying that emphasis on computation alone without regard to its implementation, neglects the special properties of the brain as biological material, which in some way uniquely could achieve intentionality. The problem can be formulated in this way: what do you have to add to, or have instead of, symbol manipulation in order to achieve intentionality? The answer probably has something to do with biology. But to respond: 'the brain (as opposed to an inanimate system)', is to give a disappointingly empirical answer, even if true, to what seems more like a conceptual question.

To bring out the inadequacy of the computational theory of mind from the point of view of biology or psychology we have to consider what is fundamental to those sciences, specifically in what they have to say about intentionality. There are reasons to expect a deep and large-scale paradigm clash between the computational theory of mind and the bio-psychological sciences, one which can hardly be resolved just by appeal to the special material composition of the brain. The concept and theory of computation on which the computational theory of mind was based was developed in formal logic, a context quite distinct from the concerns of biology and (most) psychology. Specifically, biology is concerned with animal functions necessary for successful action (survival) and the structures which realize them, including sensory, mediating, and motor systems, systems for digestion, energy production, internal temperature regulation, etc. , all these being designed to work in (being selected in) particular environmental conditions. All this, with the implications concerning functions, designs, and implementation of biological information-processing has nothing to do with formal logic. Or put the other way round, formal logic, the classical theory of computation, and the computational theory of mind, have nothing to say about the functions of and design contraints on information-processing in biological systems. We pass by the details here, which are excellently clarified by Clark (1989), in order to highlight the very general feature of information-processing (intentionality) as conceived in biology and psychology, namely, that it essentially serves action.

2.3.2 Reply: symbols are linked to activity and hence carry meaning

If we bring the aforementioned conception of intentionality, basic to biology and psychology and adopted throughout this essay, to bear on the problem identified by Searle, we arrive at something like the following: what you have add to, or have instead of, symbol manipulation, in order to achieve intentionality is the regulation of action, that is, meaningful (goal-directed, plastic) interactions with the environment. In his discussions of the Chinese room, Searle (1987) rejects this frequently made response, on the grounds, roughly, that robots don't understand anything either. Probably not, but still there are abundant reasons for keeping in mind the connection, fundamental to biology and psychology, between meaning and action.

Explanation in terms of intentional states get a grip on artificial systems in so far as they 'behave intelligently' (e.g. solve problems), even though for *many* reasons we would not be inclined to say that they 'really' understand or mean anything. These many reasons mostly, or perhaps all, have to do with the fact that we human beings are paradigms of intentionality, and AI systems are not like us: they are simpler, more circumscribed; they are inanimate (they do not show the behavioural signs of being alive), including that they don't mind what happens to them, that they are not made of biological material, that they don't look like us; and so on. All these sorts of background considerations support the intuition that AI systems do not have 'real' intentionality as we do, but they concern what is open to view, including appearance and particularly behaviour, and they are therefore consistent with the main idea that attributions of meaning are based in behavioural considerations. No other criterion of meaning is involved here. It is in particular misleading to suppose that the critical question is whether machines do, or can, have the 'subjective feeling of understanding (or meaning)', in so far as this is an updated AI version of the outdated problem of other minds. As already discussed in the first chapter (subsection 1.2.4) this problem turns on the remnants of Cartesian dualism, and has no proper place in the cognitive-behavioural paradigm, which posits intentional states essentially as regulators of activity, not as subjective experiences.

In biology and cognitive-behavioural science, cognition (or information-processing) is regarded as being primarily in the service of action, and hence also the content of cognitive states (the information picked up, processed, and utilized) is likewise to be understood in terms relevant to action. This assumption is found in one form or another in the various domains of psychology. Cognitive learning theory defines cognitive states as mediating between stimulus and response. Developmental psychology has long taken cognition to be grounded in sensorimotor capacities (Piaget 1950). This same connection is apparently supported by general considerations about neural structure. Sensory and motor pathways permeate into and pervade the cortex (Brodal 1991), and were these to be stripped away, there would be practically no cognitive processing system left which could be engaged in the manipulation of uninterpreted symbols. Within the framework of cognitive-behavioural science, with its primary aim of explaining sensorimotor capacities such as discrimination, recognition, manipulation, and catagorization, cognitive states and processes will be, in general, defined as precisely serving such capacities, and hence cannot be adequately characterized as manipulation of meaningless symbols. At the very least, the symbols must have (for the agent) semantic interpretation, namely, as being about action. But the point is better made in this way: the 'symbols' already have meaning, because they are linked intrinsically to sensori-cognitive-motor capacities. A detailed response to Searle's problem along these lines, using traditional symbolic and connectionist modelling, has been made out by Harnad (1989, 1990).

It should be emphasized that the point here is not that connectionist models of mental function automatically avoid or solve the general problem identified by Searle, the problem of how to model intentionality and not just syntax (symbolism). According to connectionist models of neural function, the brain encodes information, though not in symbolic form, but as patterns of activity. However as noted above (subsection 2.2.2), these patterns are indeed 'symbols', precisely in so far as they encode information. But the point is that we can ask of any proposed model of encoding information: 'In what sense is there anything *semantic* here?' It is always possible to raise the question identified by Searle: 'Why is there intentionality here, over and above "symbol manipulation" (in a broad sense)?' The point is then, as Harnad argues (1989, 1990), that connectionist modelling can provide an answer to this question in so far as the 'symbols' (the patterns of activity within the system) already have meaning. The 'symbols' are essentially involved in the regulation of intentional (rule-guided) system/environment interaction, intrinsically linked to sensori-cognitive-motor capacities.

It is significant that the AI models of sensori-cognitive-motor capacities are typically connectionist, not those of symbolic AI, of the kind presupposed by the computational theory of mind. On the other hand, just as connectionist models do not automatically solve Searle's problem, but only when they accomodate a theory of meaning, so too symbolic AI models do not necessarily fail to solve the problem.

However, they do indeed get off to a poor start, particularly in their usual context of the computational theory of mind. For this theory fails to make axiomatic the link between symbolism and meaning, particularly meaning as grounded in (rule-guided) system/environment interactions. It defines mental states in terms of syntactic properties, not semantic ones. It can add (on) a semantics, but typically this involves no essential link between the semantics of mental states and action. The computational theory of mind can approach the idea of mental states having semantic properties in two main ways. First, following the classical theory of computation, it can construe semantic properties as dependent on (mirrored in) syntactic properties, and secondly, it defines the semantic properties in terms of the causal role of mental states. Both approaches, in the context of mind–brain identity theory, help to make up Fodor's language of thought hypothesis as already discussed (section 2.2). However, and as Fodor is well aware, this otherwise ingenious combination of several plausible doctrines leaves open the possibility that, so far as concerns the causal explanation of behaviour, semantic properties of mental/neural states are irrelevant, that what does the explanatory work are their syntactic properties. We turn now to consider this problem, in McGinn's formulation.

2.4 OBJECTION TO THE PROPOSED SOLUTION, 3: 'IF THERE IS NEURAL SYNTAX, THEN THIS IS WHAT CAUSES BEHAVIOUR AND ENCODED MEANING DROPS OUT AS IRRELEVANT'

2.4.1 McGinn's statement of the argument

There is a plausible line of thought in this area to the effect that semantic properties cannot play a causal role, or at least, not unless they correspond to synactic ones. Let us consider this, beginning with a lengthy quote from McGinn (1989, pp. 132–4):

> I come now to what I take to be the most serious and challenging argument against content based psychology. . . . The argument proceeds from certain principles about causation (so let us call it 'the causal argument')—specifically, about how mental causation must be seen to work. . . . (It) presupposes externalism, . . . according to which contentful states are identified by reference to entities that lie outside the subject's body (including, of course, his head): . . . Now this implies that contentful states are (as we might say) extrinsically relational: they essentially consist in relation to extrinsic non-mental items (objects, properties, etc.). . . . For example, for John to have the concept *square* (and so to be capable of believing that the box is square) is for John to stand in a certain relation to the *property* of being a square. So when we ascribe that concept to John we report him as standing in this extrinsic correspondence relation to that objective property. And now the causal objection to citing such contents in psychological explanations is just this: *if such explanations purport to be causal, then these correspondence relations cannot themselves be implicated in the causal transaction being reported* [italics added]. This is because what happens at the causal nexus is local, proximate, and intrinsic: the features of the cause that lead to the effect must be right there where the causal interaction takes place. Causation is the same with brains and minds as it is with billiard balls.

In brief, and to use an illustration closer to the cognitive explanation of action, if we cite in explanation of the rat's running to the goal-box its belief that there is food there, this explanation can only be causal, the belief can only be a causal item, if it is local to the rat's movements. It cannot be part of the causal power of the belief state that it relates to something external. This is, roughly, what McGinn refers to as the 'causal argument'.[7]

The argument under consideration here points back to where we started at the beginning of this chapter. Whatever might be going on under the name of meaningful, mental causation, we know in any case, practically for certain, that the causes of behaviour are in the brain. Brain processes are at least the local causes, the disruption of which, for example, puts paid to action. So somehow, whatever mental meaningful causation is, it has to be compatible with this fact. But this is of course where the encoding thesis comes in. It enables us to formulate a resolution along the following lines: local brain events cause behaviour, but they encode meaning; or even, the causes are 'encoded meanings'.

McGinn outlines this sort of response as follows (1989, pp. 136–7):

Since only the 'shape' (syntax, orthography) of internal symbols can be relevant to their causal powers, not their semantic relations to items in the world, we need, if we are to save content for psychology, to find a way of *linking* shape with semantics. We need, that is, to suppose that content is somehow reflected in intrinsic features of the symbol: that distinctions of content are mirrored by distinctions of shape. Let us call the claim that there are such shape/content links the *encoding thesis*. The encoding thesis says that semantic properties are perfectly matched by syntactic properties—semantics is coded into syntax. . . . And it is in virtue of this one–one correspondence that content gets a causal foothold. For whenever a content enters into a causal explanation we know that there exists some intrinsic syntactic property of the underlying symbol that is turning the wheels of the causal mechanism. In other words, content attributions can occur legitimately in causal explanations because they are guaranteed to have syntactic *proxies*.

McGinn defines the encoding thesis in a strong form, as proposing something like a structural similarity between syntax and meaning. This strong form of the thesis is in the area of Fodor's language of thought hypothesis discussed in Section 2.2. We saw connectionist reasons to be less literal about how meaning may be neurally encoded. McGinn cites a different reason for doubting such a strong structural similarity between syntax and semantics, namely, that it is plainly absent in the case of natural languages (McGinn 1989, p. 138; see also subsection 1.3.2). In any case, McGinn goes on to allow a weaker version of the encoding thesis (loc. cit.):

> A less literal construal would be more charitable. By 'syntax' is meant whatever intrinsic states underlie the causal dispositions associated with an internal symbol—presumably brain states at some level of description.

This more liberal reading of the notion of encoding is of the kind being endorsed here. It would be compatible, for example but in particular, with connectionist models of neural encoding.

To recapitulate, the so-called causal argument proposes that while (neural) syntax can cause behaviour, semantic features, being non-locally defined, cannot. Faced with this consideration the encoding thesis tries to retain semantics as causally relevant by saying that meaning is encoded in syntax. McGinn argues, however, that this attempt to secure the causal relevance of meaning fails (1989, p. 137):

> If (content) does its causal work by proxy, then it seems redundant to invoke it—we could simply stick with syntax. (This would be) an application of Occam's razor: keep your theoretical entities down to a minimum, compatibly with preservation of explanatory power. The encoding thesis, by guaranteeing a translation from content to syntax, invites the elimination of talk of content in favour of syntactic talk.

Thus, the alleged causal role of meaning depends entirely on the causal role of syntax, and in this case we can, and should, invoke the latter only, and the former drops out of consideration as redundant.

McGinn presents this objection to the encoding thesis in its strong form, but essentially it applies to the weaker form as well. However loose the notion of 'neural syntax', even if it means 'whatever neural organization encodes meaning', the point apparently still stands, that these local states and processes will be doing the causal work, and there is no need to invoke encoded meaning in the causal story.

2.4.2 Reply: semantic concepts are essential when what is to be causally explained is action

In the preceding subsection we presented the so-called causal argument against the causal role of meaning, and the alleged failure of the encoding thesis to meet it. Such a failure would contradict the main idea of this chapter, so we have to respond.

We have already in the first chapter (subsection 1.3.6) considered reasons for rejecting the hypothetical conclusion of the argument, that explanation of action can be run in terms of non-semantic concepts. The point is in brief that *if* the goal is explanation and prediction of intentional behaviour (complex organism–environment interactions), *then* the methodological assumption has to be that the agent is regulated by information about the environment, that is, by intentional states, either mental, or encoded in the brain, or both. It is, on the other hand, perfectly possible to do away with intentional concepts, but then only non-intentional behaviour can be predicted, for example physical movements of the body, not intentional interactions with the environment.

This main point holds regardless of the interpretations given to the notion of encoding, whether strong or weak, regardless whether semantic properties are or are not mirrored in the syntactic structure of symbols.

The claim against which the causal argument is directed is that explanations of behaviour which invoke meaningful content, correspondence to what is external, are causal. The argument can be summarized as follows, to quote again McGinn (1989, p. 134):

> If such explanations purport to be causal, then these correspondence relations cannot themselves be implicated in the causal transaction being reported [italics added]. This is because what happens at the causal nexus is local, proximate, and intrinsic: the features of the cause that lead to the effect must be right there where the causal interaction takes place. Causation is the same with brains and minds as it is with billiard balls.

And our reply may be summarized as follows. It depends what is to be explained. What can be explained in terms of causes defined intrinsically, proximately, and locally is behaviour defined intrinsically, proximately, and locally, for example a leg moving. But if what we want to explain is extrinsically defined goal-directed, plastic behaviour, for example an animal finding its way to a goal-box, then the causes we need to invoke have to be defined extrinsically, as intentional states. But are these extrinsically defined states invoked for this purpose proximate and local? Yes of course, that is the point of the notion of encoding. The intentional, semantic property of representation is encoded in the local, proximate neural state.

As to whether causation is (all) the same with brains and minds as it is with billiard balls, probably it isn't. Causal explanations run in non-intentional terms apply to billiard balls and to brain–behaviour interactions, but in the latter case, unlike the former, there is also the possibility of constructing causal explanations in intentional terms; indeed this is mandatory when what is to be explained is intentional behaviour. This distinction between two forms of causality is developed through Chapter 4 and elaborated in Chapter 5.

The conclusion that explanation of intentional behaviour in terms of intentional states is causal was drawn in Chapter 1. The argument in the present chapter is that this conclusion is compatible with neural causation because neural states, in so far as they regulate intentional behaviour, themselves have (encode) intentional features. This ensures that causation is material, and proximate to the effects.

The implication is that the causal role of these material, proximate states depends on the semantic features that they encode. This implication can hardly be understood while we have in mind as a model of causation, in seventeenth-century style, interactions between billiard balls. The causal role of semantic features can be seen clearly at one level, in AI models of mental function, in so far as those structural and functional characteristics that encode information vary with the information they encode, and these same variable features also determine how such characteristics interact with one another and eventually cause certain outputs of the system. This is obvious enough, but it invites the response, which we have been considering under the name of the 'causal argument', that all we are really seeing here is the causal role of syntax, not the causal role of semantics. To get at semantics we need to stand back and take a broader view, taking in not just what is going on inside the system, but also the intentional activity of the system within the environment.

Intentional activity is best explained and predicted by attributing to the agent systems of intentional states. The inference about causality, drawn in the first chapter, can be expressed by saying either that the intentional states posited are casual, or that the explanations that invoke them are causal explanations. These two formulations are more or less equivalent, at least in the sense that it would be unattractive to have to argue for one and against the other. However, probably they can be understood with different emphases or connotations, and perhaps particularly when it comes to handling the critical implication that causality here turns on intentionality. In one of the two formulations, this implication will read: it is the intentional properties of intentional states which determine their causal role. Obvious though this implication may look, and indeed it is obvious, it becomes obscured by the so-called causal argument which we have been considering. All we see when we look at intentional states, for example in AI models, is syntax not semantics, and it is unclear how semantic features can play, or need to play, any causal role; still less, then, is it clear how or why such a causal role should depend on particular semantic features rather than others.

For the particular purpose of getting unstuck here, we need to remind ourselves of the other route, the other formulation of the claim that intentionality involves causality. That is: explanations that attribute intentional states to an agent and thereby predict intentional activity, are causal explanations. From here, it is not at all difficult to see that causal explanations of this kind run differently, generate different predictions, as a function of the particular semantic contents attributed to the agent. This is really obvious.

Of course it is possible to reach the same conclusion by the other route, by considering the causal role of intentional states. But this is more complicated and therefore hazardous. The complication is that it has to go via the idea that material states encode information, and the proposal that reference to the fact that such states do encode information cannot be omitted *while the purpose is to explain and predict intentional activity*. In brief, *for this purpose*, semantic talk cannot be eliminated in favour of syntactic talk. The critical turnings here are easy to miss, or are controversial. They lead away from the intentional states in themselves, and the causal role they have in virtue of intrinsic, syntactical, physical features. We take into account rather what else such states have to be credited with if we are adequately to explain and predict intentional activity, namely: semantic contents, and causal roles which are a function of the particular contents that are encoded.

2.4.3 Overview of the problem of syntax and semantics

The previous three sections have all been involved with the problem of syntax and semantics, in the attempt to defend and clarify the encoding thesis. Let us at this stage take a broad view of the problem.

Syntax may be defined as being a physical property of a symbol, such as the shape of a letter or numeral. In the context of mind–brain identity theory, the physical property would be such as the electromagnetic characteristics of neuronal networks. But this kind of definition alone, though suited to formal logic (particularly of course with the usual example of shape), does little work in logic understood as the a priori theory of representation. For logic in this sense, the notion of syntax is generally invoked in the service of semantics, of the theory of meaning. The problem of meaning can be put simply like this: how can one thing—a sign—signify another, its object? And the notion of syntax can play a role in answering this question.

One kind of solution to the problem of meaning, discussed already in the first chapter (subsection 1.3.2) appeals to something like *resemblance* between sign and signified. In some applications of this very general theory, particularly in the philosophy of language, the notion of the syntax of a sign readily plays a crucial role. The syntax of a sign, its intrinsic structure or shape, represents possible structures in reality. This kind of theory, of which Wittgenstein's *Tractatus* (1921) is probably the best worked-out example, illustrates the general point that what matters about the sign is fundamentally only what contributes to its having meaning (i.e. is only what makes it a *sign*). In this sense syntactic definitions of signs presuppose or imply a semantic theory. In particular, then, if we define syntax in terms of shape, we are presupposing that what matters to meaning (what achieves meaning) is shape, and this is a *massive* assumption in the theory of meaning, linked indeed to the resemblance theory just mentioned. But, important for our purposes, the assumption stands opposed to the definition of representation endorsed here, in terms of the regulation of action (subsection 1.3.3).

Before going on to consider what notion of 'syntax' belongs with this semantic theory, let us note a further very general point which is plain enough in the resemblance theory. Sign and signified have something *in common*, a form, the possibility of having such-and-such a structure, in virtue of which the sign can be a correct or incorrect (true or false) representation of reality. This idea is, again, worked out clearly in the *Tractatus*, in its doctrines of the identity between pictorial form, the form of thought, and the form of reality.[8] Form here means something like 'order', the fact that things are this way rather than that, or are truly or falsely represented as being this way or that. Sign and signified have something—a form—in common. In the case of picture-representations it is the (possibility of) structural configuration, and this is apparent in the syntactic description of signs. But what is 'form' in the case of representations as regulators of activity?

We have, as discussed in the first chapter (subsections 1.3.3–4), abandoned the theory of resemblance, and supposed rather that signs represent reality in so far as they are used in rule-following activities, activities which are 'right' or 'wrong'. Because the order is now seen as a property of the activity, that is, of the interaction between agent and environment, we do not *also* have to assume that there has to be some structured sign (sign with a shape) which achieves the representation of reality. The essential feature of a sign is now its use in rule-following activity, not its shape. The analogue of the theory of syntax in the new theory of representation naturally presupposes or implies a semantics. How does a sign refer to something in reality? Basically, because the users of the sign interact with things in reality. To take Wittgenstein's example at the start of the *Philosophical investigations* (1953): men are building, one man calls out the word 'slab', and another picks up and brings a certain kind of building stone.

The question arises as to how, in what sense, the use of a sign is 'right' or 'wrong'? One possibility is that the distinction between correct and incorrect uses of signs is based partly in the fact that the activity in which they are used goes right or wrong. For example, some kinds of building stone can be fitted together to make a wall, others cannot. This line of thought will be pursued in this essay, although it is not to be found in Wittgenstein. Its plausibility can be seen as follows. Action essentially admits of normative distinctions: 'right'/'wrong', 'successful/unsuccessful', 'achieves goal'/ 'fails to do so', etc. This is a reasonable enough claim in philosophy, but it is in any case axiomatic in the bio-psychological sciences. It would be extraordinary, then, if normative distinctions in the use of signs were not linked to those in practice, especially given the background theory that it is use in practice that gives a sign meaning.

The shift from the *Tractatus* theory of meaning to the one in the *Philosophical investigations*, from pictures to rule-guided activity, may be expressed as the replacement of the notion of spatial form by form of activity, or again, by 'form of life' (Bolton 1982). Continuing in the terminology of the *Tractatus*, normative distinctions can be made out in the new theory in the following way. The 'form of the sign' is the activity of the agent, and the form of reality is the interwoven movement of objects in reality, and these two are in more or less agreement: action either works in reality or not. This 'pragmatic' approach to the true/false distinction is elaborated in the next chapter (Section 3.2).

If the notion of syntax were to be retained in this context, it would refer primarily to the order in intentional activity, not the physically defined order in a sign, such as a sentence, on paper, or in the brain. Indeed, and this is the main point, sentences (on paper or in a neural code) are not yet, according to this theory, *signs* at all. They become signs only when, and only in so far as they are, involved in rule-guided activity. This point is pivotal in the shift from the resemblance theory of meaning to the understanding of meaning as use in activity (subsection 1.3.2). It can indeed be used to launch a critique of the idea that the brain encodes meaning, and we shall discuss it further in this connection later, in Section 2.6. But here the point is that the notion of *order* which is central to the theory of representation is already captured in the notion of activity according to a rule: actions are 'right' or 'wrong', subject for example to positive or negative feedback, either from reality itself, or in the form of judgements from other people. In this context we do not *also* need the idea that the order in action emanates from a more fundamental order inside the brain. On this issue, anticipating some themes in the shift from symbolic to connectionist AI modelling, Wittgenstein remarked (1967, §608):

> No supposition seems to me more natural than that there is no process in the brain correlated with or associating with thinking; so that it would be impossible to read off thought-processes from brain processes. I mean this: if I talk or write there is, I assume, a system of impulses going out from my brain and correlated with my spoken or written thoughts. But why should the *system* continue further in the direction of the centre? Why should this order not proceed, so to speak, out of chaos?

The issue in this area most directly relevant to the problems tackled in this chapter is the following. The syntax of a sign may be defined as that by virtue of which it has meaning (and the particular meaning it has). The resemblance theory in its various forms, consistent with classical computation theory, implies that the syntax of a sign is a matter of physically defined properties, specifically shape. This is obviously compatible with physicalism, which envisages only such properties as being fundamental. In the case of encoding of information in the brain, it is obviously necessary to extend the range of physical properties constituting syntax to neural properties. This line of thought can be made to mesh with the idea that information-carrying neural states cause behaviour, and with the assumption that all causation is a matter of physical events following physical laws. In brief, information-carrying neural states will have causal power by virtue of their physically defined syntactic properties of neural states. Thus, (Fodor 1987, p. 5, with an Endnote):

> Here ... is how the new story is supposed to go: You connect the causal properties of a symbol with its semantic properties *via its syntax*. The syntax of a symbol is one of its higher-order physical properties. To a metaphorical first approximation, we can think of the syntactic structure of a symbol as an abstract feature of its shape.
>
> *Endnote: Any* nomic property of symbol tokens, however—any property in virtue of the possession of which they satisfy causal laws—would, in principle, do just as well. (So, for example, syntactic structure could be realized by relations among electromagnetic states rather than relations among shapes; as, indeed, it is in real computers.)
>
> [*Text continued*] Because, to all intents and purposes, syntax reduces to shape and because the shape of a symbol is a potential determinant of its causal role, it is fairly easy to see how there could be environments in which the causal role of a symbol correlates with its syntax. It's easy, that is to say, to imagine symbol tokens interacting causally *in virtue of* their syntactic structures. The syntax of a symbol might determine the causes and effects of its tokenings in much the way that the geometry of a key determines which locks it will open.

This story backs up Fodor's position as outlined in subsection 2.2.1, but the powerful assumptions it makes about semantics, syntax, and causality are questionable.

It is possible to tell a different story. It begins with the kind of semantic theory being endorsed here, to the effect that neurally encoded semantic states essentially regulate intentional action. We then have to construct a syntactic theory compatible with this. As already noted, 'syntax' always, in any theory, has to be defined in a way that makes sense of semantics. Definition in terms of shape will do if representation is essentially a matter of spatial resemblance. Definition in terms of relations between electromagnetic states will do if semantics can be defined in terms of such relations. But according to the story we are now running, semantic properties cannot defined in those or any other physical terms. Semantic properties *and therefore also syntactic properties* have to be understood in terms of the regulation of intentional action. Hence the view of neural syntax arrived at in subsection 2.3.2: neural 'symbols' are essentially involved in the regulation of intentional system–environment interaction, and are linked intrinsically to sensori-cognitive-motor capacities.

The proposal that synactic properties are not physically definable hangs together with the point made earlier (subsections 1.3.6, 2.1.4) and which will be made again (subsection 2.5.6), that causal explanation of intentional as opposed to non-intentional behaviour has to posit intentional states in the acting system. Invoking physically defined properties will not do the required work.

The implication of diverging in this way from Fodor's account of semantic causation is that we have to envisage causal laws that are not couched in terms of physical properties, but rather in terms of semantic ones. This idea, already anticipated for example at the end of subsection 2.4.2, is worked out in chapters 4 and 5. Another aspect of this implication is that information-carrying neural states have causal generating power by virtue of being semantic states, or again, that there is something like 'semantically defined energy'. This sort of conclusion was anticipated in earlier discussion of the intimate link between cognition and affect (subsection 1.2.3). The connection between information and the generation of order in functional, intentional systems appears also as a consequence of the shift from causal to functional semantics in Chapter 4 (subsection 4.6.3).

2.5 OBJECTIONS TO THE PROPOSED SOLUTION, 4: 'ARE MEANINGS IN THE HEAD?'

2.5.1 Introduction

In this section we discuss Putnam's highly influential claim that 'meanings ain't in the head' (Putnam 1975). Putnam's proposal, based on so-called 'twin-Earth' thought-experiments, along with variations, interpretations, and elaborations of its implications, are the subjects of a very large literature in philosophy and some theoretical cognitive science. Our interest here is partial and selective, concerning specifically implications for meaningful, mental causation. Putnam's proposal can be used to construct an argument against the idea that meaningful, mental states are causal, and so we need to consider it here.[9]

Among the various ways of approaching Putnam's claim and its implications, let us start with the issues discussed in the preceding section, to do with whether semantic characteristics can be causal. In subsection 2.4.1 we considered a line of thought which may be summarized briefly as follows: the meaning of any 'sign' in the brain (of any information-carrying neural state) must involve a relation between the brain and something external, the reality represented. But causality has to be local. Therefore meaning can't be causal.

To which the reply, given in subsection 2.4.2, was, in brief: if you want to explain non-local behaviour, that is behaviour which is environment directed, then you need to cite non-locally defined causes, which can be done while preserving local causation by positing that brain states encode meaning. This solution was meant to follow the lead of the information-processing paradigm within the behavioural sciences. The aim is to explain action in terms of information-carrying (cognitive) states, and these are regarded as encoded in the brain.

Essential to this explanatory paradigm, however, is a particular way of defining the informational content of cognitive states, namely, in terms of the interactivity between agent and the environment. The conceptual linkage between meaning and action is already implied by the fact that cognitive states are posited for the purpose of explaining action. This has been implicit or explicit throughout the first chapter and the present one. However, quite different assumptions about meaning can be made, so that there is in particular no conceptual linkage between meaning and action, in which case the proposal that meaning is encoded in the brain is lost, and with it the compatibility between material (neural) causation, and mental, meaningful causation, the latter of which then has to be jettisoned. This move belongs with the idea that meaningful characterizations of behaviour are in some business other than causal explanation, and runs counter to what is being argued for throughout this essay.

In brief, what we will be considering in this section of the chapter is the way that a definition of meaning that precludes interaction between the agent and what is represented undermines the idea that meaning is encoded in the brain and thereby has a causal role. We will in effect be arguing that in the context of cognitive explanation of behaviour such a definition of meaning, omitting agent–environment interactions, is a mischief-maker.

The position is, however, somewhat complicated by the fact that the view of meaning that we will be arguing against is frequently combined with a plausible proposal that we endorse, namely, that meaningful mental states are 'broad' or 'world-involving'. This is to say that their definition makes reference to the world other than the subject. This proposal is correct, and adopted, and indeed emphasized, here, but the 'world-involving' nature of meaningful states is compatible with the causal role of meaning, assuming these states are encoded in the brain. But, to repeat, this reconciliation only works if meaningful content is defined in terms of agent–environment interactions. Without this definition, the world-involving nature of meaningful states precludes their being encoded in the brain, and precludes their having any causal role.

One more issue, a matter of terminology prominent in the literature, has to be mentioned in this introductory subsection. The dictum 'meanings ain't in the head' may be taken to sum up the claim that the meaningful content of mental states is not dependent solely on the state of the brain. The notion of dependence at work here is defined using the technical term *supervenience*. The claim is that the meaningful content of mental states does not supervene on states of the brain. The notion of supervenience may be defined, roughly, as follows: states of type X supervene on states of type Y if and only if there is no difference among X states without a corresponding difference among Y states.[10]

In what follows we shall assume that there is a link between the technical notion of supervenience and the notion of encoding familiar in cognitive science. At least in this sense: that the supervenience of states of type X on states of type Y is a *necessary* condition of states of type Y encoding states of type X. While nothing in the arguments to follow depends on this linkage between supervenience and encoding, it helps to make explicit connections between Putnam's thesis and the philosophical literature to which it has given rise, and the cognitive science paradigm which is our main concern here.

The claim to be considered is that meaningful states do not supervene on brain states, with its implication that they cannot be causes of behaviour. In terms of encoding, the claim would be that such states are not encoded in brain states: meanings are not '(encoded) in the head'. The implication, again, being that meaningful states cannot be causes of behaviour. This in effect is the contraposition of the argument being proposed here, namely: since meaningful mental states are causes of behaviour they are encoded in brain states.

We have to consider, then, the basis of the claim that meaningful states do not supervene on brain states. Putnam came to this conclusion by means of what have come to be called twin-Earth thought-experiments, to which we turn next.

2.5.2 A twin-Earth thought-experiment and its standard interpretation: meaning does not supervene on the brain

In order to answer the question whether mental states with meaning supervene on brain states we have to consider the variation. We have to conduct an 'experiment' which holds brain states constant, and then see whether meaningful mental content can nevertheless vary: if it does, then there is no supervenience. It is of course important that the 'experiment' here is not, and cannot be, an empirical one. There is the practical impossibility of finding two identical brains and knowing that they are identical. But further, it is unclear what scientific test would show whether or not meaningful contents were identical under these conditions; apparently we should have to use 'intuitions' about meaning. So for more than one reason we are squarely in the philosophical arena here: the experiment has to be a thought-experiment, and it is heavily dependent on intuition.

Consider, then, the following thought-experiment, due to Putnam (1975), which seems to show that meaning fails to depend on states of the brain.

We are to imagine there to be in another world a person P* who is an exact replica of person P on Earth; in particular their brain states are identical. Further, the world P* inhabits is exactly similar to Earth in all respects except one: it has a substance with physico-chemical composition XYZ where we have the substance with composition H_2O. XYZ is the same as H_2O according to any casual test, though they can be distinguished in a chemical laboratory. Given this imaginary situation, we are invited to share the intuition that P and P* differ in semantic characteristics, that the meaning of their words differ, and the meaningful contents of their thoughts. Specifically, the suggestion is that the words 'water is wet' means something different when uttered by P than when uttered by P*, and that the content of P's thought that water is wet is different from the the corresponding thought entertained by P*. Indeed the intuition is meant to be that P* can neither say nor think that water is wet. The source of the alleged difference in meaningful content is due to the difference in the environments, defined in physico-chemical terms. Since the meaningful content of the *doppelgänger's* thoughts differs even though their brain states are identical, the conclusion is that meaningful content does not supervene on the brain. In brief, meaning ain't in the head.[11]

The intuitions that support this conclusion are of a piece with the physicalist or materialist criterion of meaning which refers to the physical (or physico-chemical) nature of what is represented. On this basis we reach the conclusion that mental states, individuated by meaningful content, do not supervene on brain states.

The same conclusion is reached by means of a different type of thought-experiment, formulated by Burge in a series of papers (1979, 1982*a*, *b*, 1986 *a*, *b*). In this type of case, the difference in mental contents between the *doppelgänger* is not due to a difference in their (physical) environments, but is due rather to a difference in their linguistic communities. Burge's arguments (or intuitions) have a broad range, unresricted to contents which can plausibly be construed as referring to physico-chemical kinds. They point to the conclusion that *no* mental contents (expressible in language) supervene on brain events. We shall assume in what follows that if the *doppelgänger* thought-experiments exclude content–brain supervenience at all, they do so for all content. However, we shall not discuss Burge's type of thought-experiment, since our comments on the Putnam type apply to what both types have in common, namely, the claim that meaningful content can differ notwithstanding identity of brain states. We shall call this claim the 'standard interpretation' of the *doppelgänger* thought-experiments.

We shall argue in the next section that the standard interpretation of the thought-experiments is mistaken; or, to put the point more cautiously, that it is incompatible with the criterion of mental content required for a cognitive-behavioural science. First let us consider the drastic consequences of accepting the standard reading of the *doppelgänger* thought-experiments, and proposals which have been made for handling them. These consequences, as anticipated at the beginning of the section, concern primarily meaning and causality.

2.5.3 Lack of supervenience implies that mental states are not causal; or they have no (ordinary) meaning

According to the standard interpretation of the twin-Earth thought-experiments, mental states identified in terms of meaningful content do not supervene on states of the brain. Now we introduce a premise to the effect that all causes of behaviour supervene on local material events, namely, in the brain. This plausible premise serves only to exclude both non-material causation (whatever that might be), and distal causation (unmediated by local). Thus from a combination of the standard interpretation of the thought-experiment plus a plausible premise about causality, it follows that mental states identified in terms of meaningful content are not causes of behaviour.

The meaningful content at issue is that as specified in folk psychological ordinary language. The problem with meaningful content as envisaged by folk psychology and ordinary language is that it is 'broad', or 'world-involving': it supervenes on (varies with) the states of the world, not only on states of the brain (see, for example, Stich 1983; McGinn 1982, 1989).

The argument is, then, that the broad, world-involving mental states posited by folk psychology cannot play a role in the causal explanation of behaviour, and therefore in particular have no role to play in the causal explanations of cognitive-behavioural science.

The conclusion that broad content does not supervene on brain states and therefore cannot be causal threatens the cognitive-behavioural explanatory paradigm. If the paradigm is to be preserved, desperate remedies are required and have been proposed. Roughly, the saving principle has to be that cognitive states can have a causal role, but broad content has to be irrelevant to it. In which case, either cognitive states have causal role but content drops out altogether, or some notion of content is retained as relevant to causal role, namely 'narrow' content as opposed to 'broad'. Narrow content is not world-involving, does supervene on the brain, and therefore can be causal. Hence we find proposed both theories of content-less (meaning-less) cognitive causation (Stich 1983), and narrow content theories (Fodor 1980; McGinn 1982).

The idea of narrow content appears, however, highly problematic. Content, one supposes by definition, has intentionality, aboutness, hence is world-involving, and so broad. The idea of narrow content seems at best extraordinary and at worst self-contradictory. On the other hand, narrow content can be defined in terms of causal role. In this case narrow content theories become similar to the proposal to define cognitive states in terms of causal role, omitting reference to content altogether. This shifts the problem, however, rather than solving it. The cognitive-behavioural explanatory paradigm, like the folk psychological, describes not only the content of mental states in broad, world-involving terms, but also in those terms the behaviour that such states cause. We say, for example, 'having learnt that the goal-box contained food, and being hungry, the rat ran towards it'. The causal role of cognitive states is to be defined in terms of interactions among them and the behaviour they generate, but in the kind of explanation in question, the behaviours generated are typically world-involving, or broad. Hence the causal roles of the cognitive states are defined in broad terms, so also then is any notion of content tied to causal role. There seems to be no way of managing without our familiar broad, world-involving characterizations of intentional activity and the cognitive states that regulate it. Attempts to do so have to envisage an extraordinary, not yet invented, behavioural language. In Stich's terms, what is required are 'autonomous' behavioural descriptions. Stich admits to difficulties clarifying their nature, and remarks negatively: 'there is no reason to expect that the autonomous behavioural-description terminology ultimately to be found most useful will be a purely physical description of movements of the sort that behaviourists sought but never found' (1983, p. 169). Elsewhere he notes that 'perhaps an appropriate autonomous behavioural descriptive language does not yet exist' (1983, p. 136fn).

But this is, we suggest, a problematic solution to an ill-conceived problem.[12] There is no need to jettison our familiar broad, world-involving definition of the mental content involved in the regulation of action. On the contrary, this is just what is required for the causal explanation of intentional action. Basically this just repeats the point made earlier, for example in reply to the so-called casual argument in subsection 2.4.2.

We have to reassess the problem. As remarked at the beginning of this subsection, the conclusion that mental states identified in terms of meaningful content are not causes of behaviour follows from two premises. First, the standard interpretation of the twin-Earth thought-experiments, according to which mental states identified in terms of meaningful content do not supervene on (depend on) states of the brain. Secondly, that all causes of behaviour supervene on local material events, namely, in the brain.

Since we are rejecting the conclusion, we have to reject one of the premises. Attempts have been made to manage without the second premise, by distinguishing between types of causal explanation and in particular by defining a type that depends on content in the absence of supervenience. Jackson and Pettit (1988) distinguish between causal explanations which cite a *causally efficacious feature* and those which cite a *feature which 'causally programmes' without causing*. Explanations of behaviour in terms of broad mental content are then held to be indeed legitimate causal explanations, but of the causal programming variety. This proposal ensures the relevance of broad mental states to causal explanation and seems to avoid the problems inherent in the idea of narrow content. On this last point, however, the difficulty is that causal programming explanations generally seem to presuppose causal efficacious explanations, so that in particular, causal programming explanations of behaviour in terms of broad mental states apparently presuppose causal efficacious explanations in terms of narrow mental states (Rowlands 1989). A related suggestion is Dretske's distinction between 'triggering' and 'structuring' causes of behaviour, again designed to show how content can be causal even though it fails to supervene on brain states (Dretske 1988, with critical commentary in McLaughlin 1991).

Our suggestion is, however, to retain the principle in question, namely that causes of behaviour supervene on local material events in the brain. It is an apparently plausible principle, and is embraced by the idea characteristic of the information-processing based behavioural sciences and adopted here, that semantic characteristics are encoded in brain states. This means that what has to be rejected is the standard interpretation of the twin-Earth thought-experiments, according to which mental states identified in terms of meaningful content do not supervene on (depend on) states of the brain. From the point of view of the general account being proposed here, this is the real culprit.

The encoding thesis makes it possible to hold both that meaningful states are world-involving and that they act as local causes, the implication being that they satisfy the supervenience condition. This in turn implies that semantic content involves interaction between the subject of the mental states and what is represented. Such a definition of meaning is suited to the cognitive-behavioural sciences, but it is not captured by the standard interpretation of the twin-Earth experiments. Let us consider these issues in more detail.

2.5.4 Reply: meaning stands in need of behavioural criteria

The standard interpretation of the thought-experiments is that the *doppelgänger*, while identical in brain states, nevertheless have mental states with different meaningful content. As against this we can say that in the circumstances envisaged, mental contents are indeed identical, at least according to behavioural criteria of content, since the behaviours of the *doppelgänger* are the same. Use of behavioural criteria is appropriate to cognitive-behavioural science, which posits mental states with semantic contents in order to explain behaviour.

The obvious reply to this suggestion is that the *doppelgänger* do indeed differ in behaviour: one drinks, tries to find, etc. H_2O, while the other drinks, tries to find, etc. XYZ. Just as mental content varies with the environment, so does the appropriate description of behaviour. This reply serves as a quick defence of the standard reading of the thought-experiments, but it fails to recognize the point behind the suggestion that we have in these cases identity of behaviour. The suggestion is not simply the superficial one that the relevant behaviours can be described in the same way; this can indeed be met with a flat denial, consistent with the standard reading of the thought-experiment. The important point is rather that there is identity of behaviour *because a critical behavioural difference is missing, namely, behaviour which discriminates between H_2O and XYZ.*

Fundamental to the standard interpretation of the thought-experiments is that it discriminates between mental contents in the absence of corresponding discriminative behaviour. Since the *doppelgänger ex hypothesi* do not (and could not) discriminate between H_2O and XYZ in their behaviour, there is no justification for ascribing to them mental states with content H_2O as opposed to XYZ, or vice versa. At least, there is no justification from the point of view of a cognitive science of behaviour, which on the grounds of parsimony posits only those mental states and contents required for an adequate explanation of behaviour, including of discriminative behaviour. In this sense, the standard reading of the thought-experiments invokes a criterion of mental content different from, and incompatible with, the criterion appropriate to psychology.

This line of thought has some similarities with Fodor's more recent argument for the notion of narrow content in cognitive science, the so-called modal argument (Fodor 1987, 1991). Fodor criticizes the standard reading of the *doppelgänger* cases on the grounds that it invokes a difference in mental content which does no causal-explanatory work. Fodor goes on to suggest that specification of mental content should be relativized to context, in such a way that the *doppelgänger* share mental states. Fodor and his twin-Earth replica share the same mental state, the content of which is H_2O in case of being on Earth, or XYZ in case of being on twin-Earth. Content so defined would be 'narrow' in the sense of being supervenient, and causal. But it would at the same time be 'broad' in the sense of referring to a disjunctively specified environment. Fodor's argument and the notion of narrow content which it defends has been much discussed (Burge 1989; Block 1991; Crane 1991; McGinn 1991; Wilson 1992; Adams 1993*a,b*; Manfredi 1993; Russow 1993).

The position being proposed in this section is similar to Fodor's in key ways. We endorse the behavioural criterion of content suited to the cognitive-behavioural explanatory paradigm, and hence in particular the methodological principle: no difference in content to be invoked which does not explain a behavioural difference. On the other hand, our emphasis in the notion of 'behavioural difference' is not essentially concerned with differences in the environmental scene of behaviour, but is specifically to do with *discriminative* behaviour. Our proposal is to define content *only* in terms of what makes a difference to behaviour, to organism–environment interactions, in which case neither the term H_2O nor the term XYZ, nor therefore thier disjunction, has a role to play in the characterization of mental states in the twin-Earth experiments as described. This proposal delivers broad meaning and causal power, jettisons only the idea of broad content defined by reference to what makes no difference to behaviour, and in this context the idea of narrow as opposed to broad content drops out as redundant. These implications are discussed below.

The proposal, then, is to use a behavioural criterion of content with the emphasis, as indicated, on discriminative behaviour. Such a criterion stands in clear contrast to the one at work in the setting up of, and the standard interpretation of, the type of thought-experiment we are considering, which has to do with the physico-chemical nature of the environment.

On the other hand, it can be argued that the physicalist (or materialist) criterion of mental content is supported by considerations of causal history, the supposition being that the causal history of the pyschological states in question involves causation by H_2O in the one case and XYZ in the other (Davidson 1989). However, since the thought-experiments are set up in such a way that the brain states of *doppelgängers* are identical, H_2O has effects on the brain indistinguishable from those of XYZ. So whatever it is about these substances that has to be invoked in order to explain their causal effects on the brain, it is not their chemical composition. Presumably, then, within the terms of the causal theory of mental content, there are no grounds for distinguishing between the causal histories of the *doppelgänger's* mental states. In this way the causal criterion of mental content seems to point to the same conclusion as the behavioural criterion, and for similar reasons.

If mental content in the *doppelgänger* cases is not to be identified in physico-chemical terms, how else should it be specified? The line of thought in the preceding paragraph provides one approach to this question. We take it as obvious that living beings are sensitive to only some of the properties of water; obvious because we are speaking of beings with particular needs and aims, with limited sensory and cognitive capacities, not of God. Expressed in the information-processing language of biology and psychology, the point is that livings beings are sensitive to and encode only part of the hypothetical totality of information pertaining to water. In the case of human beings, and the *doppelgängers* in the thought-experiments in particular, let us call this subset of information IE: information encoded. IE includes, say: fluid, colourless, drinkable, fire-extinguishing. But in particular it excludes, *ex hypothesi* in the *doppelgänger* cases, being composed of H_2O rather than XYZ, or vice versa. Then we may say that the *doppelgänger* have the same information-bearing states, the content of which is characterized in terms of IE. The general proposal is that the mental content which regulates behaviour is to be defined in terms of encoded information, which is essentially a product of organism–environment interactions.

As indicated, such a definition of mental content in terms of encoded information is distinct from what is presupposed in the standard reading of the thought-experiments. It is the kind of definition appropriate to biology and psychology, and it hangs together with behavioural criteria of mental content. Living beings are sensitive to some features of the environment but not others: they encode particular information, salient to their activity. The criterion of whether a certain type of information is or is not encoded and used in the regulation of activity is precisely behavioural, including specifically evidence of discriminative behaviour. Thus, for example, a creature's behaviour may show that it possesses information that a pool of water is drinkable, or is polluted, but may show that it does not possess the information that water is composed of the chemical elements hydrogen and oxygen as opposed to others; and so on.[13]

2.5.5 Behaviourally defined content supervenes on the brain, is 'world-involving', and is causal

The definition and criteria of mental content being proposed are unlike those at work in the standard reading of the thought-experiments. It may be expected, then, that they give no support to the (apparently paradoxical) implications of the standard reading. According to the account proposed here, mental content does supervene on brain states, even though it is 'world-involving', and thereby it is relevant to the causal role of mental states. Let us consider these points in turn.

The content of cognitive states as identified by this method supervenes on brain states. According to behavioural criteria of content, which attend specifically to discriminative behaviour, there is no reason to distinguish between the mental contents of the *doppelgänger*. In the thought-experiment we have been considering, distinction between mental contents is based on differences in the physico-chemical nature of the environments. But the reply is that the physico-chemical nature of their environments is irrelevant to the *doppelgänger*: they simply do not detect it. This is how the thought-experiment is set up. By contrast, consider the environmental features which, as shown in their behaviour, the *doppelgänger* do detect, that water is fluid, drinkable, etc. In respect of these features, the environments of the *doppelgänger* are indeed identical, and this identity hangs together with the identity of their behaviour, brain states, and mental contents.[14]

Let us consider the dictum that meaning ain't in the head, in relation to the argument in the above paragraph. The meaning in question is tied to the physico-chemical composition of the environment. However, the thought-experiments are set up precisely in such a way that the *doppelgänger* fail to detect this feature of the environment. No wonder, then, that meaning ain't in the head! When the basis of this dictum is spelt out as above, it is (more or less) tautological. As is the following proposition: meaning is encoded in, and hence is supervenient on, states of the brain (is 'in the head') in so far as it pertains to features of the environment to which the living being is sensitive. Thus, according to the way the thought-experiment is set up, meaning pertaining to such as fluidity is in the *doppelgänger's* heads, but there is nothing in their heads about chemical composition.

Nothing in the above argument, of course, precludes there being mental states with meaningful content individuated in terms of concepts of physics and chemistry. Anyone who has learnt these sciences has them; the *doppelgänger* apparently haven't. Further, mental states with such content, according to the present argument, supervene on brain states; they are 'in the head'. The point is not that concepts of physics and chemistry cannot be used to individuate mental states, but is rather that the use of any concepts for this purpose stands in need of justification by behavioural criteria.

Mental content, defined by behavioural criteria, not only supervenes on the brain, but is essentially 'world-involving'. Contrary to the standard reading of the thought-experiments, this latter characteristic of mental content does not preclude supervenience.

According to the proposed analysis, mental content is 'broad', or 'world-involving', in the sense that it is defined and individuated by reference to features of the world. These may include, in the thought-experiment we have taken as example, features such as fluidity or transparency. It is essential to our notion of mental content that environmental properties enter into its definition. This correct insight, however, has been misconstrued in the standard interpretation of the *doppelgänger* thought-experiments as being incompatible with content–brain supervenience. It has been wrongly supposed that if content is world-involving then it cannot supervene on states of the brain, and vice versa.

The conclusion that mental content is both world-involving and supervenient on the brain belongs straightforwardly with the assumption characteristic of biology and psychology that information about the environment is encoded in the brain. This assumption is fundamental to the causal explanation of behaviour in terms of information-processing. The main point is that the contents of information-bearing states, mental or material, have to be characterized by reference to environmental features precisely in so far as they are invoked to explain behaviour as interaction between the organism and its environment. In other words, content is world-involving because of its role in the explanation of behaviour. This understanding of the world-involving character of mental content is, however, quite distinct from, and opposed to, the conception at work in the thought-experiments. In that context, the world-involving character of content is entirely irrelevant to behaviour, and this is the reason why the thought-experiments give rise to conundrums.

Meaningful content defined as information encoded within the living being supervenes on states of the brain and its effects are evident in behaviour. Given these propositions, there is apparently no reason to deny, while there is reason to affirm, that the content of cognitive states is relevant to their causal role. The causal effects of cognitive states on other such states and on behaviour depend on what information they encode. We consider these points further in the next subsection.

2.5.6 'Individualism' and causal role

We are proposing that content is attributed to the subject's mind or brain, even though it is individuated broadly, with reference to features of the environment. This conclusion may be compared and contrasted with the doctrine of 'individualism' against which Burge has argued in a number of papers (1979, 1982*a,b*, 1986*a,b,c*, 1989).

This doctrine may be stated briefly in the following form: that intentional states are fixed by, supervene on, bodily states the nature of which are specifiable without reference to external, environmental conditions. Burge has taken individualism to be refuted by the *doppelgänger* thought-experiments, his own (which have not been discussed here) and Putnam's. The standard interpretation of the thought-experiments apparently refutes individualism by the two claims, first that intentional states are individuated with reference to external conditions, and secondly that such states do not supervene on the brain.

The view proposed in this section affirms the first of these claims but not the second. According to what we are proposing, individualism is correct: the states of the brain on which intentional states supervene may be described in intrinsic terms, even though the intentional states that they encode are specified with reference to extrinsic conditions.

That said, and here we return to a line of thought already discussed in several places so far (for example, subsections 1.3.6, 2.4.2): for the purpose of causal explanation of behaviour in the environment (as opposed to behaviour as motor movement), descriptions of brain processes will be couched in the language of information-processing, including specification of information about the environment which is coded. When this language is used, brain processes themselves are characterized broadly, with reference to external conditions.

This possibility of choice between (to put it briefly) intrinsic and extrinsic description exists in the case of brain states, but probably not in the case of mental or cognitive states: here extrinsic (information-processing) description only is possible. This is connected with Brentano's thesis, that the mental is essentially characterized by its intentionality, its 'aboutness'. In the context of cognitive-behavioural science, the point is that cognitive states are posited essentially in order to explain behaviour in the environment, and so they have to specified by reference to (actual or possible) environmental states. Cognitive-behavioural science does not have as *explanandum* behaviour as motor acts, considered in isolation from the environment. Or again, there is no need to posit *cognition* in the explanation of behaviour so defined: explanation in (non-information -processing) neurophysiological terms will suffice, and is appropriate.

The suggestion is, then, that non-intentional characterization of mental states is an impossibility, or at least is useless for the purpose of cognitive-behavioural explanation. Functionalism, in so far as it is committed to a non-intentional, 'narrow', definition of the causal role of mental states, then appears as mistaken. Burge takes functionalism to be a contemporary version of individualism, and hence false. The present argument endorses this criticism. The only viable version of functionalism would define the causal role of mental states essentially in terms of information-carrying and -processing. This link between the notion of causality applicable in psychology and biology and the concept of information-processing will be argued for in detail in Chapter 5.

We have argued that mental content has the following three characteristics: it supervenes on states of the brain and is relevant to the causal role of mental states, but also it is 'world-involving', individuated in terms of environmental features. The standard interpretation of the *doppelgänger* thought-experiments, by contrast, splits these characteristics of mental content apart, making the third appear incompatible with the first two: but all three are essential for adequate causal explanation in biology and psychology.

In the way the thought-experiments are set up and standardly interpreted, the world-involving nature of mental content is indeed incompatible with supervenience and causal role, precisely because it is defined in such a way as to make no difference to the brain or to behaviour. But the incompatibility inferred from this kind of case shows up as problematic when we consider world-involving characteristics of mental states which are reflected in behaviour and which therefore presumably do supervene on the brain. This kind of case is encountered as soon as we turn from the imaginary world of the thought-experiments to consider a working psychological theory.

In support of his claim that content is world-involving, Burge cites the fact that 'the best empirical theory that we have [Marr's] individuates the intentional content of visual representations by specific reference to specific physical characteristics of visible properties and relations' (1986c, p. 38). So such content is broad and world-involving. But then let us raise the critical questions: 'Is content so defined relevant or not relevant to the causal role of representations, and do representations with content so defined supervene on brain states or not?' We take it that the answer to both these questions is going to have to be 'Yes'. However, Burge cannot give this answer, because it contradicts the standard conclusion drawn from the thought-experiments, to which Burge remains heavily committed, that mental states individuated broadly are neither causal nor supervenient on the brain. This conclusion, when applied to the theory of visual perception, leads to what appears to be the puzzling position that while the content of visual representations is individuated by reference to visible environmental conditions, this fact is irrelevant to the causal role of the representations, is unreflected, for example, in discriminative behaviour, and fails to supervene on physical states of the visual system. This is the kind of problematic position which Burge seems obliged to formulate and defend (Burge 1986c, 1989; Francescotti 1991).

It makes sense in the thought-experiments to suppose that broad, world-involving content is non-supervenient and lacks causal role because their aim is not to explicate causal explanation, and indeed they define content in such a way that it makes no difference to (discriminative) behaviour. But in working cognitive psychology, the aim is to explain intentional activity, including discrimination, and in this context it is to be expected that content will play a causal role, and will be neurally encoded (will supervene on the brain), while being at the same time 'world-involving', that is, specified as being about such-and-such an object or feature in the environment as opposed to some other.

In this context of cognitive-behavioural explanation the claim that broad content is neither causal nor supervenient creates paradoxes because the kind of content such explanation invokes is typically a matter of perceptible properties, that is, properties which can be perceived, and which when perceived make a difference to the brain and to behaviour. Of course 'perceptible' here does not mean 'consciously perceptible': what is required is that the agent be sensitive to the properties in question, consciously or otherwise. Some of these properties may coincide with the categories of physics and chemistry, such as shape and mass (within certain ranges), or oxygen in solution. Others are plainly relative to the living being, such as being non-poisonous or dangerous. In biology and psychology, the environment that is represented in information-carrying states cannot be defined without reference to the sensitivity, aims, and interests of the living being.

2.5.7 Meaning and action: post-empiricist qualifications

Mental content supervenes on brain states, has causal role, and is world-involving, individuated by reference to environmental features, these being of a particular sort, namely, features which matter to, and may be frankly relative to, the subject. The standard reading of the thought-experiments fails to insert this qualification concerning features that individuate content, indeed flatly contradicts it, and therefore leads to the conclusion that meaningful content, broadly individuated, fails to supervene on brain states and has no causal role. Meaningful content is then irrelevant to cognitive-behavioural science. At this point it may be recalled that the meaningful content that is and has been in question is meaningful content as specified in folk psychological ordinary language. The standard reading of the thought-experiments thus threatens to consign ordinary language, and folk psychology with it, into scientific oblivion.

The arguments in the preceding three subsections, against the standard interpretation of the thought-experiments, serve, if correct, to counter this attack. Moreover, they bring out that the folk psychological method of specifying mental content is, in form, correct. For the purpose of explaining intelligent behaviour in the environment, as opposed to motor movements in a vacuum, the meaningful content of cognitive states is appropriately specified by reference to (perceptible) environmental conditions. This is precisely the method used in folk psychology. The fact that mental content as specified in ordinary language is broad, or world-involving, is not at all a drawback in the context of cognitive-behavioural explanation, rather it is a virtue. Further, broadly individuated, world-involving mental contents of the sort familiar in folk psychology presumably supervene on brain states, in so far as they make a difference to behaviour, that is, in so far as the explanations which invoke them are effective in the prediction of behaviour.

An implication of the view being proposed is that the meaning of ordinary language, used among other purposes for specifying the meaningful content of mental states, is grounded in behaviour. The meaning of a sign derives from its use in action, not from, for example and in particular, the fact that it is used within an environment with such-and-such physico-chemical constitution (save in so far as such constitution makes a difference to the activity of the users of the sign, hence to the use of the sign within that activity). The contrast in the philosophy of language and meaning here is between the view proposed by the later Wittgenstein, and subsequent theories that seek to anchor linguistic meaning in a materialist reality. There is much to be said on either side of this debate, but the philosophy of language is not our primary concern here. What does follow, however, from the above arguments in the philosophy of mind is that it is Wittgenstein's view of meaning as use in activity which belongs with cognitive-behavioural science; in this context the other definition of meaning leads to paradoxes.

As it stands, the proposed definition ties meaning to the sphere of interaction between the living being and the environment, hence to experience (though not necessarily conscious experience). In this sense the claim that meaning is grounded in action is close to empiricism. On the other hand, as outlined in the first chapter (subsection 1.4.1), empiricism neglects theoretical representation of realities that cannot be reduced to experience. Human beings at least, beyond a certain level of cognitive maturation, can represent a greater reality which includes but exceeds what is given in experience; we represent, for example, events in distant regions of space and time, perhaps also spirit worlds, and so on. Plausibly such representation is dependent on our use of language; in any case, we are less inclined to attribute such world-pictures to creatures without language, to animals or infants. So what remains of the idea that meaning must be grounded in action? At the very least, it has to be qualified and elaborated to allow for the kind of case just described: meaning is grounded in interaction between the living being and its environment, though on that basis, representation may be made of reality which exceeds what is immediately encountered in action.

An elaboration of this general kind can be seen in Wittgenstein's work, by comparing the *Philosophical investigations* with *On certainty*. The former introduces the new theory of meaning in connection with simplified examples of simple activities, such as shopping and building (Wittgenstein 1953, §§1–37). The latter deals with daily activities, simple but no longer simplified, and these are now shown as surrounded by systems of belief, or world-views (Wittgenstein 1969; see also subsection 1.4.4).

The gradual freeing of concepts from action is also a prominent theme in psychological development, to be considered later (Chapter 6). Whether looked philosophically or psychologically, however, the roots of meaning in action and experience remain evident. Our conception of realities that lie beyond experience typically uses images, categories, and analogies from experience, and they presuppose that those realities interact with what is nearer to hand, so that experience contains signs of what lies beyond it. It follows from this last point that some kinds of activity require for their cognitive explanation the ascription of mental content concerned with 'distant realities'. In order to understand and predict the behaviour of a physicist, chemist, palaeontologist, priest, or tribal magician, it is necessary to suppose that their beliefs and actions concern (what they take to be) signs of realities beyond what is directly experienced in practice.

2.6 OBJECTIONS TO THE PROPOSED SOLUTION, 5: 'PEOPLE NOT BRAINS HAVE MEANING'

2.6.1 The objection

We have proposed that meaning is encoded in the brain, and thereby plays a role in the regulation of action. This proposal is intended to reconcile meaningful with neural causation, and to follow the lead of the information-processing paradigm in the brain-behavioural sciences. We have considered so far four interconnected objections to this proposal, and we turn now to the fifth and final one.

It has some superficial similarities to the one just discussed, in so far as it invokes the general idea that meaning involves the world and is therefore not the kind of thing that can be in the brain. But instead of being based in materialist preconceptions about reality and meaning, or in ultimately problematic thought-experiments, the objection in the form to be considered next is based in what may be called a Wittgensteinian view of language and meaning, as being essentially involved in forms of life.

As discussed earlier (subsection 2.4.3), Wittgenstein in his early work, the *Tractatus* (1921), proposed that the pictorial structure of the sign alone (its syntax) has meaning, is a true-or-false representation of reality. This view is given up in the later period: signs have meaning not because they are distributed in a spatial or quasi-spatial structure, but because they are 'distributed in' a rule-guided activity. Our activities are typically social, and are surrounded by cultural theories, in the way described by post-empiricist epistemology (subsection 1.4.1). In short, meaning is embedded within human social practices and culture.

Whereas the view articulated in the *Tractatus* fits well with the idea that there are signs in the brain, 'picturing' the world, Wittgenstein's later view makes this idea look odd. How can the sign with meaning be in the brain? Is it not rather in practices and culture? It seems that the idea of encoding, and all the information-processing language that goes along with it, might be something like a muddled category mistake.

Considerations along these Wittgensteinian lines have been made by various philosophers, such as Hacker (1987).[15] After quoting distinguished biologists and psychologists working within the information-processing paradigm, Hacker writes (1987, p. 488):

> The general conception at work involves the supposition that the brain has a *language* of its own, which consists of *symbols* that *represent* things. It uses the *vocabulary* of this language to *encode information* and it produces *descriptions* of what is seen . . . .

This general conception is then dismissed as a 'mythology of neural processes' (Hacker 1987, p. 490).

So on what grounds? Hacker goes on to remind us of familiar facts about language, to do with natural languages, the speakers being human, showing rule-following skills, using words in the course of diverse activities, explaining meanings, correcting errors, etc. He continues (1987, p. 492):

> I mention these platitudes because they are easily forgotten. For if one remembers them it should be obvious that it *makes no sense* to speak of the brain as having or using a language. Only of a creature that can perform acts of speech does it make sense to say that it has, understands, uses, a language. But it is literally unintelligible to suggest that a brain, let alone a part of a brain, might ask a question, have or express an intention, make a decision, describe a sunset, . . .
> To have, and to have mastered a language is to have a repertoire of behaviour.
> . . . But the repertoire of 'behaviour' of a brain or part of a brain does not lie on the same parameters as the behavioural repertoire of language users.

Hacker concludes that neurophysiologists and biological scientists are muddled, conceptually confused, etc. (1987, p. 500, *et passim*).

This sort of objection would of course silence just about the whole of behavioural/ brain science.

2.6.2 Agreed, but still . . .

The objection presented above is based on something correct, and endorsed in the essay, namely the broadly Wittgensteinian view that meaning is grounded in social practices, embedded in culture. But, as against Hacker's line of argument, we propose that this view of meaning can be combined with the information-processing paradigm, and in particular with the claim that meaning is encoded in the brain. Indeed we have to stress here that the encoding thesis *has been explicated and defended* by appeal to the broadly Wittgensteinian view of meaning just referred to.

Throughout this chapter we have steered away from the idea that there are signs (signs with syntactic structure) in the brain doing the representing, as it were, all on their own. This strong formulation of the encoding thesis is in fact what provokes the various objections to the thesis, which has therefore to be rescued from it. The strong formulation of the encoding thesis runs into trouble because it is incompatible with connectionist models (section 2.2), because it tries to reduce (neural) semantics to (neural) syntax (section 2.3), and because it fails to explain why (neural) semantic properties rather than syntactic properties do any work in the causal explanation of behaviour (Section 2.4). At each stage of the defence of the encoding thesis we have had to restrain the presumption that meaning, specifically meaning encoded in the brain, is essentially a matter of syntactic, language-like, structures, and to substitute the view that meaning essentially pertains to rule-guided activity, or again, of intentional agent/environment interactions.

The route we have taken to the notion of neural encoding has several steps. The first step, argued for throughout Chapter 1, is that explanation of action in terms of meaningful states has predictive power; the second is the conclusion of that chapter, that such explanation is causal; the third is the assumption taken for granted in this chapter that the brain causally regulates action, all of which can be made compatible on the methodological assumption that the meaning (information) that regulates action is encoded in the brain. This route to the encoding thesis does not end at 'sentences in the head', but with the proposal that the brain encodes meaning *somehow or other*. This proposal is of course much weaker empirically, but this is appropriate enough given its philosophical, conceptual origins. But in return for (appropriate) empirical vagueness, it makes the strong a priori claim that an adequacy condition of any theory of encoding is that the critical connection between meaning and the regulation of action is not lost. The strong interpretation of encoding, which posits signs with syntactic structure in the brain doing the representing, inevitably neglects this connection between meaning and action, and indeed runs the risk of neglecting meaning (in favour of syntax) altogether.

Thus we have, through sections 2.2–2.4 of this chapter, proposed a notion of meaning *and of encoded meaning* as being essentially involved with activity. This same idea was, of course, used again to protect the encoding thesis in Section 2.5, in considering whether meaning supervenes on brain states.

In brief, then, the claim that the brain encodes meaning, as defended and explicated here, far from being incompatible with the kind of view of meaning proposed by Wittgenstein, actually presupposes it.

Rule-following activity, activity which can be performed 'rightly' or 'wrongly', is what warrants the attribution of meaning to the agent, or to the brain, which as a matter of fact is the material system most of all involved in the regulation of action. To take a relatively simple case, we attribute to a rat, and in particular to the rat's brain, information about the maze, on the grounds that the animal relates to the maze in an ordered, methodical, goal-directed way. In the indefinitely more complicated case of human beings, actions have many and various meanings, and these include (perceived) relationships to realities defined by theories embedded deep in the culture. As remarked at the end of the previous section, in order to understand the actions of such as a physicist, or tribal magician, we have to understand their theories about reality and their relation to it, for these theories guide what the people do. In brief, action is regulated here by meaning as much as in the much simpler cases, and there is as much reason to invoke meanings encoded in the brain.

But of course in this context it is clear, as stressed throughout the chapter, that it is not the brain in isolation which carries meaning, but the brain in its role as regulating action. If the brain is described in intrinsic, non-relational, non-intentional terms, in terms of physical or physico-chemical processes, without reference to information-processing, then all that can explained and predicted is intrinsic, non-relational, non-intentional behaviour: the motion of the body, not the meaning of the act, which depends on nature and culture. If one is to explain and predict behaviour in relation to these realities, then the regulating neural processes have to be credited with information relating to them.

Before leaving the current objection to the idea of encoding, presented in the preceding subsection, one further point should be remarked, concerning the attribution of intentionality to parts as opposed to the whole.

While folk psychology in general attributes meaningful states to the person, cognitive psychology need not be so restricted. The concept of encoded meaning does not have to be based in the activity of the whole person, but can be based in the interaction between functional subsystems and their local environments. If an information-processing system is described as encoding information, this description is based on interaction between the system and whatever it is that the encoded information is about. This 'environment' may be the scene of action of the person as a whole, in which case the proper subject of the ascription of information is the person as a whole, and is to subpersonal systems only secondarily. The belief that this is the bus to Clapham, for example, belongs to the person, and only thereby to a subpersonal system, in particular to the brain. But the 'environment' may be less than the scene of action of the person as a whole, in which case the proper subject of the ascription is some subpersonal system, and is to the person only secondarily. To cite examples that will be discussed later, in Chapter 5, it is in this sense the retina that encodes information about light intensities (and only thereby the person); or again, it is the baroreceptors of the cardiovascular system (and probably not the person at all) that pick up information about blood pressure. And so on.

The idea that meaning belongs to the person as a whole, participating in cultural practices, and not to the brain, is linked to the 'hermeneutic' separation of meaning from anything familiar in the sciences, as if there were nothing like it lower down, in the phylogenetic scale for example, or in biological subsytems. This hermeneutic idea is the alternative to the approach being adopted and explored in this essay, which emphasizes continuities rather than dichotomies. In the present context the claim is that some meaning, and certainly some information, can be attributed to something less than the whole.

2.7 SUMMARY

The main claim of the first chapter was that explanations of action in terms of meaningful mental states are effective in prediction, and the inference was drawn that such explanations are causal. The main burden of the present chapter has been to reconcile this conclusion with the material causation of behaviour by the brain.

In Section 2.1 we saw that mind–brain identity theory promises a quick reconciliation, but it runs against several obstacles, chief of which in the present context is that mental states have intentionality while brain states arguably do not. It was suggested, on the other hand, that brain processes can be legitimately regarded as carrying (encoding) information, and indeed are so regarded at the interface between cognitive psychology and neuroscience, particularly for the purpose of explaining the role of the brain in regulating action. Subsequent sections were devoted to explication of this idea that brain states encode information, or meaning, and in particular to defending it from various lines of thought much discussed in the current literature.

In Section 2.2 we considered Fodor's language of thought hypothesis, according to which there are sentence-like structures in the brain, which serve both to encode meaning and to regulate (cause) behaviour. However, as noted in subsection 2.2.2, this particularly literal reading of the encoding thesis is apparently incompatible with connectionist models of cognitive function and its implementation in the brain. In these models, there are, at least at a micro-level of analysis, no physical (hardware) counterparts to meaningful symbols, or sentences. The relation between connectionist models of cognitive function and those of traditional, symbolic AI, the ones conducive to the language of thought hypothesis, is complex. The philosophical assumption relevant here is that, if attribution of meaningful mental states is valid, in particular if it affords causal explanations of action, then such attributions must pick out corresponding states in the brain. This assumption can be combined with affirmation of its antecedent in order to derive its consequent, in the (sophisticated) form of the language of thought hypothesis. Alternatively, the assumption can be combined with denial of its consequent (on connectionist grounds), leading to denial of its antecedent, to the 'elimination' of folk psychology. Either way the assumption is problematic, and reasons for rejecting it were presented in Section 2.2.3. Psychological descriptions attribute meaningful states to the brain, or better, to the person as agent. However, they are based on (high-level) regularities in organism–environment interactions, and it is on this basis that they predict such interactions well (enough). There is no reason to suppose that in accomplishing this task, psychological descriptions also have to pick out neural structures that correspond to them. The assumption that folk psychology seeks to define the neural structures that serve information-processing and action, still more that this is its primary aspiration, is based on a misconception of the logic of psychological description, and hence of its ontological commitments.

The upshot of these considerations is that the brain can be said to encode meaning, or information, though not because there is a one–one correspondence between meaningful states and neural states. The language of meaning and of encoded meaning is based in organism–environment interactions, and can be applied to the brain only in so far as the brain serves in the regulation of those interactions. The main claim of the chapter—that meaningful mental causation can be reconciled with neural causation by appeal to the idea that the brain encodes meaning—can thus be preserved, though with these qualifications.

We turned next to related issues in AI theory, concerning the relation between syntax and semantics. In Section 2.3 we considered Searle's well-known 'Chinese room argument' against the conflation of semantics with syntax: symbol-manipulation is not enough for intentionality. As to what is, we invoke again the claim, as throughout the essay, that intentionality is grounded in activity. Made in terms of semantics and syntax, the point would be that the 'symbols' that carry meaning must be essentially involved in the mediation of sensorimotor pathways.

The considerations in the next two sections, 2.4. and 2.5, have to do particularly with the idea that meaning encoded in the brain plays a causal role. This claim about causality is, as indicated in the first section, the main rationale of the encoding thesis. In Section 2.4 we consider a line of argument pervasive in the literature, the main thrust of which is that it would have to be neural syntax that causes behaviour, not the alleged neural semantics, because only the former is local to the effects. Semantic properties, so the argument runs, are about distal features and therefore cannot be causes. Our reply is that locally defined neural causes will have locally defined effects, namely motor behaviour which is not about the environment. By contrast, causal explanation of intentional behaviour has to cite intentional causes, causes that are about what the behaviour is about. Such causes are identified in non-local terms, though they are local to the behaviour that they regulate. This combination of intentional features with local realization is, of course, precisely the point of the thesis that meaning (information) is encoded in the brain.

We turned in Section 2.5 to a distinct though related argument which would refute the main proposal, an extremely influential argument based on Putnam's so-called twin-Earth thought-experiments. It leads to the conclusion that 'meanings ain't in the head', and hence (among other things) are not causes of behaviour. The argument, presented in some detail in subsections 2.5.2 and 2.5.3, seeks to establish the claim that mental states as individuated by meaningful content can (be imagined to) vary while brain states remain the same, this variation being due to variation in the represented states of affairs. This claim has been accepted by most commentators, leading either to the more or less reluctant dismissal of folk psychological meaning as being irrelevant to causal explanation, or else to the problematic attempt to define a 'narrow' as opposed to a 'broad' content. Putnam's argument was criticized in the remainder of the section. The standard reading of the twin-Earth thought-experiments, the one that supports the conclusion that meanings 'ain't in the head', posits differences in mental contents which are not reflected in behavioural differences, in particular, not in discriminative behaviours. This dissociation between mental content and behavioural criteria, whatever can be said for it on other grounds, is at odds with what is required in the context of a cognitive-behavioural science. In this context, the postulate of meaningful states serves the purpose of explaining and predicting action, in particular discriminative behaviour, and is otherwise unjustified. The implication is that meaningful content is to be defined essentially in terms of organism–environment interactions. Given this kind of definition of content, several features of folk psychological meaning which are problematic or incompatible according to the standard reading of the *doppelgänger* thought-experiments appear as valid. Folk psychological meaning, intentionality in general, is and should be all of the following: 'world-involving', supervenient on neural states which regulate action, and invoked in the causal explanation of action.

We considered in Section 2.6 a Wittgensteinian kind of objection to the encoding thesis. The objection emphasizes the basis of meaning in human practices and culture, and resists the idea that meaning is 'in the brain'. The underlying point is accepted, and indeed has been emphasized throughout the chapter to rescue the encoding thesis from the various objections to it. However, the language of encoding, appropriately understood, remains valid in this context. Meaningful psychological 'states' are manifested in action. It is possible to describe these states as being encoded in the brain, but this description presupposes that the brain is functioning within the person, and that the person is acting in the environment. In this sense, the subject of psychological states is primarily the person (as agent). Nevertheless it is possible and legitimate to say that the brain encodes these meaningful states: this is the way in which brain function has to be described when the task is to explain how it regulates action.

The main claim of the present chapter, that meaningful mental causation is compatible with neural causation, is thus defended against various lines of alleged refutation. Attempts to invalidate the notion of causation by meaningful mental states in effect assume that such states are either too tied to the subject or too tied to the object, with interaction between the two being ignored in both cases. The assumption has been that meaningful states have to be found in the brain (in neural syntax), independently of action, or else defined by what is outside the brain, or person, again independent of action. The replies to the objections, in Sections 2.2–2.5, were all variations on the theme that meaning (intentionality) has to do essentially with action, that is, with higher-order invariants in organism–environment interactions. For in this case there is no need to find symbolic syntax in the brain divorced from the regulation of action, and nor can meaning be defined in terms of reality independent of the sensitivity of the representing being.

The claim that attribution of mental states with meaningful content is based on, and is concerned with, regularities in organism–environment interactions hangs together with the point, made in the first chapter, that such attribution serves to predict action. This theory-driven predictive power apparently makes unavoidable the conclusion that explanations that invoke meaningful mental states are in some sense causal, and it lies at the basis of replies to all arguments to the contrary. The conclusion stands, but we have so far said little about 'in what sense'! Consideration of this major issue will occupy us in chapters 4 and 5. In the next chapter we turn to an issue that has been pressing more or less strongly in the discussions so far, namely relativity and the problem of objectivity.

NOTES

1. These issues to be addressed in this chapter, along with many ramifications neglected here, are the subjects of a large and expanding literature. Selective references will be made as we proceed. Useful collections of papers covering many of the issues to be raised include Silvers (1989), Tomberlin (1989, 1990),

Cole *et al.* (1990), Lycan (1990), Loewer and Rey (1991), and Heil and Mele (1993).

2. Davidson has emphasized the holistic and normative characteristics of mental state ascriptions, in support of his doctrine of 'anomalous monism' (Davidson 1980, Essays 11–13). Commentary includes Vermazen and Hintikka (1985), Antony (1989), Evnine (1991), Bickle (1992), and Malpas (1992). The irreducibility of the mental to the physical, and the problems of reducibility to the physical in general, are the subjects of a large literature: recent papers and collections include Crane (1990), Lennon (1990), Montogomery (1990), Charles and Lennon (1992), and Robinson (1993).

3. On points in this paragraph see, for example, Block (1980*b*) and other papers in Block (1980*a*), Part Three. A recent discussion of multiple realization is given by Kim (1992).

4. AI is a mathematical and experimental discipline of great complexity, and is beyond the concerns as well as the competence of the present essay, except to the limited extent indicated in the text. The literature in and surrounding AI is extensive and rapidly expanding. A useful sourcebook is Partridge and Wilks (1990). On AI applications to cognitive psychology see, for example, Boden (1988, 1989), Johnson-Laird (1993), and Broadbent (1993). Collections of papers on philosophical issues in AI theory include Graubard (1988), Boden (1990), and Cummins and Pollock (1991). Further references will be made to selected topics below.

5. Detailed consideration of connectionism is beyond the scope of this essay. Source material and material on applications in neurobiology and psychology include McClelland *et al.* (1986), Rumelhart *et al.* (1986), Boden (1988, 1989), Morris (1989), Arbib and Robinson (1990), Hanson and Olsen (1990), Bechtel and Abrahamsen (1991), Hinton (1991), Quinlan (1991), Davis (1992), Nadel *et al.* (1992), Broadbent (1993), and Johnson-Laird (1993). Discussion of connectionism and its philosophical implications may be found in Churchland (1986), Graubard (1988), Clark (1989), Bechtel (1990), Boden (1990), Cummins and Pollock (1991), Ramsey *et al.* (1991), and Churchland and Sejnowski (1992).

   The main point at issue in the present context is the very general one that in connectionist models there are no, or no clear, counterparts to (meaningful) symbols. This fact can be developed into an argument against Fodor's Language of Thought hypothesis particularly, and generally against the idea that folk psychological meaning has anything corresponding to it in the brain, and hence, anything corresponding to it at all. This line of thought and replies to it are the subject of the remainder of this section.

6. On the possible relations between the two kinds of model see, for example, Fodor and Pylyshyn (1988), Russell (1988), Smolensky (1988), Clark (1989, 1989–90, 1990), Hawthorne (1989), and Bechtel (1990). Power and Brewin (1991) discuss the issues particularly from the perspective of clinical psychology.

7. For another formulation see, for example, Jacob (1992). Generally this line of thought pervades the literature around Putnam's claim that 'meaning ain't in the head', to be considered in the next section.

8. See Wittgenstein (1921), for example 2.01–2.04, 2.1–2.2. Secondary sources include, for example, Folgelin (1976), Bolton (1979), and Pears (1987).

9. Recent critical commentaries on the issues around Putnam's claim include McGinn (1989) and Bilgrami (1992). Selected further references relevant to points discussed in the text will be cited as we proceed. It is fair to say that the twin-Earth thought-experiments, sketched after this introductory subsection, represent a peculiarly philosophical methodology, not user over-friendly to non-philosophers. This introductory subsection links the issues to the rest of the chapter, and some main points are summarized at the end of the chapter. Perhaps the best known application to theoretical psychology is Fodor's 'methodological solipsism' (1980), which will be discussed in the fourth chapter (subsection 4.4.2). The crucial point for the present essay is that the twin-Earth thought-experiments have been widely accepted in the philosophical community as showing that meaningful mental states do not supervene on brain states and hence cannot be causes of behaviour. Any proposal that there is causality here has to find a way around or through this standard reading of the thought-experiments, and this is the main aim of the current section.

10. This brief formulation of supervenience is Fodor's (1987, p. 30), and suffices in the present context. There are alternative, related definitions; see, for example, Stich (1983), Kim (1984), and Lennon (1990). The notion of supervenience of the mental on the physical has been invoked to accomodate anti-reductionist considerations of the kind cited in subsection 2.1.3, and to save some plausibility for physicalism (see, for example, Von Kutschera 1992; Poland 1994). Our interest in this section is the supervenience of mental content and specifically the causal role of content.

11. Putnam's original argument had a form which may be summarized as follows. Consider two plausible assumptions: first, that knowing the meaning of a term is just a matter of being in a certain psychological (dispositional) state, and secondly, that the meaning (intension) of a term determines its extension. From these it follows that the psychological state that consitutes knowing the meaning of a term determines the extension of the term. But this is the claim that the thought-experiments show to be false, demonstrating the possibility, in the case of using words, of the same psychological (subjective, mind/brain) state, but different extension. In brief, in the sense of meaning which determines extension, meaning ain't in the head (Putnam 1975, especially pp. 215–27). This line of thought was turned into a problem for the cognitive science explanatory paradigm, which invokes cognitive states as having a causal role dependent on their meaning, by Fodor (1982). This problem is our main concern and will be considered in the next subsection.

12. Dale (1990) also criticizes Stich's attempt to run the causal story with only syntax and no semantics. The general problem for the narrow content theorist of describing either content or behaviour in a useful, or indeed in any, way is well-stated by Owens (1987). A later version of narrow content theory which avoids this sort of criticism has been proposed by Fodor (1987, 1991) and will be discussed in the next subsection.

13. The contrast drawn in this subsection between behavioural criteria of mental

content and the one presupposed in the standard reading of the *doppelgänger* thought-experiments was anticipated in Chapter 1 in connection with self-knowledge and error (subsection 1.4.3, Note 16).

The connected proposal that the mental content regulating behaviour is defined in terms of interactions is approached by another route, by way of causal to functional semantics, in Chapter 4. This proposal has some connections with Dennett's notion of the 'notional world' of the organism/agent in his complex discussion in 'Beyond belief' (Dennett 1982).

14. This statement and defence of the supervenience thesis ignores the issue of demonstrative terms, such as 'this' and 'that'. It is likely that demonstratives play a critical role is specifying mental content for the purpose of explaining action (Peacocke 1981). But this specification by reference to something external is not incompatible with supervenience, as least so far as the *doppelgänger* thought-experiments are concerned. It is true that my replica cannot see, think of, or touch *this* (very same) keyboard. But by the same token, he does not have this (very same) brain. In these cases, in the sense in which *doppelgänger* have different mental contents they have different brains as well, and there is nothing of interest here about supervenience (encoding, causality, etc.).

15. See also Hamlyn (1990) for distinct though related criticisms of the information-processing cognitive science paradigm from a broadly Wittgensteinian perspective, and compare also Mendonca (1988).

REFERENCES

Adams, F. (1993*a*). Fodor's modal argument. *Philosophical Psychology*, 6, 41–56.

Adams, F. (1993*b*). Reply to Russow. *Philosophical Psychology*, 6, 63–5.

Antony, L. (1989). Anomalous monism and the problem of explanatory force. *Philosophical Review*, 98, 153–87.

Arbib, M. A. and Robinson, J. A. (ed.) (1990). *Natural and artificial parallel computation*. MIT Press, Cambridge, Mass.

Bechtel, W. (1990). Connectionism and the philosophy of mind: an overview. In *Mind and cognition: A reader*, (ed. W. G. Lycan), pp. 252–73. Blackwell, Oxford.

Bechtel, W. and Abrahamsen, A. (1991). *Connectionism and the mind: an introduction to parallel processing in networks*. Blackwell, Oxford.

Bickle, J. (1992). Mental anomaly and the new mind–brain reductionism. *Philosophy of Science*, 59, 217–30.

Bilgrami, A. (1992). *Belief and meaning: the unity and locality of mental content*. Blackwell, Oxford.

Block, N. (ed.) (1980*a*). *Readings in philosophy of psychology*, Vol. I. Methuen, London.

Block, N. (1980*b*). Introduction: what is functionalism? In *Readings in philosophy of psychology*, (ed. N. Block), Vol. I, pp. 171–84. Methuen, London.

Block, N. (1991). What narrow content is not. In *Meaning in mind: Fodor and his critics*, (ed. B. Loewer and G. Rey), pp. 33–64. Blackwell, Oxford.

Boden, M. (1988). *Computer models of mind*. Cambridge University Press, Cambridge.

Boden, M. A. (ed.) (1989). *Artificial intelligence in psychology: interdisciplinary essays*. MIT Press, Cambridge, Mass.

Boden, M. (ed.) (1990). *The philosophy of artificial intelligence*. Oxford University Press, Oxford.

Bolton, D. (1979). *An approach to Wittgenstein's philosophy*. Macmillan, London.

Bolton, D. (1982). Life-form and idealism. In *Idealism, past and present*, (ed. G. Vesey), pp. 269–84. Cambridge University Press, Cambridge.

Boyd, R. (1980). Materialism without reductionism: what physicalism does not entail. In *Readings in philosophy of psychology*, (ed. N. Block), Vol. I, pp. 67–106. Methuen, London.

Broadbent, D. (ed.) (1993). *The simulation of human intelligence*. Blackwell, Oxford.

Brodal, P. (1991). *The central nervous system: structure and function*. Oxford University Press, Oxford.

Burge, T. (1979). Individualism and the mental. *Midwest Studies in Philosophy*, **IV**, 73–121.

Burge, T. (1982*a*). Two thought experiments reviewed. *Notre Dame Journal of Formal Logic*, **23**, 284–93.

Burge, T. (1982*b*). Other bodies. In *Thought and object*, (ed. A. Woodfield), pp. 97–120. Clarendon Press, Oxford.

Burge, T. (1986*a*). Cartesian error and the objectivity of perception. In *Subject, thought and context*, (ed. C. Pettit, and J. McDowell), pp. 117–36. Oxford University Press, Oxford.

Burge, T. (1986*b*). Intellectual norms and foundations of mind. *Journal of Philosophy*, **83**, 697–720.

Burge, T. (1986*c*). Individualism and psychology. *Philosophical Review*, **95**, 3–45.

Burge, T. (1989). Individuation and causation in psychology. *Pacific Philosophical Quarterly*, **70**, 303–22.

Charles, D. and Lennon, K. (ed.) (1992). *Reduction, explanation, and realism*. Clarendon Press, Oxford.

Churchland, P. M. (1989). *A neurocomputational perspective. The nature of mind and the structure of science*. MIT Press, Cambridge, Mass.

Churchland, P. S. (1986). *Neurophilosophy: towards a unified science of the mind–brain*. MIT Press, Cambridge, Mass.

Churchland, P. S. and Sejnowski, T. J. (1992). *The computational brain*. MIT Press, Cambridge, Mass.

Clark, A. (1988). Critical Notice of Fodor's *Psychosemantics*. *Mind*, **97**, 605–17.

Clark, A. (1989). *Microcognition: philosophy, cognitive science and parallel distributed processing*. MIT Press, Cambridge, Mass.

Clark, A. (1989–90). Connectionist minds. *Proceedings of the Aristolelian Society*, **90**, 83–102.

Clark, A. (1990). Connectionism, competence, and explanation. In *The philosophy of artificial intelligence*, (ed. M. Boden), pp. 281–308. Oxford University Press, Oxford.

Cole D., Fetzer, J. and Rankin, T. (ed.) (1990). *Philosophy, mind, and cognitive enquiry*. Kluwer, Dordrecht.

Crane, T. (1990). There is no question of physicalism. *Mind*, 99, 185–206.

Crane, T. (1991). All the difference in the world. *Philosophical Quarterly*, 41, 1–25.

Cummins, R. and Pollock, J. (1991). *Philosophy and AI: essays at the interface*. MIT Press, Cambridge, Mass.

Dale, J. (1990). Intentionality and Stich's theory of brain sentence syntax. *Philosophical Quarterly*, 40, 169–82.

Davidson, D. (1980). *Essays on actions and events*. Clarendon Press, Oxford.

Davidson, D. (1989). What is present to the mind. In *The mind of Donald Davidson*, (ed. J. Brandl and W. L. Gombocz), pp. 3–18. Rodopi, Amsterdam.

Davis, S. (ed.) (1992). *Connectionism: theory and practice*. Oxford University Press, Oxford.

Dennett, D. (1982). Beyond Belief. In *Thought and object*, (ed. A. Woodfield), pp. 1–95. Clarendon Press, Oxford. (Reprinted with an addition in Dennett, D. (1987). *The intentional stance*, pp. 117–211. MIT Press, Cambridge, Mass.)

Dretske, F. (1988). *Explaining behaviour: reasons in a world of causes*. MIT Press, Cambridge, Mass.

Evnine, S. (1991). *Donald Davidson*. Polity Press, Cambridge.

Fodor, J. (1975). *The language of thought*. Crowell, New York.

Fodor, J. (1980). Methodological solipsism considered as a research strategy in cognitive psychology. With peer commentary. *The Behavioural and Brain Sciences*, 3, 63–109.

Fodor, J. (1982). Cognitive science and the twin-Earth problem. *Notre Dame Journal of Formal Logic*, 23, 116–17.

Fodor, J. (1987). *Psychosemantics*. MIT Press, Cambridge, Mass.

Fodor, J. (1991). A modal argument for narrow content. *Journal of Philosophy*, 87, 5–26.

Fodor, J. and Pylyshyn, Z. (1988). Connectionism and cognitive architecture. *Cognition*, 28, 3–71.

Folgelin, R. (1976). *Wittgenstein*. Routledge and Kegan Paul, London.

Francescotti, R. (1991). Externalism and Marr's theory of vision. *British Journal for the Philosophy of Science*, 42, 227–38.

Graubard, S. R. (ed.) (1988). *The artificial intelligence debate: false starts, real foundations*. MIT Press, Cambridge, Mass.

Gray, J. A. (1987). Mind–brain identity as a scientific hypothesis: a second look. In *Mindwaves. Thoughts on intelligence, identity and consciousness*, (ed. C. Blakemore and S. Greenfield), pp. 461–83. Blackwell, Oxford.

Hacker, P. (1987). Languages, minds and brain. In *Mindwaves. Thoughts on intelligence, identity and consciousness*, (ed. C. Blakemore and S. Greenfield, pp. 485–505. Blackwell, Oxford.

Hamlyn, D. W. (1990). *In and out of the black box*. Blackwell, Oxford.

Hanson, S. J. and Olsen, C. L. (1990). *Connectionist modeling and brain function: the developing interface*. MIT Press, Cambridge, Mass.

Harnad, S. (1989). Minds, machines and Searle. *Journal of Experimental and Theoretical Artificial Intelligence*, 1, 5–25.

Harnad, S. (1990). The symbol grounding problem. *Physica*, D 42, 335–46.

Hawthorne, J. (1989). On the compatibility of connectionist and classical models. *Philosophical Psychology*, 2, 5–16.

Heil, J. and Mele, A. (ed.) (1993). *Mental causation*. Clarendon Press, Oxford.

Hinton, G. E. (ed.) (1991). *Connectionist symbol processing*. MIT Press, Cambridge, Mass.

Hornsby, J. (1986). Physicalist thinking and conceptions of behaviour. In *Subject, thought and context*, (ed. P. Pettit and J. McDowell), pp. 95–115. Clarendon, Oxford.

Jackson, F. and Pettit, P. (1988). Functionalism and broad content. *Mind*, 97, 381–400.

Jacob, P. (1992). Externalism and mental causation. *Proceedings of the Aristotelian Society*, 92, 203–19.

Johnson-Laird, P. (1993). *The computer and the mind: an introduction to cognitive science*, (2nd edn revised). Fontana, London.

Kim, J. (1984). Concepts of supervenience. *Philosophy and Phenomenological Research*, 65, 153–76.

Kim, J. (1991). Dretske on how reasons explain behavior. In *Dretske and his critics*, (ed. B. McLaughlin), pp. 52–72. Blackwell, Oxford.

Kim, J. (1992). Multiple realization and the metaphysics of reduction. *Philosophy and Phenomenological Research*, 52, 1–26.

Lennon, K. (1990). *Explaining human action*. Duckworth, London.

Loewer, B. and Rey, G. (ed.) (1991). *Meaning in mind: Fodor and his critics*. Blackwell, Oxford.

Lycan, W. G. (ed.) (1990). *Mind and cognition. A reader*. Blackwell, Oxford.

McClelland, J. L., Rumelhart, D. E. and the PDP Research Group (1986). *Parallel distributed processing: explorations in the microstructure of cognition* Vol. 2. *Psychological and biological models*. MIT Press, Cambridge Mass.

McGinn, C. (1982). The structure of content, In *Thought and object*, (ed. A. Woodfield), pp. 207–58. Clarendon Press, Oxford.

McGinn, C. (1989). *Mental content*. Blackwell, Oxford.

McGinn, C. (1991). Conceptual causation: some elementary reflections. *Mind*, 100, 573–86.

McLaughlin, B. (ed.) (1991). *Dretske and his critics*. Blackwell, Oxford.

Maloney, J. C. (1990). *The mundane matter of the mental language*. Cambridge University Press, Cambridge.

Malpas, J. E. (1992). *Donald Davidson and the mirror of meaning: holism, truth, interpretation*. Cambridge University Press, Cambridge.

Manfredi, P. (1993). Two routes to narrow content: both dead ends. *Philosophical Psychology*, 6, 3–21.

Mendonca, W. P. (1988). Brain and mind: on the sequences of conceptual confusion in cognitive psychology. *Epistemologia*, 11, 29–54.

Montgomery, R. (1990). The reductionist ideal in cognitive psychology. *Synthese*, 85, 279–314.

Morris, R. G. M. (ed.) (1989). *Parallel distributed processing: implications for psychology and neurobiology*. Clarendon Press, Oxford.

Nadel, L. N., Cooper, L. A., Culicover, P. and Harnish, R. M. (ed.) (1992). *Neural connections, mental computations*. MIT Press, Cambridge, Mass.

Newell, A. (1980). Physical symbol systems. *Cognitive Science*, 4, 135–83.

Newton, N. (1988). Machine understanding and the Chinese room. *Philosophical Psychology*, 1, 207–16.

Owens, (1987). In defense of a different doppelganger *Philosophical Review*, 96, 521–54.

Partridge, D. and Wilks, Y. (ed.) (1990). *The foundations of artificial intelligence: a sourcebook*. Cambridge University Press, Cambridge.

Peacocke, C. (1981). Demonstrative thought and psychological explanation. *Synthese*, XLIX, 187–217.

Pears, D. (1987). *The false prison: A study of the development of Wittgenstein's philosophy*, vol. 1. Clarendon Press, Oxford.

Piaget, J. (1950). *The child's construction of reality*. Routledge and Kegan Paul, London.

Poland, J. (1994). *Physicalism. The philosophical foundations*. Clarendon Press, Oxford.

Power, M. and Brewin, C. (1991). From Freud to cognitive science: a contemporary account of the unconscious. *British Journal of Clinical Psychology*, 30, 289–310.

Putnam, H. (1975). The meaning of 'meaning'. In *Mind, language and reality*, pp. 215–71. Cambridge University Press, Cambridge.

Pylyshyn, Z. W. (1980). Computation and cognition: issues in the foundations of cognitive science, with peer commentary, *Behavioral and Brain Sciences*, 3, 111–69.

Pylyshyn, Z. W. (1984). *Computation and cognition*. MIT Press, Cambridge Mass.

Quinlan, P. (1991). *Connectionism and psychology*. Harvester, New York.

Ramsey, W., Stich, S., and Garan, J. (1990). Connectionism, eliminativism and the future of folk psychology. In *Philosophy, mind, and cognitive enquiry*, (ed. D. Cole, J. Fetzer, and T. Rankin) pp. 117–44. Kluwer, Dordrecht.

Ramsey, W., Stich, S. and Rumelhart, D. (ed.) (1991). *Philosophy and connectionist theory*. Lawrence Erlbaum Associates, Hillsdale, N. J.

Rey, G. (1986). What's really going on in Searle's 'Chinese Room'? *Philosophical Studies*, 50, 169–85.

Robinson, H. (ed.) (1993). *Objections to physicalism*. Clarendon Press, Oxford.

Rowlands, M. (1989). Discussion of Jackson & Pettit. *Mind*, 98, 269–76.

Rumelhart, D. E., McClelland, J. L. and the PDP Research Group (1986). *Parallel distributed processing: explorations in the microstructure of cognition*, Vol. 1. *Foundations*. MIT Press, Cambridge, Mass.

Russell, J. (1988). Cognisance and cognitive science. Part one: the generality constraint. *Philosophical Psychology*, 1, 235–58.

Russow, L. (1984). Unlocking the Chinese room. *Nature and System*, 6, 221–7.

Russow, L. (1993). Fodor, Adams, and causal properties. *Philosophical Psychology*, 6, 57–62

Searle, J. (1980). Minds, brains and programs. With peer commentary. *Behavioral and Brain Sciences*, 3, 417–57.

Searle, J. (1982). The Chinese room revisited. *Behavioral and Brain Sciences*, 5, 345–8.

Searle, J. (1984). *Minds, brains and science*. BBC Publications, London.

Searle, J. (1987). Minds and brains without programs. In *Mindwaves. Thoughts on intelligence, identity and consciousness*, (ed. C. Blakemore and S. Greenfield), pp. 209–33. Blackwell, Oxford.

Silvers, S. (ed.) (1989). *Rerepresentation. Readings in the philosophy of mental representation*. Kluwer, Dordrecht.

Smolensky, P. (1988). On the proper treatment of connectionism, *Behavioral and Brain Sciences*, **11**, 1–74.

Stich, S. (1983). *From folk psychology to cognitive science*. MIT Press, Cambridge, Mass.

Tomberlin, J. E. (ed.) (1989). *Philosophical Perspectives, 3. Philosophy of Mind and Action Theory*. Ridgeview, Atascadero, CA.

Tomberlin, J. E. (ed.) (1990). *Philosophical Perspectives, 4. Action Theory and Philosophy of Mind*. Ridgeview, Atascadero, CA.

Vermazen, B. and Hintikka, M. (ed.) (1985). *Essays on Davidson: Actions and Events*. Clarendon, Oxford.

Von Kutschera, F. (1992). Supervenience and reductionism. *Erkenntnis*, **36**, 333–43.

Warmbrod, K. (1989). Beliefs and sentences in the head. *Synthese*, **79**, 201–30.

Wilson, R. (1992). Individualism, causal powers, and explanation. *Philosophical Studies*, **68**, 103–9.

Wittgenstein, L. (1921). *Tractatus logico-philosophicus*, (trans. D. F. Pears and B. F. McGuiness, 1961). Routledge and Kegan Paul, London.

Wittgenstein, L. (1953). *Philosophical investigations*, (ed. G. E. M. Anscombe and R. Rhees, trans. G. E. M. Anscombe). Blackwell, Oxford.

Wittgenstein, L. (1967). *Zettel*, (ed. G. E. M. Anscombe and G. H. von Wright, trans. G. E. M. Anscombe). Blackwell, Oxford.

Wittgenstein, L. (1969). *On certainty, (ed. G. E. M. Anscombe and G. H. von Wright, trans. D. Paul and G. E. M. Anscombe). Blackwell, Oxford.*

3
Relativity in knowledge of mind and meaning; and in knowledge generally

3.1 INTRODUCTION: INTENTIONALITY IS OBSERVER-RELATIVE

To a large extent philosophical preconceptions determine whether or not the theory of knowledge of mind is of scientific interest. In Cartesian theory knowledge of mind other than one's own is problematic, at best an inference from mindless, mechanical behaviour, with no possibility of checking its validity. Such an inference is also scientifically idle: it has no incremental explanatory/predictive value. This position shifts once non-Cartesian assumptions are brought to bear, specifically the assumption that mental states serve in the regulation of intentional activity. The behaviour that signifies mind is already mind-like, characterized by intentionality, and the regulation of action is more epistemically accessible than private, immaterial, parallel processes. In so far as knowledge of mind facilitates prediction of the behaviour of living beings, then it becomes of scientific interest, appearing not only in the methodology of the behavioural sciences, but also among the objects of study. There are developmental issues in the epistemology of mind, along the phylogenetic scale, studied in biology and ethology (Byrne and Whiten 1988; Whiten 1991), and along the ontogenetic scale, studied in developmental psychology (Astington *et al.* 1988; Whiten 1991). Clinical psychology also has an interest in knowledge of mind, specifically radical gaps and errors of various kinds (Fonagy 1991; Baron-Cohen *et al.* 1993; Hobson 1993; see also subsections 1.4.2, 1.4.3, and 8.2.2, pp. 311–12).

However, problematic aspects of knowledge of mind, particularly from the point of view of the sciences, do not disappear easily. It was remarked at the beginning of the previous chapter, in relation to dualism and mind–brain identity theory, that philosophical dichotomies generally are not resolved by dogmatic assertion of one side or the other. Rather, something like a compromise is required, the deeper aspect of which is deconstruction of the terms of the dichotomy. In the present case, the point is that resolution of the problem of knowledge of mind requires deep shifts in seventeenth-century assumptions concerning both knowledge and mind. The latter have already been indicated: mind has to be seen not as a Cartesian parallel process, but as involved in the regulation of intentional activity. Likewise, shifts have to made in traditional epistemological dichotomies, specifically between subjective knowledge (of mind), and objective knowledge (of matter). We shall be working towards a position in which this dichotomy (as a dichotomy) cannot be recognized at all.

Once dualism is abandoned, with the acknowledgement that mind is involved in meaningful behaviour, there is no longer space for a radical scepticism about mind. On the other hand, as noted already in the Preface and chapter 1 (subsection 1.3.8), there arises a different though related problem, concerning the objectivity of perceptions of intentionality. This lack of objectivity, compared with the objectivity in the natural sciences, was one ground of the turn-of-the-century distinction between meaningful and causal connections. Attribution of intentionality tends to be subjective and unreliable, and hence so far inadequate for the purpose of scientific explanation, as noted, for example, by Jaspers in relation to clinical intuition (1923, p. 2). The problem is at least that inter-observer reliability in perceptions of meaningful phenomena can be poor. The corollary is that their (objective) validity is no better. In other words, the appearance of subjectivity in the purported knowledge of the phenomena casts doubt on their objective reality.

In clinical psychology and psychiatry, debate of the problem of objectivity has focused largely on psychoanalytic theory, as has frequently been the case with other problems of meaning. Psychoanalytic theory has been accused of being able to find not only different but mutually incompatible meanings in the same set of phenomena, the implication being that attribution of meaning in the theory has no objective validity (see subsection 1.4.1). The problem of objectivity of meaning is, however, a general one, not confined to psychoanalysis.

A related point is that the problem is not especially about unconscious as opposed to conscious mental states. It is tempting to suppose that attribution of conscious mental states based on subjective self-report is relatively unproblematic, but this assumption is misconceived. It presupposes that subjective self-reports are infallible, and we have already noted in the first chapter (subsection 1.4.3) that this assumption is not generally valid. The problem of determining objective criteria for ascription of mental states cannot be solved just by appeal to what the subject is inclined to say.

Knowledge of mind, and of the intentional behaviour regulated by mental states, is not 'purely objective', like knowledge of the physical movements of bodies. Rather there is an element of subjectivity in our knowledge of mind, as recognized, though exaggerated, by the Cartesian theory. This subjectivity shows up as a variation in attributions of intentionality between observers: different people viewing the same activity may see different patterns of intentionality at work, including the vacuous case of seeing no such patterns. In brief, knowledge of intentionality involves *observer-relativity*. Inevitably this has been cited as among the main reasons why the notion of meaning should have no role in a mature cognitive science (for example, Stich 1983, p. 136; discussed in subsection 1.3.8). The nature and implications of this relativity need explication, and this is the main theme running through this chapter. We approach the problem in two main ways, both already marked out as critical in the first chapter, one concerning theory of mind, and the other rule-following.

Mental states can be 'known' in the sense that they are posits in a theory of behaviour. In other words the idea explored in various ways in the first chapter, that mental states are invoked in order to explain and predict behaviour, constitutes the core of an epistemology. We might expect clear objectivity here, as usually in scientific theories, specially when we think of cognitive learning theory (discussed in subsection 1.2.2). In contrast, perhaps, it is the folk psychological theory of mind, our day-to-day way of knowing the mental states of others (subsection 1.4.2), which shows relativity and subjectivity. There may be, however, something left out by the proposal that knowledge of mind is an exercise in theory, and we consider in the next section an alternative, or complementary, epistemology based in empathy. This theory of knowledge of mind has a long history, but has recently been revived in terms of so-called 'mental simulation'.

Our second approach to the epistemology of mind is via the question of what it means to follow a rule. We shall consider Wittgenstein's arguments to the effect that rule-following involves agreement, specifically participation in a form of life.

Both routes lead to similar conclusions, including that attributions of intentionality depend on the intentional states of the one making the attributions. This observer-relativity of these judgements calls into question their objective validity, as already remarked. The question whether intentional states have objective reality, and if so, of what kind, interacts strongly with issues of brain–mind identity, discussed in the previous chapter. But the discussion in this chapter will focus more on the epistemological problem of the observer-relativity of intentional state ascriptions. This problem will be considered with reference to the relativity involved in the move from the lower-level to the higher-level sciences, from physics through to psychology.

3.2 THEORY OF MIND AND EMPATHY ('MENTAL SIMULATION')

3.2.1 The empirical basis includes intentional behaviour

In the first chapter (subsection 1.2.2) we noted that cognitive psychology posits cognitive states in order to explain and predict goal-directed, flexible behaviour. We went on to remark, in subsection 1.2.5, that folk psychology can be plausibly regarded in a similar light, as being a quasi- or proto-scientific theory used to explain and anticipate behaviour. The behavioural phenomena constitute the empirical basis of cognitive psychological and folk psychological theory: they are evidence for ascription of mental states, and they are what is predicted from such ascriptions.

The empirical basis of any scientific theory should be defined as objectively as possible. This means at least that there should be high levels of agreement between observers as to the empirical facts. Further, it is plausible to require that the empirical basis be defined independently of the theoretical constructs used in its explanation. This may be seen as a special case of the first requirement: observers with competing theories of the phenomena should at least be able to agree on the nature of the evidence which could distinguish between them. In application to the case of cognitive-behavioural science, the fundamental requirement is that there should be high levels of agreement between observers as to what behaviour is being observed. Further, it is plausible to require that behavioural evidence should be definable without explicit or implicit reference to mental states. That is to say, behavioural description should be couched in non-intentional language. These two connected requirements are apparently met by behavioural descriptions of motor and speech acts. The proposal that mental state ascriptions are, or at least should be, for the purposes of cognitive-behavioural science, based on behavioural evidence of this kind constitutes a 'purely objective' epistemology of mind.

The proposal, however, has its problems. Behaviour to which mental state ascriptions are relevant already has intentionality: it cannot be described in non-intentional language (alone). The intentional stance generally explains and predicts behaviour under intentional description, as noted in subsection 1.3.6. This characteristic was discussed further in the second chapter (subsection 2.4.2, 2.5.6) in terms of the 'world-involving' nature of mental states and their role in the causal explanation of behaviour. It was argued that mental states are 'world-involving', defined by reference to (encoded) environmental features, precisely because behaviour itself is world-involving. The *explanandum* of cognitive-behavioural explanation is not isolated motor acts, but is rather interaction between the living being and its environment. Such interactions are patterns extended through time, the actual or attempted achievement of goals, plasticity of mean to ends, depending on circumstances, etc. The terms used to describe these patterns re-appear in specification of the mental (informational) content invoked to explain and predict them. The language is in both cases intentional: mental states are about the environment, but so is behaviour. The implication here is that non-intentional behaviour is inadequate as a basis for ascription of mental states. Or, put differently, the point is that it is only when behaviour is perceived as, or conceived as, intentional, that there is need to postulate regulation by mental states.

The behavioural evidence relevant to any theory of mind already has intentionality, or meaning. It may be anticipated that this bears directly on the issue of reliability of ascriptions of meaningful, mental states. Generally observers agree as to the occurrence or non-occurrence of motor acts, such as the lifting of an arm, or movement from one place to another. On the other hand, in the case of behavioural patterns extended through time and across varying circumstances, manifesting more or less apparent goals, and more or less apparent plasticity of means to ends, etc., it is less obvious that all observers will see the same. In so far as the behavioural evidence includes intentionality, agreement between observers becomes less certain; there is more scope for interpretation.

It can be said that attributions of intentionality involve subjectivity, and are thus not entirely objective. But note how this subjectivity arises. Primarily it arises out of *individual differences* between observers, of a sort that leads to variation in the results of observation. Individual differences are typically on a continuum rather than in dichotomous categories. The implication is that the contrast between 'subjective' and 'objective' ways of knowing is wrongly conceived as a dichotomy, but is rather a matter of degree.

Relativity in ascriptions of intentionality are apparent even in the case of predicting the behaviour of artificially intelligent systems. As generally in the discussion of mind and meaning, many critical points do not turn on the mind/matter distinction, nor on the animate/inanimate distinction, but rather on the distinction between behaviour that is and behaviour that is not functional, rule-guided, mediated by information, etc. Consider the example of the chess-playing computer, used already in the first chapter (subsection 1.3.5). In order to describe its moves in intentional terms we use observation by the senses no less than if we wish to describe just the movements of pieces from squares to squares. However, it is clear that something more is required for the use of intentional descriptions, namely, *knowledge of the game*. In the absence of such knowledge, descriptions and explanations from the intentional stance are unavailable. Someone who is ignorant of the game will be able to record the moves made, but not the logic behind them. In this case, attempts at prediction would remain at the purely 'behavioural' level, proceeding by induction from past observations, and typically this method would have little success, particularly as the game develops. Recognition of intentionality in sequences of moves, the attribution of strategy and the formulation of prediction on that basis, requires familiarity with the game, over and above the ability to see what (physical) movements are being made.

3.2.2 Recognition of intentional behaviour involves empathy

The question arises as to what is involved in knowledge of a game, or generally, any rule-guided, goal-directed activity. There are, broadly speaking, two kinds of answer, with a complicated and contentious relationship between them. One draws on the notion of *theory*. This epistemology has been the one assumed and endorsed through the essay so far. It is highly suited to cognitive science (subsection 1.2.2), belongs clearly with post-empiricist epistemology (subsections 1.4.1–2) and has generated much research in various areas of psychology (section 3.1). The core of this epistemology is that attribution of intentionality is driven by a theory that posits intentional states of various kinds and contents, and interactions among such states and between them and stimuli and activity. There is, however, a different kind of epistemology of intentionality, which has less to do with using theory.

In the case of chess-playing, especially when the game develops beyond a certain stage, into positions so far unencountered, the ability to perceive strategies apparently depends increasingly on the ability to play the game oneself. The recognition of intentionality in the other's moves draws on one's own inclinations to adopt this or that strategy at a given stage in the game. It can be seen here, in this simple case, that something like 'empathy' is involved in the attribution of intentional states. Consider now the more complicated, psychological case. A particular kind of cognitive-affective state has characteristic causes and characteristic expressions in behaviour. An observer who knows the emotion in his or her own case may recognize it in another, and thereby form expectations concerning the other's behaviour. In contrast, the observer who is unfamiliar with the emotion in herself will at best be able to record the other's behaviour, and not the emotion as cause (or reason): the various expressions of the emotion will pass unnoticed, or will appear as unconnected phenomena, without underlying psychological unity. Expressions of grief, for example, would be ignored, or attributed, say, to influenza, or to other stresses. In general, perception of intentional states and connections in the other person is facilitated by the perceiver's familiarity with such states and connections in his or her own case.

Theories of knowledge of mind in which a notion something like empathy plays a critical role have recently been proposed in the philosophical literature (Gordon 1986; Heal 1986; Ripstein 1987; Goldman 1989). This kind of epistemology was soon taken into developmental psychological theory (Harris 1989; and below, subsection 3.2.6) although it is yet to appear in scientific clinical psychology. The idea that the therapist uses himself or herself to understand (and anticipate) the patient is, of course, fundamental to psychoanalysis and its derivatives, but it can hardly be envisaged in the scientific paradigm of knowledge.

The recent formulations of the theory of empathy vary among themselves, and some explicitly use the term 'empathy' while others, particularly Gordon's (1986) relies more on the technical term 'mental simulation'. Interestingly, this epistemology has been generally understood as being an *alternative* to the proposal that knowledge of mind is an exercise in theory. For example, in introducing his version of the theory in a more recent paper Gordon characterizes it as follows (1992, p. 5):

> Human competence in predicting and explaining behavior depends chiefly on a capacity for mental simulation, particularly for decision-making within a pretend context. . . . The Simulation Theory competes with the so-called 'Theory' Theory, the view that a common-sense psychological theory, a 'folk psychology', underlies human competence in explaining and predicting behavior and implicitly defines our concepts of the various mental states.

In exploring the notion of empathy or mental simulation in what follows, however, we shall not be suggesting that there is here an alternative to the epistemology that invokes theory. We shall propose that the exercise of theory, emphasized in the first chapter, and the role of empathy, endorsed here, are not at all incompatible, but are, on the contrary, interwoven. This falls out as a clear consequence of interpreting empathy, or mental simulation, as belonging to the empirical basis of the theory of mind, specifically as a form of thought-experiment, an idea to which we turn next.[1]

3.2.3 Empathy as thought-experiment, interwoven with theory

The recognition of patterns of intentionality in behaviour is part of the empirical basis for the theory of mind. But information from observed cases alone has a number of limitations. It so far fails to apply to novel, unfamiliar circumstances, and it may not permit discrimination between causal and accidental associations.

Now it is well known in the case of knowledge of (inanimate) objects that experiment, that is, intervention into what is observed, is typically more powerful than simply observation of what happens to happen. Experimentation permits observations of phenomena which might, or would otherwise, not occur, and may, in particular, facilitate definition of necessary and sufficient causal conditions, using Mill's methods of agreement and difference. A by all means *very special* sort of experiment is the so-called 'thought-experiment', that is, manipulation of reality and observation of results, all in the imagination. While thought-experiments have limited, though interesting, application in relation to knowledge of (inanimate) objects, it can be said a priori that they are particularly suited to knowledge of subjects, to knowledge of, as it were, intentional objects. The reason is just that in this case, the subject of knowledge is also among the objects of knowledge, and information dependent on the nature of the subject alone also provides information about the objects of knowledge. Since thought-experiments can, in this special case, enhance information from cases observed in reality, and since thought-experiments are easier and faster to run than experiments in reality, there is a priori reason to suppose that they figure in the empirical basis of the theory of mind.

Suppose, then, that the task is to judge how someone is feeling or would be feeling in such-and-such circumstances, hence to anticipate what she is, or would be, inclined to do; or, that it is to make a judgement as to what emotional state is giving rise to such-and-such behaviour, hence again to anticipate what the person is likely to go on to do. A possible method is to run thought-experiments along the following lines: imagine, consciously or otherwise, the initial conditions in question, and the feelings, inclinations to behaviour, etc. to which they (in the imagination) give rise.

It is clear that thought-experiments, in so far as they are experiments, go hand in hand with theory. Empirical knowledge generally requires both theory and experience. Theory requires an empirical basis, which in the special case of the theory of mind, the suggestion is, includes the results of thought- or imagination-experiments. Of course such results, like those of any experiment, are of varying reliability and validity, depending on the accuracy of the surrounding theory. There is a complementary relationship here. On the one hand, experimental manipulation in the imagination of experiences, mental states, and behavioural tendencies provides information relevant to knowledge of mind. And on the other, (use of) this information is theory-dependent: thought- or imagination-experiments, as experiments, involve assumptions and interpretations.[2]

3.2.4 Sources of error, and infallibility

The fact that information from one's own case is like the result of an experiment, and involves theory, is connected with the fact that the method as a whole is fallible. Let us consider in more detail this issue of error, which here as always is fundamental to epistemology. At the same time we shall have to address the issue of *infallibility*, the necessary absence of error, which has a special role in the case of self-knowledge.

One source of error in attribution of intentionality to others, as with all empirical hypotheses, is insufficient evidence. But there are further interconnected possibilities of error created by use of information from one's own case: this information is partial (incomplete), fallible, and subjective. Let us consider each of these points in turn.

Consider the case of failure to recognize grief. The problem may be that the observer has no information available from his or her own case concerning the psycho-logic of the emotion, or has but fails to use it. The observer's information, or theory of mind, is incomplete. Then an incorrect intentionality will be attributed, such as malingering; or a non-intentional causal attribution will be made, such as post-viral syndrome.

Suppose, on the other hand, that the observer does draw on self-knowledge in the attempt to understand the other. It cannot be assumed that this self-knowledge is infallible: we make mistakes about our own mental states, as noted already in the first chapter (subsection 1.4.3). It is likely that the use of language in articulating psychological theory, in representing relations between experience, belief, feeling, and action, is a particularly potent source of error. Theory expressed in language very often misrepresents, for example, the 'natural expression' of the emotions. A child in grief, for example, may not be helped to articulate the emotion, its causes and effects: the emotion is left unremarked, or called by the wrong name, for example weakness, illness, or boredom. The resulting incompletness or error in self-knowledge will then reappear as incompleteness or error in the child's, or later the adult's understanding of others.

It should be remarked in passing that it would be hazardous to assume that the information from the observer's own case has to be explicitly or implicitly formulated in (coded in) language. Pre-linguistic infants, and perhaps non-linguistic animals, demonstrate in their social behaviour the ability to recognize intentionality in others, and in so far as this depends on information about their own reactions, it is non-linguistic information. The way of knowing here would be primarily analogic: patterns of intentionality in the other would be compared with those in the observer. In our own case, as mature human beings, pre- or non-linguistic, analogical coding of information relevant to the perception of intentionality may be assumed to exist alongside, more or less compatibly, theory expressed in language.

Even if self-knowledge, however derived, is valid, still its use in understanding others remains a further source of error. Attribution of intentionality to another, straightforwardly on the basis of one's own, will be valid only to the extent that the other is like oneself. Otherwise it will lead to the wrong result. For example, I may correctly interpret the other's crying as the expression of perceived loss because that is how I respond in those circumstances. But equally, I may fail to recognize the experience of loss in another if I assume that the experience is always expressed in this way. There are individual differences in the expression of emotion, and in the case of difference between myself and the other, identification will be invalid. In case of difference the use of empathy has to be modified. I have to represent what it is like to be someone unlike myself. The implied paradox here is a genuine one: *I* do indeed have to imagine being *someone else*. This modified form of empathic identification involves subtle interplay between acknowledgement of difference and presumption of similarity.

There has to be acknowledgement of difference. On the other hand, in order to make sense of what it is like to have different experiences, beliefs, and feelings, I still have to draw on information from my own case. I remember having been in similar, though still distinct, circumstances, and my responses in them, or I imagine what my responses would be were I hypothetically to be in the other's position; or, to obtain the best result possible for me, I use both methods in combination. I remember, for example, what it is like to be bereaved, and I imagine what it would be like to be bereaved while at the same time believing that one should not show signs of distress to others; I then notice what I am inclined to feel, say, and do in this position.

Experience and imagination are used together in 'knowing'—more or less well—the mind of another. The method is certainly subjective, but this is appropriate and necessary: knowledge of another's subjectivity is going to have to involve one's own. The method is by all means prone to error, and leads us into much trouble. On the other hand, whatever is prone to error is also capable of being right. If there are (objective) criteria for the one, there are (objective) criteria for the other. We make mistakes, more or less serious, in our understanding of others, and these mistakes show up as failure to anticipate each other's actions, and in particular as failure in co-operative endeavour. But equally, and here we return to the theme of the first chapter concerning attribution of intentionality and prediction: we are right often enough to make social life possible.

Knowledge of mental states, one's own or someone else's, is highly prone to error. On the other hand, there is some infallibility in self-knowledge. As noted in subsection 1.4.3, reports of the mental states regulating, or about to regulate, one's own current (salient) activity tend to be correct. These self-reports, when infallible, were construed not as beliefs about one's behaviour, but rather as expressions of intent to put such beliefs into practice.

This construal of self-report is linked to a point due to Wittgenstein: if a statement is (functioning as) a description of a process, mental or otherwise, then it can go wrong; so conversely, if a statement cannot go wrong, then it is not functioning as a description of a process.[3] Arguably this appeal to non-descriptive uses of language is the only way of making sense of incorrigible statements, but in any case it cannot be done in Cartesian terms, by appeal to mental states being manifest to the self. Even if (all or some) mental states are manifest to the self, still they are not manifest with verbal labels attached, still less with (necessarily) the right verbal labels attached. There is no way through here to the notion of an infallible description. To explain infallibility we need to invoke, rather than description, something like affirmation, or commitment.

This point is in turn linked to others previously discussed with reference to Wittgenstein. They may be collected together here as all relevant to the knowledge of mind, specifically in one's own case. We saw in subsection 1.4.4 in the context of post-empiricism that some propositions hold fast as methodological rules necessary for action and thought itself. Some of these refer to the world in which we live, but some refer to oneself, and specifically to one's capacity to act. We cannot afford to be wrong about (sincerely made) statements such as 'I see the door in front of me', 'I will go out of the door', 'This is my hand', and so on. I cannot be wrong about this sort of thing, not *in normal circumstances*. This means roughly: not if my basic faculties are working as they seem to be. What lies on the other side of this qualification is so far unthinkable to me. There is a commitment here to belief, to putting aside doubt, which is necessary in order to continue to act (cf. also below, subsection 6.4.5).

In summary then, there is something like infallible self-knowledge, but only in so far as we express a resolution to act, or to respond, in such-and-such a way. Once we *describe*, we make a true-or-false representation of a process (a pattern of intentionality), and then inevitably there is the possibility of error.

Another way of making this point is to say that infallible self-report is not based on information. Hence the information from one's own case used in empathy is not infallible self-knowledge. This conclusion leads on to an issue that has been pressing for some time, concerning the relation between self-knowledge and knowledge of the other.

3.2.5 Empathic knowledge is originally subject-less

So far we have talked of empathy as using information about oneself as a way of trying to know another person. We ask, for example, 'What would I feel if I had just experienced such-and-such?', intending the answer to help in knowing what the other might be feeling given the experience in question. This a natural description, but superficial. Behind it lies the epistemological point that empathic knowledge is originally subject-less, that is to say, is not about a (particular) subject at all. This point has the corollary that knowledge of the other is not based on knowledge of the self: rather both arise in the same way and on the same basis.

In terms of the proposal being developed here, simulations as thought-experiments are not primarily a source of self-knowledge, though they can be used for this purpose. The theory of mind required to run thought-experiments has to include methodological assumptions covering the move from current results to predictions about other cases. The simplest such assumption uses the straight rule: it will be in other cases just as it is in the present one. More sophisticated rules take into account differences between cases, such as differences in spatio-visual perspective, in ways of expressing emotion, or in beliefs, etc. It is, by all means, tempting to describe the methodological assumption of the straight rule as being that the other is like the self, while the more complex rules allow for differences between oneself and others. This way of describing the assumption behind the straight rule, however, presupposes that the distinction between self and other is being made, and the point is that this distinction comes into operation only with the more complex rules, which allow for differences in perspective. The thought-experiments are not about mental states of the self as opposed to mental states of the other. They provide information which is, so far, subject-less. The information is primarily about intentional states and their (apparent) connectedness, but these are not yet states of the self as opposed to states of the other. Attribution of patterns of intentionality to the self as opposed to the other requires recognition of, and allowances for, features that distinguish the self from others, and vice versa. This is to say, self-knowledge is not the basis for knowledge of the other, but rather they share the same origins, and develop in parallel.

Rules are required to make predications about other cases from the present observation or experiment. The rules become more sophisticated as they take into account relevant differences between the current case and others, but these differences are not correctly characterized in terms of differences between self and other. The first distinction to be drawn is between *this present* case and *other* cases. The 'other cases' by all means include other people, but they also, and equally, include myself in conditions other than those in the present case, for example, myself at different times, places, or with different relevant beliefs and goals, etc. The aim is to use the current observation or experiment to predict as accurately as possible what will or would happen in other cases. Accuracy will be achieved to the extent that the rules of inference become increasingly sensitive to differences in perspective, in the broadest sense. This increasing sensitivity plausibly involves increasing capacity or skill in imaginative manipulation of perspectives (visual, cognitive, emotional, etc.), in other words, increasing aptitude for thought-experiments of the sort already discussed. But it seems equally plausible to suppose that sensitivity to perspective depends on a theory, concerning at least the idea that perception and belief do indeed depend on perspective, as opposed to being determined just by reality as it appears (at present) to be. It would be reasonable to suppose, further, that these two capacities, for thought-experiments with perspectives, and for theory about perspectives, are inextricably linked.

3.2.6 Perspectives on psychological development

The epistemological points made in the previous subsection can be applied to the question of what is involved in the child's acquisition of knowledge of mind. As remarked earlier, there has been a tendency in the philosophical literature to assume that the theory of empathy, or mental simulation, stands opposed as an alternative to the epistemology which construes knowledge of mind as an exercise in theory. This opposition has carried over into psychological theories of the child's acquisition of knowledge of mind. We find, on the one hand, developmentalists emphasizing the child's increasing theoretical sophistication (Gopnik and Wellman 1992; Perner and Howes 1992), while proponents of the Simulation Theory emphasize the child's increasing understanding of the role of perspective (Harris 1992). An advantage of combining the two epistemologies is that one does not have to choose between these two themes in psychological development, both of which are apparently major. Indeed, the implication of the line of argument proposed in the preceding subsection is not just that these two kinds of maturation are compatible, but is more that they are inextricably interwoven. Development in scientific theory characteristically goes hand in hand with innovations in techniques of observation and experimentation; by all means at times one jumps ahead of the other, which then catches up, but in general and in principle they are interdependent.

A particularly crucial development in the theory of mind, highlighted by proponents of the 'theory-theory', is towards the idea of mental states as true-or-false representations (for example, Gopnik and Wellman 1992). This important theoretical development is, however, intimately linked, as a matter of logic, to recognition of and facility with variation in perspective. The main point, which will be presented in more detail below (subsections 3.3.3–4 and 3.4.3), is that the distinction between true and false cannot be made out on the basis of the present point of view alone, still less is it made out by comparing the present point of view with an absolute reality; rather it arises in comparison and contrast between perspectives. The distinction between true and false, as also between appearance and reality, depends on the power of discriminating between me-now/me-then and me (-now)/him (-now). In effect, what is required is discrimination between the current perspective and others, and this in turn requires that the current perspective is construed precisely *as a perspective*. Thus, what appear to be advances in theory, concerning true-or-false representation, or the difference between appearance and reality, intimately involve the idea of perspective, and hence plausibly both facilitate and are facilitated by experience and imaginative play with perspectives. The argument leads, once again, round and round: from theory to experience or experiment, back to theory, and so on.

A further consequence of the mutual dependence here between theory and experiment is that prior to the development of the idea that the current perspective (whether visual, or more elaborately cognitive-affective) is a perspective, there cannot be any imaginative play with perspective. This type of experiment cannot be run; or again, the question it is designed to answer cannot be asked. Without distinction between true and false, appearance and reality, or indeed between self and other, rudimentary attribution of intentionality would be determined by what was being experienced at the time. In this developmental stage, or state of mind, attribution would use a very straight rule: primitive, and powerful.[4]

The suggestion is that development in the theory of mind is interwoven with development of imaginative play with perspectives. It should be noted at this point that in children this imaginative play is most apparent indeed in *play*. The implication here is that children use play to improve their knowledge of mind, whether in theory or simulation (Leslie 1987; Harris 1989; Hobson 1990).

The proposal in subsection 3.2.3 that the empirical basis for the theory of mind included thought-experiments was supported by the remark that experiments, that is, concerning the relation between experiences, mental states, and behaviour, were difficult and time-consuming to conduct in reality. But some of the difficulties do not arise in play, and, all being well, the child has plenty of time. Play can be used to experiment with diverse circumstances, emotions, beliefs, capacities, tasks; to try out perspectives and activities different from the child's own. This play is in a space between reality and the imagination. The experiments are neither in reality nor in thought alone; the simulations are neither on-nor off-line. Experimentation in play seems to occupy the child as much as, or more than, experimentation in the mind alone; or perhaps skill in the latter is acquired by practice in the former. These observations on the significance of play qualify earlier remarks that have focused exclusively on thought-experiments.

Experimentation with perspectives, whether manifestly in play or covertly in thought alone, is a source of self-knowledge and of knowledge of others equally. As has already been argued, the information provided is so far subject-less. It is a matter of what it is (or seems) like to have such-and-such experiences, including being in certain kinds of social role or interpersonal relationship, what it is like to have such-and-such feelings, beliefs, tasks, inclinations to action, etc. The initial conditions of the experiment can be at any point along this continuum, and the experiment is to investigate what these give rise to, or what gave rise to them. Hence the child plays at being for instance a carer, a baby, a teacher, a goody or a baddy, kind or nasty; and so on, and on. What the child finds out in this play is so far not about herself rather than anyone else, or vice versa. It is primarily, and precisely, about the mental (intentional) states themselves: particular experiences, feelings, tasks, intentions, inclinations to actions. Application of information of this sort to understanding another person, or oneself, in a real situation involves further judgement, that is, attribution of the mental states, and estimation of their interaction with others operating at the same time.

3.3 RULE-FOLLOWING

3.3.1 The role of rules: order through time

There is a close connection, already remarked in the the first chapter (subsection 1.3.4), between mental states, regulation, and rule-following. We describe behaviour as caused by mental states in so far as it is goal-directed and adaptive, and this 'causation' involves regulation, the modification of behaviour according to circumstances towards a goal. These intentional behaviour sequences are hence also typically subject to normative decriptions: appropriate/inappropriate, successful/unsuccessful, right/wrong. This normative quality can be captured by saying that the behaviour in question is subject to a rule, or is rule-following. So the central questions for this chapter concerning the epistemology of mind can be framed using the notion of rule-following. How do I know that someone is following a rule? How do I know which rule? What is this knowledge knowledge of? In this section we consider aspects of Wittgenstein's influential discussion of rule-following in the *Philosophical investigations* (1953).[5]

At the beginning of his *Investigations*, Wittgenstein criticizes the general idea that signs have meaning because they stand for objects; rather their meaning derives from use in activity (1953, §§ 1 to *c.* 37). He proceeds to criticize various doctrines familiar in the philosophical tradition which express the idea that meaning is correlation with an object, in such a way as to exclude the use of signs in activity as redundant, or even as incomprehensible. These include doctrines which invoke universals (ibid. *c.* §§ 57–78), and various logical theories, including Wittgenstein's own in the *Tractatus* (ibid. *c.* §§ 39–64 and 89–116).

Before considering briefly Wittgenstein's treatment of such doctrines below, we should note that the issues here are not only of interest to the history of philosophy, but are relevant to contemporary theories of meaning and mental content. Highly influential theories still draw on, or make a virtue of, the view that meaning and reference do not essentially involve human activity. These include the materialist theory of mental content, discussed in the context of the problem of supervenience in the previous chapter (Section 2.5), and the causal theory of semantics, to be discussed in the next chapter (Section 4.3).

Meaningful signs, whether written or spoken language, or mental representations, or information-carrying neural states, pick out, *in some sense*, the order (or *form*) in reality. It is possible to conceive this order as already given, both in the sense of already given in time, and in the sense of given without contribution from the activity of an agent. At least until the Kantian revolution, such an absolute conception of order has been dominant in the tradition. It has had various expressions, which fall broadly into two categories, concerning classes and spatial relations. In both cases the notion of resemblance between sign and signified, discussed in subsection 1.3.2, is fundamental.

The various theories of universals in ancient thought, and the theories of general and abstract ideas in modern thought, all seek to explain the unity of classes in terms of an object which is, or which resembles, what all and only members of the class have in common. Such a special and problematic 'universal (or general) object' is the meaning of any sign which represents a class.

Relation between objects in space is a different kind of order, which assumed paramount importance in the modern period. In seventeenth-century philosophy of nature it too was conceived as given absolutely: independently of time, of experience, of frames of reference, to be measured by rigid rods. The order of objects in space, the natural order, could perhaps be represented in perception, though the details were irredeemably problematic. In particular, perceptual experience is relative, dependent on the nature and position of the subject, and further, it was meant to be mental, and hence not spatial. In brief, perceptions are not rigid rods, indeed they are not rods at all. Such paradoxes point to the murky incoherence of this modern world-picture. In the *Tractatus* (Wittgenstein 1921) the problems of relativity and mind were bypassed by logic: spatial states of affairs are represented by (more) spatial states of affairs, configurations of signs, involving no relativity, nothing at all which could be called contribution by the subject. As discussed in Chapter 1 (subsection 1.3.2), the picture theory of thought and language is derived in the *Tractatus* as a solution to the problem of how a sign can be meaningful (can stand for something in reality) while yet being false (while failing to correspond to reality). The pictures are the 'real signs', hidden beneath the surface of language, which does indeed conspicuously not look like what is represented.

The theory that the meaning of a general term is a feature common to all members of a class, and the theory that a true-or-false proposition is something like a picture of a state of affairs, though otherwise distinct, both affirm the idea that meanings are essentially static, object-like structures which resemble or reflect the pre-given order in reality. These structures—universals, ideas, pictures—do all the work of representation. Or rather, there is no need for work: the 'real signs' simply *are* what reality is like. In this general picture there is no use for such concepts as time, the creation of order, activity, relativity, and subjectivity (and still less, of intersubjectivity). These excluded concepts are all intimately related to one another.

During this century, theories of meaning that turn on the notion of resemblance have become unattractive, particularly, but not only, because they fare badly when applied to language. The theories posit signs that 'resemble reality', but the signs of (everyday, natural) languages typically do not. If we persist with the question: 'How does a sign signify reality?', and if we do *not* allow ourselves to invoke resemblance, then we are led towards the idea that some *form of activity*, specifically human activity, is required to link the two. This reading inevitably introduces relativity into the theory of meaning and reference, a relativity to human activity and the community of language-users. These are familiar themes in Wittgenstein's later philosophy.

This line of thought will be resisted by those who want to preserve a non-relativistic, (purely) 'objective' philosophy. One such resistance is provided by causal semantics, probably in combination with the materialist theory of content: the dynamic relation between sign and reality is defined in causal terms, and the reality in terms of the basic natural sciences. No subjectivity or relativity here. These alternative approaches are considered and rejected elsewhere (sections 2.5 and 4.4–4.6). In this section we shall pursue the Wittgensteinian approach, which as indicated soon leads us towards relativity. In the next section, however, we go on to argue that this relativity does not dispose of, but rather re-defines, the notion of objectivity, in a way, moreover, suited to the sciences.

Wittgenstein begins his *Philosophical investigations* very simply, by citing the fact that people engage in co-operative activity, such as building, using language for communication. This is to be the starting-place for the theory of meaning and language. Starting-place means: it is not derived from deeper assumptions. In particular, it is not to be *explained away* by other theories (such as the ones described above). Philosophy always begins with what is obvious, beyond all reasonable doubt. The starting-place that Wittgenstein adopts may be contrasted with others in the philosophical tradition. Of particular relevance in the present context is the contrast with the dominant (though noriously problematic) axiom of modern epistemology, namely, the certainty of subjective experience, used, for example, by Locke as the basis for the empiricist theory of representation (ideas). The proposal underlying Wittgenstein's choice of starting-place is that the reality of action, community, and language is now more obvious, more clear, than the reality of subjective experience. Plausibly this same assumption characterizes most contemporary psychology, and it has been adopted in the present essay: our conception of mind and meaning is based in their relevance to action and mutual understanding, not in contemplation of one's own mental states.

Wittgenstein's proposal is, then, that the meaning of a sign derives from its use in activities such as making requests, sorting out one kind of thing from another, fetching and carrying, etc. This claim may indeed appear as relatively innocuous, but in fact it contradicts presuppositions about meaning and the order in reality which pervade the tradition, and which still influence our current thinking.

Given that meaning is grounded in action, the notion of *order* makes its appearance in the following way: the activity which is the origin of meaning is not random, but is ordered, essentially 'right' or 'wrong'. We may express the fact that practice is ordered by saying that it proceeds in accordance with a rule. This concept of ordered practice, practice that follows a rule, is what replaces the traditional concepts of static representation, expressed in the theories of universals, ideas of perception, picture-propositions, of truth-conditions as states of affairs; and so forth.

In their most pure expressions, these traditional theories of meaning are alien to the idea that signs are used through time, in practice, according to a rule. Nothing needs to be done to create meaning. But, if something has to be said about the use of (ordinary) signs in practice, it will be this: the order —the distinction between right and wrong—in practice and in our use of signs will be secondary to, based in, an order which is already given; either in the nature of 'real signs', or in some mental *act*. Deconstruction of various expressions of this general idea is the main negative theme in Wittgenstein's treatment of judgement and rule-following in the *Investigations*, beginning at about § 134. The contrary and new conclusion for which Wittgenstein argues may be summarized briefly thus: *meaning—the rule—is not determined in advance.*

3.3.2 Rule-following as creation of order

The simplest account of the rule for using a sign would be that the sign itself determines its application. This account does not refer to the ordinary signs of language, but rather to pictures or exemplars of things. Even so, the attempt to explain meaning in terms of the instrinsic nature of a sign only works if it is supposed that the sign is not *used* at all. For the idea was that the picture simply represents how things stand; nothing is *done* with the picture, so there is no question of doing different things with it. But once we grant that signs are used, for example in our activities of collecting things together, it becomes apparent that signs themselves can dictate no method of application, and hence no meaning. Any sign, whether verbal or pictorial, can be used in a variety of ways. This use is the source of meaning, not the object itself (Wittgenstein 1953, §§139–141; cf. above, subsection 1.3.2).

Another possibility is that the rule for the use of a sign is simply what its use *is intended to be*. According to this kind of account, a child who is learning the use of the word 'chair' by being shown examples, must try to see what meaning the teacher has in mind. And if the child goes on to make a mistake, applying the word to a sofa, say, the suggestion is that this counts as a mistake because it conflicts with the meaning that was intended, and which has been already given to the word.

Wittgenstein considers this suggestion using an analogy with continuing an arithmetical series (1953, §§ 143f., 185f.). Suppose we teach a child to expand the series '+2', giving examples at the beginning. The child then proceeds alone, correctly up to 1000, but then continues: 1004, 1008, 1012. We could point out the mistake, and the child may make corrections. What requires definition, however, is the sense in which a 'mistake' has been made. Or: 'Why is 1002 the *right* number to write after 1000?' According to the suggestion under consideration, the answer is that this is what we meant the pupil to do when we gave the instruction to continue the series '+2' from the examples given. Meaning is conceived here as a kind of intention which defines in advance the expansion of the formula, or, in general, the correct use of a sign. But the objection is that we cannot lay down all the steps in advance, because there are infinitely many of them. It may be true to say that when we gave the instruction to expand the series we *meant at the time* that 1002 should be written after 1000. But even though we meant the step then, still we did not take it then; and if we did, there are indefinitely many others that we did not take. We meant the step at the time in so far as, if the child had asked at the time how to continue after 1000, we should have replied '1002'. And we can affirm this counter-factual proposition because as soon as the issue is raised, we reply without hesitation: write 1002 after 1000. But to say that the issue can be settled at any time without hesitation does not mean, and cannot mean, that it has been settled already, in advance.

We are evaluating the idea that the correct use of sign is determined by the meaning that we give the sign. And the conclusion is that the opposite is so: it is the correct use of a sign which determines its meaning. The correct use of a sign cannot be defined in advance, but is created as we proceed. What can seem as it if were an 'act of meaning', is rather a *process*.

On the other hand, perhaps the analogy between using a sign and being able to expand an arithmetic formula is misleading in an important respect. The series of numerals associated with a formula such as '+2' is a conventional one. It is perhaps for this reason that knowing the formula alone is no help in knowing the series, that the series has to be made up—albeit with no hesitation—as we go along. But by contrast, *judgement made about the world* is not just a matter of convention. It is plausible to suppose that a series of such judgements, say the classification of many things into one class, is held together by an independent, objective regularity. So that, for example, repeated uses of the sentence 'This is red' mark a regularity in the world, and understanding how to use the sentence is a matter of perceiving and representing this regularity. It would follow then that there would be a truly informative expression of the rule for using the sentence, namely, a table with the word written opposite a sample of red. Understanding the word would then be acquaintance with such a table in the mind, a mental state that underlies and explains the practice of making judgements.

The suggestion is, then, that to follow a rule is to read off judgements from some expression of the rule, perhaps in the form of a table relating signs to samples. Wittgenstein shows, however, that this kind of suggestion does not work (1953, §§ 156 to *c.* 171). The problem is that expressions of rules, such as tables, can be 'read' in various ways, that they can determine no unique usage. Or again, expressions of rules, of whatever kind, admit of many 'interpretations'. These interpretations can be expressed by more expressions of rules, for example by more tables, perhaps with more or less complicated systems of arrows linking signs and samples, but such further expressions of rules are again open to various interpretations, to diverse applications. So one difficulty is that a particular expression of a rule, together with any number of expressions for its interpretation, can be used in various ways. But the further and related difficulty is that they can also be used in entirely random ways, *in ways which are not rule-following at all.*

The conclusion is, then, that we cannot capture the notion of following a rule in terms of intended use, nor in terms of expressions of rules. This is the negative conclusion of Wittgenstein's discussion of rule-following.[6]

This negative conclusion may be expressed also by saying that nothing short of order *in practice* will count as rule-following; that is, nothing short of making judgements (in words or in action) which are right as opposed to wrong. And this points towards a more positive doctrine, to the effect that following a rule is a practice.

In § 201, Wittgenstein refers to the difficulties that arise when we try to define action according to a rule in terms of interpretations of expressions of rules, which in turn require further interpretations, and so on. But he continues (1953, §§ 201–2):

> What this shows is that there is a way of grasping a rule which is *not* an *interpretation*, but which is exhibited in what we call 'obeying the rule' and 'going against it' in actual cases.
>
> Hence there is an inclination to say: every action according to the rule is an interpretation. But we ought to restrict the term 'interpretation' to the substitution of one expression of the rule for another.
>
> And hence also 'obeying a rule' is a practice . . . .

Nothing short of ordered practice will count as obeying a rule. In particular, no amount of mental manipulation of expressions of rules is sufficient. There are, of course, mental processes, conscious and unconscious, involved in rule-guided practice: processes such as feelings of recognition of items in the environment, feelings of being guided by samples, inspection of samples, tables, formulae, etc. But the activity that results from such processes may or may not be ordered (rational, intelligent). Whether someone is or is not following a rule depends on what they do in practice; for example, on what items they call or treat as the same. Only if a person's judgements and actions are of a certain kind do we say that she is 'going by regularities in the world'. Our concept of regularities in the world is of a piece with our concept of regularities in action. This is an aspect of the correspondence between reality and thought.

The concept of following a rule cannot be explained in terms of perception of regularities in the world, since following a rule and perceiving regularities come to the same thing. In a similar way, the practice of following a rule cannot be explained in terms of *reason*. Here the point is not that we have no reasons for proceeding as we do, but rather that our reasons run out. Wittgenstein writes (1953, § 211):

> How can he *know* how he is to continue a pattern by himself—whatever instruction you give him?—Well, how do *I* know?—If that means 'have I reasons?' the answer is: my reasons will soon give out. And then I shall act, without reasons.

Reasons come to an end once we have described, in the various ways in which we can describe, the fact that we are following the rule. We can, for example, refer to our training, saying that we are carrying on as we were taught, or we may point to a sample, saying that it guides us, etc. But if someone were to press the question: 'But why call *this* the same way as before?' or 'Why is *this* near enough to the sample?' then sooner or later we run out of answers, and carry on regardless, in the way we are inclined. The concept of following a rule—of ordered judgement and practice—is (of course) a very fundamental one, and does not rest on any more fundamental notion of reason. To say that someone is following a rule so far means, among other things, that they are acting rationally.

The rules followed in practice and in our use of signs are not laid down in advance, by pictures, or by acts of mind; rather they are formed in practice, as we take action which is right or wrong. Nor can following a rule be explained in terms of an independently defined 'following of regularities', nor in terms of independently defined 'reasons'. Right or wrong practice is not derived from a more fundamental principle of order: the practice itself is what is fundamental. The conclusion is that the origin of the rule—of meaning, of the measure of reality—is neither more nor less than *our natural inclination to proceed in one way rather than another.*

But now the paradox is: in what sense is there a *rule* here at all? We have considered attempts to define an order already made, but apparently there is none. But then, what kind of order is it that can be made up as we go along? Why is one way of proceeding any more 'correct' than any other?

3.3.3 The role of agreement

Towards the end of his discussion of rule-following, Wittgenstein begins to speak of shared practice and judgement. Thus, obeying a rule is a custom (Wittgenstein 1953,

§ 198); a rule cannot be obeyed privately (ibid. § 202), the word 'agreement' and the word 'rule' are related to one another, they are cousins (ibid. § 224).

The implication of Wittgenstein's remarks here may be that a person's practice accords with a rule in so far as it is shared with other people. However, the justification for such a move at this stage of Wittgenstein's discussion of rule-following is far from clear. So far it has been established what following a rule *is not*; it is not to follow what is laid down in advance in some act of meaning, or in some expression of a rule. But what is the justification of a move from this negative conclusion to the positive conclusion that following a rule is a matter of being in accord with other people? Why is agreement in practice either a necessary or a sufficient condition of following a rule?

It is difficult to see why *mere numbers* should make a difference to the issue. On the one hand, we can imagine a group of people all acting and speaking in similar ways, but apparently without rhyme or reason. On the other, we can presumably imagine a person on his own—perhaps on a desert island—acting and using signs in an orderly way, regardless of any relation to a present, past, or hypothetical community.[7] It is by all means the case that people (usually) do live in communities, and that their rule-following practices are shared. It may also be true to say, on biological and psychological grounds, that children have to be taught how to act and how to use signs, so that in fact no human being could ever come to follow a rule in isolation from others. But such empirical considerations and speculations so far fail to bring out the conceptual connection between rule-following and agreement. Nor is it clear that the empirical facts unformly support such a connection. Frequently we do have to follow rules on our own; others are not so preoccupied with us that they attend to, offer guidance on, or pass opinion on our every move.

We suggest that the point is *not* that we ascribe rule-following to groups as opposed to individuals; rather, we make the ascription in both cases and on the same grounds, namely, to the extent that we find practices, whether group or individual, comprehensible.

This point about grounds for ascription of rule-following indicates a radically different way of introducing the notion of agreement into the arena. The notion of agreement is relevant to the judgement whether a person's practice is rule-governed, not because a person cannot follow a rule without others there to share it, but because, if the judgement is made at all, it is made by other people, and then on the basis of whether they can follow and share in the person's activity. This can be expressed by saying that agreement is relevant to judgement about rule-following because *one person is the measure of another*. When a person is inclined to make a judgement, he or she supposes that the judgement is correct. What seems right, is right, so far as the person is concerned. Under what conditions, then, do we say that the other is following the rule? The answer is clear: when the other does what we are ourselves inclined to do. In this way, so far as a person is concerned, the notion of agreement with his or her own judgement is intertwined with the notion of following a rule. Agreement is critical in the same way to related notions such as intentionality and rationality.

The clearest cases of agreement are those in which two people are inclined to proceed in the same way, but there are of course other, critical possibilities related to these straightforward cases. In order to judge that the other is following some rule or other, it is not necessary that their practice be the same as one's own; it is enough to see some sense in what the person is doing. This involves acknowledgement that the other's action is right (reasonable, understandable), given his or her purposes and experience. Understanding of the other is like, and is based on, understanding of oneself: both are a matter of acknowledging inclinations to action. We experience tendencies and responses in directions other than those in which we act. These inclinations to action—these meanings—can be seen at work in the actions of others, which therefore make sense, even though these actions are unlike our own. Mutual understanding has to be achieved in the midst of individual differences.

Thus we come by this route to conclusions similar to those already reached in the previous section, namely, that understanding of intentionality in others is based in empathy (straightforward or otherwise). This coincidence is to be expected, in view of the intimate connection between intentionality and rule-following. Examination of the concept of rule-following leads to the conclusion that subjective inclinations form the basis of expectations about the behaviour of others.

However, unlike the considerations in the previous section concerning empathy in knowledge of intentionality, the considerations so far in this section concerning rule-following do not apply only to expectations about social behaviour, but rather to *judgement in general*, including about the natural (apart from the social) world. This great generality is of course typical of philosophical enquiry, and is to be expected of Wittgenstein's analysis of what it means to following a rule.

The argument that rules are formed in practice, outlined in subsection 3.3.2 included the point that the concept of following a rule cannot be explained in terms of perception of regularities in the world: following a rule and perceiving regularities come to the same thing. This means that subjective responses to reality, the inclination to act in one way rather than another (e.g. to treat *this* as the same as or different to *that*) form the basis of judgements about sameness and difference, classes and properties, in the natural world.

This conclusion stands opposed to those various doctrines described at the start of this section, according to which meanings are static measures which reflect pre-given order in reality. If we were to speak in the present context of measures, it would be ourselves, our responses to reality.

The implication is that our concept of reality is thoroughly interwoven with interpersonal relations, with the comparison of views. The position is not, however, that the notion of reality collapses into the notion of agreement. This is too simple, and it neglects the role of reality as independent of judgement. In the course of action through time, a person proceeds in the way she judges to be right. If another person agrees, then what seems right to the one seems right also to the other; but this does not yet mean that they *are* right. Agreement does not turn 'seems' into 'is'. But then, what is the relation between appearance and reality? All we have concluded so far, in the absence of rigid, fixed measures, is that human responsiveness is the vehicle of representation. And so far as this measure is concerned (and in fact the same would apply to any measure), what seems right, is right. These points are pursued below.

3.3.4 Relativity and the independent contraints on action

By considering Wittgenstein's treatment of rule-following we have arrived at the conclusion that the human being is the measure of things, with its puzzling and disturbing implication that the distinction between 'seems' and 'is', between appearance and reality, seems to collapse. Although it represents a diversion from the mainly contemporary focus of the present essay, it can hardly be allowed to escape our attention that this problem had a lively, though brief, airing at the beginnings of Western philosophical thought. Since, for reasons to be indicated below, the problem in this form has only recently been revived, it is worthwhile to consider briefly its fate in Plato.

The claim that man is the measure was one of the three interconnected doctrines criticized and rejected by Socrates in the *Theaetetus*:

> And it has turned out that these three doctrines coincide: the doctrine of Homer and Heracleitus and all their tribe that all things move like flowing streams; the doctrine of Protagoras, wisest of men, that Man is the measure of all things; and Theaetetus' conclusion that, on these grounds, it results that perception is knowledge. (*Theaetetus*, 160D–E; translation from Cornford 1935.)

Socrates criticizes all of these doctrines, but the most sustained argument is directed at the doctrine of Protagoras, that the human being is the measure of things. This doctrine means, according to Socrates, that individual things are to me such as they appear to me, and to you such as they appear to you (152–152C). Socrates argues that this doctrine has no place for the concept of falsity, and is therefore wrong. The claim is that the doctrine can give no account of false judgement, since it implies that all judgements are true. Or again: if the human being is the measure of things, there would be no distinction between subjective appearance and reality, indeed there would be no concept of objective reality. Socrates' claim, in brief, was that if the human being is the measure of things, then there is *loss of objectivity*.

This Socratic interpretation has been of enormous significance, setting the scene for struggles between scepticism, the claim that knowledge is impossible, and various forms of dogmatism, which claimed for knowledge an absolute, non-relative, and therefore non-human, basis. Common to both scepticism and dogmatism was the assumption that knowledge, if it exists at all, must have absolute foundations. Behind this was the assumption that beliefs acquired by relative measures involved subjectivity, that is to say, absence of objectivity. The relative measures delivered results dependent on the point of view: on sensory capacity, on relative position; on culture and ideology; and so on. But these shifting, apparently incompatible representations could hardly be representations of the one, independent reality. If this was to be known at all, there had to be absolute measures. Reason, as conceived in rationalist epistemology, and experience as conceived by empiricism, were the two absolute measures in modern thought. As these lost credibility through the nineteenth century, relativity has made its appearance in this. This long-lost, newly re-discovered relativity has been both resisted and welcomed, both on the grounds that it involves loss of (absolute) objectivity.

But what is lost is neither more nor less than the idea of an absolute, non-relative object. The idea of a 'relativistic object' remains, involved in the relativistic epistemology, though by all means such a notion of object is not the traditional one. But in any case it is wrong to suppose that relativity implies subjectivity without objectivity; on the contrary, it is obvious enough in general terms that relativity involves both subject and object in interaction.

The notion of objectivity which belongs properly with relativity is in fact familiar to common sense and language, but it is obscured by deep theoretical preconceptions. Socrates in the *Theaetetus* criticizes Protagoras' doctrine because it offers no account of false judgement, but the everyday examples of being right rather than wrong, or vice versa, which are cited, do not turn on absolute standards. Rather, the distinctions turn on mundane features of judgement that turn out to be quite compatible with the claim that human beings are the measure. Socrates cites cases in which a person is skilled at a practice, is good at achieving an intended result, as for example a physician at healing the body, or a gardner at cultivating plants (167B–C). He also cites cases of disagreement, addressing Theodorus as follows (170D–E, translation from Cornford 1935):

> When you have formed a judgement on some matter in your own mind and express an opinion about it to me, let us grant that, as Protagoras' theory says, it is true for you; but are we so to understand that it is impossible for us, the rest of the company, to pronounce any judgement on your judgement; or, if we can, that we always pronounce your opinion to be true? Do you not rather find thousands of opponents who set their opinion against yours on every occasion and hold that your judgement and belief are false?

To which Theodorus replies:

> I should just think so, Socrates; thousands and tens of thousands, as Homer says; and they give me all the trouble in the world.

Finally, Socrates cites cases where we know that not every person's opinion can be correct; as for example when a patient disagrees with his physician about the future course of his illness, or when legislators dispute whether some law will be advantageous to the state (177C–179C).

Thus Socrates illustrates the ways in which a person's judgement can be, or can be judged by others to be, false, even though it seems right to the person at the time. The examples are, of course, taken from everyday life, in which activities achieve or fail to achieve their goals, and in which expectations are realized or not, and in which people agree with one another or not. But then, it is not at all obvious that Protagoras' doctrine cannot account for the notion of false judgement defined in these ways. On the contrary, the doctrine arguably comprises such a notion, in the following way. If the human being, specifically in activity, is the measure of things, then this measure will be 'right' or 'wrong' according to whether it fulfils its goals or not. Further, since the measuring activity is extended through time, results obtained at one time may accord or conflict with results obtained later: judgements as predictions turn out 'right' or 'wrong'. Further, the human measures are multiple, and in so far as human beings differ from one another, they will disagree in the results of their measurement.

Judgement, whether in words or action, is made from a particular perspective, on the basis of particular sensory mechanisms and information, and on the basis of certain background expectations. Judgement, which consists in the inclination to say or do something, is to the effect that *this* is how things are. At the time, there is no distinction between 'seems' and 'is', between appearance and reality. It can be thought at the time, however, for example with the words: 'It seems so me now, but I may be wrong'. But what enables this thought, and what enables the distinction to be made, is the fact that judgement made from one perspective may conflict with judgement made from another, for example by another person, or by oneself at a later time. In brief, the appearance/reality distinction is based in comparison between appearances. This central point was anticipated above (subsection 3.2.6) in discussing the relation between theory and empathy in the developing mind, and it recurs again in subsection 3.4.4, in the definition of the objectivity in intentional attributions.

The relativistic way of making out the distinction between appearance and reality, in terms of comparison between appearances, stands in contrast to the idea common to dogmatism and scepticism alike, that reality lies behind the appearances, independent of them. This idea by all means holds on to a fixed reality behind the flux, but the cost is typically that knowledge of this reality tends to be insolubly problematic, at least for human beings. The relative measures are apparently all we have, and it is not clear how they signify a non-relative reality. This problematic was manifest in Classical thought and is also one way of expressing the modern (Seventeenth century) problem of knowledge (Subsection 1.2.1).

The relativistic account of appearance and reality gives a central place to agreement between appearances, between observers. On the other hand, agreement is not all that is at issue here. In general terms, the aim of judgement is not just to agree with others, but is also, or is primarily, to find agreement *with reality*. So far, particularly in consideration of Wittgenstein's discussion of rule-following, the focus has been on agreement between people rather than on correspondence with reality. This emphasis may arise particularly when we have in mind the use of language. In so far as language is a conventional means of representation, and particularly in so far as we do share language, it may seem as if agreement on the rule is primarily what matters. But according to Wittgenstein's own account, language has meaning (*is* language) because it is used *in activity*, for example, in the course of building. When we turn attention to the practical consequences of using signs in one way rather than another, then we see what is obvious, that our use of language is not at all subject only to conventional constraints, a matter of agreement with others. On the contrary, language is used in our activity, and it is subject to the same constraints in reality, as is our practice.

For example, imagine a person building a shelter. She makes separate collections of different kinds of stone, each kind with its own name. On one occasion she makes a mistake, putting a round stone in the pile of square ones. When she comes to put this stone in place in the building, it does not fit; she has to start again; or perhaps, in a more complicated case, she is bewildered, and gives up. So the person made an error, in her action and her use of words. But this is not simply in the sense that other people would call it an error, nor indeed only because the person concerned would call it an error. Rather, the error shows up because her course of action goes astray; it is disrupted.

The importance of practical constraints have sometimes been neglected in commentary on Wittgenstein's discussion of rule-following. Kripke, for example, imagines the strange case of a person who insists that the sum of 68 and 57 is 5, and he goes on to discuss in what sense this is an error, if not because of facts about past usage, then in terms of our inclination to disagree with him (Kripke 1980). But the *application* of arithmetic is not brought into the discussion. If someone used such a calculation in planning how much water he needs to cross a desert, then he would soon come to see that he had got it wrong—and if he remained adamant until the end, then he would be slow to learn as well as dead. In any case the error speaks for itself.

The consequences of incorrect judgement are evident, and they run their course regardless whether we agree among ourselves or not. A person's judgement by all means is measured by others: they agree or disagree. But also, judgement is measured by reality itself. Reality passes judgement on our judgement. By all means it does not speak English! But rather, the order of reality is involved in the ordered activity that underlies our use of language. Between these two, there is correspondence or lack of correspondence. Human activity is the measure of reality. This reality is not a state, but is rather modes of movement and interaction, and hence it is encountered directly in practice. Judgements guide activity; they lead us to anticipate certain events, certain patterns of action and consequence, and we plan our activity accordingly. If a judgement misleads us, so that our action is confounded, then that judgement has turned out to be wrong. Reality lets us know when we are in error; we take notice, and adapt, if we are to carry on.

Another way of making this point is to say that action is interaction between the living being, the means of representation, and independent reality. Not everything in this interaction depends on the living being; and what is independent in the interaction is 'reality'. Thus reality already appears in the appearances, which are therefore not 'merely subjective'. I cannot, for example, make a closed door appear immaterial by walking through it.

Acknowledgement of relativity does not entail subjectivity or scepticism, an abandonment of the idea of objectivity. Objectivity can be defined in relativistic terms. In so far as thought and language are used in practice, in the organization and planning of action, there are 'objective' constraints on them, and hence distinctions between getting it right and getting it wrong, or more or less right or wrong.

It is dialectically necessary to emphasize that there are real, practical constraints on judgement as well as, and as opposed to, accord or discord with other people. The relativistic point stands, however, that other perspectives, in the form of other people, help make up the individual's view as to what is real and what is not. Our knowledge of reality is inextricably bound to interpersonal relations. In development, the point is the general one that social processes interact with individual cognitive development (Vygotsky 1934; Butterworth and Light 1982; Hinde *et al.* 1985; Gellatly *et al.* 1989). At any age the point remains that much of our activity is social, dependent on mutual understanding and help: we cannot construct a tower, for example, if we cannot communicate about the building.

3.4 RELATIVITY AND REALITY IN THE NATURAL AND BIO-PSYCHOLOGICAL SCIENCES

3.4.1 Is what is relative really real?

Relativity in the knowledge of intentionality raises problems concerning its objectivity. In so far as relativity is taken to mean subjectivity as opposed to objectivity, then this purported knowledge will seem illusory, more apparent than real, particularly in comparison with what we expect from and find in the natural sciences.

The observer-relativity in folk psychological attributions of meaning is cited by Stich, for example, as one reason why cognitive science had better do without them (Stich 1983, p. 136). It was argued in the first chapter (Subsection 1.3.8) that this avoidance strategy has to make the dubious assumption that the information-carrying states posited by cognitive psychology can be characterized without references to meaningful content, and would deny cognitive science access to the predictive utility of explanations which invoke meaningful content. We have argued that cognitive science can, and has to, use such explanations, at least when modelling intentional behaviour. But here, as it were, we pick up the tab. If the argument is going to be that cognitive science can, and has to, use the notion of meaning (for the purpose of explaining and predicting intentional behaviour), then we owe an account of how science can include a relativistic epistemology.

It may, on the other hand, be possible to grant the predictive utility of intentional explanations without supposing that they posit anything objectively real. This would be a so-called *instrumentalist* (or perhaps 'interpretationist') as opposed to a *realist* construal of intentional language. It has advantages particularly if it is supposed that the only real states that intentional states could be are brain states, but it turns out, for example on connectionist grounds, that there are no brain states of the requisite kind (cf. above, subsection 2.2.2).

Dennett's views on these matters are appropriately complicated, and this is one way in which he sets off to explain his position (1988, p. 496):

> Sometimes attributions of belief appear entirely objective and unproblematic, and sometimes they appear beset with subjectivity and infected with cultural relativism. Catering to these two families of cases are two apparently anti-thetical theoretical options: *realism*, the view that beliefs are objective things in the head which could be discovered . . . by physiological psychology; and *interpretationism*, the view that attributing a belief is a highly relativistic undertaking . . .—'it all depends what you're interested in'.
>
> It is a common mistake to see these alternatives as mutually exclusive and exhaustive. . . . My thesis is that while belief is a perfectly objective phenomenon (which apparently makes me a realist), it can be discerned only from the point of view of someone who adopts a certain predictive strategy, the *intentional stance* (which apparently makes me an interpretationist).

Dennett's version of realism emphasizes the grounding of intentional attributions in patterns of activity more than correspondence with in-the-head items (Dennett 1988; cf. also above, subsection 2.2.3). These patterns are typically not captured by physicalist descriptions: they are higher-order invariants which cut across physically (geometrically) defined movements, concerning such as variable routes to the same goal (Dennett 1988; also below and subsection 1.3.6). Referring to hypothetical super-physicists who predict everything on the basis of a completed physical theory, using therefore only the physical stance and not the intentional stance, Dennett writes (1987, p. 37):

My view is, I insist, a *sort* of realism, since I maintain that the patterns the Martians miss are really, objectively there to be noticed or overlooked. How could the Martians, who 'know everything' about the physical events in our world, miss these patterns? What could it mean to say that some patterns, while objectively there, are visible only from one point of view?

Now of course invariance relations as such are not problematic in science or philosophy, but in the present case the particular problem is their *relativity* to the observer. On this point Dennett writes (1987, p. 39):

> I claim that the intentional stance provides a vantage point for discerning . . . useful patterns. These patterns are objective—they are *there* to be detected—but from our point of view they are not *out there* entirely independent of us, since they are patterns composed partly of our own 'subjective' reactions to what is out there; they are the patterns made to order for our narcissistic concerns . . .

The question is whether our patterns of intentionality are objectively real (like the invariance relations recognized in physics and chemistry), or whether they are more like beauty. Dennett steers a course here between objectivity and subjectivity, though one indeed that he has had repeatedly to explain and defend. Thus Dennett, (1987, p. 37):

> Perhaps the major source of disquiet about my position over the years has been its delicate balancing act on the matter of the observer-relativity of attributions of belief and other mental states. On my view, is belief attribution (or meaning) in the eye of the beholder? Do I think there are *objective truths* about what people believe, or do I claim that all attributions are just *useful fictions*?

In what follows we propose a position like Dennett's in that it tries to define a notion of objectivity as well as of subjectivity in attributions of intentionality. It rests on relativistic definitions of the kind invoked so far in this section. By all means we are unlikely to have as much success as Dennett, let alone more, in vindicating such a view!

The assumption that relativity involves subjectivity as opposed to objectivity was criticized in the preceding subsection. It was argued there that with relativity we lose the notion of *absolute* objectivity, but we gain instead a relativistic notion. Fundamental to the relativistic definition are the following points: the 'object' is that which in an interaction is independent of the subject's control, and further, is that which appears from different points of view (in different interactions). The absolute object, by contrast, is defined independently of any interactions with the subject of knowledge. In the context of a relativistic epistemology, finding relativity in any particular domain of knowledge is so far nothing to get excited about. Relativity looks problematic, of course, only against the background of absolutist preconceptions, only if we think that knowledge ought to be, or in the paradigm case is, relativity-free. And this is where a certain view of the sciences makes its appearance. The idea would be that the best or most fundamental science, physics (and perhaps chemistry), just describe reality *as it is*, untainted by anything like relativity (subjectivity). Such a view assigns physics (and perhaps chemistry) a privileged position as compared with the rest of the sciences, and suggests that any theory that wants to envisage intentionality, with its manifest observer-relativity, is in danger of falling off the edge of the scientific world.

The question that presents itself here is therefore this: 'What notion of objectivity belongs to the natural sciences, the absolute or the relativistic?' The latter answer is at least superficially suggested by the fact that we live in the age of relativity theory, as opposed to Newtonian mechanics. Is the notion of relativity in the new physics anything to do with the relativity evident in psychology, or is all that there is here just verbal coincidence?

In order to tackle this question we consider briefly at the start of the next subsection some aspects of relativity expressed at the start of twentieth-century physics, arguing that the new physics is indeed relativistic in the sense defined so far. The inference then is that, just so far as concerns the involvement of relativity, knowledge of mind is in the same position as knowledge in the natural sciences.

In effect the argument is that relativity is implicated in *all* knowledge, whether in physics or elsewhere. The generality of this conclusion is consistent with conclusions reached in the preceding section by considering what is meant by saying that someone is following a rule (as opposed to behaving randomly). The enquiry ended with relativistic conclusions, but the route went by way of considering what is involved in making judgement, including about natural regularities. In brief, and as was anticipated at the beginning of the section (subsection 3.3.1), the remit of the notion of rule-following is very wide, concerning judgement as such. It is, then, not likely that some judgement is a matter of rule-following activity, while other judgement is a matter of static structures resembling possible states of affairs. This would be peculiar hotchpotch philosophy—just a mistake. But it would be equally a mistake, indeed it would be the corresponding mistake in the theory of knowledge, to suppose that much, or even most, forms of knowledge were relative, involving (activity of) the subject, while some special type, inevitably alone considered 'genuine', managed to avoid this altogether. There would just be two epistemologies here, unconnected except in their anachronistic juxtaposition.

On the other hand, there are *differences* as well as similarities to account for. In some sense which awaits explication, the methods of physics and the phenomena with which it is concerned are more objective, less subjective, than empathic methods and the intentional phenomena which are thereby known. After briefly considering relativity in physics we shall go on to argue that there is a matter of degree here, a continuity in the sciences which can be accomodated by a relativistic epistemology. By contrast, epistemologies that posit absolutes typically dictate choices: (absolutely) objective, or else (absolutely) subjective.

3.4.2 Relativity in physics, and on upwards, with increasing differentiation

Within the special theory of relativity, observers in different positions in space-time measure spatio-temporal relations with different results.[8] The results of measurement depend partly on the nature of the observer with respect to the quantities being measured. In this sense, measurement is an 'interaction' between observer and observed. Differences in results are apparent in so far as the observers differ (with respect to the quantities being measured). However, these differences do not imply that the various results obtained are incompatible with one another: the apparent incompatibility is resolved by taking into account the differences between observers.

There are rules linking results obtained from one spatio-temporal framework to results obtained from another, these being the so-called Lorentz transformations. Contrary to what is presupposed in Newtonian mechanics, there is no priviledged framework for measurement, and no corresponding 'absolute' length of an object, nor 'absolute' time of an event: spatio-temporal relations are always relative to one or another framework from which they are measured.

In the beginnings of modern science, the great division between absolute and relative qualities was imposed by prising apart the primary qualities of objects, including mass, shape, and velocity, from the so-called secondary qualities, the sensory qualities of colour, smell, etc. The primary qualities were absolute properties of objects, independent of human perception of them. The secondary qualities, on the other hand, were relative (involved interaction). Hence they belonged not to the (absolute) object, but rather to the subjective 'mind', created for this purpose, to be the bearer of the non-absolute qualities. One sign of the problem in all this was the fact that properties of mass, space, and time were, as much as the secondary qualities, evident in sensory perception and hence, of course, appeared just as relative. This point was made early on by Berkeley as part of his attempt to dismantle mind–matter dualism (Berkeley 1710).

There are, no doubt, interesting differences as well as similarities between primary and secondary qualities of objects (for recent discussion see, for example, McGinn 1983; Hacker 1987), but whatever these differences may be, it is not possible, in the context of relativity physics, to define them in the seventeenth-century way, in terms of what is or is not absolute. In contemporary physics the primary qualities are measured by interactions, and the results of measurement are relative to the measure. The critical difference between primary and secondary qualities therefore cannot turn on the absence of interaction and relativity in the former case.

Distinctions here will have to be made out in *another* way, specifically, in terms of the nature of the measures involved. Space and time are measured by rods and clocks, whereas colour, for example, is apparent only to more complicated, specialist measuring instruments. Within a relativistic framework it is possible to make discriminations between *more or less general* measures and realities. This line of thought is pursued below.

Let us take what is, by all means, a long jump, from physics to psychology, to the 'measurement' of mental states. Knowledge of such states depends partly on the nature of the observer with respect to the qualities being measured, that is, on the mental states of the observer. In this sense knowledge of mental states is an interaction between observer and observed. Different results will be obtained to the extent that observers differ. But this apparent incompatibility can be resolved by taking into account differences between observers. There is no absolute truth concerning mental states on particular occasions: their measurment is always relative to the mental state of one or another observer.

So far, then, the epistemology of mental states is formally similar to the epistemology of space-time. In this case there is no reason to say, indeed there is reason to deny, that psychology is committed to a form of knowledge second-rate compared with that in physics; neither is there reason to doubt the reality of its objects, any more than there is to doubt the reality of spatio-temporal relations.

On the other hand, the argument has, by all means, made a long jump: knowledge of mental states seems and is very different from knowledge of physical magnitudes, in particular because subjectivity and relativity are much more apparent. Let us put down some stepping-stones.

Subjectivity and relativity become apparent to the extent that observers differ in respect of what is being measured. Since generally we share the same spatio-temporal framework, we agree in measurement of spatial and temporal relations. Likewise, we have in common basic perceptual systems, so there is broad consensus concerning familiar perceptual properties of objects, including the so-called secondary qualities. The focus of the present discussion is, by contrast, the lack of agreement between observers in the attribution of intentionality, the manifest appearance of subjectivity and relativity. However, lack of agreement here is just what is expected from the point of view of a relativistic epistemology. To the extent that the measures differ (with respect to what is being measured), the results of measurement also vary, and in the particular case of mentality and intentionality there are high degrees of individual differences. Along the phylogenetic scale there is increasing systemic organization and increasing differentiation of species. Along the ontogenetic scale in humans, there is also increasing systemic organization and increasing differences among individuals. There is in both cases a logical connection between increasing complexity of systemic function and increasing differentiation (individuality). The 'higher' behaviour of humans, and the mentality that regulates it, represent the extreme of biological, or bio-psychological, differentiation. This differentiation characterizes both the 'object' of measurement and the measuring instrument. Here, then, we find most disagreement. But this does not mean that subjectivity and relativity arise in knowledge *for the first time*, still less that there can really be no *knowledge* here. On the contrary, subjectivity and relativity characterize all (empirical) knowledge. It is just that what was before hidden among what we have in common becomes apparent in our differences. Disagreement in judgement concerning the intentionality at work in higher behaviour is a logical consequence of individual differences in cognitive organization.

3.4.3 Reliability, validity, and the subject/object distinction

Agreement in judgement is greatest in those respects in which people are alike in constitution and competence, for example in judgement whether a needle is at a certain position on a dial, or whether such-and-such is red. But as perception, cognition, and emotion become more complex, individuality is increasingly apparent. And since the perception of psycho-logic depends on psychological characteristics of the perceiver, this perception may vary from person to person. Indeed a person may fail entirely to register a desire, say, in another, if the person knows no such motivation in his or her own case. The measurement of higher cognitive-affective phenomena will certainly be less reliable in a group picked at random than measurement of, say, the number of ticks on a questionnaire. This reflects the individuality of human beings in the relevant respects. But agreement will be apparent in so far as observers are alike in respect of the qualities being observed. The implication is that even the most complex psychological interpretation of behaviour can be reliable among observers, provided they are similar with respect to cognitive-affective characteristics.

The above remarks concern reliability. Let us consider now validity, which refers to accuracy of measurement, or truth, and is not secured by reliability alone. In epistemology that takes interaction as fundamental, there is no place for a conception of truth as static correspondence between measure and what is measured (cf. Subsections 1.3.2–3). The appropriate conception of truth is dynamic, to do with interactions and relations between them, and indeed turns out to be closely connected to reliability.

All attempts at measurement, as interactions, are valid in the restricted sense of providing information. The procedure of observation produces a certain result, which is real, and which in principle at least is repeatable. The result depends on qualities in the measure and qualities in the object measured. The question then arises as to what is due to one or the other. This question, however, cannot be answered on the basis of a single case. The distinction between objective and subjective arises not in one appearance but in many. Roughly, features that are common in many interactions are defined as due to qualities in the object, and those that are particular to any one are defined as due to qualities in the subject. The concept of interaction is fundamental, and the concepts of 'subject' and 'object' are derivative. This idea is fundamental to theory in various areas of psychology (Hundert 1989), including development (Piaget 1955; Russell 1995) and personality (Bowers 1973; Mischel 1979).

A valid observation may be defined as one that correctly represents the object. Bearing in mind the above conception of object, we may say that a reliable observation, that is, one constant between several observers (or conditions of observation), is already valid. On the other hand, we have the idea that reliable observation can still be wrong. However, according to relativistic epistemology, this possibility of error is not to be understood in terms of failure to correspond to an absolute object. It concerns rather failure to predict correctly the results of further measurement. The 'object' is revealed in, and is defined in terms of, its interactions with measuring instruments. Thus the valid measurement—the one true to the object—is that which correctly predicts the results of other measurements. In brief, validity is a matter of generalizability, and the distinction between validity and reliability becomes blurred. The intimate connection between agreement and truth falls out as a natural consequence of relativistic philosophy, whereas according to a simple correspondence theory of truth it has to remain fundamentally obscure. This relativistic idea is clearly expressed in contemporary statistical theory of reliability and validity. Generalizability theory blurs the distinction between the two, in contrast to the so-called classical definition of validity in terms of the 'true score' (Cronbach *et al.* 1963).

The above remarks concern judgement generally but, of course, apply to attributions of intentionality, the topic of this chapter. The implication is that any attribution of intentionality (or meaning) provides information concerning the observer and what is observed. To the extent that the judgement provides the former only, it tells us nothing about the object of judgement; it is subjective and invalid. Still, we may infer something, concerning the one making the judgement, for example that he or she always sees the same meanings, and is inclined always to say roughly the same thing. Conversely, to the extent that a judgement provides information about the person being observed, we may infer correct predictions concerning what he or she will do in various circumstances. To the extent that a judgement supports such predictions, it is objective and valid. Thus we arrive at the unsurprising conclusion (implicit throughout the first chapter) that attribution of meaning is objectively valid in so far as it takes account of, and successfully predicts, the relevant observable phenomena.

In practice our opinions will differ more or less as we attempt to see the meaningful connections at work in behaviour. But the appearance of disagreement is no reason for scepticism about our endeavours. The issue of truth runs deeper than agreement or disagreement in opinions. Science aims not at agreement, but at correct representation of the phenomena.

In relativistic theories, the phenomena are conceived as being fundamentally interactions between the subject and object of measurement. Within this framework, it is predicted that there will be differences in the results of measurement made from different points of view, but these differences are subsumed under rules that take into account the different points of view from which measurements are made. In the special theory of relativity, these are the Lorentz transformations. An adequate psychological theory of intentionality, one which accurately represents the phenomena, should seek coherence in conflicting interpretations of intentionality among different individuals, by taking into account their diverse psychological characteristics. There is no reason why the theory of intentionality should become paralysed when faced with disagreement in judgement: on the contrary, conditions of agreement and of disagreement become part of its subject-matter. In other words, one aim of cognitive psychology is to find 'invariance laws' in the midst of individual differences (cf. Shaw and McIntyre 1974).

3.4.4 Bio-psychological measures and realities

The proposal is, then, that relativity in knowledge of intentional states does not in itself imply that the objects of such knowledge are less real than the objects known to physical theory. Perception of patterns of intentionality depends partly on our subjective reactions and concerns, that is to say, on intentional characteristics of the perceiver. But results of measurement of spatio-temporal magnitudes also depend partly on the observer's relevant characteristics, namely, position in space and time. In both cases subjectivity is combined with objectivity: measurement made from one point of view can be right or wrong, this distinction being drawn by reference to measurements made from other points of view.

It is true that patterns of intentionality do not appear as such in physics, nor would they appear (let us suppose) in a completed physics. A physical description of a chess game would not distinguish between intentional strategies and random sequences of moves, or indeed between either of those and the table being overturned by the wind. So if (a completed) physics describes all that is in reality, then patterns of intentionality are excluded as unreal, as perhaps fictions useful for prediction but no more.

But what is the basis for the claim that physics describes all that is real? Presumably this claim rests partly on the idea that physics describes reality free of any reference to subjectivity and relativity of measurement. But it does not: this idea is a leftover from seventeenth-century science. A completed physics, if current trends are any indication, will include reference to observers in space-time using rods and clocks, etc. To say that physics is free of observer-relativity, while higher-level sciences such as psychology are not, marks the distinction in entirely the wrong way, in any case in a way long past its sell-by date, and to say on these grounds that the one deals with reality (or real reality) while the other deals with convenient (or inconvenient) fictions compounds the error.

Another way of marking the differences is needed now, and it has nothing to do with the reality of physical objects as opposed to the unreality of everything else. Rather, it falls out of what is fundmental to the new epistemology, namely, the nature of the measure and its sensitivity. The distinction between physics and the behavioural sciences lies not in the absence as opposed to the presence of observer-relativity, but rather in the nature of the measuring instruments and consequently in the nature of what is measured; and this distinction is not absolute, but is a gradation. Measurement of spatio-temporal relations presupposes observers within space-time using spatio-temporal measures. But there are more and different kinds of measures in reality which are not the concern of physics. Biology and psychology study sensory and cognitive systems of increasing complexity which are sensitive to patterns of similarity and difference in the environment relevant to life, action, and social intercourse (cf. Chapter 6). Along the phylogenetic and ontogenetic scales, these measures of reality become increasingly differentiated, diverse, and individual, with consequent manifestation of subjectivity and relativity of measurement. However, what is perceived by the bio-psychic measures are no less real from the point of view of those measures than space and time are to the observer limited to the use of rods and clocks. The point is rather that the bio-psychic measures are sensitive to aspects of reality which are inaccessible to the measuring instruments of physics.

The central problem for this chapter has been knowledge of mind and meaning, in particular its apparent subjectivity which compares unfavourably with the objectivity of the natural sciences. We have argued, however, that this subjectivity is properly described as relativity, and that relativity characterizes all knowledge, including the physical sciences. Relativity pervades one subject's knowledge of another, but also the subject's knowledge of the object. By the same considerations, objectivity is also relativistic, defined in terms of invariance in interactions. It is inevitable that if the measure is relative, so is what is measured; just as absolute measures belong with absolute objects.

While it would be fair to say that concepts of absolutes are being replaced by concepts of relativity, still the influence of the former remains strong. Conceptions of representation and reality as absolute characteristically define them in advance, a priori; they circumscribe the limits of thought and reality. Relativistic definitions, by contrast, are more fluid and flexible.

Empiricism and materialism, both aspects of positivism, are examples of dogmatic philosophies that define the nature of reality and thought in advance. Empiricism proposed an account of thought and the reality represented in terms of sense-experience. It is now acknowledged, however, that in general the content of thought and language cannot be so defined (Chapter 1, subsection 1.4.1).

The materialist world-picture, however, remains pervasive in contemporary thought, and it exerts powerful pressure to adopt the materialist definition of content. Materialism claims that ultimately or fundamentally all that exists is the reality postulated by (a completed) physics. An apparent consequence of this view is that ultimately or fundamentally this reality is alone what is available for representation in thought. However, since many or most familiar concepts apparently do not coincide with physical categories, the materialist definition of content tends to be restricted to so-called 'natural kinds'. For example, the meaning of 'water' is taken to be anchored by its reference to H_2O, as in the thought-experiments discussed in Chapter 2 (subsection 2.5.2). The use of the expression 'natural' rather than 'physical' kind here signifies the materialist preconception that nature is to be identified with physical nature (with nature as defined by physics).

The materialist definition was, however, rejected (in subsection 2.5.4), as being inappropriate for biology and psychology. These are the sciences that (unlike physics and chemistry) use the concepts of functional behaviour regulated by information processing and informational content. They invoke such concepts in order to achieve adequate explanation of interactions between living systems and their environment, and the criterion of content appropriate to such explanation is fundamentally behavioural. Physical or physico-chemical kinds define informational content only to the extent that sensitivity to such kinds shows up in behaviour (in some behavioural response of the system), including specifically in discriminative behaviour. In general, the content of informational states, what they are about, is defined in terms of interaction, with explicit or implicit reference to the capacities and aims of the living being (subsection 2.5.4, also Section 4.5). In the context of the present discussion, the point is that this definition of meaning broadens out the notions of representation and what is represented beyond what can be described in terms of the natural sciences, to include also the bio-psychological measures and the realities they represent. The bio-psychological measures—living beings—are sensitive to aspects of reality which are salient to action; these aspects may include, though in any case they certainly exceed, those aspects accessible to the measures of physics.

A working assumption of cognitive-behavioural science is that ('higher') behaviour is to be explained in terms of regulation by mental states which carry processed information. Definition of the processed information carried by mental states involved in the regulation of action will include reference to its regulatory, or causal, role. Now it is also a conceptual truth that mental states represent reality. Integrating these two characterizations of mental states leads towards the idea that reality is—to put it briefly—*that which is encountered in action*. Another way of putting this point is to say that the reality represented in perception and thought is relative to cognitive processes within the living being, processes that serve in the regulation of activity.

This kind of approach to the definition of reality belongs with cognitive-behavioural science. However, it runs counter to several preconceptions of the traditional scientific world-picture. It is incompatible with materialism, since the reality encountered as relevant to action cannot generally be defined in the terms of physics. Beneath materialism lies a still deeper metaphysical prejudice, that reality should be defined independently of any reference to the subject. But the reality of action obviously cannot be defined in this way: it is an interaction between subject and object, between the living being and its environment.

If there are a priori categories of thought, they will be determined by what it means to be a living being; they will be biological and psychological categories, not primarily categories of physics and chemistry. Here would be included, for example, information concerning orientation in space and time, consumption of food (energy), threat, reproduction, and so on, and also, where appropriate, information necessary to social interaction, for example concerning the meaning of conventional signs.

Underlying such definitions of content are assumptions concerning the aims of action. It is a moot point, however, whether the aims of action, and therefore the categories of thought, can be circumscribed a priori. As noted above (subsection 3.4.2), the phylogenetic and ontogenetic scales are characterized by increasing complexity and differentiation of function: ends become served by increasingly diverse means, and new ends and means appear. For human beings in particular, the purposes of action and the contents of thought are diverse and unlimited.

The impossibility of circumscribing the content of human thought is connected partly to our use of language: in language diverse and unlimited 'meanings' become available as guides for action. This claim follows on from rejection of attempts to define the meaning of language and thought a priori, in particular from rejection of empiricist and materialist (positivist) definitions of meaning. Further, the content of thought as expressed in language apparently exceeds what is relevant to the necessities of life as envisaged by (evolutionary) biology.

To illustrate this point, consider the case of a person perceiving a shadow in the darkness. This perception may cause the belief that something rectangular-shaped is present, or further, the belief that there is danger, but also, given the requisite pre-existing system of thought, for which presumably language is required, the perception may give rise to the belief that there is concealed in the shadows an angel carrying a message. The first content can be defined in terms of physics, and can be envisaged by empiricist and materialist accounts of meaning; the first and the second content can be envisaged by (evolutionary) biology; but the third is the thought of a reality far removed from what can be defined in the terms of those philosophical and scientific theories.

All three types of content, however, have to be envisaged by psychology as a cognitive-behavioural science. The third is no less relevant than the first two to the cognitive explanation and prediction of behaviour. Psychology has to acknowledge whatever mental content makes a difference. The logic of psychological explanation and prediction is, of course, all the same whether the cognitive states invoked are true or false, scientifically valid or otherwise. For the purposes of explanation, psychology is not committed to the reality of the object of thought, only to the reality of the thought and its effects in action.

The answer to the general question as to how we determine mental content is that we observe what people do and listen to what they say, and compare the one with the other. The content of thought revealed by these methods exceeds what is countenanced by traditional attempts to circumscribe the objects of thought a priori. In general the behavioural criterion of mental content is an empirical one, dependent on observation. It stands opposed to preconceptions about what thought and the reality represented in thought *must* be like.

The proposal is, then, that it is impossible to prescribe the meanings at work in the regulation of action. The point is not that no categories of thought are fixed for us, only that not all are. Our position in the nature described by physics, and our position as living beings within nature as described by biology, provides the basis for, and places constraints on, all action and therefore all meaning.

As already noted in the previous and in the present section, intersubjectivity is fundamental to the relativistic definition of thought and reality. This aspect of relativity is still further removed from, and alien to, empiricist and materialist theories. They conceive thought solipsistically: the subject represents sense-experience or physical reality, in which realms other people appear as a special, though according to fundamental theory not so special, case.

The appearance of conflict here between relativistic and dogmatic philosophies over the role of intersubjectivity is genuine, not superficial. It is specifically *not* a matter of a philosophical theory of cognitive content (e.g. a materialist one) running parallel to, above or below, empirical theory which recognizes the role of the interpersonal in cognition. The empirical theory (such as was mentioned at the end of the preceding section) does not belong with empiricism and materialism, but with a priori principles which make fundamental the role of the interpersonal in cognition. The concept of 'reality' can be defined generally as that which determines the correctness or otherwise of thought. If reality is defined as an absolute object, the only constraint on thought is the independent nature of the absolute object represented. This idea if found in all dogmatic philosophies, including materialism in its current form. There is no essential connection between the true-or-false representation of reality and intersubjectivity. In relativistic conceptions of measurement, however, what determines the correctness or otherwise of measurement is not correspondence or lack of correspondence with an absolute object, but is rather comparison, agreement or otherwise, between points of view. This communication is fundamental to reality, taking the place of the dogmatically postulated object.

3.5 SUMMARY

The observer-relativity in knowledge of mind and meaning, and the various problems to which it gives rise, have long been recognized (Section 3.1). The issues were approached in Section 3.2 by considering the role of empathy (mental simulation), as well as theory, in our knowledge of mind. The behaviour which signifies mental states itself has intentionality (subsection 3.2.1), and perception of this plausibly involves the observer's own intentional states (subsection 3.2.2). Mental simulations construed as thought-experiments provide a fast, easy to perform means of experimenting with the causal relations among mental states and between mental states and tendencies to behaviour, and hence, along with observation of actual cases, can be part of the empirical basis of the theory of mind (subsection 3.2.3). Knowledge of mind, like other forms of empirical–theoretical knowledge, is surrounded by the possibility of error (subsection 3.2.4). The theory of empathy seems to give priority to first-person knowledge, with knowledge of oneself being the basis for understanding the other, but this appearance is deceptive: the simulations (or thought-experiments) in question are about intentional states and their connectedness, and attribution of the states and connections to this or that subject is a further step (subsection 3.2.5). This attribution involves both facility with perspectives and theory, the implication being that in developmental theory we do not have to choose between the child's increasing theoretical sophistication and the child's increasing facility with perspectives: both are fundamental and they are linked logically (subsection 3.2.6).

In Section 3.3 we approach knowledge of intentionality, and its observer-relativity, by way of Wittgenstein's discussion of rule-following. The notion of rule-following serves to capture the concept of *order* in reality and thought, as being through time, in activity, as opposed to being static, in the form of objects (subsection 3.2.1). The negative conclusion of Wittgenstein's analysis of rule-following is that the rule is not laid down in advance; the positive implication is that it is created in practice (subsection 3.3.2). The concept of agreement enters here as critical. This is not, however, because agreement is a necessary or a sufficient condition of someone's following a rule. The point is rather that one person's judgement about another that they are following a rule, is based on the observer's inclination to agree with what the other is doing (subsection 3.3.3). Relativity has traditionally been thought (since Plato's critique in the *Theaetetus*) to imply subjectivity and the collapse of objectivity. What is lost, however, is (only) the notion of an *absolute* object. The object makes many appearances, and in particular in those cases not under the control of the observer (subsection 3.3.4).

The relativity of attributions of intentionality, particularly in contrast to the objectivity in the physical sciences, seems to suggest that they describe no objective reality (subsection 3.4.1). However, consistent with the conclusions reached in the preceding section, it is argued that relativity pervades all the sciences, including physics. However, with increasing differentiation in phylogenesis and ontogenesis, subjectivity in the form of individual differences increasingly appears, both in the measures and in what is measured (subsection 3.4.2). In the context of relativity, validity and objectivity are defined in terms of multiple measurements made from different points of view, with comparisons and contrasts between them being dependent on invariance relations (subsection 3.4.3). Bio-psychological measures are sensitive to more and different aspects of reality as compared to those in the physical sciences. Contrary to what is envisaged by dogmatic philosophies such as empiricism and materialism, the implication of relativistic epistemology is that the reality we represent cannot be determined in advance, and is in its foundations interpersonal (subsection 3.4.4).

NOTES

1. We assume that this interpretation of empathy, or mental simulation, as being a form of thought-experiment, is plausible and interesting, but it is only more or less compatible with the various detailed proposals to be found in the literature. Recent collections of papers on comparisons and contrasts between empathy and theory-based epistemologies of mind are those of Davies and Stone (1995*a,b*). These include reprints of original papers and commentaries that appeared in a special issue of *Mind and Language* in 1992, as well as new papers. One of these is by one of the present authors (Bolton 1995) and it brings together themes running through this chapter and chapters 1 and 8.

2. In brief, thought-experimentation interweaves with theory, and hence the conclusion anticipated at the end of the previous subsection, that in so far as empathy or mental simulations involve anything like thought-experiments, they cannot be run without theory. If this interpretation of empathy is valid, the assumption of incompatibility

between empathy-based and theory-based epistemologies is mistaken. As already noted, this assumption is common, among proponents and opponents of simulation theory alike (for example, Gopnik and Wellman 1992; Gordon 1992; Stich and Nichols 1992). On the other hand, other commentators have seen it as obvious that simulations are going to require theory (Blackburn 1992). We endorse this line, and also the converse, that the theory of mind would work better if it made use of simulations in its empirical basis.

3. See Wittgenstein (for example 1953, sections 244 and 288ff.), and for commentary, for example, Bolton (1979, pp. 194–208) and Pears (1988, pp. 346–50).

4. The reference here is to Klein's notion of projective identification (Klein 1946; Sandler 1988). Klein described projective identification as being a basis for fundamental distinctions, as between self and non-self, as well as being among the mechanisms of defence, to be discussed in Chapter 8 (subsection 8.2.3).

5. Commentaries are numerous, and include, for example, Folgelin (1976), Kripke (1980), and Pears (1988). The treatment in the text of rule-following is most similar to the one in Bolton (1979), and discussion of the closely related problem of *form* (or *order*) summarizes some points in Bolton (1982).

6. In his influential commentary, Kripke (1980, Chapter 2) argues that Wittgenstein's analysis of rule-following leads to a major sceptical paradox about meaning, to the effect that there really is no such thing as meaning anything by a word. Kripke focuses on Wittgenstein's negative arguments, concerning what following a rule is not, and in particular, on the conclusion that the rule is not laid down in advance. Kripke then infers that, according to Wittgenstein's arguments, there is no rule, and hence no meaning. But he neglects Wittgenstein's positive proposal, that the rule is made in practice, to which we now turn in the text. Similar rejoinders to Kripke have been made by other commentators, for example McGinn (1984), Pears (1988).

We may remark briefly on interesting positive proposals that Kripke goes on to make, which interact with the topics of the present chapter, and of the essay as a whole. He suggests (1980, Chapter 3) that Wittgenstein does not rest content with the alleged sceptical paradox about rule-following and meaning, but rather offers a 'sceptical solution' to it, involving reference to the community. Kripke uses the expression 'sceptical solution' to recall Hume's famous treatment of causality. Kripke notes (1980, pp. 66f.) that Hume's sceptical solution involved two features of causal inferences: first, that they are based in custom (habit, or natural inclination), and secondly, that they pertain essentially to a number of cases, not to one in isolation. Plausibly, considerations of these kinds play a role in Wittgenstein's account of rule-following, as we shall see. However, it is not *these* features that make Hume's solution a *sceptical* one. Hume's positive account remains 'sceptical' because, according to it, causal inference is is based in custom *as opposed to reason* (Hume 1777, V, I, 35–8). By contrast, Wittgenstein draws on a notion of custom (and natural inclination) in his account of rule-following, but such a notion is *not* opposed to reason. On the contrary, the account of rule-following is at the same time an account (or part of an account) of rationality, as discussed below in the text. A preconceived absolute definition of reason, against which the human measure is adversely compared, is a (or the) sure route to scepticism. And conversely, one way of avoiding scepticism is to countenance non-absolute, relativistic methods of representation and knowledge, as through this chapter.

7. The question whether an isolated individual, a Robinson Crusoe, could or could not follow a rule has been much debated in commentaries, usually in connection with Wittgenstein's 'private language argument', for example Ayer (1954), Rhees (1954), Kripke (1980), Peacocke (1981), McGinn (1984), Davies (1988), Pears (1988), and Budd (1989).

8. The following sketch is, of course, highly simplified and selective, emphasizing points to be taken up subsequently. For the interested reader unfamiliar with relativity theory, Einstein's own popular exposition (1920) is the best introduction. Berstein's commentary (1973) is excellent on the philosophical background of Einstein's revolution. A purely philosophical treatment, emphasizing relations between relativity theory in physics and the 'relativistic' conception of measurement and knowledge generally, can be found in Bolton (1979); this gives a more detailed version of the argument in the text. The main proposal to be made is that observer-relativity characterizes the theory of measurement in contemporary physics. This point is made in connection with the special theory of relativity because it appears there simply and clearly. The same point in much the same form appears also in the extended general theory. The issue of observer-relativity in the other great foundation of contemporary physics, quantum mechanics, requires a different kind of treatment, even superficial consideration of which is beyond the scope of the present essay. That said, it may be noted at least that the issue arises there in a radical form.

REFERENCES

Astington, J. W., Harris, P. L. and Olsen, D. R. (ed.) (1988). *Developing theories of mind.* Cambridge University Press, Cambridge.

Ayer, A. J. (1954). Can there be a private language? *Proceedings of the Aristotelian Society Suppl.*, 28, 63–76.

Baron-Cohen, S., Tager-Flusberg, H., and Cohen, D. (ed.) (1993). *Understanding other minds: perspectives from autism.* Oxford University Press, Oxford.

Berkeley, G. (1710). *The principles of human knowledge.* Reprinted in *The works of George Berkeley*, (ed. A. A. Luce and T. E. Jessop), vol. ii. Thomas Nelson and Sons, London, 1949.

Berstein, J. (1973). *Einstein.* Fontana, London.

Blackburn, S. (1992). Theory, observation, and drama. *Mind and Language*, 7, 187–203. (Reprinted in Davies, M. and Stone, A. (ed.) (1995). *Folk psychology: the theory of mind debate*, pp. 274–90. Blackwell, Oxford.

Bolton, D. (1979). *An approach to Wittgenstein's philosophy.* Macmillan, London.

Bolton, D. (1982). Life-form and idealism. In *Idealism, past and present*, (ed. G. Vesey), pp. 269–84. Cambridge University Press, Cambridge.

Bolton, D. (1995). Self-knowledge, error and disorder. In *Mental simulation: evaluations and applications*, (ed. M. Davies and A. Stone), pp. 209–34. Blackwell, Oxford.

Bowers, K. S. (1973). Situationalism in psychology. *Psychological Review*, 80, 307–30.

Budd, M. (1989). *Wittgenstein's Philosophy of Psychology*. Routledge, London.

Butterworth, G. and Light, P. (ed.) (1982). *Social cognition: Essays on the development of understanding*. Harvester, Sussex.

Byrne, R. W. and Whiten, A. (ed.) (1988). *Machiavellian intelligence*. Clarendon Press, Oxford.

Cornford, F. M. (1935). *Plato's theory of knowledge*. Routledge and Kegan Paul, London.

Cronbach, L. J., Rajaratnam, N., and Gleser, G. C. (1963). Theory of generalizability: a liberalization of reliability theory. *British Journal of Statistical Psychology*, 16, 137–63.

Davis, M. and Stone, A. (ed.) (1995a). *Folk psychology: the theory of mind debate*. Blackwell, Oxford.

Davies, M. and Stone, A. (ed.) (1995b). *Mental simulation: evaluations and applications*. Blackwell, Oxford.

Davies, S. (1988). Kripke, Crusoe and Wittgenstein. *Australian Journal of Philosophy*, 66, 52–66.

Dennett, D. (1987). *The intentional stance*. MIT Press, Cambridge, Mass.

Dennett, D. (1988). Precis of *The intentional stance*, with peer commentary. *The Behavioral and Brain Sciences*, 11, 495–546.

Einstein, A. (1920). *Relativity*, trans. R. W. Lawson. Methuen, London. (University Paperback, 1960.)

Folgelin, R. (1976). *Wittgenstein*. Routledge and Kegan Paul, London.

Fonagy, P. (1991). Thinking about thinking: some clinical and theoretical considerations in the treatment of a borderline patient. *International Journal of Psychoanalysis*, 72, 639–56.

Gellatly, A., Rogers, D., and Sloboda, J. (ed.) (1989). *Cognition and social worlds*. Clarendon Press, Oxford.

Goldman, A. (1989). Interpretation psychologized. *Mind and Language*, 4, 161–85. (Reprinted in Davies, M. and Stone, A. (ed.) (1995). *Folk psychology: the theory of mind debate*, pp. 74–99. Blackwell, Oxford.)

Gopnik, A. and Wellman, H. (1992). Why the child's theory of mind really is a theory. *Mind and Language*, 7, 145–71. (Reprinted in Davies, M. and Stone, A. (ed.) (1995). *Folk psychology: the theory of mind debate*, pp. 232–58. Blackwell, Oxford.)

Gordon, R. M. (1986). Folk psychology as simulation. *Mind and Language* 1, 158–71. (Reprinted in Davies, M. and Stone, A. (ed.) (1995). *Folk psychology: the theory of mind debate*, pp. 60–73. Blackwell, Oxford.)

Gordon, R. M. (1992). The Simulation Theory: objections and misconceptions. *Mind and Language*, 7, 11–34. (Reprinted in Davies, M. and Stone, A. (ed.) (1995). *Folk psychology: the theory of mind debate*, pp. 100–22. Blackwell, Oxford.)

Hacker, P. (1987). *Appearance and reality*. Blackwell, Oxford.

Harris, P. L. (1989). *Children and emotion: the development of psychological understanding*. Blackwell, Oxford.

Harris, P. L. (1992). From simulation to folk psychology: the case for development. *Mind and Language*, 7, 120–44. (Reprinted in Davies, M. and Stone, A. (ed.) (1995). *Folk psychology: the theory of mind debate*, pp. 207–31. Blackwell, Oxford.)

Heal, J. (1986). Replication and functionalism. In *Language, mind and logic*, (ed. J. Butterfield), pp. 135–50. Cambridge University Press, Cambridge. (Reprinted in Davies, M. and Stone, A. (ed.) (1995). *Folk psychology: the theory of mind debate*, pp. 45–59. Blackwell, Oxford.)

Hinde, R., Perret-Clermont, A. N., and Stevenson-Hinde, J. (ed.) (1985). *Social relationships and cognitive development*. Oxford University Press, Oxford.

Hobson, R. (1990). On acquiring knowledge about people and the capacity to pretend: response to Leslie (1987). *Psychological Review*, 97, 114–21.

Hobson, R. (1993). *Autism and the development of mind*. Lawrence Erlbaum Associates, Hillsdale, NJ.

Hume, D. (1777). *An enquiry concerning human understanding*, (ed. L. A. Selby-Bigge, 1902, (2nd edn). Oxford University Press, Oxford.

Hundert, E. (1989). *Philosophy, psychiatry and neuroscience. Three approaches to the mind*. Oxford University Press, Oxford.

Jaspers, K. (1923). *Allgemeine Psychopathologie*. Springer Verlag, Berlin. (English translation by Hoenig, J. and Hamilton, M. W. (1963). *General Psychopathology*. Manchester University Press.)

Klein, M. (1946). Notes on some schizoid mechanisms. *International Journal of Psychoanalysis*, 27, 99–110.

Kripke, S. (1980). *Wittgenstein on rules and private language*. Blackwell, Oxford.

Leslie, A. (1987). Pretense and representation: the origins of 'Theory of Mind'. *Psychological Review*, 27, 412–26.

McGinn, C. (1983). *The subjective view: secondary qualities and indexical thoughts*. Oxford University Press, Oxford.

McGinn, C. (1984). *Wittgenstein*. Blackwell, Oxford.

Mischel, W. (1979). On the interface of cognition and personality. *American Psychologist*, 34, 750–4.

Peacocke, C. (1981). Rule-following: the nature of Wittgenstein's arguments. In *Wittgenstein: to follow a rule*, (ed. S. H. Holtzman and C. M. Leich). Routledge and Kegan Paul, London.

Pears, D. (1988). *The false prison: a study of the development of Wittgenstein's philosophy*, Vol. 2. Clarendon Press, Oxford.

Perner, J. and Howes, D. (1992). 'He thinks he knows': and more developmental evidence against the simulation (role taking) theory. *Mind and Language*, 7, 72–86. (Reprinted in Davies, M. and Stone, A. (ed.) (1995). *Folk psychology: the theory of mind debate*, pp. 159–73. Blackwell, Oxford.)

Piaget, J. (1955) *The child's construction of reality*, (trans. M. Cook). Routledge and Kegan Paul, London.

Rhees, R. (1954). Can there be a private language? *Proceedings of the Aristotelian Society, Suppl.*, 28, 77–94.

Ripstein, A. (1987). Explanation and empathy. *Review of Metaphysics*, 40, 465–82.

Russell, J. (1995). At two with nature: agency and the development of self-world dualism. In *The body and the self*, (ed. J. Bermúdez, A. J. Marcel, and N. Eilan), pp. 127–51. MIT Press. Cambridge, Mass.

Sandler, J. (ed.) (1988). *Projection, identification, projective identification*. Karnac Books, London.

Shaw, R. and McIntyre, M. (1974). Algoristic foundations for cognitive psychology. In *Cognition and the symbolic processes*, (ed. W. Weimer and B. Palermo), pp. 305–62. Erlbaum Associates, Hillsdale, NJ.

Stich, S. (1983). *From folk psychology to cognitive science*. MIT Press, Cambridge, Mass.

Stich, S. and Nichols, S. (1992). Folk psychology: simulation or tacit theory? *Mind and Language*, 7, 35–71. (Reprinted in Davies, M. and Stone, A. (ed.) (1995). *Folk psychology: the theory of mind debate*, pp. 123–58. Blackwell, Oxford.)

Vygotsky, L. (1934). *Thought and language*, (Trans. Hanfmann, E. and Vakar, G. (1962). MIT Press, Cambridge, Mass).

Whiten, A. (ed.) (1991). *Natural theories of mind: the evolution, development and simulation of everyday mindreading*. Blackwell, Oxford.

Wittgenstein, L. (1921). *Tractatus logico-philosophicus*. (Trans. Pears, D. F. and McGuiness, B. F. (1961). Routledge and Kegan Paul, London.)

Wittgenstein, L. (1953). *Philosophical Investigations*, (ed. G. E. M. Anscombe and R. Rhees, trans. G. E. M. Anscombe). Blackwell, Oxford.

4
The definition of meaning: causal and functional semantics

4.1 INTRODUCTION

In the first chapter it was remarked that explanations of action in terms of mental states with meaning are effective in prediction, and the conclusion was drawn that such explanations must be, in some sense, causal. In the second chapter it was argued that the causal status of such explanations is compatible with the fact that the material causes of behaviour are in the brain, provided we assume that mental states are realized in brain states, and in particular that the brain encodes meaning. In the third chapter we turned to issues concerning mind, meaning, and objectivity. To some extent this was a diversion from the problem of meaning and causality, although emphasis in that discussion on the close connection between meaning and relativity belongs with the emphasis throughout the essay on action, on organism–environment interactions. In this chapter we return to meaning and causality.

Our task, pursuing the conclusion of the first chapter, is to explicate the sense in which explanations in terms of meaningful mental states are causal. In accordance with the conclusion of the second chapter, the task here is not to explicate a notion of immaterial as opposed to material causality, but is rather to explore the relation between causal explanation which does, and causal explanation which does not, appeal to the notion of encoded meaning (or information).

Meaningful states appear to be causes of behaviour, but also, they appear as effects of environmental causes. In the language of cognitive-behavioural psychology, cognitive (information-carrying) states mediate between stimuli and responses, being effects of the one and causes of the other.

At this stage of the argument, with the conclusion that meaningful or information-carrying states enter into causal relations, there is a powerful pressure to construe this 'semantic causation' as being simply 'causation' of the kind known in the physical sciences. Otherwise there is apparently a threat to the 'unity of science' and perhaps also to the physicalist assumption that all causing ultimately goes on at the physical level.

The pressure here is linked to the fast and plausible route to mind–brain identity considered at the beginning of Chapter 2, running as follows: 'so if, after all, mental states are causes of behaviour (if they figure in good scientific explanations), then, since we already know from physical theory that the material brain causes behaviour, mental states must be material brain states'. The parallel line of thought concerning causality runs roughly as follows: 'if, after all, semantic states are causes of behaviour (if they figure in good scientific physical causes, best identified in the physical sciences, then causal explanation that invokes semantic states must ultimately be, or be like, causal explanation in those sciences'.

On the other hand, there is an old problem here, the difference (dichotomy) between meaningful and causal connections. It was noted in the Introduction and first chapter (subsection 1.3.8) that the dichotomy between meaning and causality drawn in the cultural sciences at the turn of the century was based on what appear to be genuine differences between explanations in terms of beliefs, desires, reasons, etc., and causal explanations of the sort familiar in the natural sciences and physics in particular. The differences include that meaningful connections are evident already in particulars, while causal connections as determined in the natural sciences essentially involve generality: repeated or repeatable events, covered by general laws. It is difficult, in other words, to construe meaningful explanations as being causal in the sense familiar in the natural sciences, and entrenched in the scientific world-picture. This was the underlying problematic which prompted the turn-of-the-century dichotomy between meaning and causality.

The contemporary position, however, looks like this: respectable empirical sciences, including cognitive psychology, now envisage semantic states and their involvement in causal interactions, and hence there is pressure to break down the dichotomy between meaning and causality. There are broadly two ways of going about this: either causal explanations in terms of semantic states have to be shown to be (ultimately) the same, after all, as causal explanations in the natural sciences; or, it has to be shown that they are a distinctive, new form of causal explanation.

The first option is taken up by the doctrine known as causal semantics. It attempts to explicate the notion of meaning, or information, in terms an analysis of causality suited to the physical sciences. In Section 4.3 we see that the attempt fails. Before moving to a more positive thesis, we pause to consider in Section 4.4 a somewhat desperate suggestion, the only appeal of which is that it retains the requisite analysis of causality even though it cannot capture meaningful relations. The suggestion is that cognitive psychology should manage without semantics, and in particular should omit study of organism–environment interactions. This line of thought can reasonably be turned into a *reductio ad absurdum* argument against the assumption that the old view of causality is appropriate to meaningful connections.

In rejecting causal semantics, the argument is in effect that the original distinction between meaning and causality *as familiar in the natural sciences* is valid. It follows then that meaningful causal connections represent a distinctive form of causality. In other words, we pursue the second of the two options defined above.

Causal semantics explicates meaning using a notion of causality suited to the physical sciences. Its other distinguishing feature is that it defines meanings primarily in terms of their environmental causes rather than in terms of the interactions among them and their regulation of behaviour. This is connected with the fact that causal semantics envisages no fundamental role for systemic activity in the creation of meaning. This in turn goes along with the notion of causality at work here, in which nothing like systemic activity has any work to do. The implication is that the rejection of causal semantics involves a shift in the definition of meaning away from emphasis on 'input' towards emphasis on interactions between information-carrying states and their regulation of motor 'output'. The chief significance of this shift is that the definition of content can then take account of the contribution of the semantic processing system. Of course this kind of definition of meaning belongs with the idea invoked in all the preceding chapters, that meaningful states are invoked in order to explain (intentional) activity, and hence are to be understood essentially in terms of the difference they make to behaviour.

We consider in Section 4.5 so-called 'functional semantics', according to which information is defined with reference to the function of information-processing systems. Implicit in the discussion is the implication that the type of causal explanations that apply to functional, information-processing systems have distinctive features not apparent in the lower-level sciences. This conclusion is made explicit and explored in Section 4.6, with reference particularly to causal necessity and generality. Thus we develop through this chapter an argument for the claim that the form of causal explanation that applies to non-intentional phenomena (to phenomena under non-intensional descriptions), fails to capture the logic of causal explanation of intentional phenomena (of phenomena under intensional descriptions). In this way we will be working towards a distinction between two types of causal explanation, which may be called for convenience the non-intentional, and the intentional. This distinction will be elaborated in Chapter 5.

It should be remarked here that the distinction we are working towards is not that between non-functional and functional explanations. Functional (or teleological) explanations, which appeal to principles such as 'The function of cholorophyll in plants is to enable plants to perform photosynthesis', are characteristic of biology, and in their appeal to function, or purpose, they appear different from the non-functional explanations found in the sub-biological sciences. On the other hand, standard philosophy of science is that explanations of this type can be analysed into a set of non-functional, non-teleological statements (Nagel 1961). But this distinction and its apparent superficiality is not what is at issue here. We are concerned rather with the distinction between explanations which do, and explanations which do not, invoke semantic concepts (information-processing). A functional–teleological explanation of an information-processing system may be given in the form: 'A system of such-and-such kind encodes/processes information in order to facilitate such-and-such kind of activity'. It may be possible, along the lines of the standard analysis (Nagel 1961), to render this as a set of non-functional, non-teleological propositions, but the expression 'encodes/processes information' survives the analysis untouched. It is this expression, we suggest, that signifies a form of causal explanation distinct from what is found in the sub-biological natural sciences.

We begin in Section 4.2 by covering in more detail issues that we have sped past in this introduction, particularly concerning the analysis of causality. It should be said straightaway that the relevant issues in the philosophy of science and metaphysics are complicated, and even the 'more detail' will be exceedingly sketchy. The story has to start with Hume's analysis of causality in terms of constant conjunction (subsection 4.2.1), which prompts the problem of necessary connection (subsection 4.2.2). Consideration of Hume's problem leads to a widely accepted view that causality essentially involves *generality covered by a law of nature* (subsection 4.2.3). Further, there is a natural enough, common presupposition that the laws of nature are (ultimately) physical laws, or again, that all real causing goes on at the physical level. This presupposition leads to what will be called the 'physicalist' construal of causality (subsection 4.2.4). Causal connections, so understood, are apparently quite distinct from meaningful connections, as recognized in the turn-of-the-century dichotomy between the two (subsection 4.2.5). But this dichotomy, and the assumptions about causality that underlie it, have to be deconstructed in so far as meaningful explanations do seem to be causal. This task occupies the remainder of the chapter.

4.2 HUME'S ANALYSIS OF CAUSALITY, SOME STANDARD ELABORATIONS, AND THE PROBLEM OF MEANING

4.2.1 Correlation and generality

In his *Enquiry concerning human understanding*, Hume argued that our knowledge of cause and effect arises from experience of constant conjunction (1777, Sections IV and VII). This is to say: the judgement that event A causes event B is based in the observation that events of type A are always followed by events of type B. This aspect of Hume's analysis of causality is fundamental, and has to be kept in sight amidst the various complications that surround it, some of which we consider next.

In practice, on any one occasion we observe an event of type B preceded by complex of circumstances, C, in addition to an event of type A. To establish a causal link between A and B the relevance of those circumstances has to be determined. To establish whether A is a *necessary* condition of B we observe C without A, as naturally occurring or by contrivance, and observe whether or not B follows. To establish whether or not A is a *sufficient* condition of B we observe A without C, as naturally occurring or by contrivance, and observe whether or not B follows. These principles, elucidated by Mill (1843) in his 'methods of agreement and difference', underlie our modern idea of controlled experimentation.

In practice, particularly in the life-sciences, psychology, and the social sciences we rarely find universal generalizations, but rather partial ones, of the form: A is followed by B in a certain proportion of observed cases. Presumably whether or not B occurs following A depends on other, so far unknown factors, and the assumption is that there are universal, causal generalizations, even if we cannot determine them. One function of a universal generalization is to license the simple inductive inference: the next observed A will be followed by B. In the absence of a universal generalization, the problem is to determine the *probability* of the next A being followed by B, given that a certain proportion of As so far observed have been followed by B. This is the problem for the theory of statistical inference. Its complexity compounds in interaction with the problem cited above, that of controlling for potentially relevant variables. (The problem comes to concern the validity of the assumption that the circumstances associated with the next A are typical of those in the sample so far observed.) The life-sciences, psychological, and social sciences rely heavily, then, on statistical methodology rather than on simple induction from universal generalizations; the universal, causal generalizations are assumed rather than known.

Thus practical application of Hume's analysis of causal propositions in terms of constant conjunction between events is complicated by the need for controlled observation and statistical inference. Nevertheless, the analysis remains firm as the underlying basis of these scientific methods.

4.2.2 The problem of necessary connection

We consider now a very different kind of problem concerning Hume's analysis, philosophical rather than methodological. This is the problem, identified by Hume (1777, Section VII), as to whether constant conjunction is *all there is* to our notion of causality, whether, in particular, there is a connotation of *necessary connection* in our notion of causality which is not captured by the notion of constant conjunction.

It should be emphasized that this is not the problem frequently encountered in scientific practice, as to whether an observed association between two types of event signifies that the one causes the other, or is mere coincidence, or perhaps signifies a common cause of both. The alternatives here can be resolved in principle by application of Mill's methods, that is, by controlled observation or experiment. The distinction here between causal connection and constant conjunction is the distinction between observation of constant conjunction which does and which does not control for other relevant factors.

The *further* problem identified by Hume remains after application of the requisite scientific methodology, which is why it is philosophical rather than methodological.

Even in case it has been established that one kind of event is a sufficient (or necessary and sufficient) condition for the occurrence of another, is this all that is required to establish a causal connection between the two? Does the concept of causal connection also connote an element of necessary connection, which we could express by saying that if the one kind of event occurs, then the other *must* occur.

Hume gave a sceptical answer to the problem that he had identified: he could find no resources in his empiricist philosophy capable of explicating any such notion of (empirical) necessity. According to empiricism the phenomena are known by experience. Thus also, any correlation among the phenomena is to be known only on the basis of observation, and is simply a matter of contingent fact, not of any 'necessity'. What comes more or less to the same is that Hume supposed cause and effect to be discrete—entirely separate—events; so that we can, for example, always imagine the cause without the effect (Hume 1777, Section IV). Imaginative capacities aside, the point is that there is no logical, a priori, or conceptual linkage between the description of the cause and description of the event. There is in this sense at least no necessary connection between cause and effect, only observed association between kinds of event. This association, and no more, is all that is allowed by a strict empiricism.

The failure of empiricism to capture a priori conditions of experience, in particular necessity in causation, became a major rationale for Kant's subsequent 'Copernican revolution' in philosophy. For the present purpose, however, we omit discussion of the Kantian post-empiricist response, and consider rather a more contemporary solution.

4.2.3 The standard assumption: causality involves generality covered by natural law

It is widely acknowledged that there has to be a distinction between 'merely accidental' generalizations and generalizations with nomic, law-like necessity. For the statement 'A-events cause B-events' to be true there has to be a correlation between the two kinds of event, but also this correlation has to be, or to be a consequence of, a law of nature: it is not enough for the correlation to be merely accidental.

Braithwaite, for example, distinguishes laws of nature from 'more generalizations', and defines causal laws as a subclass of the former (1953, chapter IX).

Davidson's complex views on a range of issues concerning causation include endorsement of the following (Davidson 1967, p. 160):

A singular causal statement '*a caused b*' entails that there is a law to the effect that 'all the objects similar to *a* are followed by objects similar to *b*, . . .'

Thus also Fodor, in setting up a major argument which we shall consider in detail later (subsection 4.4.2), puts the point as follows (1980, p. 70):

If one assumes that what makes my thought about Robin Roberts a thought *about Robin Roberts* is some causal connection between the two of us, then we'll need a description of RR such that the causal connection obtains in virtue of him satisfying that description. And *that* means, presumably, that we'll need a description under which the relation between him and me instantiates a law.

The idea may be expressed briefly as being that causality implies generality covered by (natural) law. Such a view is very widely accepted and for convenience it will be called in what follows the 'standard assumption' about causality.

The next main point, to be taken up in the next subsection, is that the natural law invoked in this standard assumption is usually and plausibly taken to be *physical law*. But before going on to consider this, let us briefly make some links with empiricism and post-empiricism which will become important as we proceed.

As remarked above, empiricism was intimately involved, in Hume, with the analysis of causation in terms of correlation and the problem of necessary connection. However, the empiricist claim that all empirical knowledge is derived from experience has come to be recognized as mistaken. As discussed in the first chapter (subsection 1.4.1) post-empiricist epistemology sees that empirical knowledge typically has the form of a theory that posits unobservables, and which cannot be analysed in terms of statements about sense-experience. It may be expected that the new epistemology has implications for Hume's empiricist treatment of causality. An obvious implication is that some statements of empirical associations will have an element of necessity in so far as they are deducible from theory: they *must hold, if* the theory is correct (Braithwaite 1953; Popper 1959). In effect, the 'empirical' necessity here derives from a deduction from other propositions. While this account clearly exceeds what is envisaged by empiricism, it remains true to one fundamental aspect of Hume's empiricist analysis. The account defines a sense in which empirical generalizations 'must' hold, but this element of necessity is added, as it were, from the outside, by the covering theory. It is not a matter of internal linkage between cause and effect, which remain, as in Hume, discrete, entirely separate from one another.

The relation between the above approach to causal necessity and what has been called above the standard assumption about causality is controversial. The standard assumption links causal necessity to natural law, or 'necessity in nature', and it is not obvious that this law-like necessity can be equated with something like inferential role in theory (Armstrong 1983). The theory in question would have to be a true, yet to be discovered, representation of reality. Even so, it may be objected, the necessity of natural law derives from necessity in nature, not from necessity within the representation. This controversy is not, however, relevant to the line of argument here. From the epistemological point of view, if not the metaphysical, the status of natural law is bound up with belonging to theory. We shall assume in what follows that natural law underlies causal necessity, and that our best estimate of what is or is not a natural law is current theory.

4.2.4 Natural laws understood to be physical (the physicalist construal)

The standard assumption about causality, as involving generality covered by natural law, has the pretty well inevitable consequence that causality comes to be seen as the province of the natural sciences, of physics and chemistry in particular. After all, it is (trivially) the natural sciences which aim to identify laws of nature, and among the natural sciences physics and chemistry apparently capture unlimited generality. A connected point is that these are the sciences in which generalizations can be seen to follow from covering theory in something like a hypothetico-deductive form. The idea that the natural laws involved in causal relations are (or are ultimately) physical laws will be called for convenience in what follows the 'physicalist construal' of natural laws (or of causality).

This construal of natural law and causality belongs with the physicalist view that ultimately *all causing goes on at the physical level*. One source of this view is the metaphysical assumption that there are only physical things. The strength and the weakness of this assumption, however, is that it may stand opposed only to (often outdated) metaphysics, claims to the effect that there are, for example, minds as well as bodies, or Platonic forms outside of nature. It is plausible enough to say that there are no entities of these kinds, and that even if there were they could have no causal role in nature. This ontological approach combines with the construal of natural law and causality now under consideration, providing support for the view that ultimately all causing goes on at the physical level.

This physicalist view—that ultimately all causing goes on at the physical level—is widespread in contemporary phiolosophy, including major positions in the philosophy of mind. It is one pressure behind adopting mind–brain identity theory as soon as mental causation has been acknowledged. As discussed in the previous chapter (subsection 2.2.1), Fodor's language of thought hypothesis allows mental, meaningful causation only because it coincides with material (neural), syntactic causation. Davidson's doctrine of anomalous monism (1970) has the consequence that the laws implicated in causal interaction between the mental and the physical must be physical. Dennett appears ambiguous over the question whether intentional states are real or (merely) constructs useful for prediction, as noted in the previous chapter (subsection 3.4.1), but in any case proposes that explanations which invoke them are causal only in so far as they supervene on physical conditions (Dennett 1987, p. 57). These diverse and influential views in the philosophy of mind apparently share the assumption that ultimately causation must be physical, involving physical laws.

Although the physicalist construal of natural causality is commonly accepted, the line of thought followed in this essay runs counter to it. The view argued for in Chapter 2, intended to endorse the current paradigm in neuroscience/cognitive psychology, is that mental, meaningful causation is compatible with material causation because mental states are encoded in brain states. This proposal stays with the idea that all causation is at the physical level, at least in the sense that it posits no immaterial (e.g. Cartesian mental) causal objects, but it draws away from the presumption that the causal laws (the theoretical explanations) in question here belong to physics (or physics/chemistry). Rather, the implication is that the logic of explanation here is distinct from what we find in physics and chemistry, invoking what we find in the natural sciences only in biology and upwards, namely, systemic function involving information-processing.

According to the account to be worked towards in this chapter and the next, we find in the biological sciences upwards a form of causal explanation which in critical respects is unlike what we find in the sub-biological natural sciences. In distancing ourselves from the idea that the 'natural laws' underlying causality have to be physical laws, we move away also from corresponding conceptions of generality and necessity. Causal explanations in biology upwards are of course theory-driven, but they do not have the generality found in the sub-biological sciences: the 'laws', and the necessity, invoked concern not nature generally, but the (normal) functioning of particular kinds of information-processing system.

4.2.5 Meaningful connections apparently not causal in these commonly accepted senses

Neither the standard assumption about causality, defined in subsection 4.2.3, nor its physicalist construal, defined in 4.2.4, are a very good fit with our familiar explanations of actions in terms of meaningful mental states such as beliefs and desires. Such explanations hardly look as if they are, or are derived from, natural laws, still less physical laws. In brief, meanings apparently are not causes.

On the other hand, we do find in meaningful explanations something like generality and necessity. A person does such-and-such because of having various beliefs and wishes, and anyone else who had exactly the same beliefs and wishes, and no other contrary ones, would do the same. There is a generalizing principle here, even if the particular statement applies to just one person on one occasion! Further, if a person has reasons for doing such-and-such, in the form of the requisite beliefs and wishes, then she must, other things being equal, do it. 'Other things being equal' here includes 'has no conflicting beliefs/desires'. But the qualification also includes 'if the person is behaving rationally', which in turn can be glossed as 'if she is behaving normally as a rational agent'. This logic of necessity will be explored later, but for the moment the point is that it has apparently little or nothing to do with causal necessity due to natural laws. Further, and worse still from the point of view of familiar assumptions about causality, the necessary connections here are due to meaning, or reason, as opposed to being contingent. In all the familiar approaches to causality considered so far, whether causal necessity is seen as based only in our experience of constant conjunctions, or in natural law, or in our hypotheses about nature, there is the clear assumption that causal necessity is fundamentally contingent, based in matters of fact about nature, which in principle could be different, not in laws of reason, or the connections between meanings, which in principle could not.

In the case of reasons, or meaningful connections, putative cause and effect are apparently not entirely separate, indicated by the fact that the mental state is typically specified in the same way, with the same meaningful content, as the action that it is said to generate. Connected with this, we do not need to make field observations, still less experiments, to establish generalizations over meaningful connections: they are apparently a priori, or conceptual, in fact linked by meaning. This kind of necessary connection is quite unlike what is proposed in Hume, and in the other accounts we have considered, where the necessary connection is a posteriori. The necessity in meaningful connections apparently does not (have to) follow from a covering natural law. Similar problems arise over the issue of whether environmental events are the causes of meaningful states. It is notoriously difficult in cognitive psychology, and in folk psychology it is frankly impossible, to define the stimulus as cause of a mental state without reference to (the meaningful content of) the mental state itself.

Meaningful connections are apparently not causal according to the standard assumption about causality, that it involves generality covered by natural law. *A fortiori*, they are poor candidates for being causal connections according to the physicalist construal of natural law, where also new problems arise, namely, that it is hard or impossible to conceive the causes of meaningful states, the states themselves, and their effects in action, in the terms of physics, in order to being them under covering physical laws.

In brief, for all these reasons (at least), meanings are not causes, and hence the turn-of-the-century dichtomies between meaning and causality, understanding and (causal) explanation.

Before proceeding, a note on terminology is necessary. The problem of the relation between meaning and causality arises under a particular interpretation, or set of interpretations, of causality, namely, those sketched in this section so far. In brief, the interpretations are to the effect that causality involves generality and natural laws, particularly laws of physics. The arguments to follow in this chapter require specification of causality as understood in these ways. So widespread are these interpretations that the term 'cause' in the literature, though used in these senses, is usually used unqualified. Where there is no ambiguity we shall follow this briefer, customary usage, in arguing for example that meaning is not causal, that it cannot be viewed as causal relation. But the sense of causality here is as outlined above: generality covered by natural, particularly physical law. Another sense of causality will be defined as we proceed, one in which meaningful connections are causal.

4.3 NEVERTHELESS, CAUSAL SEMANTICS: MEANING DEFINED AS A CAUSAL RELATION

4.3.1 The theory and overview of what is wrong with it

The conclusion that meaningful explanations are not causal may not matter much if the only 'body of knowledge' that employed them was folk psychology. But in so far as they are invoked by sciences, particularly applied sciences, which aim to make a difference, the conclusion is problematic and controversial. Much of the controversy here, as remarked earlier (subsection 1.3.8), has revolved around psychoanalysis. From the hard-headed scientific point of view, psychoanalysis can be grouped together with the folk psychology that it extends, and disposed of as non-science. But the position looks different, and becomes again thoroughly problematic, with the turn of events in which authentic, experimentally based psychological science has become involved with something very like mental states with meaning (semantic information). It is (almost) quite impossible to dismiss cognitive psychology as pseudo-science, and it is a very univiting prospect to suppose that this behavioural science is dealing not with causes but with meanings, as if it, too, were a hermeneutic exercise, along with psychoanalysis and textual criticism. This line of thought suggests that the meaning/causality distinction really has to go. It is a polemical argument, by all means, but this is suited to the fact that the distinction between meaning and causality has often enough been used and abused in polemical arguments.

In this chapter we consider various responses to the dilemma in its contemporary form, as outlined in the introductory section, starting here with *causal semantics*. Causal semantics tries to capture meaning within the familiar net of causal relations, preferably in terms consistent with physicalism. This involves dismantling the dichotomy between meaning and causality by defining the former in terms of the latter. In general terms the problem with this proposal is that it tries to dismantle a philosophical dichotomy by acknowledging only one of its terms. We have come across this philosophical strategy earlier, mainly in connection with (simple) mind–brain identity theory (subsection 2.1.2), where it was identified as one most likely to fail. The general problem is that distinctive characteristics emphasized by, though exaggerated by, the category to be absorbed, are not captured by the category doing the absorbing, which always was defined in opposition to the other. In the present case this means: the definition of meaning as being a causal relation omits the specificity of meaning, its relation to the subject, and the origin of its necessity within these factors. Causal semantics makes meaning too general, too objective, and too necessary, with no possibility of it 'breaking down'.

Causal semantics seeks to construe the relation between meaningful mental states (or information-carrying states generally) and what they mean, as being a matter of association covered by natural, probably physical, law. If causal semantics can be made to work, then the critical intentional concepts will be analysed in the familiar terms of causality, and then presumably explanations which invoke concepts of information and meaning could be eliminated in favour of explanations which invoke no such concepts. In brief, semantics would be 'naturalized' (Fodor 1990). However, we shall argue that causal semantics cannot be made to work. As implied in the preceding paragraph, the reason why the theory does not work is connected with the fact that the dichotomy between meaning and causality marked a genuine tension which cannot just be glossed over, a tension between meaningful phenomena and explanation, and the methodological assumptions suited to the (sub-biological) natural sciences.

Causal semantics has been much discussed in the literature (Dretske 1981, 1983; Fodor 1990; also, for example, Baker 1989; Villanueva 1990). Various forms of causal semantics have been proposed, the most rigorous and sophisticated being those of Dretske (1981, 1983), and of Fodor (1990). Some aspects of these versions will be considered as we proceed. For purposes of bringing out some critical features and problems of causal semantics, a brief statement of its main idea from Fodor will suffice, as follows (Fodor 1990, p. 57):

S-events carry information about P-events if 'Ps cause Ss' is a law.

A similar analysis can be given of the expression 'S-events *mean* P-events'. It can be applied to cognitive states or to linguistic utterances, though the distinction here is blurred. (An account of the meaningful content of the cognitive state 'believes that p' or 'possesses the information that p' will be closely linked to a theory as to the meaning of the sentence p, and vice versa.) A precursor in psychology of more recent theories of causal semantics, as Fodor remarks (1990, pp. 53ff.), was Skinner's attempt to extend operant theory to verbal behaviour (Skinner 1956), the proposal being that (meaningful) utterances are under 'stimulus control'. This proposal could be expressed in the form: utterances are caused by environmental stimuli, and thereby have meaning.

Causal semantics is subject to two main criticisms. First, its explanation of the content of meaningful states tends to be either vacuous or inadequate. The underlying problem is the one anticipated in the preceding section: it is unclear that the 'causes' of meaningful states can be identified independently of the meaningful states themselves, their alleged effects. The second main criticism of causal semantics is that it cannot adequately explain the fact that informational or meaningful states can come to represent what has no existence in reality. Two kinds of case come under this heading. One concerns our capacity to use meaningful though 'empty' terms or concepts, whether in myth or in play (e.g. 'unicorn'), or in scientific theory (e.g. 'phlogiston'). The other concerns the fact that information-carrying states can be *false*.

We suggest that the diagnoses of both failings are the same. In both cases the problem is that causal semantics (explicitly) seeks to define information entirely 'objectively', without reference to the 'subjective' contribution to information processing and content. Or again: the basic fault of causal semantics is its attempt to define information without acknowledging its relativity to a 'receiver' (and user).[1]

4.3.2 First problem: the definition of meaning is vacuous or inadequate

According to causal semantics, cognitive states (or utterances with meaningful content) are caused by events in the environment, and thereby carry information about, or mean, those events. The critical question concerns the definition of environmental events. Broadly speaking, there are two options. Either the events are defined *independently of* the contents they are alleged to cause, or they are defined by appeal to their alleged affects. In neither way, however, do we have an adequate explanation of mental content. The former option cannot account for the diversity of content; the latter can, but vacuously.

Environmental stimuli can be defined independently of the informational states which, according to causal semantics, they cause. Physical descriptions can be given, of the stimulus or of the sensory stimulation to which it gives rise. Or again, low-level phenomenal descriptions can be given, concerning shape, colour, etc. But either way there is so far no account of the richness and variety of informational states. Informational content is, in general, not determined by physical or low-level phenomenal characteristics. For example, a person sees a dog and comes to believe (with or without conscious thought) that is it dangerous, and so runs away, or that it is friendly, and so pats it. If the contents of such beliefs are determined by the stimuli that cause the beliefs, then these stimuli cannot be defined in physical terms, or in terms of perceived shapes and colours.

Since this option is unpromising, causal semantics tends to rely on the alternative: environmental stimuli come to be defined by reference to the informational states that they are held to cause. It is in making this move that the theory lapses into vacuity. The environment is populated with whatever properties are required to explain the corresponding mental states. If I see a dog and believe it to be dangerous, my belief has this content because it is caused by (an instance of) the property *dangerousness*, etc. In this way causal semantics comes to embrace a prolific realism concerning properties, the assumption being that at least all meaningful predicates of all natural languages are associated with independently existing properties. But whatever the philosophical attractions or otherwise of this realism, it is of little or no use in the explanation of meaningful states or events, mental or verbal. In general, the grounds for positing the existence of causal properties is the existence of their alleged effects, that is, meaningful mental states or linguistic utterances, not the other way round. The postulate of environmental causes becomes merely an *ad hoc* device for explaining the content of representational states. The classic statement of this kind of objection to causal semantics is Chomsky's critique of Skinner's proposal that verbal behaviour is under 'stimulus control', already discussed in the first chapter (subsection 1.2.2). Fodor's recent rigorous formulation of causal semantics (Fodor 1990), to be discussed below, continues to rely on the same kind of prolific realism as was exploited by Skinner.

Causal semantics seeks to capture meaning within the notion of causal association by identifying the meaning of information-carrying states with their environmental causes. But the problem is how to determine these environmental causes without reference to their alleged effects. Let us contrast the causal approach to semantics with another, which draws essentially on the notion of information-processing. What does a cognitive psychological, information-processing, story about the production of informational states look like? A rough answer will serve the present purpose:

At the input end, in stimulation, information is picked up by sensory systems. The information picked up depends partly on the physically defined nature of the stimulus, and partly on characteristics of the sensory system. As a rule, sensory systems are designed to pick up information of kinds relevant to the animal's behaviour and needs, at least to its survival. This information is then processed, which includes assimilation into innate or acquired patterns of association or expectation, of greater or lesser complexity, these being again of kinds relevant to the animal's behaviour and needs. Processing eventually produces informational states which serve in the regulation of behaviour. The more information becomes processed, the more it differs from the low-level information picked up at the periphery. The information that this is thirst-quenching water, for example, is not what is encoded on the retina. The processed information not only does not allow definition in terms of physics (e.g. the content 'water' cannot be defined as H_2O), but it essentially implicates the animal's needs (drives), which have even less to do with physics. The environment has to be defined in physical terms to tell the first part of the information-processing story, in specifying what can be and is picked up at the sensory level, but after that physical definition of informational content becomes decreasingly relevant. What becomes relevant in its place is the way in which low-level information is interpreted, the criterion of which, at any given stage, is a matter of behavioural responses of information-processing subsystems, eventually of the animal (as a whole) as it acts in the environment.

We assume, crude though the above sketch is, that it captures some essential features of the cognitive psychological account of the causal history and content of information-carrying states, and it is apparent that in such an account physical descriptions of the environment represented in cognitive states (as opposed to bio-psychological descriptions) play a limited, though by all means a fundamental, role.[2]

Cognitive psychology acknowledges that there are properties of environmental stimulation which can be specified without reference to information-carrying states, physical properties such as shape, orientation, energy patterns, etc. But it proceeds to explain how these are processed in ways dependent on the living being (the receiver, perceiver, and agent), producing cognitive states with content which cannot be defined in physical terms, which is richer and more diverse.

It is in this critical respect that the information-processing story in cognitive psychology diverges from causal semantics, which seeks to explain content by reference to environmental causes. If causal semantics acknowledges that the environmental causes sufficient to explain content cannot be captured by physical definitions, then it has to define them, in a circular way, by reference to the content of the information-carrying states themselves. In this way the environment is credited with properties corresponding to mental states which involve much interpretation or processing of physical characteristics, mental states concerning, for example, dangerousness. In effect, the results of interpretation and processing are explained in terms of ready-made features of the world. In this sense the subjective contribution to concept-formation (meaning) is denied.

There is nothing wrong with attributing to the environment characteristics such as dangerousness. Certainly this is what the frightened animal does, notwithstanding the fact that physics countenances no such property. The issue is rather how we proceed in scientific explanation. The *explanation* of how the animal becomes frightened is not simply that it 'sees an instance of the property *dangerousness*'. The explanation has rather to cite information-processing capacities of the animal, and the interests that they serve. The postulate of the property of dangerousness can be added as an after-thought to the account in terms of interpretation and processing, but it does no explanatory work. The significance of such a postulate is in fact metaphysical rather than scientific. The claim that meaningful content is caused by ready-made, independently existing properties ensures that the results of interpretation are 'objective' rather than 'subjective'. The effect is that the subjective contribution to meaning is denied. In this way the theory of causal semantics stands in the venerable (and diverse) realist tradition, which posits reality as ready-formed, then simply impressed on the mind (or brain), with nothing for the mind (or brain) to do except register the way things are. Empiricism was a theory of representation and knowledge of this kind, and causal semantics is one of its not so distant descendents. Causal semantics is true to the realist tradition in two related ways. First, in that the mode of representation is objectively defined (i.e. as a causal association); second, in that the representational content is objectively defined, in terms of already-made, independent properties.

Causal semantics, in the version that makes profligate appeal to environmental properties, has difficulty in remaining causal, in so far as the criterion for the existence of such properties is the existence of their alleged effects, mental states with the corresponding content. Further, the theory seems to have little to do with the information-processing account characteristic of cognitive psychology. In brief, causal semantics in this version seems to be neither causal nor scientific.

4.3.3 Second problem: no explanation of empty terms or false propositions

The above problem for causal semantics is intensified when the theory has to deal with 'empty' content, signified by terms such as 'unicorn' or 'phlogiston'. Up to this point, causal semantics can appeal to the causal role of *instances* of properties in generating mental states which mean, or carry information about them. But in the case of empty concepts, there are no such instances. To cope with this kind of case, causal semantics has to run the causal story in terms of properties, not instances of properties (Fodor 1990, p. 100). The idea would be that, for example, beliefs about phlogiston were caused by the *property* 'phlogiston'.

The theory has to run in the same way even in case of mental content that is not empty. This is partly to achieve simplicity and consistency in the theory, but also, and more importantly, because we have to allow for the possibility in principle that a concept such as 'electron' may turn out to be empty after all, in some future physical theory. Even well-entrenched notions are replaceable. Generally, theories of meaning have to secure meaning in the absence of truth. Beliefs about phlogiston, though false, never were meaningless; no more would beliefs about electorns turn out to be senseless, and to have always been senseless, in case the theory in which those beliefs are embedded came to be superceded. This general point applies in the theory of linguistic meaning and in the theory of mental content, and specifically, in the theory of the role of mental content in regulating action. Explanation of Lavoisier's and Priestley's 'experimental behaviour' (their behaviour as they conducted their critical experiments on burning) in terms of their beliefs and conjectures has to include reference to the content *phlogiston*. It is, of course, entirely irrelevant to the cognitive-behavioural explanation that this content is, and always was, empty.

To handle the problem of empty content, casual semantics tells the causal story in terms of properties, not instances. But in making this move, causal semantics is not only forced to rely heavily on the problematic notion of properties, it is also faced with the additional problem of explaining their causal role. What are properties (as opposed to their actual instances), and how do they exert causal influence? How should we proceed to investigate the processes by which a property, such as *phlogiston*, or *electron*, gives rise to beliefs?

Neither in common-sense psychology nor in cognitive psychology do these baffling questions arise. Both theories proceed in a different way. Beliefs are acquired by *interpretation of* relatively simpler experiences or stimuli, and are empty or otherwise, true or false, according to whether the interpretation is correct or incorrect. Thus, for example, the story of the acquisition of the concept *phlogiston* involves reference to a plausible though mistaken interpretation of the fact that usually, that is in open systems, the products of combustion are less substantial than what is burnt. False belief is understood here in terms of mistaken interpretation. This is the approach taken in common sense, or at least, in the philosophy of science. Cognitive psychology can appeal to such interpretative processes which are open to view, and also to others which are not, concerning, for example, the pick-up of low-level physical stimulation and its subsequent (largely unconscious) processing. But in neither case is there anything about properties causing mental states with corresponding contents.

As a version of realism, causal semantics allows no fundamental role for creation of meaning by the subject, whether in construction of scientific theory or in imaginative play. But this drive for what may be called an excessive objectivity is exactly what makes the theory inadequate. What requires explanation, including from the point of view of a cognitive-behavioural science, is that mental states with informational or meaningful content determine behaviour (and affect) regardless of whether or not they correspond to anything in reality. It is just at this stage that we require subjective contribution to meaning as well as objective determination. This is the natural route taken by common sense and cognitive psychology. But this subjectivity cannot be envisaged by realism, which therefore postulates that (possibly) instance-less properties are the objectively real determinants of meaningful content. This postulate, however, affords nothing recognizable as a scientific explanation of the origin of meaning.

Let us consider briefly another way in which causal semantics might approach the problem of empty concepts, other than by appeal to instance-less properties. The proposal would be that ideas that are, or that might be, empty, are essentially *complex*, that is to say, composed of simpler ideas, such as colour and shape, which do derive from real instances. This proposal is characteristic of empiricism (Locke 1690, II, Chapter XII; see also Fodor 1990, p. 101). It has advantages compared with prolific realism about properties, including that it posits activity within the mind, this activity being the generation of complex ideas from simple, according to the principles of association elaborated by empiricism and later by conditioning theory. So we work here towards the idea of subjective contribution to meaning, which can be described in a general way as interaction among representations, or as information-processing, which results in the production of something new. Note, however, that while the complex idea is produced by mental activity, its ultimately simple constituents are not, but are simply impressed on the mind by reality. In *this* sense nothing new is ever produced, only rearrangements of what is already given. What has to added to this picture, or what has to transform it, is the post-empiricist critique, which brings out the theory-dependent nature of experience and the hierarchical functioning of theory, in the light of which it cannot be maintained that all concepts are analysable into simple, given, ideas (see above, subsection 1.4.1). Perhaps the concept *unicorn* is composed of simple ideas such as colour and shape, but this is only to the extent that we have no (not much) theory about them. If we believed in unicorns, and they mattered to us, we presumably would want a theory about them, about their signs, appearances, and effects, and about their activities behind the scenes, and the concept then would exceed what is envisaged by empiricism. A main thrust of the post-empiricist critique is that propositions about theoretical entities, for example about phlogiston in the theory of combustion, typically cannot be reduced to propositions about observational data.

The post-empiricist account of concept-formation provides another perspective on the main point of this section, namely, that information depends on the information-processing system, and that this relativity is denied by causal semantics. In its clearest form, causal semantics posits properties in reality, no matter how complex or abstract, which just 'cause' representations with that content. There is no need here for any activity within, or contribution by, an information-processing system. Indeed in the fundamentals of the theory the notion of such a system does not appear. Causal semantics is in this sense akin to S–R psychology, which proposes a direct, one–one, relation between environmental causes and effects in the organism, without mediation by the mind (or brain), which concept has little, if any, theoretical use (see above, subsections 1.2.1–2).

We have been discussing the fact that meaningful content can be about what does not exist. Content expressible by empty terms is one kind of case, another is content expressible by false propositions. The two kinds of case are connected, but we turn now to consider briefly the second in its own right. The falsity of meaningful content, like the presence of empty concepts, presents causal semantics with a probably insurmountable problem.

The problem can be expressed as follows: according to causal semantics, an event A means or carries information about an event B in case A is caused by B, but, if A is not caused by B, then A carries not false information about B, but rather carries no information about B at all. Correlations between types of event can be more or less reliable, but there seems to be no apparent sense to the notion of a *miscorrelation*, and hence none so far to the notion of false or incorrect information. In brief, the problem is *how to obtain a distinction between right and wrong in terms of the notion of causal association*. Attempts by proponents of causal semantics to solve this fundamental problem have not met with much success.[3]

The problem of empty content (of concepts) and the problem of false content (of judgements) are closely linked together, both arising from the fact that what is represented need not exist. This feature is, of course, none other than the *intentionality* of representation (subsection 1.3.1). Any aspiring theory of content has to account for this; it constitutes a very clear adequacy condition for the theory of meaning. The problem for causal semantics is that it seems to fail just this critical test.

We first considered the problem of error, which is as just remarked another name for the problem of intentionality, in the first chapter (subsection 1.3.2). We began to tackle the question: how can one item represent, or mean (or carry information about) another? We saw that the simplest answer would be just that sign and signified are 'correlated' in some way or other, so that the one stands for the other. But even at this superficial level the problem of error makes itself felt. An empty or false sign stands for nothing, but then what is the difference between this and not being a sign at all? How can a sign be meaningful even though there is nothing it is correlated with? The notion of *resemblance* provides an excellent solution to this problem, though its plausibility depends on the extent to which signs do in fact resemble what they signify. Signs of language, in particular, apparently do not. In the absence of resemblance we can define meaning in terms of the *use* of signs in activity, acknowledging the distinction between right and wrong actions, and uses of signs, in terms of the notion of rule-following.

The question as to what following a rule amounts to was taken up in the third chapter, Section 3.3. The problem of making out a difference between 'right' and 'wrong' presses hard in the account of meaning in terms of rule-following, as it does in any theory of meaning. We arrived at the apparent paradox that when a person follows a rule what seems right is right, so far as the person is concerned for the time being, and so far we have defined no sense to 'but is wrong' (subsection 3.3.2). The proposed solution was a relativistic one, which made out the normative distinctions in two connected ways, in terms of agreement or disagreement between judgements made from various points of view, and in terms of success or otherwise of action (subsections 3.3.3–4). An implication of these relativistic distinctions between right and wrong, or between appearance and reality, is that the vehicle of meaning (of true or false representation) has to be a system which can compare representations from various points of view, which can predict one from another, and which can modify them as appropriate. We arrive, in brief, at a conception of the vehicle of meaning (the measure of reality) as being an active system with the capacity to process information. The contrast here is with theories of meaning which posit static, object-like measures which mirror, or resemble, absolute states of affairs (cf. subsections 1.3.2, 3.3.1).

We are working our way towards this idea from another direction, by considering what is wrong with causal semantics. The point argued so far in this section is that this theory apparently comes to grief on what is a decisive testing ground for theories of meaning, the problem of empty content. We have considered two aspects of the same problem, namely, the creativity and error in ideas and judgement. No account of these features of meaning, both aspects of the fact that meaning can run free of reality, can be gleaned simply from the idea of 'objective' causal correlation between events. So what is the alternative? A more promising account has been indicated in the discussion so far. In the course of criticizing causal semantics we have invoked an account that looks more promising, namely, one which acknowledges what causal semantics is concerned to deny, namely, that there is a subjective contribution to meaning, one that derives from the measuring system itself. This idea will be taken up in later sections. In the next section we continue to consider the consequences of trying to apply standard concepts of causality to explanations in cognitive psychology.

4.4 TRYING TO MANAGE WITH NO SEMANTICS AT ALL

4.4.1 Stich's meaning-less cognitive science

We have already mentioned in various contexts Stich's attempt to avoid the problem of meaning in cognitive science by trying to characterize cognitive states only in terms of causal role, not content. One objection was spelled out in the first chapter (subsection 1.3.8), briefly as follows: information-processing is axiomatic to cognitive psychology, but there cannot be information-processing without information to process, and once information is allowed in, so is meaning. The concepts of meaning and information are closely related: the problem of meaning and causality can be run in exactly the same way using the expression 'information' instead of 'meaning'; what matters here is what they have in common, namely intentionality (subsection 1.3.7). Another problem emerged in the discussion of so-called narrow content in the second chapter (subsection 2.5.3): without intentional language there is apparently no way of characterizing the behavioural effects of cognitive causes.

We turn in this section to consider a related, though different, recommendation to the effect that cognitive science should run without semantics, due to Fodor. Unlike in Stich, there is no wedge inserted between meaning and causal relations, on the contrary the two are held together, but since, so the argument runs, cognitive science cannot encompass causal relations, nor can it encompass semantics. As anticipated, the sense of causality presupposed here is as previously defined: generality covered by natural, specifically physical, law.

4.4.2 Fodor's 'methodological solipsism' as a research strategy for cognitive science

Causal semantics seeks to define the content of information-carrying states in terms of their environmental causes. As noted in the preceding section, this attempt runs straight on to a well-known cleft stick: either the environmental stimuli are defined independently of the mental states they are said to cause, in physical terms, or they are defined in terms of their alleged effects. The former option looks untenable because the content of mental states, the reality they mean, exceeds physically definable aspects of the environment. The latter option looks untenable because it can provide no non-vacuous, causal explanations. Moreover, it leads to a profligate realism concerning properties, and to the scientifically odd idea that properties (as opposed to their instances) have causal power.

No one is better aware of this cleft stick, and the problem of escaping it, than Fodor. This is so notwithstanding the fact that in his (1990) paper Fodor proposes a causal semantics, adopting the second of the above options, apparently choosing to ignore for the sake of argument the risk of vacuousness.

Earlier, in his well-known paper 'Methodological solipsism considered as a research strategy in cognitive science', Fodor endorses the other option open to causal semantics, definition of meaningful content in terms of its *physically defined* environmental causes.

This physicalist version of causal semantics is consistent with the physicalist construal of causality (subsection 4.2.4), as involving coverage by physical laws. It is also closely related to the idea, discussed and rejected in the second chapter (Section 2.5), that 'meaning is not in the head'. The main point in the background here is that if the key concepts of meaning and causality are interpreted in a physicalist way, they turn out to have nothing to do with cognitive behavioural psychology.

Thus we find that Fodor in his (1980) paper endorses the physicalist version of causal semantics, but he does not recommend its use in cognitive psychology. On the contrary, he argues that it offers to cognitive psychology an impossible methodology! The implication, then, is that cognitive psychology has to manage without any semantics at all. Indeed, Fodor proposes, it has to manage without any account of the (causal) interactions between organism and the environment. Rather, cognitive psychology is confined to a 'solipsist' methodology. In this way Fodor provides a salutary lesson on the consequences of applying the physicalist construal of causality to psychology.

Fodor's paper is complex, and we shall draw out for discussion only those themes relating directly to the notion of causality and causal law at work in psychological explanation.

The working assumptions in Fodor's argument are that mental states are legitimately invoked in the explanation of behaviour, and that interactions between mental states, behaviour, and the environment are essentially causal. Specifically, mental states have a causal role in the production of behaviour, and the environment has a causal role in the production of mental states. Further, it is the causal interactions between organism and the environment which fix the meaning of mental states. Granted these working assumptions (which are all of the kind endorsed in this essay) what should psychology be aiming for?

According to Fodor, one research strategy, recommended by what he calls 'naturalistic psychology', is to determine organism–environment interactions and the causal laws that govern them (1980 p. 64 et passim). Naturalistic psychology thus aims to comprise a semantics (1980, pp. 70–1).

But, Fodor's line of thought continues, causality implies nomological necessity, that is, deducibility from scientific law, in particular, from physics (loc. cit.). Granted this, determination of causal laws in general requires that the *relata* of causal connections are specified in terms of physics. Therefore, in particular, the determination of causal laws in organism–environment interactions requires specification in such terms. The requirement is at least that the environmental causes of behaviour and mental states would have to be specified in terms of physics, including such as H_2O and $NaCl$. Causes so defined would determine the content of mental states (loc. cit.). Thus causal semantics naturally belongs with the materialist (physicalist) definition of content, as remarked above and anticipated in Chapter 2 (subsection 2.5.3). In this way Fodor concludes that naturalistic psychology, with its associated semantics, has to rely on physical theory as to the nature of environmental causes. We have to wait for physical theory to tell us what it is that cognitive states are about. But this conclusion Fodor takes to be untenable; the argument apparently has the form of a *reductio ad absurdum*.

Before considering the closing step of the argument, however, let us consider what alternative Fodor offers in place of a discredited naturalistic methodology. It would have to be one that eschews the study of organism–environment causal interactions, being concerned with the organism and its representations without reference to the environment. Such a strategy is in this sense 'solipsistic'. Fodor takes methodological solipsism to be characteristic of what he calls the tradition of 'Rational' psychology, and in particular of the recent expression of that tradition, the computational theory of mind (discussed in Chapter 2, subsection 2.3.1). According to this theory, mental processes satisfy the so-called *formality condition*, that is to say: they have access only to the formal properties of representations, hence no access to their semantic properties, including truth and reference, and 'indeed, no access to the property of being representations *of the environment*' (Fodor 1980, p. 65, original italics).

In summary, Fodor assumes the standard, physicalist analysis of causality as involving coverage by natural, physical law, and argues on this basis that psychology cannot aim to determine causal interactions between organism and environment; further, since these causal interactions are what determine the meaning of mental states, cognitive psychology cannot comprise semantics. The argument sketched above, extracted from Fodor's complex discussion, apparently has the form of a *reductio ad absurdum*, though we have yet to consider the nature of the alleged absurdity.

What is wrong with naturalistic psychology's dependence on physical science? At one critical point Fodor suggests that, on the basis as set out, naturalistic psychology would have to wait for *completion* of the natural sciences, in which case the research strategy on offer would indeed be hopeless. No doubt, Fodor remarks, it's alright to have a research strategy which says 'wait awhile', but who wants to wait for ever? (1980, p. 70).

But this move is dubious. Why should psychology, in the circumstances envisaged, have to wait for a completed physics? Why could it not proceed in the meantime with the physics we have? After all, chemistry, for example, manages on this basis, as does physics itself!

Elsewhere in the paper Fodor apparently envisages another argument, to do with the division of labour between psychology and physics. The objection to a naturalistic psychology as the study of causal interactions between organism and environment is that it would have to specify relevant causal properties of the environment, but this is the task of physics, not psychology (1980, p. 70). This alternative argument also seems questionable, however. Why should the science of organism–environment interaction not make use of, and partly rest on, physical theory about the environment? It is unclear why such a science would thereby not be psychology, if this is what Fodor is suggesting, unless we assume what Fodor is seeking to show, that psychology must use a solipsistic methodology.

So far, then, Fodor's arguments against the possibility of a naturalistic psychology seem weak. That said, there is another type of argument against the possibility of a naturalistic psychology, at least in the sense defined by Fodor. The point is simply that physical descriptions of the environment as represented in thought are generally not the appropriate kind for the purpose of cognitive explanations of behaviour. Following the arguments against naturalistic psychology, Fodor writes (1980, p. 71):

> It is important to emphasize that these sorts of arguments do *not* apply against the research program embodied in 'Rational psychology'; viz., to the program which envisions a psychology that honours the formality condition. The problem we've been facing is: under what description does the object of thought enter into scientific generalizations about the relations between thoughts and their objects. It looks as though the naturalist is going to have to say: under a description that's law-instantiating; e.g. under physical description. Whereas the rational psychologist has a quite different answer. What *he* wants is *whatever description the organism has in mind* when it thinks about the object of thought, . . . It's our relation to these sorts of descriptions that determines what psychological state type we're in in so far as the goal of taxonomizing psychological states is explaining how they affect behaviour [original italics].

Fodor thus proposes that what might be called an 'organism-based' definition of mental content is what is required for cognitive-behavioural explanation. This, we may note, is the kind of definition of content endorsed in the present essay (particularly subsections 2.5.4 and 3.4.2, also Section 4.5 below). Fodor, however, takes the proposal to be characteristic of so-called rational psychology, of the computational theory of mind in particular, and of solipsistic methodology. This is certainly not the position adopted here.

But Fodor's line of thought as sketched above is dubious. It is unclear why a psychology which invokes 'organism-based' descriptions of the environment represented in thought, for the purpose of explaining behaviour, belongs with a methodology unconcerned with semantics and organism–environment interactions. On the contrary, such a psychology seems straightforwardly to be concerned with both.

Suppose we attribute to an animal thirst, and the belief that the liquid before it is thirst-quenching. These cognitive–affective states are specified in terms that the animal has in mind, and these terms may not coincide with physical descriptions of the environment. From attribution of these states, we predict that the animal will lower its head and initiate drinking-behaviour. The belief state invoked essentially has semantic properties, in particular the property of being about the environment. And the prediction concerns organism–environment interactions: it is not 'solipsistic'.

By all means truth and successful reference are irrelevant to explanation and prediction. The animal may be deceived in believing that the liquid before it is thirst-quenching, and, in conditions of illusion or hallucination, there may be no liquid there at all. Nevertheless, the explanation runs the same way: it predicts at least *attempted* behavioural interaction. For example, the animal spits out polluted water, or starts with surprise when it bends its head and encounters sand. In action, or at least in attempted action, the animal has no access to the truth or successful reference of its cognitive states; it proceeds, as it were, by appearances only. But the animal must have access to at least one semantic property of its information-carrying states, namely, that they are about the environment. Without access to this minimal but fundamental property of cognitive states, it would have no reason, or cause, (to try) to act in the way it does. Action regulated by cognitive states, whether successful or otherwise, is intentional, it has 'aboutness', and is not 'solipsistic'. This same semantic property essentially characterizes the regulating cognitive states, whether these are invoked from the outside, for the purpose of explanation and prediction of action, or whether they are accessed from the inside, for the purpose of planning and carrying out action.

The above argument amounts to a rejection of the 'formality condition' imposed in particular by the computational theory of mind, that is, the condition that mental processes have access only to formal, not to (any) semantic properties of representations (see above, and Fodor, 1980, p. 65).

The main topic of this chapter concerns causality, and the main question for this section concerns the effects of applying to cognitive psychology a familiar philosophical analysis of causal necessity, viz. that it involves coverage by scientific law, in particular by physics. Fodor shows that application of this analysis to psychology reaps havoc. In the extreme, the consequence is that cognitive psychology is prohibited from studying the causal interactions between the organism and its environment, and hence also has to exclude semantics. Since Fodor endorses the standard, physicalist view of causality, he is obliged, and is willing on other grounds (particularly the computational theory of mind), to embrace this consequence.

The consequence is, however, highly implausible! Cognitive psychology, and artificial intelligence, are pervaded by studies of organism–environment interactions, as many of the commentators on Fodor's paper were quick to point out (Fodor 1980, open peer commentary). Assuming that the interactions under study are indeed causal interactions, the inference apparently has to be that the familiar, physicalist construal of causality does not apply to cognitive psychology.

The problem is not that a physicalist theory of organism–environment interactions could never get off the ground, because of waiting for ever for physical theory to be completed. The problem is rather that for the purpose of explaining and predicting an organism's behavioural responses in terms of cognitive states, what matters is the way in which the environment is encoded and represented within the organism, and such informational content generally cannot be specified in the categories of physics.

It has already been argued, contrary to what Fodor claims, that the requisite organism-based definitions of the environment represented in cognitive states belong to a psychology of organism–environment interactions. So is a naturalistic psychology possible after all? It is, but not in the sense defined by Fodor. Naturalistic psychology as defined by Fodor is a combination of two doctrines. The first is the methodological proposal that psychology can and should study causal interactions between organism and environment. The second is the philosophical assumption that, given this aim, psychology has to describe these interactions in such a way that they can be covered by causal laws of the natural sciences (physics and chemistry). Adoption of an organism-based definition of mental content requires rejection of this philosophical assumption, but the methodological proposal remains intact.

4.4.3 Summary of difficulties and likely solution

The conclusion reached in the preceding subsection was that while it was possible for there to be a cognitive psychology of causal interactions between organism and environment, the notion of causality at work here cannot be the physicalist one. This physicalist construal of causality requires the materialist theory of mental content, and the arguments against the latter in the second chapter (subsection 2.5.3) are, as already remarked, closely connected to the arguments against the latter in this section. The fundamental problem is that the categories and explanations of physics are of very restricted value when we want to construct a cognitive-behavioural psychology, that is, a theory of the regulation of higher behaviour by cognitive states. In brief, the *meaning* in higher behaviour, in the mental states which regulate it, and in the environment as perceived and acted on, resists capture in the concepts of physics.

This 'failure' of the physical sciences appears as problematic from the point of view of the materialism and physicalism that dominates much current philosophical thinking, and there is much pressure to deny it. It is denied precisely by the materialist theory of content and the physicalist construal of causality, according to which meaningful content and connections can be captured within the physicalist net. But then the tension between meaning and the physical sciences certainly does not go away, but is manifest in various conundrums in the philosophy of psychology. Given the materialist theory of content, it appears that meanings ain't in the head and therefore aren't causes of behaviour (subsection 2.5.2). Given the physicalist construal of causality, it seems that psychological theory cannot cope with causal organism–environment transactions at all (subsection 4.4.2).

We have suggested, however, that this last, pretty implausible conclusion can be resisted, provided we abandon the physicalist construal of causality, along with the materialist definition of content. In this way we preserve as a possible and legitimate area of study for psychology the causal interactions between living beings and their environments, and in particular their mediation by semantic processing.

The question then arises as to what notion of causality psychology presupposes. The general implication of the argument so far is that causal explanations of interactions between organism and the environment have to take into account information-processing characteristics of the organism, and the functions that they serve. In brief, the causal connections in question, and the meaning they determine, are 'organism-based'. Several distinguishable though closely related points come under this heading, and will be discussed in remaining sections of this chapter:

First, informational content is relative to functional systems.

Secondly, explanations that invoke informational content and its processing are essentially relative to functional systems, and the 'laws' covering such systems must be of a kind distinct from those in physics and chemistry, concerned with the design, means, and ends of particular functional systems. The necessity in these laws will turn on the assumption of 'normal' functioning. Causal concepts and normative concepts coincide here.

Hence, thirdly, since these 'laws' are specific to particular information-processing systems, we lose the *generality* characteristic of the physical sciences.

These points are taken up in the next two sections.

4.5 FUNCTIONAL SEMANTICS: MEANING DEFINED IN TERMS OF SYSTEMIC FUNCTION

4.5.1 General principles

Causal semantics defines meaning in terms of causality as understood in the physical sciences. Further, it defines meaning primarily in terms of environmental causes rather than behavioural effects. These two features of causal semantics hang together with the fact the theory does not envisage, indeed goes out of its way to deny, that there is any systemic contribution to the production of meaning. Properties are posited as already in the environment, able to cause mental states with corresponding content, which causal process hence involves no subjective contribution (subsections 4.3.2–3). This negative conclusion is plainly demanded by the physicalist construal of causality. The implication is that the rejection of causal semantics involves not only a shift away from the physicalist construal of causality, but also a shift in the definition of meaning away from emphasis on 'input' towards emphasis on interactions among information-carrying states and their role in regulating 'output'. The chief significance of this change is that the definition of content can begin to take account of the contribution of the semantic processing system. This kind of definition of meaning belongs with the idea invoked in all the preceding chapters, that meaningful states are invoked in order to explain (intentional) activity, and hence are to be understood essentially in terms of the difference they make to behaviour.

Another way of looking at what is essentially the same point about the move from causal to functional semantics is in terms of the theory of error. We saw in subsection 4.3.3 that causal semantics flounders on the problem that information-carrying states can be false as well as true. This fundamental feature of such states apparently defines capture by the notion of causality alone: either events of one kind are causally associated with another or they are not, but there is no obvious sense in the notion of a 'mis-association'. In this section we explore the possibility indicated at the time, that solution of the problem of error requires reference to the system that picks up, processes, and utilizes information. Error will be down to something like 'misinterpretation', or 'misapplication'.

By whichever route we approach functional semantics, meaning comes to be defined with reference to information-processing systems. The first version of functional semantics to be considered retains the essential claim of causal semantics, namely, that the content of an information-carrying state is defined by its environmental causes. We shall call this version 'causal-functional semantics', and it will be contrasted later with a 'behavioural-functional' version, which defines content primarily in terms of the difference it makes to the behaviour of the system.

4.5.2 Millikan's version: content defined by normal biological/evolutionary causes

The problem for functional semantics in its causal version is to define the normative characteristic of informational content—that it can be true or false, correct or incorrect—in terms of a normative distinction among its environmental causes.

The task is to define a sense in which some causes of information-carrying states are 'right' and others are 'wrong'. Such a normative distinction between types of cause is not afforded by a straightforward causal semantics, but it can be drawn once we make explicit reference to functional systems. The basic idea of functional semantics is that error arises in informational states of a system in case they are caused by conditions unlike those in which the system has been designed to function. The required assumptions concerning design, function, and conditions can be based in considerations of evolutionary biology. Functional (or teleological) theories of content along these lines have been proposed, for example, by Millikan (1984, 1986) and Papineau (1987).[4] What follows is a brief version of some of their key features.

Biological systems and subsystems have been selected in the evolutionary process in so far as they fulfil certain advantageous functions in particular environmental conditions. These latter may be called for short the 'normal' conditions for particular systems. Consider now specifically the case of systems whose function it is to represent (carry information about) the environment. Such representational systems, like others, have evolved in normal conditions. Normal conditions define the content of a representational state, as follows: a representational state carries the information that it is caused by normal conditions. In these terms it is possible to apply a normative description to particular representational states of a system. We may distinguish between representational states which are caused by normal conditions, and those which are caused by abnormal conditions: the former are 'correct' representations, the latter 'incorrect'.

In this way we can apparently capture a distinction between correct and incorrect representations, and one, moreover, with scientific credibility. The basic idea that in incorrect representation something has gone wrong is explicated in terms of informational states of a system being triggered by conditions unlike those that the system has been designed to respond to.

4.5.3 Fodor's objection: these causes are ambiguous

An objection to the analysis outlined above has been forcibly put by Fodor (1990). Fodor makes the objection using the example of fly-detection and -snapping behaviour in the frog, the subject of the seminal paper of Lettvin *et al.* (1959), 'What the frog's eye tells the frog's brain'.

An account of the frog's behaviour according to the proposal being considered would include the following claims. There is in the frog an information-processing mechanism selected in the evolutionary process for detecting and snapping at flies. On occasion the frog detects and snaps at ambient black dots which are not flies. However, in this case the mechanism is responding to environmental conditions unlike those in which it has evolved. Thus we may say that in this case and in this sense the informational content carried in some state of the mechanism is 'incorrect'. Hence we achieve a distinction between correct/ incorrect, true/false informational content.

Fodor's objection is, however, that we can apparently run the account in another way, blocking the conclusion. We can say that there is in the frog a mechanism selected in the evolutionary process for detecting and snapping at ambient black dots. If the function of the mechanism is described in this way, detection and snapping at a non-fly ambient black dot is *not* an error. By all means, in the frog's normal ecology, all or most ambient black dots are in fact flies, so the result of the selection process is indeed a mechanism that, all or most of the time, succeeds in detecting and snapping at flies. The choice is therefore in the description of the 'intentional object' of the frog's information-carrying state, as being flies or ambient black dots. But, Fodor objects, the evolutionary story can be told either way, and in the latter case the proposed distinction between correct and incorrect informational content collapses (1990, pp. 71ff.). Dretske (1986) makes a similar point.

4.5.4 Rejoinder: evolutionary theory delivers intensional specifications of functions and stimuli

But is the objection outlined above valid? Can the evolutionary story be told either way? According to evolutionary theory a given mechanism is selected for a particular function. Plausibly this means something like: it would not have been selected unless it performed that function. So then, what function has the frog's 'fly(?)-detecting-snapping' mechanism been selected for? Surely the answer has to be: for catching flies *as food*, not for catching inedible ambient black dots. That is, the mechanism would not have been selected but that it performs the function of securing flies (as food); not, . . . but that it performs the function of catching ambient (inedible) black dots.

The point may be expressed in terms of *intensional descriptions* (as defined in subsection 1.3.1). Evolutionary theory demands an intensional description of the function of the mechanism for detecting and catching flies, as being for securing *food*, and hence also it vindicates the corresponding intensional description of the normal conditions in which the mechanism has been selected.

Nevertheless, there is something right about Fodor's objection. Its valid aspect can be brought out by asking the question: 'How could a biological information-processing system ever come to represent environmental conditions which it has not been selected to represent?' In so far as there is no answer to this question, the proposed distinction between true and false representation seems to collapse. Let us unpack this line of thought. It appeals to features of biological information-processing systems such as specialized detectors, and capacity for being deceived, which will be emphasized and elaborated on in the next chapter.

Not any state of an information-processing system counts as an information-carrying state. For example, a state of the brain caused by massive haemorrhage so far carries no information at all, and in particular none about the cause of the state. A state of an information-processing system is information-carrying only in so far as it results from the processing (coding, translation, etc.) of information picked up from the environment, characteristically by specialized detectors. The problem for the theory of error under consideration is that the only environmental states that can cause information-processing systems to go into information-carrying states *are those that the system is designed to respond to*. In the case of biological information-processing systems this means: only normal environmental conditions. So the proposed distinction between true and false information-carrying states cannot be made out.

In the particular case of the frog's behaviour there is, then, a reason for describing the regulating information as being about ambient black dots. It is simply that frogs are just as good at detecting and snapping at non-fly ambient black dots as at dealing with flies. It is hard to avoid the conclusion, endorsed by the considerations in the preceding paragraph, that the relevant mechanism is designed to process and respond to information about ambient black dots, regardless whether they happen to be flies or not.

So we have here two apparently conflicting intuitions, backed by biological and behavioural considerations. But is the conflict genuine? There is no escaping the conclusion that the frog's mechanism is designed in such a way that it detects and responds to ambient black dots, flies or otherwise. The behavioural evidence is clear. But equally, there is no escaping the demand of evolutionary theory that this mechanism has been selected because it fulfils the function of detecting and catching flies (as food). It is on the basis of theory of function that biology speaks pervasively and unhesitatingly of 'deception' in biological systems. But 'deception' is itself possible only because the system is designed in such a way as to receive and respond to information which is in fact irrelevant to, which does not serve, its function (the function for which it has been selected). The notion of deception, and in general a distinction between correct and incorrect information, can be vindicated on the basis of an (intensional) specification of systemic function. Such specification can in turn be based on evolutionary theoretic considerations, as indicated above.

4.5.5 Systemic behaviour is also a basis for intensional specifications of function

The question arises as to whether specification of systemic function has to be based in evolutionary theory, or whether it can be based in behavioural evidence alone. Plausibly behavioural evidence alone will do, bearing in mind that we are concerned here with behaviour which exhibits intentionality. To bring out the nature of the behavioural evidence sufficient to determine function, and hence to afford various normative distinctions, let us start with evolutionary theoretic considerations. It will be seen then that such evidence can stand on its own, detached from evolutionary theory.

Part of the evolutionary story about the frog's information-processing system is that it would not have evolved but for the fact that it enabled ingestion of flies as food. If the environment had been different (too few ambient black dots were flies) the system would have been de-selected and, let us suppose, replaced by another, more discriminatory one. This notion of *adaptation* is of course fundamental to evolutionary theory. As things are, the system fails to discriminate between flies and other ambient black dots. Frogs snap at and ingest the one as much as the other. They have, in particular, no 'corrective' mechanisms that arrest the routine of snapping at and ingesting non-flies at any stage. The evidence for such mechanisms would, of course, be behavioural: we would observe 'corrective behaviour', which is essentially a matter of arrest, possibly with replacement of, an initiated behavioural routine. Frogs—we are assuming—show no such corrective behaviour in the case of a non-fly; they do not desist from snapping on the basis on a closer look, nor do they spit it out. All this gives reason for saying that so far as the frog is concerned, non-flies are all the same as flies.[5]

Thus there is no evidence that an individual frog regards non-fly routines as an error; it does not behave as if it has made a mistake. We, on the other hand, because we know the function that the behavioural routine is meant to serve, that for which it has been selected, can call its application to non-flies an error. Connected with this, it might also be said, briefly and therefore in scare quotes, that the ecosystem consisting of the species frog and its environment also 'treats the non-fly routine as an error': too much in the species and it would be discarded.

The above remarks define the kind of behavioural evidence required to support the hypothesis that the frog regards catching non-flies as a mistake. Imagine an adapted frog species, members of which show either or both of the following sorts of behaviour. First, on sighting any ambient black dot, the frog prepares for snapping, but makes closer inspection (in some way): the frog then usually snaps if the dot is in fact a fly, but otherwise usually does not. Secondly, in case the frog snaps at and takes into its mouth a non-fly, it promptly spits it out. Here we would have behavioural evidence that the frog treats snapping at and/or ingesting non-flies as a mistake, the evidence being arrest of either or both the snapping and the ingestion behaviours. Such behaviour is evidence of discriminatory mechanisms, and of regulation of behavioural routines on the basis of information received at particular stages.

The discriminatory and corrective behaviour of this (hypothetical) frog constitutes evidence that it is after flies but not any other ambient black dots. The behaviour itself shows what the function of the behaviour is. In particular, the function may be determined on the basis of behavioural evidence alone, without the need for an evolutionary theoretic definition of function.

Indeed, it is arguable that even with frogs being the way they are, there is behavioural evidence that it is flies they are after, not any other ambient black dots. It is true that the frog, as it were, happily snaps and ingests non-flies. But the behavioural evidence is broader than just this. The behavioural consequences of at least persistent non-fly snaps are presumably different from those of persistent fly snaps. In the former case the frog stays hungry, an affective state which would show up in various ways; in the latter the frog is satiated, with different behavioural effects. Observation of these behavioural differences would be grounds for saying that the function of snapping behaviour is to secure flies (as food). In this case, contrary to what has been assumed so far, evolutionary theory is not required in order to define the function of snapping behaviour as being to catch flies (as food); this definition of the function can be based on behavioural evidence alone.

We may note in passing that these considerations to the effect that there are behavioural criteria of content of information-carrying states characterized intensionally runs counter to the claim that attempts to naturalize intentional explanation have failed because they have rendered intentional states non-intensional (Rosenberg 1986), but without restriction to language-users (Emmett 1989). Of course the line of argument we propose is based on the assumption, made back in the first chapter (subsection 1.3.6), that the behavioural evidence for meaningful states already has (to be seen) to have intentionality. In this sense there is here no sympathy with the aim characteristic of causal semantics, to 'naturalize' meaning (Fodor 1990, with critical commentary in, for example, Baker 1991; see also subsection 4.3.1 above).

Function may be specified using behavioural evidence, not only by appeal to evolutionary theory. Moreover, it may be argued that there is a sense in which behavioural determination of function *has to precede* evolutionary considerations. The point is the simple one that until we have determined, on the basis of observation of behaviour, the function of a behavioural routine, and hence of the information-processing mechanisms that serve it, we cannot even begin to construct an evolutionary explanation of its development.

But of course, as we may suspect given post-empiricism (subsection 1.4.1), the implied contrast here between observation and theory is artificial and unnecessary. 'Observation' of basic patterns of animal behaviour is laden with biological/evolutionary theory. The point for the present purpose is simply this: the function of functional behaviour is generally manifest in the behaviour, particularly in such characteristics as discrimination, modification of strategy, and satiation or otherwise.

The fact that we can get a handle on function, and on what counts as error, without recourse to evolutionary theory has particular importance, however, in relation to 'higher' forms of activity about which evolutionary theory has nothing definite to say. The scale of 'higher' and 'lower' forms of activity concerns at least degree of discrimination, of complexity and length of behavioural routines, and hence degree of regulation. 'Higher' behaviour is thus precisely of the kind in which function, or at least distinction between getting it right and getting it wrong, shows up in the behaviour itself. In this way behavioural criteria of function and error are increasingly available as we move up the scale from lower to higher activities, and the need for evolutionary theoretic definitions decreases. Indeed, such definitions become less and less helpful, particularly as we consider cultural practices, which constitute much of human activity, and which interact with our 'natural' behaviour. It is arguably degrading, but in any case notoriously difficult, to define the function of cultural activities, and the complex processes by which they are regulated, in terms of basic biological needs and natural selection.[6]

Let us summarize some of the main points made so far in this section. Causal semantics fails to allow the possibility of informational content being wrong. The suggested diagnosis of this failure is neglect of the contribution to informational content by the system which receives, processes, and uses information. This neglect is made good by functional semantics. Given an intentional specification of the function of a system, of what it (its response) is 'meant to achieve', we can define what counts as success or failure, and hence define other normative distinctions. If, on a particular occasion, a system fails to achieve its function, it has made an error somewhere along the line. Intentional specification of systemic function can be derived from evolutionary theoretic considerations, or on the basis of (intentional) behavioural evidence alone.

Let us grant that functional semantics in the form so far considered affords a solution to the problem of error, and in this respect improves on causal semantics. Still, in so far as functional semantics seeks to retain an essential claim of causal semantics, the claim that content is defined by its environmental causes, it inherits other problems of causal semantics, reviewed in Section 4.3. Thus, what is to be said about environmental causes that define the content of 'empty' informational states, for example those carrying information about (and regulating behaviour about) unicorns or phlogiston? There are no corresponding conditions in the environment. Or again, do we have to adopt a profligate (and vacuous) realism, ascribing to the environment whatever properties are needed in order to explain the existence of informational states with the corresponding content? Of course such problems are minimized, though certainly not removed, while we stay within the context of basic biological mechanisms and functions, the context in which the theory of functional semantics has usually been worked out. But they arise explicitly and in full force when we come to consider highly processed informational content which frankly exceeds characteristics of its environmental causes as defined in physics, or in psychological theories of perception. Here we think of content such as *dangerous*, or *edible*, but also, for example, *beautiful, democratic*, etc. In brief, in so far as functional semantics seeks to remain a genuine causal theory, to define informational content in terms of environmental causes, it continues to run up against problems of the kind faced by causal semantics.

4.5.6 A behavioural version of functional semantics: meaning defined in terms of action (again)

It was suggested in subsection 4.3.1 that the failures of causal semantics all arise from the same source, namely, its neglect of the systemic contribution to informational content. Functional semantics in the causal version so far considered, does not sufficiently free itself of this error. In order to explain this criticism, let us sketch a different form of the theory, to be called for convenience 'behavioural functional semantics', which avoids the problematic definition of content in terms of environmental causes. The basic claim of functional semantics in this form is that informational content is defined by its effects on the outputs of the system rather than by inputs (McGinn 1989; Papineau 1993). The point may be expressed by saying that behavioural functional semantics defines informational content in terms of what the information-processing system *makes of* input. Thus functional semantics captures the idea that there is indeed a systemic contribution to information, or meaning.

As we have seen, all semantic theories have to explain how information or meaningful content can be true or false. We have seen that causal semantics apparently fails in this task, while functional semantics in its causal form succeeds. But consider how it succeeds. The normative distinction applied to content is based in a normative distinction among environmental causes. This distinction in turn is based in a definition of systemic function, in considerations of what the system has been designed to achieve, of that function for which it has been selected in evolution. Systemic function has to be specified here intensionally, and we saw that such specification is indeed legitimate in the context of evolutionary biology. It was argued, however, that definition of systemic function essentially refers to the behaviour of the system, in particular to its intended effects, that is, the effects that the system has been designed or selected for. The implication, then, is that normative distinction among environmental causes of information-carrying states rests ultimately on normative distinction among the behavioural effects of these states. The implication is that the latter distinction is fundamental, and this point is what functional semantics in its behavioural version seeks to make explicit.

Let us consider in some detail how behavioural functional semantics works, and in particular how it approaches the problem of error.

How might error in informational content be defined in functional terms? Functional systems pick up information from the environment, process it, and use the result in regulating responses. It is in this systemic process that we find the possibility of error.

In brief, a functional, information-processing system *makes a mistake* if it interprets a signal P as being a sign of (as being caused by) environmental condition C1, when in fact P emanates from (is caused by) environmental condition C2.

For this proposal to work, we obviously require a definition of 'interprets signal S as a sign of C', and it is at this critical point that we need to refer to behaviour. The definition required is something like the following: a system 'interprets a signal P as a sign of C' if reception of P causes the system to respond in way appropriate to it being the case that C.

This definition in turn requires definition of when system responses are appropriate or otherwise to particular environmental conditions. This runs along the following lines. In order to know whether a systemic response is appropriate to the environment being in such-and-such a condition, we have to know what the behaviour is 'meant to achieve'. In other words, definition of what counts as a response being appropriate or inappropriate requires a theory about the function of the behaviour in question, or generally, of the system. This theory has to specify function intensionally, and we have already considered in the previous subsection the kind of principles used in such specification.

In summary, the proposed account of correctness or error in informational content runs as follows: a system emits a certain response R, regulated by an information-carrying state Si with a particular content. The response (we assume) is meant to achieve a particular result, typically some change in the environment to a condition CR. The response is appropriate to achieving CR if the initial condition of the environment is CI. In this sense the response is appropriate to it being the case that CI. The informational state Si is then true if CI is in fact the case, and is otherwise false. Whether the state is true or false will then (tend to) show up in the success or otherwise of the behaviour to which it gives rise.

As would be expected, the above account of truth and error in informational states defines also informational content. In brief, an information-carrying state Si has a particular content, C (that is, carries the information that the environment is in condition C), in case it tends to cause, other things being equal, behaviour appropriate to it being the case that C.

This kind of definition of content may seem to raise problems. Causal semantics was charged with the problem of being unable to specify the environmental causes of information-carrying states independently of the contents which they are supposed to cause (subsection 4.3.2). But now it looks as if behavioural functional semantics might be faced with a behavioural version of the same problem, namely, that of identifying the content of information-carrying states independently of the behaviour they are supposed to cause. In so far as mental content is defined in terms of its alleged behavioural effects, it seems that it cannot be taken to have a causal role. This echoes one of the considerations underlying the traditional distinction between meaningful and causal connections (subsection 4.2.5). However, this line of thought presupposes a narrow reading of what is involved in understanding cognitive states in terms of their role in regulating behaviour. The definition of content suggested above was as follows: an information-carrying state Si has a particular content, C, in case it tends to cause, other things being equal, behaviour appropriate to it being the case that C. This definition of content so far cites no specific behaviour, and therefore avoids the alleged circularity. The specific behaviours which are 'appropriate to it being the case that C' will depend on many factors, including, as already indicated, on what the system is trying to achieve, and on interaction with other relevant information-carrying states. For example, the behaviour appropriate to it being the case that there is a bull before me is a function of my desire to escape it, and my belief that this can best be done by climbing a tree, if there is one, or otherwise by running. Thus the content of my belief that there is a bull before me can be defined simply in terms of its tendency to generate behaviour appropriate to that being the case, but what this amounts to is specifiable in non-trivial ways. There is therefore so far no obstacle to saying that the belief has a causal role in relation to the behaviour generated in particular circumstances.

In the definitions given above of correctness and incorrectness, and of informational content, information-carrying is a property of states of the information-processing system, not, as in causal semantics, a property of the signal itself. Further, and related, the proposed definition of content appeals primarily not to the environmental causes of information-carrying states, but rather to their role in the regulation of behaviour. In brief, content is defined not in terms of input, but rather in terms of what the system *makes of* input. The contribution of the system to content is what gives scope for error. Also it creates the possibility of 'empty' content, content which corresponds to no reality. Both these features of informational content are problematic for causal semantics, precisely because it neglects the systemic contribution to content.

We have considered two versions of functional semantics. One defines content and the true/false distinction by reference to the role of information-carrying states in the regulation of intentional activity; the other by reference to a certain type of environmental cause of such states, namely, their normal causes as defined by evolutionary theory. In any given case, however, given the same intensional specification of function, both versions of functional semantics will deliver the same results, the same specification of content, and the same evaluation, true or false.

The behaviour-based version has several advantages, however. It avoids those problems that the causal version inherits from causal semantics *simpliciter*, namely, the problem of identifying environmental causes independently of their alleged representational effects, and the problem of empty content. Further, it is not restricted to behaviour and informational content of the limited kind addressed by evolutionary biology. But aside from these advantages, the behavioural version of functional semantics makes explicit what is misleadingly only implicit in the causal version; namely, that specification of informational content and normative description of it rest fundamentally on considerations of (intentional) behaviour.

We are led by this route, via discussion of causal and functional accounts of meaning, to themes and conclusions already familiar from the first three chapters. Attribution of meaningful content rests on behavioural criteria. The behaviour in question is essentially interactive: it already has intentionality. Hence explanations that invoke meaningful states are effective in the prediction of action. Such explanations attribute propensities to follow rules: the behaviour they predict is essentially subject to normative descriptions: correct/incorrect, appropriate/inappropriate, successful/unsuccessful, etc.

4.6 SYSTEMIC FUNCTION, MEANING, AND WHAT WE EXPECT OF CAUSAL EXPLANATION

4.6.1 Necessity, linked to norms of function and dysfuction

The main conclusion of the first chapter was that explanations of action in terms of meaningful, information-carrying states are causal, though it was left open in what sense. In Section 4.2 we outlined various familiar views about causality, noting their well-known apparent incompatibility with meaningful explanations. We sketched first Hume's analysis in terms of correlation and generality (subsection 4.2.1). This idea of causality is taken into causal semantics, but it provides no adequate basis for a definition of meaning, specifically because it is too simple to provide a theory of error, and generally because it sets out to ignore systemic contribution to meaning (Section 4.3).

Other familiar views about causality were sketched in the second section. Within the confines of empiricism, Hume could find nothing necessary in causal connections, nothing over and above mere conjunction between events (subsection 4.2.2). This apparent gap in the analysis of causality can be made good by appeal to natural laws, and in practice by deducibility from scientific theory (subsection 4.2.3), specifically by appeal to physical laws (4.2.4). But this analysis fails to apply to cognitive psychology. As noted in subsection 4.4.2, application of such a notion of causality leads to the apparently false conclusion that cognitive psychology cannot aspire to study causal interactions between organism and environment, and in particular can say nothing about those interactions that are relevant to meaning (or information-carrying). If cognitive psychology does study causal interactions, then we have to abandon the idea that causality and causal necessity must be a matter of physical laws. The implication was that such laws as are invoked in bio-psychological explanation have to do with the functioning of particular systems (4.4.3).

This implication hangs together with the conclusions reached in Section 4.5, that the shortcomings in causal semantics are addressed by functional semantics, which defines meaning essentially by reference to the functional activity of information-processing systems.

We return in this section to the problem of causal necessity, to discuss in the light of considerations so far its relation to explanations that invoke meaning.

It was noted in subsection 4.2.3 that the problem of necessary connection in causality can be solved by appeal to covering natural laws. It is tempting to construe these as physical laws (subsection 4.2.4), but as this does not suit psychology (subsection 4.4.2), why not just drop this physicalist construal, and draw back to the weaker position that causal explanation is committed to there being some covering natural law or other? This line of thought leads to the idea that the causal status of cognitive explanations derives from their place within a well-entrenched systematic empirical theory about relations between stimuli, cognitive states, and behaviour. There is something correct about this suggestion, but it is not yet complete. It omits special features of descriptions of functional systems, namely, that they essentially invoke *norms* of function, and that this accounts for their necessity.

If a person believes such-and-such, then she *must*, in appropriate circumstances, act in a way that accords with that belief. This 'must', however, has nothing to do with scientific theory or natural law. If the consequent of the hypothetical fails, no scientific theory has been refuted, still less has there been a miracle! Rather, the inference would be that, for one reason or another, the person has apparently acted irrationally. The nomological character of the prediction pertains to the 'laws' of reason, not to laws of an empirical science.

It is true that cognitive explanations are embedded in theory, but it is also true that the theory is permeated by reference to norms. Let us expand on this point in relation to Dennett's notion of the intentional stance, already described in Chapter 1, subsection 1.3.5.

Dennett is clear that use of the intentional stance as a predictive strategy involves adoption of several working assumptions: we treat the living being as a rational agent, assuming that it acts on beliefs and desires according to rational rules; we attribute the beliefs it ought to have, given its place in the world and its purposes (including here all truths relevant to its interests which are available from its experience); in a similar way we attribute desires the creature ought to have, and make predictions on this basis (Dennett 1987, for example p. 17). The critical first assumption is one of 'perfect' rationality, and this ideal is revised downwards, presumably in the light of the creature's behaviour. Attribution of what beliefs and desires the creature actually has, as opposed to those it ought to have, is presumably subject to revision downwards in the same way.

It may be seen that application of the intentional stance in the way Dennett proposes requires assumptions about the creature's sensory and cognitive capacities (which determine what is 'available from experience'), and about its purposes and interests. Some of these assumptions are presumably made in advance; for example, all living beings must have an interest in food, and information-processing capacities appropriate to its securement. Apart from such cases, however, determination of what desires and beliefs a creature has requires observation of what it actually strives for, and how.

Given that application of the intentional stance is partly based on, and is answerable to, observation of behaviour, it is tempting to suppose that the methodology could proceed straightforwardly a posteriori: we observe the behaviour of the system, find that its prediction is best served by positing drives and information-carrying states, attribute these in accord with behavioural criteria, adjusting such attributions as predictions fail. No a priori assumption of perfection in rationality would be made in this method, nor any assumption of appropriateness of beliefs and desires. In other words, it is tempting to suppose that application of the intentional stance as a predictive strategy can proceed 'bottom-up' just as well as 'top-down'. However, the supposition that attribution of intentionality can proceed entirely a posteriori, on the basis of observation alone, though plausible, is unsound. Dennett is right in claiming that non-empirical assumptions are being made, assumptions which are specifically *normative*.

Application of the intentional stance involves the assumption that the system in question has a design (natural or artificial) relevant to the achievement of certain ends. This assumption is essentially normative, presupposing distinctions between good and poor design, between function and malfunction. The non-empirical character of the assumption of design in the intentional stance shows up in the options open when its predictions fail. It is true that specification of ends and means can, and should, be based on observation of the behaviour of the system, that predictions of the theory then succeed or fail, and that, if they fail, the theory can be modified. So far, then, the theory acts simply as an empirical hypothesis. However, there are always other possibilities open when predictions fail, namely, that the system is poorly designed, or is malfunctioning. When these possibilities are considered, the assumption of design is held fast, and is used for the purpose of diagnosing failure in the system. In these contexts the assumption of design assumes an a priori role, held fast in the face of anomalies, and used in the detection of error elsewhere. The error is located, as it were, within the phenomena, not within the theory. Only in biology and psychology is such a diagnosis of error possible; there is nothing corresponding to it in physics and chemistry. This is because these basic sciences are not concerned with functional systems (as functional systems), and therefore have no use for normative descriptions of their subject-matter.

Psychological generalizations and their predictions in particular cases allow for the possibility of system failure. They are typically qualified by provisos to the effect 'if all other things are equal', by so-called *ceteris paribus* clauses, which include particularly explicit or implicit reference to 'normal' functioning. It can be said, for example, that perception of danger in the immediate environment will lead to avoidance behaviour, other things being equal. If in a particular case the creature in question fails to take evasive action, it may be inferred that other things are not equal, and one particular kind of possibility here is that the creature is not functioning normally.

It is clear, however, that while generalizations can be rescued in the face of anomaly by this method, the risk is that they become unfalsifiable, empty of empirical content, compatible with everything and excluding nothing. If this were the case, then the proposal that explanations that invoke intentional states are useful in predicting behaviour, the premise of the present essay, would be invalid: the appearance of predictive efficacy here would be an illusion.

This argument can be turned the other way round, however: since explanations that invoke intentional states are useful in prediction, they cannot be trivial or vacuous, notwithstanding their reliance on *ceteris paribus* clauses. The argument is turned this way round by Fodor (1987, chapter.1). Fodor goes on to observe that reliance on *ceteris paribus* clauses is characteristic of generalizations in other sciences, with physics being the possible exception, without lapse into triviality (Fodor 1987; see also Fodor 1991; Schiffer 1991).

It may be noted, however, that while scientific theory and prediction typically rely on *ceteris paribus* clauses, the theory and prediction of functional systems invoke them for a special reason. The point is not just that the phenomena are complicated, and generalizations in practice always partial. It is also that in the case of functional systems, theory and its predictions refer essentially to the *normal* case, and provisos are then added to allow for the abnormal.

Many examples from folk psychology and from the various fields of psychological science could be used to illustrate this point. Consider, for example, the following familiar case of a principle based in meaningful connections: intense sadness is precipitated, other things being equal, by experience of major loss. Anomalies include cases of intense sadness appearing in the absence of self-report of recent major loss, in the absence of such a loss in the recent history, or following recent experience of minor loss only, such as the death of a pet cat. In the face of such anomalies the principle can be preserved in one of two ways. It can be hypothesized that memory of past major losses, perhaps cued by one or several minor losses, is regulating current mood, consciously or otherwise. Alternatively, disruption to normal psychological function by lower-level (non-meaningful) causes, such as hormonal imbalance, can be hypothesized. In general, the explanation of breakdown of meaningful connections can proceed by positing either other meaningful connections or lower-level (non-semantic) disruption.

These points about the explanation of breakdown will occupy us through subsequent chapters. For now the point is that in the case of functional systems, including human beings, theory and its predictions refer essentially to the *normal* case, and provisos are then added to allow for the abnormal. We cited above the psychological principle: intense sadness is precipitated, other things being equal, by experience of major loss. We noted that 'other things being equal' in this case includes: unless experience of recent minor loss is intensified by memory of past major loss, and, unless there is biochemical disruption to normal psychic function.

Both of the above qualifications are reasonable. Others would (probably) not be, such as: unless the person's birth sign is Scorpio. This means, both cited applications of the *ceteris paribus* clause are plausible on the basis of current theory and empirical data. But the clause does not license salvage of the theory in any which way we choose. It has more or less specific, but in any case circumscribed, content. It leads, in case of anomaly, to more or less specific, but in any case circumscribed, predictions, concerning early learning history, or the underlying biochemistry. The psychological principle, together with its specified *ceteris paribus* clauses, serves as a methodological rule for distinguishing between normal and abnormal function, and for the investigation of apparently abnormal cases.

It can be seen here that the relation between a meaningful generalization and its *ceteris paribus* clause is an intimate, 'internal' one. In brief, the former is about what happens *normally*, while the latter is (partly) about what happens *abnormally*.

Another aspect of this point is that psychological generalizations do not even purport to hold good in *all* cases, only, and by definition, in normal ones. In this sense anomalies are not properly described as 'counter-examples' to the generalization; they are rather, and only, the abnormal cases which the generalization already envisages. The internally related *ceteris paribus* clause then serves to explain why and how conditions are abnormal. The position is different in sciences unconcerned with systemic function, and therefore with the distinction between normal and abnormal function. In these sciences anomalies for a generalization are indeed counter-examples which so far contradict it, unless a *ceteris paribus* clause can be invoked to explain away the counter-example and hence save the generalization.

In summary, then, the relative immunity of meaningful explanations from revision, their use of *ceteris paribus* clauses, and in particular the fact that they express norms of function, does not preclude their usefulness in prediction.

It is important to stress that we have here only *relative* immunity from revision. It is true that theories of meaningful content and connections, with more or less specific *ceteris paribus* clauses, are well entrenched. But in principle they can be given up, and some have been. In effect this involves radical revision in the theory of functions of particular biological or psychological (sub-)systems, and of their norms of operation.

Consider, for example, assumptions concerning the accessibility of mental states to consciousness and self-report, a topic already discussed in the first chapter (subsection 1.4.3). A principle in the Cartesian mould would run something like the following: if a person believes that p, then, other things being equal, she is aware that she believes that p, and will assent to the statement that p. 'Other things being equal' includes: all the relevant psychological functions are working normally, but also, for example, the person is being sincere. Anomalies for the generalization, disavowal, or denial of a belief apparently present according to other (behavioural) criteria, would be dealt with by invoking one or other component of the *ceteris paribus* clause. In this way the principle can be maintained, and was for a long time. However, it has been overturned, regarded now as valid only within a limited domain, by the combined operation of two factors. First, accumulation of (or attention to) anomalies that can be dealt with only by *ad hoc* explanations with no independent support, and secondly, and essentially, by the emergence of a new paradigm, according to which the definitive function of mental states is regulation of action, not appearance in consciousness. The processes by which even well-entrenched theories can be overthrown, or at least radically demoted, are described by Lakatos in his classic paper, (1970), as discussed in the first chapter (subsection 1.4.1). Lakatos was concerned with the physical sciences, but the basic rules are the same for psychological theory, whether philosophical, folk, or scientific.

It has been argued that explanations of action in terms of meaningful states are not causal in the sense of Hume's analysis and its standard elaborations, at least because they typically involve rational norms. These claims are familiar in the literature (Collingwood 1946, with commentary by, for example, Martin 1991; also Strawson 1985; Roque 1987–88; Haldane 1988; Henderson 1991). To the extent that it is assumed, then, that the neo-Humean accounts have a monoploy on causality, it follows that the explanation of action in terms of reasons, the bringing of behaviour under rational norms, must be a different kind of enterprise from causal explanation. This inference in effect preserves something like the dichotomies between meaning and causality, and between understanding and (causal) explanation. The position being argued for here is quite different. The proposal is that reason-giving explanation is causal: it is what causal explanation comes to look like in the case of the action of rational agents.

This interpretation of the general idea that reasons are causes is distinct from Davidson's very influential thesis. Davidson has argued that explanations in terms of reasons are causal, but the causal laws envisaged here are not content-based but rather refer to physical properties (Davidson 1963, with commentary in, for example, Lepore and McLaughlin 1985; Dretske 1989; Evnine 1991). Our quite different proposal is that the causal nature of explanations in terms of reasons involves precisely those reasons, and hence meaning and norms. As above, our argument is that reason-giving explanation is what causal explanation comes to look like in the case of the action of rational agents. In physics, causal laws have nothing to do with either intentionality or functional norms. These concepts make their appearance in the bio-psychological sciences, and they come eventually, as we move along the phylogenetic and ontogenetic scales, to involve beliefs, desires, and reasons for human action. But the logic of explanation which cites reasons as causes can be seen already in the foundation of biological science, the fundamental point being that the causal explanation of functional behaviour typically invokes information-processing and norms.

Dretske (1988a) has proposed an influential account according to which reasons function in causal explanations, and do so, moreover, by virtue of their content. This represents an improvement on Davidson's position, but it is again distinct from what is being argued for here. As discussed in subsection 2.5.3, Dretske's account is constructed to allow for the alleged lack of supervenience of content on neural states, whereas we are assuming that content supervenes on and specifically is encoded in such states. The assumption that information is encoded in material states of systems is evident in biology as well as psychology, and is central to our version of the claim that explanations in terms of information-carrying states, of which reasons are a particularly advanced form, are causal.

The suggestion that we should speak of *causality* in the case of meaning and reason may seem unattractive from the point of view of a philosophy which assumes that the lower-level natural sciences have a monopoly on the notion of causal law. Normative concepts pervade conceptions of psychological order, and hence also definitions of disorder (Fulford 1989). But are they implicated in causal explanation? If normative concepts such as rationality have to do with the causal explanation of behaviour, what is to prevent the involvement of the even more frankly unscientific concepts of ethics? Probably nothing, at least in the case of explanation of human behaviour, of its order and disorder, normality and abnormality. But uninviting though this prospect might be to the scientific mind, the vantage point from which it appears is unavoidable. The normative character of our conception of living beings, which reaches up to the level of rationality and morality, appears already well below that level. As Dennett's exposition makes clear, normative concepts concerning good and bad design, function and malfunction, with respect to certain ends, are presupposed in all applications of the intentional stance, and, it might be added, of the design stance. They are found in biological explanations of systemic function, and indeed in AI. It cannot be reasonably denied, we take it, that these sciences are in the business of finding causes, necessary and sufficient conditions of systemic responses. The analysis of the concept of causal explanation has to be broad enough to encompass the explanations of these sciences, which explicitly involve normative assumptions.

4.6.2 Generality, though decreasing with differentiation

Hume saw that generality is fundamental to the notion of causality. The proposition that one event has caused another implies the generalization that events of the one kind are followed by events of the other kind. How might this insight be applied in biology and psychology, to the relation between stimuli and responses? Hume's analysis would be applicable most straightforwardly in case the same stimulus always gave rise to the same response. In other words, the paradigm causal connection would be the reflex arc (as in the knee-jerk), axiomatic to seventeenth-century physiology and to bio-psychological schools which continued that tradition. The relation between stimulus and response in living systems is, however, not always one-one. Particularly as systemic complexity increases, the relation is more often one-many and/or many-one. Explanation of such variability requires postulation of mediating processes within the system, operating in a way dependent on the system's design. Therefore such generalizations, or partial (statistical) generalizations, as exist are essentially relative to the design of particular systems. Systems with different designs give rise to different correlations between stimuli and responses. Of course there is so far nothing to prevent us calling the correlations causal in Hume's sense, nor is there need to deny the implication of generality.

Generalization of this kind will be possible, however, only across systems with similar designs, and this condition severely restricts the scope of generalization in the biological sciences and upwards. By way of compensation, there can be generalizations over systems with different designs but the same function, though these generalizations are so far unconcerned with details of the mediating mechanisms. Either way, the result is that there is no 'general theory' of biological function. What we have rather is many specific (sub-) theories, concerning the function and design of such as the heart, kidney, liver, limbic system, etc., with often different theories for different species.

In psychology the same point applies, even more so as we deal with more highly differentiated cognitive-affective functions. We have (sub-) theories of vision and of memory, for example, more or less varying across different species, and often different depending on the kind of information being processed. In psychology, as in biology, there is no 'general theory' of function.

In psychology there was an attempt to construct a general theory of at least one fundamental function, learning, which would be applicable across the phylogenetic and ontogenetic scales, that is, the theory of conditioning. The theory explicitly aspired to the status of the general laws of the natural (sub-biological) sciences. But such aspiration is misconceived. Once we deal (explicitly) with systemic function, generality of the kind achieved in physics and chemistry is unattainable, and more importantly, inappropriate. Bio-psychological systems have diverse functions and fulfil them by diverse means. The scientific method appropriate in the case of such systems is investigation of specifics.

The above considerations raise the question to what extent we can expect to find generalizations concerning cognitive-affective states, their environmental causes, and their behavioural effects. Such connections are essentially relative to the perceiving, acting living being concerned. Given species' differences, individual differences within species, particularly in human beings, and given the diversity of contexts in which action occurs, it would seem so far that the prospects for generalization are slim.

That said, there is in fact no shortage of generalizations concerning cognitive-affective states, their causes and effects. However, generalization here is of a special kind, and is achieved at some cost.

Examples of generalizations over cognitive-affective states include the following. Fear is caused by (perception of) stimuli which are (interpreted as) threatening, for example because they are associated with pain, or just because they are novel; and it results, depending on many factors, including (perceived) context, in such behaviours as search, defence, avoidance, or preparation for attack (Gray 1982). Or again, the cognitive-affective state of helplessness results from persistent or traumatic (perceived) lack of control over major aversive events, such as pain, or deprivation, and ensues in behavioural inertia (Seligman 1975).

Such generalizations invoke informational content, or meaning. Stimuli are perceived as having a certain significance, resulting in a cognitive-affective state with a particular content, which in turn, generates in a way depending on perceived meaning of context and on aims, appropriate intentional, meaningful behaviour (or, in the case of helplessness in particular, appropriate cessation of intentional behaviour). In this sense, the generalizations are over 'meaningful connections'. Jaspers cites other examples: attacked people become angry and spring to the defence, cheated people grow suspicious (1923, p. 302).

So there are generalizations over cognitive-affective states, their causes and effects, and they typically invoke meaningful connections. It may be seen, however, that such generalizations are somewhat vague, or *non-specific*. This is, of course, connected to the well-known multifactorial nature of the processes involved. There is variation among species, among individuals, this in turn compounded by variation in (perceived) characteristics of particular situations. The generalizations cover many different kinds of case, and many different particular cases. What counts as threat, novelty, pain, defence, lack of control, deprivation, attack, cheating, suspicion, etc. differs, more or less, between species, individuals, and contexts.

Although the generalizations are vague, their instances can in principle be described in highly specific ways. *This* person, in *this* mental state, finds that such-and-such is intolerably offensive, and so retaliates in these ways ... Description of the details in particular cases contains much information, in principle as much as is being used (consciously or otherwise) by the agent. Hence the familiar idea that meaningful connections are by their nature highly specific, even to the extent of being 'unique', instanced in but one particular case. On this particularity Jaspers writes (1923, p. 314):

> We all know a great many psychic connections which we have learnt from experience (not only through repetition but through having understood one real case which opened our eyes) ... Such meaningful connections as we all know and as constantly conveyed by our language lose all their force if we try to give them a general formulation. Anything really meaningful tends to have a concrete form and generalization destroys it.

Compared with the particular instance, the corresponding generalization is less informative. The implication is that specificity in particular cases makes generalization problematic: it can be achieved, but at the expense of information. Generalizations concerning meaningful connections thus do not capture the data inherent in particular cases, but are rather abstractions achieved by reduction of content. In this respect such generalizations stand in marked contrast to those in the (sub-biological) natural sciences.

As summaries of observations of particular cases, generalizations concerning meaning leave much to be desired. However, summary of observations is not the only function of such generalizations. As noted in the preceding subsection, they also have a 'non-empirical' role in theory, as expressions of norms. Consider again Jaspers' examples: attacked people become angry and spring to the defence, cheated people grow suspicious. These propositions possess an element of non-empirical necessity. If they seemed not to hold in a particular case, we would be inclined to investigate further to see whether first appearances were deceptive, and in so far as investigations were negative, the generalization can still be retained, by considering the possibility that the person is not acting appropriately (meaningfully, rationally). It can be seen in these and similar examples that generalizations concerning meaning are not simply the result of observation, but rather serve as *rules* for the interpretation and investigation of the phenomena, and in particular, for the diagnosis of disorder.

Jaspers was right to emphasize the particularity of meaningful phenomena. It is a mistake, however, to suppose that generalization here is impossible. Generalization over meaningful connections is possible, though, as Jaspers again recognized, it is unlike empirical generalization. It is not grounded in induction from observed cases, nor, a related point, is it overthrown by anomalies. This non-empirical character of generalizations about meaning is not, however, derived from a covering general theory. Rather, meaningful generalizations function as expressions of norms of appropriateness (rationality) for particular kinds of cognitive-affective states, their causes and effects. They concern norms for specific cognitive-affective subsystems: trust, fear, grief, anger, curiosity, rationality, and so on. In these contexts the laws are 'logical'—'psycho-logical'—rather than empirical.

The distinction at issue here may also be drawn in this way. Empirical generalization is grounded in enumeration of instances. In meaningful, psychological generalization, by contrast, single instances already contain the general. If connections are perceived as meaningful in just one instance, the perceived meaning immediately assumes the status of a rule for the interpretation and investigation of other, similar cases. In this sense generality is inherent in meaning. Hence the inevitable although hazardousness ease with which we move here from the particular to the general.

Meaningful generalizations can be used in such a way as to be immune from revision by experience. If they seem to fail in a particular case, appeal can be made to one or another mitigating circumstance, and in particular, to failure of 'normal' function. However, as noted in the preceding subsection, what we have here is only *relative* immunity from revision. Theories of normal function can change, from pressure of empirical anomalies, consolidated by paradigm shifts, and what was at one time a rule for the interpretation of phenomena can become treated as an empirical generalization which turns out to be false.

The dual aspect of propositions that invoke meaningful connections, which function on the one hand as summaries of empirical correlations and on the other as rules of normal function, is relevant to an aspect of the issue of discreteness of cause and effect, discussed in subsection 4.2.5 and subsequently in relation to functional semantics (subsection 4.5.6). Hume's analysis emphasized that if two events are causally related they (their descriptions) must be logically independent. However, some propositions that invoke meaningful connections apparently flout this condition. We can say, for example, that if someone believes that p, then she tends to act in a way that accords with that belief. In this formulation the belief and the action fall under the same intensional description. It is tempting then to suppose that the generalization is simply true 'by definition', without substantial content; in particular that it does not specify an empirical association between two independent events, and is for that reason not a causal proposition.

However, this line of thought, which would support the dichotomy between meaning and causality, can be seen in the light of considerations in this and the preceding subsection to be oversimple and invalid. Meaningful generalizations are not true 'by definition', at least, not by definition of words. One might say that they are true by definition of the meaningfulness of psychological processes. They are true in so far as agents are behaving meaningfully: normally, appropriately, with 'everything intact'. The generalizations can fail in so far as the condition of normality is not met. We can imagine cases, indeed there are of course actual cases, in which a person shows clear signs of having such-and-such a belief, but nevertheless behaves in ways incompatible with that belief. The implication of this possibility of failure is that a belief and its normal effects can become dissociated, so that there are indeed two independent states (processes) at work here. This being so, one more support for the dichotomy between meaningful and causal connections appears invalid.

4.6.3 Agency: actions as self-caused, with 'inner necessity'

The considerations so far in this section lead to a perspective on the problem of free will and causality. This problem is in fact a set of interrelated problems, each of which and the connections between them are complicated. But consider something like the following line of thought, which brings into question not so much freedom as action itself.

In so far as we suppose that all of nature proceeds according to laws, then it seems as though what we are inclined to call human action is rather part of a larger process, following these laws of nature, in which nothing new, nothing not covered by law, could appear. Each branch of knowledge, each 'science' in the broadest sense, could give its own account of this process and the laws that it followed, as in theology, in mechanics, and to some extent also in evolutionary biology, psychology, and sociology. So we have the idea of natural law, of what happens under natural law, but no fundamentally distinct notion of *action; a forteriori*, then, no notion of *free action*.

The only concept on offer in this thought space seems to be just that *the law can sometimes be broken*. In the case of divine law, theology struggled with the problem of free will. In the case of natural law, in the modern scientific world-view picture, the idea that the law can fail, can be broken, is out of place. In any case, lawlessness, what looks at though it may be caprice or chance, may offer no attractive analysis of (free) action. Thus there seems to be a choice between action being subsumed under general laws, and its being law-less. It is possible, however, to deconstruct this dichotomy.[7]

The argument in this section has been that our notion of causality, and the notion of law-like necessity to which it is linked, is inevitably modified in application from the lower-level natural sciences, to the biological, then up into psychology. The 'laws' involved in causality become increasingly specific. At the same time, by the same considerations, the *origin of law* appears increasingly specific, from the whole of nature, to parts. This point may be illustrated as follows.

Explanation of why a living being, a dog say, when unsupported falls to the ground, appeals to the nature of the physical body as one among all others. Explanation of food-seeking appeals to the nature of the dog as a living being. More particular types of styles of action are explained in terms of the dog being a dog. To the extent that one dog behaves much like another, at least so far as we are concerned, we attribute the cause of the dog's behaviour to the nature of its species, rather than to the individual. As to human beings, there are perhaps also actions, or reactions, which are common to all, or to all human beings of a particular culture, and for these we may want to find causes within human nature, or within society, rather than in individuals. The question is where the authorship lies. The concept of individual action takes hold in cases where human beings act differently from one another. It is by experiencing the diversity of the actions of others that a human being can realize her own possibilities, between which she must chose. When a person acts in the way she has chosen, the reason for the action can be attributed to no nature other than her own. What a person does then is self-caused, with inner necessity due to the person's nature. In this sense such an action is the agent's responsibility, and 'free'.

Human action does conform to laws, but these laws become increasingly specific, reaching the point at which the law is the 'inner law' of the agent. Another way of expressing the point would be to say that human action does not simply conform with, but nor does it 'break', natural laws. Within these terms, the point would be rather that our action creates natural law, that we are in this sense small, human-size, miracles. By all means we are at this point a long way away from general natural law of the kind known in the physical sciences, but the transition here is developmental: individual agency is what general natural law has become.

This conclusion is consistent with the line of thought from Wittgenstein (1953), considered above (Section 3.3), concerning what it means to follow a rule. The argument is to the effect that the rule is made in practice, as opposed to being given in advance, in acts of mind, or in pictures, formulae, tables, and other expressions of rules. The argument is a priori, a matter of logic, and is not concerned with *causes* of action. However, at the philosophical level of generality, these various kinds of point tend to merge. If logic comes to the conclusion that action involves the creation of order, it is likely that the analysis of causal law will come to something like the same conclusion, that action is self-caused, etc. Also, in the sciences themselves there is expression of the very general idea that action involves the creation of order, for example in Schroedinger's (1967) suggestion that living systems are *local* areas in which the second law of thermodynamics does not hold. This suggestion in turn belongs with the shift from causal to functional semantics recommended in the previous section, the implication of which is that systemic functional activity creates information (cf. Sayre 1976, 1986; Oyama 1985; Wicken 1987).

There are deep and complicated connections between concepts such as order, entropy, information, action, and intentionality, anticipated early in our considerations, in the intimate link between cognition and affect (subsection 1.2.3). But let us pass these by and focus back on the particular line of argument proposed in this subsection, to note some problem areas which it implies.

The argument was that as behaviour becomes more particular and less general, then its causes are seen correspondingly as more particular and less general. This process reaches its height in the case of human action, which is seen as self-caused; that is, as opposed to being attributable to our nature as physical bodies, living beings, human beings, of a particular culture, etc. But this perception is by all means highly theory-dependent! Roughly, the methodological rule is to attribute the origins of action to the entity which is acting, ... until we find out more about the general laws under which it falls. So then it would follow that the more we know about, say, the psychological principles governing human behaviour, the less we are inclined to say that the particular person is the cause of the act. This, we have to note in passing, apparently threatens the moral idea of individual responsibility for action. So it may be that after all we have to envisage a form of determinism which seems to rule out (individual) action, not linked to mechanics, but to the twentieth-century paradigm for explaining human behaviour.

On the other side, we have the fact that there is, objectively, according to current deeply entrenched biological and psychological theory, increasing differentiation along the phylogenetic scale, and then along the ontogentic scale. Generality decreases, specificity (individuality) increases. This spectrum is not just a matter of observer/theory-relativity, a matter of what we happen to know, but is in the phenomena (in nature). Another aspect of the same point is the special characteristic of generalization which emerges as we deal with increasingly specific systems. As noted in the previous subsection, there are generalizations in biology and in psychology, but they are achieved at the expense of loss of information about specifics. They assume the role more of methodological propositions for the investigation of specifics, as opposed to being empirical generalizations which summarize individual instances. In this way, even as we learn more about the psychological principles of human behaviour, this theoretical knowledge will always be in the service of, and cannot replace, the understanding of why the individual person behaves as she or he does.

4.7 SUMMARY

The conclusion that meaningful explanations of action are causal was reached in the first chapter, based primarily on the fact that they deliver theory-driven predictive power. The explanations in question are those of folk psychology, but they include those in cognitive psychology, and indeed in biology, which share the fundamental idea that functional systemic activity is regulated by information-carrying states. The main argument of the present chapter has been that while explanations of this general kind are causal, their logic is not captured by certain familiar interpretations of causality.

The traditional analyses of causality were sketched in the second section. Hume proposed that causal propositions are based in observation of association between kinds of event (subsection 4.2.1). However, this analysis failed to capture the necessity in causal propositions (4.2.2), a gap which has to be made good by distinguishing mere generalizations from those which are, or which are covered by, natural law (4.2.3), in particular of physics (4.2.4). Essential features of causal propositions according to this kind of analysis are thus empirical correlation covered by a general physical law. Meaningful explanations do exhibit the features that are expected of causal explanation—necessity and generality—but not in the way envisaged by the views of causality already outlined (subsection 4.2.5).

Nevertheless, once it is granted that meaningful explanations are causal, there is great pressure to bring them into the domain of the physical sciences and the notion of causality appropriate to them. Causal semantics, discussed in the third section, is one way of doing this. The proposal is (briefly and roughly) that A carries information about B in case B causes A, that is, in case there is a correlation between events of kind A and events of kind B covered by a natural law (subsection 4.3.1). This proposal tends to be either vacuous or inadequate (4.3.2), and fails to capture two linked features of the representation relation, that intentional states can be empty, and false (4.3.3).

In the fourth section we considered further the point that the objects of intentional states cannot, in general, be defined in terms of physical theory. A consequence is that semantic relations cannot be captured in the net of physical theory. Fodor embraces the unattractive conclusion that cognitive psychology cannot study the causal interactions between organism and environment, and in particular not those which ground semantics (subsection 4.4.2). The correct inference is not that causal relations here are ungraspable, but rather that an inappropriate model of causality is being applied (4.4.3).

The causal processes that serve information-processing essentially involve the activity, hence the design and function, of the processing system. Neglect of the systemic contribution to information processing and content is the main failing of causal semantics, and is made good by so-called functional semantics, to which we turned in the fifth section. The main idea of functional semantics is that information (or meaning) has to be defined with reference to the (normal) function of the information-processing system (subsection 4.5.1). Two versions of functional semantics were considered. In its 'causal' version, the notion of normal function is used to make a normative distinction among the causes of information-carrying states, and hence a normative dictinction among the contents of such states, with the critical task of defining the normative distinction among causes to be performed by biological/evolutionary theory (subsection 4.5.2). Contrary to an argument of Fodor's, evolutionary theory can deliver intensional descriptions of functions and objects, and hence also a theory of error (subsections 4.5.3–4). It was subsequently argued that a behavioural version of functional semantics can deliver the same (4.5.5). Causal-functional semantics disguises the fact that the notion of normal function affords primarily a normative distinction among behavioural responses, and that it is this which grounds the distinction between true and false informational content. Functional semantics in its behavioural version makes this explicit (subsection 4.5.6).

The intimate connection between intentional states and functional systems is what gives rise to the special causal status of intentional explanations. The familiar account of causality in terms of generality covered by natural law is appropriate for the lower-level sciences, physics and chemistry, up to, but not including, biology. With the appearance of (the study of) functional systems, in biology and psychology, different principles of causality come into play. In particular, the critical principles of necessity and generality have to be re-thought. The issues are considered in the sixth section.

In subsection 4.6.1 we returned to the problem of causal necessity. If prediction from physical theory fails, and statements of initial conditions are sound, then there is an error somewhere in the theory. Either that or there has been a miracle! By contrast, if prediction from a meaningful generalization fails in a particular case, then certainly the generalization can be abandoned, but there is another possibility, namely, that the system in question is failing to function normally. This possibility is analogous to the breakdown of law, which the physical sciences never envisage. But in the case of systems, breakdown can and does occur. The 'laws' being broken are not general laws of nature, but are rather rules or norms which apply specifically to one or another kind of functional system. In this way the causal necessity in explanations of systemic function is based in norms of function, not in general laws of nature. Hence one aspect of the difference between intentional causality and the type envisaged in the standard analyses.

There are further implications concerning generalization, drawn out in subsection 4.6.2. While it is possible to make generalizations concerning systemic function, and meaning in particular, they are restricted to, precisely, one or another kind of functional system. The sciences from biology upwards are concerned with specifics. A connected point is that generalization tends to be at the expense of information about particular cases. This point increases in relevance as specificity of function increases, in particular as we make generalizations about meaningful connections among higher-level cognitive-affective states and action. On the other hand, as implied by the considerations above, summary of empirical data is not the only function of generalizations concerning meaning. The propositions function also as expressions of norms or rules. This function gives rise to the well-known difficulties in attempting to construe meaningful connections between phenomena as being empirical associations. This is a further aspect of the distinction between meaningful causation and what may be called neo-Humean causation.

Implications for the concept of agency fall out of the analysis (subsection 4.6.3). Causal power is attributed to what is specific to the agent to the extent that explanation cannot be given in terms of a more general nature. In the extreme case, the individual person is identified as the causal origin of the act.

In this chapter we have worked towards the conclusion that there are two types of causal explanation, which may be called for convenience the non-intentional and the intentional. The first of these is defined in neo-Humean terms as based in observation of empirical correlations, covered by general natural law. This notion of causality belongs to the lower-level natural sciences, physics and chemistry. Intentional-causal explanation, by contrast, is distinctively embedded within concepts of functional, information-processing systems. This type of causal explanation makes its appearance in biology, pervades psychology, and also provides the appropriate model for folk psychological explanations of action in terms of meaningful mental states. The distinction between the two kinds of causal explanation, the logic of each kind, and the relation between them, are explored in more detail in the next chapter.

NOTES

1. It may be noted that the mathematical theory of information, or communication, (Shannon and Weaver 1949) is concerned with quantities of information and explicitly not with informational content, and it is therefore irrelevant to the definition of the latter (Dretske 1981, 1983; see also above, subsection 1.2.2). That said, the mathematical theory defines quantity of information as essentially relative to the receiving system, in particular to the information already possessed. Our main objection to causal semantics to be made in this section is that it neglects this essential relativity in the case of informational content.

2. This account is intended to be relatively uncontentious cognitive psychology.

Cognitive psychological theories of vision are concerned with physical features and particularly their invariance relations, but acknowledge more advanced stages of processing which involve the 'semantics' of objects, including use and purpose (e.g. Marr 1982). The points made in the text against causal semantics, that it neglects the agent-relativity of informational content, and that content exceeds what can be specified in physicalist terms, echo the arguments in the second chapter against Putnam's claim that 'meaning ain't in the head' (Section 2.5).

3. Dretske (1981, 1983), attempted to allow for error by distinguishing between causal links between sign and signified established during learning and causal links established subsequently, and perhaps wrongly. Fodor has argued convincingly that this does not work (1987, p. 102f.). Fodor proceeds to develop a highly sophisticated causal semantic theory which does indeed afford distinction between correct and incorrect content, resting on what Fodor calls the principle of asymmetric dependence (1987, 1990). However, there are, in our view, two weaknesses in Fodor's theory. One is that it depends essentially on the idea that properties (as opposed to their instances) are the causes of mental content. This idea has already been criticized in the text for its apparent obscurity, not least from the point of view of scientific investigation and explanation. The other weakness concerns specifically the principle of asymmetric dependence. The principle solves the problem of error, and the closely related problem of ambiguity of mental content, but at the critical point of solution Fodor appeals to the behavioural characteristics, specifically to 'recovery from error' (Fodor 1990, p. 107). In this way the distinction between truth and error turns fundamentally on systemic behaviour, and the principle of asymmetric dependence, with its apparatus of properties and causal associations, appears only as an embellishment. This criticism of Fodor's solution is elaborated below, subsection 4.5.5, Note 5.

4. See also Bogdan (1988), McGinn (1989), and Papineau (1993). For critical commentary on functional semantics, in one or another version, see, for example, Dretske (1988*b*), Israel (1988), Forbes (1989), and Lyons (1992).

5. Fodor's (1990) sophisticated causal semantics seeks to secure what a simple causal semantics cannot secure, solution of the problem of ambiguity of content and of the related problem of error. Fodor's solution rests on appeal to what he calls the principle of asymmetric dependence. It was remarked above in 4.3.3 (Note 3), that while Fodor's principle succeeds, it does so only because it helps itself to criteria that go beyond what is available to causal semantics. This remark can now be justified. Fodor argues, by application of the principle of asymmetric dependence, that the intentional object of the frog's fly snaps is ambient black dots rather than flies, and hence that non-fly snaps are not errors. Crucial to the argument, however, is appeal to behavioural characteristics. Thus: frogs 'are prepared to go on going for bee-bees *forever*', they are not 'in a position to recover', they '*have no way at all* of telling flies from bee-bees', in particular no discrimination by use of another modality (Fodor 1990, p. 107 and note 19, original italics). By contrast, Fodor observes, *he* can tell the difference between a fly and a bee-bee, and if he swats at the latter he has made a mistake, from which he can 'recover' (loc. cit.), that is, presumably, he makes a mistake which he can correct. In this way Fodor appeals to discriminative and

corrective behaviour, or their absence, in his definition of content and error. The position is, then, that Fodor's sophisticated causal semantics, by use of the principle of asymmetric dependence, can indeed resolve ambiguity of content and provide a solution to the problem of error. But it rests on appeal to concepts that exceed what is permitted to causal semantics, concepts concerning (presence or absence of) discriminative and/or functional behaviour. That content and error are defined in terms of these phenomena is a claim belonging rather to functional semantics.

6. Recent critical discussion of sociobiology includes Sterelny (1992).
7. The problems here are discussed in the literature in connection with two positions, usually called compatibilism and incompatibilism (Searle 1984; Honderich 1988; Bishop 1989; Ginet 1989; Dretske 1992). According to the former, free will is compatible with the fact that our action conforms to natural laws, while according to the latter it is incompatible. The proposal to be made in the text identifies with neither of these views.

REFERENCES

Armstrong, D. (1983). *What is a law of nature?* Cambridge University Press, Cambridge.

Baker, L. R. (1989). On a causal theory of content. In *Philosophical perspectives, 3: philosophy of mind and action theory*, (ed. J. E. Tomberlin), pp. 165–86. Ridgeview, Atascadero.

Baker, L. R. (1991). Has content been naturalized? In *Meaning in mind: Fodor and his critics*, (ed. B. Loewer and G. Rey), pp. 17–32. Blackwell, Oxford.

Bishop, J. (1989). *Natural agency. An essay on the causal theory of action.* Cambridge University Press, Cambridge.

Bogdan, R. J. (1988). Information and cognition: an ontological account. *Mind and Language*, 3, 81–122.

Braithwaite, R. (1953). *Scientific explanation.* Cambridge University Press, Cambridge.

Collingwood, R. G. (1946). *The idea of history.* Clarendon, Oxford.

Davidson, D. (1963). Actions, reasons, and causes. Reprinted in Davidson, D. (1980). *Essays on actions and events*, pp. 3–19. Oxford University Press, Oxford.

Davidson, D. (1967). Causal relations. Reprinted in Davidson, D. (1980). *Essays on actions and events*, pp. 149–62. Oxford University Press, Oxford.

Davidson, D. (1970). Mental events. Reprinted in Davidson, D. (1980). *Essays on actions and events*, pp. 207–25. Oxford University Press, Oxford.

Dennett, D. (1987). *The intentional stance.* MIT Press, Cambridge, Mass.

Dretske, F. (1981). *Knowledge and the flow of information.* MIT Press, Cambridge, Mass.

Dretske, F. (1983). Precis of *Knowledge and the flow of information*, with peer commentary. *Behavioral and Brain Sciences*, 6, 55–90.

Dretske, F. (1986). Misrepresentation. In *Belief*, (ed. R. Bogdan), pp. 17–36. Oxford University Press, Oxford.

Dretske, F. (1988a). *Explaining behavior: reasons in a world of causes.* MIT Press, Cambridge, Mass.

Dretske, F. (1988*b*). Commentary: Bogdan on information. *Mind and Language*, 3, 141–4.

Dretske, F. (1989). Reasons and causes. In *Philosophical perspectives, 3: philosophy of mind and action theory*, (ed. J. Tomberlin), pp. 1–15. Ridgeview, Atascadero.

Dretske, F. (1992). The metaphysics of freedom. *Canadian Journal of Philosophy*, 22, 1–13.

Emmett, K. (1989). Must intentional states be intenSional? *Behaviorism*, 17, 129–36.

Evnine, S. (1991). *Donald Davidson*. Polity Press, Cambridge.

Fodor, J. (1980). Methodological Solipsism considered as a research strategy in cognitive psychology. With peer commentary. *The Behavioral and Brain Sciences*, 3, 63–109.

Fodor, J. (1987). *Psychosemantics*. MIT Press, Cambridge, Mass.

Fodor, J. (1990). A theory of content, I & II. In *A theory of content and other essays*, pp. 51–136. MIT Press, Cambridge, Mass.

Fodor, J. (1991). You can fool some of the people all of the time, everything else being equal; hedged laws and psychological explanation. *Mind*, 100, 19–34.

Forbes, G. (1989). Biosemantics and the normative properties of thought. In *Philosophical perspectives, 3: philosophy of mind and action theory*, (ed. J. E. Tomberlin), pp. 533–47. Ridgeview, Atascadero.

Fulford, K. (1989). *Moral theory and medical practice*. Cambridge University Press, Cambridge.

Ginet, C. (1989). Reasons explanation of action: an incompatibilist account. In *Philosophical perspectives, 3: philosophy of mind and action theory*, (ed. J. E. Tomberlin), pp. 17–46. Ridgeview, Atascadero.

Gray, J. (1982). *The neuropsychology of anxiety*. Clarendon Press, Oxford.

Haldane, J. (1988). Folk psychology and the explanation of human behaviour. *Proceedings of the Aristotelian Society, Suppl.* LXII, 223–54.

Henderson, D. (1991). Rationalizing explanation, normative principles, and descriptive generalizations. *Behaviour and Philosophy*, 19, 1–20.

Honderich, T. (1988). *A theory of determinism. The mind, neuroscience and life hopes*. Oxford University Press, Oxford.

Hume, D. (1777). *An enquiry concerning human understanding*. (Ed. Selby-Bigge, L. A. (1902) (2nd edn). Oxford University Press, Oxford.)

Israel, D. (1988). Commentary: Bogdan on information. *Mind and Language*, 3, 123–40.

Jaspers, K. (1923). *Allgemeine Psychopathologie*. Springer Verlag, Berlin. (English translation by Hoenig, J. and Hamilton, M. W. (1963). *General Psychopathology*. Manchester University Press.)

Lakatos, I. (1970). Falsification and the methodology of scientific research programmes. In *Criticism and the growth of knowledge*, (ed. I. Lakatos and A. Musgrave), pp. 91–196. Cambridge University Press, Cambridge.

Lepore, E. and McLaughlin, B. (ed.) (1985). *Actions and events. Perspectives on the philosophy of Donald Davidson*. Blackwell, Oxford.

Lettvin, J. Y., Maturana, H. R. McCulloch, W. S., and Pitts, W. H. (1959). What the frog's eye tells the frog's brain. *Proceedings of the Institute of Radio Engineers*, 1940–51.

Locke, J. (1690). *An essay concerning human understanding*. (Ed. Nidditch P. H. (1975). Oxford University Press, Oxford.)

Lyons, W. (1992). Intentionality and modern philosophical psychology, III the appeal to teleology. *Philosophical Psychology*, 5, 309–26.

McGinn, C. (1989). *Mental content*. Blackwell, Oxford.

Marr, D. C. (1982). *Vision: a computational investigation into the human representation and processing of visual information*. Freeman, San Francisco.

Martin, R. (1991). Collingwood on reasons, causes, and the explanation of action. *International Studies in Philosophy*, 23, 47–62.

Mill, J. S. (1843). *A system of logic*. John W. Parker, London.

Millikan, R. (1984). *Language, thought, and other biological categories*. MIT Press, Cambridge, Mass.

Millikan, R. (1986). Thoughts without laws: cognitive science with content. *Philosophical Review*, 95, 47–80.

Nagel, E. (1961). *The structure of science: problems in the logic of scientific explanation*. Routledge and Kegan Paul, London.

Oyama, S. (1985). *The ontogeny of information: developmental systems and evolution*. Cambridge University Press, Cambridge.

Papineau, D. (1987). *Reality and representation*. Blackwell, Oxford.

Papineau, D. (1993). *Philosophical naturalism*. Blackwell, Oxford.

Popper, K. (1959). *The logic of scientific discovery*. Hutchinson, London.

Roque, A. J. (1987–88). Does action theory rest on a mistake? *Philosophy Research Archives*, 13, 587–612.

Rosenberg, A. (1986). Intentional psychology and evolutionary biology, Parts I and II. *Behaviorism*, 14, 15–27 and 125–38.

Sayre, K. M. (1976). *Cybernetics and the philosophy of mind*. Routledge and Kegan Paul, London.

Sayre, K. M. (1986). Intentionality and information processing: an alternative model for cognitive science, with peer commentary. *The Behavioral and Brain Sciences*, 9, 121–66.

Schiffer, S. (1991). Ceteris Paribus laws. *Mind*, 100, 1–17.

Schroedinger, E. (1967). *What is life?* and *Mind and matter*. Cambridge University Press, Cambridge.

Searle, J. (1984). *Minds, brains and science*. BBC Publications, London.

Seligman, M. (1975). *Helplessness: on depression, development, and death*. Freeman, San Fransisco.

Shannon, C. and Weaver, W. (1949). *The mathematical theory of communication*. University of Illinois Press, Urbana.

Skinner, B. F. (1956). *Verbal behavior*. Appleton-Century-Crofts, New York.

Sterelny, K. (1992). Evolutionary explanations of human behaviour. *Australian Journal of Philosophy*, 70, 156–73.

Strawson, P. (1985). Causation and explanation. In *Essays on Davidson. Actions and events*, (ed. B. Vermazen and M. B. Hintikka), pp. 115–35. Oxford University Press, Oxford.

Villanueva, E. (ed.) (1990). *Information, semantics and epistemology*. Blackwell, Oxford.

Wicken, J. S. (1987). Entropy and information: suggestions for a common language. *Philosophy of Science*, 54, 176–93.

Wittgenstein, L. (1953). *Philosophical investigations*, (ed. G. E. M. Anscombe and R. Rhees, trans. G. E. M. Anscombe). Blackwell, Oxford.

5
Two forms of causality in biological and psychological processes

5.1 INTRODUCTION

We have seen in the first chapter that explanations of behaviour which invoke mental, intentional states have predictive power, and that both folk psychology and cognitive psychology exploit this fact. It was argued further that, in respect of predictive power, explanations in terms of mental states are apparently akin to causal explanations. Several major questions to which this conclusion gives rise were outlined at the end of the first chapter.

One set of issues concerns the logic of causal explanation in terms of mental states, in itself, and in relation to the type of causal explanation familiar in the natural, physical sciences. The most straightforward, the most parsimonious manoeuvre here is to suppose that explanations in terms of mental, intentional states are causal in the same sense as explanations in the physical sciences, that there is no distinct notion of causality at work in psychological explanation. A particularly clear expression of this line of thought is the theory known as causal semantics, which seeks to explicate the critical notions of meaning and information in terms of the notion of causality as it applies in the physical sciences (Dvetske 1983). This attempt was considered and rejected in Chapter 4. It was argued that while explanations which invoke intentional states have several features characteristic of casual explanation, including predictive power and (a qualified) generality, they possess other features which are not captured by the standard Humean and neo-Humean analyses of causality which apply to explanations in the physical sciences. The conclusion was drawn that it is necessary to distinguish between two kinds of causal explanation, given the names 'intentional' and 'non-intentional' causality.

The task of this chapter is to elaborate the distinctive character of intentional causality and its relation to non-intentional causality. We shall see that causal explanations that invoke mental states have many features that distinguish them from non-intentional-causal explanations. However, the proposal is far from raising any possibility of a mind–body dualism. Rather, we argue that both forms of causal explanation apply throughout biological systems, whether psychological, physiological, or biochemical. In particular, intentional-causal processes can be seen to operate throughout the phylogenetic scale, throughout biological processes of any given organism, and throughout human psychological development. This form of causality was referred to in a previous paper (Hill 1982) in terms of 'reasons', but we have preferred to use 'intentional causes' here in order to underline their causal role, and to emphasize that the concept does not refer only to psychological causality.

The proposal is biological but not 'downward', or reductionist. It runs counter to a prevalent assertion that the aim of biology is the explanation of living processes in physico-chemical terms, and instead highlights the levels of abstraction and intentionality already present in non-psychological living systems. It will be seen that this is of crucial importance in the area of psychology and psychiatry where a very specific reductionist interpretation of the meaning of 'biological' has been widely espoused (Guze 1989; Scadding 1990). It is equally relevant in other areas. For instance Ingold (1990) has outlined the consequences for social anthropology, of a psychobiology that leaves phenomena such as culture stranded as in some way 'non-biological'.

The method employed will consist first of a presentation of the characteristics of intentional causes, contrasted with non-intentional causes. We will illustrate the application of the analysis to a number of biological processes. We will then show that explanations that invoke intentional causality cannot be translated into accounts that invoke non-intentional causality, and that for the same reasons a reduction of biological and psychological processes to physico-chemical terms cannot on a priori grounds be effected. The general point to be made is that processes characterized by intentional causes cannot be redescribed in a reduction that is unable to specify the same informational content. However, it will be seen that this holds only where the system is functioning normally, and that under conditions of malfunction the explanation may be in terms of a non-intentional cause, such as that where pathology is identified in disease. This in some ways resembles a reduction in the level of explanation from the physiological or psychological to the physico-chemical.

Having established the case for biological systems in general, we will examine in Chapter 6 examples from different points in the phylogenetic scale, and at different stages in human psychological development, and this will constitute a further test, and an illustration of the utility, of the proposition. We will argue further that this and other approaches should be tested not only in relation to discrete acts of perception, or computational tasks, but should provide an analysis of real life activities, including those where there is distress or disturbance. There will be a discussion of the interplay between intentional and non-intentional causes, and a specification of conditions under which each is sought in giving an account of psychological function and dysfunction, which will lead in chapters 7, 8, and 9 to a more detailed consideration of psychiatric disorder.

5.2 INTENTIONAL CAUSALITY

5.2.1 The principles of intentional causality

The features of the operation of intentional causes can be specified generally, with reference to any biochemical or physiological processes, and the regulation of blood pressure in the cardiovascular system will be used to illustrate the points. The description of such regulation will be of the form: 'pressure receptors in the walls of the major arteries (baroreceptors) respond to changes in arterial blood pressure leading to an alteration in the frequency of impulses in the nerves which travel to the specialized (vasomotor) centre in the medulla oblongata region of the brain, resulting in an alteration in the frequency of impulses in the (sympathetic and parasympathetic) nerves running to the blood vessels and the heart. Alterations in blood pressure lead via this mechanism to changes in the diameter of the blood vessels and heart rate, with consequent compensatory changes in blood pressure.'

Normal and abnormal processes

First, we note that the description is of the normal functioning of the system. The response of the regulatory systems is referred to as 'normal', 'correct', or 'appropriate', and it follows that incorrect, abnormal, or inappropriate responses can be identified. In the absence of these or equivalent terms, there would not be an adequate explanation of the regulation of blood pressure nor of the failure to regulate blood pressure.

Goals

Secondly, the definition of normal functioning of the system requires a specification of its goals. In the absence of mention of this, when talking of the maintenance of blood pressure, we will not have criteria for normal or abnormal functioning. Ethological explanations of animal behaviours, similarly, entail a specification of their goals (Tinbergen 1948; Hinde 1982).

Purpose

Thirdly, wider reference is made to the purpose of this system. This specifies the task that is achieved in relation to survival, and places the organism within an evolutionary framework. In these second and third points it will be clear that we are talking of a teleological account, and two rather contrasting points need to be made about this. There is no doubt that this account joins those of Polanyi (1958), Tinbergen (1948), and Hinde (1982) in asserting that *descriptively* a teleological explanation is required. For many purposes this will put the ultimate purpose in terms of survival, although as we shall see, as our thesis develops, the concept of purpose in human psychological functioning changes. It does not, however, disappear. We will see that descriptions that lack teleology will also lack intentionality, and so both are crucial to the prediction of the behaviour of biological systems. Nevertheless, at no point will it be argued that the teleological account includes an explanation of the way any particular function has come about. Certainly, once the role of intentional causality is described, some questions may be posed regarding its origins in biological systems, but these are not the concern of this analysis.

Information and intentionality

Fourth, what is contained within the receptors, nerves, and brain is information about blood pressure. The physical state of each of these elements is of no causal relevance apart from its capacity to encode the level of blood pressure. Thus the events in this system have intentionality in the sense that Searle has used the term to refer to their 'directedness'. Searle (1983) has discussed intentionality primarily in terms of mental states such as beliefs, wishes, and desires. He emphasizes that they consist both of a representation and a states of affairs that is represented. Thus the mental state is systematically linked with a state of affairs, but that state of affairs may not obtain, in which case a mistake has been made. Searle argues that human perception, and some non-human psychological states, for instance those of dogs, have intentionality. In arguing for the intentionality of visual experience Searle writes, 'the visual experience is as much directed at or of objects and states of affairs in the world as any of the paradigm intentional states (such as beliefs, wishes, desires) . . .'. Searle does not allow intentionality a role in non-psychological functioning, but a central plank of our case is that it is pervasive in biological systems. Here, in the example of the regulation of the cardiovascular system, the patterning of the impulses in the regulatory system is directed at or of the blood pressure, and the system has intentionality with respect to blood pressure. This patterning is linked systematically with blood pressure, but may be found also in the absence of that blood pressure, in which case a mistake has been made.

Range of function and preoccupation

Fifth, the frequency of the nerve impulses to the brain is not defined by the blood pressure but by the preoccupation of the system, which is to monitor the blood pressure in relation to its normal level. Below an arterial blood pressure of 50 mmHg there are no impulses, the frequency increases slowly over the next 30 mmHg, and then the rate of increase accelerates between 80 and 160 mmHg, and plateaus at about 200 mmHg. Thus it shows a maximum response in relation to the point round which it is required to regulate blood pressure. Other blood pressures are of no 'interest'. Here, and throughout biological systems, we need a concept of what matters to the system. This does not amount to semantics in the usual sense of the term, nor would it be useful to stretch it this far, nevertheless it is a precursor of what we recognize as meaning when referring to the activities of the mind.

Action

Next, the response of the cardiovascular system is an action. Action here refers to behaviour that is informed by the implication of the stimulus for the system, and is an appropriate response to it. In general, intentional-causal processes, whether within the internal environment of the organism (*milieu interieur*) or in the organism in its external environment (*milieu exterieur*), have implications for action. Thus events in the environment, the preoccupations of the system or organism, and actions are closely linked elements of intentional-causal processes. As we shall see in examples of animal behaviour, and normal human behaviour, perceptual and cognitive responses generally lead to effective action. Similarly, in interpersonal functioning the capacity for appropriate action in social settings is crucial. In considering the possibility of disorder, we will be concerned with the difference between behaviour and action, and with conditions under which effective action is not possible.

Selectivity and accuracy

This leads to the seventh point, which is that the responses are selective (depending on the preoccupation of the system) and they have to be correct. There is not a response to what is 'out there' in terms of a complete objective account, but to those aspects of what is out there that are relevant to what the system is up to. When we come to a consideration of the relationship of organisms to events in the environment we shall see that the same point applies. The analysis has to place the organism as central to the process in that it determines which aspects of the environment are relevant, but having done that it must read the position accurately, otherwise for most species the consequence is death.

Differences

Eighth, the system deals predominantly in differences. It is most exquisitely tuned to departures from the normal. As we shall see in further examples, biological systems in general respond to departures from the expected in terms of key features rather than by detection or perception of the object as a whole.

Rules, convention, and agreement

The ninth feature is that the changes in blood pressure and the alterations in the frequencies of impulses in the nerves require rules that specify what the frequencies will stand for. In their absence there could be no systematic link between the pressure of the blood in the arteries and the frequencies of transmitted impulses. The tenth feature follows directly from the ninth and it is that the rules are conventionalized. That is to say, they take the form of 'let frequency X stand for blood pressure Y where X is open to a range of possibilities limited by the properties of the nerves'. Thus, the physical properties of the nerve provide some constraints, but the convention linking the frequencies to the blood pressure changes provides the specification of those frequencies. This point is easily missed because we are familiar with conventions that are created among people, but not with those that are wired in within organisms and not, in practice, subject to change. Nevertheless, the principle is the same, for we could envisage a system that conveyed the same information about blood pressure but had a starting frequency of X_1 impulses per second that corresponded to a blood pressure of up to 50 mmHg and increased to X_2 impulses per second at 200 mmHg. Provided these frequencies changed in a manner that bore the same systematic relation to blood pressure, their absolute values would not matter. It follows (principle eleven) from the specification of conventionalized rule-bound responses that this convention has to apply throughout the system. Thus the convention covering the relationship between blood pressure and frequency of impulses that are generated at the receptor has to be 'read' in the same way at the brain, otherwise the information will be lost. As we shall see, in more sophisticated sensory systems, such as that of the visual system, the convention must be shared among several elements. We can speak, therefore, of an agreement among the elements of the system about the information that is carried by a given physical state, such as the frequency of impulses in the nerves.

Physical—intentional asymmetry

The twelfth principle is that the information (about blood pressure) can be encoded in a wide range of physical entities, and the intentionality is not specifiable by the physical state of the system only. A non-neuronal system might encode the information in terms of exactly the same range of frequencies as those seen in the nervous impulses, but the physical entities along which such frequencies were transmitted might be quite different. In one sense the physical entity is seen to be the servant of the functioning of the system. This point is made intentionally in a way which underlines the abstract nature of the processes. However, it is made with a further qualification, namely that the materials do matter. The physico-chemical laws are not violated and the processes have to take advantage of these physico-chemical properties in order to perform functions. Put another way, biological systems consist of both form and substance, and a separation of the two is not sought in this analysis.

Processes not specifiable by energy equations

A further, thirteenth feature of intentional causes, which brings them into sharp contrast with non-intentional causes, is that they cannot be specified using energy equations. The energy of neuronal transmission is generated within the nerve and is not caused by the force of the blood pressure. The energy or force entailed in a change of blood pressure does not enter into the equation specifying its representation, as this is defined by the convention that we have already described. It follows that the blood pressure could, in theory, be represented by a range of frequencies each involving different levels of energy expenditure. Thus, the link between the stimulus and the response does not violate the laws of physics, nor, however, do these laws enable us to define the response.

Specialist receptors

The fourteenth distinctive element of intentional causality is that it can act only via specialized receptors. The link between the blood pressure and the impulses in the nerves, which we could now reasonably call signals, requires an apparatus that translates blood pressure into the specified frequencies of nervous impulses. This is the interface between the physical changes of blood pressure and the encoded frequencies of the afferent nerves. The change of blood pressure stretches the baroreceptors, that is to say the force of the blood causes the stretching without the mediation of intentional processes, but the output of the receptor is variable depending on the blood pressure to which it is most sensitive. Thus, the physical changes induced in the receptor by the blood pressure are exploited to provide a measure of that blood pressure over a range that is closely linked to the task of maintaining a normal blood pressure. Although changes in blood pressure can initiate frequency changes via the baroreceptors, they will not have this effect at other points in the regulatory system where these receptors are absent. For instance, pressure applied directly to the nerve will have a local effect proportional to its force that may well damage it, but will not lead to a volley of impulses that represents such a pressure.

Deception

Finally, the regulatory system is capable of making mistakes or being deceived. Stimulation of the nerves from the baroreceptors at the same frequency as that produced by the rise and fall of blood pressure would lead to a response of the vasomotor centre and the sympathetic and parasympathetic nerves the same as that which would be observed if there were a change of blood pressure. Simulation leads to the same response as the actual stimulus.

5.2.2 The interrelationship of the principles of intentional causality

The purpose of enumerating these 15 principles is to make them explicit and available for inspection as we proceed. They are, however, closely interlocking and exist in relation to each other. Two examples will illustrate the point. The notion of correct and incorrect responses can be see to be linked directly to that of rules. The rules provide the basis from which the judgement of failure or breakdown can be made. Responses either follow the rule or break them. We should note that in the absence of rules, that is to say when only non-intentional causality applies, reference is made to the general laws of nature. These cannot be definition be broken except in a miracle, or in another universe. There may be observations that depart from the laws, but these are either disregarded, or provide a basis for the revision of those laws. However, when intentional responses depart from the prevailing rules, the rules may still hold although the responses are faulty. It is important to emphasize that we are considering here only the case where one set of rules applies, so that departures from them can be taken to be incorrect. As we shall see later, the position is different where more than one set of rules may be operating.

Similarly, the concept of purpose cannot be disconnected from intentionality and convention. The intentionality of the state of the system, for instance of nervous impulses, is related to the function that is performed by the system as a whole, and the set of rules provides the conditions under which the desired outcomes can be achieved.

5.3 NON-INTENTIONAL CAUSALITY

The implication thus far has been that the enumerated features of intentional causality are not to be found in the physical sciences. It is beyond the scope of this book to explore at any length the nature of physical causality. It has, after all, merited a substantial literature of its own. In the previous chapter (Section 4.2) we considered several closely connected interpretations of causality appropriate to the physical sciences, none of which of course involved intentional concepts, noting some of the unresolved issues.

Here we will re-emphasize that the nature of causality in physics and chemistry is not straightforward. The mechanistic classical mechanics of Newton have been supplanted by uncertainty, probability, and relativity, the last of which has been discussed in Chapter 3 (subsection 3.4.2). This has led to questions about the possibility of determinist explanations in which outcomes can be predicted precisely from a given set of physical conditions, and a considerable controversy that started with Einstein and Bohr over whether physics can deal only in probabilities, or whether uncertainty about outcomes is an expression of current ignorance. Thus the question of the extent to which available explanations are a function of what is 'out there' or of the observer, or an interaction between the two are unresolved. These ideas of the new physics, with their emphasis on the fit between the physical phenomenon and the process of the mind of the scientist, are entirely consistent with the argument presented so far and the one which will be further unravelled over the next chapters. At the same time, the nature of the explanations employed in that human activity, which must significantly reflect aspects of the reality, differ in key respects from those employed in our explanations of biology and psychology. This is our current focus. Therefore, we will not attempt, even briefly, a further review of current models or ideas in physics, but highlight further the *difference* between explanations that refer to non-intentional causality and those that involve intentional causality.

Non-intentional causality makes no reference to normal or correct functioning (first principle). There may be unexpected or unusual results, but these are by definition not contained within the general law to which the explanation appeals, and lead to its modification or occasionally to its abandonment. Similarly, the concepts of goals and purposes are not required in the elaboration of physical laws or the prediction of events (second and third principles). The concept of information has no place in physical or chemical descriptions (fourth principle). All terms such as signal, representation, or language, which denote information-processing are absent. Physical states do not have intentionality, although the human preoccupation with intentionality has led to the interpretation of physical events as 'warnings' or 'indicators'. Explanations of this kind, for instance linking a fall in atmospheric pressure to cloud and rain, involve the exploitation of the regular association of events rather than the representation of one event by another in the physical world. The fifth, sixth, and seventh properties of intentional causes, referring to the preoccupation of the system, the selectivity of responses, and response to differences, have no place in physico-chemical explanations. Nor does the concept of action as directed and informed (eighth principle). The ninth, tenth, and eleventh principles refer to rules, conventions, and agreements, none of which are to be found in physio-chemical explanations. As we have seen already, the physical laws stand in a similar relationship to physical events as do rules to biological events, but they are universal, not alterable, and cannot be broken.

In relation to the thirteenth principle, explanations in physics and chemistry are contrasted with those of intentional causality in that they involve the writing of energy equations, and both Newtonian and relativistic physics make predictions on the basis of these. The fourteenth feature of intentional causality was the requirement for specialized receptors as mediators between physical events and intentional-causal links. In contrast, physico-chemical interactions can take place at any point, and depend only on the physical features, such as the spacial configuration or electrical charges of the atoms and molecules. Finally, the concept of deception or mistaken responses is absent from physico-chemical systems.

5.4 THE RELATIONSHIP BETWEEN INTENTIONAL AND NON-INTENTIONAL CAUSALITY

Having outlined the case for two distinctive types of causal process, we move to examine the relationship between the two. As we have made clear previously, there is no disguised dualism in this theory, and the operation of the two forms of causality are closely linked. This will become apparent as we survey a range of non-psychological and psychological examples. However, at this stage we can summarize the relationship by saying that intentional processes, whether psychological or not, take advantage of the physical properties of matter in order to achieve their ends. In the case of neuronal conduction, the impulses are generated by the movement of sodium and potassium ions, which alter the electrical potential across the cell membrane, which in turn leads to an alteration of the permeability of the membrane, thus leading to further movement of ions. This is done in such a way that the information is transmitted accurately. Thus although we can give a non-intentional account of the way in which the end-result is achieved, the parameters of the end-result, and the judgement about whether it is the right one, can be made only with reference to the functioning of the system, the information carried, and the ensuing action. This is the domain of intentional causality. We shall see later in this chapter that DNA makes use of the structure of nucleotides to encode genetic information, and that the structure of haemoglobin creates a spatial organization of atoms so that oxygen is transported and released to the tissues of the body. There is, therefore, a very close link between the physico-chemical properties of the ions, atoms, and molecules, and the organization of these which employs the principles of intentional causality.

This can be summarized with reference to physical-intentional asymmetry. Taking again the example of the conduction of nerve impulses in the control of the cardiovascular system, then the relationship of intentional and non-intentional causality can be expressed in the form of three statements. The same frequency of impulses may have no intentionality, the same frequency may have a different intentionality, and a different frequency may have the same intentionality. The first condition would apply where the nerves were stimulated by an electrode. The second would occur if the nerves could be transplanted and connected to receptors that monitored something different, such as the acidity of the blood, in which case the same frequencies would have a quite different intentionality. In the third condition the same information about blood pressure would be embodied in a different set of frequencies. This would be possible provided the frequencies of impulses bore the same systematic relationship to blood pressure as the existing ones.

This principle will be seen in further examples in later chapters and we do not want anticipate their working out yet. However Fodor (1981) has provided a graphic argument for the same point applied to economics, and we include it here because of its clarity, and because it provides an indication of the extent of the applicability of the principle. He assumes that some general laws of economic transactions can be stated, and considers the range of possible physical manifestations of those laws (p. 134), 'Some monetary exchanges involve strings of wampum. Some involve dollar bills. And some involve signing one's name to a check', and then, '. . . what is interesting about monetary exchange is surely not their commonalities under *physical* description. A kind like a monetary exchange *could* turn out to be coextensive with a physical kind; but if it did, that would be an accident on a cosmic scale.'

Returning to the principles of intentional causality, the intentionality of the frequency of the nerve impulses and that of money are guaranteed where there are rules that follow a convention, and these are observed by the participant elements; whether in a neuronal circuit or monetary system.

5.5 INTENTIONAL CAUSALITY CANNOT BE REPLACED BY NON-INTENTIONAL

5.5.1 Introduction

What then of the possibility that intentional descriptions could, in principle, be recast in non-intentional terms. It will be clear by now to the reader that we believe that it is not possible. After all, the starting point of this chapter, taking up themes from earlier chapters, was that attempts to describe psychological processes using the same causal principles as those of physics and chemistry have led to major problems. The proposal presented here is intended to solve these. Furthermore, we have indicated already that intentional causality entails processes that are not found in physico-chemical processes. Nevertheless, it might be objected, surely the only real causality is physico-chemical and non-intentional, and in any case it is widely assumed in areas of psychiatry and psychology that the causes of disorder are likely to be established at a molecular level.

We will come at the issue of the possible elimination of the intentional from three directions in this section. First, there are the arguments that intentional explanations could be replaced by physics and chemistry by a reduction of one to the other. Secondly, there is the case, put particularly strongly by Searle, that non-mental intentional explanations are fine as a manner of speaking, but are not really explanatory. Thirdly, the question is posed what might be the consequences of trying to describe an intentional system with reference only to its physical components?

5.5.2 Intentional explanations are not reducible

'Reductionism' has had a long history, and has been interpreted in many different ways. We are interested in the strongest form of reduction, whereby the claim is made that explanations, given in terms of intentional causality, could be replaced by the 'lower-level' explanations of physics and chemistry. Following the argument from earlier in the book, we will require a reduction to provide at least as good, and preferably a better, explanatory framework. This should enumerate the general principles by which the causal processes work, and should be effective at prediction.

As we saw in Chapter 2, there are powerful arguments against the reducibility of intentional states of mind and actions, and examples such as that provided by Fodor of the impossibility of a physical specification of the laws of economics, provide further support to the case. The question then arises as to whether non-psychological biological processes can be reduced. If they can, we will have to entertain the possibility of a dualism, whereby explanations of the mind are in some fundamental way different from those of biology more generally.

Nagel's (1961) argument for the possibility of the reduction of a 'secondary science' such as biology to the 'primary sciences' of physics and chemistry provides a useful starting point. He wrote (p. 352), 'A reduction is effected when the experimental laws of the secondary science (and if there is an adequate theory, its theory as well) are shown to be the logical consequences of the theoretical assumptions of the primary science.' However, he continues, 'If the laws of the secondary science contain terms that do not occur in the theoretical assumptions of the primary discipline . . . the logical derivation of the former from the latter is prima facie impossible.' It is clear from the example of the regulation of the cardiovascular system, and it will be apparent in further examples, that this is the case with biological processes. Numerous terms, such as 'normal', 'function', 'mistake', 'information', and 'rules', do not occur in the primary sciences. Nagel proposes that under such conditions the reduction might still be made if the secondary and primary sciences can be linked in accordance with the 'condition of connectability' and the 'condition of derivability', where the first must be satisfied before the second is applicable. Fodor (1981) has similarly argued that the reduction of one science to another requires 'bridge' laws or conditions.

According to Nagel's first conditon, the terms may be connected either if they are analysable in physico-chemical terms, or if they are associated by a co-ordinating definition, or if there are empirical connections. The intentional terms cannot be re-analysed in physico-chemical terms for the same reasons that this cannot be done in economics. Specific physico-chemical examples of normal blood pressure can be given, but the meaning of the term within a description of the cardiovascular system, and in the prediction of its behaviour, cannot be provided in physico-chemioal terms, and similarly for 'information', 'signal', 'rules', and so on. A second way in which the condition of connectability might be fulfilled is through a co-ordinating definition. It would seem, however, that in the absence of concepts corresponding to those found in intentional causality, a definition or convention that might link these to physico-chemical processes will not be possible. The third of Nagel's conditions of connectability is the presence of an empirical link. It might be tempting to suppose that where the molecular structure has been established, as is the case with many protein molecules, then an empirical link between the physico-chemical and intentional has been established. However, the protein molecule is part of a system that includes its synthesis and its actions, for instance as an enzyme. Information is required for its construction, criteria for correct and incorrect assembly are needed, and these are to be found in relation to its effective function. Empirical evidence that protein molecules assemble themselves in the absence of encoded information is lacking. Indeed, the evidence is that amino acids polymerize under certain conditions in sequences that are determined partly by the different reactivity of amino acids with different substituent groups and partly by chance (see, for example, Fox and Dose 1972). In other words, they do not assemble preferentially into functional protein molecules. It seems, therefore, that the condition of connectability cannot be met, and the reduction cannot be effected.

A somewhat less technical objection to the reducibility of biological processes can be put briefly by drawing on our earlier consideration of intentionality. Intentional states carry information about, and refer to, other states, events or conditions, and cannot be reduced beyond the point where that information has been lost.

As we saw in the previous section, our argument does not propose that there is not a relationship between the intentional and the non-intentional, but that many of those functions we expect a causal explanation to perform cannot be reduced. The point can be illustrated with reference to two opposing views on the reducibility of biochemical explanations. Kincaid (1990) has argued along similar lines to those described here, that an attempted reduction of biochemistry will not work for a range of reasons, including that the same function may be served by different physical entities, and that any one particular physical entity may serve different functions, depending upon context. Robinson (1992) countered with the assertion that 'Biological entities and processes are being equated to chemical entities and processes increasingly day by day'. This, however, does not bear directly on the issue of the reduction of causal mechanisms. The discovery of the physico-chemical structure illuminates the detail and the realization of intentional processes. Furthermore, in the process of discovery there will be an interaction between the studies of functions and structure. Robinson provides details of the relationship between a range of neurotransmitter substances and receptor sites, and describes the way in which different chemicals may have similar effects at those sites, 'For it is through examination of the structure of the *receptors* [his italics] that biochemical unity is revealed. The triumph for biochemical simplification and generalization is in recognizing that these chemically diverse mediators work through two different classes of receptors.' In spite of his emphasis on the chemistry, Robinson inadvertently demonstrates that he is interested in the physical realization of intentional processes, through reference to transmitters, mediators, and receptors. This is further illustrated in his comments on structure and function, 'Knowledge of function has been a guide and reference for biochemistry research, but, . . . the biochemical studies not only reveal common themes for achieving that function, they also can add to the catalog of functions.' The point is that biochemistry is the study of structure in relation to function, and these belong to the area of intentional causality. The study of structure may indicate further functions, and the study of function lead to the elucidation of structures.

The claim that intentional-causal explanations are reducible to physics and chemistry has been subjected to a softening by some authors, so that the case is no longer one that biological explanations can be replaced by physico-chemical ones. For instance, with reference to scientific domains, such as those of psychology and neuroscience, Hardcastle (1992) has proposed that, 'reduction merely sets out a relationship between the two domains', and Sarkar (1992) has argued for constitutive reductionsim which refers to, 'Those models of reduction that assert, at least, that upper-level (intuitively larger) systems are composed of lower-level (intuitively smaller) systems and conform to the laws governing the latter.' These 'reductionist' theories do not run counter to our thesis. They require an elucidation of the organizing principles and rules that will determine the onset, the direction, the content, the duration, the outcome, and the cessation of biological responses. This is, after all, what we demand of laws in physics, and require also of causal explanations in biology.

In concluding this section it is important to emphasize that the identity of the domains of function and explanation should not be taken to be clearly demarcated. It will be evident in later chapters that the intentional response to an external event will often be psychological, physiological, biochemical, and neuroendocrinological. Our prediction is only that in order for the causal process to take place there must be a capacity to encode information about the stimulus. Thus it will not be useful to determine whether, *in general*, psychology can be reduced to neuroscience, but rather how is the intentional state of the organism represented and placed in the service of action. As Hardcastle observes, 'no easy or obvious division of labour exists between psychology and neuroscience'.

5.5.3 Intentionality is not 'as if'

A second assault on our proposed demarcation between intentional and non-intentional causality could take a rather different form. This would argue that the proposed intentionality is spurious and that it constitutes what Searle (1984, 1990) has termed 'as if intentionality'. He has claimed that once intentionality is ascribed to biological processes other than mental processes, then there will be no limit to the phenomena that will be included, 'everything in the universe follows laws of nature, and for that reason everything behaves with a degree of regularity, and for that reason behaves as if it is following a rule, trying to carry out a certain project, acting in accordance with certain desires and so on. For instance suppose I drop a stone. The stone *tries* to reach the centre of the earth, and in doing so follows the rule $s = 1/2gt^2$.' Searle rightly objects to the ascription of mental processes to biological processes in general, but wrongly denies their intentionality. His fears that this would lead to a universal intentionality can be countered by the application of the principles that have been enumerated already in this chapter. In brief, the falling stone cannot fall incorrectly, its fall can be described without reference to information, it does not give priority to some speeds rather than others, it follows universal laws of nature that cannot in this universe be conceived of differently and do not entail a convention, the fall is described using an energy equation, there are no special receptors involved, nor could there be deception. There is, therefore, a very clear demarcation between intentionality, including non-mental intentionality, and the non-intentional world of physics and chemistry.

5.5.4 The Martian needs intentionality

In a third approach to the problem let us suppose that we wish to instruct a Martian, who knows nothing of intentionality, to assemble the regulatory apparatus of the cardiovascular system. We will assume that the mechanics of this process are fully understood. Would it be possible to assemble a working replica of the regulatory system without reference to intentional concepts? Let us suppose that we have already a conducting apparatus that can transmit electrical impulses in the same way as that of the relevant neurons, with the same frequency range as that found in the regulation of the cardiovascular system. We now need the receptors that will convert blood pressure to nervous impulses. It would be possible to tell the Martian how to construct the receptor, and he (or she) would have to carry this out on the basis of 'that goes there'. If the Martian were to ask 'why?' then the answer would be either that this must be obeyed without question, or that 'this is how it is done in order to convert a range of blood pressures into a given frequency range'. Thus the construction could be carried out either by submission to an authority, or with reference to the intentionality of the system. Further, if the Martian knew only the physical laws governing the components he would not know when he had made a mistake. This could be identified only by the instructor, or by a Martian who knew about the intentionality of the system. Similarly, he would not know when to stop, unless either he was instructed, or he was aware of when the receptor had been completed according to the function it was designed to perform. The general point is that knowledge of intentional causality would be required for the Martian to understand what he was doing and to act appropriately, and in its absence he would have to depend on the instruction of another, who did know about the intentionality of the baroreceptor.

5.6 THE PLACE OF NON-INTENTIONAL CAUSALITY IN THE EXPLANATION OF BREAKDOWN

Thus far we have focused on processes that cannot be described adequately in physico-chemical terms, and for which a reduction to such terms is not possible. Surely, it would be objected, the history of medicine especially over the past 100 years has rested on the replacement of explanations which involved intentional causes by physico-chemical and reductionist explanations. Thus syphilis is the cause of general paralysis of the insane, a brain lesion is the cause of temporal lobe epilepsy, and Alzheimer's disease is a cause of dementia. Here we come to a further element in the application of the distinction between intentional and non-intentional causes to biological systems in general. The general case was put by Polanyi (1958) who argued that we look for reasons for the way biological systems work, and causes of their failure. Restated within the terms of this book we invoke intentional causes to describe the way biological systems function, and non-intentional causes for the account of their breakdown. (It should be emphasized that although this holds for the great generality of non-psychological examples, it cannot be assumed for human psychological functioning. Indeed, possible intentional origins of psychological disorder will provide a major focus of Chapter 8.) The example of the regulation of blood pressure will serve again to illustrate the issues. When the regulation breaks down, and there is, for example, low blood pressure, we look for a non-intentional cause. The judgement that this has taken place is based on a knowledge of normal functioning and this is an issue to which we will return in the next section. At this stage it will be assumed that it has been established that the blood pressure is low. The origins of this can be found in any medical textbook under the heading of 'The causes of hypotension'. The headings from *Harrison's principles of internal medicine* include hypovolaemia (low blood volume), cardiogenic causes, obstruction to blood flow, and neuropathic (due to abnormalities in the nervous control of blood vessels). The list illustrates a number of points that provide a sharp contrast with those made regarding the way the system works. Here the causes of disruption do not act with reference to information about blood pressure. Examples include a laceration to a blood vessel, an injury to heart muscle, an obstruction to blood flow along an artery, or nerve damage. A description of the cause and effect is a physico-chemical one without the mediation of information. The amount of damage is related to the volume of the toxin, or the force of the injury. The cardiovascular system does not have a detection apparatus nor a state of readiness for such disruptive agents, and they can, in principle, have their effect at any part of the system. Finally there is no question of failure resulting from mistaken identity or deception.

It seems then that in clear cases of dysfunction or disease at least some of the causal story does not entail intentional-causal processes. However, the position is somewhat different from that of eliminating an intentional account, for instance through a reduction to physics and chemistry, because here we are seeking to explain those cases where intentionality has run out. Taking the example of low blood pressure, this is no longer performing its function adequately, and it is the departure from the correct intentional response that needs to be explained. Just as in Chapter 1 we saw that as long as behaviour was described only in terms of movement, and not as action or similar functional response, then only a physical causal story was required, so this is also the case in breakdown. If the explanandum (low blood pressure) lacks intentionality so will the explanans, at least in part. This is not therefore a reduction in the sense considered by Nagel, Fodor, and others, whereby intentional phenomena are explained in the physical sciences, but it resembles a reduction in as much as one type of event in the biological system (that representing disruption of function) may have a non-intentional explanation.

5.7 DISRUPTION OF FUNCTION AND THE CONDITIONS FOR NON-INTENTIONAL CAUSALITY

If questions of function and dysfunction, normal or abnormal, are central to the identification of intentional or non-intentional causal processes, then we need to clarify the conditions under which each is sought. Often it is quite clear that breakdown has occurred, as function has been quite dramatically disrupted. However, this is not always the case, and it may well be very unclear, especially in examples of psychological functioning. In the regulation of the cardiovascular system, if the frequencies of impulses in the nerves were not to rise in the normal rule-bound manner in relation to a rise in blood pressure, then we would look for a (non-intentional) cause of the disruption of function. However, the behaviour of a part of an intentional system does not necessarily indicate whether a disruption of the rules has taken place. Take the example of pulse rate. A low pulse rate, or bradycardia, might lead the physician to suspect dysfunction on the grounds that this was a departure from normal. One possibility would be that there had been an interruption of the functioning of the conducting tissues of the heart leading to the bradycardia. This would have involved non-intentional causality; for instance a toxin or reduced level of oxygen supplied to the tissues might have damaged the nerve. However, the same bradycardia could arise in a very fit person. In this case it would be a response to the increased capacity of the heart, and would therefore be an appropriate response mediated by information about cardiac output. Furthermore, we would find in this case that when the person exercised the pulse rate would increase in a way that was systematically linked to the increased need of the body for oxygen. The damaged heart, by contrast, would not respond appropriately. The general principle is that we pay attention to apparent disruption of normal functioning and of the operation of rules, and such an apparent disruption may originate from intentional processes or may represent breakdown arising from a physical, non-intentional cause. Either way our starting point is a study of the integrity of the intentional system. The conditions for establishing breakdown of function, and the question of whether intentional or non-intentional explanations are relevant will provide a recurring focus in later chapters.

5.8 BIOLOGICAL PROCESSES: A FURTHER EXAMINATION

Thus far we have considered only one example in order to explore the distinction between intentional and non-intentional causality and the relationship between the two. In concluding this chapter we will take further examples in order to illustrate the general applicability of the argument, and to provide, at least in part, an examination of the proposals.

5.8.1 DNA and protein synthesis

At first sight the elucidation of the role of deoxyribonucleic acid (DNA) in determining the structure and function of complex biological structures, with the accompanying possibilities of the modification of such structures through the alteration of the molecule, appear to support the physico-chemical re-analysis of living processes. However, it provides one of the most dramatic demonstrations of the opposite thesis—the one argued here. For the DNA molecule has significance only by virtue of the vast quantity of information that is stored within the molecule, and because it is linked in a systematic way with protein synthesis, a process that is characterized by intentional causality. Briefly, the sequence involves the reading (transcription) of the nucleotide triplet codes in the DNA, by the messenger ribonucleic acid (mRNA) molecule, which acts as a template for the assembly of amino acids in the synthesis of proteins. Amino acids are brought to the mRNA by smaller transfer RNA (tRNA) molecules, which have the task of delivering specific amino acids to the correct sites on the mRNA. This process is referred to as the 'translation' of the genetic code into proteins.

Taking the 15 principles of intentional causality;

1. The process can take place normally or correctly, and there can be mistakes, often with devastating results.
2. The goal of the DNA–RNA protein synthesis system is the accurate construction of protein molecules from amino acids.
3. The purpose is to provide the underpinning for living organisms, and a means whereby adaptive structure and function are passed down the generations.
4. The DNA molecule carries information about, or has intentionality with respect to, protein structure, and this in turn has intentionality in relation to a range of functions.
5. and 6. Only certain features of the DNA molecules are of interest to the

mRNA, namely the nucleotide sequence.

7. The DNA provides the information that directs the assembly of the RNA and protein molecules; it informs actions.
8. The DNA code is read as this sequence in contrast to another sequence; the system deals in differences.
9. The nucleotide code follows the rule that links particular triplets to particular amino acids.
10. This code is conventionalized. From the point of view of the physics it could take many different forms. The criterion for a fault is given by the convention. Thus some amino acids are coded by more than one triplet code, which means that in some cases a difference of nucleotide is not a mistake, but in other cases it is.
11. The crucial feature that enables the convention to work is that there is agreement throughout the sequence. For instance, amino acids are brought to the mRNA by the tRNA, molecules which have sites that fit selectively to certain mRNA triplets. Thus the structure that systematically links a particular amino acid (say AA1) to the tRNA site for AA1 must correspond to the triplet code for AA1 in the mRNA, and the triplet code for AA1 in the DNA.
12. The information about protein structure or mRNA could be encoded in a different physical structure. However the DNA, mRNA, and protein molecules make use of the physical properties of the nucleotides in order to carry out the task of protein synthesis with great efficiency.
13. The sequence cannot be specified by an energy equation.
14. Specialized receptors are involved. Notably the tRNA has a specific site at which it binds to the mRNA.
15. The system can be deceived. This can be demonstrated, for instance, in relation to the synthesis of the enzyme (a protein) lactase in bacteria. This enzyme takes part in the metabolism of lactose, and the rate of its synthesis increases in the presence of lactose. However, if a molecule is introduced that resembles lactose in some key respects, but is not metabolized by lactase, the cell is deceived into producing more lactase than is appropriate to the level of lactose.

An attempted elimination of the intentional account of DNA and protein synthesis would have to define in physico-chemical terms items such as triplet coding, the role of mRNA as a messenger, and the nature of correct functioning and mutations. Similarly, although the terms 'transcription' and 'translation' may seem to refer inappropriately to human language, in many respects the process more closely resembles that of human communication than it does physico-chemical processes.

5.8.2 The haemoglobin molecule

We can explore the relationship between intentional and non-intentional causality further using the example of a particular protein, the haemoglobin molecule. This large and complex molecule is the main component of the red blood cells which carry oxygen from the lungs to the tissues and help to carry carbon dioxide back to the lungs. The presence of the haemoglobin molecule increases the oxygen-carrying capacity of the blood by 70 times, and without haemoglobin large animals could not get enough oxygen to exist. In order to perform this function it has to operate over a very precise range of oxygen pressures, such that it absorbs oxygen in the lungs and releases it in the tissues. If this does not occur, either it will carry insufficient oxygen from the lungs, or it will release insufficient at the tissues.

Consider an attempted reduction or redefinition of the synthesis of haemoglobin in physico-chemical terms. As we have seen, according to Nagel's condition of connectability a reduction is effected if there can be a re-analysis in physico-chemical terms, a co-ordinating definition, or an empirical connection. The possibility of a re-analysis can be explored with reference to normal or correct versus abnormal or incorrect sequences of amino acids. The re-analysis of the normal sequence of amino acids in the haemoglobin molecule would simply be a recitation of the amino acid sequence. However, it is known that the substitution of one amino acid (valine for glutamic acid) has serious consequences for the functioning of the haemoglobin molecule and leads to sickle-cell disease. In this condition, the red cells become mishapen, leading to blocking of blood vessels, and reduction of blood supply and hence lack of oxygen at the tissues. The substitution of valine for glutamic acid gives rise to an abnormal or incorrect sequence. As long as the re-analysis of the sickle-cell haemoglobin molecule was simply the enumeration of a sequence of amino acids, it would be neutral as to whether it was normal or abnormal. It would not be able to specify the crucial difference which leads to malfunction and illness.

The second possibility, namely that a co-ordinating definition might enable the condition of connectability to be met, fails for similar reasons. Given that physico-chemical processes lack the features described in biological processes, a co-ordinating definition cannot be envisaged. There remains the possibility of an empirical link. However, as we have seen, the experimental evidence shows that amino acids polymerize in sequences that are determined partly by the different reactivity of amino acids with different substituent groups and partly by chance. The probability of a given sequence is very low, and the chance of the sequence appearing repeatedly is remote. Thus Nagel's criteria of connectability are not met.

The sickle-cell example illustrates very clearly the way in which abnormality is identified in relation to function, and is not given by any particular physical facts. Thus, if the shape of the red cells were not affected by the substitution of valine for glutamic acid, it would be a normal variant. Or, if the shape of the red cell in relation to the size of the blood vessels did not matter to their flow, and if the transport of oxygen to the tissues were not a central function of haemoglobin, then the substitution might not be a fault. This is to certain extent the case for individuals who live in parts of Africa where there is a risk of malaria. The sickle-cell trait, whereby only some of the haemoglobin molecules are affected, confers some protection from malaria and so if resistance to malaria is specified as a property of haemoglobin, then under certain conditions those with this trait have advantages over those that lack it. The question of which form of haemoglobin has a fault then is less clear. The general point is that the condition is determined by the function that the molecule serves in relation to particular features of the environment, and by the effect that the physical variation has on that function.

Once an abnormality has been identified, a non-intentional causal factor may be sought. For instance a protein abnormality might be traced back to faulty DNA. This would require that the mistake in the DNA had been transcribed and translated correctly in the synthesis of the protein. Once the mistake in the DNA has been identified it might be possible to give a non-intentional account, for instance where a chemical agent had, by virtue of its physical properties, affected the nucleotide sequence. It seems then that an elimination of intentionality, and reduction to physics could be achieved. However, the intentionality has already been eliminated in that what has to be explained is the abnormal behaviour of the haemoglobin and red blood cells. There is therefore not a reduction from the intentional to the non-intentional, but from abnormal behaviour to abnormal molecule. At the same time, the fault is defined by contrast with the correct behaviour and amino acid sequence, and the integrity of the rest of the intentional system is required for the chemical to be the cause of the abnormal protein.

5.9 SUMMARY

In this chapter we have sought to lay the foundations for the argument that intentional and non-intentional causal processes occur throughout biological systems, including those involved in human psychological functioning. Our purpose has been to state, and in some degree demonstrate, the differences between the two, and to anticipate ways in which this analysis will provide an account that is biological and psychological, of order and disorder in the mind.

REFERENCES

Dretske, F. I. (1983). Precis of knowledge and the flow of information. *Behavioural and Brain Sciences*, 6, 55–90.

Fodor, J. A. (1981). *Representations: philosophical essays on the foundations of cognitive science*. Harvester Press, Sussex.

Fox, S. W and Dose, K. (1972). *Molecular evolution and the origin of life*. Freeman, San Francisco.

Guze, S. B. (1989). Biological psychiatry: is there any other kind?. *Psychological Medicine*, 19, 315–23.

Hardcastle, V. G. (1992). Reduction, explanatory extension, and the mind/brain sciences. *Philosophy of Science*, 59, 408–28.

Hill, J. (1982). Reasons and causes: the nature of explanations in psychology and psychiatry. *Psychological Medicine*, 12, 501–14.

Hinde, R. A. (1982). *Ethology*. Fontana.

Ingold, T. (1990). An anthropologist looks at biology. *Man*, 25, (2), 208–9.

Kincaid, H. (1990). Molecular biology and the unity of science. *Philosophy of Science*, 57, 575–93.

Nagel, E. (1961). *The structure of science*. Routledge and Kegan Paul, London.

Polanyi, M. (1958). *Personal knowledge: towards a post-critical philosophy*. Routledge and Keegan Paul, London.

Robinson, J. D. (1992). Aims and achievements of the reductionist approach in biochemistry/molecular biology/cell biology: a response to Kincaid. *Philosophy of Science*, 59, 465–70.

Sarkar, S. (1992). Models of reduction and categories of reductionism. *Synthese*, 91, 167–94.

Scadding, J. G. (1990). The semantic problems of psychiatry. *Psychological Medicine*, 20, 243–8.

Searle, J. R. (1983). *Intentionality: an essay in the philosophy of mind*. Cambridge University Press, Cambridge.

Searle, J. R. (1984). *Minds, brains and science*. BBC Publications, London.

Searle, J. R. (1990). Consciousness, explanatory inversion and cognitive science. *Behavioural and Brain Sciences*, 13, 585–642.

Tinbergen, N. (1948). Social releasers and the experimental methods required for their study. *Wilson Bulletin*, 60, 6–51.

6
Intentional causality, neurobiology, and development

6.1 INTRODUCTION

We turn in this chapter from physiology and biochemistry to animal and human neurobiology and psychology. There is a shift from systems that respond to stimuli from the '*milieu interieur*', such as changes in blood pressure or blood sugar, to those that respond to features of the external environment. The external environment is comprised both of inanimate objects and other living creatures. Intentional-causal processes with the features described in the previous chapter, will be seen to operate throughout.

The method in the first place will be to determine whether there is a break at any point in the phylogenetic (evolutionary) or ontogenetic (human developmental) scales, whereby the analysis applied to physiological processes ceases to be appropriate. However, this alone will not be sufficient. An analysis that showed a common form of causality would provide a valuable unity of explanation, but would run the risk either of an inappropriate elevation of basic biological processes to a level analogous to that of complex human psychological functioning, or an implied reduction of such functioning to a more basic form. Our argument does neither. Rather it proposes that there is a potential inherent in the simplest biological processes which has been elaborated during evolution, and is seen at its most sophisticated in human psychological functioning. Where the operation of intentional causal processes is 'wired in', through particular neuronal connections, then the rules, conventions, and agreements and their relationship to action are fixed. However, where the organism has the capacity to learn, there is scope for different rules and representations to apply under different circumstances and at different times. Where this is the case there will be a need for the capacity to represent representations, to monitor them, and to link them to action. These requirements follow inevitably from our specification of the features of intentional causality, once they are open to acquisition, testing, and variability. The analysis will then be seen to specify functions that are fulfilled by sophisticated human capabilities, including consciousness and language. As the extent of the sophistication of this evolutionary 'play' on intentional causality becomes evident, so will the scope for its malfunction. Our discussion in this chapter will lay some of the foundations for a consideration of the basis of disordered psychological functioning in chapters 7 and 8.

6.2 NEUROBIOLOGY

6.2.1 The basic units

The basic units of the nervous system are the neurons, which are the signalling units of behavioural responses (Kandel *et al.* 1991). Neurons possess the capacity to generate all-or-none action potentials which can convey information encoded in the frequency of the impulses. Where sensory data are involved, there exist sense receptors that transduce physical events, such as pressure or light, into patterns of impulses that bear a systematic relationship to the relevant features of the stimulus. Information is passed from one neuron to another at synapses via a range of chemical neurotransmitters. The release of these transmitters is brought about by the arrival of the electrical impulses, and they act at receptor sites on the next neuron (the post-synaptic membrane) to bring about further transmission of impulses. Synapses are points of integration where several neurons from different locations, or with different actions, can converge. The transmitted chemicals are released and taken up again in a precise manner, so that the information in the signal is retained. The *raison d'être* of the neuron is information processing.

6.2.2 The visual system

This point may be illustrated with reference to the function of the visual system. Much of what is known about the visual system has been derived from work on animals, and so our analysis of intentional causality does not yet need to refer to human psychological functioning. Nevertheless, in all animals the visual system enables discriminations to be made that influence behaviour, and therefore it participates in processes that are at least precursors of human psychological functioning.

Briefly, the visual system of a wide range of organisms may be described as follows (Bruce and Green 1990). The eye contains a lens that focuses images on the retina where there are cells that are responsive to particular frequencies of light. These cells convert (transduce) light into electrical events, and these lead to the release of transmitters into synapses with bipolar cells. These bipolar cells synapse with ganglion cells which send axons via the optic nerve to the lateral geniculate nucleus and thence to the visual cortex. Horizontal cells and amacrine cells in the retina modulate the flow of information. Particular structures in the visual cortex respond to specified features of the stimulus, and a representation of the stimulus is utilized in the elaboration of action.

How do the features of intentional causality that we enumerated in the previous chapter apply to the operation of the visual system? The role of the specialized receptor is very clear. Intensity, shape, pattern, and colour are features of the stimulus that play a causal role in perception and action, but only if they are detected by receptors capable of translating the key features of the stimulus into patterns of neuronal firing. Light is absorbed by the cells and leads to a change of molecular conformation of retinal, a form of vitamin A. This molecular change leads to the separation of retinal from opsin, which is a protein, and a consequent hyperpolarization of the receptor cell membrane, and this is mediated by a messenger (cyclic guanosine monophosphate (GMP)). The hyperpolarization of the membrane leads to the release of transmitters to the bipolar cells. There is an exact correspondence between the action of one photon and the amount of cyclic GMP synthesized, and therefore, a relationship between the amount of light and the amounts of transmitter released. Much of the information about the image on the retina is contained in the spatial arrangement of the retinal receptors and their systematic connections with the visual cortical cells. Thus, the retinal receptors make use of a photochemical process to generate information about light.

It might be supposed that in the initial, peripheral processing of visual stimuli, processes that most resemble non-intentional causality might be seen. For instance it might be predicted that there would be a direct correspondence between light intensity and intensity of response of retinal cells. Then it might be possible to apply, at least initially, an analysis along the lines of causal semantics (discussed in subsection 4.3.1). However, the reverse is the case. The function and organization of retinal cells in invertebrates and vertebrates appear to be suited to the transformation of sensory stimuli into information, according to a set of rules that is tightly linked to the functioning of the organism in its environment. The extensive research into the visual apparatus of the horseshoe crab (*Limulus*) will illustrate many of the points. One of the first discoveries made by Hartline and Graham (1932) was that the frequency of impulses that pass along the optic nerve is roughly proportional to the logarithm of light intensity. This means that although the frequency is systematically related to the intensity, the changes of frequency are not uniform over the whole range of light intensities. *Limulus* is exposed to light intensities that may vary by a factor of $10^6–10^7$, and if there were a linear correspondence the frequencies would have to cover the same range. Given that the maximum rate at which impulses can pass down an axon is 1000 per second, the dimmest light would be coded by a frequency of one impulse every several thousand seconds. Thus, even in this 'primitive' organism, the most peripheral visual processes entail a rule linking intensity of light to the frequency of impulses. This rule leads to function over a wide range of light intensities, corresponding to the range of conditions experienced by the organism and in which action must be possible. It also preserves the quality of information over the range. In the absence of this mechanism it would be difficult to discriminate differences in frequency at the lowest end of the frequency range, and the time required to make that discrimination would put the crab at risk from predators.

The extent of peripheral processing is seen further in the phenomena of light and dark adaptation, and lateral inhibition. The response of the *Limulus* cell axon when light is shone on it, is first to show a rapid increase in the frequency of impulses, which rises to a peak and then falls to a steady state. Both the peak rate and the steady level are related to the intensity of the light. This therefore provides information both about the change, and the intensity of the light. Thus discrimination of some features of the environment is enhanced. Lateral inhibition (Hartline *et al.* 1956) improves spatial discrimination. When photoreceptors are stimulated they inhibit the firing of those cells that surround them. This means that if the whole eye is evenly and diffusely illuminated, excitation of receptor cells by light will be largely cancelled by inhibition from neighbouring cells. However, if there is a sharp boundary between bright and dimly lit areas, lateral inhibition will enhance the difference in rates of firing of the neurons. Thus it is clear that the *Limulus* eye does not represent the objective characteristics of what is 'out there'; rather it selects and highlights some features at the expense of others. Slow temporal changes and gradual spatial differences are not perceived, while rapidly changing, sharply contrasted stimuli elicit maximal firings of neurons. This enhances the quality of the information about events in the environment that matter to the organism. The process is both selective and places a premium on accuracy.

The vertebrate eye is, in general, more complex, but performs similar functions. The role of the peripheral visual system in selecting and discriminating is similarly striking. Each ganglion cell has a receptive field: a region of the retina in which stimulation affects the ganglion cell's firing rate. In the cat, these receptive fields are concentric (Kuffler 1953). Some ganglion cells respond with a burst of impulses when a spot of light is shone on the centre of the field, and when light ceases to shine on the surround. This is referred to as a centre-on response. Other ganglion cells respond in the opposite fashion, and are termed centre-off cells. Ganglion cells are further differentiated into X and Y cells. X cells show a graded response depending on the extent of illumination in different areas of the field. Y cells, by contrast, show a non-linear response, and respond preferentially to movement. These selective mechanisms increase discrimination and hence quality of information. Clearly, the priority of the system is once again effective discrimination of stimuli.

This example highlights also the points made earlier about rules, convention, and agreement. A stimulus with the same physical property leads to opposite responses in different neurons, and these are therefore not specified by the physical properties of the stimulus. Similarly, in the distinction between X and Y cells the same physical stimulus may lead to a response in one, but not in the other. The systematic relationship between the stimulus and the response therefore requires a rule and a convention that extends throughout the visual system, so that, for instance, bursts in some neurons are read as onset and others as offset. There will need to be in effect an agreement within the system that this is the case. This is reflected in the very precise mapping of the retinal fields in the areas of the brain to which fibres from the eye travel via the lateral geniculate nucleus and the occipital cortex. Some occipital cortex cells have concentric fields like the retinal cells, but others have excitatory and inhibitory areas which are straight lines. In some cells there are two boundaries with a central excitatory area and an inhibitory area on either side, and vice versa. Clearly these will have to be linked systematically to neurons in the visual pathway in such a way that a burst of firing is 'taken' to signify onset or offset of light.

Overall, the structure of the striate cortex shows a very precise regular arrangement of cell types. This 'functional architecture' (Hubel and Wiesel 1962, 1968) ensures that a wide range of features of stimuli are mapped on to the cortical structure. For instance, some cortical cells are arranged in columns according to their preference for the orientation of the stimulus. Each column covers approximately a 10° arc. Here, then, the responses of the cells are selective, precise, and make discriminations. They provide information about particular features of the stimulus.

Now let us turn to two broader questions in vision: possible mechanisms in the assembly of perceptions, and the relationship between vision and action. A detailed consideration of the psychophysiology of perception is beyond the scope of our discussion, but some of the recent work is highly relevant. Marr (1982) argued that an explanation of the components of the system can be provided only once its overall function has been described. This requires a computational theory that specifies what the visual system must do, a specification of the way in which problems are solved (algorithm), and an understanding of ways in which these are implemented. A specific example of Marr's approach is found in his theory of the role of the primal sketch in vision. He hypothesized that this is comprised of a number of representations of light intensity differences present in the image. Typically an image will contain numerous gradations of light intensity, not all of which are of similar significance. The task of the raw primal sketch is to identify those changes of intensity that are crucial to the identity of the image, rather like the key lines in an artist's sketch, say, of the human face. Marr and Hildreth (1980) derived an algorithm in which the gradients of intensity are measured using the second derivative of the intensity values. This mathematical operation provides a value which reflects the rate of change of intensity of light over distance, and therefore will provide specific information about the extent to which the intensity gradient in an image is changing. They implemented the algorithm using a computer, and showed how it could produce patterns of light that might constitute raw primal sketches. This, of course, does not demonstrate that such an algorithm applies in living visual pathways, and the evidence concerning this is rather conflicting (Bruce and Green 1990). The method used by Marr and his colleagues does, however, underline the distinctive nature of the intentional causal processes that are to be elucidated. The task is taken to be the identification of crucial edges or boundaries in the image, and then the algorithm refers to the method. Clearly, if there is one method, there could also be others. The method will take account of the nature of the stimulus, but equally the priorities of the organism. The method as formulated is not embodied in any paricular physical entity. Any arrangement of physical entities that could carry out the transformation of the light intensities will do. It is not that the physical entity is irrelevant, but that its definition will follow the specification of the operation. This we referred to earlier as the intentional-physical asymmetry. Interestingly, in Marr and Hildreth's algorithm the rule is defined by a mathematical procedure, but this might not have been the case. For instance, they also postulate another set of operations which are effectively filters of different widths. These determine the intensity of light to which responses are made, and their setting is not specified by a mathematical operation.

Vision is linked clearly to action. Even in a simple organism such as a fly the mechanism is quite complex (Gotz *et al.* 1979). The fruitfly, *Drosophila melanogaster*, turns to follow stripes within a rotating drum by a combination of altered wing action and a sideways deflection of the abdomen and hind legs. The visual system detects a difference in the environment and action is taken to lessen it. In more complex examples corrective action is taken to ensure that a goal is achieved. For the insect, accurate landing is crucial. Then there will be a relationship between perceptions of key aspects of the surroundings, and of the fly's speed and position in relation to them, with action taken to ensure an effective landing. The vision must be selective and accurate, and the external state of affairs must be represented and compared with current actions in order to determine what is required for the landing. The principle is the same as that for the cardiovascular system, but the goal, of landing, is one that is performed under many varied circumstances. It therefore requires the detection of differences, and corrective action, under a much wider range of circumstances. Equally, the complexity of the processes is much lower than that entailed in human action. Nevertheless, as we shall see, the human capacities for learned skills, multiple goals, and complex actions are all sophisticated elaborations of the potential in these more simple examples of intentional causal systems.

Now that we have reviewed some of the key principles of the visual system in a range of organisms, let us recapitulate on their implications for causal explanations in biological systems in general, and, more specifically, for perception and behaviour. We have argued that external stimuli, linked systematically to representations by the organism, with behavioural consequences, constitute genuine causal pathways. When we describe the visual system we cannot omit reference to any of the features that we enumerated in Chapter 5. We are referring to the normal functioning of the system and there are numerous points at which it could fail. This is not merely normative, as an infinity of other forms of functioning would not serve this purpose, with serious implications for the organism. Abnormality is not given by the physical make-up, but by the implications for functioning in relation to environment. It is defined ecologically. The visual system highlights some aspects of the environment in its representation in order to detect crucial differences between different features of the environment, and particularly those that have implications for different actions. In other words, the totality of what is 'out there' is not represented, but what it is about 'out there' that matters to action. There are no 'raw' perceptual experiences, as physical stimuli are transformed and coded via sets of rules at peripheral receptors and made available for complex processing. The transmission of information entails the coding of a wide range of features of visual stimuli in frequencies of neuronal impulses, their spatial arrangement, and their interconnections at a range of points in the visual pathway. The rules require a convention that must be preserved throughout. Marr has referred to the intentional-physical asymmetry in terms of the algorithm and the implementation.

The physical apparatus is given the task of carrying out the procedure. As we described earlier, the implications are:

(1) that the same physical events need not have intentionality—if, for instance, the same physical state of affairs were triggered by electrical or chemical stimuli;

(2) the same elements of the system could have different intentionality—this is seen in the contrast between those neurons that show bursts of activity to onset of light and those to offset of light; and

(3) that a different physical state, for instance a different frequency of impulses, could represent the same intentionality.

Where the frequency range is optimal, it is because the organism has evolved an effective algorithm in relation to need, not because of a physico-chemical definition of a specific frequency for a given stimulus. It will be evident from these considerations that the energy of the physical stimulus does not enter into the energy equation of the perceptual response or the actions. The energy of the light may be represented but that will entail a rule-bound set of processes and not a series of events that are definable by a physical equation which includes the energy of the stimulus.

6.2.3 Representation and behaviour in animals—some further examples

Our consideration of further animal examples will cover the bat, the bee, and the stickleback. Take first the bat. This mammal has poor eyesight and flies at night. It emits pulses of sound waves and is able to perceive when these are returned from objects. The auditory cortex is very large compared with that of other mammals, and it is subdivided into distinct areas, each of which provides information about some feature of the bat's insect prey (Suga *et al.* 1981). Separate regions are concerned with the distance, size, relative velocity, and wing-beat frequency of the prey. Bats compute prey distance with great precision from the delay between emission of the orientation sound and time of arrival of the returning echo reflected from the insect. The frequency of emitted impulses is greater when the bat is near the ground, which gives it better resolution for small objects. In one area of the auditory cortex, single neurons hardly respond to either the outgoing sound or the echo alone, but fire strongly to pairs of such sounds with a particular delay between them. Neurons sensitive to the same delay are grouped together, and the delay producing maximal response alters progressively along the cortex from a fraction of a millisecond (ms) to about 18 ms, equivalent to target distances ranging from just under 10 cm to 3 m.

This system has to be described in terms of what is carried out, and the fact that this can occur correctly or incorrectly, requires special senses, is capable of representing information about the physical world, and could be deceived. The reflected sound waves are the cause of the bat's behaviour, and in their absence the bat would collide with some objects, and fail to catch others. This example provides a good illustration of the way in which the properties of the physical world, here the effect of objects on sound wave, are exploited by the organism. The sequence of events from the emission of the sound waves to their return is governed by the laws covering the transmission of sound through gasses, which are not variable, but the processes whereby the emitted and returning signals are compared require rules and a convention within the bat as to how the frequencies are represented. This transforms the sounds into signals. A different species of bat could have evolved in which the same patterns of firing could have denoted a different range of target distances, say between 3 and 10 m.

The representation of key features of the external world may be transmitted among organisms, and the behaviour of bees provides a good example. Bees returning to the hive perform a dance which indicates the direction and distance of nectar-bearing flowers, in relation to the position of the sun (von Frisch 1967). The subsequent flight of other bees in the swarm is influenced by the features of the dance. The dance goes in a figure of eight, and the information is in the straight run through the middle of the figure eight. The angle from the vertical on the honeycomb gives the angle between a line from the nest to the sun, and a line from the nest to the flowers. The duration of the straight run gives the distance, at a ratio of 75 ms/100 m.

In this example of social interaction among organisms, all of the principles of intentional causality are to be found. In brief, it serves a function, it can occur normally or there can be mistakes, it has intentionality with respect to the location of nectar, only some features of the dance count as sources of information, and only certain aspects of the terrain are conveyed, namely the ones that are crucial to the finding of nectar. The dance has the relationship to the location of nectar as has a map to a geographical location, and requires a set of rules and a convention that is held in common by all the participating bees. The rules must specify not only how direction is coded in the dance, but also that it is direction to which reference is being made. Not only what distance, but also that distance is what is referred to. Not only where and how far, but also that what is referred to is nectar. However, there is no reason why a species of bees should not have evolved a convention that used, for instance, the angle with the horizontal to give direction, or a different ratio of time of run to distance of flowers, or that used the same dance to indicate a different set of information. Thus, here again, before the evolution of human minds, there evolved the operation of rules, requiring conventions, and these have been utilized within social organizations so that both what is referred to and the content of that reference is shared.

Tinbergen (1948) demonstrated the significance of the red belly of the three-spined stickleback which develops during the breeding season when the fish establishes its territory. If there is an incursion by one male into the territory of another, the threatened male will attack if the intruder has a red belly. It has been shown that very crude models of the stickleback elicit attack from other males provided the red belly is present, and conversely, life-like models that lack the red belly are relatively ineffective. There is no doubt that the red belly is the explanation for the behaviour, in that it meets all the conditions for a cause, viz. the behaviour is elicited in its presence, is not elicited in its absence, and there is a regular conjunction of antecedent and consequent under specifiable conditions. However, the process involves all the features described earlier in relation to the regulation of the cardiovascular system. There are normal and abnormal responses, the responses depend upon the capacity of the recipient to represent 'red', the response is selective and it depends crucially on the distinction 'red' versus 'non-red'. The stickleback shows no 'interest' in other qualities, such as whether the object is life-like. Referring back to the visual system, it is highly selective but has to be accurate with respect to this stimulus. There has to be a rule covering the relationship between the colour and behaviour, and this must be shared within the species. This is conventionalized in the sense that it is quite feasible to envisage that another colour, or another perceptual quality such as size, could have the same causal function if there had a evolved a convention within the species that such perceptual stimuli signified threat.

6.3 EARLY HUMAN PSYCHOLOGICAL DEVELOPMENT

6.3.1 Introduction

How will our analysis stand up in relation to human psychological functioning? To repeat, we have proposed that it should:

(1) apply without a break across biological examples both psychological and non-psychological;
(2) stand up to detailed scrutiny in relation to complex human behaviours; and
(3) make predictions about human psychological functioning, and in particular address both normal and abnormal processes.

6.3.2 The newborn infant

The newborn infant provides us with a useful starting point. He or she is in many respects helpless and incompetent. His/her survival capability is lower than that of most other animals, and this vulnerability will persist longer than that of any others. Yet, given that, for infants, adult caregivers are a normal part of the environment, they are equipped to detect and respond to those features of the outside world that are necessary for survival. Two examples will illustrate this.

Suckling is an activity that is seen in most infants from the first hour of birth. By contrast with the other motor capabilities of the newborn which are very poor, suckling is fully developed. It occurs in response to a stimulus such as a nipple, and consists of a well-coordinated activity involving sucking, swallowing, and breathing. Whether or not it is readily characterized as psychological, it entails perception, the encoding in the afferent nerves of information about a nipple-like stimulus, and a highly integrated delivery of efferent messages to a range of muscles. This highlights how a relationship between the stimulus, the assessment of the stimulus, and the behaviour may occur in a way that is closely analogous to, and involves the same principles as, those of the cardiovascular system and the stickleback, yet is higher up the continuum towards psychological processes.

The second example is of the visual capabilities of the newborn infant. Newborn infants appear to make relatively few perceptual discriminations; however, they do look preferentially at face-like patterns, compared to patterns that do not resemble faces (Fantz 1963). Here is a perception that is selective with respect to the stimuli, a receiving agent that is ready for such an input, and a response that requires a set of rules in the infant about patterns which are of interest or matter. In the light of the subsequent emergence of relationships with adults as a primary source of protection, stimulation, and affective development, this preference can be seen to perform an important function. Here is a process that most would describe as psychological and yet at a relatively low level of sophistication. It undoubtedly involves intentional causality.

6.3.3 The first months

Now let us take our account on a few weeks in the life of the infant. At around 4–6 weeks infants start to smile socially, and interactions with adults take off (Stern 1977). Infants show clearly that they enjoy contact with other people, through smiling, open facial expressions, gurgling, and excited body movements. Parents and other caregivers experience them as having elements of what appears later as mature psychological functioning. Much of the developmental research into the early months has focused on the pleasurable, excited face-to-face exchanges between caregivers and infants (Stern *et al.* 1974; Trevarthen 1980). These are constructed jointly by adult and infant and require the accurate and sensitive participation of each. The infant plays an important part in the initiation, maintenance, and termination of the exchanges. Here then in early infant development, and within the context of an environment of other people, perception and action are tied together closely. Perception leads to action which leads to further perception, and further action. And what is that draws the attention of the infant? The behaviour of adults with infants is characterized by exaggerated, repeated, and rhythmic movements and vocalizations. It is as if adults know that it is helpful in the development of perception to create well-marked regularities, and indeed infants respond to this. Equally, infants are interested in repetition only if there is variability woven into it (Kagan 1967; Kagan *et al.* 1978). As Stern has put it, 'Infants are [also] constantly "evaluating", in the sense of asking, is this different from or the same as that? How discrepant is what I have just encountered from what I have previously encountered?' (Stern 1985, p. 42). It seems that the infant is interested in the fact of regularity and departures from it, which suggests that once a set of rules about the stimulus is established the variations become of interest. The infant deals in (constructed) norms and differences from them. However, if the difference is too great then the infant is likely to pause or withdraw. The variations are welcome provided they do not undermine the background set of expectancies developed by the infant, and if there is a major difference in caregiver behaviour, a new appraisal is required. Here then perceptions are selective and related to what matters to the infant. By contrast with most of our previous examples, the sets of rules against which stimuli are judged are constructed by the infant. Even at this age we are beginning to see the exploitation of the potential inherent in all intentional-causal processes. If events can be judged within one set of rules, they can also be construed and acted upon under others.

It is evident also from the study of early infant processes that aspects of the external world are represented. We have argued (in subsection 1.3.2) against a pictorial concept of representations, and throughout earlier chapters have argued in favour of representation as construction with respect to key aspects of the environment in relation to the preoccupations and needs of the organism. Further, representation will exist at a level of abstraction whereby the information is given by the rules and patterns, rather than any given physical state of the organism. Two further examples from early infant development will illustrate this. The first relates to the capabilities of 3-week-old infants. In an experiment carried out by Meltzoff and Borton (1979) the infants were blindfolded and given one of two different dummies (pacifiers) to suck, one which had a spherical-shaped nipple, and the other a nipple with nubs protruding from various points on its surface. After an infant had sucked one nipple, both were placed in front of him/her and the blindfold was removed. Following a quick visual comparison the infants looked more at the nipple they had just sucked. Thus the infant's representation of what was sucked was sufficiently abstract that it could be related to a visual stimulus. It did not consist only of what it felt like, or what it looked like.

With age the level of abstraction becomes greater. Infants of 10 months of age were shown a series of schematic face drawings in which each face was different in length of nose or placement of the ears or eyes. Then the infants were 'asked', using a task that involved the distinguishing of familiar and novel faces, which single drawing best 'represented' the entire series. They chose a drawing that averaged the features of all the faces that had been seen, but was not one of the individual drawings of the series (Strauss 1979). The representation was related systematically to the stimuli but also took a form that was linked to the needs of the developing child. The representation had sufficient generality that it could provide a basis for future perceptions and actions, including faces that had not previously been seen. Equally it had certain defining characteristics such that some stimuli could have fallen outside its range.

6.3.4 Attachment

Between 6 and 9 months there occurs the emergence of selective attachments, a phenomenon which is particularly informative. Attachment theory and the relevant research now constitutes a major body of knowledge, and only the basic principles will be outlined here in order to illustrate a number of points. Although there is no doubt that infants distinguish between familiar and unfamiliar adults before the age of 6–9 months, at about this time the preference for their principal caregivers becomes very striking. This is manifest in a very specific way. The infant will look for comfort from attachment figures, especially when under perceived threat, or tired or ill, but will move away from that person and explore when not under threat. The attachment figure is said to act as a secure base for exploration and play, as well as a comforter at times of anticipated or actual distress (Bowby 1969). Different patterns of behaviour in relation to the attachment figure can be identified reliably using the Ainsworth Strange Situation Test, and these different patterns are related both to the preceding quality of parent–infant interactions, and a number of aspects of subsequent development (Bretherton 1985). These have been assessed several years later, and blind to the original attachment classification, and there is an association between the classification and subsequent characteristics such as quality of peer relationships, self-esteem, and effectiveness at coping with difficulties or in tackling novelty (Sroufe *et al.* 1990). It should be emphasized that an association does not ensure a mechanism, but it is reasonable to conclude that the quality of early relationships is relevant to later personal functioning.

What does this tell us about the developmental progression in intentional-causal processes? First, it underlines the importance to the infant of other people, and by this age, specific people. In the context of the points made earlier, other people matter to the infant. Secondly, it reinforces the proposition that any theory of causality in relation to the mind must encompass perceptual, cognitive, emotional, and behavioural aspects of interpersonal functioning. Thirdly, the behaviour of the infant can be predicted only on the basis of an internalized set of rules or schema. Earlier attempts to predict behaviour on the basis of frequencies of specific behaviours did not work (Sroufe and Waters 1977). Thus, for instance, smiling and laughing with mother do not predict smiling and laughter with a stranger. Indeed, typically the securely attached infant demonstrates quite different behaviours with mother and with a stranger; differences which appear to represent inconsistencies of behaviour, but which can be reliably predicted under the terms of an internalized set of rules. Fourthly, the attachment pattern is related to the preceding interactions of mother and infant (Crittenden 1992). These have entailed contributions from both mother and infant, and it is difficult to separate the relative contributions of each; however, undoubtedly the characteristics of the mother's handling of the infant play an important part. Thus the set of rules is assembled significantly from the infant's experience of his or her mother (Stern 1985). Each sequence between the mother and infant can be seen both as a manifestation of the sets of rules regarding attachment, and a test of them. It has been shown that when mothers are exposed to significant distress, the attachment category of their infants is more likely to change over a period of 6 months, than otherwise (Vaughn *et al.* 1979). It is likely that the rules and expectancies have changed in the light of experience. Fifthly, the evidence from the follow-up into later childhood indicates that the internalized attachment schema may have considerable stability, and influence subsequent sets of rules (Sroufe *et al.* 1990). Such sets of rules about the worth of the self, and about competence are likely to be crucial to an understanding of the causation of psychological states and behaviours.

6.3.5 Play

At around 18 months we see the emergence of perhaps the most dramatic demonstration of the potential of intentional-causal processes; in play. This is characterized by the creation, using convention and agreement, of identities and stories related to objects or other people. As this activity becomes more sophisticated with age, the actual physical properties of objects act increasingly only as cues for their imagined identities. The story, a series of events tied together by an intentional explanation, makes use of these imagined identities, which are conventionalized and rule bound (Garvey 1977). In general, by the age of 3 years, children are at home with repeated changes of sets of rules. Sometimes this is clarified by the words 'let's pretend . . .' or a statement that implies pretending, such as 'I'm the mummy and you're the daddy'. There is no requirement, however, that the participants are male and female, nor that the performance is an exact replica of the children's experiences. Equally, it is likely to reflect some key elements of their experiences or preoccupations. In joint play it is crucial that the participants share the same set of rules. The actions of each has a causal role in the actions of the other, which can be predicted only by reference to the agreed, conventionalized, jointly constructed frame of reference.

In order for this to work the children must have a firm grasp of what is and what is not play in their shared interactions. If this is in doubt, there needs to be the capacity to check, from outside the play.

Consider examples from Garvey (1977). The first is the following sequence. X sits on a three-legged stool that has a magnifying glass in the centre:

X. I've got to go to the potty.
Y. (turns to him) Really?
X. (grins) No, pretend.
Y. (smiles and watches X).

For this sequence to work it must be assumed that there can be a conversation in which an assertion is untrue but playful, and that there are communications which can be relied upon to comment truthfully on whether this is the case.

The capacity to play requires a high level of abstraction of joint rules, and of actions within those rules. Take this example: X and Y conduct a game that consists of X discovering a stuffed snake, Y sharing the discovery, X playing the straight man, and Y expressing fear.

X. (holds up the snake)
Y. (draws back in alarm) What's that?
X. It's a snake! (laughs at Y's exaggerated fear)
Y. Do it again.
X. (holds up snake)

Here there are clear rules, unspoken but communicated, and an understanding that 'it' refers to the sequence, and again that 'Do it again' is spoken from outside the sequence and is about it.

The extent to which children familiarize themselves with rules and conventions of communication is seen in their play with the conventions of language, in which it is used as non-play and then experimented with, and then returned to non-play again. X and Y are discussing their feelings about the playroom.

X. Don't you wish we could get out of this place?
Y. Yeah, 'cause it has yucky things.
X. Yeah.
Y. 'cause it's fishy too, 'cause it has fishes.
X. And it's snakey too 'cause it has snakes. And it's beary too 'cause it has bears.
Y. And it's hatty too 'cause it has hats.
X. Where's the hats? (X ends the game).

The conventions of social exchange may be played with and create humour. For instance, if I ask you a question the convention is either that I do not know and need the information, or that I do know and I want to test your knowledge. In the following sequence two children relaxing together enjoy a series of pointless questions and answers:

X. (picks up dress-up items) What's this?
Y. It's a party hat.
X. What's this?
Y. Hat.
X. Funny. And what's this?

Y. Dress.
X. Yuck.
Y. Tie.
X. It's all yucky stuff.

X did not need the information nor was he testing Y's knowledge. They jointly violated the convention.

There is an extensive research literature on the purposes of play which undoubtedly extend beyond our current considerations; however, they clearly include the experimentation with movement among different sets of rules of interpretation, different solutions, and their associated feelings, wishes, fears, beliefs, and actions (cf. subsection 3.2.6). This is personal and interpersonal, it requires that play and non-play are distinguished, that fantasy and reality are differentiated, and that true and false may be identified accurately.

6.4 RULE MULTIPLICITY: SELECTION AND COMMUNICATION

6.4.1 The problems and forms of solution

Consideration of rules about rules brings us to a crucial developmental issue, and one that is of great importance to our thesis. We return to our argument about intentional-casual processes. In order for these processes to be effective, their elements must operate in harmony. This is to say, the representation, the rules, the convention, the range of function, the needs of the organism, and the action must be compatible. As long as the intentional systems are comprised of fixed biological structures, these rules and the underlying conventions are also fixed. Their harmonious operation has evolved over long periods and they have an established survival value. However, now we are considering examples in which the rules are in some degree acquired, and may vary rapidly depending upon internal states and needs, and external circumstances. In other words, the appearance of novel intentional sequences, which in evolution have occurred over thousands of years, may appear as new perceptions, cognitions, or action sequences, in humans from moment to moment. It is not surprising then that the developing child practises from the first weeks of life, in play and relationships, the skills required to move among internal sets of rules, representations, and states of mind.

In the context of this variability a certain general condition has to be met if action is to be possible: there has to be means for determining which set of rules applies at any one time. The necessary functions here are closely linked, in the theory and in practice, and they may be classified and described in various ways, such as the following:

1. An executive function, to exercise some control over multiple rules, and specifically to select those used for immediate action. Presupposed here is a capacity for monitoring, so that the executive can access states of mind and relate them to external context prior to selection.
2. In the case of social, co-operative action, a method of sharing information as

to which among the multiplicity of rules are being used, or are about to the used is required. In brief, social beings need communication.

Broadly speaking, the former grouping has to do with what is within the organism, with the intrapsychic, and with consciousness specifically, while the latter has to do with intersubjectivity, including the use of language. These divisions are somewhat arbitrary in that the phenomena in question, though distinguishable, are closely interwoven.

Concepts which span all the phenomena with which we are concerned here are those of self, and person. These concepts highlight particularly continuity through time, which is at the heart of action. Action presupposes continuity through time specifically in the form of access between memory and plans. From the point of view of the agent this continuity, and the access on which it is based, may appear subjectively as the sense of self, at least for those agents who can say and think 'I'. Monitoring, selection, and communication of mental states, presuppose an I which thinks (which remembers, plans, wills). From the outside, from the point of another, co-operative agent, the continuity of self appears as the perception of an understandable, predictable-enough person.

In summary, along the phylogenetic scale we see the release of the potential within intentional processes, specifically the freeing-up of rules and conventions from what is innately fixed, the generation of multiple possibilities, which requires, if action is to continue, methods of monitoring, selection, and, for co-operative beings, communication. These hypothesized functions are closely linked to concepts of consciousness, self, communication, and language. In this way the theme of the present chapter comes across these very large ideas. They are considered in the remainder of this section, which ends with some epistemological implications. The discussions are inevitably partial, with the emphasis on connections with the current theme and with other parts of the essay.

6.4.2 Consciousness

Consciousness is a thriving research area within the cognitive psychology paradigm and has already been referred to in this context in the first chapter (subsection 1.2.4.). Some points may be summarized as follows. Most information-processing occurs without the subject's conscious awareness. Processing of incoming sensory information, for example, is monitored and selected for conscious attention under certain conditions, including relevance to the regulation of ongoing activity. Consciousness presupposes monitoring of subliminal processing and plays an executive role in the control of action. The main point to be made in the present context is that consciousness is implicated in selection from among multiple rules and representations for the purposes of action.

6.4.3. Self and personality

Continuity and consistency in conscious awareness, and control of mental states and action, are closely linked to the concepts of self, subjectively experienced, and person or personality, as experienced by others. The extent to which individuals vary from situation to situation, and the extent to which they show consistency has been a source of extended and unresolved debate (Mischel 1968, 1973, 1979; Bem 1983). However, in summary, the evidence may be taken to indicate that there is both variability and consistency, and that, in general, the consistency is less in individual behaviours than in underlying organizational principles. Personality may be seen as that which gives order and congruence to different kinds of behaviour in which the individual engages (Hall and Lindzey 1978) and personality traits are 'enduring patterns of perceiving, relating to, and thinking about the environment and oneself and are exhibited in a wide range of important social and personal contexts' (American Psychiatric Association 1994, p. 630). This is consistent with the idea that there is an overarching mechanism that provides substantial continuity over time and place. Clearly, the statement in schematic form of the need for this agency will lead to many questions that are beyond the scope of this chapter. For instance is this 'self' seen best in everyday events and encounters, or is it that which is seen under particular circumstances such as extreme passions or duress? Is self as subjectively experienced co-extensive with the monitoring and executive mechanism, the function of which we outlined earlier?

Notwithstanding these questions, the developmental findings provide considerable illumination. Stern (1985) has provided an account of the development of the self system, that draws on developmental findings and theories, and is highly pertinent to this issue. He argues that in the first weeks of life there is evident a capability for representation that reflects the first steps in the development of the self. As we saw earlier in the chapter, the infant possesses, from the first days of life, the capacity to represent aspects of the external world. Thus the perception of a difference in the shape of nipple that has been experienced only through touch is manifest when two nipples are seen. This requires a representation of difference in shape that is not tied to one perceptual route. Even at this age we see capacities of sufficient abstraction and generality that they may form the basis of what will become more recognizable as self functions, and Stern has referred to the presence in the first 2 months of life of the 'emergent self'. However, in the succeeding 4 months capabilities appear that more clearly fulfil our requirements. Here, as Stern has argued, the infant develops the senses of self-agency, self-coherence, self-affectivity, and self-history. Self-agency refers to a sense of authorship of one's own actions derived from a range of action-related processes: the formation of motor-plans for actions, feedback via nerves from joints and muscles that actions have occurred (proprioception), and the regularity of consequences for actions. Stern and colleagues carried out experiments with 4-month-old Siamese twins, which showed that although each sucked the other's fingers, they distinguished between their own and those of their twin. This reflected differences in proprioception and action plans. Schedules of reinforcement for actions carried out by the self, and those carried out by others, will be different, and infants as young as 3 months are able to make these distinctions. This experience of self-agency will provide the infant with an experience of continuity. Also in this age period, from 2 to 6 months, the sophisticated interpersonal exchanges with caregivers include many different games, and interactions which are not games, which means that they take place under different rules. Putting the two together, self-agency is a domain in which actions may be performed under different sets of rules, and are also experienced as having the same agent. It seems then, again, that action is crucial to the account. Not only is the elaboration of effective action a crucial outcome of intentional-causal processes, it also provides a basis for the organization of intentional-causal processes, representations, and plans of actions. Subjectively, it contributes to the continuity of the sense of self, with implications that where the conditions for action are significantly curtailed the sense of self-agency and continuity may be threatened.

The argument concerning self-affectivity is similar. The young infant experiences the same affects, notably pleasure, and distress, in a range of circumstances. Stern comments that 'affects are excellent high-order self-invariants because of their relative fixity: the organisation and manifestation of each emotion is well fixed by innate design and changes little over development' (Stern 1985, p. 89). Stern continues, 'mother's making faces, grandmother's tickling, father's throwing the infant in the air, the baby-sitter's making sounds, and uncle's making the puppet talk may all be the experience of joy' (Stern 1985, p. 90). The rules of engagement with each of these people are likely to be different, and with development that differentiation will become sharper, yet it is the same joy with each encounter, and this provides support for the sense of self. In this analysis innate responses are taken to provide the underpinning of the self and its metarepresentational function. Different representations are linked to a common, wired-in affective response, and this in turn leads to an overarching affectively laden representation.

Further on in development, we find an increasing capacity to formulate in language one's own mental states, in particular to give reasons for one's actions and to announce one's intentions. This capacity to give an account of oneself, in language, is fundamental to our concepts of self and person, as already noted in the first chapter (subsection 1.4.3). Some developmental aspects of the capacity are referred to in subsections 6.4.4 and 6.5.3.

6.4.4 Communication, metacommunication, and language

We have seen already that even at a few weeks of age infants are able to participate in joint activities with caregivers in which there are shared rules of engagement. At around 9 months of age it is evident that the establishment of which set of rules will apply is simultaneously personal and interpersonal. Two examples will illustrate this. Sroufe and Waters (1976) asked mothers to put masks over their faces in the presence of their 9-month-old infants, under a range of conditions. The authors described the typical responses of the infants. There was initially a cessation of previous activity and a period during which the infant looked closely at his/her mother, often with an expression of puzzlement. This was followed either by crying and other manifestations of distress, or by laughter. The type of reaction was influenced significantly by factors such as whether the infant was in familiar surroundings. Thus it seemed that the central question that the experiment presented to the child was, 'Has my mother gone and am I under threat, or is she still there and am I OK?' The cues were both internal and external, and the search was for an individual and shared frame of reference. Once the solution was established, action ensued, but prior to this it was not possible; the infant was immobile.

The second example illustrates the use of another person in order to determine which rules apply to a state of affairs in the physical world. One-year-old infants may be lured with a toy to crawl across a visual cliff (an apparent drop off on the floor which is mildly frightening to a child of this age). When infants encounter this situation they often give evidence of uncertainty; action is unclear. Emde and Sorce (1983) found that they then look towards a parent to read her face for its affective (emotional) content. If the mother has been instructed to show facial pleasure by smiling, the infant crosses the visual cliff, but if she has been instructed to show facial fear, the infant turns back and sometimes becomes upset. Thus the infant appears to find out from the other what her state of mind should be. Here the elements of intentional causality are interpersonal and the rules, convention, and agreement are shared between the participants. These also need a metaframe which has the form of shared action and commitment. Here is scope for variability and creativity, provided the communications from the other person can be relied upon. If they cannot, further disruptions of intentionality, with threats to effective action, may arise.

Increasingly, non-verbal communication, and communication about communication, is joined, to some extent covered over, and is elaborated by, the use of language. It has been emphasized throughout this chapter that early human development is characterized by finely tuned sensitivity to social interaction; that the aspects of reality that matter to the infant are largely interpersonal. Social interaction requires agreement on tasks and methods. Social animals generally require ways of communicating which, among various sets of rules, are to be applied on given occasions, rules relating to such as hunting, avoiding predators, feeding, playing, etc. It is plausible to suppose that among the functions served by the development of language phylogenetically and ontogenetically is that of facilitating communication of which sets of rules are to be used in co-operative endeavours.

It was noted at the beginning of this section that selection among multiple sets of rules is linked to consciousness within the agent, and to language (as well as non-verbal conventions) in relation to shared activities. It was anticipated that these divisions are somewhat blurred, however, and this point can be expanded upon here. There is an intimate relationship between cognition and social relationships, as was discussed throughout Chapter 3, and with particular reference to Vygotsky's developmental psychology at the end of subsection 3.3.4. Cognition here, of course, includes features of consciousness. The carer–infant relationship guides development of the infant's cognitive capacities, including aspects of consciousness itself. For example, Vygotsky proposed that the capacity for attention to aspects of the environment and to current activity, one function of consciousness, is an internalization of shared attention-behaviour within the infant–carer relationship (Vygotsky 1934). At a later stage, and more obviously, the acquisition of language depends on teaching, but this socially acquired language is internalized, as linguistically encoded rules, and these come to play an increasing role in regulating action in the developing child (Vygotsky 1934; Luria 1961; see also subsection 6.5.2). In this way, while both attention and language have social origins, both become crucial to the regulation of the individual's actions.

The connections here between individual and social, thought and language, are many and complicated. For example, joint attention-behaviour is arguably (one of) the earliest signs in the infant of the capacity for representing the other's mental states, this being in turn at the basis of acquiring the 'theory of mind', problems with which may be implicated in autism (Baron-Cohen 1991). It has already been remarked that selective attention is one aspect of consciousness (subsections 6.4.2, 1.2.4). The capacity to say what rules one is following is another aspect of consciousness, linked to what we call self-consciouness, as noted in the fuller discussion in the first chapter (subsection 1.4.4).

A further strong link between consciousness and social activity has been suggested from an evolutionary point of view by Humphreys (1983). He proposes that conscious-ness delivers information about the mind–brain states of the agent, and has evolved particularly with the function of facilitating analogic knowledge of the intentionality of others. This proposal is linked to the so-called simulation epistemology of mind discussed in Chapter 3 (Section 3.2).

6.4.5 Cognition and commitment

In the context of multiple rules and representations, what is required is a cognitive function which selects one plan of action, with its associated representations, from among various possibilities, a function which 'decides what to do'. So far in this section the need for a mental executive function has been considered from the point of view of biology and psychology. As generally in this essay, however, similar conclusions can be reached by an a priori, epistemological route. In the present case this has to do with the close connection in post-empiricism between cognition and commitment.

In the first chapter we outlined general characteristics of post-empiricism (subsection 1.4.1) and went on to discuss links between epistemology and logic, that is, between the theory of knowledge and the theory of representation (subsection 1.4.4). It was an insight of modern, seventeenth-century epistemology, in the Cartesian system, and in empiricism, that the a priori basis of certainty is to be found in logic, in the nature of thought itself. According to the logic of Wittgenstein's *On certainty* (1969), this insight assumes the form: the a priori basis of certainty lies in our methods of thinking, and beneath those, our ways of acting. Commitment to the methods being used, rejection of what is incompatible with them, is a precondition of action, and of thought itself. Doubts about the methods, indecision between alternatives, is incompatible with practice, leading to perpetual hesitation, to no action. Conversely, in so far as we do act and think, we expel doubt and proceed with certainty. This commitment, or certainty, is necessary in practice. But it also belongs to logic, to the very idea of judgement. On this, Wittgenstein remarks (1969, § 150):

> ... somewhere I must begin with not-doubting; and that is not, so to speak, hasty but excusable: it is part of judging.

We have, and must have, certainty in action, and in methods of judgement. This means that in particular procedures some beliefs have to stand fast; these beliefs are not so much assumptions, as instruments essential to the activities in question. This applies to everyday actions. For example (Wittgenstein 1969, §§ 148, 150):

> Why do I not satisfy myself that I have two feet when I want to get up from a chair? There is no why. I simply don't. This is how I act.

> How does someone judge which is his right and which his left hand? How do I know that my judgement will agree with someone's else's? How do I know that this colour is blue? If I don't trust *myself* here, why should I trust anyone else's judgement? That is to say: somewhere I must begin with not-doubting; and that is not, so to speak, hasty but excusable: it is part of judging.

The point applies also to the most cognitively complex activities, such as scientific enquiry (Wittgenstein 1969, §§ 341–3):

> ... The *questions* that we raise and our *doubts* depend on the fact that some propositions are exempt from doubt, are as it were hinges on which those turn.

> That is to say, it belongs to the logic of our scientific investigations that certain things are *indeed* not doubted.

> But it isn't that the situation is like this: we just *can't* investigate everything, and for that reason we are forced to rest content with assumption. If I want the door to turn, the hinges must stay put.

The beliefs which stand firm are those which define particular methods of interpretation and action. They have the form, typically, of affirmations of what is presupposed by application of a particular method, and at the same time they rule out alternative methods of interpretation and enquiry. Whatever activity we are engaged in, some things have to be taken for granted. The point here is of course a very general one. Thus (Wittgenstein 1969, § 344): 'My *life* consists in my being content to accept many things.'

Another expression of the same point is that methodological rules guide the interpretation of experience and the planning of action (subsections 1.4.1 and 1.4.4). These tend not to be given up in the face of anomalous experiences. Rather, these core rules are preserved by denying or reconstruing what seems to go against them. This is necessary if judgement, in general, or of particular kinds, is to continue. Related here also is the account given earlier of the incorrigibility of self-reports (subsections 1.4.3 and 3.2.4). Reports of the mental states regulating one's own current activity or the actions about to be performed function in part as statements of intent, and hence cannot, in normal circumstances, be wrong. In various ways the knowledge—or certainty—required for action and thought appears in the form of a *decision* (Wittgenstein 1969, for example §§ 516, 360–62; quoted from and discussed in subsection 1.4.4). What is needed is *commitment* by the agent, or an *executive function* within the information-processing system.

These issues are central to post-empiricism, because it frees thought and knowledge from something pre-given and fixed, from 'experience' construed as an absolute category, and thereby emphasizes creative activity. There are then many possibilities, and in the midst of these decisions are necessary.

In biology this requirement appears as sketched through this chapter. Along the phylogenetic scale, rules and representations are progessively less pre-given and fixed, becoming more acquired, created, and diverse. Hence the need for decision-making procedures and communication, appearing as aspects of consciousness and language.

In the history of epistemology the same underlying problematic can be seen at work in the problem of knowledge, particularly in its Classical form and in its present-day form. As remarked in Chapter 1 (subsection 1.2.1), the seventeenth-century problem was generated by and preoccupied with the split between sense–experience and the absolute nature posited by modern science. There is, however, a more accessible problem of knowledge, related to, though obscured by, this modern extreme. The problem arises from the *relativity* of what passes for human knowledge, relativity to the senses, to personal opinions, to culture, and may be expressed in the form: how in all this flux can we identify anything really fixed, anything that we can really know? This was the Classical problem, identified by Plato, for example in the *Theaetetus* (discussed above, subsection 3.3.4) and expounded at length by the Pyrrhonists. Thus Sextus Empiricus propounds the various modes of sceptical argument, citing many and diverse examples of variation and opposition among experiences, theories, beliefs, and customs (Sextus Empiricus *c*. AD 200 chapters 14–16). To any one may be opposed another of apparently equal validity, so that there is no way of deciding which is right, and the sceptic therefore judges neither way, saying only 'perhaps', 'possibly', or 'it seems so' (op.cit. chapters 21–2). This state of affairs invites the sophists to propose that being right or true can be a matter only of power, alleged values assigned to the opinions and interests of the dominant group. Such cynicism, which has much to be said for it, is well expounded by contemporary post-modernist writers such as Foucault (1977; and for critical commentary see for example Norris 1993).

The sceptical problem arises where there is consciousness of variety, of the many possibilities, the relativity, and the apparent absence of absolutes. One response is to believe that one's own beliefs have absolute validity, untainted, unlike everybody else's, by relativity, but this position is essentially undermined by the sceptical critique. The conclusion that there are no absolute truths may appear inevitable. There is, however, the exception that we can affirm the world which generates this conclusion, a world in which relativity and difference are recognized rather than disqualified. A further qualification to scepticism, connected because it belongs with the same relativistic episteme, is that we have to have to affirm some beliefs rather than others in order to be able to think and act at all. This is a non-sceptical thought characteristic of twentieth-century epistemology, the positive side of the relativity, found when it is in an affirming rather than a sceptical mood, as for example in Wittgenstein's *On certainty*: we know, are certain of, what we need to know in order to be able to act.

To put the point another way, the sceptical suspense of judgement is nothing for a living being. It essentially presupposes an 'I' which sits and thinks rather than does anything. This kind of criticism was made by Hume in his *Treatise* (1739, p. 160):

> He [the Pyrrhonian] must acknowledge, if he will acknowledge anything, that all human life must perish, were his principles universally and steadily to prevail. All discourse, all action would immediately cease; and men remain in a total lethargy, till the necessities of nature, unsatisfied, put an end to their miserable existence. It is true; so fatal an event is very little to be dreaded. Nature is always too strong for principle.

Central to the sceptical problem is that *more of the same*—more experience, thought, opinions, reasons—will not solve it. *More cognition* makes no difference. Rather, what is required is a decision, or commitment, to do (or believe) this rather than that. The implication here is that, at basis, activity and thought are unsupported by reason. This certainly does not imply 'irrationality'. On the contrary, it belongs to the definition of action that it is justified by reasons, with reference to beliefs and desires. Rather, reasons in the end run out, and what remains then are our inclinations, the will, to act and think in this way rather than that, according to our nature, as living beings, as human beings, and as the particular person that we are. These points have been discussed in other contexts. In Chapter 3 (subsection 3.3.2) in discussion of Wittgenstein's critique of rule-following we concluded that reasons run out, leaving inclinations. In Chapter 4 (subsection 4.6.3) we argued that explanations of action cite the nature of the agent, in terms of theories which have more or less generality, from those which cite general biological nature to those which appeal to personality.

6.5 THOUGHT AND REASON

6.5.1 Introduction

The main task of this chapter is explication of the proposal that intentionality and intentional causality run right though from relatively elementary biological processes to the most complex psychological processes, up to mature human cognition, including reason. Essential to this developmental story is the seamless transition from biology to developmental psychology as considered in sections 6.2 and 6.3. We saw in section 6.3 that principles of intentionality can be seen at work in early development, and that their creative potential begins to be realized in children's play. This creative potential, the freeing of rules and representations from fixed patterns, is of enormous significance in nature and culture, and was viewed from various perspectives in section 6.4. In this closing section we return to the developmental story of the chapter, extending it from the early stages of human cognitive development to its maturity.

6.5.2 Origins in action

Notwithstanding the evident, great differences between intentionality in the beginnings of life and in the mature human mind, the transitions are seamless. The links between early biological and psychological function in human development are made clear in the claim, fundamental to Piagetian theory, that cognition has its origin in action (Piaget 1937, with commentary in Flavell 1963). Thus Piaget (1970, pp. 103–4):

> In the common view, the external world is entirely separate from the subject ... Any objective knowledge, then, appears to be simply the result of a set of perceptive recordings, motor associations, verbal descriptions, which all participate in producing a sort of figurative copy or 'functional copy' (in Hull's terminology) of objects and the connections between them. The only function of intelligence is systematically to file, correct, etc., these various sets of information; in this process, the more faithful the critical copies, the more consistent the final copies will be. In such an empiricist prospect, the content of intelligence comes from outside, and the coordinations that organize it are only the consequences of language and symbolic instruments.
>   But this passive interpretation of the act of knowledge is in fact contradicted at all levels of development and, particularly, at the sensorimotor and pre-linguistic levels of cognitive adaptation and intelligence. Actually, in order to know objects, the subject must act upon them, and therefore transform them: he must displace, connect, combine, take apart, and reassemble them.
>   From the most elementary sensorimotor actions (such as pushing and pulling)

to the most sophisticated intellectual operations, which are interiorized actions, carried out mentally (e.g., joining together, putting in order, putting into one-to-one correspondence), knowledge is constantly linked with actions or operations, that is, with *transformations*.

Piaget here correctly suggests that the main idea, that cognition is grounded in action, stands opposed to a variety of traditional and contemporary doctrines, as has been argued throughout this essay, such as the resemblance theory of representation (subsections 1.3.1–2), the computational theory of mind (section 2.2, also 2.4), and empiricism (section 1.4).

Vygotsky, too, endorses the link between higher mental functions and action. We have noted already that he typically emphasizes social action (subsection 3.3.4), and the role of language in regulating (or controlling) action (subsection 6.4.4). Thus Vygotsky (1981, pp. 69–70):

> Children master the social forms of behavior and transfer these forms to themselves. With regard to our area of interest, we could say that the validity of this law is nowhere more obvious than in the use of the sign. A sign is always originally a means used for social purposes, a means of influencing others, and only later becomes a means of influencing oneself.
>
> According to Janet, the word initially was a command to others and then underwent a complex history of imitations, changes of functions, etc. Only gradually was it separated from action. According to Janet, it is always a command, and that is why it is the basic means of mastering behavior. Therefore, if we want to clarify genetically the origins of the voluntary function of the word and why the word overrides motor responses, we must inevitably arrive at the real function of commanding in both ontogenesis and phylogenesis.

Separation of thought and language from their beginnings in action is a major developmental task, involving creation of many distinctions, between self and object, appearance and reality, sign and signified. Such distinctions remain blurred in what may be called pre-rational, or magical thought. In this stage (or state of mind), imagination, wish, sign and reality merge, while through childhood the rational mentality draws more precise boundaries (Piaget 1937; Vygotsky 1981; Subotskii 1985; Harris 1994).

6.5.3 Cognitive maturation in adolescence

Further cognitive development occurs at or around puberty. As would be expected, this is linked to further maturation in brain structure and function, specifically in the frontal regions (Jernigan *et al.* 1991), which characteristically serve the organization and regulation of action (Luria 1966).

In his formulation of cognitive development during adolescence, Piaget emphasized the appearance of so-called formal operations, basic to which is application of propositional logic. Indeed the study was called *The growth of logical thinking* (Inhelder and Piaget 1958). The propositional calculus specifies rules for making complex propositions from simple ones, using connectives such as *not, and, or,* and *implies.*

Inhelder and Piaget's emphasis on formal logic as the high point of reason is connected to themes in early twentieth-century philosophy referred to in the first chapter. The propositional calculus had a fundamental role in both Wittgenstein's *Tractatus* (1921) (subsection 1.3.2) and logical empiricism (1.4.1). In both cases it was the structure which contained the combinations of all simple propositions which represented reality. It defined the permissible relations between propositions, and the validity of inferences between one (complex) proposition and another. In brief, and in these senses, the propositional calculus defined 'reason'. Against this logico-philosophical background, it was plausible to regard human cognitive development as culminating in competence with the propositional calculus, and other formal logical systems (such as set theory).

This whole background metaphysics was being overturned at the same time, however, giving way to post-empiricism, with its emphasis on activity and theory. Representation is seen primarily as being in the service of action, as opposed to being pictures or images of states of affairs, and it employs hierarchically organized theory, and is not simply a passive reflection of experience (Chapter 1, subsection 1.4.1). Of course, Piaget himself was a main contributor to both aspects of the paradigm shift as it has occurred in psychology. His emphasis on the intimate connection between thought and action in early cognitive development is well known, and referred to above (subsection 6.5.2), as is his emphasis on the role of cognitive structures.

The paradigm shift in the definition of cognition has immediate implications for logic in the broader sense of the theory of judgement. The inference is that what matters to logic is the role of cognition in regulating action, and the role of theory in the interpretation of experience. In the new paradigm, what matters to logic, to the a priori definition of the conditions of thought and reason, is whatever is essential to theory in the regulation of action (Chapter 1, subsection 1.4.4).

Emphasis on the development of the power to theorize can, in fact, be found in Inhelder and Piaget's theory of cognitive maturation in adolescence, but at the end, in the final chapter, after all the material on the development of formal logic. The authors write (1958, pp. 339–40):

> The adolescent is the individual who commits himself to possibilities although we certainly do not mean to deny that his commitment begins in real-life situations. In other words, the adolescent is the individual who begins to build begins to build 'systems' or 'theories', in the largest sense of the term. The child does not build systems. His spontaneous thinking may be more or less systematic . . . but it is the observer who sees the system from outside, while the child is never aware of it since he never thinks about his own thought . . . The child has no powers of reflection, i.e. no second-order thoughts which deal critically with his own thinking. No theory can be built without such reflection. In contrast, the adolescent is able to analyse his own thinking and construct theories. The fact that these theories are oversimplified, awkward, and usually contain very little originality is beside the point.

Inhelder and Piaget go on to emphasise the developmental function of the adolescent's theories (1958, p. 340):

> From the functional standpoint . . . they furnish the cognitive and evaluative bases for the assumption of adult roles . . . They are vital in the assimilation

of the values which delineate societies or social classes as entities in contrast to simple interindividual relations.

Consistent with the point made throughout this chapter, that developmental processes create also new possibilities of misrepresentation, Inhelder and Piaget remark on the fantasies of omnipotence which can accompany the adolescent's newly acquired powers of thought, a theme to which we will return in chapter 8 under the heading of psychological defences (Inhelder and Piaget 1958, pp. 345–6):

> The adolescent goes through a phase in which he attributes an unlimited power to his own thoughts so that the dream of a glorious future or of transforming the world through Ideas (even if this idealism takes a materialistic form) seems to be not only fantasy but also an effective action which in itself modifies the empirical world. This is obviously a form of cognitive egocentrism.

6.6 SUMMARY

In this chapter we have reviewed the operation of intentional causal processes in an ascent from the perceptual apparatus of primitive organisms to the complex interpersonal life of the developing child. Such processes are, we have argued, pervasive and unifying in biology. Equally, there are marked differences between the operation of non-human organisms and that of the human mind. These can be seen to be based on an extraordinary, explosive, and rich elaboration of intentionality, characterized by the capacity for the acquisition of multiple sets of rules of perception, thought, emotions, and actions. This implies immense scope for creativity and change, but also the need for the capacity to represent representations, to monitor them, and to link them to action, including social interaction. These functions are among those served by consciousness and language. As the extent of the sophistication of this evolutionary 'play' on intentional causality becomes evident, so will the scope for its malfunction.

REFERENCES

American Psychiatric Association (1994). *Diagnostic and statistical manual of mental disorders*, (4th edn). American Psychiatric Association, Washington, DC.

Baron-Cohen, S. (1991). Precursors to a theory of mind: understanding attention in others. In *Natural theories of mind: evolution, development and simulation of everyday mindreading*, (ed. A. Whiten, pp. 233–51). Blackwell, Oxford.

Bem, D. (1983). Constructing a theory of triple typology: some (second) thoughts on nomothetic and ideographic approaches to personality. *Journal of Personality*, 51, 566–77.

Bowlby, J. (1969). *Attachment and loss: I. Attachment*. Hogarth Press, London.

Bretherton, I. (1985). *Attachment theory: retrospect and prospect*. In *Growing points of attachment theory and Research*, (ed. I. & V. E. Horton and E. Waters). Monographs of the Society for Research in Child Development, 50, Serial No. 209, 3–38. University of Chicago Press.

Bruce, V. and Green P. R. (1990). *Visual perception.* Lawrence Erlbaum Associates, London.

Crittenden, P. M. (1992). Treatment of anxious attachment in infancy and early childhood. *Development and Psychopathology,* 4, 575–602.

Emde, R. N. and Sorce, J. E. (1983). The rewards of infancy: emotional availability and maternal referencing. In *Frontiers of Infant Psychiatry,* (ed. J. D. Call, E. Galenson, and R. Tyson), Vol. 2. Basic Books, New York.

Fantz, R. L. (1963). Pattern vision in new-born infants. *Science,* 140, 296–7.

Flavell, J. H. (1963). *The developmental psychology of Jean Piaget.* D. van Nostrand, New York.

Foucault, M. (1977). *Language, counter-memory, practice,* (ed. D. F. Bouchard and S. Simon). Blackwell, Oxford.

Garvey, C. (1977). *Play.* Fontana, London.

Gotz, K. G., Hengstenberg, B., and Biesinger, R. (1979). Optomotor control of wingbeat and body posture in *Drosophila. Biological Cybernetics,* 35, 101–12.

Hall, C. S. and Lindzey, G. (1978). *Theories of personality,* (3rd ed). Wiley, New York.

Harris, P. L. (1994). Unexpected, impossible and magical events: children's reactions to causal violations. *British Journal of Developmental Psychology,* 12, 1–7.

Hartline, H. K. and Graham, C. H. (1932). Nerve impules from single receptors in the eye. *Journal of Cellular and Comparative Physiology,* 1, 227–95.

Hartline, H. K., Wagner, H. G., and Ratliff, F. (1956). Inhibition in the eye of the *Limulus. Journal of General Physiology,* 39, 651–73.

Hubel, D. H. and Wiesel, T. N. (1962). Receptive fields, binocular interaction, and the functional architecture in the cat's visual cortex. *Journal of Physiology,* 160, 106–54.

Hubel, D. H. and Wiesel, T. N. (1968). Receptive fields and functional architecture of monkey striate cortex. *Journal of Physiology,* 195, 215–43.

Hume, D. (1739). *A treatise of human nature.* (Ed. Selby-Bigge, L. A. (1888). Oxford University Press, Oxford.)

Humphreys, N. (1983). *Consciousness regained.* Oxford University Press, Oxford.

Inhelder, B. and Piaget, J. (1958). *The growth of logical thinking from childhood to adolesence.* Basic Books, New York.

Jernigan, T., Trauna, D., Hesselink, J., and Tallal, P. (1991). Maturation of human cerebrum observed *in vivo* during adolescence. *Brain,* 114, 2037–49.

Kagan, J. (1967). Stimulus–schema discrepancy and attention in the infant. *Journal of Experimental Child Psychology,* 5, 381–90.

Kagan, J., Kearsley, R. B., and Zelazo, P. R. (1978). *Infancy: its place in human development.* Harvard University Press, Cambridge Mass.

Kandel, E. R., Schwartz, J. H., and Jessel, T. M. (1991). *Principles of neural science.* Elsevier, New York.

Kuffler, S. W. (1953). Discharge patterns and functional organization of mammalian retina. *Journal of Neurophysiology,* 16, 37–68.

Luria, A. R. (1961). *The role of speech in the regulation of normal and abnormal behavior.* Liveright, New York.

Luria, A. R. (1966). *The higher cortical functions in man.* Basic Books, New York.

Marr, D. (1982). *Vision: a computational investigation into the human representation and processing of visual information.* W. H. Freeman, San Francisco.

Marr, D. and Hildreth, E. (1980). Theory of edge detection. *Proceedings of the Royal Society of London, Series B,* **207,** 187–216.

Meltzoff, A. N. and Borton, W. (1979). Intermodal matching by human neonates. *Science,* **282,** 403–4.

Mischel, W. (1968). *Personality and assessment.* Wiley, New York.

Mischel, W. (1973). Toward a cognitive social learning reconceptualization of personality. *Psychological Review,* **80,** 252–83.

Mischel, W. (1979). On the interface of cognition and personality: beyond the person–situation debate. *American Psychologist,* **34,** 740–54.

Norris, C. (1993). *The truth about postmodernism.* Blackwell, Oxford.

Piaget, J. (1937). *The construction of reality in the child.* (Trans. Cook, M. (1954). Basic Books, New York.)

Piaget, J. (1970). Piaget's theory. In *Carmichael's manual of child psychology,* (ed. P. H. Mussen), pp. 703–32. Wiley, London. (Reprinted in P. H. Mussen (ed.) (1983) *Handbook of child psychology,* Vol. I, pp. 103–28. Wiley, London. Page reference to this volume.)

Sextus Empiricus (*c.* AD 200) *Outlines of Pyrrhonism.* (Selections with commentary in Hallie, P. (ed. (1985). *Sextus Empiricus: selections from the major writings on scepticism, man, and God.* Hackett, Indianapolis, Ind.)

Sroufe, L. A. and Waters, E. (1976). The ontogenesis of smiling and laughter: a perspective on the organization of development in infancy. *Psychological Review,* **83,** 173–89.

Sroufe, L. A. and Waters, E. (1977). Attachment as an organizational construct. *Child Development,* **48,** 1184–99.

Sroufe, L. A., Egeland, B., and Kreutzer, T. (1990). The fate of early experience following developmental change: longitudinal approaches to individual adaptation in childhood. *Child Development,* **61,** 1363–73.

Stern, D. (1977). *The first relationship, mother and infant.* Fontana, London.

Stern, D. (1985). *The interpersonal world of the infant.* Basic Books, New York.

Stern, D. N., Jaffe, J., Beebe, B., and Bennett, S. L. (1974). Vocalizing in unison and in alternation: Two modes of communication within the mother–infant dyad. *Annals of the New York Academy of Science,* **263,** 89–100.

Strauss, M. S. (1979). Abstraction of proto typical information by adults and ten-month-old infants. *Journal of Experimental Psychology: Human Learning and Memory,* **5,** 618–32.

Subotskii, E. V. (1985). Preschool children's perception of unusual phenomena. *Soviet Psychology,* **23,** 91–114.

Suga, N., Kuzirai, K., and O'Neill, W. E. (1981). How biosonar information is represented in the bat cerebral cortex. In *Neuronal mechanisms of hearing,* (ed. J. Syka and L. Aitkin). Plenum, New York.

Tinbergen, N. (1948). Social releasers and the experimental methods required for their study. *Wilson Bulletin,* **60,** 6–51.

Trevarthen, C. (1980). The foundations of intersubjectivity: development of inter-personal and cooperative understanding in infants. In *The social foundation of language and thought: essays in honor of Jerome Bruner* (ed. D. R. Olson) Norton, New York.

Vaughn, B., Egeland, B., Sroufe, L. A., and Waters, E. (1979). Individual differences in infant–mother attachment at twelve and eighteen months: stability and change in families under stress. *Child Development*, 50, 971–5.

Von Frisch, K. (1967). *The dance, language and orientation of bees.* Harvard University Press, Cambridge, Mass.

Vygotsky, L. (1934). *Thought and language.* (Trans. Hanfmann, E. and Vakar, G. (1962). MIT Press, Cambridge, Mass.)

Vygotsky, L. (1981). The genesis of higher mental functions. In *The concept of activity in Soviet psychology*, (ed. J. V. Wertsch, pp. 144–88. M. E. Sharpe, New York. (Reprinted in K. Richardson and S. Sheldon (ed.) (1990). *Cognitive development to adolescence*, pp. 61–80. Lawrence Erlbaum Associates, Hove. Page reference to this volume.)

Wittgenstein, L. (1921). *Tractatus logico-philosophicus.* (Trans. Pears, D. F. and McGuiness, B. F. (1961). Routledge and Kegan Paul, London.

Wittgenstein, L. (1969). *On certainty, (ed. G. E. M. Anscombe and G. H. von Wright, trans. D. Paul and G. E. M. Anscombe). Blackwell, Oxford.*

7
Psychiatric disorder and its explanation

7.1 INTRODUCTION

We turn now to order and disorder in human psychological functioning. In doing this we build on the conclusions of the previous chapters. We assume that intentional states such as beliefs and fears are genuinely causal, and that they underpin action. We expect that the analysis of intentional-causal processes which applied to non-psychological biological and psychological processes in development will apply also to descriptions of adult psychological functioning. Inasmuch as intentional processes have throughout been seen to require the specification of function and dysfunction, this will apply also to psychological order and disorder. In other words, the analysis of order in psychological functioning inevitably leads to one of disorder. We will illustrate the application of the analysis through a detailed consideration of a relatively unremarkable example of danger and fear. Even in such a simple example there is scope for a complex interplay between intentional- and non-intentional-causal processes. This will lead to a more general consideration of the ways in which we might specify physical and psychiatric disorder, and the extent to which psychiatry has borrowed a model from general medicine. It will be evident that it is the examination of intentionality, rather than the issue of biological causation, that is central. We will suggest that the failure to identify the role of intentional-causal processes in established medical diagnoses has led to a rather narrow concept of biological psychiatry.

7.2 THE OPERATION OF INTENTIONALITY IN PSYCHOLOGICAL PROCESSES

7.2.1 Introduction

Our 'ascent' through physiology, phylogeny, and development brings us to adult human psychological functioning. This forms the final part of the thesis that intentional-causal processes are seen throughout biological systems. Our initial, and most detailed example will be of human behaviour in response to an external threat. We have chosen this because it provides a very clear basis on which to illustrate quite substantial complexity. The case could be made that we need to go further, to sequences of behaviours, to relationships, families, social groupings, and societies, and some of these will be considered in relation to a range of possible mechanisms in order and disorder, in this and the following two chapters. Nevertheless, we will not in this book attempt to carry the analysis into a detailed consideration of the functioning of complex human organizations.

7.2.2 An analysis of the response to danger

Take the example of a state of fear induced in a person (who will be referred to henceforward either as 'the man' or 'the subject') standing in a field, at the sight of a bull in the same field. The state of fear is a normal or appropriate response. It is mediated by information about the bull. There is a series of physical events set in train, starting at the retina and proceeding via the visual pathways to the visual cortex, and thereafter a number of complex processes involving other cortical and subcortical structures. These events have to be described in terms of being about a state of affairs in the outside world; they have intentionality.

The response is not determined by the inherent properties of the bull but by the preoccupation of the individual. Thus the size of the bull might be a determining factor; however, it is likely that, in a manner rather analogous to that of the response of the cardiovascular regulatory system, there will be a threshold below which fear is not induced, then a range over which fear is related to the size of the bull, and a point above which fear is reduced on the grounds that at a certain weight the bull would be unlikely to be sufficiently mobile to pose a threat. The point is that the response is determined by a quality such as 'dangerousness' which is a function of the perceiving organism; the subject in relation to the stimulus.

The perception is rule-bound and conventionalized. It could be represented in many different ways provided the information were retained. Thus is would be possible to induce fear if the observer were looking in the opposite direction to the bull, at a person who had a prearranged signal which meant 'bull'. This could be any action provided it had been agreed previously what it meant. The rules governing the response of the man in the field are likely to be a combination of wired in and learnt. Those linking light impinging on the retina, bursts of impulses in the visual pathway, and visual cortical responses were considered in the previous chapter. These rules, or the capacity to acquire them, are likely to be determined genetically, although as we shall see, the experiments of Hubel and Wiesel and others have indicated that exposure to light early in development may also have an important role. Further brain processes are likely to interpret shape or movement in terms of previous experiences. Influential experiences may include seeing bulls or even having been charged by a bull, but equally may consist only of having read about, or having been told about bulls and their behaviour. Thus the internalized sets of rules may have been generated in a number of different ways. Further, there is a wide range of ways in which the link between the bull and the emotional and behavioural response could be mediated. It could be in the form of a belief of the form 'bulls are dangerous' or 'Aberdeen Angus bulls are dangerous'. Equally there could be, depending on history and culture, other internalized sets of rules that would lead to the same response, of the form 'all animals over 5 feet high are dangerous' or 'all four-legged animals are dangerous', or 'all animals with rings in their noses are dangerous', and so on. Such beliefs would be embedded in further beliefs such as that 'animals are stronger than humans', or that 'these animals move faster than humans', and beliefs such as those concerning the efficacy and the value of the self. Thus the internalized rules may vary substantially and they may be generated through very different routes.

The term 'belief' is here a shorthand for a wide range of states of mind. Thus the man in the field might be a farmer whose knowledge of bulls is based on 40 years of experience but no reading, or he may have had no experience of bulls directly but might have read extensively about cattle. The beliefs of the former might be manifested in behaviour that is systematically related to the behaviour of the bull but in few words, and the latter predominantly in conversation. Alternatively, the man in the field might be a French student with exactly the same amount of book knowledge regarding bulls as a student whose first language is English. Each of these will have used entirely different words, and hold beliefs that are expressed differently, but are linked to the phenomenon in the same systematic way. Within the context of the analysis of intentional causality, a belief is an example of the way in which we describe to ourselves the set of rules governing the construction that is to be placed on our experiences. This is true of all intentional states, including those that are predominantly cognitive, and those that are predominantly affective.

The indirect association between the energy of the stimulus and that of the response is well illustrated in this example. Clearly, a charging bull has momentum and energy. However, the response of the person to the presence of the bull is not mediated by that energy. If we suppose that the presence of the bull is indicated to the man by a third gesticulating party, then a large energetic gesture could mean 'bull standing still' whereas a small gesture might convey 'bull charging'. This will depend entirely upon the convention that has been adopted. The process is fundamentally the same whether we refer to signalling among the neurons of the visual system, or signalling among people. Just as the responses of neurons to light may be an increase or decrease of the rate of firing—via on-centre and off-centre receptors—so human signalling systems utilize increases or decreases of magnitude or energy of responses to denote the presence of the object.

The perception of the bull entails the detection of difference. We saw on p. 242 how this occurs in the peripheral visual system. Higher perceptual processes need to discriminate between numerous possibilities such as bull versus cow, and dead versus alive. The extent of the discrimination will depend upon the experience of the observer. For instance, for many people the perception of the bull would be sufficient to provide the basis for action, however a farmer might discriminate 'Aberdeen Angus' and 'Hereford', and in the latter case (because Hereford bulls are not generally aggressive) he will not be anxious. The response is based on the presence of sufficient cues to make the distinction.

Just as in the case of the baroreceptor, so here the response depends upon the presence of a specialized receptor, the visual apparatus. In the absence of this, and if no alternative sensory apparatus were used, the bull, no matter how fierce, could not be the cause of the fear.

Finally, the person in the field was capable of being deceived. Clearly this could be achieved easily by the gesticulating mediator. However, provided that the cues which were taken as crucial to make the distinction were available, so could a bull-like object. The conditions under which this requirement were met would vary. For instance at dusk, a bull-like shape may suffice, while in daylight and close up, the resemblance would have to be closer. Nevertheless the bull-like object would be the intentional cause of the fear in exactly the same way as a volley of impulses from the baroreceptors to the vasomotor centre.

7.3 THE DISRUPTION OF INTENTIONALITY

How then do we construct criteria for judging normal and abnormal responses? Thus far, we have stated that fear is a normal response to a bull which is perceived as a potentially dangerous animal. This can be further clarified with reference to the person's beliefs about bulls, about this bull in relation to bulls in general, beliefs about the self, and information about the person's current circumstances. All of these are relevant to a description of the state of anticipation or readiness of the person in the field. Let us assume that we are observing the man in the field. If he is clearly in a state of fear, as evidenced by sweating, rapid heart rate, or alteration of speech or behaviour, we would be likely to ask no further questions. This is because we have used the information about the situation and our knowledge of the concerns, perceptions, and beliefs of other people in general, and concluded that the response is consistent with the set of rules under which we expect it to take place.

7.3.1 The identification of an apparent break in intentionality

Suppose, however, the man does not show fear under these circumstances. The observer cannot provide an account according to the set of rules, or expectations that he assumes are operating. *There is a discontinuity in the account that can be given*. However, if the observer then notices that the man in the field is carrying a rifle, he is less likely to be puzzled, because he has further information that tells him about the assumptions or expectancies of the person in the field. The rifle can be said to be the intentional cause of the lack of fear, provided the observer can interrogate the man further to establish that the gun is loaded, and he knows how to use it, or, following the point about deception, that he believes the gun is loaded, and he believes he knows how to use it. The observer can only account for the behaviour if he has the same information as that which is influencing the man in the field.

Suppose now that there are no such observable items which might enable the observer to give a satisfactory account. There are four possibilities:

(1) that the observer does not have sufficient knowledge of the sets of rules or expectations that inform the behaviour;
(2) the man in the field has not seen the bull and so does not have relevant information;
(3) the man in the field does not have the relevant set of concerns, expectancies, or beliefs; and
(4) that there has been disruption of the functioning of his perceptual, cognitive, or motor capabilities.

The first explanation would apply if the man turned out to be a Spanish bullfighter who relished an encounter with a bull. In terms of Dennett's analysis, which we reviewed in Chapter 1 (Dennett 1987), this would be a design stance explanation, in that this was the framework in which the response could be predicted. The man had been trained to perceive bulls as a challenge and source of excitement, and the intentionality of his response could be described within that framework. This would have nothing to do with design in the sense of an immutable wired-in feature, but as an acquired set of rules and expectancies, an issue to which we will return later in this chapter.

In the second case the man in the field has not received the information about the bull and so there cannot be a response which has intentionality with respect to the bull.

The third type of account would apply if the animal were unfamiliar to the man, either from direct experience or through other sources of information, in which case he would not have the 'equipment' with which to respond. The experience of the bull would then fall outside the range of the information-processing capability of the man, and this would be another modified 'design stance' explanation.

There remains the possibility that function has been disrupted. This may have been the result of disease or trauma to one or more elements of the pathway linking perception and action. For instance, there may have been damage to the optic nerve, to the visual cortex, or he may have a condition that affects thinking or emotional responses. The damaging agents operate in the same ways as those that might disrupt the cardiovascular system. For instance, a blow to the head or a tumour may disrupt the functioning of the optic nerve by virtue of its physical force or pressure. The energy of the trauma does enter into the equation, no special receptors are required, and the system does not have a set of rules that underpin the representation of the trauma. If a blow to the head is the cause of injury to the optic nerve, there will be no requirement that the man 'saw it coming' or that he in any sense perceived the blow. Indeed it could have had the same effect if it were administered while he was asleep or under an anaesthetic. Here then, the cause of the disruption would be non-intentional and would depend crucially on the physical make-up of the nerve and the extent of the injury. Thus far we need make no reference to intentional processes; and only to physico-chemical laws. The significance of the physical injury would, however, depend upon the role of the molecules, atoms, or ions in the intentional system. If the change of physical state had no implications for functioning, then it would not be a significant injury, and equally a small change of physical state might have serious consequences. Here then, the envisaged link between the disruptive agent and the visual system does not entail intentional causality, but its significance does.

7.3.2 The experience of the individual

We turn next to the experience of the man in the field. In the straightforward case, he is likely to provide an explanation of his fear in similar terms to those that have been used by the observer. Common-sense, or folk psychology, accounts are close to those of intentional-causal explanations. He would be likely to explain similarly his lack of fear if he possessed an object such as a gun which made him feel safe. His explanation of those instances where he did not show fear, and there were no aspects of the circumstances that were hidden from the observer, are of great interest. Here, to a greater or lesser extent, the man is likely at the time to have been unaware of the cause of his lack of response. The Spanish bullfighter might, if asked subsequent to the event, say that when he was younger he was afraid of bulls, or that he knew of people who were afraid of bulls. Then he would be able to refer to a different set of rules in which bulls were seen as fearsome, but it would be crucial to his competence as a bullfighter that the contradictory sets of rules, 'I must fight' and 'I must run away' did not operate together if effective action were to ensue. We will return at length to the consequences of the operation of contradictory sets of rules in the next chapter.

If he did not see the bull, then only afterwards when we say something like 'You seemed very calm in the field with the bull', and he replies 'Oh my God was there a bull? I probably didn't see it as the sun was in my eyes', does the cause of the lack of fear become apparent. Where bulls fall outside the range of experience or knowledge of the man, at the time he will have nothing to report. Questioned afterwards he will report the perception but not its significance. Once the significance of bulls is explored, it is likely that he will be able to provide the explanation of his lack of fear.

The physical cause of disruption of vision is similar. The man is not aware that the disruption has occurred. It is, however, different in that neither can he perceive its origins. Although he has an intentional apparatus which perceives the sun as the origin of the blinding light, this is not the case for the physical agent. Thus he cannot give an account of the way in which his perceptual apparatus was disrupted. This is an example of the general principle, which is that non-intentional-causal agents have their effect without the awareness or the activity of the person, who has the experience of something happening to him. This follows from our observation that non-intentional-causal agents do not require sensory or information-processing facilities, which in relation to psychological functioning means forms of perception.

Before taking our example further, we will summarize the general points covered so far. Human psychological responses are explained in terms of states of mind which entail intentional-causal processes. These require internalized sets of rules and frames, and where responses are seen to be consistent with these, there will be many questions to be addressed about the origins and mechanisms, but there will not be doubt about the functioning of the system. Where the observer notes a discontinuity between the stimulus and the expected response then further questions will be asked. Answers may entail further information about circumstances, further information about the subject's perceptions, expectations or beliefs; or they may specify stimuli outside the range of the subject's perceptual or cognitive range; or there may be disruption of functioning. Where the apparent discontinuity has arisen from lack of information its provision will remove the discontinuity and provide an explanation of the apparent dysfunction. Where the stimulus is outside the range of functioning or there has been a disruption, then the discontinuity will remain. The subject, on interrogation, may be able to provide an account of the intentional origins of the discontinuity where, for instance, he was using a set of beliefs that were unknown to the observer. Where there has been disruption of the intentional processes, the origins of discontinuity will be outside the awareness of the subject, at the time, and on subsequent reflection.

7.3.3 Accounting for a change in behaviour

Now let us return to our example and consider a change of behaviour, for this eventually is one of the key issues to be addressed in the area of psychological disturbance. The man looks at the bull, he starts to sweat and look around for an escape route; suddenly he stops. Now the discontinuity is clearly a feature of the man in the field. Provided the observer is correct in assuming that up to the change of behaviour the man was responding appropriately, then we cannot postulate the modified design stance explanation whereby the stimulus is outside the range of the subject's experience or expectations. The explanation could still be that this is only an apparent discontinuity in that he believes, for instance, that the best strategy for dealing with the bull is first to show fear and then indifference. However, other possibilities are more likely. The first is that he has remembered, following the initial response, that the best strategy is not to show fear, and has put this into practice. In other words he has employed a new set of rules to govern the response. The second possibility is that he has acquired or discovered that he has an agent that makes the position safer. For instance, he has reached into his pocket and there has found a pistol. Thirdly, in a revision of the perceptual processes of the sort described earlier, he may have discovered that it is not a real bull, or only a Hereford bull. Fourthly, there may have been a disruption of his appreciation of the situation. Thus an agent which induced clouding of consciousness, such as epilepsy, or a drug administered unknown to him, could have been the cause. The general point is that disruptions or apparent disruptions in the account that can be given can arise from the intrusion or introduction of another set of rules, additional information, or a disruption of the intentional apparatus by a physical agent. In the latter case the search for further rules or information will not remove the disruption. Of crucial interest here is the fact that from the observer's point of view an apparent disruption in the rule-following may arise either from the interaction of sets of rules, or from the acquisition of new information by the subject, or a disruptive cause, and the extent to which the observer considers alternative sources of such rules or information, will influence his or her explanation.

7.4 LEVELS OF EXPLANATION AND THE REDUCTION OF MENTAL PROCESSES

We have seen that intentional causality makes reference to principles that are not found in chemistry and physics, but the operation of the principle takes advantage of physical processes to achieve their ends. Intentional causality is not reducible to the non-intentional where the system is functioning, but dysfunction can arise from disruption that can be explained at least in part by non-intentional-causal processes. There is implied in this analysis a concept of levels of functioning that needs to be spelt out in relation to psychological functioning.

Intuitively, it would seem, and many authors have proposed (Nagel 1961; Darnell *et al.* 1990), that a hierarchy of levels may be constructed which places physics at the bottom and proceeds via chemistry, biochemistry, physiology, and neuropsychology to psychology and psychiatry. This has led to a continuing discussion regarding the reducibility of mental processes (Fodor 1983; Putnam 1983; Dennett 1987; Hardcastle 1992). We have argued that if biological causality is not reducible to physico-chemical processes, then by the same argument neither will that branch of the biological, referred to as the psychological. The argument against reduction of the psychological therefore in part borrows from that in Chapter 5.

Many recent authors have also argued against the reduction of mental processes (e.g. Davidson 1980; Fodor 1983), but, as we have seen, the accompanying danger is that mental processes are stranded without a causal story, or one that separates them from other biological processes. However, once the case for the pervasiveness of intentional processes in biology is presented, then explanations of psychological processes are no more stranded than those of molecular biology. Nevertheless, we do need to be quite specific about what can and cannot be reduced, and how far. We need also to be clear about levels of causal processes, for we are not referring to distinctions such as those of mental versus non-mental, or neuroscience versus biochemistry. That would be to create a dualism (or multilevelism) that is totally at odds with our analysis. For instance a rapid heart beat is part of the intentional response of fear, and an erection is part of male sexual excitement. These physiological responses have intentionality with respect to the stimulus in just the same way as mental processes.

In one sense then, the concept of 'level' becomes redundant. This is, however, different from the concept 'level' that emerges from our proposition; one that is defined by the nature of the analysis of information. Just as intentional explanations cannot be reduced to chemistry and physics where the words and concepts have no parallel, so they cannot be reduced to a point where the rules of interpretation of information no longer exist. The location of this point will depend upon the way in which information is encoded, and the relevant rules are stored. Take the distinction between the neurosciences and psychology. These may be taken to denote different levels of explanation whereby one might be invoked to explain the other. In our analysis the relevant issue is, how is the representation and its link with action elaborated?

Often, this means that reduction will not be the appropriate way to characterize the link between the neurosciences and psychology (Hardcastle 1992). Thus the rules for transforming light from the bull into patterns of neuronal firing are present throughout the visual system and underpin the intentionality of the system with respect to features such as dark and light, orientation and movement. The specification of these rules belongs to the neurosciences. However, the determinant of the response is the perception of 'bull' or 'particular breed of bull' and this will require the representation of the person's knowledge of the bull also under a range of relevant beliefs and expectations about them. As we have argued earlier, such mental events are genuinely causal in the mediation of stimulus and response, and here it is clear that the response requires the internalized rules which underpin the perception and discrimination. The question of level of analysis relates only to the level at which such rules are present and capable of being utilized in perception and judgement.

The identification of level requires a specification of the intentional 'work' that is entailed. For instance, what would be entailed in envisaging a lower-level account of perceptions or beliefs? It would be necessary to specify how the same information could be represented without these psychological entities. This would, in effect, require a parallel system with the same ability as a psychological system but non-psychological. It would need to have access to the information derived from sources such as reading, talking, and direct experience, and it would have to partake of the generation of internalized rules, and of the movement among them, while not being psychological. Further, if we take consciousness to be a key feature of psychological functioning, and the monitoring of the wide range of internalized rules to be an important function of consciousness, this lower level activity would have to do without that facility to monitor movement among sets of rules. Thus in postulating a lower-level capability we would have to envisage it functioning without some of the capacity that appeared in our developmental account to be crucial to the handling of multiple sets of rules. It is likely that such a system would be inefficient and mistake-prone. Further, from our perspective, it would not do any explanatory work. To return to the fundamental point, 'level' here refers to level of intentional analysis and response, and this may correspond to a range of academic disciplines.

The interplay between different levels of intentionality may be illustrated using two further variations of the story of a man in the field with the bull. In the first he is not anxious, and there is no explanation, and when asked about it subsequently the man says he was surprised at his response because previously he had been very frightened by bulls. The explanation is that unknown to him he has been given a drug which reduces anxiety. This drug interrupts the intentional link between the stimulus, the perception, emotional and physiological responses, and the behaviour. It acts like other physical agents without the subject's perception.

Drugs are interesting agents in relation to the intentionality of physiological and biological systems. For instance, many antibiotics mimic the features of molecules that are important for the synthesis or division of bacteria, and hence fool the organisms into absorbing them. However, they do not perform the usual function of such molecules and the biochemistry of the bacteria is disrupted. In other words, they make use of intentional features to cause interruption.

Anxiety-reducing agents, such as beta-blockers, use the same principle. The molecules of these drugs are similar to those of the receptors for the naturally occurring transmitters. Interestingly, there is more than one receptor, and the effect of the transmitter differs depending on the nature of the receptor. The beta-blocker sits on beta-receptors so that the apparatus is effectively 'blinded'. The effects of the sympathetic nervous system transmitters to stimulate nervous impulses and hence sympathetic activity, which is a part of the anxiety response, are therefore decreased. Here then, the blockade has an intentional component in that the beta-blocker mimics to some degree the transmitter, but lacks the features required to stimulate a response. It therefore acts to deceive the system. If the receptor only accepted the correct molecule, that is, made finer discriminations, the blockade could not work. Function is disrupted because of the interruption of the intentional causal link. This is then observed and experienced as an interruption of the link between the bull and fear. That part of the link we call psychological has been interrupted and the effect of the drug does not entail psychological processes such as awareness and perception. Therefore in relation to psychological processes and the relevant information for them, there is a non-intentional-causal effect. However, inasmuch as sympathetic activity is also part of the intentional response to the bull, and the blockade requires mimicry at the receptor site, it performs the same function as that which a cardboard bull might if it were to deceive the man into being afraid.

The second case makes a different point. The man is in the field and there is no bull, or at least he hasn't seen it. Nevertheless he feels anxious and has a tachycardia. The explanation is that he has not eaten for some time, and is hypoglycaemic (has low blood sugar). In this case his state has intentionality with respect to glucose metabolism, but not anxiety-provoking agents. There is then an intentional cause of his state, but not in relation to anxiety-provoking agents. Inasmuch as he is not anxious about anything, the anxiety does not have an intentional cause. In this example we see the intrusion of the effect of intentional processes at one level (physiology) into another level, the psychological.

The purpose of these examples is to underline two rather contrasting points. The first is that the concept of levels of functioning is misleading if it obscures the extent to which responses with the same intentionality may occur at multiple levels. Equally, there are differences in levels of representation such that intentionality with respect to 'dangerous bull' has a different logic and degree of complexity than intentionality with respect to 'lack of glucose'.

7.5 DISORDER

We have, earlier in this chapter, considered the possibility that a medical condition might account for a disruption in the function of perceptions, emotional states, cognitions, or behaviours in response to the presence of a potentially dangerous animal. We turn now to the general description of illness or medical condition, before going on to psychiatric disorder. The definition of physical illness is not straightforward because, depending on the condition, different features such as pain, disability, or threat to life will be more or less prominent. However, frequently, abnormality of biochemistry or physiology will be crucial, and the concept of abnormality will refer to the elements of intentional-causal processes outlined in Chapter 5. Conditions such as diabetes, renal (kidney) failure, high blood pressure, and various endocrine conditions such as Addison's disease or Cushing's disease, entail their failure to regulate the relevant systems appropriately.

It is crucial to emphasize that frequently specification of the physical state of a system does not give the diagnosis. Take the example of a tachycardia (rapid pulse). This may have intentionality, for instance with respect to a decrease in atmospheric oxygen, or vigorous exercise. Thus if a physician were working in Cuzco (Peru) at a height of 12 000 ft, and a patient came to her with a pulse rate of 100, she would ask them how long they had been at this altitude. If the answer were 'one day' she might well look no further. This would be because she had made the judgement based on the normal functioning of a system that is able to detect a change of oxygen and respond with appropriate action. However if this were a long-term resident of the town she might look for another explanation. One possibility might be that a disturbance in the conducting mechanism of the heart could have led to the tachycardia, and this would have taken place via non-intentional-causal links. The tachycardia would not have intentionality with respect to the effective functioning of the cardiovascular system, and evidence of this disruption might be found in the form of an identifiable lesion.

The account of physical disorder is, however, not so straightforward, because in medical conditions non-intentional causality is seldom found in isolation from intentional causality. Indeed, it is one of the most striking features of living organisms that they detect and respond to agents such as infections or injuries, which may present threats to their integrity. They have available compensatory (intentional) responses. Take the example of blood-clot formation and the healing of tissues in response to injury. Here the injury that occurs by a non-intentional mechanism is detected and a response is elaborated that restores normal functioning. All of the criteria of intentional causality apply, but the stimulus is breakdown of functioning. In general, although we can point to pathology or noxious agents as the cause of breakdown, it is rare that this is seen in the absence of compensatory mechanisms. In the examples of healing, it is usually clear which components arise from the disruptive agent, and which are part of the compensatory mechanism (although scar tissue can cause considerable damage), but in other examples they may be closely related. For instance, a further explanation for a tachycardia might be that substantial blood loss has taken place, in which case the increased pulse rate forms part of an adaptive response to a fall in blood volume, which is designed to maintain blood pressure in the face of this reduced volume of circulating blood. In some susceptible individuals this tachycardia might lead to chest pain due to relative insufficiency of the oxygen supply to the heart, so that the clinical picture arises from a complex interplay of intentional and non-intentional causality. Where there is injury there also is compensation, and where there is threat there also is adaptation.

Another source of complexity arises from the fit between the organism and the environment. We noted in Chapter 5 that where intentional causality operates, there is a normal range of function that is defined in terms of fit between the system and the environment. Where this is the *milieu interieur* there is little scope for change, but where it is the external environment there is considerable scope. In general the environment relevant to the range of functioning will be that in which the animal evolved, 'the environment of evolutionary adaptiveness' (Bowlby 1969). It is evident that in Westernized societies the physical and social environment is substantially different from that in which humans evolved. It seems also that the nutritional environment is different and that this has consequences for physical health. It is not within our scope to examine the evidence for and against such explanations; however, the emerging role of diet in disease is illuminating. Research over the past 20 years has focused on the role of diet in the genesis of diseases of Western society such as large bowel cancer and coronary heart disease. Western diets differ from those of more traditional societies, in having less fibre and a higher proportion of animal fat. In some cases, such as those related to high transit times for low fibre food through the gut, there may be a toxic effect; in other words a non-intentional cause. However, in other cases, such as that of raised blood cholesterol, with its associated increased risk of coronary heart disease, there may be a greater demand placed on the regulatory system than that for which it was designed (and in which it has evolved), or an alteration of the setting of that mechanism. The mechanism would be that the intake of dietary animal fat is greater than that which can be metabolized without an increase of blood cholesterol, and the system is overloaded, or that there is, in effect, an adjustment of the normal level, that is to say of the one the system seeks to restore. In either case, intentional processes are important. Once the cholesterol has persisted at an abnormal level it may in turn lead to other processes that proceed beyond their normal range of functioning, and hence lead to atheroma (fat deposits in the blood vessels) and coronary heart disease. Similarly, the normal regulatory process for cholesterol may include exercise and in its absence the regulation may be impeded.

Mechanisms that entail functioning at the limits of the range of the intentional apparatus and alteration of setting can be illustrated through two further examples. Many individuals who live at high altitudes have a condition called polycythaemia, in which there is an increased number of red cells in the blood. This is a response of the red cell manufacturing system to lack of oxygen at altitude and therefore mediated through intentional-causal processes. However, these individuals also have an increased risk of stroke, a condition that arises from blockage of an artery to the brain consequent upon the thickness of the blood, and secondary to the polycythaemia. The explanation of the stroke therefore includes intentional and non-intentional causality. A mechanism which is adaptive over some ranges of oxygen levels, may be maladaptive when humans live under conditions which are near the limits of their physiological design.

An alteration in the 'setting' of the system is seen in sufferers with chronic lung disease who often have a permanently raised level of carbon dioxide in their blood, to which their brains have become accustomed. When there is a worsening of the condition, usually because of chest infection, the carbon dioxide level rises and they become more breathless. Thus the intentional system continues to work, but over a different range. The aim of treatment is to return the patient to his or her previous state, including the previous carbon dioxide level in the blood and not to a more general normal level.

In summary, we may say that medical illnesses are characterized by disruption of functioning which often entails an interplay between intentional and non-intentional-causal processes. These processes are equally physiological but radically different. The intentional processes entail causal links in which there may be correct or incorrect responses, there is rule-following, there is a detection apparatus with rules for the interpretation of events, there is a range of functioning, there is effective action, and there could be deception. Explanations such as those involving a blow to the head or laceration of a blood vessel are also physiological but do not entail any of these elements, and refer to the disruption of the integrity of the intentional system.

7.6 PSYCHIATRIC DISORDER

7.6.1 The definition of psychiatric disorder

Over the past 20 years there has been a substantial international effort to create a effective classification of psychiatric and psychological disorder. The two principal systems, those of the World Health Organization (1992) and the American Psychiatric Association (1994) have provided detailed criteria for disorder, and research questionnaires and interviews based on them have been developed. These have introduced substantial comparability among studies of psychiatric conditions. However, a number of problems remain unresolved, and it is important to review these briefly before going on to the explanation of psychiatric disorder.

First, the definitions of psychiatric syndromes are, in many respects, arbitrary. For instance, definitions of depression differ over the symptoms that are required, their duration, and whether they have to be associated with impaired functioning before a diagnosis is made.

Secondly, 'comorbidity' between psychiatric conditions is very common. People with one psychiatric condition often have two or more (Cloninger *et al.* 1990). For instance, depression and panic disorder are classified separately but they occur together commonly (Andrade *et al.* 1994). Clearly this could deflect two or more conditions with a common cause, or that one condition confers vulnerability for another, or that there is a lack of distinctiveness between the hypothesized diagnostic categories.

Thirdly, it is not clear that psychiatric disorders are best captured by a categorical model. This assumes that the subject either has a condition or he/she has not. Clearly this is appropriate where there is a definable pathology with a clear clause, which is the case for many medical conditions. However, most psychiatric conditions may also be satisfactorily characterized by scores on a dimension such as depression, anxiety, or aggression.

Fourthly, even when the syndrome definition may appear to be reasonably satisfactory, the condition may be heterogeneous. For instance, it has been argued that schizophrenia may be heterogeneous, with genetic and environmental factors playing a role to different extents in different subgroups (Murray *et al.* 1985, 1991).

It may be that these difficulties will prove so substantial that a quite different approach to psychological disorder will be required. It is more likely that the classification system will be modified gradually. We are interested here to understand what it has borrowed from medicine and what are the *implied* causal processes.

Psychiatric diagnoses are generally characterized by a mixture of 'abnormal' beliefs, experiences, emotions, or behaviours, and often include impaired social functioning as part of the definition. These features are referred to as symptoms, with the implication that they signify illness or disease. Thus psychiatry has borrowed from general medicine the concept of symptom constellations with clearly identifiable pathologies. This has been supported by medical findings of the early twentieth century:

> ... the clinical correlations between postmortem pathological findings and the behavioural sequelae of strokes, and the identification of the basis of general paresis (syphilis) filled the imagination of a generation of psychiatrists who believed that the application of such approaches would yield similar results for other psychiatric conditions. (Tsuang 1993.)

The conditions referred to here are clearly the result of a disruption of functioning by a physical agent. The explanation of a discrete condition could be provided by reference to a non-intentional cause, together with the functioning of the system in which there is a specification of the role of blood supply to, or neuronal circuits in, the brain.

Thus psychiatric classification has borrowed the assumption that intentionality has run out, that there has been a disruption of functioning, and that a non-intentional-causal process is responsible. Let us review the requirements that this is the case. There will be a disruption of the intentionality of states of mind or behaviours in relation to external stimuli, or in relation to previous behaviour, or both. There must be an identifiable disruptive agent that is absent in subjects who do not show this condition and in those that do prior to its onset, and this agent should have identifiable physical properties, such that a mechanism for the prediction of mental states or behaviours via bridge conditions can be envisaged. It will be evident as we consider a range of examples that these conditions are not met for any psychiatric diagnosis, but that some elements of the requirement may be present in some conditions.

7.6.2 The disruption of intentionality

Our analysis starts with a further consideration of the intentionality of mental states and behaviour. In one sense the judgement about intentionality looks as though it might be rather uncertain. After all, an extensive analysis of the man in the field with the bull was based upon the judgement of the observer as to what might be expected. If that judgement is highly individual, then my analysis and yours may differ substantially, and our capacity to describe what is going on will be limited. However, for most purposes our judgements of the expected behaviour of others is good, because we are good at guessing at their thoughts, attitudes, and emotions. Indeed, if it were not so, our capacity to cope socially would be very limited as we would not be able to predict the behaviour of others, nor moderate our behaviours in relation to the expectations of others. We are generally good monitors of the intentionality of other people. (Some indication of the consequences of a deficit in this ability may be seen in conditions such as autism or Asperger's syndrome, where the capacity to understand the rules of social interaction and the likely state of mind of others is limited. Sufferers make serious errors in social situations and require special educational and social supports. Many are of average or above-average intelligence and so it seems that the capacity to understand the intentionality of others is distinctively different from that of a general problem-solving capacity (Hobson 1993).)

The judgement of the intentionality of possible psychiatric disorder, such as anxiety or depression, may not be as straightforward as that of the man in the field. Where symptoms follow a major loss, such as the death of a close relative or friend, the link will be clear. Suppose, however, that the depressed mood and associated difficulties, such as poor concentration, poor sleep, and lack of appetite, come on apparently unexpectedly. From the perspective of the sufferer the episode has the characteristics of an illness, in which he/she is the passive recipient of a state which has intruded inexplicably into his/her life. One possibility is that the depression has intentionality that was not immediately apparent to the person. George Brown and Tirril Harris and colleagues have made an explicit approach to this possibility through the investigation of life events and depression in women (Brown and Harris 1978; Brown 1989). In measuring life events they assumed that their meaning would be important, and they operationalized this in terms of the extent of contextual threat. Threat was taken to be comprised of a combination of the nature of the event and the circumstances of the person, so that the same event could have a different rating of threat depending on circumstances. In order to avoid the possible 'colouring' effect of depressed mood, their ratings were made by trained researchers who were given details of the event and the circumstances, but not whether the person had become depressed. These assessors made a rating based on what might be expected under those circumstances. Thus the method explicitly assumed that there exist general sets of rules of perception and interpretation of events, provided circumstances can be specified adequately. The prediction of depression was strongest where there was a combination of vulnerability factors such as lack of confiding partner, and life events. Brown and Harris have not reported on the extent to which the women in their studies themselves believed these factors were important; however, they showed that for a substantial group of women with depression there may be intentionality with respect to current adversities and circumstances. (We say 'may be' because some evidence indicates that the association between provoking agents and depression may be due to a 'third variable', namely an influence that leads both to increased life events and depression (McGuffin *et al.* 1988). This does not, however, undermine the strategies used by Brown and Harris in the investigation of the intentionality of depression.)

If these findings endure, will it mean that depression should not be considered a psychiatric condition? Clearly other factors, such as the extent of distress or inability to function adequately, will be relevant to that judgement. However, they do indicate that in some cases the assumption of disrupted intentionality, which has been borrowed from the concept of illness, may not be appropriate.

A second approach to the ascertainment of intentionality was that of Jaspers (1963) who sought to drive a wedge between meaningful and causal connections, and argued that meaningful connections are accessed for the self through introspection and in others through empathy. Our concept of intentional causality is much wider than that of Jaspers' concept of meaningful connections; however, our approach has much in common with his. He proposed that some beliefs, both normal and abnormal, were understandable in the context of the person's history and beliefs and current circumstances. These were to be contrasted with primary delusions which are direct, intrusive, unmediated by thought, and not understandable. Jaspers defined personality as, 'the term we give to the individually differing and characteristic totality of understandable connections in any one psychic life' (Jaspers 1963, p. 428), and against this background a primary delusion is one that intrudes into and distorts existing understandable connections (Walker 1991). Jaspers is here making two claims together; that the question of understandability is central, and that it can be resolved by reference to the form of the mental phenomenon. The latter claim remains uncertain. Schneider proposed that 'first rank symptoms', ones which are least likely to be understandable, will demarcate schizophrenia from other psychotic disorders (Schneider 1959). These first rank symptoms are, however, found in association with other symptom constellations which are not typical of schizophrenia, and their utility is not proven. Nevertheless, within Jaspers' framework the use of understandability is clearly central to the determination of the intentionality of mental states and behaviours.

7.6.3 Non-intentional-causal explanations

An alternative approach to the question of intentionality and disorder may be made from the other end of the hypothesized causal chain. If possible candidates for non-intentional causation of psychiatric disorder could be identified, then perhaps a non-intentional explanation would be supported. Depression provides us with an example of a condition in which a wide range of candidates for such an explanation has been identified. These have included neuroendocrine abnormalities in the regulation of thyroid and adrenal functioning. The results have, however, been rather inconsistent, and have not discriminated consistently between depressed and non-depressed adults. Let us suppose that further research provides firmer evidence for an association between endocrine abnormalities and depression. What would we require if they were playing a causal role? At least that the administration of the relevant hormone increased the risk of depression, that a reduction in the circulating hormone was associated with remission, and that where people became depressed the changes in hormone level preceded the mood changes.

Some supporting evidence comes from Cushing's syndrome. Here the pituitary gland at the base of the brain produces excess adrenocorticotrophic hormone (ACTH) which stimulates the adrenal gland to produce excess corticosteroids. There is a non-intentional cause of the increased steroids. Depression is seen in roughly half the cases of Cushing's syndrome and usually remits after treatment for the Cushing's disease (Kelly *et al.* 1980). Thus increased corticosteroids *may* have a causal role in depression, but given that Cushing's syndrome is a very rare cause of depression, unless there exists a more covert form of the disease, it is not the usual explanation.

Numerous studies have demonstrated an association between depression and abnormalities in the regulation of corticosteroids (Checkley 1992). Mere association between hormonal changes and depression will not, however, provide us with the causal story. Altered corticosteroid levels may be a consequence either of other causally relevant factors or they may form part of the physiological component of the depressive syndrome. It has been demonstrated in animals that corticosteroid levels in the blood rise in response to stress, and this introduces (the as yet untested) possibility that an increase in corticosteroids might provide part of the intentional-causal link between stressful life events and depression (Checkley 1992). Such a possibility serves to underline, yet again, that in an examination of intentional- and non-intentional-causal links the division between psychological and physiological, or mental and neuroendocrine, ceases to be appropriate.

Two further examples make the point. Patients with panic attacks have been shown, using positron emission tomography, to have significant increases in cerebral blood flow in a number of regions of the brain during lactate (chemically) induced attacks. It would be tempting, therefore, to deduce that the altered cerebral blood flow represents a non-intentional cause of the panic attacks. However, normal individuals during states of anticipatory anxiety (when awaiting an unpleasant stimulus) have also been shown to have significant increases in cerebral blood flow in identical regions of the brain (Reiman *et al.* 1989). Here the altered cerebral blood flow was a consequence of the state of anxiety, or at least an integral part of it, and the mechanism entailed intentional causality. In the case of the patients, the altered cerebral blood flow may have been a cause, consequence, or integral part of the anxiety state, which was induced by a non-intentional-causal route. One possible explanation could bring the findings together along the lines of: repeated episodes of anxiety for which there are intentional-causal explanations, could lead to an altered sensitivity of cerebral blood vessels (in other words an altered setting of the cerebral blood vessels) to the blood chemistry, and that this instability might lead to the triggering of alterations of cerebral blood flow, possibly when the acidity of blood changed, giving rise to further episodes of panic. This explanation would invoke an intentional explanation with respect to anxiety, leading to alterations of the physiology of cerebral blood vessels, with consequent panic episodes of non-intentional origin with respect to anxiety.

A similar mechanism may well operate in the association between levels of aggression and raised levels of male hormones in young men. In non-human primates, individuals who are dominant within a troop show a rise in androgen levels in response to a challenge, and socially dominant non-aggressive delinquent boys have higher levels of androgens in their blood than less-dominant peers (Ehrenkranz *et al.* 1974). It seems then that androgen levels may *reflect* social position and behaviour, and there is an intentional-causal explanation. However, delinquent aggressive boys have higher levels of androgens than either of the other two non-aggressive delinquent groups. These levels may simply reflect the aggression, or it may be that androgen levels were, in the first place, increased as a consequence of their social behaviour, and this in turn led to, or contributed to, aggressive behaviour. This would mean that there was an intentional-causal link for the raised androgens, which in turn contributed to the level of aggression via a non-intentional-causal route.

7.6.4 Interactions between intentional- and non-intentional-causal processes

We have seen so far that our investigation of intentional- and non-intentional-causal links will need to focus on mental states and behaviours and their relationship with preceding or concurrent events, and on the physiological accompaniments of these states and behaviours. Throughout, the analysis will be of the extent of, and possible disruption of, intentionality. We can illustrate this further by reference to the same mechanisms as those that we considered earlier in relation to physical conditions. First there was the role of compensation in response to non-intentional disruption. Such a mechanism might operate in schizophrenia. Neuropsychological theories of schizophrenia have postulated that sufferers have difficulty in sorting out which features of a situation should be attended to, and which can be taken for granted or are irrelevant (Gray *et al.* 1991). They therefore have to deal with more uncertainty than most people. One possible explanation for the fixed ideas of delusions is that they create certainty, and that because testing or questionning these beliefs would open the person to substantial uncertainty, a better strategy is to insist on their truth. Support for the proposal that delusions have a value to individuals, comes from a study by Roberts (1991). He compared patients who were deluded with a group that had recovered from delusions, and comparison groups of psychiatric nurses and trainee priests. The deluded patients and those who had recovered showed marked contrasts. The deluded scored much higher than the recovered patients on a measure of meaning and purpose in life, and were less depressed with fewer suicidal ideas. In all the measures, the deluded patients resembled closely the nurses and the trainee priests. This study suggests that symptoms may have intentionality with respect to difficulties, of which cognitive deficits would be one example. We will consider this in more detail in Chapter 9.

Next we reviewed mechanisms that entailed functioning beyond the normal range. 'Normal' here referred to the environment of evolutionary adaptiveness and the design features of the organism. A similar mechanism may be envisaged in the case of schizophrenia. Numerous studies have shown that individuals with schizophrenia are more likely to relapse if they are living in a family where there is a high level of expressed emotion, which is characterized by high levels of criticism, hostility, or overinvolvement. Cross-cultural studies have demonstrated that the level of expressed emotion is lower in non-Westernized societies, such as that of rural India, and that schizophrenia runs a more benign course in these societies (Kuipers and Bebbington 1988). Putting the neuropsychological theory and these findings together, it may be that information-processing which has been adaptive in environments experienced during evolution, is not adequate in the altered interpersonal climate of contemporary Western societies.

Finally, we considered mechanisms which entail alterations in the 'setting' of the system. These may be considered alterations of the design features such that responses have intentionality, but over a different range. For instance, there is good evidence that psychotic episodes are linked to life events as well as to high expressed emotion (Norman and Malla 1993). Equally, only a minority of individuals who are exposed to these experiences develop psychotic episodes. It may be that the critical issue is the level of stress that can be handled, and that for some individuals the threshold is low and for others high for responding with psychotic symptoms. Those with a low threshold may have a design fault with non-intentional origins, but episodes are provoked via an intentional-causal mechanism.

7.7 GENETICS, 'DESIGN', AND DISORDER

7.7.1 Introduction

We have referred in earlier chapters to 'design fault' as one type of origin of disorder. In doing this we have made use of the framework described in Chapter 1 and outlined by Dennett (1987). Thus far Dennett's proposal *re* design and the chess-playing computer has served us well. We return to it at this point because, in the light of our discussion of intentional causality and development, it requires some additions and some modifications. The concept of 'design' provided a useful framework against which intentionality could be understood to have run out. Further, design stance explanations might seem to resemble genetic explanations. By analogy with the chess-playing computer it might be that in human psychological development the design would refer to genetically determined, 'hard-wired' constitutional factors. The match between these and the demands of the environment would then provide us with part of the description of function, and design faults with part of the explanation of disorder. However, neither the application of the concept of design, nor the operation of genetic influences are so straightforward.

7.7.2 Dennett, development, and design

The concept of design

In order to examine this we need to start by explicating the meaning of the term 'design'. We will follow Dennett in considering a non-biological example, but one that is adapted to a rather more extensive range of conditions than the chess-playing computer, the aeroplane. The term 'design' refers to a number of features of construction and operation. First, it refers to the objective of the construction of the object, namely that it should be able to fly. Just as in the biological examples, this leads immediately to criteria for normal or correct design and construction and to criteria for mistakes. Secondly, it refers to the means by which this will be achieved, and therefore to the functioning served by components and their intentionality. Thirdly, it provides a specification in relation to the environment. Here this might include temperature, wind speeds, height of flying, and length of runways. The physical construction can be judged only in relation to these environmental demands. Fourthly, the design refers to what goes in at the outset, in the construction, and remains constant. It therefore provides a reference point against which any particular event can be judged. Fifthly, it has a high degree of generality in that it covers most or all of what the aeroplane is up to. We can see that in many respects this analysis conforms with that implied by Dennett's chess-playing computer. Nevertheless, the complexity of the computer may obscure the extent to which its functioning is defined very narrowly. Its relationship to the environment is defined by a keyboard input and by an agent that understands the rules of chess. This is in marked contrast to the range of environments that might be encountered by the aeroplane, or indeed by a biological organism. Dennett's example does not contradict this, but it may obscure it, and it is crucial at this stage to bring out the relationship of 'design' to complex environments.

Biology and design

How might the concept of 'design' stand up in relation to human psychological functioning? We can examine this using the 'method' used so far in the book. We first require that it works in non-psychological biological examples on the grounds that it must work here if it is to succeed with psychological functioning, and then examine it in relation to the observation that psychological functioning is subject to development during which there is a complex interplay between person and environment. This will lead to a consideration of design in relation to multiple sets of rules, and the generation of these within human functioning.

Taking examples from previous chapters, the term 'design' could be applied to the cardiovascular system, the genetics of protein synthesis, or the visual system. In each of these it would refer to the purpose of the system, and to the means by which it is achieved. The means would include the specification of the rules, and the convention and agreement within the signalling and control systems. As we have seen earlier, the environments of the cardiovascular system and the DNA are the *milieu interieur* which have further links with the external world, and that of the visual system is the external world. The example of haemoglobin and sickle-cell disease provided an illustration of the intimate relationship between structure, function, and environment in the definition of 'correct' or 'incorrect', and these could all be taken to be aspects of 'design'. As in the example of the aeroplane the 'design' of these biological examples will often refer to what is there from the start, and what remains constant, although in more complex perceptual systems this may not be the case. Finally, the design can be taken to refer to the functioning of the system in general. It would seem then that the concept of 'design' will apply to many biological systems, and it is entirely compatible with our analysis of intentional causality.

Design and 'wiring'

The position is rather different when we come to development and multiple sets of rules. How are we to interpret the notion of what is 'wired in', stable, and general? Take first the issue of wiring. In human development, in contrast to that of other organisms, the neuronal connections of the brain develop substantially after birth (Changeux 1985). Evidence from animal experiments, where postnatal neuronal development is more limited, indicates that neuronal connections are influenced by experience. Hubel and Wiesel (1962) showed that cats or monkeys that have been reared with one eye sutured closed have no vision in that eye and there is shrinkage of the area of the lateral geniculate body devoted to that eye, with a corresponding diminution in the number of branches sent by the deprived cells to the cortex. At the cortex there is a shift in the number of connections from the deprived to the non-deprived eye. This effect is seen only following monocular deprivation in the first 3 months of life, and after that age even extended periods of deprivation seem to have little effect. Furthermore, the effect of environment on neurodevelopment can be quite specific. Blakemore and Cooper (1970) showed that kittens raised in environments in which there were only horizontal stripes are blind to other orientations, and this is reflected in the preferential responses of neurons in the visual cortex. Human infants show a loss of visual capacity in an eye that has been subject to 'monocular deprivation', for instance where there is a squint. It is probable that this is accompanied by similar brain changes to those demonstrated in cats and monkeys. It seems therefore likely that, given the greater level of postnatal development of neuronal connections in humans during the first years of life, there may be a similar process whereby connections that are required for a wide range of psychological functioning are influenced by environmental experiences. Wiesel (1982) wrote:

> ... deprivation experiments demonstrate that neuronal connections can be modulated by environmental influences during a critical period of postnatal development. We have studied this process in detail in one set of functioning properties of the nervous system, but it may well be that other aspects of brain function, such as language, complex perceptual tasks, learning, memory and personality, have different programmes of development. Such sensitivity of the nervous system to the effects of experience may represent the fundamental mechanism by which the organism adapts to its environment during the period of growth and development.

It seems then that the wiring might be influenced by organism—environment interaction through a process that is similar to learning. If we are to retain the concept of design, we will at least need to talk of a succession of designs each related to, but different from, the previous one, and we will need to understand the relationship between them, and the environment.

Design, stability, and generality

The question of stability brings us back to the generation of sets of rules and expectancies, and their role in providing the basis for action, and further testing of the rules in development. Theories of the development of intimate (attachment) relationships and of cognitive development have emphasized the interplay between internal mental models or schemata, and experience, whereby sometimes new evidence may be incorporated into existing schemata, and at others may contribute to the development of new ones. The implication is that the internalized general models will be more or less stable, depending on:

(1) the extent to which they are tested;
(2) the extent to which experience supports or undermines them;
(3) the extent of the person's need to hold on to them, for instance in order to maintain the basis for actions; and
(4) their general utility.

We will refer to points (1), (2), and (3) extensively in the next chapter as they provide an important basis for further considerations of disorder. However, we should note here, and will return to the point, that (4) has a resemblance to that made by Polanyi (1958) and Popper (1969) in relation to beliefs in the sciences. Theories or 'laws' will be held strongly and persist, even in the light of contradictory evidence, if their wider utility is great and there is nothing to replace them; indeed one might argue, provided they are effective in directing further action. So that we can say at this point that the candidates for the persistence of sets of rules or schema, especially those with great generality, may relate to considerations other than those of whether they are wired in.

The developmental story leads to further inroads into the straightforward concept of 'design'. Development clearly entails the generation of succeeding sets of rules, schemata, cognitive-affective models, and ways of interpreting and feeling. Developmentalists of diverse origins, including Freud, Klein, Erikson, Piaget, Kagan, Bowlby, and Stern, have all postulated such successions. Each has striven to articulate the *differences* in *general* frameworks within which children operate at different phases of development, and to provide an account of what links these. While not opposing this proposal, Rutter and Rutter (1992) have argued that in development the identification of what constitutes a continuity or discontinuity is not straightforward. Thus the emergence of a butterfly from a chrysalis preceded by a caterpillar is clearly in many respects a discontinuity, but in that the information for the butterfly is already present in the caterpillar this is a continuity. Indeed, it must be assumed that the design information for the butterfly is present in the caterpillar. Similarly the child may take one set of expectancies from an environment in which they were appropriate to one in which they are not. What might be generated then is a different set of expectancies and behaviours, that can be understood best as the outcome of the interactions between the previous ways of seeing things and the current environment. Where then does this leave the concept of design? Either that it will have to be reserved for those aspects of psychological functioning that are not subject to such changes, or it will be necessary to talk of successive designs. Our analysis must, however, go further in relation to multiple sets of rules. The chess-playing computer is just that until a further design feature is built it. But what of the chess-playing human being? Strikingly, he or she can perform that function for a relatively brief period, and simultaneously perform other functions, such as that of being a parent. Indeed, a feature of the behaviour of young children in play is the way they experiment with different 'designs'. Clearly it would be possible to subsume this under the overall description of a 'playful child', which might then be referred to in terms of the design. However, clinical experience suggests that if such a child were to experience a major trauma his/her play might decrease quite dramatically. Would we then refer to a 'new design' or revise the design to be 'playful child, sensitive to trauma'? The point is that in development and in maturity human psychological functioning operates under a range of sets of rules, schemas, or assumptions, all of which have some of the features attributed to design in machines or non-psychological biological systems. However, they vary in the extent of their generality and stability.

In summary, it seems that the concept of 'design' can provide a useful shorthand, and we will use it, together with the caveats reviewed here, in relation to examples of disturbance. However, the analysis presented earlier provides a different emphasis. It suggests that although rule-bound responses probably evolved in ways that have clear survival value, there is inherent in the use of rules a creative potential whereby goals and activities can have their own intrinsic value. In other words, if it is possible to see the same thing in many different ways, then those different ways of seeing may become the focus of interest, for instance in play. This is not to propose a mechanism but to point out that the freeing of sets of rules, assumptions, or ways of seeing, and of the accompanying emotional states and behaviours, from being wired in, has potential for the elaboration of goals which might not be essential to survival. Once psychological states are conceptualized in terms if rule-bound processes there is no prediction as to whether or not they are wired in, or to the extent to which they are the outcome of an interaction with the environment. Similarly, there is no prediction as to their stability or generality. They may be wired in and stable in the case of physiological and some psychological processes, or patterned in ways that are open to change. They may have great generality, or they may be quite specific. Thus it may be more valuable to talk of sets of rules governing internal models of relationships, beliefs, or patterns of emotional response, which have greater or lesser degrees of generality, are related to a greater or lesser extent to previous experiences, and are more or less stable.

7.7.3 Genetic influences

Genes and environment

Genetic influences enter into our account in a fascinating and somewhat paradoxical way. This arises from the frequent contrast that is made between genetic and environmental influences, as if each were a separate commodity that taken together could explain outcome. As we shall see, this may fit some particular cases but does not work well in the general analysis.

Our argument will again start with non-psychological examples. The genetic code contains information about structure and function, both of which have a close fit with the environment of the organism. Indeed, the analysis of the principles of intentional causality when applied to the perceptual apparatus, specified that the system must anticipate and detect key aspects of the environment. The performance then is that of the 'organism in the environment'. This means that what has to be understood is the process whereby structure and function relate to the environment, and in that sense the questions are not primarily or necessarily genetic.

We will return to the example of sickle-cell trait and sickle-cell disease. Under some atmospheric conditions it will be apparent that the inheritance follows a straightforward recessive pattern, and it might be understood purely as a genetic condition. However, in a country in which people lived at different altitudes it might emerge that the prevalence of the symptoms was substantially different in one area compared to another, thus indicating an important environmental effect. In one environment the contribution of the environment would be practically zero, but when comparing the two environments it would be substantial. Furthermore, the environments could differ substantially in all respects other than that of the pressure of oxygen in the air and make no difference, and similarly the two altitudes might be indistinguishable in all respects except for atmospheric oxygen and still make a major difference. Thus the feature of the environment that *matters* is that which is specified in the structure and function of the system, which in this example is directly and simply related to genetic structure. The contribution of the genetic influence could be elucidated *only* in relation to that structure and function.

Just as we saw in Chapter 5 that the physical contribution of the haemoglobin molecule does not provide a definition of 'fault', so the definition of genetic fault is not given by the physical fact. This is seen particularly clearly in the example where in one area of the world the sickle-cell trait confers resistance to malaria and so is advantageous. Thus the same physical fact may be either a deficit or advantageous depending on the relationship between the structure, function, and environment. Differences can be destructive or creative! That physical differences may have such contrasting consequences depending on the relationship between the structure, function, and environment may introduce some unwished for complexity; however, if they did not, we would be without a theory of the way in which mutations can have survival value.

The extent to which genetic influences have consequences that are environmentally sensitive varies. Some, it seems, are destructive of structure and function irrespective of environments; for instance those that give rise to cystic fibrosis or Huntington's chorea. Others, such as sickle-cell disease, cause symptoms and damage only under certain environmental conditions. When we come to human psychological functioning there are extensive possibilities for organism–environment interactions.

Genes and 'design'

As we have seen, the term 'design' describes well what is encoded genetically for the haemoglobin molecule, and 'design fault' refers to a difference that is stable and that interacts in a relatively straightforward manner with the environment. Where studies show greater concordance for a condition among those who are genetically more related than those who are genetically less similar, this may be interpreted as reflecting a design fault.

The interpretation of such studies in relation to human psychological functioning is not, however, so straightforward. To some extent this follows from our previous examination of the concept of 'design' in the developing person. In particular, we saw that the brain develops substantially after birth and that the interaction with the environment is probably very important. Most of the evidence comes from experiments with the visual system of cats and monkeys, in which it is evident that the development of the brain is related in very specific ways to environmental stimuli. It is possible that similar considerations apply to social development in some animals. Perhaps the strongest evidence for an effect of experience on 'wiring' comes from studies of imprinting and critical periods in birds and animals. Birds, such as geese, will become imprinted on to a moving object if they are exposed to it at a particular time early in development (Lorenz 1965). These objects are, in the environment of evolutionary adaptiveness, adult birds, but have included Konrad Lorenz and other humans, and other animals. The young birds then follow the animal or object on which they have been imprinted. Imprinting takes place only over a defined (critical) period, and if exposure does not occur at this time, imprinting does not take place. It seems likely that the critical period is determined by a neurodevelopmental process, and that the identity of the object of the imprinting is then similarly wired in. In lower animals the stimulus acts only as a releaser of the imprinting and its qualities are relatively unimportant; however, in higher animals, such as monkeys, the quality of the experience matters. Newborn monkeys exposed to punitive artificial 'maternal' figures show increased clinging behaviour (Harlow 1961). Monkeys reared in social isolation for the first 6 years of their life have been shown to display substantial and persistent abnormalities of social and sexual behaviour in adult life (Harlow and Harlow 1969). An effect of early social experience on brain development would be difficult to demonstrate in monkeys, and probably impossible in humans. However, it is possible that early social experiences may affect brain development. As we have seen, at about 9 months the infant forms selective attachments and this is a phenomenon seen throughout a wide range of cultures. Assessments of the quality of attachments during this period have substantial predictive capability up to 10 years later (Sroufe *et al.* 1990), which suggests that a relatively enduring 'design' feature is established early in life. In a study of children who were in institutions for the first 4 years of their lives, and then adopted, Hodges and Tizard (1989) showed that in adolescence these early institutionalized individuals still had interpersonal difficulties. This was in spite of the very advantageous circumstances of their adoptive homes. This does not demonstrate an effect of early experiences on the 'wiring' of the brain but is consistent with it.

Whatever the role of external environmental experiences in brain development, it is clear that the genetic code cannot specify the wiring of the brain. It is striking that only 1 per cent of the human genome differs from that of the ape, which suggests that the enormous differences in intellectual, aesthetic, and interpersonal capabilities are encoded in a general strategy for brain development which unfolds in relation to experience. There is substantial evidence that this proceeds via the creation of an internal environment in which a complex signalling process guides the formation of neuronal connections (Jones and Murray 1991). It is possible that, as Wiesel proposed, this internal environment takes its cues from the external; after all, the function of the brain is to mediate through beliefs, emotions, and actions, between internal and external worlds (Hundert 1988).

Genetics, development, and disorder

Now we turn to the interpretation of studies of genetic influences on development and disorder. Until recently, strategies for the assessment of genetic influences have used predominantly twin and adoption studies. Although there has been some criticism of these, much of the evidence for genetic influences has been derived from such studies. Both strategies depend upon the comparison of groups that can be predicted to differ in a consistent way in their genetic make-up. Twin studies entail an estimation of the co-occurrence of a condition in both twins (concordance) and a comparison of identical (monozygotic) and non-identical (dizygotic) twins. If there is a difference in the concordance between the identical and non-identical twins, this is taken to reflect the extent of genetic influence. This is based on the assumption that twins in general have a shared environment, and that higher concordance among monozygotic twins will reflect the fact that genetically, they are identical. There is now considerable evidence that twins do not experience identical environments in the same family, and so the interpretation will become more complex (Plomin and Daniels 1987; Goodman 1991). Adoption studies compare the rate of a disorder in children of parents with that disorder who have been adopted, with other adopted children whose parents do not have this disorder. A significant difference between the two groups is taken to result from genetic factors. This method also has its limitations. For instance, adopted children may not be representative of the wider population of the children of parents with the disorder. It could be that the parents of children who are adopted have a variant of the condition that is more severe or has some different features, compared with parents whose children are not adopted. This may not therefore provide an examination of wider genetic mechanisms in the condition.

We will focus on issues that arise from our earlier discussion. In the account of the intentionality of behaviour there cannot be a specification of the environment independent of the selective perceptions, needs, and functioning of the organism. This means that genetic influences will be definable only in relation to specific aspects of the environment. Let us consider this point in relation to twin studies. This method requires first the identification of an affected twin, and then the assertainment of whether the other has the condition. If environmental factors play a part in the genesis of the condition, then it is possible that by identifying an affected twin one is at the same time identifying a particular environmental feature. This would then mean that the comparison of monozygotic and dizygotic twins was a study of genetic influences under certain environmental conditions. By environment, we mean not the general characteristics of families and other important social influences, but those which matter to the condition. For instance, adoption studies of schizophrenia suggest that there is a genetic effect but only where the adoptive parents show particular characteristics (Tienari 1990). Given the care with which adoptive families are generally chosen, it is unlikely that this represents global dysfunction, but rather specific features of relevance to the condition. Where such a specific feature is influential, it may contribute to the genesis of vulnerability early in development; that is to say, through a relatively persistent design difference; or in the presence of such a vulnerability it may affect whether the condition is manifest. The extent of specificity in the fit between organism and environmental features means that genetic studies have to specify environments quite precisely.

As we saw earlier in our discussion of the concept of design, a physical difference may have design implications, depending on function, and a design difference may, under some conditions, lead to a functional deficit, and in others confer advantage. The difference between genetic fault and useful mutation is not given by the physical fact but by the organism and environment fit. Thus the investigation of genetic vulnerability will not be straightforward. Let us suppose that the quality of 'sensitivity to others' is a genetically determined trait. This trait would include an awareness of the state of mind of others, and a concern about it, combined with a difficulty in ignoring other people. This is likely to be an asset in a family where there is mutual concern and respect, but a disadvantage where there is discord and violence. The trait might emerge as a valuable quality in a study of the normal range of family functioning, and an inherited 'vulnerability' in a study that included adverse family environments.

The concept of range of function is of relevance to our discussion. As we have seen, in some cases quite specific aspects of the environment may influence outcome. However, the environmental demands may be so great that avoidance of disorder requires an exceptional capacity to cope. This is likely to be the case where there is parental violence or physical or sexual abuse. Then genetic studies may find no apparent effect because genetic differences are overwhelmed by a level of adversity that is outside of the range normal psychological experience. The effects of such traumas will provide an important focus for the next chapter. Conversely, there may be detectable genetic effects whose operation is quite different from those seen in studies of less severe experiences. The genetics of resilience may be different from the genetics of vulnerability.

Finally, intentionality entails representation and action. This opens up important interactional possibilities in the relationship between genetic influences and environmental factors. This is illustrated by the role of attachment in development. It is probable that the security of attachment of the young infant (see p. 250) is related to the contribution of the mother or other principal caregiver, but maternal behaviour is also influenced by the temperamental characteristics of the infant. Given the genetic influences in temperament, it is likely that the security of attachment is related to genetic processes via temperament and maternal behaviour. In turn, securely attached infants are treated differently by teachers later in life (Sroufe *et al.* 1990). So they continue to have an effect on their environment. Thus a twin study might find a significant genetic effect, but in the absence of an examination of developmental processes, might omit crucial elements in the story.

7.8 'BIOLOGICAL' PSYCHIATRY AND PSYCHOLOGY

In psychiatric research the field of biological psychiatry has expanded rapidly, and although the causal assumptions are rarely spelt out, 'biological' here is generally taken to refer to the disruptive effect of biochemical or neuroendocrine abnormalities on psychological functioning. Thus Scadding (1990) writes 'I will take it that "biology" is being used here to mean the study of living organisms directed towards explanation in physicochemical terms'. He goes on, 'some disorders of behaviour can already be explained in this way, and it is to be expected that with advances in knowledge, more and more of psychology and behavioural science will become biological'. These quotations come from an editorial in a leading psychiatric journal. The same journal contains an editorial by Guze (1989) entitled 'Biological psychiatry: is there any other kind?' in which he emphasizes that human evolution has been substantially the evolution of the brain and its capacity for thought, language, and culture. He acknowledges the complex interaction between individuals and the environment. He argues that in relation to psychiatry:

> [if] it could be asserted that few if any of the states or conditions that constitute the forms of psychiatry are the result of differences in the development or physiology of the brain, biology would be of only marginal interest. If it could be argued that all or most of our patients develop their disorders primarily, if not exclusively through normal learning processes, that are independent of human variability, the emphasis on biology might justifiably be seen as excessive and unjustifiable.

He goes on to suggest that, 'if environmental factors play a part in psychiatric conditions, these putative causes of psychiatric disorder seem to reflect only the normal range of human trouble that most people experience without becoming ill'. Later in the paper he writes, 'the conclusion appears inescapable to me that what is called psychopathology is the manifestation of disordered processes in various brain systems that mediate psychological functioning. Psychopathology thus involves biology'.

Reference to these papers has been included in some detail in order to indicate the particular ways in which the term 'biological' is being used. How does it stand up in relation to the analysis presented here? Let us first take Scadding's assertion, implied also by Guze, that 'biology' can be taken to refer to the study of living organisms 'directed towards explanation in physicochemical terms'. We have seen throughout that biology consists of the elucidation of the processes whereby environments are represented, functioning is regulated, and responses are elaborated. These processes have intentional properties and a level of abstraction, none of which is available in physico-chemical descriptions. The examples of DNA and protein synthesis were emphasized in order to highlight how the description in terms of molecules may distract us from paying proper attention to the information processing and representational processes.

Guze makes a central point of the explanation of disorder arising from differences in brain function. It should be pointed out that his assertion about the effects of environmental influences is incorrect and a considerable body of research has demonstrated the effects of childhood experiences on adult psychiatric functioning (Rutter *et al.* 1990; Bifulco *et al.* 1992). However, no developmentalist would argue that individual differences do not matter. The central issue is, what is the brain up to? As we have seen, it is crucially concerned with the elaboration of sets of rules, in the form of beliefs, wishes, fears, and of internal models of relationships. These may be more or less wired in. The extent to which this is the case has nothing to do with 'more or less biological'. Inasmuch as the brain elaborates these intentional processes, and the intentional processes are the explanations of behaviour, brain function has to be considered in relation to these processes. Just as the molecular mechanism that is employed to translate blood pressure into efferent impulses has to be described in terms of its successful transmission of the information, so the brain processes invoked in perception have to refer to the information transmitted to the visual cortex. According to the analysis presented earlier in Chapter 5, the biological view should not anticipate the relative importance of innate versus processes, nor can it predict the source of variation among individuals.

A third point concerns the distinction between function and dysfunction. Scadding appears to have assumed that because 'some disorders of behaviour' can already be explained in terms of physical agents, that 'with advances in knowledge more and more psychological and behavioural science will become biological'. We see here a failure to distinguish function from dysfunction which leads to an unjustified generalization from cases that involve breakdown to those that do not.

There is to be found in such analyses of 'biological psychiatry and psychology' an implicit reductionism or implicit dualism. Thus Scadding takes biology to refer to a study which will eventually yield physico-chemical descriptions, and Guze looks forward to a time when psychology and psychiatry will be replaced by neuroscience. However Guze, hinting perhaps that the enterprise might not work, argues that if learning turned out to be central to the origins of dysfunction, then psychiatry would have less need for neuroscience and more need for cultural anthropology, sociology, and social psychology. Presumably these are seen as 'non-biological' and therefore refer to aspects of brain function which are 'non-biological'. Ingold (1990), a social anthropologist, has argued that the effect of sociobiology has been to account for some phenomena as biological by reference 'down' to neurological structures, while explaining others with reference to culture, by implication a phenomenon that is non-biological. Once it is clear that intentional processes pervade biological systems, then biological psychiatry will expect to refer to disciplines such as anthropology and social psychology without abandoning the biological stance.

7.9 SUMMARY

We have now taken our account of intentional-causal processes into the explanation of adult human behaviour. As was the case with non-psychological and non-human examples, the description of the normal or functional response is inseparable from that of the abnormal or dysfunctional, and the key is the integrity of the intentional-causal process. In human psychological functioning this is more complex but the principles are the same.

The definition of psychiatric disorder is essentially descriptive and probably refers to a heterogeneous set of phenomena, but the apparent disruption of intentionality is central to its identity. The explanation may entail further, previously unidentified, intentional contributions, or disruption arising from a non-intentional-causal agent. In many respects psychiatric practice has borrowed from general medicine the assumption that in disorder intentionality has been interrupted, or run out, and in some instances this will be the case. In general, even where there is a non-intentional cause of breakdown, both in psychological and non-psychological systems there are compensatory, intentional-causal responses.

The interplay between intentional- and non-intentional-causal processes, and between developing individuals and specific environmental factors, are important in a consideration of genetic influences. The concept of genetically influenced 'design fault' is useful once it has been modified to take account of the developmental issues that we reviewed in Chapter 6. In the light of our analysis of causal processes, 'biological psychiatry' is seen to have made use of a restricted sense of the term 'biological'. Further, where it has assumed that biological processes are reducible to physics and chemistry, it has departed from an intentional-causal analysis which is needed both in biology and psychology.

REFERENCES

American Psychiatric Association (1994). *Diagnostic and statistical manual of mental disorders*, (4th edn). American Psychiatric Association, Washington, DC.

Andrade, L., Eaton, W. W. and Chilcoat, J. (1994). Lifetime comorbidity of panic attacks and major depression in a population-based study. Symptom profiles. *British Journal of Psychiatry*, **165**, 363–9.

Bifulco, A., Harris, T. O., and Brown, G. (1992). Mourning or early inadequate care? Reexamining the relationship of maternal loss in childhood with adult depression and anxiety. *Development and Psychopathology*, **4**, 433–49.

Blakemore, C. and Cooper, G. F. (1970). Development of the brain depends on the visual environment. *Nature*, **228**, 477–8.

Bowlby, J. (1969). *Attachment and loss: I. Attachment*. Hogarth Press, London.

Brown, G. W. (1989). Introduction: life events and measurement. In *Life events and illness* (ed. G. W. Brown and T. O. Harris). Guilford Press, New York.

Brown, G. W. and Harris, T. (1978). *Social origins of depression: a study of psychiatric disorders in women*. Tavistock Publications, London.

Changeux, J. P. (1985). *Neuronal man: the biology of mind*. Pantheon, New York.

Checkley, S. A. (1992). Neuroendocrine mechanisms, life events and depression. *British Journal of Psychiatry*, **160**, (Suppl. 15), 7–15.

Cloninger, C. R. *et al.* (1990). The empirical structure of psychiatric comorbidity and its theoretical significance. In *Comorbidity of mood and anxiety disorders*, (ed. J. D. Maser and C. R. Cloninger), pp. 439–62. American Psychiatric Press, Washington, DC.

Darnell, J., Lodish, H., and Baltimore, D. (1990). *Molecular cell biology*, (2nd edn). Freeman, New York.

Davidson, D. (1980). *Essays on actions and events*. Clarendon Press, Oxford.

Dennett, D. (1987). *The intentional stance*, pp. 43–68. MIT Press, Cambridge, Mass.

Ehrenkranz, J., Bliss, F., and Sheard, M. H. (1974). Plasma testosterone correlation with aggressive behaviour and social dominance in men. *Psychosomatic Medicine*, **36**, 469–75.

Fodor, J. (1983). *Representations: philosophical essays on the foundations of cognitive science*, pp. 127–45. MIT Press, Cambridge, Mass.

Goodman, R. (1991). Growing together and growing apart: the non-genetic forces on children in the same family. In *The new genetics of mental illness*, (ed. P. McGuffin and R. Murray), pp. 212–24. Heinemann Medical Books, Oxford.

Gray, J. A., Feldon, J, Rawlins, J. N. P., Hemsley, D. R. and Smith, A. D. (1991). The neuropsychology of schizophrenia. *Behavioural and Brain Sciences*, **14**, 1–84.

Guze, S. B. (1989). Biological psychiatry: is there any other kind? *Psychological Medicine*, **19**, 315–23.

Hardcastle, V. G. (1992). Reduction, explanatory extension, and the mind/brain sciences. *Philosophy of Science*, **59**, 408–28.

Harlow, H. F. (1961). The development of affectional patterns in infant monkeys. In *Determinants of infant behaviour*, (ed. B. M. Foss), Vol. 1. Methuen, London.

Harlow, H. F. and Harlow, M. K. (1969). Effects of various mother–infant relationships on rhesus monkey behaviours. In *Determinants of infant behaviour*, (ed. B. M. Foss), Vol. 4. Methuen, London.

Hobson, R. P. (1993). The emotional origins of social understanding. *Philosophical Psychology*, **6**, (3); 227–49.

Hodges, J. and Tizard, B. (1989). IQ and behavioural adjustment of ex-institutional adolescents. *Journal of Child Psychology and Psychiatry*, **30**, 53–75.

Hubel, D. H. and Wiesel, T. N. (1962). Receptive fields, binocular interaction, and the functional architecture in the cat's visual cortex. *Journal of Physiology*, **160**, 106–54.

Hundert, E. M. (1988). *Philosophy, psychiatry and neuroscience*. Clarendon, Oxford.

Ingold, T. (1990). An anthropologist looks at biology. *Man*, **25**, (2), 208–9.

Jaspers, K. (1963). *General psychopathology* (transl. J. Hoenig and M. W. Hamilton). Manchester University Press, Manchester.

Jones, P. and Murray, R. M. (1991). The genetics of schizophrenia is the genetics of neurodevelopment. *British Journal of Psychiatry*, **158**, 615–23.

Kelly, W. F., Checkley, S. A. and Bender, D. A. (1980). Cushing's syndrome, tryptophan and depression. *British Journal of Psychiatry*, **136**, 125–32.

Kuipers, L. and Bebbington, P. (1988). Expressed emotion research in schizophrenia: theoretical and clinical implications. *Psychological Medicine*, **18**, 893–909.

Lorenz, K. Z. (1965). *Evolution and modifications of behaviour*. University of Chicago Press, Chicago.

McGuffin, P., Katz, R., and Bebbington, P. E. (1988). The Camberwell Collaborative Depression Study: III. Depression and adversity in the relatives of depressed probands. *British Journal of Psychiatry*, 152, 775–82.

Murray, R. M., Lewis, S., and Reveley, A. M. (1985). Towards an aetiological classification of schizophrenia. *Lancet*, i, 1023–6.

Murray, R. M., Jones, P., and O'Callaghan, E. (1991). Fetal brain development and later schizophrenia. In *The childhood environment and adult disease*, CIBA Foundation Symposium 156, pp. 155–70. Wiley, Chichester.

Nagel, E. (1961). *The structure of science*. Routledge and Kegan Paul, London.

Norman, R. M. G. and Malla, A. K. (1993). Stressful life events and schizophrenia. I: A review of the literature. *British Journal of Psychiatry*, 162, 161–6.

Plomin, R. and Daniels, D. (1987). Why are children in the same family so different from one another? *Behavioural and Brain Sciences*, 10, 1–60.

Polanyi, M. (1958). *Personal knowledge: towards a post-critical philosophy*. Routledge and Keegan Paul, London.

Popper, K. R. (1969). *Conjectures and refutations*, (3rd edn). Routledge and Kegan Paul, London.

Putnam, H. (1983). Reductionism and the nature of psychology. In *Mind design: philosophy, psychology, artificial intelligence*, (ed. J. Haugland), pp. 205–19. MIT Press, Cambridge, Mass.

Reiman, E. M. *et al*. (1989). Involvement of temporal poles in pathological and normal forms of anxiety. *Journal of Blood Flow and Metabolism*, 9, (Suppl. 1), S589.

Roberts, G. (1991). Delusional belief systems and meaning in life. *British Journal of Psychiatry*, 159, (Suppl. 14), 19–28.

Rutter, M. and Rutter, M. (1992). *Developing minds: challenge and continuity across the life span*. Penguin, London.

Rutter, M., Quinton, D., and Hill, J. (1990). Adult outcome of institution reared children: males and females compared. In *Straight and devious pathways from Childhood to adulthood*, (ed. L. Robins and M. Rutter), pp. 135–57. Cambridge University Press, Cambridge.

Scadding, J. G. (1990). The semantic problems of psychiatry. *Psychological Medicine*, 20, 243–8.

Schneider (1959). *Clinical Psychopathology* (transl, by M. W. Hamilton), Grune and Stratton, New York.

Sroufe, L. A., Egeland, B., and Kreutzer, T. (1990). The fate of early experience following developmental change: longitudinal approaches to individual adaptation in childhood. *Child Development*, 61, 1363–73.

Tienari, P. (1990). Genes, family environment or interaction? Findings from an adoption study. In *Etiology of mental disorder*, (ed. E. Kringlen, N. Lavik, and S. Torgersen), pp. 33–48. University of Oslo, Vindern.

Tsuang, M. T. (1993). Genotypes, phenotypes, and the brain. A search for connections in schizophrenia. *British Journal of Psychiatry*, 163, 299–307.

Walker, C. (1991). Delusion: What did Jaspers really says? *British Journal of Psychiatry*, 159 (suppl. 14), 94–103.

Weiner, I., Feldon, J., and Ziv-Harris, D. (1987). Early handling and latent inhibition in the conditioned suppression paradigm. *Developmental Psychobiology*, 20, 233–40.

Wiesel, T. N. (1982). The postnatal development of the visual cortex and the influence of environment. Nobel Lecture report. *Bioscience Reports*, 2, 351–77.

World Health Organization (1992). The ICD-10 classification of mental and behavioural disorders—clinical descriptions and diagnostic guidelines. WHO, Geneva.

8
Intentionality in disorder

8.1 TWO APPROACHES: LOGIC AND BIOLOGY

In psychological disorder we find apparent disruption at one or more stages in the intentional-causal pathways linking stimulus, perception, thought, emotion, and behaviour. Another aspect of this point is that psychological disorder essentially involves disorder of (intentional) action (cf. Fulford 1989). Physical disruption will be a major candidate for the explanation along the lines discussed in Chapter 7. In this chapter we examine the possibility that interruption of intentionality could have intentional-causal origins. In doing this we find ourselves considering questions and solutions formulated at the beginnings of the psychological theory of disorder. Freud can be regarded as starting from the same central question: could psychological phenomena that display the same qualities as those seen in unequivocal cases of physically caused conditions, of persistent, intrusive disruption of normal function, have their origins in psychological processes? This is to say, in the terms used here: could they have their origins in intentional-causal processes? In his analysis of hysterical conversion syndromes, Freud postulated disruption of normal function by states of mind deriving from early intolerable, traumatic experiences and impulses. Similar principles were being invoked at around the same time in an otherwise very different psychological theory of disorder, namely Watson's account of phobias. In this account, the disorder was due to the inappropriate generalization of learnt fear, this learning having occurred in a one-trial traumatic experience. Thus at the beginnings of clinical psychological theory at the turn of the century, in the two early models which, it would be fair to say, gave rise to all the rest, what we find is the fundamental idea that memories of traumas intrude into, and hence disrupt, normal function. The notion of trauma is fundamental to the explanation of breakdown of intentionality in terms of intentional processes, though broader concepts are also required.

We shall take two approaches to the problem. One draws on general logical and epistemological considerations of the sort discussed in the first chapter. In that chapter we, in effect, gave an outline definition of a family of concepts including representation, thought, and intentionality. The linkage to action, and the organization into theory, were critical to the definition. In this chapter we show how from these very general considerations it is possible to derive conditions of psychological disorder with particular characteristics. This is done in Section 8.2.

The second approach takes further the account given in the previous chapter of disruption of function, which placed emphasis on the disruption of intentionality. Just as intentional causality was seen to operate throughout biological systems, both psychological and non-psychological, so disruption of intentionality was seen to be the hallmark of disorder throughout biological systems. The consideration of possible intentional origins of such disruption will draw on our consideration of intentional causality in biological systems given in Chapter 5 and of our proposition in Chapter 6 that the psychological development of the child may be seen to represent the exploitation of a potential inherent in the simplest biological processes. In particular, the development of multiple internalized rules and representations with their immense potential for flexibility and creativity, will be seen also to entail substantial risks.

8.2 THE LOGIC AND EPISTEMOLOGY OF DISORDER

8.2.1 Radical error

Persistent misrepresentation and rule-conflict

We have defined representations as being involved essentially in the regulation of action, and we have remarked that they are typically hierarchically organized, in the way highlighted by post-empiricist theory of knowledge. From these assumptions it is possible to derive general features of psychological disorder and general principles for its explanation.

We will be working towards defining a form of explanation of disorder in intentionality which is couched at the level of the intentional processes themselves. Such a form of explanation therefore has to derive from the definition of intentionality, in this sense from logic. It turns out that it has basically the following form: radical failures of intentionality arise in case intentional processes subvert their own nature, that is to say, their role in the planning of action. Post-empiricist epistemology provides the framework for elaborating this basic idea. The investigation will take us close to familiar psychological models of disorder, from conditioning models to those in the more cognitively elaborate psychoanalytic tradition.

We begin with a priori remarks on psychological disorder. In so far as intentionality is the defining characteristic of mind, all mental disorder involves breakdown of intentionality. Intentionality is, of course, a broad concept here, concerning the representational (cognitive) capacities of mind. We may provisionally distinguish two kinds of way in which representation may fail: it may fail to represent reality correctly, or it may fail to regulate action appropriately. This distinction is blurred, however, in so far as misrepresentation leads to inappropriate action.

We make mistakes all of the time, however, and so far this has nothing to do with what we mean by 'mental disorder'. To begin to capture this notion, we need some idea of *radical* misrepresentation. We may expect that the understanding of 'radical' here should follow from the nature of representation itself. In so far as representation regulates action, and action is extended though time, it belongs to the nature of representation that error is subject to discovery and correction through time, in the course of action. This general idea underlies the definition of at least one kind of radical misrepresentation, namely, as being misrepresentation that fails to be corrected through time. In the phenomena of persistent error we begin to recognize something of what is meant by 'mental disorder'.

However, regulation of action may fail even if representation of the environment is correct. The circumstances are simply those in which two or more representations are correct, but give rise to incompatible plans for action. In brief, the circumstances involve one or another kind of *rule-conflict*. As outlined in Chapter 6, human psychological functioning is characterized by a multiplicity of sets of rules, with the implication that there is ample scope for rule-conflict. While misrepresentation can in principle be due to lower-level disrupting causes, rule-conflict is generally unamenable to this type of explanation. This is to say, it arises generally in the context of normal psychological functioning. The representations and their regulation of action are individually in order, but in combination they are in disorder. Once again, as in the case of misrepresentation, it should be noted that rule-conflict is common, and has nothing to do yet with what is meant by 'mental disorder'. Again as in the case of misrepresentation, we begin to capture this notion when we envisage *persistence* despite continuing failure of action. In other words, in persistent, unresolved rule-conflict, leading to persistent disarray in action, we begin to recognize signs of 'mental disorder'.

Avoidance and re-enactment (re-experiencing)

What stands in need of explanation, then, is persistent misrepresentation, and persistent, unresolved rule-conflict. Various forms of explanation are possible a priori, of which our main interest here are those that run in terms of the intentional processes themselves, those that may be called 'psychological'.

As already remarked, in rule-conflict representations are in order, but only opposed, and there is typically no lower-level, reductive explanation. Persistent misrepresentation, on the other hand, may have an explanation in terms of physical disruption of information-processing systems, as when, for example, visual images are produced by electrical stimulation of the visual cortex. On the other hand, persistent misrepresentation may essentially involve intentional processes, specifically the fulfilment of a wish, or the enactment of fear, as in the case of Don Quixote, who in search of adventure perceived windmills as monstrous giants, or Macbeth, who falsely perceived the image and ghost of his murderous action. Something like hallucination may occur from either kind of cause. In the framework of Dennett's three explanatory stances (subsection 1.3.5), hallucination admits of explanation from the physical and the intentional stances.

Persistent error in representing the environment may be explained also from Dennett's design stance, in the sense that it is innately determined. Consider, for example, the case of the frog's fly-snapping behaviour discussed in Chapter 4, (Section 4.5). The frog may mistake an ambient non-fly black dot for a fly, this being a mistake at least from our point of view, and the mistaken representation is due to innate features of cognitive design, in particular to the absence of a mechanism for discriminating between flies and other fly-like objects.

Error in representing the environment is also an intrinsic risk during learning. The principle is relatively simple: representations acquired in and appropriate to one environment are wrongly applied to another, different environment, and the error naturally shows up in failure of action. For example, a rat learns its way though a complicated maze to the goal-box, and is then put in a more or less subtly different maze, where cues lead to unexpected results, for example dead-ends. Consequently action is thwarted, desires remain unsatisfied. Breakdown of function shows up in, for example, frustration-behaviour, randomness, repetitiveness, or inertia.

However, the fact is that we are continuously exposed to new situations, more or less different from what we have experienced before, and we are not constantly falling into confusion. Normally we change the old rules, or learn new ones. What has to be explained in clinical psychology, as we have already noted, is precisely the *persistence* of maladaptive rules and representations, their failure to respond to new information.

Broadly speaking, the explanations of this failure invoke the fact that new information is *avoided*. Avoidance includes the straightforwardly behavioural variety, but may also include complex forms of mental denial and disqualification. But further, whatever type of avoidance is used, there is typically a kind of experience, after all, of what is being avoided, and this experience confirms the old rules and representations, even if they are, otherwise, quite invalid. This may be called *re-enactment* (or re-experiencing).

These points, in one form or another, are familiar in clinical psychological theory, and the main aim of this section is to explicate them from the more general, philosophical perspectives presented in the first part of this essay. Before embarking on this task, a sketch of some examples of what is to be explained, and the kinds of explanation in question, may be helpful.

Consider for example phobias, irrational fears and avoidance, regulated by the (persistent) representation of an object as extremely dangerous, when in fact it is not. A psychological explanation of the phobia, for example of enclosed spaces, would run as follows: in the past the person has been exposed to real danger in a situation from which escape was or was thought to be impossible, and this representation of enclosed space as dangerous has generalized to all other (similar) enclosed spaces. The question arises as to why the representation is not modified by subsequent exposure to safe enclosed spaces.

That example is of the kind emphasized by conditioning or behavioural theories. Consider another example of the kind emphasized in psychoanalytic theory, with its characteristic concern with interpersonal relations. A person experiences persistent breakdown in intimate friendships. Examination reveals a pattern, one theme in which is that the person begins to act as if she were about to be rejected, in circumstances in which there is apparently no objective evidence for this expectation. An obvious psychological explanation of this theme, one which draws again on simple principles of learning, is that the person has experienced rejection in past intimate relationships, and the representation of them as involving rejection has generalized to all other (similar) intimate relationships. But again, the problem for theory is this: why has the representation not been modified by subsequent exposure to friendships that work?

Answers to the problem of persistence run in terms of avoidance. Phobias are characterized by behavioural avoidance, so one reason why a learnt fear of enclosed spaces would not be modified by subsequent contrary experience is simply that the person avoids enclosed spaces and therefore never experiences them as safe. By the same principle, someone who has experienced devastating rejection in past important relationships may subsequently avoid similar relationships, and hence the representation of them as involving rejection is never put to the test.

On the other hand, in the second case as described we are supposing that the person continues to try, and still the earlier acquired representation persists. So explanation of persistence in terms of avoidance does not apply here. Implicit in the sketch of the case is that the person responds in accord with the earlier acquired representation. She selectively attends to (the slightest) signs of rejection, or interprets behaviour of her partner as signifying rejection, even though (we are supposing) no rejection is intended. The perception of rejection leads by psychologic to emotions of hurt and anger, hence to such as irritation and withdrawal, which in turn, we may surmise, prompts similar responses in her partner. In short, the relationship progresses into difficulties, and the outcome is one that readily lends itself to the interpretation by the person that she is being rejected. In this way the representation that is brought to the relationship from the beginning generates a pattern and sequence of responses the outcome of which is confirmation of the representation. This kind of pathway to persistent misrepresentation is distinct from avoidance. The same principle can operate in phobia, in case the person does not avoid the feared situation completely. Here the representation of the situation as dangerous gives rise to anticipatory anxiety, which may intensify when in the situation to the extreme of panic. In this way the situation comes to be experienced after all as threatening and dangerous, even when objectively it is not. The expectation is fulfilled: the representation is confirmed.

The examples of persistent misrepresentation outlined above involve expectations that, in some way or other, action will not achieve desired goals. In the first case there is fear of physical danger, in the second fear of rejection by significant others. The proposed explanation of persistent misrepresentation turns on this feature. If the results of action are represented as threatening or useless, then there will tend to be either avoidance, or generation of confirming experiences in situations which might otherwise be disconfirming.

We can, on the other hand, envisage something like inappropriate and uncorrected representations which involve expectations of success. For example, the child is likely to persist for a considerable time in the expectation that her parents or other adults in charge will take care of her, notwithstanding ample evidence to the contrary. But here we have a plausible case of an expectation, a hope, which is innately determined, and which therefore stands relatively firm no matter what experience is like. As remarked earlier, persistent error in representation arises in case of inadequate match between the design of the living being, between the reality for which it is designed, and the world into which it is born.

All the examples cited above involve conflict among representations. In phobic anxiety, the person (usually) also believes that the feared situations are safe, that the fear is irrational. Otherwise, indeed, there would be no disorder, at least not so far as the person was concerned. Similarly, we tend to persist in the expectation that action, for example in relation to others, can and should satisfy needs, notwithstanding evidence to the contrary. The conflict generally is between the need to act, the expectation that action can and must succeed, and the perception that in one way or another it does not work. The conflict is among the cognitive-affective representations, in so far as they are to be used in the regulation of action. Conflict may arise in various ways: if the same object is perceived as both desirable and undesirable; if two objects, which cannot both be achieved, are both desired; or if two objects, which cannot both be avoided, are both undesired. Normally such conflict can be resolved, but it stays unresolved, persistent, if there is unpreparedness to tolerate negative consequences of action, these being either some kind of punishment, or at least failure to achieve one of two desired ends. It may be inferred that from the point of view of the agent action is impossible: it would would lead to intolerable danger, or to intolerable loss.

It is here that we return to the proposal made at the beginning of this subsection. Radical failure of intentionality arises in case intentional processes subvert their own nature, that is to say, their role in the planning of action. The point is that representation incompatible with action is in some sense also impossible. This is the origin of the paradox already implied in the juxtaposition of avoidance and re-enactment.

8.2.2 Threats to action and thought: trauma and paradox

Introduction: a priori approaches

The distinction between conditions that are conducive to the agent and those that are not, between 'pleasure' and 'pain', and the interaction between them, has a long history in attempts to understand and explain behaviour. Severe pain, or threat, appears typically under the name of 'trauma' in psychological theories of disorder. We shall make use of something like this notion, emphasizing, in accord with our approaches up to now, intentional and developmental perspectives.

The distinction between conditions favourable to action, and conditions that make action difficult to impossible, is relevant not only to psychology and clinical psychology, but also, given a certain assumption, to philosophy, specifically to the a priori theory of representation. The assumption in question is that representation essentially serves action. In terms of the cognitive-behavioural paradigm defined by this assumption there arises the prospect of profound paradox in case representation is of conditions in which action cannot proceed. The underlying logical problem is that there are conditions of reality which cannot be represented.

It is possible to see from within logic the logical form or forms that psychological disorder can assume. The critical point is that thought is for the planning of action, and therefore it must represent the possibility of action: if it cannot do this it undermines itself. Thought goes on, but is impossible. This defines the central, paradoxical idea of psychological disorder.

We will approach this idea in two ways. First, via post-empiricist epistemology, and secondly via the idea of the limits of thought.

Core theory and negative critical experiments

According to post-empiricist epistemology, as outlined in the first chapter (Section 1.4), beliefs are hierarchically organized, in the form of a theory. The theory interprets experience and is used in the planning of action. It typically has a core of working assumptions, which define essential characteristcs of reality and knowledge. These core assumptions are essential to the theory: without them the theory, the interpretation of experience, and the planning of action would fall into disarray. If the theory makes a prediction that turns out to be false, it can be inferred that there is a mistake somewhere in the system, but not yet where. There is room for manoeuvre in the diagnosis of error. A sound methodological rule is to make as little adjustment as is necessary, though in the case of repeated, or serious failures of prediction, major revision in the theory may be indicated. In any case, there has to be resistance to giving up core beliefs, which are fundamental to the whole enterprise. Thus apparent anomalies are deflected away from the core, to be handled in some way or other elsewhere. Occasionally in the sciences there are attempts to construct a so-called critical experiment, which has the aim of putting the core of a theory to the test. Generally, however, this can happen only when there is an alternative theory standing by to pick up the pieces: in the absence of a viable alternative theory which can handle the recalcitrant data, no experiment is likely to be regarded as critical (Lakatos 1970).

In the first chapter (subsection 1.4.4) we applied post-empiricist epistemology to the theory of action. Action presupposes at least the following beliefs, or expectations: that the self is competent (enough) to act, that the world is predictable (enough), and that the world provides (enough) satisfaction of needs. Such expectations have to be preserved if activity is to continue. If they were to be abandoned, action would appear to be either impossible or pointless: there would be, so far, no reason to act.

We may ask, then, what would happen if fundamental convictions of these kinds were to be apparently challenged by experience? Suppose they were put to the test by apparently critical experiences, in the absence, moreover, of an alternative theory which could handle them. There would be major cognitive problems, in both representation and knowledge. From the point of view of the theory, particularly the core theory, apparent anomalies have a highly peculiar status. On the one hand, they represent an enormous threat, signifying the downfall of the theory and the end of action itself, and have maximum salience. But on the other hand, they cannot be true, or really true, according to the theory, and so should be only discounted. So the theory of action in relation to these apparently critical anomalies gets into profound confusion.

The limits of thought

The same idea can be approached by considering the idea that there are limits of thought. It is natural enough to presuppose that whatever exists, or at least whatever is known to the subject, can be represented. We find this assumption in the philosophical tradition, but alongside it we find also the recognition that there are limits to representation, deriving from the nature of representation itself. The most rigorous working out of this idea is by Wittgenstein in his *Tractatus logico-philosophicus* (1921). We considered the *Tractatus* account of representation in the first chapter (subsection 1.3.2) as a particularly clear expression of a theory which has a long history, namely, that representation is a matter of *resemblance* between sign and the reality signified. In the *Tractatus* theory, thoughts and linguistic propositions alike are pictures, or combinations of pictures, of possible states of affairs. The general form of proposition is: This (the picture) is how things stand. This account implies limits to representation, namely: only what can be pictured can be represented in thought or in language.

However, the *Tractatus* account also implies that there are things that cannot be pictured. Pictures cannot represent, for example, that the relation between representation and reality is pictorial, nor that the world is the totality of facts, nor any of the philosophical theory of the *Tractatus*. The paradoxical implication, which the young Wittgenstein was quite prepared to embrace, was that his book expressed what was inexpressible in thought and language, and was therefore itself nonsense. The appearance of paradox here is inevitable, however, because definition of the limits of thought requires that we think both sides of the limit. (The primary material referred to here includes mainly Wittgenstein 1921, 4.11s, 4.12s, 4.5s, 5.1–6.1 and 6.1–7, the last proposition in the book. Unfamiliar readers would, however, be advised to consult commentaries, practically all of which address the major and integral theme of the 'inexpressible'.)

As noted in the first chapter (subsection 1.3.3), the *Tractatus* picture-theory has little to do directly with the theory of representation at work in the present essay. We explicate representation not in terms of pictures (or images) but rather primarily with reference to the regulation of action. We adopt, in other words, the axiom of cognitive psychology, and indeed of biology, that information-processing generally is in the service of action. But just as the *Tractatus* theory recognizes that there are limits to what can be represented, limits that derive from the nature of representation itself, so too the present theory of representation implies corresponding limitations, and indeed also the paradoxes to which such limitations inevitably give rise.

The key here is the definition of representation as serving action. Suppose that there are circumstances in which action is, or is perceived to be, impossible. Suppose that these circumstances are represented as such. But then the representation cannot be used to facilitate (to regulate, to plan) action, which is, according to the representation, not possible. But in so far as the representation cannot be used in the service of action, in so far as it is incompatible with action, it is not a possible representation. The paradox here can be expressed by saying that the reality in question has to be both represented and not represented.

The considerations in this and the preceding subsections are closely connected, and in the end come to the same. Definition of the limits of thought, in terms of thought itself, and its paradoxical consequences, are of the general form clarified in the *Tractatus* account. But in order to apply these insights to the theory of representation adopted here, we leave behind the *Tractatus* idea of passive pictures, and consider representation in the form of action. This takes us to post-empiricism.

Post-empiricism, like the empiricism that it replaced, is as much a theory of representation as a theory of knowledge. As a theory of representation it emphasizes the active nature of cognition, in a variety of senses. These include that beliefs are flexible in relation to experience, organized in a theory, and also that beliefs are used to plan action. We considered in the preceding subsection what happens in case such a theory, such a vehicle of representation, comes up against what it defines as its limits, which involves acknowledging the other side, the possibility of critical experiences which would refute the core of the theory.

Trauma

We have invoked the notion of experiences that constitute a major threat to the conditions of action, and which lead to radical disorder in cognition. The concept in clinical psychology and psychiatry that comes closest to this idea, sketched so far in a purely a priori way, is the concept of (psychological) *trauma*. The concept of trauma is a broad one, and is invoked in whole or partial explanation of many kinds of psychological disorder. It is of relevance, however, not only to clinical psychology and psychiatry but also to logic, the a priori theory of representation, provided that logic defines representation essentially as serving in the regulation of action. The underlying problem, logical and psychological, is that representation of reality in which action is impossible or pointless subverts itself: it makes itself impossible, or pointless.

The most apparent traumas are experiences that threaten life itself, as in war, fires and other disasters, and serious physical attacks on the person. The most immediate effect is terror; fear of death or damage. It is clear that the traumatic events are experienced and represented; otherwise there would be no (psychological) problem. Indeed, typically they are persistently *re-experienced*, in one way or another. On the other hand, in some sense (or senses) the trauma is not and cannot be represented. For example, there may be amnesia for critical periods in the sequence of events, or the events are remembered, but not the terror; or the events are recalled with a third-person perspective, as though observed from the outside rather than experienced from within them; or the memory images have an unreal, dream-like quality. These points will be discussed further in the next chapter, under the heading of Post-traumatic Stress Disorder (subsection 9.3.3).

The points made so far in this section apply to manifest traumas such as involvement in disasters. It has to be emphasized, however, that 'trauma' in the sense at work in this section, namely, experience that radically subverts the conditions of intentionality, is not confined to such cases of obvious 'psychological shock'. In a developmental context particularly, a broader notion is required. The development of action and cognition requires certain forms of experience, and is inhibited in their absence. Children have to learn how to how to relate, how to act, how to think, and how to speak. Children are no doubt biologically designed for these tasks, but they require the right kind of help from adults. They need, for example, a secure space for action (for play), encouragement and help in planning and in achieving goals, and in finding the right descriptions of, predictive patterns for, reality. Parent–child interactions that include patterns such as neglect, excessive prohibition on, or rejection of, the child's spontaneous attempts to act and speak, excessive (for example age-inappropriate) demands, confused or contradictory communications, may be expected, on a priori grounds alone, to inhibit or distort development of the child's capacity to act and to think. As in the case of manifest disaster, the result will tend to be experience of a world in which action is perceived as impossible, or pointless, or both. This broader notion of what subverts conditions of intentionality, based in developmental considerations, will be explored in more detail in the next section (8.3).

Theory of mind: further possibilities of disorder

We have been discussing so far in this section threats to core beliefs in the theory of action which have to do with apparently disconfirming experience. There are other kinds of threat, however, involving apparently opposed socially acquired beliefs. Here belongs the fact, already discussed in the first chapter (subsection 1.4.2), that we use an explicit theory of mind and action which is, like theories generally, socially acquired. In this case the possibility arises that children are taught to have beliefs which seem to contradict the assumptions required for action to be viable. A child may be taught in words as well as in practice that he or she is too demanding, or is incompetent, or that the world is too dangerous, or unsatisfying; and so on. Thus we can envisage threats to the core assumptions underlying action arising not only from acute or chronic traumatic experiences, but from conflicting propositions which come with the force of parental authority. In these circumstances there is a similar adverse and paradoxical effect on the capacity for thought: the assertions assault what has to be believed if action is to continue, and hence they have to be both taken seriously and ignored. This kind of threat to intentionality will be discussed also in the next section (8.3), where the focus is explicitly on developmental processes.

Wherever there is threat to what is fundamental to action, whether in the form of obvious or hidden disasters, or breakdown in the conditions of child development, including perverse instruction, the assault has to be dealt with in some way if action is to carry on. Protection is needed.

8.2.3 Psychic defences

Behavioural strategies, mental analogues, and elaborations

In the previous section we considered threats to the core of the theory presupposed by action, to assumptions or expectations of safety, competence, and satisfaction of needs, for example. Such attacks require defensive manoeuvres. At their simplest, these are behavioural. Living beings respond to threats to their integrity by escape or fighting. And if the environment fails to provide for needs, alternative sources of satisfaction are sought. In so far as living beings have the capacity for representation, however, there are alternatives to these real actions: they can create analogues within the realm of representation itself. Threats can be denied representation, or they can be attacked and destroyed in thought. Satisfaction of needs can likewise be thought, even if not really achieved. Such strategies operate within the mind as opposed to reality: they are acts of the imagination, and they involve departure from, or distortion of, reality.

Pursuing this line of thought rapidly leads to points of a kind familiar in psychoanalytic theory. However, our aim in this section is not to explicate or endorse specific psychoanalytic models of particular psychic defences, but is rather to sketch some principles for understanding the concept which belongs with proposals made so far in this essay. The reason that we come across here points familiar in psychoanalytic theory is just that Freud was the first to see clearly the problem-space in question. Its definition required various conceptual assumptions which contradicted and superceded what was envisaged by mainstream scientific psychology until fairly recently. These assumptions included the following, all of which were discussed in the first chapter: preparedness to use the intentional stance, the language of intentional states, in psychological explanation and prediction, as in common-sense folk psychology; but departure from common sense (Cartesian common sense) by not restricting intentionality to what is available to consciousness and expressed in self-report; the post-empiricist recognition that some intentional states constitute the core of belief, to be protected from counter-evidence, and the inevitable conclusion then that while such protection averts perceived catastrophe, it involves at least distortion of reality, and perhaps manifest disorder.

As indicated above, there is a model for intrapsychic defences in the post-empiricist conception of scientific theories discussed in the first chapter (Section 1.4). In this context, unlike the unconscious mind, cognitive maneouvres to protect the core of theory are open to view. The defensive strategies have been well documented by Lakatos in his seminal paper (1970) and discussed in subsections 1.4.1 and 1.4.4. They include simple denial of the anomalies, which works well until replication, and degenerating theory changes, such as *ad hoc* elaborations which involve restriction of scope. We should note also an extreme reaction to pressure within theory, namely, the splitting of the scientific community, where one side takes the old theory and all its evidence, ignoring, disqualifying the new, and the new school envisages only its domain of evidence. In these circumstances there can be little (genuine) communication between the two schools of thought. An example would be the splitting of psychoanaltyic and scientific paradigms in psychology under the weight of the dichotomy between meaningful and causal connections. All these sorts of manoeuvre under radical pressure, which are familiar in science—denial, theory-restriction, and splitting—have intrapsychic analogues.

Simple denial in the face of unwanted or inexplicable phenomena is common enough. It is likely to be unsustainable, however, in any form in the face of trauma, whether a single catastrophe, or chronic adverse experience. One way of responding to undeniable conflict involves what may be called splitting: the traumatic experiences, and in particular their apparent meaning, are kept isolated from the convictions presupposed by action. Cognitive responses to gross and subtle trauma may include that the trauma is represented, indeed persistently re-experienced and re-enacted, but it is split off from the representation of reality as one in which it is possible to live. This splitting off is a form of denial, of not allowing the trauma to access basic, necessary beliefs. Splitting, and the dissociation which it implies, thus present as relatively simple ways of protecting fundamental assumptions. The precise nature and modelling of these and related psychic mechanisms has been, and remains, a subject of debate (Breuer and Freud 1895; Klein 1946; Hilgard 1977/1986; Power and Brewin 1991; Gardner 1993).

Denial and splitting can be readily identified within a post-empiricist philosophy of mind as possible defensive manoeuvres. The possibility of dissociation belongs with the idea explored in detail in Chapter 6, that human cognition is characterized by multiple sets of rules, concerning subsystems of cognitive-affective-behavioural states. Coherence and integrity among these subsystems are not a given, but have to be achieved, and this process can be threatened, as will be discussed in more detail in the next section. Also, however, dissociation can be conscripted into use as a defence. As generally with cognitive phenomena, even otherwise maladaptive mechanisms can be made use of, including as defences, a point that will recur through the remainder of this section.

Other types of defence familiar in psychoanalytic theory have a more complicated, though still strong, relation to the kind of assumptions we have been using in this essay. Consider, for example, projection (or projective identification), one of the main primitive defences posited in Kleinian theory (Klein 1946; Sandler 1988). To understand projection from the standpoint of the considerations adduced so far in this chapter, we need to elaborate on the view of the self which is essential for action. It includes competence, or power. However, if the self is seen as *too powerful* further problems arise, in particular in case the self is perceived as capable of destroying the source of needs, and is inclined to because that source is not sufficiently satisfying. The idea of an 'impossible reality' is then complicated by the idea of an 'impossible self', that is to say, a self that is inclined to attack and destroy the source of satisfaction of its needs. Destructive attack is a familiar, effective response to threat. It is, however, a particularly problematic response in the specific case of frustration of needs. In early development, it would appear as destructive impulses, anger or rage, against the carer, prompted by perceived deprivation. In general, and at any developmental stage, intolerable destructive impulses would include those directed at any outside object, or any aspect of the self, which is valued. Such impulses are bound to create conflict. One solution to the conflict is to project the destructive impulses into the source of needs. Projection then appears as a primitive defence against such impulses, by ascribing them not to the self, but to the outside world, either to a natural object, or to another subject. In this way projection presents as a radical misuse of the 'theory of mind'. As in the case of all defences there is a cost. In this case the cost is that the self is stripped of power, and confronts a frightening reality.

So far we have considered the defences of denial, splitting, and projection. More positive strategies include self-gratification. If the real world fails as a source of satisfaction of needs, such as for comfort and affirmation, it is possible to create an imaginative world in which the self can please itself. Pleasure in this state of mind may include sexual self-satisfaction as an expression of power to elicit comfort and love. At another level, there may be dreams of praise and acclaim. Reality is given up as a source or object of love, and the self is substituted. Such are the procedures involved in the so-called narcissistic defence (Freud 1914). On the surface is the thought that the world is inferior and unworthy of love; beneath is the fear that the self has these awful qualities. As with other defences, there is dissociation, with more or less rapid switching between contrary states of mind.

Failure of self-knowledge as defence

So far we have considered psychic defences which are in effect developmentally primitive, without any essential dependence on language. The issues, here as elsewhere, become complicated by the use of a theory about one's own mental states. More sophisticated, 'rational' forms of denial of unacceptable states of mind become available, including such as re-construal, intellectualizing, and explaining away. These defences are typically added to the repertoire with the theorizing that makes them possible during adolescence (Freud 1936, see also Chapter 6, subsection 6.5.3). These intellectual responses to intolerable mental states are akin to the defensive, degenerating strategies used in scientific theory when it is faced with anomalies. As in scientific theory, the cost is typically restriction of scope and predictive power, but what is secured is at least certainty within the restricted domain. Once there is an explicit, working theory of mind, moreover, primitive defensive strategies such as straightforward denial, splitting, projection, and narcissism, can all be elevated into theoretical form. The theory of the self and others can be conscripted into the service of defence, by selective attention to, and distortions of, the phenomena.

We described self-knowledge in the first chapter (subsection 1.4.3) as having the form of a theory. The account belongs with post-empiricist epistemology, and stands opposed basically to the Cartesian idea of introspection. We noted that failure of self-knowledge leads to confusion and rule-conflict, endorsing the long-recognized close connection between failure of self-knowledge and psychological problems. On the other hand, we did not in the earlier discussion refer to the defensive function of failure of self-knowledge, a further point emphasized by Freud and subsequent psychoanalytic theorists. We noted that the theory of mind, applied to the self as well as to others, is, like all theories, acquired in education, which thus appears as a major source of error. Hence this new model of self-knowledge apparently differs from the psychoanalytic view in implicating education rather than defensive function in the production of error. And to this we may add another apparent difference, that Freud viewed the processes involved in self-knowledge and ignorance as intrapsychic, whereas the account endorsed here emphasizes their interpersonal nature. On the other hand, while it is true that psychoanalytic theory has emphasized the intrapsychic nature of processes involved in self-knowledge and its failure, the contrast with interpersonal accounts is not that sharp. Psychoanalytic theory has always been concerned with interpersonal relations, whether internalized in the mind of the individual or played out in reality. This is connected with the fact that there is no tension between Freud's insight that failure of self-knowledge typically serves a defensive function, and the view of self-knowledge and its failures as originating in social and family life. It has been emphasized by family therapists working within a psychoanalytic framework that the blind spots and error intrinsic to the family's psychological theory typically have a defensive function (for example, Byng-Hall 1973). The theory includes rules, explicit or implicit, which systematically promote ignoring, disqualification, or distortion of certain beliefs and desires. Moreover, among the methods for achieving this result are the developmentally primitive defence mechanisms described in psychoanalytic theory. These mechanisms may be called 'intrapsychic', and they may indeed be subjective in origin, but in any case they are also modelled, selectively reinforced, and maintained by family function. Children have ample opportunity to learn from parents the use of various forms of denial, such as splitting and projection.

Defence benefit/cost analysis: avoidance and re-enactment (re-experiencing)

We have been considering the proposal that certain core assumptions have to be preserved if action is to be possible. They concern a view of the self as competent, of the world as safe and predictable, and sufficiently gratifying. If this view is threatened in some way, the first response is to act so as to remove the threat. But of course special problems arise in case intervention is impossible or unsuccessful, when the circumstances for some reason cannot be altered. The living being is then obliged to remain in a situation in which action is either impossible or pointless or both. In this condition the tendency will be for action to become random, or irrelevant, or it may cease altogether. Such are the signs in behaviour. As to cognition, it may be inferred a priori that there are similarly radical disorders: thought may cease altogether, or may become random, or it frees itself from reality.

The risks involved in abandoning core beliefs testify to their necessity, to the importance of defending them at practically any cost. The consequences of giving them up, in more or less circumscribed areas of life, include the two most common themes in psychological disorder: profound anxiety, and depression. The anxious person lives in fear of danger, and has to restrict his or her sphere of activity more or less drastically. In depression the view of action is hopeless: the self is powerless, the world provides no pleasure, and there is no prospect of change. To the extent that the depressed person sees no point in it, she does not act. The extreme is suicide, the act that brings action to an end.

Anxious or depressed beliefs signify the failure of attempts at defence, the failure to preserve convictions that action can carry on. As discussed in the previous section, they may arise from traumatic experience of some kind, or they may have been acquired from parental instruction, or both.

Depressed and anxious beliefs are maladaptive in the sense that they inhibit action. But there is another possiblity here, that maladaptive beliefs may themselves function as defences, as protection of something considered necessary to carry on. This complicated and paradoxical possibility is consistent with the general assumption used in this essay, that the fundamental direction of mental phenomena is to ensure the continuation of action. The methodological assumption is that this continues to be true even in, and indeed plausibly *especially* in, the most difficult bio-psychological circumstances. This implies that 'symptoms' may well be serving functions, an idea that has always been central to psychoanalytic theory and its derivatives.

Consider, for example, one of the well-known psychoanalytic models of depression, as being aggression towards the carer, as a response to perceived neglect or abuse, turned against the self. The view of the self as weak and useless may serve as a defence against the view that the self is too powerful, and in particular inclined to assault the one who should be helping. Further, helplessness may be expected to elicit care. The point here is that maladaptiveness, like threat, admits of degrees, and is hierarchically organized. Certain assumptions will be given up, even valued ones, in order to preserve what is still more important.

Or again, consider the issue of excessively contradictory parental instruction, which is closely connected to themes of this chapter (p. 308 and subsection 8.3.5). The child is persistently given contradictory instruction, information, and commands, so that, for example, statements of affirmation are combined with verbal or non-verbal rejection, or the child is informed that what he or she experiences is not really happening; and so on. In such circumstances the distinction between right and wrong judgement is not made out clearly enough, and so far there are no rules by which to act or to think. Doing nothing, the giving up of action and thought, may be the most viable response in the circumstances. This solution works but only until independent action is required, which becomes increasingly unavoidable through adolescence. Moreover, the adolescent is faced with the task of constructing a theory of this apparently nonsensical world. What kind of theory would this be? One option would be construction of solipsistic independence from reality, especially from other people, and a theme in the theory would inevitably be profound fear of chaos.

The psychic defences serve to protect core assumptions perceived as necessary for action. If these assumptions are abandoned, in the light of experience or parental instruction, the result is that action is perceived as in some way impossible, or pointless. Further, some basic assumptions may be given up in order to preserve others perceived as even more essential. Whatever the origin of the maladaptive cognitions, they likewise assume the status of rules for the interpretation of experience, to be held with certainty, and protected from apparent counter-evidence.

The psychic defences are self-perpetuating; their aim is to preserve the status quo. This means: core beliefs are to be maintained, contrary experience is to be kept at a distance by forms of denial and distortion. It is reality itself which is being denied and distorted. But reality being what it is, that in experience and action which is independent of the will, it continues to have its effects, to make itself known. What is feared is continually re-experienced and re-enacted. In anxiety states, reality is avoided, but is still represented and feared; in depression, inaction fails to elicit enough care and maintains absence of reward; the narcissistic personality acts so as to extinguish love from others; in delusion, the person may seem to make sense to himself, but communication with others fails drastically.

The psychic defences have the benefit of protection of the view of the world and the self as tolerable. The costs involve distortion of the phenomena, restriction of theory and consequently life style, and re-experiencing (re-enactment) of the original threat, typically without comprehension.

It was remarked at the beginning of this section that radical failure of intentionality has two connected forms: persistent misrepresentation and persistent rule-conflict. These are what require explanation. We went on to note, in subsection 8.2.2, that the explanation invokes the notion of trauma, broadly conceived. Persistent misrepresentation and persistent rule-conflict appear as the re-experiencing, or re-enactment, of the orginal threats to the integrity of action. We then went on, in the present subsection, to consider psychic defences, and we have arrived at the conclusion that these defences characteristically involve persistent misrepresentation and persistent rule-conflict, these being, again, the re-experiencing, or re-enactment, of the original traumatic experience. The solution to the problem plays out the problem. The disorder is an attempt to preserve order by the repetition of disorder. The position here is thus a matter of complex identities and paradoxes, inevitably, since we are considering the undermining of cognition by cognition, and its reconstruction.

Integration

Traumatic experience, broadly conceived, undermines conditions of action. The conflict may be resolvable, depending on many factors and circumstances. Resolution requires a single frame of reference in which, first, danger and safety are acknowledged, and secondly, the world is construed as, on balance, safe enough. As already discussed, in the absence of such a meta-frame, there remains a split between two conflicting systems of representation, affect and behaviour. The two systems run in parallel, without communication between them. In particular, the fear that the world is as experienced in the trauma remains split off from the expectation and evidence to the contrary. In this way the fear persists, notwithstanding subsequent experience that may contradict it.

Change in these circumstances is, needless to say, not easy to achieve. It is necessary to distinguish between kinds of change. As implied throughout this discussion, we characteristically find in psychological disorder conflicting systems of cognition, affect, and behaviour. The conflict is generally between what is tolerable and what is intolerable. Shifts between these states of mind, more or less rapid, constitute what may be called first-order change. Second-order change, by contrast, requires integration, and is more difficult to achieve. It requires dismantling of defences, whether these be simple avoidance, or more subtle mental strategies. With this dismantling, the feared outcome is realized, namely, threat to core assumptions about the self and its relation to reality. These core assumptions have to be adjusted to take account of, to make sense of and predict, what before was denied or distorted. A new and better theory is required. The kind of change required here is akin to what occurs in scientific theory, when under the weight of anomalies, and on condition that a more powerful theory can be constructed, it shifts from one paradigm to another.

8.3 INTENTIONAL CAUSALITY AND DISORDER

8.3.1 Introduction: threats to the integrity of intentional causality

In the previous section possible intentional origins of psychological disorder were considered in relation to representation, cognition, motivation, and action. Our method was essentially philosophical and psychological. We pursue now the same issues taking our discussion of chapters 5, 6, and 7 as a starting point. We will, in effect, press our account of intentional causality and show that it leads to similar proposals as those of the previous section, and further supports the convergence of accounts from epistemology and philosophy of mind on the one hand, and biology and development on the other.

It was evident in our earlier discussion that where intentional causal processes are wired in then elements are likely to be harmoniously linked. Provided the environment remains roughly that in which the organism evolved, representation and action will be possible. Humans are physiologically adapted to a narrow range of environmental conditions, but they possess the capacity to devise a wide range of strategies for action, and hence are able to live in very varied environments. The possession of multiple and acquired internalized rules for action, which may be matched to contrasting environmental demands, has therefore been of considerable survival value. However, with the capacity to acquire rules of perception, thought, and action, there has arisen the possibility that the operation of intentional-causal processes will not be smooth. In contrast to non-intentional causality, the elements of intentional-causal processes that we specified in Chapter 5 do not necessarily work in harmony. This point may be obscured where the process is biochemical or physiological, because the elements are not acquired or multiple. There is also a dramatic difference in the time periods over which the intentional processes of biochemistry and physiology, and those of the child, develop. If we assume that the efficient function of an intentional-causal sequence in a physiological system has evolved over several million years, then the learning of new rules for perceptions and actions over hours, days, months, or even a few years, may seem to be a precarious truncation of the process!

In the next sections we examine some of the ways in which the elements of intentional causality might not be in harmony, and hence give rise to psychological disorder. Our discussion is derived directly from that of Chapter 5. We need only take the features of intentional causality as seen in biological processes generally and ask what will happen if these are inappropriate, contradictory, or in competition.

First, there are those conditions in which accurate representation and action are incompatible. We ask what will be the consequences when accurate representation does not create the grounds for action, and what are the consequences if accuracy of perception must be sacrificed for action to take place? Just as when we took a philosophical starting point, we are interested in coping and psychological survival in the face of severe adversity and trauma. Secondly, there are risks arising from the requirement that internalized sets of rules should be both sufficiently general that they may inform action in different circumstances, and sufficiently differentiated that they can distinguish among different environmental demands. Thirdly, acquired internalized rules require stability if they are to inform action, and need to be available to revision in the light of experience. Threats to the integrity of representation and action will arise where either there is insufficient stability or there are conditions under which testing is not possible. Finally, intentional processes may be threatened where the monitoring and metarepresentational capacity is undermined. Each of the first three types of threat may be so persistent and pervasive that this more radical breakdown occurs, or there may be a direct assault on the basic sense of self and the experience of the external world.

8.3.2 Incompatibility between representation and action

Take first the requirement that representation is in the service of action. This is unlikely to contain a contradiction provided that accurate perceptions and effective actions have evolved together in harmony with the needs of the organism. As we have seen, problems arise where events in the outside world do not fall within the range of representations that an organism is able to link to action; for instance, where a threat is so great that neither fight or flight are possible. Then the alternatives are either that the animal reprocesses the threat as falling within the usual scope of representation and action, or that action is not possible. A further possibility arises where the individual is capable of generating multiple representations. This is seen in animals, especially non-human primates, but to a much greater extent in humans, and we have reviewed in Chapter 7 the flexible and creative potential of such a capability in activities such as play. There exists then in human development the possibility that this capacity for multiple representations will provide a means of coping with trauma and other circumstances under which action is not possible. The child may cope by generating two representations, one which omits reference to the threat but is compatible with action, and the other which includes the threat and the accompanying thoughts and emotions and is split off in the mind so that it does not underpin action. There is then the scope for an inaccurate representation which is compatible with action, and an accurate representation that is incompatible with action. Having considered this possibility in detail earlier in relation to post-empiricist theory of knowledge, we encounter it now as a risk pursuant on the freeing-up of elements of intentional causality in human development. The evolutionary perspective enables us to see clearly how dangerous this could be. For children, psychological and physical survival depends upon the capacity to act in relation to caregivers. Actions will need to preserve close contact with those who might provide for the child, and this will be straightforward if the representations of the behaviours of the caregivers are compatable with these actions. But suppose they are not. Suppose the perceptions of the child are of neglect, hostility, or physical or sexual abuse. How is the child to act and still retain the link with caregivers? The child has a need to be looked after, and to find a reasonably tolerable emotional state, but accurate perception reveals something different.

Then there is the possibility of an undermining of the flow of intentional causal sequences with a consequent inability to act, or incoherence of action. We have referred already to the possibility that this may contribute to some clinical pictures, but it is also evident in development. The study of infants with their caregivers in the Strange Situation Test (Ainsworth *et al.* 1978) has indicated that most have a strategy in their relating; that is to say they act in ways that are related systematically to the behaviours of their parents. A minority, comprised predominantly of those who come from families at risk for mental health or parenting problems, show a different pattern. Their behaviours with their parents are characterized by sudden cessation of actions, freezing, and actions that are contradictory either together or in sequence. The behaviours of the parents of these infants have been described as unpredictable or frightening (Main and Hesse 1990). The context is that the infant is with the person who, above all others, should be a source of protection and care, but who is also frightening. The consequence of the preservation of accuracy of perception is an undermining of the conditions of action.

It seems from the evidence so far that this 'disorganized' attachment pattern does not generally persist beyond infancy, and is replaced by others in which actions are possible. The evidence from non-human primates is that in a competition between accuracy of perception and the need for care, the latter will prevail. Baby monkeys will cling to surrogate 'mothers' that punish them (Harlow 1961) and children have often been observed to continue to seek comfort and care from parents who reject them (Bowlby 1969). If we assume that representations of some kind are required for these actions to take place, then they must omit whatever information is incompatable with the actions. It might be argued that this information could simply be forgotten, but the act of forgetting some specific items of information is likely also to entail their representation. Not only that, but there will be required the mental effort of making sure that this information is not used in the regulation of action. Put simply, the forgetting of painful and frightening information is probably not an option. Thus in effect there are established two different sets of internalized rules, one that preserves accuracy but does not meet the needs of the individual, and one that sacrifices accuracy but allows those needs to be met, both in terms of personal comfort and the survival of the relationship with key caregivers. It is likely that the one that meets some needs will prevail, whereas the other is predominantly non-operative. The non-operative perceptions, affects, and cognitions will then be unconscious, untested, and in contradiction to those that underpin actions. It will be evident that where this mechanism applies, the task of the overarching agency, of the self, or representer of representations, will be made particularly complex because of the contradictions between the schemata. Contradictions between representations, especially partial representations, will provide important examples of possible sources of disruption of functioning.

We return, then, to an analysis which is similar to that of the previous section, albeit via a somewhat different route. We find ourselves again, in some respects, in agreement with Melanie Klein's view that the child may separate representations which, broadly speaking, may be 'good' or 'bad'; while not espousing her particular developmental account. Here the inactivation of a representation of some aspects of the environment, in order to permit action, arises as a prediction from the operation of intentional-causal processes.

How might such inactivated representations operate? Suppose the accurate perception is 'I am being abused' there will be many associated perceptions such as 'I am in pain', 'I am angry', 'I am helpless'. If the relationships of the child demand that these are not acknowledged, then they cannot provide the basis for action, and it is likely that they will be maintained out of consciousness, and will not be available for testing that might establish their truth and their range of applicability. It is then possible that such a constellation of beliefs and emotions may be activated later, perhaps by events or people that in some way resemble the original, and then they may intrude into the life of the individual. The extent of generalization, the lack of relationship with the severity of the precipitating event, and the subjective experience of intrusion will arise from the extent to which this state of mind has been kept separate and untested. Pain, hopelessness, and helplessness erupting in this way might lead to an episodic disorder such as depression. This proposal assumes that the observing capacity of the self remains relatively intact. That is to say, the individual reports the intrusion into the continuity of his/her life. Often this is the case in depression where the state of mind is experienced as different from the person's usual self, unwanted, something that is suffered. Those elements of self, of the identification with, and commitment to, the depressed state of mind are lacking. The observing capacity retains its contact with that prior to the episode, and encounters a state of mind which is experienced as unfamiliar.

Repetition of traumatic experiences, especially in childhood, might lead to a rather different state of affairs which may have implications for the integrity of the self. We saw in Chapter 6 that the self probably develops out of a combination of innate capabilities and the repetition and generalization of emotional states, perceptions, and actions across situations and over time. This in turn allows for a benign diversity of states of mind and behaviours that may vary considerably but do not contradict or undermine each other. If, however, the young child's experiences require a repeated splitting of perceptions, thoughts, and emotional states, then what is split off may become a representational framework with so great a generality and commitment that it resembles that of the self. Nevertheless it will remain split off from the 'day to day' self. Here then, is a possible mechanism for intrusions into the activity of the self which are not apparent from the individual's perspective because there is a different observing agent. Those close to the individual often refer to 'Jekyll and Hyde' or to 'two people', and for the individual one state of mind and accompanying behaviours is strikingly inaccessible from the other. Here the commitment to, and conviction of the rightness of, each is very strong. Examples might include outbursts of relatively unprovoked violence, the rapid changes of state of mind of 'borderline' functioning (Chapter 9), and some types of psychotic episodes.

8.3.3 The generalization and differentiation of representations

Our second possible mechanism is derived from a consideration of the extent of generalization and differentiation of rules of perception, thought, and action. As we have seen, this changes with development. The young infant is responsive to human faces in general, but at around 9 months he/she makes a very sharp distinction between familiar adults (attachment figures) and strangers. However, this is not rigid, and the infant acquires new attachment figures through interaction and familiarity. The recognition of the difference between relating to special people and others underpins relationships throughout life. Similarly, the ability to judge the different interpersonal requirements of settings such as parties, job interviews, or funerals is crucial to effective social functioning. This requires sets of rules of sufficient generality that they may provide a guide for action under these different conditions, and sufficient differentiation that they are able to support appropriate behaviour. Difficulties may arise where there is either too restricted a range, or overgeneralization of the representations.

Clearly overgeneralization may simply arise from faulty learning. Fear or salivation may be elicited by association with conditioned stimuli that are, in themselves, not threatening nor nutritious. Such conditions should be open to relatively straightforward corrective action. Equally, overgeneralization may appear as a strategy in order to cope with difficult circumstances. Take the dilemma of the child for whom accuracy and need are in conflict, in relation to parents. If the representation that has to do with emotional needs is widened to include other adults, then potentially some further needs may be met. This is seen in some children who are insecurely attached, and in particular in children who have been in institutions where there have been many caretakers (Hodges and Tizard 1989). Here the overgeneralization may be linked clearly to survival, and may not be open to such ready revision. Such an overgeneralization may have consequences for the accurate perception of the differences between different relationships, and varied social circumstances.

Sets of rules, or schemata, that are too narrow may have implications for the development of the self and the metarepresentational systems. As we have seen, generalizations of a sense of agency and of affects are likely to be crucial mechanisms in the development of the self. In the case of affects this will require a reciprocal process. Joy is experienced with different people in relation to different joint frameworks but is the same experience, thus supporting the continuity of the sense of self (Stern 1985). Experiences of sorrow may be linked in similar fashion. However, crucially, there will also be required the sense of self that is capable either of joy or of sorrow. This may be provided by other indicators of continuity, such as continuity of a sense of agency and memory. However, where the child's experiences are predominantly of a narrow range of affective states, and where only these affective states are reinforced or permitted in the family, then these may generalize to the point where the self and its narrow range of emotional states are closely identified. If we assume that a priority for the self is ensuring the conditions for action, problems may arise if these have been clearly identified with a particular restricted constellation of affective states. Circumstances that have implications for emotional states outside this range, such as bereavement, may lead to representations that undermine these conditions, and hence helplessness and possibly depression.

8.3.4 The stability and testing of representations

A further, third, source of disruption of intentional causality may arise if the conditions that sets of rules should both be testable but also relatively enduring are threatened. If they are not testable, they are likely to become inappropriate to the demands of the environment. If they are open continuously to revision, then they will cease to provide a map or model in relation to which testing can take place. As we have seen, the interplay between relatively enduring and general hypotheses and testability is prominent in many theories, including those of Piaget, in relation to cognitive development, and Lakatos, in relation to the development of scientific paradigms. In each of these cases the hypotheses not only provide the bridge with reality, but also the conditions for thought, and for action. During development, children continually test internalized sets of rules concerning beliefs, fears, wishes, and motives. The test may concern the truth of a belief, for instance about the cause of an event. It is common for children to blame themselves for events that have, in fact, been accidents, or have been brought about by adults. Expression of that belief through talking about it, or through play, will be important if it is to be examined. Where a child faces harsh or critical parents, the truth of her beliefs may be particularly difficult to establish. For instance, a child may blame herself for the abuse that a sibling has received. If she is to locate the harm as coming from a parent, this may need to be identified by a trusted adult; however, she will take a risk in seeking to check that perception with the perpetrator, or the other parent. So she may continue to blame herself. Similarly, for the abused child there is often a requirement that the acts be kept secret, so it may be impossible for the child to test the belief 'I am being abused' and so an important truth may not be available to the child. We will return to this issue in the next chapter.

A need for constant revision of expectations is likely to be necessary where the behaviours of parents or other caregivers are inconsistent and unpredictable. Inconsistencies of parenting are common in the families of children with behaviour problems (Patterson 1982). Plans for effective action are then likely to be difficult to establish, and this may be reflected in the high frequency of impulsive and aggressive responses of the children.

8.3.5 The integrity of the metarepresentational system

So far, we have traced possible mechanisms for the disruption of function from contradictions among the elements of intentional causality in human psychological functioning. It seems that the more repeated and generalized these are, the greater the scope for a more radical malfunction of the metarepresentational and organizational agency. However, it is possible that there are routes to disruption that primarily affect this organizing process.

Take first the processes described by Stern (1985) in relation to the development of the self after around 6 months of age. At this stage the infant refers to the parent for guidance as to which set of rules applies, for instance regarding the visual cliff. But what do the infant and mother have to achieve? They have to establish their joint frame of reference, along the lines of 'I (the infant) am asking you a question and need guidance'. And then the content of that communication has to be applied to the task. Of course, the infant cannot check with the parent whether they do have that joint frame of reference because the checking would require that framework. In other words, interactions require an organizing principle that frames them, and establishes their rules, just as do individual states of mind. These are established by metacommunications, which convey what are the rules of social exchange. It is interesting to note that the a priori nature of the statement of the rules often is provided by the explicit or implicit rules of institution, dress, titles, or architecture. These are especially useful where the individuals do not know each other well. Where they do, the metacommunications are likely to be more particular to the relationships.

There will normally be a reciprocal support between the metacommunications and the content of the communications. Thus to take an everyday example, the child stands on the table and checks with the parent whether this is permissible. The parent answers 'no' using the metacommunication (through posture, facial expression, and tone of voice), 'this is serious and I mean it'. The child continues, falls off, and discovers both that the content was correct, and that he had read correctly the rules underpinning his relationship with the parent. Now suppose the parent does not indicate unequivocally that she is serious, perhaps by smiling, or walking out of the room while saying 'no'. Then the child ignores the content but follows the metamessage 'I am not serious' and falls of the table. If he is blamed, then either he has to point out that there was another component to the message (i.e. you did not appear to mean it), or accept what the parent says and deny that component. If the metacommunication has been experienced along the lines of 'I don't care whether you fall off the table' it will remain an unacknowledged hostile element in the relationship. The general point is the same as that considered earlier in relation to split off aspects of individual representations. The child has to find a basis for action in the relationship. If the content and the metacommunication are in conflict, he must choose which to follow, otherwise he has to tolerate contradictory elements in the intentional-causal processes, and this will preclude action. It is likely, with the parent, that he will choose the route that least threatens the relationship, and in this case it is hypothesized to be the one that does not mention a possible lack of care or hostility. Where the majority of exchanges do not contain such contradictions, and where it is clear that angry or hostile emotions can be acknowledged, such interactions are not likely to have a major impact. Where they are repeated then the child may develop split off states of mind of the form 'I hate my mother' which are not accessible or testable.

A second source of disruption to the observing and overarching representational agent may arise from a direct assault. It is likely that this high-invariant agent, or self, contains some general and some core assumptions. These, as our discussion of Stern's work has indicated, are related to the sense of self as having continuity, and to a differentiation of the continuity of the self from that of the external world. In other words, the predictability of the physical world, the world of other people, and of the individual, with their different rhythms, promotes the differentiation into the distinctive sense of self. Crucially, a central assumption is that action is possible. Where elements of intentional-causal processes are contradictory, and hence do not provide the basis for action, elements of that contradiction may be ignored in the service of action. Suppose, however, that action is not possible. Severe trauma may pose a threat to the self because of the break in the continuity of experience, and by creating conditions in which action is not possible. Disasters, such as those seen in football stadia or on ships, entail a breakdown of the predictability of the physical world, of the individual's relationship to it, and of the conditions for action. There has then occurred a break in the basic condition for intentionality. For some individuals a solution may be found in denial that would create or recreate conditions for action, but for many the representation is so powerful that it persists and includes the representation that action was not possible. As we have seen, such a paradoxical representation may provide the basis for the repetitive intrusive thoughts in reaction to trauma. These phenomena are seen also after sustained childhood sexual abuse where usually the child has been helpless, and following bereavement when, at least in relation to one person, action cannot change the circumstances.

8.4 PSYCHOLOGICAL MODELS OF DISORDER AND TREATMENT

8.4.1 Introduction

We are now in a position to explore similarities and differences between the analysis proposed so far in this chapter and current theories of psychological disorder. Our account has not emphasized a particular theoretical framework in psychology and psychiatry. It is not our purpose to do so, nor to attempt to elaborate a new theory. Rather, we have been examining the kind of account of order and disorder that follows from bringing together considerations in the philosophy of mind and knowledge, and in the theory of causal processes in biological systems. Nevertheless, this has led us to a point where it is possible to be quite specific about mechanisms, and the question arises as to the relation of this account to the available theoretical frameworks, of which we consider six briefly below. There is no attempt to do justice to the models, but only to indicate links with the proposals made so far in this chapter.

8.4.2 Conditioning theory

The principles of classical and operant conditioning supported models of various kinds of psychological disorder. Among the most elaborated and important was the formulation of phobic anxiety as a conditioned fear response. Conditioning theories of phobic anxiety invoked intentional processes of the kind described so far in this section, including hypothesized origin in traumatic experience (or in at least repeated, adverse, subtraumatic experiences), inappropriate generalization of fear, avoidance which precludes unlearning, and/or re-experiencing of the original fear in similar situations (Eysenck 1979).

Conditioning models, and particularly the behavioural therapies to which they gave rise, remain important, but generally they have been superseded by more sophisticated theories within the cognitive psychological paradigm outlined in the first chapter (subsection 1.2.2).

8.4.3 Social learning theory

Social learning theory extends conditioning theory by acknowledging social influences on learning, including the acquisition of behaviours by observation of others, and by recognizing cognitive processes in behaviour, including the regulating role of verbally expressed rules (Bandura 1977; Hodgson 1984).

One of the main applications of social learning theory has been to severe and persistent aggressive and disruptive behaviours in children. There is ample evidence that behaviour problems in children often occur against a background of inconsistent parental discipline, a high level of instructions, a high level of criticism or hostility, inadvertent reinforcement of aggressive behaviours, and a lack of explanation of the reason for instructions or reprimands (Patterson 1982). This may lead to a set of internalized rules in which the actions of others are readily construed as aggressive and aggressive responses are seen as appropriate. In studies that made use of videotapes of cartoon characters, young children who had been physically abused and showed high levels of aggressive behaviour, when compared with non-abused, non-aggressive children, construed the actions of the participants as more aggressive, and were more likely to indicate that aggressive solutions to interpersonal encounters were preferable (Dodge *et al.* 1990). This would indicate that the children had stable coherent representations and action plans that were inappropriate. Equally it is possible that inconsistency of experiences will not provide the setting for consistent internalized sets of rules, in which case contradictory schemata might be established along lines described earlier. This process may be more likely where, as Patterson has shown for some parents, discipline is determined by the mood of the parent, rather than the objective characteristics of the behaviour. This will make it difficult for the child to identify under which sets of rules the parental injunction falls. Is it to be understood as a function of the parent's mood, and therefore requiring a response that falls within a general strategy for dealing with mood changes, or is it to be construed as linked to the child's behaviour? In opting for one, the child may leave the other unexpressed, untested, and unexplored.

Interventions based on the teaching of new skills to parents, and thereby creating a setting in which children may acquire new internalized rules for behaviour, have had significant success (Kazdin 1993). These techniques focus also on effective action. It is characteristic of children with aggressive and disruptive behaviours that though they 'act' frequently, they provoke aversive responses from, or frustration by, others. Thus their experience of effective action is low. Parent training techniques place considerable emphasis on the creation by the parents of situations where the child has more control, and hence is able to act effectively; for instance in periods of play in which the parent is encouraged to follow the child's requests. A further way in which the child's experience of being able to act effectively is undermined arises where interactions have become so negative that her helpful or competent behaviours are no longer noticed by the parents. They are not acknowledged to be making an effective contribution to the relationships. The therapeutic approaches help the parents to notice, and then to praise prosocial behaviours. Through the reinforcement of such behaviours they become effective agents of social (inter)action. For some children the restoration in this way of a sense of agency may have important consequences for the recovery of the experience of a coherent self.

8.4.4 Cognitive therapy

Cognitive therapy is based on the assumption that cognition, in the form of beliefs and expectations, has a causal role in the generation of affect and behaviour. This proposal has been applied particularly in models of depression and anxiety (Beck 1976; Beck *et al.* 1986). Cognitions said to be implicated in the generation of depression include such as: 'I will be ineffective at this task, I am generally ineffective', 'Other people are better at doing things than I am', or 'I did not do that well, I don't do things well'. While cognitive therapy is clearly related in some ways to cognitive psychology (Brewin 1988), its scientific basis is not yet clearly elaborated (Teasdale 1993).

Cognitive therapy was developed partly to add value to behaviour therapy. Behaviour therapy confronts cognition with experience: irrational (inappropriate) fear is treated by safe, contained exposure to feared stimuli; depression by promoting activity which may bring satisfaction. Such experiences serve to disconfirm anxious or depressed views of the world, and also as evidence, despite expectations to the contrary, that the person can cope. On the other hand, behavioural methods can fail if a person uses theory to re-construe the relevant experiences. If a person is convinced that he and the world are hopeless, then any experience which seems to contradict this assumption is at risk for being avoided, denied, reconstrued, or rationalized away. Such cognitive manoeuvres fall outside the scope of behavioural intervention, but they are precisely what can be addressed and questioned in cognitive therapy. On the other hand, a possible weakness of cognitive therapeutic intervention at the level of verbally expressed beliefs alone is that it may fail to engage with, make a difference to, the underlying cognitive-affective states. For these sorts of reason, a combination of the two kinds of approach, under the name of cognitive-behavioural therapy, is commonly indicated.

Recently an extension of this idea has been recommended, on the basis of a complex model, in the direction of using active, 'experiential' therapeutic methods, such as those usually associated with Gestalt therapy (Teasdale 1993).

Cognitive therapy focuses on the person's theory of his or her own mental states, through attempting to make explicit underlying assumptions and rules, at first unavailable for self-report. Beck (1976) writes:

> These [cognitive schemata] will operate without the person's being aware of his rulebook. He screens selectively, integrates, and sorts the flow of stimuli and forms his own responses without articulating to himself the rules and concepts that dictate his interpretations and action.

How do these internalized sets of rules explain the disruption of functioning which occurs with the onset of a depressive episode? The theory is that the cognitions have developed prior to the episode and often are unconscious. At some point these sets of rules or schemata are then triggered into action, where they become the predominant set of rules that determine mood and behaviour, resulting in depression. A central assumption in the treatment is that these sets of rules of interpretation of events and other people may not have been tested, and the therapist examines the basis for them jointly with the patient. Therefore in cognitive therapy an explicit link is made between the monitoring and observing capacity of the individual and the therapist. On the basis of the thesis discussed earlier (subsection 8.3.2) it might be expected to be effective only where that observing agency appears to be intact. This is a prediction that remains to be tested.

Cognitive therapy is not much concerned with the origins of maladaptive cognitions, though it is presumably likely that in some cases they have an understandable connection to previous experience. There is, similarly, relatively little attention to the other aspect of the intentionality of maladaptive cognitions, namely, that they may in some cases serve a function. As remarked above (p. 313), maladaptive cognitions, for example in depression, may serve as protection from some greater threat, such as an assault on a valued other.

8.4.5 Psychoanalytic theories

Freud's early career was as a physician, working with neurological disorders which had clear, non-intentional, organic origins (Glymour 1991). He found himself attempting to explain apparently identical conditions for which no organic pathology could be identified. In his therapy of women with hysterical conversion syndromes Freud sought to establish whether an intentional account might be found for a disruption of functioning, which to the person and to an observer appeared intrusive and lacking in intentionality. He concluded that the activity of unconscious wishes which for much of the individual's life had been maintained inactive could provide an explanation (Izenberg 1991). Furthermore, the conflict between the conscious representation, and the separate unconscious representations created the conditions in which action was not possible, and hence paralysis.

The general principles underlying this proposal include ones that we have considered earlier in this chapter, such as the preparedness to invoke intentional states in explanation of disorder, departure from (Cartesian) common sense by not restricting intentionality to what is available to consciousness and expressed in self-report, and recognition that some intentional states constitute the core of belief to be protected from counter-evidence at any cost, including sacrifice of perceptions of reality or aspects of the self.

Psychoanalytic theories, and especially that of Freud, have been criticized for using a nineteenth-century hydraulic model of the effect of unconscious processes. This is seen to attribute qualities of force and energy inappropriately to brain states which might be better understood in terms of information-processing. While it is quite evident that information-processing is going on, intentionality entails also the registering of what matters to the organism, especially in its emotional charge, and action in avoiding or countering threat, or achieving a goal. The concepts of force and energy capture graphically what it is that energizes the response of the organism, whether animal or person. Furthermore, they provide pointers to the implications of conditions under which these states of mind and actions are disallowed. When we consider that the disallowing or splitting off of representations together with their very powerful emotions may have arisen in the context of painful, frightening, and immobilizing experiences, then their psychological impact when they are reactivated may be best described in the language of force and energy. Such an activation of a set of unconscious, untested, unintegrated, beliefs, wishes, and fears is likely to be experienced as intrusive, uncontrollable, and not understandable, in the same way as a physical (non-intentional) disruption of functioning. It seems then that Freud saw how intentional processes could, while remaining intentional, lead to causal pathways that produce phenomena with the same form as those arising from non-intentional origins, and hence apparently share their force, energy, and lack of intentionality.

The importance of early interpersonal experiences in psychological development was argued for by Melanie Klein (1946), and subsequent object-relations theorists. Klein's proposition that representations may be split into good and bad, and that if these are not in contact with each other there is a ·price to be paid, is a form of explanation that is highly compatible with a consideration of the consequences of threats to intentionality. However, and with hindsight perhaps surprisingly, Klein assumes that this is the basic universal human condition in early infancy which is 'cured' by good parenting. The evidence, which we reviewed briefly in Chapter 6, would suggest that infants possess substantial integrative capabilities from birth, and that disorder is more likely to arise from threats to the integrity of intentionality. Notwithstanding this difference, both analyses lead to the conclusion that parents, or other committed caregivers, are important to the developmental processes whereby a child comes to represent reasonably accurately key aspects of the external world, and his/her own internal world, and to elaborate appropriate and effective actions. In the absence of such development there arise the risks of inaccurate or partial representations, for instance where aspects of reality are split off, and an unintegrated and therefore more unpredictable and frightening mental life. This explicit linking of accuracy of representation of the external world and integration of mental life is clearly consistent with our previous considerations of epistemology and intentional-causal processes.

Winnicott (1971) also belonged to the object-relations school of psychoanalysis and his writings continue to exert a powerful influence on psychoanalytic theory. We find in them glimpses of ideas rather than an explicit and overarching framework. Two particular aspects of his work illuminate a consideration of function and dysfunction. He proposed, using extremely confusing terminology, that the infant needs to make the move in development from 'relating to' an object to 'using' an object. Roughly speaking, this means that the child ceases to need to control the other person, normally the parent, and becomes able to have a more mature multifaceted connection that is intimate but not controlling. The route is via an attack on the person, that he/she survives. Although Winnicott does not use the same language, he is referring to the testing of internalized schemata of the form 'I fear that my aggression is too dangerous for you', 'I will be rejected if I show aggression', 'I fear you will retaliate if I show aggression'. The survival of the parents, the lack of retaliation, and the absence of rejection provide containment for the child through the creation of a sense of safety. In addition, they may be seen to serve the function of contributing to the frame in which multiple, and often anxiety-provoking representations may be explored. They have the quality of commitment, and stating 'here are the boundaries', that are needed in order to promote the development of the metarepresentational system, the self. Put another way, the parent is a source of certainty and of what has to be to some extent just asserted, in order to provide a framework in which uncertainty and multiple rules of interpretation and action can be explored. The containment offered by parents has both an emotional and an epistemological function.

Winnicott's emphasis on the role of play has similar implications. He refers to play as taking place in a 'transitional space', that is to say in a domain of experience that is neither subjective and therefore unconnected to reality, nor objective and therefore representational of reality. In play crucial issues are explored with intensity and in detail, but without the consequences that would occur in the real world. These issues concern sex, loss, death, aggression, fears, wishes, and adult roles. Here the representations and their implications for action can be given life within the containing boundary of the 'this is play' metacognitions and communications. One side of a conflict, such as that concerning love and hate for a parent, may be worked out to the point of action, in the knowledge that the consequences may be enacted but will not actually ensue. This might entail a benign form of splitting in order to explore the consequence of the actions, but within a containing frame. Thus in Winnicott's theory play provides another epistemological and emotional container for the development, explanation, and testing of sets of rules and representations.

8.4.6 Family systems theories

The theories that we have considered thus far take as their starting point that disruption of function has taken place, and that this is the individual's problem. Family therapy has in some respects proposed that this is a case of mistaken identity. We say 'in some respects' because currently there is a wide diversity of emphases in family therapy (Hoffman 1982; Boscolo *et al.* 1987), and some will not be captured in this brief overview.

A major influence on the analysis of psychological problems has come from systems theory and the work of Gregory Bateson (1971). It is agreed that disruption of function is a key issue, but that the disruption is only apparent. By analogy with the physician who may ascribe a tachycardia to the effects of altitude, systems theory and family therapy have led therapists to examine further sources of intentionality within a person's context. For instance, a person may suffer from depression and there may be no apparent precipitants in the form of life events that involve loss or threat. We may then look for an agent that might have disrupted function, or for the intrusion of affective/cognitive representations along the lines described earlier. A family systems approach might lead to an interview with the family, in which the pattern of relationships prior to the depression and after its onset provide the focus for investigation. Take the example of a woman in her thirties who is married with children. It might be that her own mother had been widowed and that the depression provided a focus for the maternal grandmother's care for the patient, and hence brought them closer, without overtly challenging the marriage between the patient and her spouse. This would not provide an explanation of the intentionality of the origin of the depression, but would suggest that its maintenance was linked to the family relationships. The depression that had been seen previously as malfunction would then be 'reframed' as forming an important component of the family functioning. The behaviour is therefore seen to come under a different set of rules from that which the patient and the family first envisaged. Previously these rules, approximating to 'she is ill' placed the action in the hands of the physician, whereas under the new sets of rules, which include the question of how to care for the mother and preserve the marriage, the possible actions are in the hands of the family members. The family systems model can be widened in order to emphasize, that, before it is assumed that intentionality has run out, many contexts will need to be examined. However, the application of systems theory to therapy has a major difference from the analysis presented in this chapter in that it does not have a theory of breakdown. It is claimed that all apparent disorder may be analysed in terms of context. Whether this is the case is an empirical issue; however, at this stage it seems unlikely that such a position will be tenable. Serious individual psychological dysfunction can be substantial and seen across many contexts, each of which no doubt creates the setting for the disturbed behaviour, but also to which that individual contributes significantly.

Although family therapy has generally stopped short of an attempt to understand the implications of family functioning for the individual's development, different schools of family therapy have focused on some of the features of intentional causality that we have described. Much early interest centred on the origins of schizophrenia and the role of double-bind communications (Bateson *et al.* 1956). Bateson argued that communication has a content and a frame (metacommunication) and if the recipient is not to be confused, these must be congruent. Where they are contradictory and there is an implied prohibition on accurately reading one of the elements of the contradiction, then the participants will be confused. Bateson suggested that some symptoms of schizophrenia might represent attempts to bring order to the confusion, for instance through the generation of a clear fixed delusional belief, and others might reflect the confusion, for instance in the disturbed logic of formal thought disorder. This is close to our discussion of the possible impact on the developing child of confusing and contradictory communications, with implications for the integration of states of mind and the self (subsection 8.3.5; cf. also the discussion at the end of subsection 1.4.3). However Bateson's theory was expressed in terms of an attempted solution to current relationship difficulties, rather than a developmental process. His theory of schizophrenia is almost certainly incorrect. However, subsequent family systems approaches, especially those of the 'Milan School' have analysed family functioning in terms of communication deviance (Palazzoli *et al.* 1978), and have derived interventions that have been designed to lead to clarity.

Another 'school' has placed emphasis on the organization of the family (Minuchin 1974; Minuchin and Fishman 1981). Presenting problems are analysed in terms of current relationships, and are postulated to arise where the patient occupies a position that is inappropriate to his/her developmental stage and that of the family. For instance, in the example of the depressed woman, her role as mother of young children might have been taken over by the grandmother, leaving the mother functioning more like one of the children than a parent. The maintenance of the depression might then be seen to be related to this position in the family, and the solution might be for the mother to regain some of her role. This approach emphasizes the importance of family structure for children, and therefore addresses containment in development in a way that has points of contact with approaches based on psychoanalytic and social learning theory.

Recent developments in family therapy have included the system of the family and therapist in the analysis (Boscolo *et al.* 1987; McNamee and Gergen 1992). This has therefore moved away from a description of the intentionality of the presenting problem, to one that addresses behaviours seen in therapy. This is clearly related to an issue that arises in all psychotherapeutic approaches, namely one of the identity of the metaframe. As an observer I may be able to identify the frame and set of rules within which a person is functioning; however, when I engage in the therapeutic relationship a joint frame must be established. This, after all, will provide the container in which different representations of actions may be explored. In doing this, however, the therapist enters the frame that he/she is attempting to understand. Family therapists have for a long time made use of one-way screens and teams of observers in an attempt to commentate from the outside, but of course at the point where such groupings also participate in the therapeutic process the same considerations will apply. While it is the case that in order to understand the intentionality of behaviour within therapy it will be important to include the metarules of that engagement, including the role of therapist variables such as age, gender, and professional identity, our analysis would predict that behaviours seen in therapy can also be understood in relation to individual and family biography. The therapeutic task then is one of determining which sets of rules, representations, and actions are most relevant.

8.4.7 Attachment theory

Attachment theory (Bowlby 1969) differs from those discussed so far in that it has not developed in relation to psychological treatments. However, some of the research findings, to which we referred also in subsection 8.3.2, are of direct relevance to the issue of the intentional explanation of disorder. Infants who have been been assessed as 'secure', and those who have displayed behaviour that may be classified 'insecure avoidant' and 'insecure ambivalent' appear to have a coherent strategy with respect to attachment. It is not clear whether these insecure patterns have implications for subsequent disorder. On the one hand, they do not appear to be adaptive ways of dealing with distress and it is possible that, with repetition, lack of containment and splitting along the lines that we have outlined might occur. Equally there may be sufficient flexibility for change. A third 'disorganized' insecure category may signify already at 12 months of age an organization of internalized representations which has the intrusive and unpredictable qualities that we have associated with disorder. Infants in this group are described as showing sequential displays of contradictory behaviour patterns, especially on reunion with the parent. Examples include 'immediately following strong proximity seeking and a bright full greeting with raised arms, the infant moves to the wall or into the centre of the room and stills or freezes with a "dazed" expression' (Main and Solomon 1990). Disorganized infants are described as also showing simultaneous displays of contradictory behaviour patterns. An infant approaches her mother 'by moving backward towards on her stomach, face averted'. It seems that either in sequence, or simultaneously these infants show behaviours that reflect incompatible, intrusive representations. Each may separately preserve the conditions for action; however, 'freezing' or 'dazed expressions' lasting for 20 seconds or more, even while being held by a parent, are common. Thus it seems that the conditions for action here are not maintained. The category 'disorganized' is common in high-risk groups, especially where there has been maltreatment (Main and Hesse 1990). The developmental path of disorganized infants is of great interest to the account proposed here, in that often it is replaced at 4 or 5 years of age by a 'controlling' pattern. This is characterized by taking control of interactions with the parent through bossing her about, insulting her, or controlling through caregiving (Cassidy and Marvin 1991; Wartner *et al.* 1994). It seems that in these children the imperative to act has taken over, but at the expense of reciprocity and of receipt of care in the relationship. It is likely that representations of the unpredictable or frightening parental behaviours are now inactivated or split off.

Parental attachment representations can be assessed using the Adult Attachment Interview Schedule (Main and Hesse 1990). This yields a classification of 'secure autonomous', 'insecure dismissing', 'insecure preoccupied', 'insecure unresolved with respect to loss or trauma'. The ratings are made on the basis of the way in which the adult describes relationships with his or her own parents in childhood. The secure autonomous account is characterized by significant realistic detail, emotional content that does not become overwhelming, and a capacity to reflect on experiences. The insecure dismissing category is characterized by brief and emotionally neutral descriptions, and the insecure preoccupied by long, emotionally entangled accounts. The unresolved category is rated where there is a lack of coherence of the account, lapses in the metacognitive monitoring of reasoning processes or of the process of the discourse, or where the account is derailed by the intensity of emotion, associated with loss or trauma. Here then, the research instrument has taken the intrusion into the account, and disruption of the observing capacity, to which we have attached great importance, as the key to the rating. Studies of mothers and infants have shown a strong association between this unresolved category and the disorganized infant status, which suggests that adults who are prone to such intrusions and failures of metarepresentations may, as parents, behave in ways that contribute to similar development in their children (Ward 1990; Ward and Carlson 1995). Recent attachment research has therefore provided an indication of the role of intrusive disruptive internalized sets of rules in relation to adverse childhood experiences, and this provides a promising avenue for the understanding of the intentional basis of psychiatric disorder.

8.5 SUMMARY

In this chapter we have considered explanation of psychological disorder in terms of intentional processes. We approached the problem in two ways, first, in Section 8.2, as it were top-down, via consideration of the logic of representation, and secondly, in Section 8.3, as it were bottom-up, by considering conditions of intentionality in biological systems. We noted in subsection 8.2.1 that radical error in intentionality is a matter of persistent misrepresentation or persistent rule-conflict, and that these admit of psychological explanation in terms of avoidance and re-enactment of unacceptable outcomes. This idea was taken up and explored at some length in subsection 8.2.2. The broad notion of trauma and the cognitive paradoxes to which it gives rise was approached from the direction of post-empiricist epistemology (pp. 305–6), and via Wittgenstein's early work on the limits of thought (pp. 306–7). Reference was then made to post-traumatic stress reactions, to be taken up in the next chapter. Along with the notion of threat to psychic integrity comes the notion of psychic defences, and this was explored in subsection 8.2.3, using two quite different sources. First, analogy with threats to scientific theory, relatively open to view and well understood. And secondly, with reference to psychoanalytic theory, where the psychic defences have been first identified and explained. Several defences were discussed (pp. 308–11), including simple denial, splitting, projection, and narcissism. More intellectualized defences, and intellectualization of the primitive defences, become possible in the context of an explicit theory of mind (pp. 311–12). Defences typically entail costs as well as benefits, and in the special case of psychic defences these costs involve perpetual movement between avoidance and re-enactment. In this paradoxical sense the problem coincides with the solution (pp. 312–14).

From a biological perspective it was evident that where rules of interpretation are wired in, or there is limited scope for the acquisition of new representations, events that fall outside the range of the rules that are able to underpin action are not recognized as such, or lead to disorganized action or inaction. The position is different where multiple sets of rules of intentional processes can be generated. The elaboration of these intentional processes in psychological and social development, seen most dramatically in childhood, provides the basis for flexible, intelligent, and creative development. The integrity of intentional processes is, however, no longer guaranteed. The child may cope with trauma and other threats in development through the creation of contradictory representations, some that are accurate but cannot underpin action, and others that are inaccurate but lead to action, and especially action that retains crucial relationships with adults (subsection 8.3.2). This creates the possibility of internal disruptions of the integrity of intentional processes and hence intentional origins of psychological disorder. Further mechanisms include the generation of mental representations that are either insufficiently differentiated or too narrow (subsection 8.3.3), representations that are either lacking in sufficient stability or unavailable for testing and revision (8.3.4), and a metarepresentational system that is unable to monitor and integrate individual and interpersonal processes (8.3.5).

In Section 8.4 the nature of explanations of disorder in a range of theoretical, research, and therapeutic frameworks was discussed in the light of the operation and disruption of intentional processes.

REFERENCES

Ainsworth, M. D., Blehar, M. C., Waters, E., and Wall, S. (1978). *Patterns of attachment*. Erlbaum, Hillsdale, NJ.

Bandura, A. (1977). *Social learning theory*. Prentice Hall, Englewood Cliffs, NJ.

Bateson, G. (1971). *Steps to an ecology of mind*. Ballentine, New York.

Bateson, G., Jackson, D., Haley, J., and Weakland, J. (1956). Toward a theory of schizophrenia. *Behavioural Science*, 1, 251–64.

Beck, A. T. (1976). *Cognitive therapy and the emotional disorders*. International Universities Press, New York.

Beck, A. T., Emery, G., and Greenber, R. C. (1986). *Anxiety disorders and phobias: a cognitive perspective*. Basic Books, New York.

Boscolo, L., Cecchin, G., Hoffman, L., and Penn, P. (1987). *Milan systemic family therapy: conversations in theory and practice*. Basic Books, New York.

Bowlby, J. (1969). *Attachment and loss:I. Attachment*. Hogarth Press, London.

Breuer, J. and Freud, S. (1985). *Studies in hysteria*. Standard Edition 2, (1964). Hogarth Press, London.

Brewin, C. (1988). *Cognitive foundations of clinical psychology*. Lawrence Erlbaum Associates, London.

Byng-Hall, J. (1973). Family myths used as defence in conjoint family therapy. *British Journal of Medical Psychology*, 46, 239–49.

Cassidy, J. and Marvin, R. S., with the Working Group of the John D. and Catherine T. MacArthur Foundation on the Transition from Inancy to Early Childhood (1991). Attachment organization in three- and four-year olds: coding guidelines. Unpublished manuscript, University of Virginia, Charlottesville.

Dodge, K. A., Bates, J. E., and Pettit, G. S. (1990). Mechanisms in the cycle of violence. *Science*, 250, 1678–83.

Eysenck, H. (1979). The conditioning model of neurosis. *The Behavioral and Brain Sciences*, 2, 155–99.

Freud, A. (1936). *The ego and the mechanisms of defence*. International Universities Press, New York.

Freud, S. (1914). *On narcissism: an introduction*. Standard Edition 14, (1957), pp. 73–102. Hogarth Press, London.

Fulford, K. W. M. (1989). *Moral theory and moral practice*. Cambridge University Press, Cambridge.

Gardner, S. (1993). *Irrationality and the philosophy of psychoanalysis*. Cambridge University Press, Cambridge.

Glymour, C. (1991). Freud's Androids. In *The Cambridge companion to Freud*, (ed. J. Neu), pp. 44–85. Cambridge University Press, Cambridge.

Harlow, H. F. (1961). The development of affectional patterns in infant monkeys. In *Determinants of infant behaviour*, (ed. B. M. Foss), Vol. 1. Methuen, London.

Hilgard, E. (1977/1986). Divided consciousness: multiple controls in human thought and action. Wiley, New York. (Expanded edition 1986.)

Hodges, J. and Tizard, B. (1989). IQ and behavioural adjustment of ex-institutional adolescents. *Journal of Child Psychology and Psychiatry*, 30, 53–75.

Hodgson, R. (1984). Social learning theory. In *The scientific principles of psychopathology*, (ed. P. McGuffin, M. Shanks, and R. Hodgson), pp. 361–82. Academic Press, London.

Hoffman, L. (1982) *Foundations of family therapy*. Basic Books, New York.

Izenberg, G. N. (1991). Seduced and abandoned. The rise and fall of Freud's seduction theory. In *The Cambridge companion to Freud*, (ed. J. Neu), pp. 25–43. Cambridge University Press, Cambridge.

Kazdin, A. E. (1993). The treatment of conduct disorder: progress and directions in psychotherapy research. *Development and Psychopathology*, 5, 277–310.

Klein, M. (1946). Notes on some schizoid mechanisms. *International Journal of Psychoanalysis*, 27, 99–110.

Lakatos, I. (1970). Falsification and the methodology of scientific research programmes. In *Criticism and the growth of knowledge*, (ed. I. Lakatos and A. Musgrave), pp. 91–196. Cambridge University Press, Cambridge.

McNamee, S. and Gergen, K. (1992). *Therapy as a social construction*. Sage, London.

Main, M. and Hesse, P. (1990). Lack of resolution of mourning in adulthood and its relationship to infant disorganization: some speculations regarding causal mechanisms. In *Attachment in the preschool years*, (ed. M. Greenberg, D. Cicchetti, and E. M. Cummings), pp. 161–82. University of Chicago Press, Chicago.

Main, M. and Solomon, J. (1990). Procedures for identifying infants as disorganized/disorientated during the Ainsworth Strange Situation. In *Attachment in the preschool years*, (ed. M. Greenberg, D. Cicchetti, and E. M. Cummings), pp. 161–82. University of Chicago Press, Chicago.

Minuchin, S. (1974). *Families and family therapy*. Harvard University Press, Cambridge, Mass.

Minuchin, S. and Fishman, H. C. (1981). *Family therapy techniques*. Harvard University Press, Cambridge, Mass.

Palazzoli, S., Boscolo, L., Cecchin, G., and Prata, G. (1978). *Paradox and counterparadox*. Jason Aronson, New York.

Patterson, G. R. (1982). *Coercive family process*. Castalia, Eugene, OR.

Power, M. and Brewin, C. (1991). From Freud to cognitive science: a contemporary account of the unconscious. *British Journal of Clinical Psychology*, 30, 289–310.

Sandler, J. (ed.) (1988). *Projection, identification, projective identification*. Karnac Books, London.

Stern, D. N. (1985). *The interpersonal world of the infant*. Basic Books, New York.

Teasdale, J. (1993). Emotion and two kinds of meaning: cognitive therapy and applied cognitive science. *Behaviour Research and Therapy*, 31, 339–54.

Ward, M. J. (1990). Predicting infant–mother attachment from adolescent mother's prenatal working models of relationships. Paper presented at the International conference on Infant Studies, Montreal, Canada.

Ward, M. J. and Carlson, E. A. (1995). Associations among adult attachment representations, maternal sensitivity, and infant–mother attachment in a sample of adolescent mothers. *Child Development*, **66**, 69–79.

Wartner, U. G., Grossman, K., Fremmer–Bombik, E., and Suess, G. (1994). Attachment patterns at age six in South Germany: predictibility from infancy and implications for preschool behaviour. *Child Development*, **65**, 1014–27.

Winnicott, C. (1971). *Playing and reality*. Basic Books, New York.

Wittgenstein, L. (1921). *Tractatus logico-philosophicus*. (Trans. Pears, D. F. and McGuiness, B. F. (1961) Routledge and Kegan Paul, London).

9
Psychiatric conditions

9.1 INTRODUCTION

We are now in a position to take further our consideration of causal processes in biology and psychology in relation to disorder. The purpose of this is to outline the way in which these causal processes might operate. Emphasis will be on causal routes for which there is good evidence. Where the evidence does not point strongly in any particular direction, we shall rely on theory and some speculation. After all, if this enterprise is to be useful or valid, it should be able to go beyond the evidence. We shall consider three kinds of syndrome: schizophrenia; anxiety disorders, mainly obsessive-compulsion and post-traumatic stress disorder; and personality disorder. We have selected these, obviously not with any aim of covering all of psychopathology, but because they illustrate various kinds of issue in the explanation of disorder. Schizophrenia has been addressed by all, or most, orientations in psychiatry and clinical psychology, with theories about it from practically every point of view, invoking non-intentional- and intentional-causal pathways of various kinds. The task is set, therefore, of assessing which are valid and how they hang together. Obsessive-compulsive disorder is less researched, but it has the special interest of suggesting alternative aetiological models, one of which emphasizes intentionality while the other posits non-intentional-causal pathways. Post-traumatic stress disorder is included because of the clarity of its intentionality, its relation to environmental stressors, which is indeed (unusually) built into the definition of the disorder. The relatively transparent nature of post-traumatic stress reactions may serve as a partial model for more obscure problems, as will be discussed. Personality disorder represents both a problem and an opportunity for research and clinical practice. The problem arises from the attempt to encompass the complexity of personality functioning in diagnostic categories, and the opportunity from the recognition of the role of the person in our understanding of psychiatric disturbance. This demands an analysis that is developmental, and that attends to the interplay between intentional and non-intentional processes.

In what follows we use diagnostic terms because they will orient the reader and provide general pointers to boundaries between conditions. However, this does not imply a commitment either to the assumption that each is unitary, or that explanations might not cross their boundaries.

9.2 SCHIZOPHRENIA

9.2.1 Introduction: syndromes

Schizophrenia has a central place in the practice, theory, and research endeavours of psychiatry and clinical psychology. The term probably covers a range of conditions with different aetiologies, although their separation has not been achieved with any certainty. A distinction that has had substantial utility is that between Type 1 and Type 2 syndromes (Crow 1985; Tsuang 1993). The Type 1 syndrome refers typically to the symptoms of acute episodes characterized by delusions (firmly held, culturally inappropriate erroneous beliefs), hallucinations (perceptual experiences without basis in the external world), and disorders of thinking. The Type 2 syndrome is comprised of the so-called negative symptoms of restriction of emotional range, poverty of thought and speech, decreased motor activity, apathy, lack of spontaneity, and diminished interpersonal interactions. These syndromes are not distinct and the same individuals often show signs of both. However, there is some evidence that the inheritance of each may be distinctive and that there may therefore be differences in aetiology. In this consideration of schizophrenia (and this caveat will become familiar throughout this chapter) we cannot assume that our review of possible causal explanations will apply equally across all cases. Nevertheless, studies to which reference is made have used a standardized definition of schizophrenia, either that of the World Health Organization or the American Psychiatric Association, so that, in general, the clinical pictures presented by subjects in the investigations will be broadly comparable.

9.2.2 Biochemical contributions

Some of the earliest 'biological' explanations of schizophrenia provided examples of non-intentional-causal accounts. The 'dopamine hypothesis' contained the following propositions. Amphetamines can lead in normal individuals to a disturbed state that closely resembles that seen in sufferers with schizophrenia. Amphetamines increase the level of dopamine in the relevant parts of the brain (see later) and drugs that are effective in episodes of schizophrenia also block the effects of dopamine at receptor sites. It is therefore possible that an episode of schizophrenia is the result of excess dopamine. The explanation is that the level of dopamine in the system will be outside the normal range, or that there is deception of the system, with levels of dopamine that might be expected in the presence of certain sensory stimuli, but occurring in their absence. With respect to this biochemical system there would be an intentional explanation (e.g. deception), but with respect to stimuli that are relevant to the intentionality of beliefs or experiences there is an intrusion and a non-intentional explanation. Episodes might be precipitated by psychological factors if, for instance, these led to increased arousal that was associated with a consequent alteration of dopamine levels. Then there would be an intentional explanation for the altered dopamine level, and a non-intentional explanation of the altered state of mind and behaviour. The origin of this susceptibility to altered dopamine might be genetic. Evidence from twin and adoption studies indicates a substantial heritability for schizophrenia, although the nature of the genetic contribution is unclear (Roberts 1991).

9.2.3 Neuropathology and neuropsychology

Evidence for a neuropathological deficit in schizophrenia is increasing. The area of the brain that is most consistently identified is the parahippocampal gyrus on the median side of the temporal lobe (Jakob and Beckman 1986; Falkai *et al.* 1988). How might this contribute to the development of schizophrenia? Medial temporal lobe structures are believed to have a crucial role in the integration and processing of the inputs from a wide range of areas of the brain. They act as a kind of 'gate' for information, selecting only certain items for further processing (Frith and Done 1988; Gray *et al.* 1991). It is possible, then, that at least some patients with schizophrenia have deficits in information processing. Gray *et al.* (1991) have proposed that a central deficit in the functioning of the schizophrenic patient is found in a problem in the linking of stored memories to current stimuli. As we saw in Chapter 6, the ability to do this is present in very young infants. Repeated stimuli are of great interest provided they are accompanied by variations. Clearly, variations may be detected only by comparison with previous, remembered stimuli. This theory suggests that for the schizophrenic patient each stimulus appears as if new. The authors cite, in support of this, findings that schizophrenic patients show deficits in experimental conditions that test the influence of stored memories of regularities of previous input on current perception. It is hypothesized that in the acute schizophrenic state the individual is unable to determine which aspects of sensory stimuli are familiar and which are novel, and so attends to incidental stimuli. Those aspects of monitoring the surroundings and the self that are usually carried out unconsciously have to be done consciously and the individual is overloaded by the task. This leads to disorientation of thought and speech.

This theory is linked to the dopamine hypothesis via results of experiments on learning in rats. Rats, like other animals, including humans, can be trained to respond to a conditioned stimulus when it is paired to an unconditioned stimulus. Famously, Pavlov's dogs learned to salivate to the sound of a bell, after the bell had been paired with the sight of food. However, if rats have been exposed to the conditioned stimulus in the absence of the unconditioned stimulus prior to the pairing of the two, they take longer to link the conditioned to the unconditioned stimulus. In other words, their previous experience of the conditioned stimulus has taught them that it is not linked to a reward (such as food) and so they take longer to adopt a different 'interpretation'. In the language of our previous discussion, they have one internalized set of rules for the interpretation of the stimulus, and take time to replace it with another. This phenomenon of latent inhibition can be abolished with amphetamine and restored by the administration of a drug that blocks the effect of dopamine; a drug of the same type as that used in the treatment of schizophrenia.

Gray and colleagues (Gray *et al.* 1991) have argued that these deficits arise from an interruption of the brain's capacity to integrate sensory inputs with a person's current motor state and stored memories, which is required in order to make judgements about current circumstances and the possible need for action. They propose that this deficit is caused by excess dopamine activity and so they postulate a non-intentional origin for the limited information-processing capacity of the brain. This reduces the ability of the individual to generate internalized sets of rules, and to use them in perception and the regulation of action. Under certain conditions, say those where the perceptual demands are high, the task may be too great and thoughts and behaviour become disorganized. Thus against this background, any particular episode may have intentional origins in the extent of sensory overload. As we saw in Chapter 7 the concept of 'design' is derived from a consideration of organism and environment. This model postulates a combination of the two in the generation of the psychotic (schizophrenic) breakdown. Whether environmental factors appear to be important will depend upon the critical range over which they make a difference. It is possible that, at least for some individuals, the limitation of information processing is so profound that all or most levels of environmental demand will be sufficient to lead to psychosis, and for others that it is of an order that some commonly encountered environmental requirements can be accommodated whereas others cannot. Then differences in environment will be seen to be critical to the incidence of psychosis. Clearly, the earlier non-intentional account and this one may be combined. For instance, a deficit in the regulation of dopamine might lead to an increase in its level, thus impeding the information-processing capability of the individual and hence precipitating psychosis.

What then of the origins of the hypothesized deficit? We return to the neuropathology of schizophrenia. One possibility is that neuronal damage occurs shortly prior to the onset of the first psychotic episode, so that the episode is an immediate consequence of the development of the lesion. This would suggest a degenerative brain condition; however, the evidence does not support this (Murray *et al.* 1988). It is more likely that there is a disturbance in brain development, either before birth, or in the first few months of life. Here we enter an area of some controversy. The case has been made that environmental factors, such as viral infection or perinatal injury, may contribute to the neurodevelopmental deficit (Jones and Murray 1991), and conversely that the deficit generally arises from genetic influences (Roberts 1991).

9.2.4 Neurodevelopment and psychological development

The proposition that schizophrenia may arise from a neurodevelopmental deficit takes us back to our consideration of development, design, and intentional-causal processes. If the deficit is present at an early stage, what might be the consequences in childhood? Further neuropsychological hypotheses are of great interest in this respect. Frith (1992) has argued that an important deficit in schizophrenia is in the link between willed intentions and the monitoring of actions. Under experimental conditions schizophrenic patients have been shown to be poorer than other individuals at correcting their actions when they are unable to see their effects, which suggests that their central monitoring is poorer (Mlakar *et al.* 1994). A consequence of such a deficit is likely to be that the schizophrenic sufferer does not recognize that he is the cause of his own actions, and this may form the basis of the experience of having one's actions controlled by another agent, and by analogy with action, the experience of thoughts being controlled. There is a failure of (meta)representation of the individual's own mental activities. Frith has also emphasized that a problem for many schizophrenics is to understand context. In human communication it is necessary to understand the meaning of the words, and also the way in which they are being used in a particular context, and schizophrenics tend to be bad at this. In other words, they have difficulties in identifying metacommunications accurately. If these hypotheses are correct, and at this stage they must be viewed as informed speculations, the person with schizophrenia suffers from deficits in processes which in infancy appear to be crucial to the development of the self, and its metarepresentational capabilities. The linking of memory to event provides a sense of continuity over time, the sense of agency repeated over time and place creates continuity, and the accurate identification of context links self to different circumstances.

If it is hypothesized that the neurodevelopmental deficit is present in infancy, is it possible that analogous psychological deficits might be present also early in development? If so, what would be the implications for the infant's experience of the caregiver, and the caregiver's experience of the infant? We do not know the answer to these questions, but our speculations will focus on information-processing and the development of the self. We may guess that the infant whose capacity to generate internalized regularities and to detect and enjoy novelty is impaired might appear rather puzzled and unresponsive, which might impede the development of pleasurable, rhythmic, face-to-face interactions which are so characteristic of the first months of life, and appear to form the basis of subsequent forms of communication and relating. Difficulties in understanding interpersonal context might have similar consequences. We do not know whether the hypothesized deficit might be overcome, at least in part, by the use of appropriate strategies. Clearly, the generation of expectations and departures from them arises both from the capacity of the infant, and the nature of the stimuli, provided predominantly in infancy by a caregiver. Might some parents be more able than others to provide sufficient scaffolding on which to create such internalized rules, perhaps through substantial repetition, or more marked variations against such a background? Conversely, might some parents give up the task of close sustained interactions in the face of an apparently uncomprehending infant? Consideration of such possibilities highlights the way in which the development of representations and metarepresentations might be impeded or facilitated. They entail variants of the design stance explanation, in the sense outlined in Chapter 7. The common strand is the acquisition of the rules for the interpretation of events. The extent to which these are wired in, how pervasive they are, and extent to which they are open to modification is not prejudged.

We should make clear that there are other possibilities. For instance, it could be argued that the neurodevelopmental deficit, although present from early childhood, is not expressed until the time when schizophrenia is commonly first seen, in adolescence, perhaps as a result of neuronal maturation at that age. Then our analysis might not apply. It seems, however, that at least a significant number of children who are at risk for schizophrenia do show differences from other children. Studies of the children of parents with schizophrenia have shown that they have more attentional deficits, and that these are associated with subsequent social insensitivity, social indifference, and social isolation (Cornblatt *et al.* 1992). Clearly studies such as this are complicated by the presence of parents with schizophrenia who might have the same or similar hypothesized deficits as their children; however, they provide some preliminary evidence that deficits may be present in childhood which could disrupt early parent–child interactions, with implications for subsequent development.

In our discussion of the design stance, it was emphasized that even where intentional causal processes are wired in, in humans the 'wiring' may be influenced by experience. If the development of the visual system is influenced by visual experience then why not information-processing? In rats the phenomenon of latent inhibition is not seen if they have not been handled during the first days of life (Weiner *et al.* 1987), which suggests that early experiences may have long-term structural implications. This does not lead us away from the role of genetic influences, but rather to an interactive theory in which the information-processing capacity is central and the origins are in genetically determined variability and variability in early intentional-causal processes.

Further indirect support comes from studies where both inheritance and environment have been assessed. In the Finnish Adoption Study the rate of schizophrenia or schizophrenia spectrum disorders in the adopted children of schizophrenic parents was 30 per cent, with 15 per cent in a control group. However, these differences were apparent only in a comparison of adopting families which were rated (without knowledge of the adopted children's mental health) as showing confusing patterns of communication. These might be expected to make difficult the identification of metacommunications concerning the rules of social interaction and hence, in vulnerable individuals, lead to an impaired understanding of the actions of others (Tienari *et al.* 1994).

In the context of a developmental interactional account, the capacity for multiple representational systems may be important to outcome. Thus the infant with the hypothesized deficit may, as a result of a parent's ability to compensate, develop a secure attachment relationship, which will increase the chances of instrumental and interpersonal competence. This may act as a protective factor in relation to a persistent deficit and the risk of psychosis. Conversely, the development of insecure attachment may increase the risk. Children who as infants have been classified as 'insecure', later in life elicit less supportive responses from their teachers than those rated 'secure'. If a similar effect applies between parents and children, and if the vulnerability of infants makes it more difficult for parents to establish a secure attachment relationship, then these parents might later be less supportive and more critical of their children. There is ample evidence that the emotional atmosphere in the home, and especially the level of criticism, hostility, and over-involvement (which together are termed 'expressed emotion'), influences the course of schizophrenia (Bebbington and Kuipers 1994), and the relapse rate can be reduced substantially if the expressed emotion of the parents is lowered through a family-based intervention (Jesus Mari and Streiner 1994). It is not clear whether expressed emotion is a factor in the onset of schizophrenia, however if developmental processes of the kind described here are important, it is likely to be the transaction between vulnerability and parenting style that matters.

9.2.5 Psychosis, certainty, and action

Is it possible to take further the account of the formation of psychotic symptoms, especially those of the acute phase, delusions and hallucinations? The simplest dopamine hypothesis would predict that the symptoms are the consequence of overstimulation of neurons; a non-intentional explanation. However, it may be that the origin and nature of these abnormal beliefs and experiences is not qualitatively different from those of individuals who are not psychotic. The diagnostic classifications and research instruments create a sharp distinction but in practice it is not clear-cut (Strauss 1992). If we put this together with the neuropsychological theories of schizophrenia, we may emerge with a different formulation. The theory provides an explanation of disordered, chaotic, overwhelmed, and unpredictable thoughts and behaviours. Delusions and hallucinations are, by contrast, clear, unambiguous, and relatively or absolutely uninfluenced by evidence. Consider further contrasts. The experience of self predicted by the neuropsychological theory is fragmented and discontinuous in time; the experience of self in relation to delusions and hallucinations is likely to be coherent, and to have continuity. The experience of external reality where stimuli require constant reassessment, and where context is indecipherable, is likely to be one of uncertainty in which high vigilance is required. The experience of external reality through delusions and hallucinations is likely to contain substantial predictability. The neuropsychological theory predicts a deficit in information-processing which renders action impossible or at best fragmented and inconsistent; delusions and hallucinations will often have clear implications for action. For these reasons the symptoms, at least of some sufferers, may be seen as the outcome of coping strategies which restore coherence to representations, and provide a basis for action. They are possible attempts to restore the integrity of intentional-causal processes. Evidence in support of this proposition comes from several sources.

Studies of the attributional style of deluded and hallucinated patients have shown that, compared to non-psychotic individuals, they make use of less evidence in coming to conclusions, and when making causal inferences they ascribe more global, stable, and external origins to events (Bentall *et al.* 1991). This is evident in relation to tasks that have nothing to do with their abnormal beliefs. It seems possible therefore that they are using a particular strategy for making inferences; that they have a characteristic set of internalized rules for the interpretation of events. This is a style which restricts attention to incoming stimuli and creates certainty. The attributions have much in common with depressive (global, stable) cognitions, but favour externality over internality. It could be argued that such external (paranoid) attributions provide a better basis for action than the depressive.

Roberts (1991) compared currently deluded patients, with patients who had recovered from delusions, and with psychiatric nurses and Anglican ordinands, on measures of purpose in life and depression. The groups with the highest purpose in life scores were the deluded and the ordinands, with the nurses slightly lower, and those who had recovered from delusions substantially (and statistically significantly) lower than all other groups. The recovered patients were also the most depressed. The explanation could be in part that the content of more of those with persistent delusions was grandiose or erotic, although persecutory delusions were equally common in both groups. It seems then that the delusions, although in some respects maladaptive, also provided coherence and meaning. Strauss (1992) has similarly described contrasting examples from a major follow-up study of schizophrenic patients:

> At the two year follow-up, a woman who was still very delusional was functioning socially in a way better than many 'normal' people. She was working, looking after her child, and taking care of her house on a relatively limited income, all while frequently being psychotic. Another patient I saw, a woman whose symptoms had essentially disappeared, was sitting in darkened room in her house, and had not worked or had contact with friends for most of the time since I had seen her at the initial evaluation, two years before.

This does not demonstrate that the delusions were important to effective functioning and action, but it is consistent with that proposition. However, a patient from the study of Roberts, who had recovered from delusions, expressed himself directly on the issue, 'I always felt everything I said was worthless, but as Jesus everything I said was important—it came from God . . . I just want to hide away, I don't feel able to cope with people . . . I always feel lonely, I don't know what to say.'

In these examples we see the operation of compensatory mechanisms, comparable to those of the increase in heart rate in response to blood loss. However, there is the added element that we described in the previous chapter. Intentionality in psychological processes entails the experience of continuity, coherence, and efficacy. Where the environment is reasonably benign and decipherable, and where action is possible and effective, these experiences are supported. Threats arising either internally or externally or in combination, may be countered via mechanisms that entail sacrifice in order to restore meaning and action. The sacrifice of accuracy of perception in the pursuit of clarity and action may be a particular (but not exclusive) schizophrenic strategy.

9.3 ANXIETY DISORDERS

9.3.1 Intentionality, development, and content

Central to the anxiety disorders is excessive or unrealistic anxiety. Various kinds of anxiety disorder may be distinguished according to the object of the fear and the behavioural and physiological responses. The main kinds of anxiety disorder defined by DSM-IV (American Psychiatric Association 1994) include phobias, characterized by avoidance; obsessive-compulsion, in which anxiety is relieved by compulsive neutralizing rituals; generalized anxiety disorder, involving persistent worrying; panic disorder, comprising unexpected anxiety attacks; and post-traumatic stress disorder, involving persistent re-experiencing of the trauma, avoidance, and emotional numbing.

In this section we consider anxiety disorders using the approach to psychological function and dysfunction proposed in previous chapters. The approach to psychological function takes intentionality, embedded in developmental processes, to be fundamental. Underpinning this core assumption is the very general idea that it is principles of intentionality which are going to deliver causal explanations of bio-psychological phenomena. Without this background philosophical assumption, intentionality, involving meaningful connections between the contents of intentional states and processes, will tend to be neglected or regarded as secondary, and in particular will not be put to work in the explanation of psychological disorder, where meaning seems, in any case, to have run out.

In the case of anxiety disorders, unlike some other kinds of psychopathology, we can begin with a good grasp of the relevant 'normal' function and its intentionality. As discussed under the heading of functional semantics in Chapter 4. (subsection 4.5.2), 'normal' is most readily understood in this sort of context in terms of evolutionary biology: the normal function of a biological or biopsychological system is that which it was selected in evolution to serve (Millikan 1984, 1986). The normal function of anxiety is relatively easy to define in broad terms, as involving detection of danger to the living being. Thus for example, Eysenck (1992, p. 4):

> In considering the potential value of a cognitive approach to anxiety, it is important to consider anxiety from the evolutionary perspective. Anxiety is an unpleasant and aversive state, and it is perhaps not immediately obvious what (if any) biological significance it might have. However, it is clear that rapid detection of the early warning signs of danger possesses considerable survival value . . . The key purpose or function of anxiety is probably to facilitate the detection of danger or threat in potentially threatening environments.

Given the function of detection of danger, anxiety typically involves intensification of, and selection in, various pre-attentional and attentional processes, including hypervigilance towards and mental preoccupation with danger, and danger and safety signals (Gray 1982; Oatley and Johnson-Laird 1987; Eysenck 1992).

It has been assumed throughout this essay that psychological functions generally are dedicated to action. In the case of anxiety this means generating solutions to the problem of the perceived danger. Once detected, threat has to be appropriately responded to. Relatively primitive (from the evolutionary point of view) ways of doing this include behavioural avoidance and physical destruction of the source of danger. Avoidance and destruction have in common that they get rid of the danger: they get the living being out of harm's way, or vice versa. A different kind of coping strategy can be called 'problem-solving', as opposed to problem avoidance or problem destruction. It involves interacting with the source of danger in such an adaptive way that, after all, it does no harm to the agent.

It is also relatively easy to see ways in which the function of anxiety is elaborated in phylogenesis and ontogenesis. Danger comes to include not only assaults on physical integrity and deprivation of biological necessities, but also, for example in social beings, threat to status in the group, and in human beings, threat to various aspects of 'self-esteem'. Development also elaborates the response side of anxiety. Increased cognitive resources create more possibilities of problem-solving. Specifically, the behavioural coping skills of avoidance and attack find mental analogues (analogues in mental representations) in living beings with the requisite congnitive capacity. This means, roughly, that some possible dangers need not be thought about at all, or if at all, that they can be disqualified in the imagination. There are also problem-solving analogues within the realm of mental representations, which involve making plans as to how to cope with the difficult situation if and when it arises.

The detection of danger and the solving of the perceived problem are intimately linked. This implies that along with detection of danger, appraisal of coping skills is fundamental to anxiety (Lazarus and Averill 1972; Eysenck 1992). Hence perceived absence of being able to cope, in the form of perceived unpredictability or uncontrollability of significant events, is critical in the generation of anxiety, in animals (Mineka and Kihlstrom 1978) and in human beings (Olah *et al.* 1984; Edwards 1988; Endler and Parker 1990). If, in the face of threat, no coping skills can be found which work, the result tends to be runaway anxiety (panic).

According to the approach taken here, principles of intentionality and development of the kind sketched above make up the foundations of the theory of anxiety. They constitute the core of theory in the sense of post-empiricist epistemology (subsection 1.4.1). Core assumptions, it may be recalled, are less concerned with particular facts established by particular methods, and more concerned with defining the nature and aetiology of the phenomena, and formulating critical questions about them. They are at work in the selection and interpretation of data, and they typically drive research programmes.

The assumptions about anxiety sketched so far are intended to be relatively uncontroversial in the sense that they are supported by a great deal of empirical data and are compatible with many other relevant, well-supported approaches. The question concerns rather what is at the core of the theory. We have begun with intentionality in the context of development, but there are certainly other places for the theory of anxiety to start. For example, Gray (1982) takes as his main problem the question as to what brain systems serve anxiety, and approaches this by studying the operation and effects of anxiolytic pharmacological agents. Eysenck (1992) applies another paradigm to anxiety, namely the explanation of individual differences in terms of personality traits. Another approach is study of what are inevitable side-effects of the normal function of anxiety, such as lowered interest in (lowered concentration on, and motivation for) other situations and tasks (Williams *et al.* 1992). Important though all these models and accompanying methodologies are, they are designed to focus on issues other than the intentionality of anxiety and its developmental complexities. While such differences in emphasis and direction are already in the models of normal anxiety, they are perhaps most apparent in application to the problem of disorder.

When applied to disorder, the model proposed here defines the primary problems as being in the area of intentional and non-intentional processes and possible interactions between them. Critical questions include: to what extent are biologically normal, intentional processes operating in cases of anxiety disorder? At what point if any are they disrupted by non-intentional-causal processes?

The assumption that the anxiety system functions to facilitate detection of, and response to, threat is a methodological principle rather than an empirical generalization (a distinction discussed in subsection 4.6.2). It defines the 'normal' case, and by implication the 'abnormal', this distinction being most readily understood in this sort of context in terms of evolutionary biology, as already indicated. The methodological principle envisages that normal function can break down. This is to say, the anxiety system may run free of the detection of danger. In this case the system is functioning abnormally, that is, it is not serving the function for which it was selected. Abnormal function can be caused in various ways, but all are variations on abnormalities in the physiological structures and functions which realize the anxiety system, such that this system operates in the absence of appropriate (in the sense of evolutionary theory) information-processing.

At this point, of course, we encounter squarely the problems posed by anxiety disorder. Commonly the person will say what his or her anxiety is about, will describe the intentional object of the fear, but the anxiety is inappropriate to this object, being either excessive or unrealistic in relation to it. It may be inferred that in such cases the anxiety system is operating in a biologically abnormal way, in the absence of appropriate (in the sense of evolutionary theory) information-processing, in which case it would be appropriate to look for neurological or cognitive 'design flaws' (cf. Gray 1982; Eysenck 1992; Williams *et al.* 1991).

On the other hand, it would be agreed that the person's self-report is no infallible guide here. Absence of an account of perceived real threat by the person so far hardly counts against there being one. The cognitive processing which permeates anxiety is not necessarily conscious, in the sense of conscious awareness or verbal report (Tyrer *et al.* 1978; Dixon 1981; Kemp-Wheeler and Hill 1987). The assumption that anxiety has intentionality, specifically perception of threat, is thus independent of whether or not the person is aware of, or can say, what the perceived danger is. In general, the information-processing which mediates between perception and action (affective responses and behaviour) may be unconscious, in the sense of being unavailable for, and perhaps misrepresented by, self-report (subsections 1.2.4, 1.4.3).

The question arises, therefore, as to how we get a hold on the intentional objects of psychological states without reliance on self-report. Earlier discussions of the epistemology of mind and meaning (subsection 1.4.2, Section 3.2, subsections 4.5.4–5) focused on three closely interwoven methods: observation of intentional behaviour, application of a theory of mind, and perhaps mental simulation (thought-experiments) in one's own case. A fourth source of information is, of course, other relevant self-reports which may be assumed to be reliable.

Consider, for example, the case of a child presenting with excessive and unrealistic fear about his own health. Assessment of such a case, described in more detail in, for example, Bolton (1994), would involve gaining information about events in the family, the child's patterns of intentional behaviour, application of theory about the kind of thing that would make a child really afraid, perhaps supplemented by use of empathy, and information about the child's relevant beliefs and views, and all of these in combination could lead to an hypothesis about the real object of the child's fear, for example, in the context of medical anxieties in the family, that the father is in danger of having a heart attack.

In general, not only is there no reason to assume that the self-report of the intentional object of fear (what it is about) is accurate, but there is reason positively to doubt it. This is just because real causes of anxiety have to be dealt with, and one great way is avoidance, including in its mental form, denial. As indicated earlier, gaps and error in the theory of mind are frequently in the service of defence, in the individual and in the family (pp. 311–12).

The approach proposed here is based simply on the methodological assumption that normal biopsychological function is *persistent*. And normal function has, of course, to do with detection of *real* danger, not imagined. The evolutionary hypothesis is that the anxiety system would not have been selected had it not served the function of detecting danger, but it makes no sense to interpret 'danger' in this context as things that really represent no threat at all. The search is for something that *really matters to* a human being of such-and-such a kind. If a toddler, for example, seems to get into something like a panic state when a toy is taken from him, it is plausible to suppose that the appropriate intensional description of the event is one that brings out its highly threatening nature for the child, so that it means to him, for example, the collapse of plans and the disintegration of action, or his powerlessness. A second-choice hypothesis in this case is that the child's anxiety is excessive or unrealistic, that the anxiety system, the detection of significant threat, is functioning abnormally due to some design fault.

This is not to say, of course, that the anxiety system, or any other bio-psychological system, cannot go wrong. As already discussed, the methodological assumption of normal function may have to be given up in particular cases or kinds of case. There may be direct evidence of non-intentional causation of activity of the autonomic nervous system, and in this case hypotheses about intentional causation would be discounted, or there may be interactions between the two kinds of causal pathway. Otherwise the reason for abandoning the assumption of normal function is likely to be the negative one, that is, failing to find any plausible hypotheses about real threats to the person which the expressed intentional object means. What guides the search for meaning here is primarily bio-psychological theory, in which developmental issues are fundamental.

Threat is, of course, readily understandable in the form of, for example, a predatory animal, as is the response of fleeing or attacking. For social beings, particularly slowly maturing ones like ourselves, the role of carers is equally a matter of life and death. For the infant, avoidance or attack by carers constitute major, life-threatening, dangers. Given the vulnerability of infants, it is plausible to envisage no lower limit to the age at which patterns of anxiety and its management are generated. Psychoanalytic theory has emphasized that these patterns belong from the beginning to the mother–infant interaction, and the first critical type of coping task is attributed naturally enough to mother. Mother has to contain the infant's anxiety, which means, briefly, that her task is to not, out of her own anxiety, avoid or panic in the face of the child's, but is rather to stay with the baby, physically and mentally, holding him calm (cf. Winnicott 1971; see also subsection 8.4.5). This kind of task and its vagaries become apparent enough as the child grows older. The theme of dependence on adults runs through all the variety in the child's developmental and life-tasks, and the evolving child–carer relationship therefore remains closely implicated in fear and coping.

A related approach to the objects and causes of anxiety concerns the development of self. The general principle is that perceived threats to self-preservation generate high anxiety (Oatley and Johnson-Laird 1987). What that amounts to depends on what is essential to, or perceived as essential to, the self, and this is a complicated matter for human beings. As discussed in Chapter 6 (subsections 6.4.3, 6.5.2), the foundations of various aspects of the sense of self are established early in life (Stern 1985), and these are developed and elaborated at least through childhood and adolescence (Erikson 1963). Formation of the sense (or senses) of the self depends on the accomplishment of a wide and complex variety of tasks, including physical actions, affective responding, interpersonal relating, speech, education, and so on. Tasks generate anxiety, and solutions require effective coping skills.

Psychological theory here moves into social theory. It is impossible to know what is essential to the sense of self in human beings, and therefore what signifies a major threat to them, without understanding culture. Superficially the same event may have very different meanings between societies. A certain kind of practice may be innocent according to one set of values, but sin in another, and so on. If an event generates high anxiety, it can and should be construed in a way that brings out its highly dangerous significance. Failure of a child at school, to take another kind of example, may signify to an immigrant family loss of hope of improvement for generations.

The issues in meaningful explanation encountered here have been discussed in previous chapters. The meanings available in culture, and which guide human activity, are diverse and cannot be circumscribed, exceeding what is visible from the point of view of evolutionary biology (subsections 2.5.7, 3.4.4, 4.5.5). It is possible to make generalizations about meaningful connections, but they are achieved by abstraction from specific cases, with loss of information and explanatory/predictive power concerning specific cases (subsection 4.6.2). The generalizations are less like summaries of the data and more like methodological principles for the investigation of cases. Thus we can say in very general terms that anxiety involves detection of threat, but what this comes to in particular cases stands in need of further investigation. The specifics are differentiated in phylogenesis and ontogenesis. Some things, such as physical assault and deprivation of nutrition, are dangerous to us, as to all living beings. More specific dangers arise for us as social beings. Also, different dangers can arise for women as opposed to men, and vice versa, for one kind of social group rather than another, and so on. Meaningful explanations can be made progressively more particular, referring eventually to a particular person (subsection 4.6.3).

Another aspect of the investigation and definition of meaning lies on the borderline between psychological theory and epistemology. Empiricism envisaged several ways in which one event may signify another, according to principles of resemblance and learned association. As discussed in subsection 1.4.1, post-empiricism makes this picture much more complicated. The perception of events is theory-laden, as is the perceived connection between events. Appreciation of the meaning that events have for a person requires study of his or her system of beliefs.

These points may be applied to the methodological assumption that unrealistic content in anxiety disorder may stand for something realistic. Empiricist conditioning principles may do some work here. Simple phobias may be caused by one or more really threatening, traumatic experiences of the feared object. In post-traumatic stress disorder the overgeneralization of realistic fear, the overinclusiveness of resemblance, is manifest. In other cases the link may be less evident in content, due to contiguity in time and place only, as when a person fears a particular smell, for example, because of its previous coincidence with real danger. The *meaning* in such a case is just an association, in the context of a particular conditioning history. Alongside such cases, emphasized in the conditioning theory/behavioural paradigm, are those involving more complex symbolism and theory, as for example fear of contamination meaning guilt. These are familiar more in psychoanalytic theory, which has always worked with characteristic post-empiricist principles, including specifically the idea that there are core features of self which the person seeks to preserve (pp. 308–11). However, all these various types of case encountered in the anxiety disorders involve meaning and intentionality. All can be brought under the heading: the person is anxious about something which means to him or her something really threatening. Intentional-causal pathways are involved, and clinicians of diverse psychological persuasions are alike engaged in trying to track them.

We have been discussing the search for meaning in the case of anxiety and the anxiety disorders. Biological, psychological, and social theory guide the search for real threats which the person is perceiving. They include involvement in gross disasters such as serious accidents or war. Real threats include also the more subtle developmentally defined traumas discussed in the previous chapter (pp. 307–8 and Section 8.3). In general terms these developmental traumas involve deprivation of what the growing child needs in order to be able to learn to how to act. Of specific relevance in the present context, the child may fail to learn adequate, effective coping skills. These considerations suggest that life in the family is likely to be critical in the generation and maintenance of anxiety in various ways.

The child begins with practically no coping skills, so starts off, according to our working definitions of anxiety, highly prone to anxiety, being dependent more or less entirely on adults to get things to work. To the extent that the adults have poor coping skills, the child has no experience, no modelling, of adaptive problem-solving. At a more complex level, including theory explicit in language, carers' appraisal of the child's attempts at problem-solving is likely to influence the child's self-appraisal of his coping skills. Pessimism, worry, disqualification, criticism of the child's attempts to work out solutions (for example in making friends, or learning to read) are all bound, other things being equal, to make or keep the child anxious.

Another aspect is learning from parental modelling. Two main kinds of cases come under this general heading: learning excessive anxiety reactions, and failing to learn appropriate coping strategies to carry into adult life. As emphasized above, failure to cope with anxiety-provoking situations is an important aspect of anxiety, but it has particularly strong relevance under the plausible assumption that many childhood fears are innate, or least an inevitable theme in bio-psychological maturation. For, in this case, what stands in need of explanation in the case of disorder is not so much the appearance of anxiety but failure to handle it and the situations that give rise to it. This learning process, like most others, is highly sensitive to parental example and instruction.

A further, major way in which family function may be causally linked to childhood anxiety disorder concerns the content of the anxiety. Family life may be a source of major stressors, including death or serious illness within the family, parental mental illness, chronic marital conflict, and of course sexual abuse.

The hypothesis that family function plays a major role in the aetiology of anxiety disorders, both in childhood and in continuations into adulthood, is well supported. Evidence from a wide range of studies, using a variety of designs, supports the general conclusion that anxiety disorders, and related difficulties such as depression, tend to run in families. A high proportion of the mothers of children with anxiety disorders themselves have a lifetime history of anxiety disorder (Last *et al.* 1987), and children of anxious parents are at increased risk for anxiety disorder (Sylvester *et al.* 1987; Turner *et al.* 1987). There is raised incidence of anxiety disorders and other types of psychopathology in the relatives of individuals with anxiety disorders (Carey and Gottesman 1981; Harris *et al.* 1983), and there are relationships between anxiety and depression and familial patterns of psychopathology (Leckman *et al.* 1983; Weissman *et al.* 1984; Livingston *et al.* 1985; Bernstein and Garfinkel 1988; Bernstein *et al.* 1990).

Evidence of a genetic contribution to anxiety disorders is relatively weak, although the story may be different for different anxiety disorders. Where physiological signs dominate, there may be a constitutional, genetically based, low threshold for functioning of the anxiety system. There is evidence of more genetic contribution to panic disorder than to generalized anxiety disorder (Torgersen 1990), where the evidence so far is for purely environmental familial transmission (Eysenck 1992). Adult patients with generalized anxiety disorder reported more trauma in the family as children than patients with panic disorder (Torgersen 1986).

The methodological assumption that even in excessive or unrealistic cases anxiety may still be fulfilling its normal biological function, applies not only to the detection of significant threat but also to the generation of solutions. This implies that the symptoms of anxiety disorder are unsuccessful attempts to solve real problems. The anxiety presents as a persistent perception of danger, and the cognitive and behavioural symptoms are the accompanying persistent attempts to find a solution.

Coping strategies include avoidance, destruction of the problem, and problem-solving. Such strategies may work in given circumstances, but if the perceived threat cannot be managed satisfactorily, they tend in one way or another to get out of hand, leading to the exaggerated and persistent combinations of avoidance, perhaps destructive acts, at least in the imagination, vain attempts at problem-solving, and panic, which are the anxiety disorders. Overreliance on coping with anxiety by avoidance, physical and mental, tends to alternate with surprise panic, as in panic disorder. Physical avoidance is an efficient strategy for keeping safe and therefore calm, but is maladaptive in case the feared situation is also desired for some reason, as usually in agoraphobia, or social phobia. The worry characteristic of generalized anxiety disorder, verging on panic, endless and fruitless, appears as a form of cognitive avoidance in adults (Borkovec *et al.* 1991), and in children, once they develop the prerequisite cognitive capacities (Vasey 1993). Avoidance is mandatory when situations are seen as really dangerous, as life-threatening, but for the very same reason they demand attention and vigilance: paradoxical attempts to do both at the same time, in reality and in the imagination, are seen most clearly in post-traumatic stress disorder. Obsessive-compulsive disorder may represent a pre-rational coping style getting out of hand, exhibiting the characteristic, paradoxical combinations of coping and not coping, being in and out of control, and panic. The fundamental fear is of being out of control where coping is essential, and this leads to excessive, out-of-control coping. In general, the problem and the solution become timelessly muddled, this being characteristic of intentional processes in disorder (pp. 312–14).

In this opening subsection we have considered in general terms intentional-causal models of anxiety disorder, based in assumptions about the biologically normal function of anxiety. In what follows we consider the points raised in more detail in relation to two particular anxiety disorders, obsessive-compulsion and post-traumatic stress. In the first of these, intentional and non-intentional theories are both plausible in the current state of research, and the form of solution to this inter-theoretic tension is unclear. By contrast, an intentional-causal model is clearly appropriate for post-traumatic stress disorder, and may have application to other kinds of mental state involving recurring, intrusive, distressing cognition.

9.3.2 Obsessive-compulsive disorder

It is very plausible to view obsessive-compulsive disorder (OCD) as an anxiety disorder, and it is so classified in all the standard nosologies. Anxiety is typically involved in the phenomenology: the person has preoccupying, anxiety-provoking thoughts, usually about some unrealistic danger, and compulsively attempts to neutralize these thoughts and to relieve the anxiety they engender by activities such as counting, cleaning, or checking, carried out in stereotyped or ritualized ways. Anxiety is apparently implicated also in normal, non-clinical phenomena which may be akin to obsessive-compulsion phenomena, in children's magical thinking and actions, and in adult life, particularly in people with so-called obsessional traits.

Broadly speaking, the classification of OCD as a kind of anxiety disorder goes along with emphasizing its intentionality. Obsessional fears are typically quite irrational, but it may be hypothesized that they have meaning, along the lines discussed in the previous subsection. Profound fear of losing control, perhaps specifically with destructive results, is a plausible candidate for a general theme in many cases of obsessional anxiety. The obsessive-compulsive rituals have obvious intentionality so far as the person is concerned: they are about preventing feared catastrophe. At a more symbolic level, it may be that rituals serve to produce the feeling of control in otherwise senseless activities, in response to the perception of being out of control in a realistic area of life. This function of ritualistic behaviour was noted by Freud (1913) and by later theorists (Rachman and Hodgson 1980; Leonard 1989). Psychoanalytic theory also emphasizes the developmentally early fear that the self may become uncontrollably aggressive, making mess, or chaos (Freud 1966). More recent theorizing in the cognitive-behavioural tradition has retained the assumption of intentionality while emphasizing the person's appraisal of the thoughts concerned. It has been hypothesized that fantastic thoughts, for example of causing great harm, are found also in the non-clinical population, but an abnormally exaggerated sense of responsibility for these otherwise ordinary thoughts, negative evaluation of the self for having them, can give rise to recurring distressing thoughts and attempts to neutralize them (Salkovskis 1985; Rachman 1993).

All these psychological theories characteristically point to continuities between the clinical and the non-clinical phenomena, between the abnormal and the normal case. This hangs together with accepting the intentionality of obsessive-compulsive phenomena, in which case the search is for meaning in the otherwise apparently meaningless. The 'meaning' of the obsessional thoughts for the person may be to do with being out of control in some suitably profound sense, or, or as well, it may be that they signify a negative evaluation of the self.

So far, so understandable. On the other hand, there has recently been an accumulation of evidence to suggest that intentional-causal connections of such kinds can hardly be the whole story about OCD. In the past 5 years evidence has accumulated of neurological soft signs and neuropsychological deficits in OCD (Cox *et al.* 1989; Denkla 1989; Head *et al.* 1989; Hollander *et al.* 1990, 1993; Hymas *et al.* 1991; Christensen *et al.* 1992). More direct evidence of neurological structural abnormalities has been detected using computed tomography (CT) and magnetic resonance imaging (MRI) (Luxenberg *et al.* 1988; Scarone *et al.* 1992). There are also associations between OC phenomena and known kinds of neurological disorder, including postencephalitic Parkinson's disease (von Economo 1931), Sydenham's chorea (Swedo *et al.* 1989), and brain injury (McKeon *et al.* 1984), and some response to psychosurgery (Chiocca and Martuza 1990). The range of evidence indicated above has been plausibly cited in support of the hypothesis that OCD has an abnormal neurological basis, probably specifically in the basal ganglia (Wise and Rapoport 1989; Rapoport 1990). This model is complex in various ways, comprising both neurological and psychological hypotheses. It proposes that the basal ganglia serve sensory and cognitive, as well as motor functions, and that specified neurological dysfunctions cause psychological dysfunctions characteristic of OCD. Specifically, the model regards OC symptoms as *displacement activities* (in the ethological sense) 'run wild', triggered in the absence of, or in any case unregulated by, normal processing of external stimuli.

Wise and Rapoport introduce the notion of displacement activities as follows (1989, pp. 336–7):

> [Our hypothesis] is based on a simple model of an innate releasing mechanism in the basal ganglia: a detection mechanism for recognizing specific aspects of stimuli (key or sign stimuli) and a releasing mechanism for the species-typical behavioral response (sometimes known as a fixed-action pattern). Usually detection of the key stimulus causes release (i.e. execution) of the appropriate behavior. But two sorts of behavior can occur in the absence of a key stimulus. Vacuum behaviors . . ., for example, are often actions which would be appropriately directed toward a specific object but when the object is not present. A bird may snap at insects absent and go through the motions of preparing the non-existent bugs for its meal . . . Similarly, displacement behaviors are released when there are 'conflicts between two strongly activated antagonistic drives', or 'when the normal outlet for a certain motivation is blocked'.

The authors go on to remark that displacement activity is of particular relevance in the case of OCD, and quote the following passage from Lorentz (1981, p. 251):

> A vast majority of motor patterns appearing as displacement activities are common 'everyday' activities ... the so-called comfort activities of birds and mammals, such as scratching, preening, shaking, furnish the most common examples of displacement activities; when embarrassed, even humans tend to scratch behind the ear—and in other places.

Wise and Rapoport proceed on the basis of neuroanatomical considerations to conjecture that in OCD hyperactivity in the cingulate cortex causes execution of displacement activities in the absence of the appropriate sensory input and in the absence of motivation to perform them (1989, p. 338).

It may be seen that the ethological strand in this model of OCD is compatible with a psychological story invoking intentional causality. Strong drive conflict or blocking may trigger 'easy', innate behaviour patterns with a low performance threshold, but such behaviours would then acquire the function of reducing the high anxiety generated by the drive frustration (Stein *et al.* 1992). The processes involved here would be biologically normal, and indeed suggestive of the psychological models of obsessive-compulsion already discussed. The assumption would be that displacement activities acquired anxiety-reducing functions as just outlined, and this relatively simple biological beginning was elaborated in development into something like a coping strategy in salient situations perceived as uncontrollable: otherwise senseless routines would serve at least to create the 'illusion of control'. An obsessive-compulsive disorder in intentionality would thus come about within the intentional processes themselves, in the way described in general terms in the previous chapter.

So far, then, there is nothing in the ethological approach to OCD incompatible with the psychological, and there may indeed be developmental connections between the two. In the ethological model, as in the psychological, there is so far nothing to do with neurological deficit. The further step proposed in Wise and Rapoport's model, is the claim that displacement activities are not being triggered by intentional-causal processes, but by lower-level, non-intentional, interference with normal information processing. This shift in the model from intentional- to non-intentional-causal explanation has the consequence that it says nothing about compulsive behaviour having functional, specifically anxiety-reducing, properties.

There are anomalies for the basal ganglia hypothesis, acknowledged by its proponents, including less than perfect fit between known basal ganglia damage and OCD, and also anomalies for the general hypothesis of neurological deficit: the course of OCD (sometimes late onset, sometimes episodic), cognitive-behavioural specificity in the disorder (certain thoughts and actions only), and the efficacy of behaviour therapy, including anxiety-reduction techniques (Wise and Rapoport 1989).

The position in the current state of OCD research is thus that we have two apparently conflicting types of aetiological model of OCD: one type invokes only intentional-causal mechanisms, the other only, or mainly, non-intentional-causal mechanisms. Apparently they are each consistent with different sorts of evidence. The psychological models with their emphasis on anxiety and anxiety reduction are plainly consistent with the typical phenomenology of OCD, and with the efficacy of behaviour therapy. The neurological deficit model is more consistent with a variety of evidence of neurological impairment as listed above. What is evidence for the one, is anomalous for the other. Thus efficacy of behaviour therapy is at least superficially analomous for hypothesis of neurological deficit, while there is apparently no way that the psychological models (in their current form at least) predict neurological impairment. The fact that there are differential predictions here shows that the conflict between the two kinds of model is a genuine one. It is not that the two sorts of model 'say the same thing in two ways', in neurological and psychological language. This reflects the general point, made back in the first chapter (subsection 1.3.5), that intentional stance explanation of breakdown of function is distinct from physical stance explanation of breakdown: they invoke quite different sorts of causal pathway, and point to different sorts of remedy.

The most elegant solution to the conflict is that OCD is heterogeneous in the appropriate respects. According to this line of thought, OCD would exist on a spectrum. At one end we would have an anxiety disorder, blending into non-clinical phenomena of similar kinds, akin to other neurotic disorders in various ways, while, at the other end of the spectrum would be found disorder associated with neurological dysfunction. The prediction is that markers of functional neurosis cluster together and markers of neurobiological deficit cluster together, and the two clusters are dissociated. The hypothesis of such a neat solution is worth testing, though by all means it is not necessarily the most likely. It puts to sea among known anomalies, including conspicuous lack of correlation between neurological soft signs and neuropsychological test abnormalities in the many studies referred to above. Preliminary analysis from a study designed for the purpose of testing this heterogeneity hypothesis also indicates more or less entirely negative results (Shafran, Bolton, and Gray, in preparation).

Alternatives to this kind of solution to the conflict between 'psychological' models of OCD, which invoke intentionality, and 'neurological deficit' models, which do not, will have to be more complicated, even messy, though none the less likely for that. In one way or another, the different kinds of evidence will have to be reassessed and/or reinterpreted. It is possible that, for example, soft neurological signs in OCD signify comorbidity rather than abnormal neural aetiology. As to neuropsychological test abnormalities, a recent study by Cohen *et al.* (in press), not yet replicated, has shown that some are associated with anxiety not OCD specifically, and hence may not, after all, signify any neurological deficit. On the other side, it may be necessary to re-frame in some kinds of case the response of OCD to behaviour therapy: perhaps it is misleading to speak of cure here, or of remission, it being rather that the person learns how better to manage a chronic neurological disability.

9.3.3 Post-traumatic stress disorder and other cases of recurring, instrusive, distressing thoughts

Trauma is a most fertile ground for psychological theory, and it is no accident that right at the start of clinical psychology it figured prominently in the two paradigms that were to set the scene for the century to come: Freud's and Watson's. Irrational fear lends itself to the simple explanation of inappropriate generalization. This model is at its simplest in Watson, and at its most complex in Freud, complicated by cognitive and developmental processes. Of course, backwards trauma hunting has been problematic in both traditions: Freud didn't know whether he had found real or fantasized trauma, and the behaviourists often failed to find the hypothesized one-trial learning in the history of patients with irrational fears. In trying to model post-traumatic stress disorder (PTSD) we do not have this sort of problem, because generally matters are much more open to view. In the paradigm case envisaged by the standard diagnostic systems (such as DSM to be discussed below) the traumatic shock is clear in time and in broad outlines in nature. It is, generally speaking, clear enough whether a person has experienced trauma, when, and of what kind.

Post-traumatic overgeneralization of fear, with physiological arousal and behavioural avoidance, can be explained relatively straightforwardly in conditioning theory. Trauma also affects more complex cognition. We have already considered (in sub-section 9.3.1) the effects of anxiety on information-processing. The main function of the anxiety system is detection of and response to danger, and hence involves intensification of and selection in various pre-attentional and attentional processes, including hypervigilance towards and mental preoccupation with danger, and danger and safety signals. Inevitable side-effects of anxiety then include lowered interest in (lowered concentration on, and motivation for) other situations and tasks. All of this is plausibly a natural reponse to a major, life-threatening experience. The development of core post-traumatic stress symptoms following major trauma appears as biologically normal. The problem is not so much understanding why they develop, but is rather explaining why they are so persistent, sometimes over many, many years.

We consider these sorts of issues in what follows, bringing to bear proposals from previous chapters. To begin with, it may be helpful to readers unfamiliar with post-traumatic stress disorder to see a summary of standard diagnostic criteria.

DSM-IV introduces the diagnostic criteria for post-traumatic stress disorder in the following way (American Psychiatric Association 1994, pp. 427–8):

> The person experienced, witnessed, or was confronted with an event or events that involved actual or threatened death or serious injury, or a threat to the physical integrity of self or others . . . [and] the person's reponse involved intense fear, helplessness, or horror. **Note:** In children this may be expressed instead by disorganized or agitated behaviour.

The core of PTSD is then persistent re-experiencing of the traumatic event, in one or more of the following ways (loc. cit.):

- recurrent and intrusive distressing recollections of the event including images, thoughts, or perceptions. **Note:** In young children, repetitive play may occur in which themes or aspects of the trauma are expressed.
- recurrent distressing dreams of the event. **Note:** in children there may be frightening dreams without recognizable content.
- acting or feeling as if the traumatic event were recurring (includes a sense of reliving the experience, illusions, hallucinations, and dissociative flashback episodes, including those that occur on wakening or when intoxicated). **Note:** In young children trauma-specific reenactment may occur.
- intense psychological distress at exposure to internal or external cues that symbolize or resemble an aspect of the traumatic event.

- physiological reactivity upon exposure to internal or external cues that symbolize or resemble an aspect of the traumatic event.

A second group of symptoms has to do with persistent avoidance of stimuli associated with the trauma or numbing of general responsiveness, at least three of which are required for diagnosis, as follows:

- efforts to avoid thoughts, feelings or conversations associated with the trauma
- efforts to avoid activities, places, or people that arouse recollections of the trauma
- inability to recall an important aspect of the the trauma
- markedly diminished interest or participation in significant activities
- feeling of detachment or estrangement from others
- restricted range of affect (e.g., unable to have loving feelings)
- sense of a foreshortened future, e.g., does not expect to have a career, marriage, or children, or a normal life span

A further diagnosic criterion is persistent symptoms of increased arousal, as indicated by at least two of the following:

- difficulty falling or staying asleep
- irritability or outbursts of temper
- difficulty concentrating
- hypervigilance
- exaggerated startle response

What is described here as the diagnostic criteria for PTSD are responses to trauma which are, for the most part, readily understandable from a bio-psychological point of view. It would be difficult to imagine contrary responses to trauma as being normal. Any living being that narrowly escaped death and, as it were, shrugged it off, would so far be taking chances, would be at risk for being less lucky the next time. If a person experiences severe threat, then she should be anxious about what may have happened, what she could have done, if anything, to avoid or escape the danger, and whether it may happen again. In other words, cognitive resources would be focused on the trauma and its possible recurrence. In effect this comprises the cognitive symptoms in the first group, persistent re-experiencing, and the consequent symptoms of physiological arousal in the third group. Symptoms in the second group, significantly, pull the other way: traumatic experience, as well as demanding constant attention, also, and for the same reason, makes us want to avoid it like anything. The avoidance of trauma-like memories, feelings, and situations can generalize, so as to cover practically any stresses, including otherwise normal demands, such as interpersonal relationships and future planning.

Before considering approach-avoidance conflict further, we may note in passing the signs of tension here between bio-psychological normality and the notion of disorder. Emphasis on the bio-psychological normality of post-traumatic stress reactions suggests that any disorder here has more to do with these reactions failing to decay over time. The position would be akin to the distinction between bereavement and depressive episode. Grief can give rise to thoughts, emotions, and behaviour barely, if at all, distinguishable from a depressive syndrome, but diagnosis of major depressive episode is excluded in case the disturbance is a normal reaction to the death of a loved one (American Psychiatric Association 1994, p. 323). Signs of bereavement becoming complicated by depression include morbid preoccupation with worthlessness, suicidal ideation, marked functional impairment or psychomotor retardation, or prolonged duration. It would be possible in a similar vein to envisage a 'normal' post-traumatic stress reaction which could become complicated by 'disorder', signs of which would include, for example, high degrees of generalization of fear reactions, or of withdrawal, or prolonged duration. These remarks, by the way, are not at all a criticism of the standard definition of post-traumatic stress disorder, but are intended only to clarify what otherwise might seem odd, that bio-psychological normality and the appearance of disorder can be closely linked, particularly following major stressors.

The theme in the background here has to do with the paradoxes inherent in the experience of and response to trauma, discussed in Chapter 8 (Section 8.2), in subsection 9.3.1, and further below. A sign of paradox is that bio-psychologically normal coping strategies when applied to apparently insoluble problems can themselves become maladaptive, disrupting normal activity. The symptom follows from and re-enacts the perception of the impossibility of carrying on. Lines between normal response and disorder are, in these circumstances, difficult to draw sharply. Death of a loved one is distinguished as a normal cause of what otherwise could be called depressive disorder, but other major losses which also lead to grief reactions, such as loss of physical capacity following serious accident or illness, are not so distinguished. The issues here are complicated, and the lines to be drawn are bound to be vague.

These considerations, however, point to the fact that what needs explanation in the case of post-traumatic stress disorder is not so much the appearance of the signs of post-traumatic stress, but their failure to decay over time. Why is the trauma persistently re-experienced, often over many years?

PTSD can be regarded as a phobic reaction, and modelled accordingly in conditioning theory. Recurring re-experiencing is accounted for by this model, for example as a result of a high degree of generalization which makes avoidance impossible (Keane *et al.* 1985). The CS–CR link is preserved because the CS is endured with great anxiety, that is, is never perceived as (responded to as) safe, and anxiety incubates rather than decays (Eysenck 1979). A broadly similar, though more explanatory story can be told in terms of more complex information-processing models. The task for the person traumatized in, for example, a shipping disaster, is to acquire the information that, nevertheless, ships are really safe (enough), but assimilation and accomodation of this information from experience is ruled out in so far as there are expectations of danger, leading to search for danger signals, leading to lowered threshold for such interpretations, leading to the perception that ships are dangerous after all. A model along these lines, applied to the post-traumatic stress of war veterans, is worked out by Chemtob *et al.* (1988). A related formulation is proposed by Foa and Steketee (1989), to be discussed further below; and see also Creamer *et al.* (1992).

The idea, then, is that traumatic experience produces a massive effect on information-processing, on the anxiety system specifically, so that it becomes, as it were, permanently on, sensitive to danger signals and unprepared to recognize security. This is very likely to be a major part of the story. But so far it does not easily address the persistent re-experiencing of the trauma itself, in waking thought, in dreams, or other re-enactments. Why does the victim go through it over and over again? Here we come across the idea that the traumatic experience is in some way 'unresolved'. But what does this mean, and why does it happen?

Directly relevant to this central question is Rachman's (1980) notion of *failure of emotional processing*. He invoked it to explain a variety of phenomena: obsessions, the return of fear, incubation of fear, abnormal grief reactions, failures to respond to fear-reducing procedures, and nightmares. Although Rachman was not concerned in the paper explicitly with post-traumatic stress disorder, the notions could be applied to it, and have been by Foa and Steketee (1989), using a model proposed by Foa and Kozak (1986). Much discussion in all these papers concerns the criteria or signs that emotional processing has or has not occurred. There is a risk, of which the proponents of the model are aware, that signs of its failure coincide with the phenomena to be explained. This issue is basically one of operational definition of a highly theoretical construct. In fact two sorts of definition are required: theoretical and operational. In his original paper Rachman concentrated on the latter somewhat at the expense of the former. He suggested that, 'as a start, emotional processing is regarded as a process whereby emotional disturbances are absorbed, and decline to the extent that other experiences and behaviour can proceed without disruption' (Rachman 1980, p. 51). The notion of emotional processing in this way rests heavily on the theoretical construct of 'absorption'. But what is this?

Further progress was made by Foa and Kozak, who defined emotional processing as the modification of memory structures that underlie emotions, particularly acquisition of new, incompatible information (Foa and Kozak 1986, p. 22). Concerning post-traumatic stress disorder in particular, Foa and her colleagues proposed that what distinguishes it from other anxiety disorders is that the traumatic event was of monumental significance and violated formerly held 'basic concepts of safety' (Foa and Steketee 1989, p. 166). They propose that this violation establishes massive fear structures (information-processing biased towards danger) which then inhibit new learning, specifically of safety (Foa and Steketee 1989, pp. 167–70).

This was the proposal discussed above. It is likely to be correct, but, as already suggested, it apparently does not directly address the issue of repeated re-experiencing the trauma itself. The hope was that the concept of 'failure of emotional processing' would cast light here, but it is not yet clear how.

We suggest that some very general consideration about the nature of cognition can be brought to bear on these issues, mainly the post-empiricist assumption that we use hierarchically organized systems of belief for the purpose of action. This was discussed in the first chapter (subsections 1.4.1, 1.4.4) and linked to trauma in the previous chapter (pp. 305–6). In these terms it is possible to elaborate on key theoretical notions such as 'basic concepts of safety', 'size' of fear structures, and resistance to change. It is specifically possible to gain a distinctive theoretical grip on the key problem of persistent re-experiencing of the trauma through time, of failure to decay.

The basic idea, as outlined in the previous chapter (Section 8.2, 8.3), is that trauma comes into conflict with core assumptions in the theory of action, such as that the world is a safe enough place for action, and that the self is competent enough. The conditions of action include 'safety' in the broadest sense, a notion invoked by Foa and her colleagues (Foa and Steketee 1989). If reality is being represented as incompatible with the conditions of action, then representation itself is confounded, having to both exist and not exist. The paradox of representation and non-representation, extended through time, finds dramatic expression in the most characteristic of post-traumatic signs, namely, in persistent and intrusive re-experiencing of the traumatic events. These points will be expanded on later, but first we may consider another theoretical approach close to what we are proposing, one that relies heavily on the notion of 'basic assumptions'.

Janoff-Bulman (1985) argues that the stress syndrome of PTSD is largely attributable to the shattering of victims' 'basic assumptions' about themselves and their world. She cites various theorists in explanation of the notion of basic assumptions at work in daily life, and notes that traumatic experience clashes with these on a scale comparable to threats to 'paradigms' in Kuhn's sense. This passing reference to post-empiricist philosophy of science directly points in the direction we are taking. As basic assumptions threatened by traumatic experience Janoff-Bulman cites three, as follows (1985, pp. 16f.):

- the belief in personal invulnerability
- the perception of the world as meaningful and comprehensible
- the view of ourselves in a positive light.

And she goes on to discuss their implication in post-traumatic stress disorder.

We do not disagree with the proposal that these three assumptions can be fundamental and involved in the response to trauma. However, in accord with the general approach of the essay, we would start by viewing the 'basic assumptions' of action from a more biological perspective, and indeed from a more general epistemological one. This approach points to assumptions of action being more like the following:

(1) the world is safe enough;
(2) predictable enough;
(3) satisfies enough needs; and
(4) the agent is competent enough.

If these assumptions were to be given up, action would appear as either impossible or pointless, or both. The assumptions, the consequences of giving them up, and the need to hang on to them have been discussed earlier (subsections 1.4.4, 8.2.2).

This second set of assumptions we are proposing stands in contrast to the first set, listed above as proposed by Janoff-Bulman, in three main ways. First, the second set applies down the phylogenetic scale, without restriction to specifically human characteristics such as positive self-image or perceived invulnerability. The theory of anxiety certainly has to be applicable early in phylogenesis, but arguably animals can also show something specifically like post-traumatic stress syndrome, including learned helplessness aspects (Foa *et al.* 1992; Peterson and Seligman 1983). Secondly, the concept of 'good enough', due famously to Winnicott (1971), peremeates all these matters: it is not necessary to have perfect control, competence, and so on. Thirdly, as already mentioned, the second set of assumptions *have to* be preserved if action is to continue. Giving them up means that it is either impossible to perform (intentional) behaviour, or pointless to, which implies, for example, random behaviour, freezing/ paralysis, or withdrawal. In brief, the second set of expectations are minimal, attributable to animals, and essential to action as such, and all these features hang together.

On this basis we can develop our proposals further. It was remarked above that traumatic experience on the one hand demands attention from the victim, but on the other hand avoidance is also an adaptive response. This certainly includes behavioural avoidance of similar situations, but also mental avoidance of the terror. Mental approach-avoidance conflict in effect means that the same phenomena *have to be both thought about and not thought about*. The paradoxical effects of traumatic experience on cognition were considered in some detail in Chapter 8, in relation to post-empiricist epistemology (pp. 305–6) and the philosophical notion of limits of thought (pp. 306–7).

The key here is the *definition of representation (thought) as serving action*. Consider circumstances in which action is, or is perceived to be, impossible, and which are represented as such. The representation cannot be used to facilitate (to regulate, to plan) action, which, according to the representation, is not possible. But in so far as the representation cannot be used in the service of action, in so far as it is incompatible with action, it is not a possible representation. Thus the reality in question has to be in some way thought about and not thought about. It is clear that the traumatic events are experienced and represented; otherwise indeed there would be no (psychological) problem. But they also have to be in some way not represented.

The paradox here shows up in various ways. For example, there may be amnesia for critical periods in the sequence of events, or the events are remembered but not the terror; or the events are recalled with a third-person perspective, as though observed from the outside rather than experienced from within; or the memory images have an unreal, dream-like quality. All of these are ways of remembering the trauma and not remembering the trauma at the same time. Another form of the paradox is to alternate remembering with not remembering through time. This involves mental avoidance some of the time, feeling fine, as if nothing had happened, or as if the self had not really been affected, with this fragile sense of well-being repeatedly being interrupted by intrusive, distressing preoccupation with the traumatic experience, or by unexpected panic attacks.

Persistent and intrusive re-experiencing of the traumatic events is the dramatic core of post-traumatic stress. It can appear in several forms, as in DSM-IV's first group of diagnostic signs listed above: in waking thought, in dreams, in re-enactment (for example in children's play), and in situations which resemble or symbolize the trauma. The representation is thus clearly in evidence, though it may be partial in one or more of the ways described above (e.g. remembered as if unreal), and it has the special quality of intrusive repetition. The intrusiveness here can be seen as a measure of the salience of the experience for the bio-psychological being—it demands attention—and the repetition can be seen as the expression through time of the paradox of representation and non-representation. It is forgotten during the day, say, when life continues more or less as usual, and provides distraction, but it is remembered as soon as cognitive resources are available, at night, or when the mind wanders off some other task. The energy involved in both preoccupation with the trauma (trying to understand it, trying to withstand the fear) and in mental avoidance of the trauma (trying to forget, to keep oneself engaged in distracting tasks) is substantial. These mental tasks typically leave the person exhausted, much less able to cope with the stresses of daily living, which he or she may then avoid.

In terms of post-empiricist epistemology, as discussed in the previous chapter (pp. 305–6), the point is that traumatic experience contradicts deep convictions in the theory of action, to the effect, for example, that the world is predictably a possible place in which to act, or that the self is able to cope. This creates two cognitive responses. On the one hand, the traumatic experience is impossible, according to these convictions, and thus cannot have happened (to me), and warrants only being put out of mind. On the other hand, still more powerfully, the traumatic experience is, according to the same convictions of massive importance, apparently signifying the impossibility of action (life) itself, so not only cannot be forgotten, but has to be attended to above all else.

The trauma and the core of the theory of action are incompatible, so they cannot both be believed, and this leads to circular cognitive sequences which may be schematically represented as follows:

Step 1: trauma occurred,
Step 2: therefore the core theory is false,
Step 3: but the theory must be preserved: or else 'life is unbearable',
Step 4: so the trauma cannot really have happened,
but, Step 5: it certainly did, that is, back to Step 1 again, and so on.

Traumatic experience signifies that core theory presupposed in action is wrong. But if it is wrong, action comes to an end. But this is impossible (we are inclined to carry on). But if the theory that action is possible is retained, then the traumatic experience cannot have happened. On the other hand, it is remembered. There is a massive conflict here between theory—theory that we have to hang on to—and experience. And paradoxes press: if the experience happened, the theory is wrong, but it can't be wrong . . . Or the other way round, if the theory is right, the experience cannot have happened, but it did . . . and is of huge significance (i.e. overthrows the conditions of survival), therefore needs much attention, cognitive resources. But it implies that action is impossible, which is impossible . . .. And so round and round. This is by all means confusing. The fundamental problem is that traumatic experience apparently contradicts the conditions of action, and will therefore be both rejected, and attended to, both for dear life.

Another way of putting the problem is that core convictions and the trauma cannot both be believed, but must be each believed. Solution of this problem requires drastic mental measures. Both cannot be believed at the same time, with the same mind. One kind of solution is dissociation, as discussed above, in third-person memories or dreams of the event, in remembering without affect, in memories experienced as unreal, in forgetting the worst times. These are ways of believing that the trauma was experienced, and believing that it was not, at the same time. The alternative is persistent re-experiencing, alternating with persistent forgetting/denial, thus achieving beliefs in each side of the contradiction at different times.

There is in post-traumatic stress reaction a *failure to integrate the trauma into the system of belief about the self and reality*. There is frequently, in fact, resistance to such integration, taking the form of explicit thoughts to the effect that the trauma cannot, or should not, have happened. This protest of despair and outrage marks the contrast between reality as it is and reality as it must be, or ought to be. Life requires that reality is benign enough, and the thought that it is not is not a possible thought, at least, not one that can be used as a basis for action. This thought has no use; its meaning cannot be understood. Hence there is a pattern of repetition in which the trauma is persistently re-experienced and its apparent meaning, that core beliefs are false, is rejected.

The proposed explanation of re-experiencing and re-enactment is partly, then, that it cannot be accomodated within the core of theory. This amounts to a theoretical definition of the idea of failure of emotional processing discussed earlier. However, this negative feature exists alongside a more positive mechanism. As indicated above, it is very plausible to suppose that following narrow escape from serious danger cognitive resources should be dedicated to understanding what happened and how, with a view to making sure that it never happens again, or if it does, that the person knows what to do. This problem-solving may be a function of persistent re-experiencing and re-enactment of the trauma. This possibility was envisaged in Freud's notion of attempts at 'completion' following trauma, interestingly discussed in the context of more recent theories by Horowitz (1986, Chapter 6). The person may, for example, think or dream about the disaster, with alternating endings, some worse than what actually happened, but some better. A successful resolution, in representations unmarked by time, may even serve to undo the traumatic experience, or it may restore a positive view. However, unsuccessful attempts to work out a better ending, in dreams, in waking thought, or in patterns of behaviour, in effect only re-enact the trauma, over and over again. In this case, the attempts to find a solution have become the problem, a typical sign of intentional processes in disorder as discussed earlier (pp. 312–14, 348–9).

Attempts to work out a more successful, tolerable outcome of a traumatic experience may also, however, be a kind of denial, a refusal to accept that the experience was as awful as it was. This denial would then characteristically alternate with the repeated realization through re-enactment that it was, after all, that bad. This pattern persists in so far as the representations of past and present lack distinctive time or context markers, and are hardly distinguished.

A quite different strand in the attempt to adapt to traumatic experience is construction of a representation which acknowledges how awful it was, but which forsees the possibility of a different, better outcome next time. Or, what comes close to the same thing, construction of a representation in which the the trauma is recognized as both awful but despite that somehow possible to survive. Either way, what is envisaged is a world, or a self and a world, which is both dreadful and yet possible.

Here we come across the key idea of integrating the traumatic experience into the person's system of belief, noted in the previous chapter (p. 314). The psychological conflicts and tasks of adjustment here can be compared with the problems of anomalies and theory adaptation which are manifest in the progress of the sciences. As noted above, Janoff-Bulman (1985), in introducing the idea of basic assumptions with a view to conceptualizing the effects of trauma, refers to Kuhn's (1962) notion of paradigm in science. We also suggest that the epistemological principles linking theory and experiment, visible in science, are similar to those operating in the case of psychological adjustment to trauma. The principles are specifically those of post-empiricism (subsections 1.4.1, 1.4.4., pp. 305–6).

Trauma may be defined as experience which scores pretty well a direct hit on the core of the theory which regulates action, contradicting the conviction that the world is, in various senses, safe enough. To achieve this the event has to be one which cannot simply be ignored. It may be experienced fast and dramatically, in one trial, as in disasters. Or it may be experienced repeatedly, as for example child sexual abuse in the family. Either way the trauma is forcibly experienced. As already discussed, a natural response to this blatent conflict between the undeniable force of the trauma and the unmoveable core of belief is something like dissociation, or splitting (pp. 309–10, and above). Both are held on to, but in different states of mind, through time, or even at the same time. What is required in these circumstances if the trauma is not to be repeatedly re-experienced, is construction of a representation which can accomodate both the traumatic experience and the view of the self and the world as, on balance, secure enough. This kind of resolution following a disaster may be apparent in thoughts to the effect: 'It did happen, I nearly died, I was terrified; but I survived (without too much loss), it is over, and all being well, taking into account reasonable estimation of probabilities, it is unlikely to happen to me again'. Or following sexual abuse: 'It did happen, but it was not my fault; my mother did not stop it, or did not believe me, but she is not all bad'. And so forth.

By all means whether such a resolution can be achieved in practice depends on many circumstances and factors. Some of these will have to do with the severity of the trauma and the losses sustained. Thinking particularly of trauma experienced in adult life, it may be expected that pre-existing personality characteristics are also relevant, specifically concerning core assumptions about the self and world. We can envisage several broad kinds of case here. One is the kind emphasized by Janoff-Bulman (1985), in which the person's core assumptions are somewhat extreme, such as the assumption of personal invulnerability, or super-competence. Highly successful men and women may 'fall apart' following trauma and fail to recover, often developing depression. In such cases the person simply cannot stand the vulnerability and failure to cope, or the loss of function in the initial post-traumatic reaction. Adjustment to trauma against the background of excessively self-confident assumptions can be extremely difficult, and Janoff-Bulman is right to draw attention specifically to them. Something critical to the person's view of themselves is lost, and post-traumatic stress can be then complicated by depression in response to this loss. The task in such cases is to achieve a view of the self as 'good enough'. Similar sorts of considerations apply to cases in which the pre-existing core assumptions about the world are overoptimistic. Experience contradicting this is quite unprepared for, and is particularly devastating. This is one aspect of the reason why young children are so vulnerable to traumatic abuse in the family: they have, and they have to have, more or less unquestioning trust in those meant to be looking after them.

Another kind of case is that in which pre-traumatic core assumptions are already of a balanced, not black-and-white kind. Here one would find already in the one scheme of things acknowledgement that there was safety and danger, coping and not coping, succeeding and failing, and so on. The prediction would be that such a view, or way of thinking, would serve to facilitate adjustment to trauma, other things being equal.

A third kind of case might be in people whose view of the self and world was already pretty negative, as the result of experiences and achievements that were perceived as not good enough. Here it might be predicted that the adjustment to trauma, or certain kinds of trauma, might be facilitated, in so far as it did not in fact contradict basic assumptions. But, on the other hand, the trauma would serve to give massive confirmation to the person's depressive outlook.

It can be assumed that variations in the theory of self and world are highly conditioned by learning. In other words, we suppose that from the beginnings the child's view of the world and self is shaped by experience and education to become more or less like the three kinds described above. The child may come to have a highly negative view of carers, or other people, or the self. He may be competent, and brought up so as to believe that he is wonderful, and that everything goes and should go his way. In certain circumstances these two views can even coexist, unintegrated, reflecting unresolved ambivalence in the family and in the mind. A different possibility is development of a view of the self and world as positive and negative, and on balance good enough. This would require a combination of not too much adversive experience, enough good experience, together with help from carers to do the integrative work of containing positive and negative, security and anxiety, possession and loss, success and disappointment, in the one mental space.

The concept in developmental cognitive psychology which comes closest to what is at issue here is that of attachment representation, discussed previously (subsections 6.3.4, 8.4.7). We have suggested that post-traumatic stress reactions will more readily decay to the extent that the person's pre-existing core beliefs about the self and world already contain positive and negative features with negotiation among them. Assuming that core beliefs are associated specifically with secure attachment representation, the prediction would be that secure attachment representation facilitates recovery from post-traumatic shock. As with all hypotheses about personality variables as protective or risk factors in post-traumatic stress, there is the problem that they are measured after the event and hence are confounded by the post-traumatic effects themselves. However, the methodological problem is soluble using large samples and control groups.

We have proposed that trauma is persistently re-experienced or re-enacted in so far as it contradicts the representation of a tolerable, secure reality. The traumatic experience is remembered alongside the experience of safety, with persistent, recurring alternation between the two states of mind. This cycle resolves to the extent that the traumatic experience can be integrated into a representation of the self and world as being, on balance, safe enough.

Finally in this subsection we consider briefly other possible applications of the model sketched so far. As remarked above, Rachman (1980) invoked failure of emotional processing in order to explain a variety of cases of repetitive, intrusive distressing thoughts, including obsessions and abnormal grief reactions. The model proposed here applies most transparently to post-traumatic stress disorder. It applies readily also to persistent grief reactions, unsurprisingly since bereavement typically involves trauma. In grief the loss of the loved one is both represented and not represented. Representation may take the form of persistent memories of aspects of the death or discovery or news of the death. Alternating with this is non-representation of the loss, by seeing the dead person, in hallucination, or mistaken first appearances, and by other diverse forms of denial, including the wish to carry on as before as though nothing had changed. So far, as remarked in connection with trauma in general, this is normal. The problem is more when this splitting persists, when there is no integration, when the person does not adjust to the loss, but carries on alternating between a fragile sense of well-being, and depressive episodes.

A problem much more challenging to the model is explanation of the obsessions in obsessive-compulsive disorder. The model as outlined works best in cases of real traumatic experiences contradicting reasonable basic assumptions about the self and the world. It is so far unclear that this could have anything to do with the fantastic world of obsessional beliefs and rituals. On the other hand, even if destined for failure, it is worthwhile considering possibilities here.

The core ideas would be as before. The proposal would be that obsessional thoughts signify something quite contrary to basic assumptions about the self and the world, that they repeatedly, intrusively recur in the absence of any integration of the thoughts, or what they mean, into a tolerable self- and world-view. Aspects of these hypotheses fit fairly readily with the clinical presentation. According to psychological formulations, the best candidates for the meaning of obsessional thoughts have to do with fear of uncontrolled loss, or destruction, for which the self is in some way responsible (subsection 9.3.2). This interpretation is an example of construing the intentional object of apparently irrational fear in such a way as to bring out its bio-psychological significance (subsection 9.3.1). Apparently irrational compulsions would be construed in a corresponding way, as symbolizing the person's capacity to keep things in order. It is also plausible to hypothesize something like splitting or dissociation in at least some people with obsessive-compulsive disorder. Fear of being out of control shows up alongside, alternating with, keeping in precise control, these two contradictory themes being timelessly entangled together in the compulsions themselves.

A critical feature of obsessive-compulsive disorder is as yet untouched by this approach, however. This is the characteristic blurring of the distinction between mind and reality. Obsessions are expressions of fear of serious harm, typically some catastrophe to the self, or destruction of (the person's) world by the self. The person is unclear (in this state of mind) between imagined destruction (or destruction in the imagination) and real destruction. At the same time the individual believes that his or her special stereotyped, ritualized actions can avert the feared catastrophe.

At this point it is possible, in line with themes in previous chapters, to introduce a developmental aspect into the model of recurring, intrusive thoughts when applied to obsessive-compulsive disorder. 'Irrationality' can be construed as *pre-rationality*. All the above-listed irrational characteristics of the obsessive-compulsive have early developmental analogues, concerning blurring of the distinctions known to reason and the reliance on 'magical' thinking (Piaget 1937; Vygotsky 1981; Harris 1994; see also Chapter 6, subsection 6.5.2). There are in pre-rational thought in children inflated views of the power of the self, linked to egocentricism, including feelings of omnipotence, linked then to perceived responsibility, the other side of which is fear of helplessness and destruction. There is also blurred appearance/reality distinction, and belief in the power of ritual (in thought or action) to influence otherwise uncontrollable reality. In the face of possible catastrophe, pre-reason uses magic. Mind is experienced as powerful, which has the following implication: if the mind can destroy reality, it can also save it. Apparent similarities between pre-rational thought and activity and obsessive-compulsive phenomena have long been recognized (Freud 1913; A. Freud 1965). There are also, of course, differences, specifically in persistence and in distress caused, which are emphasized by those who see obsessive-compulsion as a neurological disorder (Leonard 1989; see also subsection 9.3.2).

It may be possible, then, to apply the model of intrusive, distressing thoughts worked out in the case of post-traumatic stress to obsessive-compulsive disorder. The adult experiences trauma in reality. The young child, by contrast, is a world in which fantasy and reality are not yet reliably distinguished, in which imagined catastrophe might be real catastrophe, or in which real catastrophe, such as loss or prolonged separation from a carer, might be due to his imagination. The adult responds to real catastrophe by cognitive preoccupation alternating with avoidance. The young child (the mind in that developmentally early stage) responds also by preoccupation, and the problem-solving strategy is the exercise of magical powers of control.

9.4 PERSONALITY DISORDER

9.4.1 Introduction

The concept of personality disorder has a long and rather chequered history. At worst its use has been pejorative, non-developmental, and anti-therapeutic. Notwithstanding the difficulties, it provides a pointer to important aspects of disturbance that are not characterized by episodic occurrences of relatively clearly defined syndromes, such as depression. The two main classificatory systems include a number of different categories of personality disorder, but they assume that there is a unified underlining concept which is characterized by the presence of abnormal traits. The *Diagnostic and statistical manual of mental disorders*, (4th edn) (commonly known as DSM-IV) states that:

> Personality traits are enduring patterns of perceiving, relating to, and thinking about the environment and one's self that are exhibited in a wide range of social and personal contexts. Only when personality traits are inflexible and maladaptive and cause significant functional impairment or subjective distress do they constitute personality disorders. (American Psychiatric Association 1994, p. 630.)

In practice, the different personality disorder categories include very widely differing kinds of items, including those that refer to states of mind (e.g. uncertainties of self-image), mood states, (e.g. marked shifts from normal mood to depression, irritability or anxiety), interpersonal difficulties (e.g. a pattern of unstable and intense interpersonal relationships), and specific behaviours, such as failure to accept social norms. Given this heterogeneity, attempts to provide one explanatory framework are likely to prove frustrating. It is clear also that each personality disorder category is not distinct, and co-occurrence of several diagnoses is common (Oldham *et al.* 1992), so that in considering one particular category we cannot be confident of its separate identity. These limitations, combined with the tendency for the concept to be misused, might make it seem a poor subject for our concluding chapter. However, from a mental health perspective, its value lies in drawing our attention to the presence of recurring maladaptive patterns of attributions, emotional states, cognitions and actions. These persistent patterns of personal dysfunction are found in over 50 per cent of patients referred to mental health facilities with problems such as depression and other non-psychotic conditons, such as anxiety and eating disorders (Pfohl *et al.* 1984; Gartner *et al.* 1989; Shea *et al.* 1990). When we turn to the possible intentionality of personality disorder, the most striking findings are those that indicate that frequently it is preceded by behavioural disturbance, or severe adversity in childhood, or a combination of the two (Robins 1966, 1986; Ogata *et al.* 1990).

9.4.2 Borderline personality disorder

Notwithstanding the problems of definition, we will examine one particular personality disorder, 'borderline personality disorder', in relation to intentionality and development. Borderline personality disorder is characterized by intense and unstable intimate relationships, rapid changes of mood, and impulsive aggressive behaviour often towards the self, in the form of overdoses or cutting the wrists or other parts of the body. It is commonly preceded by a history of physical or sexual abuse (Ogata *et al.* 1990). How might these childhood experiences be related to the adult disorder?

We start with an examination of borderline processes in relation to our earlier considerations, particularly those in Chapter 8. Clinical experience and a range of psychotherapeutic formulations (e.g. Kernberg 1984) have provided a valuable picture of borderline processes. The mind of the individual is characterized by sharp and unpredictable shifts of mood and perceptions. The contrast is often between a view of the self and those around that is optimistic and confident, and one dominated by anger and unhappiness. In the happy state of mind, often it seems that facts that do not fit that state are not recognized, or if they are, they lead to catastrophic change to pessimism and anger. These facts may be derived from current circumstances, or from reference to the person's previous states of mind or behaviours. When in one state of mind the individual appears not to have access to others. This applies also in the other direction, so that when he/she is pessimistic and angry, good experiences are forgotten and angrily denied, and there appears to be little scope to consider some modification of that way of seeing things. Here then, representations and the rules of perception and experience are contradictory and are subject to rapid, intense, and unpredictable change. Furthermore each will tolerate only certain kinds of information, so that its range of function is narrow and open to catastrophic failure.

Relationships are subject to a similar roller-coaster effect as the individual. Typically they are seen as filled with love and perfection, or as useless or destructive, and they may become violent. Then relationships seem to reflect in part the individual's need to keep states of mind pure and lacking in doubt or difficulty, and in part a particular pattern of communication. As long as a relationship is in one state or another and the individual can keep hold of it that way, communication of departures from this are ignored or are not tolerated. Communication, as a means of adding new information to interactions between people, is eliminated. Put another way, there is a lack of negotiation of a joint frame of reference between the individuals, and instead a demand by at least one of the participants of what has to be the case, for instance that it is a perfect relationship. Thus both the individual and his/her relationships are characterized by rapid shifts between contradictory states, and a lack of individual or interpersonal metarepresentational systems.

Repeated injury to the body is common in borderline functioning. Sometimes this represents a suicide attempt, but usually it does not. Often the individual will cut him/herself when frustrated or angry. This is a complicated phenomenon and many different explanations have been offered for it. Here we will focus on one aspect, the attack on a part of oneself. In evolution, anger and attack appear to be part of an intentional response which has survival value for the individual and species through reducing danger. They form part of effective action with respect to the environment. In self-injury it seems that part of the intentional sequence, entailing the emotion and the action, is subverted so that action is not effective in bringing about change. It is an example of a contradiction in the intentional process, (referred to earlier, subsection 9.3.3), of action both occurring but not occurring, simultaneously. The way this is achieved may be through a split in the representation of the self (or at least of the body) so that a part of oneself can become the object of action. In one sense that creates the appearance of effective action, but in reality it is ineffective because it is part of the same person. In summary, in borderline processes we have contradictory unpredictable states of mind and relationships, lack of effective communication and negotiations, and action that is not action.

9.4.3 Sexual abuse and borderline processes

How might these be related to childhood experiences of adversity? We reviewed some of the relevant mechanisms in the previous chapter, and return to them here in more detail. We will focus on sexual abuse, although many of the processes are likely to be found in other forms of abusive, punitive or neglectful parenting. Sexual abuse of young children is usually painful, intrusive, confusing, and frightening. Typically it occurs under conditions of secrecy with threats from the perpetrator of injury or loss, for instance through break-up of the family, if the child discloses. Whether it is carried out by a parent or an adult from outside the family, it involves a transgression of the assumed protective role of adults. It may well be carried out in a perverse manner within the day to day events of family life. Furniss (1992) described a father who signalled to his daughter that the abuse was about to take place with the words, 'Go and wash your hands', and once it was over would say, 'Now it is time to do your homework'. Abused children may show signs characteristic of trauma in general, of hyperarousal, irritability, and flashbacks, but may manage to hide the distress and maintain an appearance of normality. Then, in spite of severe trauma, they continue to act in ways that preserve their relationships, including those in the family. How does the child cope? He/she is faced with representations of the facts of what are going on, and with the accompanying emotions of fear and anger, without a means of acting on them. These representations would, under other circumstances, lead to report of the act, but as physical danger and loss of family are threatened if that happens, the secrecy is preserved. Furthermore the actions that are required, to behave as if nothing is happening, require quite different representations in the mind. So here are the conditions under which the child may split off cognitive-emotional states of the form 'I am being hurt, I am frightened' which cannot be linked to action, and 'I am fine', which is inaccurate but may provide the basis for survival and action. He/she learns to segregate the components of the mind so that what is known is not known. Here then, may be the conditions for the development of contradictory states of mind, that are maintained separate in order to preserve the conditions for action in childhood.

Not only is sexual abuse likely to lead to segregated thoughts and feelings, but also ones that are not linked systematically to external events. The scope for establishing their applicability, and for their testing and modification, is likely therefore to be limited. Thus if the child learns to split off the emotions labelled 'I am frightened' when being abused, the question arises as to how to deal with the same emotions arising at other times. How is he/she to distinguish those times when the state of mind can be registered and talked about, and when this is not possible? It is unlikely that there will be help available from adults in sorting this out, and so there is the possibility that events which might not usually be frightening will come to be feared. Similarly, if such a state cannot be registered and talked about, there will be little scope for exploring those conditions under which being frightened might be modified. This is the reverse of the benign exploration of perceptions, fears, and wishes that goes on in the play and relationships of most children, and may lead to mental representations that are inflexible, inappropriate to external circumstances, and not readily open to modifications.

The example of the father's use of everyday language to signal the beginning and end of episodes of abuse, illustrates the way in which trust in what is said can be undermined, in abuse. If some sentences are uttered under one set of metarules and others under different rules, but the difference cannot be acknowledged, then the child is likely to feel uncertain about the meaning of apparently straightforward communications. This will have implications for the monitoring of the individual's state of mind, and for his/her understanding of what is happening between people. In contrast to the infant who looks to the parent for help in deciding whether to cross the visual cliff (subsection 6.4.4), the child who is being abused may not have adults with whom communications are sufficiently unambiguous that such checking could be possible. One possible solution then is to attempt to constrict the range of individual and interpersonal emotions, thoughts, and actions in order to reduce uncertainty, and enable actions to be preserved. This, in turn, is likely to reduce the scope for negotiations in relationships, as these require confidence that what is said is what is meant, and that areas of uncertainty can be entered with relative safety. This constricting of communication may provide another basis for the splitting of representations. If communications allow only 'normal' family life to be acknowledged, then the unacknowledged aspects have to be kept separate in the minds of the participants, and hence for the child this may become an habitual way of coping.

The child not only has to cope with the knowledge that the abuse is taking place, but also with the fact of it. This frequently involves physical pain and revulsion and many survivors have described dividing their mind from their body so that, in effect, what happens to the body is not experienced as happening to them. This is yet a further division in the representation of what is going on, but with somewhat different consequences. If the child comes to see the body as in some ways not part of the self, then the body can be treated as if it is that of someone else, and in particular may be neglected or attacked. Not only that, by creating a split between mind and body, the child runs the risk of separating representation and the agent of action, the body.

9.4.4 Development, intentional, and borderline processes

Let us summarize now the developmental processes that may be impaired when a child is abused sexually or in other ways, and underline the links with the function and dysfunction of intentional processes. First children need to register the presence of perceptions, thoughts, and emotions, and their differences, and to move among them without fear, just as happens in their play. When certain states of mind are not allowed they may become disconnected, unintegrated, and disruptive. Secondly, the content of these representations needs to be tested for their applicability, truth, and possible modification. In the language of our earlier discussion, the underlying rules have specificity and generality so that they can mediate between events and actions. Where such mental representations cannot be tested, for instance through play with other children, or through being brought into relationships with adults, they are likely to become rigid, and inappropriate. The child, and the adult, is likely to find none reflects reality satisfactorily so that one is held until it can no longer bear the strain of the evidence, only to be replaced by another with similar limitations. Thirdly, children need to be confident of the truth of communications within their social networks, and in particular that they can be clear about the convention that is being followed in the use of language. The metarepresentational framework in which communications take place must have clarity. Then language can be used to express needs, state views, and enter areas of uncertainty, in short to negotiate effectively within relationships. This basic assumption that what is said is meant often cannot be made by the child who is being abused. Fourthly, the child needs an integrated experience of mind and body. Our accounts of development and of post-empiricist thought have underlined the close connection between thoughts and action, and of the experience of effective agency as crucial to the sense of self. Under conditions of repeated helplessness and of dissociation from the body, this link in intentional processes is likely to be undermined, leading to inaction, or action that is ineffective and turned on the person's own body. In many ways the child is faced with representing the unrepresentable, acting the impossible action, and dividing the basis of intentionality. The features of borderline functioning that we considered earlier, the intense unstable relationships in which negotiation and communication are limited, and the rapid changes of moods, beliefs and actions, can be seen to follow from these processes.

Of all the borderline phenomena, self-injury is perhaps one of the most striking and puzzling. We see now several ways in which the person who has been abused may come to injure herself repeatedly in adult life. The child searches for an explanation and blames herself, but the conditions for testing her explanations are undermined by secrecy and fear. Her experience of her body is separated from her experience of herself because she has coped with the trauma by dissociating herself from her body. Then via a similar mechanism she may blame parts of her body for the abuse. Her sense of self does not include an experience of her body as an agent of effective action, through the impossibility of action being linked to representation. With subsequent development the 'choice' when faced with stress, loss, or maltreatment is either to deny the difficulties, hence using the childhood coping strategy; or to allow them to be represented with implications for action. Where she sees herself or her body as the cause of the difficulties, where she does not have the previous experience of action as effective, where her body has not been integrated into her sense of self, action may be turned on to her own body.

9.4.5 Protection and resilience

Our account has so far indicated ways in which threats to intentional processes may arise through coping with experience, with possible borderline functioning later in life. It is important to keep in mind that at this stage we do not know why some people show this kind of disturbance in adult life following child sexual abuse, while many do not, nor whether sexual abuse has specific effects when compared to other forms of abusive and neglectful parenting. The implications for the intentionality of adverse experiences may vary considerably. For instance, some children may be able to keep some areas of relatively integrated mental life alive, while still coping in ways that we have discussed here. If that is the case, that might be a function of constitutional factors, early pre-abuse experiences, or other valued previous or current relationships. Here the fit between the child and the experience may be crucial. For instance, some children who are abused are preoccupied with the welfare of other members of the family and do not disclose in order to protect them from the knowledge. Then a sensitivity to others may be a greater risk factor for coping later in ways that are maladaptive, than lack of sensitivity. Such a difference of sensitivity might have its roots in earlier experiences, or in inherited differences.

The capacity of a parent to envisage the infant or child as a mental entity may be a further source of resilience (Fonagy *et al.* 1994). Then the child will experience her wide range of intentions, feelings, and desires as contained within her parent's mind, within the relationship, and therefore containable within her own mind. Containment, as we saw in Chapter 8, is both epistemological and psychological. This may enable the child to reflect emotionally and cognitively on her own states of mind, even in the face of trauma, so that she may then be less vulnerable to the radical undermining that we have considered earlier. Fonagy and his colleagues have provided evidence that this self-reflective capacity may confer resilience in the face of adversity, and its role in protection from severe consequences of abuse will be an important focus of future research.

9.5 CONCLUSION

In reviewing psychiatric syndromes, some themes recur. This does not lead to a general theory of disorder, but to an analysis that has some general features. When seen against a developmental background, disorder is viewed in relation to the tasks that must be achieved where multiple sets of mental rules are possible. These include the monitoring of internal and interpersonal rules, the maintenance of the individual's experience of continuity in the presence of multiple states of mind, and the capacity to understand the mental states and actions of others. Many of the overarching, metarepresentational functions could also be characterized as functions of the self, and these appear to be disrupted in conditions that are as widely different as schizophrenia and borderline personality disorder. In schizophrenia the monitoring of the individual's own thoughts or actions may be impaired, whereas in borderline functioning the continuity of states of mind is undermined. If the sense of self is derived from the awareness of being the author of one's own actions or thoughts over time, then in these conditions it is undermined in different ways. In as much as the coherence of the self is in turn central to action, disturbances of action are the result of these different forms of disruption of the self.

In both conditions further contrasting factors may undermine action. In schizophrenia inefficient information-processing may lead either to action based on incidental aspects of a situation, or to inaction based on information overload. In borderline personality disorder experiences in which action has been impossible may lead to action turned on itself, in self-injury. However, in both, there may be elements that represent the attempt to preserve action in the face of such threats. In schizophrenia delusions and hallucinations may, in part, be compensatory mechanisms that reduce uncertainty, hence providing the basis for action. In borderline personality disorder the splitting of mental representations may similarly, by excluding elements that are incompatible with action, provide (partial) representations that provide the basis for action. Thus in both conditions elements of accurate representation are sacrificed, in order for action to continue.

Conditions in which action is preserved may be contrasted with those, such as depression, where it is not. In either case a range of intentional and non-intentional origins may be envisaged. In situations of helplessness, depression may be seen to be an appropriate and accurate representation that action is not possible. Depression seen in the absence of such a threat may result from the intrusion of cognitive and emotional states that undermine action, arising from a physical, non-intentional interruption of perceptions, thoughts, feelings, or actions. Equally, depression may arise where mental representations that have been maintained inactive or out of consciousness are activated, and are incompatible with action.

In post-traumatic stress disorder there appears to be a lack of resolution in favour of either representation or action. While some of the elements, such as denial of aspects of the trauma, seem to be attempts to limit the scope of the representation, this is not as comprehensive or complete as that seen for instance in borderline processes. Instead there is a circular repeated movement back and forth between the representation of the trauma and hence threat to action, and an assertion that action and therefore life is possible and so the representation must be denied or limited: and so on. Perhaps in this 'disorder' we find the clearest statement of the need to represent and to act, and the price paid when these requirements are in conflict.

We conclude by revisiting our starting point. Mental entities, perceptions, feelings, thoughts, and wishes are genuinely causal and must provide sufficient certainty that the individual can act effectively. Throughout biology, intentional states of organisms, from the simplest cellular creatures to non-human primates, have provided the basis for action, and in general the certainty has been derived from the evolution of those intentional states over long periods of time. In this and the preceding chapters we have seen how, in the activities of the human mind, is seen an infinite elaboration of the potential inherent in all intentional processes in biology. This has introduced novelty, creativity, and flexibility, which are seen in the achievements of language, custom, technology, and culture. It has also increased the risks of uncertainty, confusion, and the undermining of action. These are reduced through an interplay between the sophisticated integrative capacities of the human brain and the continuities of human relationships, skills, beliefs, and social organizations. Disorder is found in the failure of intentional states to underpin action, either where these are undermined by the external world, or where they are distorted, contradictory, or unintegrated, and action is undermined or ineffective.

REFERENCES

American Psychiatric Association (1994). *Diagnostic and Statistical Manual of Mental Disorders*, (4th edn). American Psychiatric Association, Washington, DC.

Bebbington, P. and Kuipers, L. (1994). The predictive utility of expressed emotion in schizophrenia: an aggregate analysis. *Psychological Medicine*, **24**, 707–18.

Bentall, R. P., Kaney, S., and Dewey, M. E. (1991). Paranoia and social reasoning: an attribution theory analysis. *British Journal of Clinical Psychology*, **30**, 13–23.

Bernstein, G. A. and Garfinkel, B. D. (1988). Pedigrees, functioning, and psychopathology in families of school phobic children. *American Journal of Psychiatry*, **142**, 1497–9.

Bernstein, G. A., Svingen, P. H., and Garfinkel, B. D. (1990). School phobia: patterns of family functioning. *Journal of the American Academy of Child and Adolescent Psychiatry*, **29**, 24–30.

Bolton, D. (1994). Family systems interventions. In *Handbook of phobic and anxiety disorders of children*, (ed. T. Ollendick, W. Yule and N. King), pp. 397–414. Plenum, New York.

Borkovec, T. D., Shadick, R., and Hopkins, M. (1991). The nature of normal and pathological worry. In *Chronic anxiety: generalized anxiety disorder and mixed anxiety-depression*, (ed. R. Rapee and D. H. Barlow), pp. 29–51. Guildford Press, New York.

Carey, G. and Gottesman, I. (1981). Twin studies of anxiety, phobic, and obsessive disorders. In *Anxiety: new research and changing concepts*, (ed. D. F. Klein and J. Rabkins), pp. 117–33. Raven Press, New York.

Chemtob, C., Roitblat, H. L., Hamada, R. S., Carlson, J. G., and Twentyman, C. T. (1988). A cognitive action theory of post traumatic stress disorder. *Journal of Anxiety Disorders*, **2**, 253–75.

Chiocca, E. A. and Martuza, R. L. (1990). Neurosurgical therapy of obsessive-compulsive disorder. In *Obsessive-compulsive disorders: theory and management*, (ed. M. A. Jenicke, L. Baer and W. E. Minichiello), pp. 283–94. Year Book Medical, Chicago.

Christensen, K. J., Kim, S. W., Dysken, M. W., and Hoover, K. M. (1992). Neuropsychological performance in obsessive-compulsive disorder. *Biological Psychiatry*, **31**, 4–18.

Cohen, L., Hollander, E., DeCaria, C. M., Stein, D. J., Simeon, D., Liebowitz, M. R., and Aronowitz, B (in press). Specificity of neuropsychological impairment in obsessive compulsive disorder: a comparison with social phobic and normal controls. *Journal of Neuropsychology and Clinical Neuroscience.*

Cornblatt, B. A., Lenzenweger, M. F., Dworkin, R. H., and Erlenmeyer–Kimling (1992). Childhood attentional dysfunctions predict social deficits in unaffected adults at risk of schizophrenia. *British Journal of Psychiatry,* **161,** (suppl. 18), 59–64.

Cox, C., Fedio, P., and Rapoport, J. (1989). Neuropsychological testing of obsessive-compulsive adolescents. In *Obsessive-compulsive disorder in children and adolescents,* (ed. J. L. Rapoport), pp. 73–85. American Psychiatric Press Inc., Washington.

Creamer, M., Burgess, P., and Pattison, P. (1992). Reaction to trauma: a cognitive processing model. *Journal of Abnormal Psychology,* **101,** 452–9.

Crow, T. J. (1985). The two syndrome concept: origins and current status. *Schizophrenia Bulletin,* **11,** 471–86.

Denckla, M. (1989). Neurological examination. In *Obsessive-compulsive disorder in children and adolescents,* (ed. J. L. Rapoport), pp. 107–15. American Psychiatric Press Inc., Washington.

Dixon, N. F. (1981). *Preconscious processing.* Wiley, Chichester.

Edwards, J. R. (1988). The determinants and consequences of coping with stress. In *Causes, coping, and consequences of stress at work,* (ed. C. L. Cooper and R. Payne) pp. 233–63. Wiley, Chichester.

Endler, N. S. and Parker, J. D. A. (1990). Multidimensional assessment of coping: a critical evaluation of coping. *Journal of Personality and Social Psychology,* **58,** 844–54.

Erikson, E. (1963). *Childhood and society.* Norton, New York.

Eysenck, H. (1979). The conditioning model of neurosis. *The Behavioral and Brain Sciences,* **2,** 155–99.

Eysenck, M. W. (1992). *Anxiety: the cognitive perspective.* Lawrence Erlbaum Associates, Hove.

Falkai, P., Bogerts, B., and Rozumek, M. (1988). Limbic pathology in schizophrenia: the entorhinal region — a morphometric study. *Biological Psychiatry,* **24,** 515–21.

Foa, E. B. and Kozak, M. J. (1986). Emotional processing and fear: exposure to corrective information. *Psychological Bulletin,* **99,** 20–35.

Foa, E. B. and Steketee, G. (1989). Behavioral/cognitive conceptualizations of post-traumatic stress disorder. *Behavior Therapy,* **20,** 155–76.

Foa, E. B., Zinbarg, R., and Rothbaum, B. (1992). Uncontrollability and unpredictability in post traumatic stress disorder: an animal model. *Psychological Bulletin,* **112,** 218–38.

Fonagy, P., Steele, M., Steele, H., Higgitt, A., and Target, M. (1994). The Emanuel Miller Memorial Lecture 1992. The theory and practice of resilience. *Journal of Child Psychology and Psychiatry,* **35,** (2), 231–57.

Freud, A. (1965). *Normality and pathology in childhood: assessments of developments.* New York: Interbational Universities Press.

Freud, A. (1966). Obsessional neurosis: a summary of psychoanalytic views as presented at the Congress. *International Journal of Psychoanalysis,* **47,** 116–22.

Freud, S. (1913). *Totem and taboo*. Standard Edition **13**, (1953), pp. 1–161. Hogarth Press, London.

Frith, C. D. (1992). *The cognitive neuropsychology of schizophrenia*. Lawrence Erlbaum Associates, Hove.

Frith, C. D. and Done, D. J. (1988). Towards a neuropsychology of schizophrenia. *British Journal of Psychiatry*, **153**, 437–43.

Furniss, T. (1992). Lecture, First European Conference of the Association of Child Psychology and Psychiatry and Allied Disciplines, York, England.

Gartner, A. F., Marcus, R. N., Halmi, K., and Loranger, A. W. (1989). DSM-III-R personality disorders in patients with eating disorders. *American Journal of Psychiatry*, **146**, 1585–91.

Gray, J. A. (1982). *The neuropsychology of anxiety*. Clarendon, Oxford.

Gray, J. A., Feldon, J., Rawlins, J. N. P., Hemsley, D. R., and Smith, A. D. (1991). The Neuropsychology of Schizophrenia. *Behavioral and Brain Sciences*, **14**, 1–84.

Harris, E. L., Noyes, R., Crowe, R. R., and Chaudery, M. D. (1983). A family study of agoraphobia. *Archives of General Psychiatry*, **40**, 1061–4.

Harris, P. L. (1994). Unexpected, impossible and magical events: children's reactions to causal violations. *British Journal of Developmental Psychology*, **12**, 1–7.

Head, D., Bolton, D., and Hymas, N. (1989). Deficit in cognitive shifting ability in patients with obsessive-compulsive disorder. *Biological Psychiatry*, **23**, 323–7.

Hollander, E. *et al.* (1990). Signs of central nervous system dysfunction in obsessive-compulsive disorder. *Archives of General Psychiatry*, **47**, 27–32.

Hollander, E., Cohen, L., Richards, M., Mullen, L., Decaria, C., and Stern, Y. (1993). A pilot study of the neuropsychology of obsessive-compulsive disorder and Parkinson's Disease: basal ganglia disorders. *Journal of Neuropsychiatry and Clinical Neurosciences*, **5**, 104–7.

Horowitz, M. (1986). *Stress response syndromes*, (2nd edn). Jason Aronson, New York.

Hymas, N., Lees, A., Bolton, D., Epps, K., and Head, D. (1991). The neurology of obsessional slowness. *Brain*, **114**, 2203–33.

Jakob, H. and Beckman, H. (1986). Prenatal developmental disturbances in the limbic allocortex in schizophrenics. *Journal of Neural Transmission*, **65**, 303–26.

Janoff-Bulman, R. (1985). The aftermath of victimization: rebuilding shattered assumptions. In *Trauma and its wake*, (ed. C. Figley), Vol. 1, pp. 15–35. Brunner/Mazel, New York.

Jesus Mari, J. De and Streiner, D. L. (1994). An overview of family interventions and relapse on schizophrenia: meta-analysis of research findings. *Psychological Medicine*, **24**, 565–78.

Jones, P. and Murray, R. M. (1991). The genetics of schizophrenia is the genetics of neurodevelopment. *British Journal of Psychiatry*, **158**, 615–23.

Keane, T. M., Zimmerling, R. T., and Caddell, J. M. (1985). A behavioral formulation of post-traumatic stress disorder in Vietnam veterans. *The Behavior Therapist*, **8**, 9–12.

Kemp-Wheeler, S. M. and Hill, A. B. (1987). Anxiety responses to subliminal experience of mild stress. *British Journal of Psychology*, **78**, 365–74.

Kernberg, O. (1984). *Severe personality disorders*. Yale University Press, New Haven.

Kuhn, T. S. (1962). *The structure of scientific revolutions*. University of Chicago Press, Chicago.

Last, C. G., Hersen, M., Kazdin, A. E., Francis, G., and Grubb, H. J. (1987). Psychiatric illness in the mothers of anxious children. *American Journal of Psychiatry*, **144**, 1580–3.

Lazarus, R. S. and Averill, J. R. (1972). Emotion and cognition: with special reference to anxiety. In *Anxiety: current trends in theory and research*, (ed. C. D. Spielberger), Vol. 2, pp. 241–83. Academic Press, New York.

Leckman, J. F., Weissman, M. M., Merikangas, K. R., Pauls, D. L., and Prusoff, B. (1983). Panic disorder and major depression. *Archives of General Psychiatry*, **40**, 1055–60.

Leonard, H. (1989). Childhood rituals and superstitions: developmental and cultural perspective. In *Obsessive-compulsive disorder in children and adolescents*, (ed. J. L. Rapoport), pp. 289–309. American Psychiatric Press Inc., Washington.

Livingston, R., Nugent, H., Rader, L., and Smith, R. G. (1985). Family histories of depressed and anxious children. *American Journal of Psychiatry*, **142**, 1497–9.

Lorentz, K. Z. (1981). *The foundations of ethology*. Springer-Verlag, New York.

Luxenberg, J., Swedo, S., Flament, M., Friedland, R., Rapoport, J., and Rapoport, S. (1988). Neuroanatomical abnormalities in obsessive-compulsive disorder detected with quantitative X-ray computed tomography. *American Journal of Psychiatry*, **145**, 1089–93.

McKeon, J., McGuffin, P., and Robinson, P. (1984). Obsessive-compulsive neurosis following head injury: a report of four cases. *British Journal of Psychiatry*, **144**, 190–2.

Millikan, R. (1984). *Language, thought, and other biological categories*. MIT Press, Cambridge, Mass.

Millikan, R. (1986). Thoughts without laws: cognitive science with content. *Philosophical Review*, **95**, 47–80.

Mineka, S. and Kihlstrom, J. (1978). Unpredictable and uncontrollable aversive events. *Journal of Abnormal Psychology*, **87**, 256–71.

Mlakar, J., Jensterle, J., and Frith, C. D. (1994). Central monitoring deficiency and schizophrenic symptoms. *Psychological Medicine*, **24**, 557–64.

Murray, R. M., Lewis, S. W., Owen, M. J., and Foerster, A. (1988). The neuro-developmental origins of dementia praecox. In *Schiziphrenia: the major issues*, (ed. P. Bebbington and P. McGuffin), pp. 90–106. Heinemann/Mental Health Foundation, Oxford.

Oatley, K. and Johnson-Laird, P. N. (1987). Towards a cognitive theory of the emotions. *Cognition and Emotion*, **1**, 29–50.

Ogata, S. N., Silk, K. R., Goodrich, S., Lohr, N. E., Western, D., and Hill, E. M. (1990). Chidhood sexual and physical abuse in adult patients with borderline personality disorder. *American Journal of Psychiatry*, **147**, 1008–13.

Olah, A., Torestad, B., and Magnusson, D. (1984). *Coping behaviours in relation to frequency and intensity of anxiety provoking situations*. Reports of the Department of Psychology, 629. University of Stockholm.

Oldham, J. M., Skodol, A. A., Kellman, D., Hyler, S. E., Rosnick, L., and Davies, M. (1992). Diagnosis of DSM-III-R personality disorders by two structured interviews: patterns of comorbidity. *American Journal of Psychiatry*, **149**, (2), 213–20.

Peterson, C. and Seligman, M. (1983). Learned helplessness and victimization. *Journal of Social Issues*, **2**, 103–16.

Pfohl, B., 'Stangl, D., and Zimmerman, M. (1984). The implications of DSM-III Personality disorders for patiients with major depression. *Journal of Affective Disorders*, **7**, 309–18.

Piaget, J. (1937). *The construction of reality in the child*. (Trans. Cook, M. (1954). Basic Books, New York.

Rachman, S. (1980). Emotional processing. *Behaviour Research and Therapy*, **18**, 51–60.

Rachman, S. (1993). Obsessions, responsibility and guilt. *Behaviour Research and Therapy*, **31**, 149–54.

Rachman, S. J. and Hodgson, R. (1980). *Obsessions and compulsions*. Prentice Hall, Englewood Cliffs, N. J.

Rapoport, J. L. (1990). Obsessive compulsive disorder and basal ganglia dysfunction. *Psychological Medicine*, **20**, 465–9.

Roberts, G. (1991). Delusional belief systems and meaning in life. *British Journal of Psychiatry*, **159**, (Suppl. 14), 19–28.

Robins, L. N. (1966). *Deviant children grown up*. Williams and Wilkins, Baltimore.

Robins, L. N. (1986). The consequences of conduct disorder in girls. In *Development of antisocial and prosocial behaviour*, (ed. D. Olweus, J. Block, and M. Radke-Yarrow), pp. 385–414. Academic Press, Orlando.

Salkovskis, P. (1985). Obsessional-compulsive problems: a cognitive-behavioural analysis. *Behaviour Research and Therapy*, **23**, 571–83.

Scarone, S. *et al.* (1992). Increased right caudate nucleus size in obsessive-compulsive disorder: detection with magnetic resonance imaging. *Psychiatry Research, Neuro-imaging*, **45**, 1115–21.

Shea, M. T. *et al.* (1990). Personality disorders and treatment outcome in the NIMH treatment of depression collaborative research program. *American Journal of Psychiatry*, **147**, 711–18.

Stein, D., Shoulberg, N., Helton, K., and Hollander, E. (1992). The neuroethological approach to obsessive-compulsive disorder. *Comprehensive psychiatry*, **33**, 274–81.

Stern, D. (1985). *The interpersonal world of the infant*. Basic Books, New York.

Strauss, J. S. (1992). The person — key to understanding mental illness: towards a new dynamic psychiatry, III. *The British Journal of Psychiatry*, **161**, (suppl. 18), 19–26.

Swedo, S. E. *et al.* (1989). High prevalence of obsessive-compulsive symptoms in patients with Sydenham's chorea. *American Journal of Psychiatry*, **146**, 246–9.

Sylvester, C., Hyde, T. S., and Reichler, R. J. (1987). The diagnostic interview for children and personality interview for children in studies of children at risk for anxiety disorders and depression. *Journal of the American Academy of Child and Adolescent Psychiatry*, **26**, 668–75.

Tienari, P., Wynne, L. C., Moring, J., Lahti, I., Naarala, M., Sorri, A., Wahlberg, K.–E., Saarento, O., Seitamaa, M., Kaleva, M., and Laksy, K. (1994). The Finnish adoptive family study of schizophrenia. Implications for family research. *British Journal of Psychiatry*, **164** (suppl 23), 20–6.

Torgersen, S. (1986). Childhood and family characteristics in panic and generalized anxiety disorder. *American Journal of Psychiatry*, **143**, 630–9.

Torgersen, S. (1990). Genetics of anxiety and its clinical implications. In *Handbook of anxiety*, Vol. 3: *The neurobiology of anxiety*, (ed. G. D. Burrows, M. Roth and R. Noyes), pp. 381–406. Elsevier, Amsterdam.

Tsuang, M. T. (1993). Genotypes, phenotypes, and the brain. A search for connections in schizophrenia. *British Journal of Psychiatry*, **163**, 299–307.

Turner, S. M., Beidel, D. C., and Costello, A. (1987). Psychopathology in the offspring of anxiety disorders patients. *Journal of Consulting and Clinical Psychology*, **55**, 229–35.

Tyrer, P., Lewis, P., and Lee, I. (1978). Effects of subliminal and supraliminal stress on symptoms of anxiety. *Journal of Nervous and Mental Disease*, **166**, 88–95.

Vasey, M. W. (1993). Development and cognition in childhood anxiety: the example of worry. In *Advances in clinical child psychology*, (ed. T. H. Ollendick and R. J. Prinz), Vol 15, pp. 1–39. Plenum, New York.

von Economo, C. (1931). *Encephalitis lethargica: its sequelae and treatment*. Oxford University Press, Oxford.

Vygotsky, L. (1981). The genesis of higher mental functions. In *The concept of activity in Soviet Psychology*, (ed. J. V. Wertsch), pp. 144–88. M. E. Sharpe, New York. (Reprinted in Richardson, K. and Sheldon, S. (ed.) (1990). *Cognitive development to adolescence*, pp. 61–80. Lawrence Erlbaum Associates, Hove.

Weiner, I., Feldon, J., and Ziv–Harris, D. (1987). Early handling and latent inhibition in the conditioned suppression paradigm. *Developmental Psychobiology*, **20**, 233–40.

Weissman, M. M., Leckman, J. F., Merikangas, K. R., Gammon, G. D., and Prusoff, B. (1984). Depression and anxiety disorders in parents and children. *Archives of General Psychiatry*, **41**, 845–52.

Williams, J. M. G., Watts, F. N., Macleod, C., and Matthews, A. (1992). *Cognitive psychology and emotional disorders*. Wiley, Chichester.

Winnicott, D. W. (1971). *Playing and reality*. Tavistock, London.

Wise, S. and Rapoport, J. (1989). Obsessive-compulsive disorder: is it basal ganglia dysfunction? In *Obsessive-compulsive disorder in children and adolescents*, (ed. J. L. Rapoport), pp. 327–44. American Psychiatric Press Inc., Washington.

Index

action
  basis of intentionality and cognition 21–3,
      260–1; *see also* meaning, definition in terms
      of action
  creation of order and 97–8, 142–4, 210
  intentional causality and 222–3, 244
  invariants in; *see* invariants
  mind, meaning, and explanation of 1–71
  non-intentional behaviour distinct from 9,
      27–9; *see also* invariants relativity and
      independent constraints on 146–50
  representation and, incompatibility between
      306–7, 316–18, 358
  rule–following and 23–4, 139–41
  self–caused 209–11, 254
  theory of in terms of mind, *see* theory of mind
  theory fundamental to, *see* theory fundamental
      to action
  thought and, threats to 304–8
adaptation 194, 260
adolescence, cognitive maturation in 39, 261–3,
      313, 346
adoption studies 291, 292, 336, 339
Adult Attachment Interview Schedule 329
affect
  basic emotions 14
  cognitive psychology and 13–15, 58, 59
  cognitive therapy and 323–4
  communication and 255–6
  early development and 255
  energy and 325
  failure of emotional processing 356, 360
  generalizations about cognitive–affective states
      206–9, 346
  implications of narrow range 319
  post traumatic stress disorder and 354, 358–9
  self-affectivity 255
agency
  causal laws and 209-11
  in development 254, 323
  see also self; responsibility
aggression
  children's attributions and 322
  dealing with threat and anxiety 345, 348
  social and hormonal factors 283
agreement
  between parents and infants 255–6
  concept of reality and 148–50, 155–7, 161
  in play 250–2
  in visual system 242–4
  intentional causality and 223–4

rule-following and role of 144–6
  self-knowledge and 46–7
Ainsworth Strange Situation Test 249
analogical knowledge 31, 39, 112, 134; *see also*
      empathy
animal learning theory 5, 6, 7, 12
animals
  anxiety reactions in 343, 357
  communication in 256; *see also* bees
  learned helplessness in 55, 357
  representation and behaviour in 240–7, 357–8;
      see also cognitive learning theory
  see also bats; bees; frogs; fruitfly; sticklebacks
anti-psychiatry critiques xiv, xvi
anxiety
  containment and 326, 345
  definition, evolutionary theory and 342–3
  intentional explanations of 268–74, 342–3,
      347, 348-9
  levels of intentionality and 275–6
  psychic defences and 312–13
  see also danger; fear
anxiety disorders 303–4, 323, 341–64, 348–9; *see
      also* obsessive–compulsive disorder; phobias;
      post traumatic stress disorder
appearance/reality distinction 188, 207, 261,
      362, 363
  in modern (seventeenth century) thought 4, 16,
      147, 154
  in relativistic thought 17, 137–8, 146–50, 155,
      162, 184
approach–avoidance conflict 354, 358
artificial intelligence (AI) 10–11, 24, 81, 84, 87,
      90, 91; *see also* connectionism
association 36, 260, 346–7
attachment 249–50, 291, 316–17, 328–30, 339
autism 26, 49, 256, 280

bees 246
behaviour therapy 323, 351, 352
behavioural criteria and mental content 104–8,
      110–12, 194–9
behavioural functional semantics 194–9
behaviourism xiii, 1, 4–5, 9, 11, 16, 36, 41, 48, 81
beta-blockers 276
biochemistry
  arguments regarding reduction of 230
  schizophrenia and 335–6
'biological' psychiatry and psychology
      293–5